Rodney Brazier was born in 1946. He was educated at Buckhurst Hill County High School, Essex, and at the University of Southampton, where he graduated in 1968. He was called to the Bar in 1970, being a major scholar of Lincoln's Inn, and is a Fellow of the Royal Historical Society. He has taught at the University of Manchester since 1968, where he is a Professor of Law. He has published widely on constitutional law and practice and has been an editor of de Smith's *Constitutional and Administrative Law* since its third edition, published in 1977. His other books include *Constitutional Practice* (2nd edn, 1994) and *Ministers of the Crown* (1997). He is married with a daughter and lives in Manchester.

Stanley de Smith was Downing Professor of the Laws of England at the University of Cambridge.

CONSTITUTIONAL AND ADMINISTRATIVE LAW

Stanley de Smith and Rodney Brazier

EIGHTH EDITION BY
RODNEY BRAZIER

PENGUIN BOOKS

PENGUIN BOOKS

Published by the Penguin Group
Penguin Books Ltd, 27 Wrights Lane, London w8 5TZ, England
Penguin Putnam Inc., 375 Hudson Street, New York, New York 10014, USA
Penguin Books Australia Ltd, Ringwood, Victoria, Australia
Penguin Books Canada Ltd, 10 Alcorn Avenue, Toronto, Ontario, Canada M4V 3B2
Penguin Books (NZ) Ltd, 182–190 Wairau Road, Auckland 10, New Zealand

Penguin Books Ltd, Registered Offices: Harmondsworth, Middlesex, England

First published 1971
Second edition 1973
Reprinted with minor revisions 1974
Third edition 1977
Fourth edition 1981
Fifth edition, published in Pelican Books, 1985
Reprinted with minor revisions 1986
Sixth edition 1989
Seventh edition 1994
Eighth edition 1998

1 3 5 7 9 10 8 6 4 2

Set in 9½/11½ pt Bembo
Typeset by Rowland Phototypesetting Ltd, Bury St Edmunds, Suffolk
Printed in England by Clays Ltd, St Ives plc

Contents

Preface

In this eighth edition I attempt to provide a new portrait of the British constitution. That aim has required the incorporation of developments which have taken place since early 1994 when the last edition was completed.

As always both Parliament and the courts have altered constitutional law in numerous ways. It would be tedious and not especially helpful to list those changes here: all the most significant of them are noted in the appropriate places in the text. As I write, the Labour Government is beginning to implement its major programme of constitutional reform. During the course of the present Parliament the shape of the British constitution will be altered by legislation in a number of important respects. But – of course – the British constitution consists of much more than a body of laws: the legal rules are moderated by conventions and practices, some of which are changed through the operation of politics. In recent years political necessity has led to the appointment of several official inquiries which have prompted the adoption of new procedures, of which the Scott inquiry and the Committee on Standards in Public Life are primary examples.

A number of chapters have been left out of this edition. First, given the demise of the nationalized industries there is no case for keeping the treatment of public boards and the economy, and I have dropped it. Secondly, because few students these days need to cope with the organiza-tion of the police that chapter has been excised. Thirdly, the sketch of local government was never intended to provide a comprehensive account: local government can be studied in its own right using specialized works, and to reduce the pressure on space that chapter has been omitted. In the result this edition is fifty pages shorter than it would have been otherwise.

I have tried to state the law and to describe constitutional developments down to December 1997.

Rodney Brazier

PART ONE

GENERAL FOUNDATIONS

The first chapter asks some elementary questions and indicates answers. What do we mean by a constitution? What matters are dealt with in the constitutions of other countries? Why have we no written constitution in Britain? How can constitutions be classified?

Chapter 2 outlines the main features of the British constitution today. It touches very briefly on the theory of the rule of law and the doctrine of separation of powers. It reviews the sources of British constitutional law. And then it goes on to deal at some length with conventions of the constitution, those rules of political practice which have played such an important part in the British system of government. How do they differ from rules of strict law? In what sense are conventions 'rules'? How does one identify conventions? It is easier to ask some of these questions than to answer them. A number of individual conventional rules will be examined in later chapters. In this chapter a preliminary indication is given of the impact of European Community law on the constitutional law of this country, and various ideas about constitutional reform are reviewed.

The integral parts of the United Kingdom and of the British Islands (two quite separate concepts in our law) are examined in chapter 3. The continued attempts to provide a satisfactory constitutional framework for Northern Ireland are described. And plans to provide for legislative devolution to Scotland and Wales are noted.

In chapter 4 still more awkward questions are asked. In other countries the constitution is the supreme law. In this country Parliament is traditionally supposed to be entitled to pass any law whatsoever on any subject whatsoever. What makes a constitution valid and supreme? Why is (or was) Parliament sovereign? How do judges behave in other countries when a revolutionary change of government takes place and the new rulers act in ways unauthorized by the constitution? This is a basic question about the foundations of a legal system. Can Parliament's law-making authority ever be restricted? If so, how? Is it really entitled to legislate for any part of the world? Can it effectively limit its own powers in any way? To what extent are its powers limited by Britain's membership of the European Union? Here we take a closer look at Community law doctrine and its repercussions on the legal concept of parliamentary sovereignty. The suggested answers to quite a lot of the questions posed in this chapter are somewhat speculative. Students may find parts of it difficult. They should not be despondent. The subject-matter of later chapters will be more down-to-earth. Anyone who feels so inclined can read chapter 4 again, and more closely, at a later stage. But what is said about Community law needs to be noted.

Chapter 5 examines in more detail the relationship between the United Kingdom and the European Union. The political background, purposes and institutions, and the law of the Union are surveyed and the effects of the Single European Act and the Maastricht Treaty are explained.

CHAPTER I

Constitutions[1]

WHAT ARE CONSTITUTIONS?

When de Tocqueville observed that the British constitution did not exist, few people took his remark at its face value. Lawyers have not been deterred from writing books about constitutional law, nor are books by non-lawyers on the British constitution in short supply. Dicey's assertion that we had no administrative law in Britain was a more serious matter; it frightened writers away from the subject for many decades, and only in the last thirty years or so has the practising side of the legal profession come to regard administrative law (or the law relating to public administration) as a living reality, wholly worthy of study. But the study of the law of the constitution earned respectability long ago.

In the vast majority of modern states or political societies there exists an identifiable document, or a group of documents, called the constitution, embodying a selection of the most important rules about the government of the country. Books on constitutional law in these countries are usually commentaries on this special document or group of documents – on the historical circumstances in which a constitution came to be adopted, on the political and philosophical assumptions underlying it, on the special position of authority enjoyed by the constitution within the legal order, on the individual provisions of the constitution and their implications, on their amendment, interpretation and practical operation. Insofar as these commentaries stray beyond the bare text of the constitution, they show that the terms 'constitution' and 'constitutional law' can be and often are used in a wider sense, to describe matters which are thought to be of 'constitutional' importance – importance, that is to say, in understanding what lies behind and beyond the 'constitution', so that the constitution

1 Several of the points made in this chapter are set out with exemplary lucidity by Sir Kenneth Wheare in his *Modern Constitutions* (2nd edn, 1966).

3

can be understood as a central feature, but not the sole feature, of the rules regulating the system of government.

And so studies of constitution law are likely to range into history, political and legal theory, political science, and legislative and political practice. In those countries where courts have power to inquire into the compatibility of legislative and administrative action with the constitution, books and lecture courses on constitutional law will include a lot of material about judicial review. This is the position in, for example, the United States, Canada, Australia and India. In the United States today it would be absurd to consider the meaning of constitutional expressions such as 'freedom of speech', 'due process of law', and 'the equal protection of the law', except by scrutinizing recent judicial interpretation, which happens to be far more significant than what the framers of the constitution and its amendments meant or thought they meant by those expressions. Similarly, in Canada the general power of the Federal Parliament to make laws for the 'peace, order and good government of Canada'[2] loses its deceptive simplicity when viewed in the context of restrictive judicial decisions. In Australia the meaning of the important constitutional guarantee of absolute freedom of interstate trade and commerce has been moulded by the High Court in a series of leading cases by a process of unavowed judicial legislation.

Sometimes the text, or much of the text, of a constitution is not intended to be taken literally. It sets out the framework of government, postulates how it ought to operate, and makes declarations about the purposes of the State and society and the rights and duties of citizens; but no real sanction is provided against violation of particular provisions of the constitution. Much of the constitution is 'programmatic', an affirmation of dogma or of objectives to be realized one fine day.[3] In such countries the study of constitutional law may be hardly distinguishable from jurisprudence or political theory; the books on the subject can still be bulky and verbose.

Although written constitutions differ widely in their purposes, form and content, they will normally be found to have two characteristics in common. They will be the fundamental law of the land; and they will be a kind of higher law. They will be fundamental law in so far as they designate the principal organs of government and invest them with authority; thus, they will constitute and define the Legislature, and state what is the scope of its law-making power and the procedure for exercising that power. In other

2 Constitution Act 1867, s. 91.
3 This was the case in Communist states in particular: see J. F. Triska (ed.), *Constitutions of the Communist Party States* (1968).

words, they will be the law behind the law – the legal source of legitimate authority. They will also, as a rule, be a higher form of law, in that the law (or some of the law) set out in the constitution will be hierarchically superior to other laws and will not be alterable except by a specially prescribed procedure for amendment. In a number of countries, courts have jurisdiction to pronounce laws inconsistent with the constitution to be invalid.[4] In order to escape such a fate, a law will have to be properly adopted as a constitutional amendment; and the same procedure will normally apply to a measure designed to 'amend' the constitution by way of addition without subtraction. Procedures for constitutional amendment differ widely from one another, but they usually require the amending measure to be passed by special majorities in the Legislature, or to be submitted to the people voting at a referendum, or both. It is perfectly possible, and is indeed not uncommon nowadays, for various provisions of a constitution to be alterable in different ways; some may be alterable by an ordinary legislative enactment, and others 'entrenched' at various levels against legislative encroachments, depending on the degree of importance originally attached to particular parts of the constitution. In West Germany and Cyprus, certain constitutional provisions were expressed to be unalterable by any means. To this extent the constitutions of those countries were, of course, rigid. But the rigidity or flexibility of written constitutions cannot be ascertained merely by comparing procedures for constitutional amendment. A constitution containing a cumbersome procedure for its own amendment may in fact be very flexible if there is no effective opposition to the party in power; and several modern states have authoritarian regimes. The constitution of Sri Lanka (formerly Ceylon)[5] on the other hand, remained remarkably stable for nearly twenty-five years, although most or all of it could be changed, quite simply, by a bill commanding the support of two-thirds of the members of the House of Representatives. The main reason for its durability was the existence of a volatile multi-party system, in which governments were preoccupied with

4 Judicial review of the constitutionality of legislation is not accepted in a number of other countries (for example, France). Unconstitutional legislation may consequently be deemed to be valid for the purposes of application and enforcement in the courts. The only remedy against this usurpation of legislative power will be political.

5 A republican constitution was adopted in 1972, by a Constituent Assembly, not following the procedure for amendment prescribed by the independence constitution. This was a deliberately contrived 'breach of legal continuity', designed to give Sri Lanka an 'autochthonous', or home-grown, constitution. See p. 69.

sustaining their own position in a usually unsuccessful attempt to avoid defeat at the next election.

As every beginner knows, the United Kingdom has no 'constitution' in the narrower sense of the term. There is no document or group of documents called the British constitution. But since Britain has a regular system of government, with a complex of rules defining the composition, functions and interrelationship of the institutions of government, and delineating the rights and duties of the governed, Britain does have a constitution and a body of constitutional law, if these terms are used in a broader sense. Even if Britain did have a formal written constitution, this would not necessarily determine the boundaries of the study of British constitutional law, for many rules of constitutional interest would not be found in the written document itself. In the absence of such a document, an author's selection of topics has to be conditioned by what he personally regards as relevant or instructive.

Why, then, have we no 'constitution'? Why does nearly every other country in the world have one? What topics would probably be dealt with in a constitution for Britain, and why? Before trying to offer answers to these questions, one must touch upon a preliminary problem. Some English lawyers will say that to adopt a written constitution would be pointless. It would be pointless because such a constitution would have no higher sanctity than an ordinary Act of Parliament; it could be amended or repealed the next day by another Act of Parliament, just as if it were an Act for the licensing of rat-catchers. For it is (or has been) a fundamental rule of British constitutional law that the United Kingdom Parliament is incapable of restricting its own omnipotence.

Now the question of parliamentary sovereignty raises some extremely difficult issues, which will be examined in chapter 4. For example, how 'fundamental' are the rules about the omnipotence of Parliament? For the moment it is enough to say that an orthodox opinion does not become unassailable merely because it is widely held by distinguished authorities.

WHAT GOES INTO CONSTITUTIONS?

Constitutions are primarily about political authority and power – the location, conferment, distribution, exercise and limitation of authority and power among the organs of a State. They are concerned with matters of procedure as well as substance. More often than not they also include explicit guarantees of the rights and freedoms of individuals. And sometimes they incorporate ideological pronouncements – principles by which the State ought to be guided or to which it ought to aspire, and statements of the citizens' duties.

There is no preordained stereotype of an ideal constitution. The form and content of a constitution will depend first on the forces at work when the constitution is established and amended, secondly on common-sense considerations of practical convenience, and thirdly on the precedents available to the politicians and their advisers who draw up the constitution. The first and third points may be particularly important. For instance, there was a very big difference between Ghana's independence constitution of 1957 and its republican constitution of 1960. The 1957 constitution was incorporated in an Order in Council drafted in London after an Independence Conference. The 1960 constitution was drafted in Ghana. The former was a 'Westminster model' type of constitution, an agreed compromise package-deal[6] embodying a parliamentary executive and various safeguards for individual and minority group interests. The latter was made to suit the requirements of the then President alone; it provided for a presidential form of government and included no significant safeguard for the interests of individuals or groups which might have resisted the wishes of the President's party. In 1964 the constitution was further amended to make Ghana a single-party state. Clearly the changes made in 1960 and 1964 were strongly influenced by constitutional precedents set in neighbouring French-speaking African states. After a change of regime in 1966, local opinion swung away from single-party authoritarianism, and the constitution adopted in 1969 included a wide range of devices designed to prevent serious abuses of legislative and executive power. To put the matter in another way, Ghana had reverted, at least for the time being, to 'constitutionalism' or the idea of limited government. But in less than three years the regime was overturned by a military coup. Constitutions in developing countries can be frail structures, mainly because so much value is attached to the acquisition and retention of political power. Changes of government are likely to be usurpations of power, followed by the suspension or supersession of the constitution.

6 See generally, Y. P. Ghai and J. P. W. B. McAuslan, *Public Law and Political Change in Kenya* (1970), chs. 5, 13.

WHY IS THERE NO WRITTEN BRITISH CONSTITUTION?

Every independent Commonwealth country has a written constitution, with the exception of Britain itself. Israel[7] and a few countries which are in the process of reconstructing new constitutions in place of old ones that have been overturned lack written constitutions. All British colonies have had a written constitution. Indeed, so has nearly every country in the world.[8] Why does Britain stand out as an anomaly?

The answer lies above all in the facts of history. In other countries constitutions have been granted or adopted to mark stages in a progression towards (or a regression from) self-government, to establish the foundations of the machinery of government in a newly independent State (for example, the United States, Cyprus) or a reconstituted State (for example, Malaysia, Tanzania), or to rebuild the machinery of government following the wreckage caused by defeat in war, or to start afresh after a revolutionary upheaval or because of widespread disillusionment with the existing regime, or even to signify a change in ideological attitudes. With very few exceptions, governments in the modern world feel it necessary to point to a constitution as the source of their authority – if only as a badge of legitimacy or respectability.

In Britain none of these factors has been effectively at work. England has not been unambiguously defeated in war, or at least has not been successfully invaded (save by special invitation) since 1066. There were, it is true, two revolutions in England during the seventeenth century. The Civil War of 1642–8 ended with the execution of Charles I in 1649 and the establishment of a republican Commonwealth. From the ferment of political ideas there emerged in 1653 an authentic written constitution, skeletal but readily identifiable, the Instrument of Government. But in the welter of controversy this document (which was to be influential in the North American colonies) was soon reduced to the status of a scrap of paper; the revolution petered out and Charles II was restored in 1660. In 1688 James II was deposed after a reign of three years; the Crown was offered to a usurper, William of Orange, who accepted it jointly with his wife Mary, James II's daughter, and the Glorious Revolution triumphed.

---

7 See E. Likhovski, *Israel's Parliament: The Law of the Knesset* (1971). New Zealand had no written constitution until 1987: her constitution now consists of a consolidation of previously scattered enactments, together with some new law. See Constitution Act 1986 (New Zealand).

8 See A. Blaustein and G. Flanz, *Constitutions of the Countries of the World*.

The revolutionaries, however, were insistent that they were nothing more than the conservators of the ancient rights and liberties of the people, which James had been seeking to subvert. James, moreover, was deemed to have abdicated. Apart from changing the line of succession to the throne, and enacting, in the Bill of Rights 1689, some fairly important limitations on the royal prerogative, Parliament attempted no fundamental restatement of the constitution. To have made such an attempt would have been politically imprudent,[9] and in any event this was not a time when constitutions had become fashionable. And, indeed, instead of laying the foundations of a written constitution, it formed a base for the concept of untrammelled parliamentary sovereignty. Since then the serenity of historical continuity has survived Jacobite revolts, the French Revolutionary and Napoleonic Wars, riots at home and some bloodied noses in far-away encounters; and the two World Wars of the twentieth century have ended in victory. In modern times Britain has known neither the humiliation of conquest nor the turmoil of full-scale revolution.

Since England was a sovereign State for many centuries, the question of adopting a constitution on the attainment of independence did not arise. But in 1707 England ceased to be an independent State. It entered into union with the independent State of Scotland. This union was founded on Articles of Union negotiated by commissioners representing the two Parliaments, and it was consummated by separate Acts of Union merging the two Parliaments into a new Parliament of the United Kingdom of Great Britain. The Articles of Union, incorporated with the Scottish Act in the English Act of Union, were expressed to be fundamental and unalterable conditions of the Union. They provided a rudimentary framework of a written constitution. Yet south of the border the Act of Union has not been regarded as enjoying any greater binding force in strict law than other statutes of major constitutional importance.[10]

There are other reasons why the question of adopting a written constitution has not been embraced by the main political parties – insularity, a lack of interest in political philosophy, a dearth of enthusiasm among politicians for restraints that might impede their freedom of action when

9 Immediately after the Revolution, when the conditions under which the throne should be offered to William and Mary were being discussed, more radical views were canvassed, but they were shelved because an ensuing controversy would have delayed the settlement; see T. P. Taswell-Langmead's *English Constitutional History* (11th edn, 1960), p. 447; J. R. Western, *Monarchy and Revolution* (1972), ch. 9.

10 See further, p. 77. The legal effect of the Act of Union with Ireland 1800 has also been a matter of controversy.

in office, a relatively high degree of homogeneity, and a widely diffused acceptance of traditional forms, gradualism and parliamentary methods. Britain's one intractable political (and religious) problem was Ireland; and it is significant that it was in relation to Ireland, in 1885, that fundamental thinking about the restructuring of the British constitution came to the surface. Only after the First World War, with the partitioning of Ireland and the creation of a separate Irish Free State (later Eire, and now the Republic of Ireland), was it possible to sweep this embarrassing problem under the carpet – till 1969.[11]

ASPECTS OF CLASSIFICATION[12]

Written and unwritten

This mode of classifying constitutions has already been discussed. Among liberal democracies, only the United Kingdom and Israel lack a written constitution in the narrower sense of the term. But the law of the constitution in those countries can be found in writing – in statutes, law reports, parliamentary standing orders, works of authority, and so on, although an authoritative and reasonably comprehensive document called the 'Constitution' is lacking.

Flexible and inflexible

Constitutions for which no special procedure for amendment is prescribed are *prima facie* more flexible than others. But flexibility is a matter of degree, and will not necessarily be predetermined by the formal procedure for constitutional amendment. And some constitutional rules will in practice be more flexible than others. In the United Kingdom the 'constitution' is, in theory, entirely flexible, but (for example) legislation to abolish the monarchy or to extend the maximum duration of a Parliament could only be passed in very extraordinary circumstances.

11 On whether the United Kingdom should acquire a written constitution, see p. 46.
12 For a more elaborate classification see Leslie Wolf-Phillips, *Comparative Constitutions* (1972). See also Leslie Wolf-Phillips, *Constitutions of Modern States* (1968), Introduction.

Monarchical and republican

This is no longer a difference of any general importance, because it tells us nothing worth knowing about the form or substance of government. One can have an absolute monarch or one with extensive personal discretionary powers (as in Nepal), or one with very limited personal powers (as in the United Kingdom and several Commonwealth and Western European countries). One can have a President who is head of State but is not the effective executive head of Government (as in India and Germany), or one who is both head of State and head of Government (as in the United States and a great many other countries).

Presidential and parliamentary

This method of classification is concerned with the executive branch of government and its relationship with the Legislature. Under a 'presidential' system the head of the executive branch is also head of State, and is not a member of or directly responsible to the Legislature. In a parliamentary system the chief executive is a Prime Minister who is a member of and is responsible to the Legislature. Thus the American system and its imitators are distinguishable from the Westminster model of responsible government. But this kind of classification is not very illuminating, because of the wide variations within each type of system. For example, in Kenya there is an executive President, but he has to be a member of the Legislature; in Tanzania and several of the other presidential regimes in Africa, the President cannot be a member of the Legislature but (in contrast to the United States) his Ministers must be members of the Legislature, though they are not fully responsible to it. Again, whereas the President of the United States has no power to dissolve Congress, the power of dissolution is vested in Commonwealth executive presidents; and whereas the constitutional powers of the American President are hedged about by checks and balances, presidential heads of governments in new States are usually freer from restraints. And the constitution of the fifth French Republic is both presidential and parliamentary.

Single-party and other constitutions

Obviously a constitution under which only one party can legitimately operate tends to differ from one in which, at least ostensibly, freedom of political association is permitted. A constitution for a single-party State is apt to be something of a political manifesto. In such a constitution, lip-service may still be paid to the basic freedoms of the individual. Again, however, constitutional forms may give little indication of what happens in practice. In some states with single-party constitutions there is more freedom of expression than in nearby countries with impeccably liberal constitutions.

Federal and unitary

The difference between a federal and non-federal constitution will often be clear-cut; sometimes it will be only one of degree; sometimes it will be positively misleading. The United States, Australia, Canada, Germany and Switzerland are manifestly federal States. The relationship between the United Kingdom and Northern Ireland under the Act of 1920 was strictly non-federal, since Northern Ireland had no exclusive field of competence, but in practice the degree of regional autonomy till 1970 was substantially greater than that of the republics of the old Soviet Union or even the states of Malaysia, both of which countries have nominally federal constitutions. Tanzania is a part-federation, since Zanzibar has exclusive fields of competence both in theory and in practice; but for political reasons the term 'federal' does not appear in the constitution inasmuch as it implies a degree of disunity as well as diversity. The word 'federal' has caused some difficulty during debates and negotiations about the development of the European Union. Federalism means different things to different Europeans: to some it threatens a strong central Executive; for others it implies the retention by Member States of the maximum degree of autonomy.

Diarchical and other constitutions

A diarchical constitution can be defined as one in which there is a division of governmental competence between two or more authorities in the State otherwise than on a regional basis. For instance, law-making powers may be divided between the Legislature and the Executive, the former having power to pass laws within a defined field and the latter having an autonomous and exclusive power, derived directly from the constitution, to issue decrees, ordinances or regulations within a defined field; this, broadly speaking, is the position under the French constitution.[13] Such divisions of competence have certain affinities with the separation of powers doctrine, of which

13 John Bell, *French Constitutional Law*, (1992), ch. 1.

more will be said later; they also indicate that the concept of unitary, as distinct from federal, constitutions is not particularly illuminating in some political systems.

CHAPTER 2

The British Constitution

CHARACTERISTICS

Here will be stated, or restated, very briefly the main features of the British constitutional system. All the characteristics to be listed differentiate the British constitution from *some* other constitutions.

Unwritten character. The British constitution is not written in a basic document or group of documents.

Continuity of development. It has evolved over the centuries with but few sudden or dramatic changes, and a high degree of historical continuity has been maintained as the constitution has been brought up to date. Of the modern institutions of government, some are still rooted in medieval origins. Among the existing rules of British constitutional law, quite a number were laid down in the seventeenth century or earlier. Our history is still with us. But the constitution is not a museum piece. The greater part of our constitutional law has been made this century.

Parliamentary sovereignty. Subject to the law of the European Union, Parliament as a legislative body can enact any law whatsoever on any subject whatsoever in the eyes of United Kingdom courts, according to the generally held view[1]. Changes in rules of constitutional law can be effected by ordinary legislation.

Law and convention. Particularly in the working of the executive branch of government and its relationship with the Legislature, the constitution is regulated to a large extent by rules which do not belong to the normal legal categories. These rules are called constitutional conventions. They

---

1 For this basic rule, see ch. 4.

are rules of political conduct or binding usages, most of which are capable of being varied or of simply disappearing as political conditions and ideas change. If conventions are to be classified as rules of constitutional law, then the term 'law' must be given a very broad meaning. To use the term 'law' in more than one sense is not in itself unusual. Sometimes it is convenient to contrast convention with 'strict law'. Thus, in strict law (by virtue of the royal prerogative) the Queen can dismiss her Ministers at pleasure. By convention this legal power is exercisable only in very extra-ordinary circumstances. And because it is well understood that, save in exceptional situations, the Queen must act in accordance with ministerial advice, Parliament still adopts the form of conferring discretionary powers on Her Majesty. This dichotomy of law and convention pervades much of our constitutional law.

Flexibility. The absence of a cumbersome procedure for altering rules of constitutional importance, the omnicompetence of Parliament and the pliability of many constitutional conventions tend to make the British consti-tution flexible and easily adaptable. But, as has been pointed out, flexibility is a question of degree. It would be easier in practice to enact legislation to abolish the House of Lords or the hereditary peerage or the Privy Council than, say, to abolish the remedy of habeas corpus. Moreover, not every consti-tutional convention is flexible in practice; some conventions are very rigid.

Unitary nature. The United Kingdom is a unitary, not a federal, State at the present time. If it were a federal State, Parliament would not be omnicompetent.

Freedom of political activity. The legitimacy of organized dissent and oppo-sition to the Government is recognized by convention; and nowadays there are few oppressive legal restrictions on freedom of expression and associations in political controversy. Elections are freely conducted (although whether through a fair electoral system is another matter).

Limited monarchy. Succession to the throne is hereditary. The functions of the head of State are primarily ceremonial, and despite their amplitude in strict law they are now of little or no political significance in normal times.

Bicameralism. The upper House of Parliament, the House of Lords, still constituted mainly on a hereditary basis, is of minor importance; the lower House, the elected House of Commons, is the focus of political attention.

Parliamentary Executive. The political arm of the executive branch of government is recruited from and located within Parliament, and the Cabinet is collectively 'responsible' to Parliament in general and the House of Commons in particular. A Government would either have to go to the country or resign if it were to lose a vote of confidence in the Commons.

Executive dominance in the Legislature. Because of the structure of modern British parties, and the operation of the electoral system and certain constitutional rules, the Government in office is normally able to command parliamentary support for the implementation of almost any policy that it is in practice likely to adopt. The Government has indeed to be *responsive* to parliamentary opinion, as well as to the weight of opinion in the electorate at large, but one must not imagine that it is in any real sense a delegate or agent of Parliament. Parliamentary government is not government by Parliament. The Government governs in and through Parliament. At the same time, it would be erroneous to speak in terms of 'Cabinet dictatorship'. A Government operates within a complex network of constraints, restricting its freedom of manoeuvre.

Impartial public service. The civil service is non-partisan except in so far as it serves the Government in office. Its insulation from political involvement, and the security of tenure enjoyed by its members, have been the product of convention, not of strict law.

Judicial independence. The Judiciary is appointed by the Executive, but it is conspicuously independent both of the Executive and of the Legislature, partly because of rules of strict law but mainly because of extra-legal factors. The prestige of the superior judges in Britain is exceptionally high by any international standard, although the appalling miscarriages of justice which have come to light in recent years, and the Court of Appeal's role in them, have somewhat tarnished the image of the senior English Judiciary.

Constitutionalism. Despite the absence of constitutionally entrenched guarantees and prohibitions or impregnable institutional bulwarks against the abuse of power, serious encroachments on basic individual freedoms are rare in times of peace,[2] and the protection of dissenting minorities in Britain is more efficacious than in many states which enjoy a superabundance of

2 But note the anti-terrorist legislation which has been in force since 1974. See below, pp. 433–4.

devices designed to achieve this end. Those rules and practices which do restrain abuses of public power under the British constitutional system are generally observed. The formal restraints are not always as effective as in some other liberal democracies – for instance, Parliament is a less formidable body than the United States Congress; the powers of the courts are significantly narrower than in America; civil liberties are not buttressed by a bill of rights – but there is a widely diffused acceptance of the principle that the restrictive rules of the political game are more important than the retention of power, or the pressing of legal power to the ultimate limit at the expense of individual liberty. In this sense we can say that constitutionalism, or limited government, or the rule of law – the meanings of these expressions overlap – exists in Britain.[3]

THE RULE OF LAW AND THE SEPARATION OF POWERS

Dicey[4] saw the rule of law as a central feature of the British constitution. He had his own idiosyncratic ideas of what the concept of the rule of law implied. His ideas, rooted in Whiggish libertarianism, were very influential for two generations;[5] today they no longer warrant detailed analysis. Nor would it be justifiable to examine the general concept of the rule of law at length in this book. The concept is one of open texture; it lends itself to an extremely wide range of interpretations. One can at least say that the concept is usually intended to imply (i) that the powers exercised by politicians and officials must have a legitimate foundation; they must be based on authority conferred by law; and (ii) that the law should conform to certain minimum standards of justice, both substantive and procedural. Thus, the law affecting individual liberty ought to be reasonably certain or

3 The readers who feel that these assertions show an establishmentarian bias may wish to consult as correctives Harold Laski, *Parliamentary Government in England* (1938); Ralph Miliband, *The State in Capitalist Society* (1973); Paul O'Higgins, *Censorship in Britain* (1972); D. N. Pritt, *Law, Class and Society* (1970); Keith Ewing and Connor Gearty, *Freedom under Thatcher* (1989).

4 A. V. Dicey, *Introduction to the Study of the Law of the Constitution* (10th edn, 1959), pt 2, especially ch. 4. The first edition was published in 1885. See R. A. Cosgrave, *The Rule of Law: Albert Venn Dicey* (1981).

5 Sir Ivor Jennings's *The Law and the Constitution* included a sustained critique of Dicey's views, moderated, however, in the later editions. See Appendix 2 to the 5th edn. For more sympathetic assessments, see E. C. S. Wade, Introduction to the 10th edn of Dicey, pp. xcvi–cli (1959); Lawson (1959) 7 *Political Studies* 109, 207, cf. Ford (1970) 18 *Political Studies* 220; and All Souls – *Public Law* seminar, 'Dicey and the Constitution' [1985] *Public Law* 583. For further comment see below, pp. 503–7.

predictable; where the law confers wide discretionary powers there should be adequate safeguards against their abuse; like should be treated alike, and unfair discrimination must not be sanctioned by law; a person ought not to be deprived of his liberty, status or any other substantial interest unless he is given the opportunity of a fair hearing before an impartial tribunal; and so forth. The concept has an interesting characteristic: everyone who tries to redefine it begins with the assumption that it is a good thing, like justice or courage. When Communist theoreticians extolled the merits of 'socialist legality', they could simply have substituted the term 'rule of law', though their conceptions of what was connoted would have differed from those of liberal democratic ideologists.

The doctrine of the separation of powers, like the rule of law, has usually been discussed as one which *ought* to be embodied in a system of government. But whereas commentators are almost unanimous that the rule of law (whatever it may mean) is splendid, the virtues of the separation of powers do not evoke so enthusiastic a chorus. Perhaps this is partly because the doctrine has acquired a harder core of generally accepted meaning, and because some constitutions survive adequately without relying on it for sustenance.

This is not to say that the quintessence of the separation of powers is easy to distil. The doctrine has emerged in several forms at different periods and in different contexts.[6] It is traceable back to Aristotle; it was developed by Locke; its best-known formulation, by the French political philosopher Montesquieu, was based on an analysis of the English constitution of the early eighteenth century, but an idealized rather than a real English constitution; the disciples of Montesquieu, particularly numerous in the North American colonies, added their own refinements; and today the doctrine survives in a number of curious manifestations. No writer of repute would claim that it is a central feature of the modern British constitution. However, a brief survey of the doctrine brings out more clearly some features of the British system of government.

The doctrine, as propounded by Montesquieu and his followers, may be stated briefly as follows.

1 There are three main classes of governmental functions: the legislative, the executive and the judicial.
2 There are (or should be) three main organs of government in a State: the Legislature, the Executive and the Judiciary.

6 For the fullest analysis, see M. J. C. Vile, *Constitutionalism and the Separation of Powers* (1967).

3 To concentrate more than one *class* of function in any one person or organ of government is a threat to individual liberty. For example, the Executive should not be allowed to make laws or adjudicate on alleged breaches of the law; it should be confined to the executive functions of making and applying policy and general administration.

Even if one accepts the first two propositions, one is not obliged to accept the third. To concentrate a large *quantity* of power in the hands of one person, in the absence of proper safeguards, is surely more dangerous than to combine a few powers analytically different in *quality* in the same hands, if adequate safeguards exist. And a rigorous segregation of functions may be highly inconvenient. In many countries subscribing to versions of the separation of powers doctrine, rule-making powers have been vested in the Executive because it is manifestly impracticable to repose such powers exclusively in the Legislature. The third proposition stated above is therefore both extreme and doctrinaire, and is not taken literally by all proponents of the theory.

One of the implications commonly read into the separation of powers doctrine is that the three branches of government ought to be composed of different *persons*. In the United States for instance, the President and his Cabinet cannot be members of Congress (although the Vice-President presides occasionally over the Senate). It does not inevitably follow that the one branch of government should not be in a position to dominate the others. Matters may be so designed that each branch operates as a check on the others. Again the United States provides an illustration. The President may veto legislation but has no power to dissolve Congress; although he holds office for a fixed term and is not dependent on the support of a Congressional majority, he can be impeached by Congress,[7] he appoints federal judges but his appointments need to be confirmed by the Senate,[8] the courts can determine the constitutionality of legislative enactments and administrative action, but judges cannot validly be given powers totally alien to the judicial office; federal judges cannot be removed by the Executive but they can be impeached by Congress. In France, on the other hand, the separation of powers has been understood to preclude the ordinary

7 Impeachment of a President is, however, rarely embarked upon. President Andrew Johnson was impeached in 1868 but escaped conviction by one vote; impeachment proceedings were started against President Nixon but were pre-empted by his resignation in 1974 in the aftermath of the Watergate scandal, on which see Philip Kurland, *Watergate and the Constitution* (1978).
8 President Lyndon Johnson's choice for Chief Justice, Justice Fortas, two consecutive nominations to the Supreme Court, of Judges Haynsworth and Carswell, by President Nixon and one by President Reagan, of Judge Bork, were rejected by the Senate.

courts from determining the constitutionality of legislation; yet judicial and administrative functions are commingled in the *Conseil d'État*, and legislative and executive powers in the Presidency.

In Britain we have Cabinet government with a parliamentary Executive; the Law Lords act both as judges and as legislators; the Lord Chancellor is a Minister as well as head of the Judiciary and an active member of the House of Lords in its legislative capacity. Legislative powers are delegated by Parliament to members of the Executive (the Queen in Council, and Ministers); powers to determine justiciable controversies are also confided in Ministers and other non-judicial agencies. Indeed, there never was a time in English constitutional history when the functions of government were neatly compartmentalized. The medieval *Curia Regis*, the King's Council, exercised all three classes of functions. Parliament was a High Court as well as a legislative body. For several centuries the local government authorities in the counties were judicial officers, the justices of the peace. But the modern Judiciary does stand in a special position. Professional full-time judges are disqualified from membership of the House of Commons because any other arrangement would hardly be compatible with the judicial office; the Law Lords generally abstain from politically controversial debate in the upper House, and only the Lord Chancellor and former occupants of that office have a free rein. Moreover, a number of rules and practices insulate judges in office from political pressure.

If we had a written constitution, this insulation of the Judiciary might be more complete. Two examples bring out this point. In the Commonwealth of Australia the constitution allocates the legislative, executive and judicial powers to the corresponding organs of government. There is a parliamentary Executive, as in Britain, and the Australian courts have declined to hold that parliamentary delegation of legislative powers to the Executive is unconstitutional; but they have held that the judicial power of the Commonwealth can be vested only in 'courts' within the meaning of the constitution, and that powers wholly alien to the judicial cannot be vested in those courts.[9] In Sri Lanka (Ceylon)[10] the constitution did not allocate judicial powers in the same form, and it would be reasonable to

---

9 See *Att.-Gen. for Australia* v. *R. and the Boilermakers' Society of Australia* [1957] AC 288 (PC) affirming the decision of the High Court of Australia *sub nom. R.* v. *Kirby, ex p. Boilermakers' Society* (1956) 94 CLR 254. See also *Hinds* v. *R.* [1977] AC 195. The *Boilermakers'* case was followed (with some reluctance) by the Australian High Court in *R.* v. *Joske and Others* (1974) 130 CLR 87.

10 For a general commentary on the 1972 constitution, see J. Cooray, *Constitutional and Administrative Law of Sri Lanka* (1973).

infer that the separation of powers doctrine had no place in the constitutional jurisprudence of the island. But in a famous case the Judicial Committee of the Privy Council held that implicit in the constitution lay the principle that the province of the Judiciary was immune from the grosser kinds of encroachment by the Executive and the Legislature; hence, retroactive legislation designed to secure the conviction and punishment of particular persons for specified conduct was declared unconstitutional, for it approximated to a non-judicial judgment.[11] One wonders how the War Damage Act 1965, which reversed a judicial decision of the House of Lords[12] with retroactive effect, would have fared if it had been measured against a written British constitution in which judicial review of the constitutionality of legislation was accepted.

It is easy to see, therefore, that the immunity of the Judiciary from interference by the political organs of government could be fortified by a written constitution; and such a constitution would certainly entrench the judges' security of tenure. To that extent the doctrine of the separation of powers, and the climate of thought of which it is a part, has practical value. Whether it would be helpful, as a means of restoring the vitality of Parliament, to separate the Executive from the Legislature in Britain is an interesting but academic speculation. The blending of Executive and Legislature is a fundamental characteristic of the British system of government. To discard it would be a more startling change than the introduction of federalism and entrenched civil liberties in a written constitution.

SOURCES OF BRITISH CONSTITUTIONAL LAW

The law of the constitution, though in one sense unwritten, is traceable to written sources, some of which are recognized as authoritative law-making agencies.

Legislation

This is by far the most important single source of constitutional law. In the first place, there are Acts of Parliament such as the Bill of Rights 1689, the Act of Settlement 1701, the Act of Union with Scotland 1707, and the European Communities Act 1972, embodying rules of major importance

---

11 *Liyanage* v. *R.* [1967] 1 AC 259; cf. *Kariapper* v. *Wijesinha* [1968] AC 717 (*Liyanage's* case distinguished).
12 *Burmah Oil Co.* v. *Lord Advocate* [1965] AC 75.

in the history of the constitution. There are numerous Acts dealing with the electoral system and the composition and functioning of Parliament (for example, the Representation of the People Acts, the Parliamentary Constituencies Act 1986, the House of Commons Disqualification Act 1975, the Life Peerages Act 1958, the Peerage Act 1963 (permitting the disclaimer of hereditary peerages), the Parliament Acts of 1911 and 1949 (asserting the primacy of the House of Commons in conflicts between the two Houses), and the Royal Assent Act 1967). There are statutes relating to the monarchy, regulating the succession to the throne, authorizing the adoption of new forms of the royal style and titles, and providing for a regency; but there are not many statutes of general importance defining the authority of the political executive branch. Acts of Parliament have made big changes in the law relating to civil liberties (for example, the Habeas Corpus Act 1679, the Administration of Justice Act 1960, the Public Order Acts, the Defamation Act 1952, the Obscene Publications Acts, the Race Relations Act 1976, the Theatres Act 1968, the Police and Criminal Evidence Act 1984 and the Prevention of Terrorism (Temporary Provisions) Act 1989). We have legislation relating to British nationality, the status of aliens, and immigration and deportation; regulating the conditions under which fugitive offenders may be extradited; conferring diplomatic and kindred privileges and immunities. In the general area of administrative law we have major enactments such as the Crown Proceedings Act 1947, the Parliamentary Commissioner Act 1967, and the Tribunals and Inquiries Act 1992 (consolidating earlier legislation), and a host of statutes regulating particular fields of administrative action. And then there are numerous Acts concerning Commonwealth relations, such as the Statute of Westminster 1931 (setting the seal on the concept of Dominion status) and independence Acts. One has only to glance through the statute book for any year since the late 1960s to appreciate how much legislation of constitutional interest is enacted by Parliament. The overwhelming bulk of this legislation has been introduced by Ministers.

Subordinate legislative instruments are also a source of constitutional law. For example, Orders in Council are made under the Ministers of the Crown Act 1975 to transfer functions between Ministers and to alter their titles; Orders in Council and regulations of constitutional importance can be made under the European Communities Act 1972. Orders in Council (made by the Queen in her Privy Council) and rules and regulations made by Ministers under statutory authority are called statutory instruments within the meaning of the Statutory Instruments Act 1946. In a narrow field, the Crown has an inherent law-making power exercisable by virtue of the royal prerogative; examples of the use of this non-statutory power are Orders regulating the civil service.

Common-law sources

Beneath this general rubric are subsumed rules widely different in character from one another.

(a) There is a small group of customary rules, now partly modified by statute, determining what is an Act of Parliament and enunciating the principle of parliamentary sovereignty. Clearly these rules are of fundamental importance in our legal system. Their origins and present status will be examined in chapter 4.

(b) The royal prerogative is the gradually diminishing residuum of customary authority, privilege and immunity, recognized at common law as belonging to the Crown, and the Crown alone. In the great *Case of Proclamations* (1611)[13] the judges of the common-law courts emphatically asserted their right to determine the limits of the prerogative; and since the Revolution of 1688 this claim has not been contested by the Crown. Among the prerogatives still exercised by or in the name of the Crown are the appointment of Ministers, the dissolution of Parliament, the power of pardon and the award of honours and dignities; these powers must, as a matter of constitutional convention, normally be exercised on ministerial advice. The immunity of the monarch from prosecution in the courts is another aspect of the royal prerogative.

(c) Judicial decisions are also a significant source of constitutional law. Indeed, Dicey went so far as to assert that the British constitution was 'a judge-made constitution'.[14] He was thinking particularly of the rules relating to the liberty of the person, freedom of expression and freedom of association, which had been demarcated largely by binding precedents set by the superior courts. The law of civil liberties is still to a large extent judge-made, though statutory restatement has become increasingly important in recent years. The law relating to judicial review of administrative action is predominantly judge-made, and it has probably developed faster since 1963 than in any comparable period. Again, judicial decisions have set limits not only to the royal prerogative but also to the ambit of parliamentary privilege.

13 12 Co. Rep. 74.
14 Dicey, op. cit., p. 196.

(*d*) Legislation of constitutional importance may be moulded by judicial interpretation; and there are common-law presumptions of legislative intent (for example, that major constitutional innovations cannot be introduced,[15] and taxation cannot be imposed,[16] save by virtue of clear and express statutory language) which conserve what are understood to be constitutional principles against casual erosion.

Conventions of the constitution

In order to avoid tedious repetition, and in an attempt to do justice to the complexity of the topic, the role of conventions as a source of law will be considered in a separate section.[17] Here it is enough to say that if conventions are regarded as a source of law, then it is inappropriate to affirm that the law of the British constitution is part of the ordinary law of the land; for it has at least one source which is extraordinary inasmuch as it begets rules unaccompanied by judicial sanctions or relief.

The law and custom of Parliament

This comprises the rules relating to the functions, procedures, privileges and immunities of each House of Parliament. To a small extent it is statutory, and to a still smaller extent judge-made. For the rest, it is either to be found in resolutions of each House (recorded in the official Journals, in *Hansard*, and on some important matters in standing orders) or not to be found in any authoritative source because it rests on informal understandings or practices. For example, the functions of the Leaders of the two Houses and the party whips, the duty of impartiality cast on the Speaker of the House of Commons and the convention that the chairman of the Public Accounts Committee shall be a member of the Opposition, are not formally recorded, though they

---

15 See, for example, *Nairn* v. *University of St Andrews* [1909] AC 147 (votes for women could be conferred only by a direct grant); *Re Parliamentary Privilege Act 1770* (1958) AC 331 (important provision of Bill of Rights 1689 not impliedly repealed by generally worded subsequent Act).

16 See, for example, *Att.-Gen.* v. *Wilts United Dairies Ltd* (1921) 37 TLR 884, though see now pp. 283–4. The courts also adopt presumptions against so construing legislation as to oust the supervisory jurisdiction of the superior courts to determine the rights and liabilities of individuals, or to authorize deprivation of private property without compensation; see generally D. L. Keir and F. H. Lawson, *Cases in Constitutional Law* (6th edn, 1979), pp. 15–22. The force of the last-mentioned presumption has been weakened: *Westminster Bank Ltd* v. *Beverley BC* [1971] AC 508.

17 See pp. 27–46.

can be elicited from a reading of parliamentary debates. In any event, the internal proceedings of the two Houses are not cognizable by the courts. For this reason, large tracts of the law relating to parliamentary privilege have never been subject to judicial appraisal. And so a great deal of the law and custom of Parliament lies outside the scope of the *ordinary* law of the land.

Community law

With the accession of the United Kingdom to membership of the European Community on 1 January 1973, Community law became a source of the constitutional law of Britain. Although the European Community has become the European Union, it remains correct to refer to European Community law.

Community law[18] is to be found in the Community treaties;[19] in regulations, directives and decisions of European Union organs (the Council of Ministers, a political body composed of Foreign Ministers; or the European Commission, a supranational body composed of top European Union officials); and in rulings and decisions of the Court of Justice of the European Communities (the European Court of Justice). It is applied *mainly* by courts of the Member States, but authoritative rulings are given by the European Court. According to that Court, Community law is distinct from national law but exists alongside it; and where Community law is in conflict with national law, Community law prevails. By section 3 of the European Communities Act 1972, the United Kingdom accepted the binding authority of the rulings and principles laid down by the European Court. The Court has stated quite clearly several times that no Parliament of a member State can legislate inconsistently with Community law, and that proposition has been unambiguously applied by United Kingdom courts. Hence our acceptance of Community law has affected the doctrine of parliamentary sovereignty. This matter will be considered more fully in chapter 4. But the importation of Community law brings with it a constitutional innovation of the highest importance.

At various points in the book we shall note the actual or likely impact of Community law on the law of this country. In fact the content of

18 For a good and concise outline, see PSRF Mathijsen, *A Guide to European Community Law* (5th edn, 1990). See below, ch. 5.
19 A shorthand expression covering the three original treaties establishing the three Communities (ECSC, EEC and EURATOM), the instruments by which the United Kingdom acceded to the Communities, and various other Community agreements. See the European Communities Act 1972, s. 1.

Community law has up to now mainly concerned agriculture, free trade, fair competition, transport regulations, social security and so on. But on certain matters – for example, immigration and aspects of public finance – it bears directly on specific areas of constitutional law.

One very important point needs to be made at this stage. Some rules of Community law are 'directly applicable' in the sense that they confer rights or impose duties on individuals, rights and duties which are enforceable in national courts without being re-enacted by the governmental organs of Member States. These rules are, in the main, *regulations* made by the Council of Ministers or the Commission. Section 2(1) and part of section 2(4) of the European Communities Act give effect to the concept of direct applicability. The relevant Community rules are applied by the courts of this country 'without further enactment', as if they were Acts of Parliament. This was a major constitutional innovation. These regulations are made in Brussels in consequence of decisions taken in Brussels. And they are *primary* rather than delegated legislation.

Community law will be considered further in chapter 5.

Authoritative works

Literature on the constitution has only persuasive authority. Sometimes unusual and abstruse questions of constitutional law arise before a court – for instance, peerage law,[20] or aspects of the royal prerogative,[21] or the law of treason,[22] or the definition of an act of State,[23] or the jurisdiction of the English courts in British protectorates[24] – and reference may then be had to the views of writers of repute for the purposes of guidance. When a particularly awkward question relating to the scope of parliamentary privilege was referred to the Judicial Committee of the Privy Council for an advisory opinion, the opinions of constitutional historians in the eighteenth and nineteenth centuries were copiously cited in order to explain the mischief which an obscure and ambiguous Act of 1770 was designed to cure.[25] In controversies about the existence and scope of individual constitutional conventions – controversies which usually take place outside

20 *Re Parliamentary Election for Bristol South-East* [1964] 2 QB 257.
21 For example, *Burmah Oil Co.* v. *Lord Advocate* [1965] AC 75; *Council of Civil Service Unions* v. *Minister for the Civil Service* [1985] AC 374.
22 *Joyce* v. *DPP* [1946] AC 347.
23 *Nissan* v. *Att.-Gen.* [1970] AC 179.
24 *Ex p. Mwenya* [1960] 1 QB 241.
25 *Re Parliamentary Privilege Act 1770* [1958] AC 331.

the courts of law – the views of writers such as Jennings, Anson, Dicey, Maitland, Keith, E. C. S. Wade, Hood Phillips, Amery, Mackintosh and others are frequently prayed in aid. On issues of parliamentary privilege, Erskine May[26] is regarded as an exceptionally persuasive authority. It is fair to say that in the diffuse field of constitutional law the opinions of authorities are resorted to more often than in other branches of English law. They are a useful subsidiary source of constitutional law in the broad sense of the term. In administrative law cases the opinions of modern writers – especially those of the late Stanley de Smith – have come to be quoted in argument and are occasionally cited in judgments. In cases involving points of Community law, recourse is occasionally made to the opinions of specialist writers.

CONVENTIONS OF THE CONSTITUTION[27]

There is no rule of statute or common law to the effect that there must be a Prime Minister and a Cabinet, though legislation providing for the payment of ministerial salaries rests on the assumption that these institutions do exist. But clearly the Prime Minister and the Cabinet are cardinal features of the British constitution. They are creatures of convention, not of strict law.

Again, as has been noted, the Queen has enormously wide powers, prerogative and statutory, but she is obliged by convention to exercise these powers on and in accordance with ministerial advice, save in a few very special situations. This is the most important convention of the British constitution. The main exceptions to the general rule will be considered in chapter 6.

There are many other major conventions of the constitution, dealing with relations between the Executive and the Legislature (for example, the rules about ministerial responsibility to Parliament), relations between the two Houses of Parliament (for example, the rule that money bills have to be introduced into the House of Commons), the working of each House (for example, the rule that the Speaker of the House of Commons shall behave impartially), the civil service and the Judiciary.

It is obvious that *some* constitutional conventions are far more important than most of the statutory and common-law rules connected with the British system of government. The convention that the Queen must assent to bills duly passed is overwhelmingly more important than her strictly

---

26 Sir Thomas Erskine May, *Parliamentary Practice* (21st edn, 1989).
27 See generally Dicey, op. cit., chs. 14 and 15; Sir Ivor Jennings, *The Law and the Constitution* (5th edn, 1959), ch. 3; Geoffrey Marshall, *Constitutional Conventions* (1984).

legal prerogative power to withhold her assent. Since the rules of strict law, in this context and many others, give a grotesquely misleading picture of the rules actually observed, and observed on the assumption that they are binding, constitutional conventions ought to be treated as part of constitutional law.

At once we are in terminological difficulties. In one aspect conventions are law; in other aspects they are not. Dicey was quite clear that they were not ' "laws" in the true sense of that word, for if any or all of them were broken no court would take notice of their violation'.[28] In other passages he observed that laws were 'rules enforced or recognized by the courts', whereas conventions were 'a body not of laws, but of constitutional or political ethics', the 'constitutional morality of the day', 'not enforced or recognized by the courts'.[29]

Dicey's distinctions between strict law[30] and constitutional convention were too clear-cut and have been severely criticized,[31] but they have substance.[32] For instance, if the Queen were to refuse her assent to a bill of which she disapproved, no court would deem the bill to be an authentic Act of Parliament. If a Government, defeated on a vote of confidence in the House of Commons, neither resigned nor advised a dissolution of Parliament, no court would take cognizance of this gross breach of convention by granting a declaration that any of the Ministers was not legally entitled to exercise his office. No form of judicial redress is obtainable purely for a breach of convention. And in the eyes of the courts, Parliament is competent to legislate in unequivocal disregard of conventional limitations on the exercise of its powers.[33]

Distinctions of substance between constitutional conventions and rules of strict law are well illustrated by the evolution of Dominion status within the Commonwealth. By 1926 most of the self-governing Dominions were in effect independent States, equal in status, for most purposes, to the United Kingdom. They had achieved this status not by legislation but by the development of conventions, many of which were formally recorded

28 Dicey, op. cit., p. 27.
29 ibid., pp. 417, 422. See also Hood Phillips (1966) 29 Mod. L. Rev. 137.
30 The term aptly employed by Sir Kenneth Wheare in *The Statute of Westminster and Dominion Status* (5th edn, 1953), ch. 1.
31 Notably by Sir Ivor Jennings, op. cit., ch. 3. See also J. D. B. Mitchell, *Constitutional Law* (2nd edn, 1968), pp. 26–39.
32 For a subtle defence of the basis of the distinction, see Hood Phillips (1964) 8 *Journal of the Society of Public Teachers of Law* (NS) 60. For an attempt to say the last word, see Munro (1975) 91 *LQR* 218.
33 *Madzimbamuto* v. *Lardner-Burke* [1969] 1 AC 645 at 722–3 (legislation dealing with internal affairs of Southern Rhodesia).

(or created) in resolutions of Imperial Conferences. There remained a few elements of formal inequality. Some of those (for example, the procedure for appointing a Governor-General) could be and were removed by the formulation of new constitutional conventions. Others could not be removed by convention. In strict law the Dominions were still colonies. They were prohibited by section 2 of the Colonial Laws Validity Act 1865 from legislating repugnantly to United Kingdom enactments extending to them as part of their own law. Among these enactments were the Judicial Committee Acts 1833 and 1844, under which the prerogative power of the Crown to grant special leave to appeal from colonial courts to the Privy Council was placed on a statutory footing. This power to give leave to appeal and to hear appeals was not expunged by convention; and in 1926 the Judicial Committee of the Privy Council held[34] that the Canadian Parliament was incompetent to abolish the appeal by special leave from Canadian courts in criminal matters. The necessary legal authority could be conferred only by United Kingdom legislation. Some of the Dominions pressed for the enactment of enabling legislation, and Parliament passed the Statute of Westminster 1931. This excluded the Dominions from the definition of 'colony', abolished the repugnancy rule and empowered Dominion Parliaments to legislate inconsistently with United Kingdom legislation extending to their countries.[35] Thereafter the Canadian Parliament was able to pass legislation abolishing criminal appeals to the Privy Council.[36]

The distinction blurred

These examples suggest that the distinction between law and convention is reasonably clear. But in a number of contexts the distinction is blurred. In particular, Dicey was exaggerating when he said that conventions were 'not recognized' by the courts. The courts do sometimes take cognizance of conventions;[37] sometimes they use them as aids to interpretation. Thus,

34 *Nadan* v. *R.* [1926] AC 482.
35 ss. 1, 2, 11; see generally, Wheare, op. cit., and R. McG. Dawson, *The Development of Dominion Status 1900–1936* (1937).
36 British Coal Corporation v. *R.* [1935] AC 500. See also *Att.-Gen. for Ontario* v. *Att.-Gen. for Canada* [1947] AC 127 (abolition of appeals in civil matters; see below).
37 In *Att.-Gen.* v. *Jonathan Cape Ltd* [1976] QB 752 Lord Widgery LCJ referred extensively to the convention of collective ministerial responsibility (on which see below, p. 195); in *Air Canada* v. *Secretary of State for Trade* [1983] AC 394 reference was made to the convention that Ministers do not see certain papers of a previous Administration of a different political party without the agreement of its Prime Minister (on which see below, p. 183).

English courts have occasionally supported their refusal to review the grounds on which executive discretionary powers have been exercised by pointing out that a Minister is responsible to Parliament for the exercise of the power.[38] In one Privy Council appeal, Canada's accession to independence, and the convention of equality of status recited in the preamble to the Statute of Westminster, were primary reasons for so interpreting an ambiguous section of the Canadian constitution as to empower the Federal Parliament to abolish appeals to the Privy Council from all Canadian courts in civil cases.[39] In another appeal it was contended that appeals from Ceylon courts had been impliedly abrogated by the grant of independence, because the report of the Judicial Committee on such an appeal was issued in the form of an Order in Council affecting the law of Ceylon. The Judicial Committee held[40] that although a *legislative* Order in Council purporting to alter the law of Ceylon would have been invalidated by the Ceylon Independence Act 1947, a *judicial* Order in Council was, by convention, no more than the formal promulgation of a determination by a court of law which had not yet been deprived of jurisdiction by the Parliament of Ceylon. Again, the High Court of Australia has used constitutional conventions as an aid to statutory interpretation, holding that United Kingdom amendments to copyright legislation in 1928 and 1956 did not alter Australian law in the absence of any indication that they purported to extend to Australia with Australian concurrence; the original legislation passed by the United Kingdom Parliament in 1911 had undoubtedly extended to Australia as part of its law, but conventional limitations on the territorial competence of the United Kingdom Parliament and Government had evolved since that time.[41]

A striking illustration of a constitutional convention having as much effect in practice as strict law comes from Canada. The Canadian Govern-

---

38 See, for example, *Liversidge* v. *Anderson* [1942] AC 206 (where the Home Secretary was expressly required by regulations to make reports to Parliament); *Carltona Ltd* v. *Commissioners of Works* [1943] 2 All ER 560; *Robinson* v. *Minister of Town and Country Planning* [1947] KB 702.

39 *Att.-Gen. for Ontario* v. *Att.-Gen. for Canada* [1947] AC 127.

40 *Ibralebbe* v. *R.* [1964] AC 900. Appeals from Sri Lanka (Ceylon) were terminated in 1972.

41 *Copyright Owners Reproduction Society Ltd* v. *EMI (Australia) Pty Ltd* (1958) 100 CLR 597; see Gray (1960) 23 *Mod L. Rev.* 647; Bennion (1961) 24 *Mod. L. Rev.* 355. The amendment made in 1956, after Australia had adopted the Statute of Westminster, was held moreover to be inoperative in Australia because it was not *expressed* to have been made at the request and with the consent of the Commonwealth of Australia, as was required by section 4 of the Statute. See further pp. 80–81. The power of the United Kingdom Parliament to legislate for Australia was finally ended at Australia's request by the Australia Act 1986, s. 1.

ment sought patriation of the constitution in the early 1980s, but agreement on the new settlement could not be reached with the provinces. When the Government decided to proceed without it some of the provinces challenged the legality of the Government's actions in the courts. The Supreme Court held that, although no rule of law existed which established provincial consent as a prerequisite to any constitutional amendment, there was a convention that such consent would be obtained.[42] The Government thereupon delayed its plans and held further negotiations in which nine of the ten provinces agreed to revised Federal proposals which formed the basis of Canada's 1983 constitution.[43]

These examples[44] show how constitutional conventions may materially influence judicial decisions. In this sense they may be compared with recitals in the preamble to an Act of Parliament. The terms of preambles are not directly enforceable in court, but the facts and purposes (and occasionally conventions)[45] there set out may be used as aids to the interpretation of ambiguous provisions in the main body of the Act. Alternatively conventions may be compared with the Directive Principles of State Policy, which are an integral part of the constitution of India but are expressed not to be 'enforceable by any court';[46] they are nevertheless used as guides to constitutional interpretation.

Some conventions, then, may be indirectly justiciable. And some rules of strict law may be non-justiciable. The latter point can be illustrated in constitutional and administrative law.

1 General duties to provide efficient services were cast by statute on public corporations administering nationalized industries. These duties were often formulated in terms so broad that no person would be able to obtain a judicial pronouncement that the corporation had failed to carry out its duty.[47] Sometimes the nationalization Act stated explicitly that these general duties were not enforceable in any court of law.

---

42 *Reference re Amendment of the Constitution of Canada* (1982) 125 DLR (3d) 1.
43 See Canada Act 1982, and Laskin [1982] *Public Law* 549; Sharpe [1987] *Public Law* 48.
44 See further, *Ryder* v. *Foley* (1906) 4 CLR 422; *Commercial Cable Co.* v. *Government of Newfoundland* [1916] 2 AC 610.
45 Notably in the preamble to the Statute of Westminster 1931, reciting basic conventions about equality of status in the Commonwealth. A preamble is part of an Act and can be debated and amended during the passage of the bill. Each clause will begin 'Whereas . . .'
46 Constitution, art. 37.
47 cf. *Watt* v. *Kesteven C. C.* [1955] 1 QB 408 (duty of local education authorities to have regard to the general principle that as far as possible children are to be educated in accordance with parental wishes (Education Act 1944, s. 76) unenforceable by aggrieved parents in legal proceedings).

2 Under the Parliament Act 1911, a money bill passed by the Commons can be presented for the royal assent after one month although it has not been passed by the Lords. The Act defines a money bill and provides that a certificate given by the Speaker of the House of Commons that the bill is a money bill shall not be questioned in any court. If the Speaker's certificate were based on an erroneous interpretation of the statutory definition, no way of raising the issue before a court would be feasible, unless possibly the error was so flagrant as to raise doubts as to the Speaker's good faith.

Examples could be multiplied. It is enough to say that non-compliance with statutory norms is not necessarily coupled with the possibility of judicial sanctions, even the sanction of nullity.

3 There is the curious case of section 1 of the Northern Ireland Constitution Act 1973: '. . . it is hereby affirmed that in no event will Northern Ireland . . . cease to be part of . . . the United Kingdom without the consent of the majority of the people of Northern Ireland voting in a poll held for the purposes of this section . . .' This reads like a particularly solemn affirmation of a constitutional convention,[48] binding on the United Kingdom Parliament and Government but placed in the main body of an Act instead of in the preamble. Here the distinction between strict law and convention not only lacks substance but is tenuous in the matter of form.

4 Written constitutions in other countries often embody non-justiciable rules. Some are non-justiciable because the constitution says so. To this category belong those provisions in a number of Commonwealth constitutions requiring the Governor-General to act on ministerial advice. In the constitution of Ceylon, British conventions concerning the exercise of discretionary functions by the Queen's representative were incorporated by general reference; and it was expressly stated that the question whether these conventions had been observed was not to be inquired into by any court.[49] Was this constitutional provision not

---

48 See also Cmnd 534 (NI 1969), referring to the 'clear pledges made by successive United Kingdom Governments that Northern Ireland should not cease to be a part of the United Kingdom without the consent of the people of Northern Ireland' (§56(1)). Section 1 of the 1973 Act replaced section 1 (2) of the Ireland Act 1949 which had referred to 'the Parliament of Northern Ireland'; that Parliament was abolished by section 31 of the 1973 Act and the formula cited in the text was enacted. For an argument that section 1 (2) of the 1949 Act was in law a redefinition of the meaning of the United Kingdom Parliament, see Harry Calvert, *Constitutional Law in Northern Ireland* (1968), pp. 23–33.

49 Jennings, op. cit., pp. 120–21; see also his *Constitution of Ceylon* (3rd edn, 1949). Sir Ivor Jennings was the main architect of the Ceylon constitution. See generally S. de Smith, *The New Commonwealth and its Constitutions* (1964), ch. 3, on methods of incorporating 'conventional' rules into Commonwealth constitutions.

'law'? Are the Directive Principles of State Policy in the Indian constitution (which are only indirectly justiciable) and the corresponding
statements of principle in the constitutions of the Republics of Ireland
and Malta not part of the law of constitution? And what is one to make
of those constitutional provisions, common enough in non-
Commonwealth countries (for example, France), which impose limitations on legislative competence but cannot be the subject of adjudication
because judicial review of the constitutionality of legislation is not an
acceptable doctrine?

Why not codify conventions?

It may be argued that the illustrations cited above are marginal or anomalous
cases which do not significantly weaken the general proposition that conventions are not directly enforceable in courts whereas obedience to rules
of strict law is directly enforceable through courts. This is broadly correct.
But why is a distinction between strict law and convention maintained
at all in the United Kingdom? Why not codify conventions in a strictly
legal form? After all, conventions and rules of strict law alike are binding
rules.

The answers to these questions are not simple. The reasons for retaining
the distinction are various. In the first place, there is the constitutional role
of the monarch. Most of the main conventions of the constitution were
originally evolved in order to ensure that the monarch exercised his
prerogative powers on the advice of Ministers responsible to Parliament.
This end could be and was achieved by a gradual process in which royal
discretion was quietly eroded. Abrupt changes in the law should, it was
felt, be avoided unless the monarch behaved like James II. As long as the
monarch played, or thought he was entitled to play, a significant role in
the making of policy decisions, it might have been politically imprudent
to urge that his dwindling personal influence should be attenuated by
statutory restrictions, for example by requiring him to act on the advice of
the Privy Council or the incipient Cabinet or a named Minister. No
obvious harm was done by leaving the monarch with wide prerogative
powers exercisable in strict law in his personal discretion; and unnecessary
friction could have been caused by trying to take them away, particularly
as long as a large section of the general public thought of the monarch as
the executive head of Government. A prerogative power might be converted into a statutory power or duty exercisable under prescribed conditions, but these conditions would not include an obligation to act on

ministerial advice. *New* statutory powers and duties could be vested in the monarch, the Crown in Council or a named Minister without breaking away too blatantly from historical tradition. And the tradition was not valueless. To involve the monarch personally in the making of important decisions on matters of State lent greater dignity to the business of government; and there were exceptional situations, not easily definable, where the monarch's personal views ought to be taken into account, or even to prevail in a time of constitutional crisis. Even today, time-honoured formal tradition is not easily eradicated unless there are obvious reasons why it should be. If there is urgent pressure for clarification or change, conventions may be explicitly set down as conventions in their existing or a modified form, or rules of strict law may replace them.

Secondly, it would be difficult or even harmful to define a number of important conventions. For example, some of the conventions about ministerial responsibility or the working of the Cabinet system are blurred. Codification would purchase certainty at the expense of flexibility; informal modifications to keep the constitution in touch with contemporary political thinking or needs would be inhibited.[50] Evolution by conventions is still needed in countries with written constitutions. In some contexts the rules ought *not* to be crystal clear. Clarification would tend to stultify one purpose of conventions – keeping the constitution up to date. Again a situation may arise in which a convention ought, in the public interest to be waived; waiver would be more difficult if the convention were set down in unambiguous language. These are, of course, admissions that many conventions are significantly different from typical rules of law.

Thirdly, as long as a conventional rule is regularly observed, there is no apparent reason for codifying it.[51] Lay peers regularly comply with their conventional obligation not to present themselves to sit with the Law Lords to hear an appeal in the House of Lords; the Speaker of the House of Commons regularly behaves impartially.[52] If these conventional rules were

50 This was one of the reasons why the Radcliffe Committee on Ministerial Memoirs (Cmnd 6386 (1976)) rejected the proposition that the rules concerning the publication of former Ministers' autobiographies or diaries should be put into statutory form. Instead it recommended that the rules should be drawn to Ministers' attention, and amended as needs be, by the Prime Minister. See further below, pp. 199–201.
51 One could equally say that there is no sound reason for not codifying it. The reasons, sound or unsound, are characteristic inertia masquerading as veneration for unwritten constitutional tradition, and the absence of political pressure for change.
52 There are customary rules of the House of Commons directing the manner in which the Speaker is to use his or her casting vote in the event of a tie.

to be broken, they could simply be restated in formal terms or superseded by statutory rules. In 1909 the House of Lords disregarded its somewhat vague conventional duty to defer in the last resort to the will of the Commons; the sequel was the Parliament Act 1911, redefining relationships between the two Houses on a statutory basis.

Nevertheless, it is highly unsatisfactory that the content, and indeed the very existence, of some of the most important conventions should be indeterminate. There is no consensus of opinion on the *conventional* powers of the Queen to remove a Prime Minister, to require a dissolution of Parliament or to refuse a request for dissolution. Clarification may be brought about by the march of events in a time of political turbulence; but the Queen may then be criticized for having acted 'unconstitutionally' or for having failed to discharge her constitutional duty to act; she will be unable to answer back, and those who will speak for her may have to rely on dubious precedents, debatable opinions of writers, and principles deduced from a concept of the constitutional system with which some are bound to disagree. An authoritative statement, prepared by an expert body, of the conventions regulating the constitutional functions of the monarch might therefore be useful, difficult though it would be to formulate.[53] But if such conventions were to be codified, they ought not to be made directly justiciable,[54] even if they were written into an Act of Parliament or a new British constitution. Experience in some Commonwealth countries has shown that whilst the embodiment of such rules in the texts of constitutions makes for greater certainty, so that people have a clearer idea of what may, must or cannot be done, the burden thrust upon the courts when they are called upon to determine whether prescribed rules have been complied with in a politically sensitive situation is liable to be excessive. Whatever the outcome, the prestige of the Judiciary will probably suffer. If the rules of the game are to be set down, they do not require the courts to decide whether, for example, a Prime Minister has been validly dismissed. This is pre-eminently a question about the reins of power. If the constitutionality of such an act is disputed, the controversy is unlikely to be resolved by

---

53 The Australian Constitutional Convention, which was made up of delegates from the Commonwealth and State Parliaments, formally declared 34 conventions in 1983. Not surprisingly it could not agree on the Governor-General's power to dismiss Ministers (on which see below, p. 122). See C. Sampford and D. Wood [1987] *Public Law* 231.

54 For discussion of this matter, see H. V. Evatt, *The King and his Dominion Governors* (2nd edn, 1967), chs. 29–33; Geoffrey Marshall and G. C. Moodie, *Some Problems of the Constitution* (5th edn, 1971), pp. 34–6; de Smith, op. cit., pp. 86–7; Keith (1967) 16 *ICLQ* 542.

the pronouncement of a court.[55] However, clarification of the rules by codification may reduce the area of potential conflict.

One point must be made to avoid misunderstandings. Some rules of political behaviour, or standards of conduct in public affairs, have in fact been 'codified', or promulgated in an authoritative form. For instance, the principles governing the private financial interests that a Minister of the Crown can properly retain after appointment can be found in a statement by Sir Winston Churchill published in 1952.[56] These principles embody constitutional conventions because they state rules that ought to be followed by Ministers; and enforced resignation would be the sanction for breaking them. Each incoming Prime Minister gives his new team written guidelines, entitled *Questions of Procedure for Ministers*: this was published for the first time in 1992; Tony Blair republished it in 1997 as the *Ministerial Code*. Some other assertions about what is right and proper in public affairs do not enjoy the same degree of importance; or the standards of conduct they lay down may be more elastic; or their original or continuing authority may be disputed; or the consequence of deviating from them may be no more than adverse criticism from political opponents. It may, therefore, be doubtful whether such statements are to be regarded as embodying conventions (or rules) at all. Nearly all discussions about the existence and scope of the *lesser* constitutional conventions include arguments of dubious authenticity.

Interrelationship between law and convention

Law and convention are closely interlocked. To quote Jennings, constitutional conventions 'provide the flesh which clothes the dry bones of the law; they make the legal constitution work; they keep in touch with the growth of ideas'.[57] Conventions presuppose the existence of a framework of strict law; they do not exist in a legal vacuum. For example, conventional

---

55 Dismissals were held valid in *Adegbenro* v. *Akintola* [1963] AC 614 (Western Nigeria) and invalid in *Ningkan's* case [1966] 2 *Malayan LJ* 187 (Sarawak). See, on the latter case, Thio (1966) 8 *Malaya L. Rev.* 283; Keith (1967) 16 *ICLQ* 542. The decision in the former case was reversed locally by a constitutional amendment having retroactive effect, followed by the abolition of appeals from Nigerian courts to the Judicial Committee. The decision in the latter case was accepted, but a state of emergency was proclaimed, the constitution amended (validity upheld in *Ningkan* v. *Government of Malaysia* [1970] AC 379) and the Chief Minister dismissed.

56 496 HC Deb. 701–3 (25 February 1952). See also p. 190 and *Ministerial Code* (Cabinet Office, 1997), paras. 111–29.

57 Jennings, *The Law and the Constitution* (5th edn, 1959), pp. 81–2.

rules about the functions of the Cabinet Office presuppose the existence of a Cabinet, which presupposes the existence of a Privy Council and Ministers appointed by the Crown. In turn, some rules of strict law presuppose conventions. Statutes dealing with ministerial salaries presuppose the existence of a Prime Minister, a Cabinet, Leaders of the Opposition and party whips, though they do not define their functions.[58] And when Parliament gives Her Majesty powers of appointment to offices of State and other statutory discretions, it acts on the tacit assumption that she will use her powers only on ministerial advice.

Again, as we have seen, the line between strict law and convention is sometimes uncertain. Legal duties are not always justiciable, and conventions may be justiciable in so far as the courts use them as aids to construction.

None of these comments is likely to be regarded as controversial. If, however, one asks the question: Are rules of strict law and constitutional conventions obeyed for similar reasons? problems at once arise.

1 Dicey contended that 'the sanction which constrains the boldest political adventurer' to obey a convention he might feel inclined to break was his fear that breach would almost immediately bring him into conflict with the courts and the law of the land.[59] Thus, if the convention that Parliament be summoned each year, or that a Government which has lost a vote of confidence in the House of Commons must go to the country or resign, were to be broken, legal authority for collecting the most productive taxes, for spending money and for maintaining and disciplining a standing army would soon expire, for such authority is granted by Parliament only for a year at a time. Since the Government would have to perform acts devoid of legal authority, Ministers and officials would soon find themselves in the dock or mulcted in damages. Obedience to conventions was therefore buttressed by the sanctions of strict law.

The weaknesses of Dicey's argument are familiar. Some political adventurers may indeed have been deterred from breaking certain conventions for fear of indirectly incurring legal sanctions; but who knows? The boldest adventurer will (as Dicey himself conceded) carry out a *coup d'état* and defy the law. The not-so-bold is far more likely to be deterred by fear of the *political* consequences – justified charges of unconstitutional

---

58 See especially the Parliamentary and other Pensions Act 1972; Ministerial and other Salaries Act 1975; Parliamentary and other Pensions and Salaries Act 1976; Parliamentary and other Pensions Act 1987.
59 Dicey, op. cit., pp. 445–6.

conduct, public ridicule or odium, loss of office or even the precipitation of revolution. Moreover, many conventions are not buttressed by the threat of legal sanctions. If the Queen were to refuse her assent to a bill because she disapproved of it, this could not entail breach of any legal rule; but it might lead to *changes* in the law – the abolition of the power to refuse assent, and imposition of statutory duties to exercise other royal discretionary powers on ministerial advice; or enforced abdication, or abolition of the monarchy. If the majority of the House of Commons voted to expel the Opposition, or if a lay peer were to insist on sitting with the Law Lords, or if the Speaker were to make a party political speech in the Commons, conventions would be broken and the consequences might be very unpleasant for those concerned; but obedience to the existing conventions is not explicable in terms of legal sanctions.

2 Conventions are normally observed for a variety of mundane reasons – force of habit, inertia, desire to 'conform', belief that it is 'right' to obey them and wrong to disobey them because they are reasonable rules or because they are part of a reasonable structure of rules which ought to be preserved and upheld. In so far as they are observed by persons involved in politics who feel inclined to break them, obedience can usually be attributed to fear of disrepute and its political implications. Now, most of us obey the criminal law for much the same set of reasons.[60] If, for example, one finds a purse containing a large sum of money in the street, one is likely to resist any temptation to appropriate and keep it because one feels one *ought* not to behave in such a way. If one's decision to hand it in to the police station is materially influenced by fear of being prosecuted and convicted for theft, the probability is that one will be more concerned with the *social* disgrace involved in a publicized conviction than with the prospect of being fined or sent to prison. The sense of obligation and the fear of disagreeable consequences which tend to induce people to comply with conventions are broadly similar to the corresponding feelings which conduce to observance of the criminal law. There are, of course, many people who will not feel any sense of obligation to return the purse, who will be deterred from dishonesty only by the prospect of detection, and who will fear imprisonment but not loss of social esteem. And some politicians will cheerfully break a hallowed convention (for example, about ministerial responsibility to Parliament) if they think they can carry if off without adverse personal repercussions. Again, some of us will break certain rules of strict

60 cf. Jennings, op. cit., Appendix 4.

law, for example, speed limits on a clear road in a built-up area, without compunction provided that a police patrol car is not in the vicinity, because we do not feel a sense of obligation to obey the rule to the letter. Awareness that a patrol car is close behind us will slow us down, not because we are overcome by a sense of moral obligation but because we do not want to be stopped and perhaps have to pay a fine.

This is not a jurisprudential essay and these points will not be elaborated. It is enough to repeat that the sense of legal obligation is often much the same as the sense of obligation to obey constitutional conventions. One difference between strict law and conventions is that legal obligations are on the whole more complex, technical and exactly defined; another is that where there are direct sanctions for breach, strictly legal sanctions tend to be more specific and can be imposed by authoritative tribunals endowed with powers of interpretation. These differences are not trivial. But are they really fundamental?

Identification of constitutional conventions

If one can borrow from the vocabulary of H. L. A. Hart, constitutional conventions, in so far as they impose duties,[61] are primary rules of obligation unaccompanied by an adequate apparatus of secondary rules of recognition, interpretation (or adjudication) and change.[62] And the tests for the ascertainment of conventions are neither universally agreed nor, when agreed, easily applied in a large number of marginal cases. Some conventions are clear-cut; some are flexible; some are so elusive that one is left wondering whether in fact the 'convention' is an ethereal will-o'-the-wisp. It is often particularly hard to say whether a political practice has crystallized into a constitutional convention and, if so, what is its scope.[63]

1 Most of the conventions of the constitution are binding usages, understandings or practices.[64] They are forms of political behaviour regarded

---

61 Some confer powers – for example, the special powers of a Prime Minister.
62 *The Concept of Law* (1961), ch. 5. Hart does not himself characterize conventions in this manner. For him, a system of 'primary rules' unaccompanied by the 'secondary rules' referred to above is exemplified (p. 99) by the customary law of some simple (or primitive) societies.
63 See Sir Kenneth Wheare, *Modern Constitutions* (2nd edn, 1966), ch. 8; cf. Marshall and Moodie, op. cit., pp. 26–31.
64 See, for example, the discussion of the conventions on ministerial responsibility (pp. 190–202).

as obligatory. When or how does a non-binding *usage* become binding? General acceptance by everybody whom the usage affects (the Queen, Ministers, Members of Parliament, civil servants or judges) and by authorities on the constitution that there is an *obligation* to continue to behave in that way is, of course, the most satisfactory answer. Such an answer is not always forthcoming. The difficulty can be illustrated by reference to two major conventions. The first is that the Queen is obliged to assent to a bill of which she personally disapproves, unless presumably she is advised by the Cabinet to withhold her assent. The last time the royal assent was refused was in 1708: Queen Anne was not prepared to agree to the creation of a Scottish Militia. But a century later it was still thought imprudent to support bills for the removal of the disabilities attaching to Roman Catholics, on account of George III's personal objections. In 1829 George IV grudgingly gave his assent to such a bill; this can be regarded as an unequivocal normative (or rule-constitutive) precedent, the balance of the constitution having shifted away from independent royal discretion; but in the years between, who can say when usage had hardened into convention? Secondly, it is a convention that the Prime Minister should be chosen from the House of Commons (or from among persons elected to the House if a change of Prime Minister becomes necessary as a result of a General Election). The last Prime Minister to sit in the Lords was Lord Salisbury in 1902. In 1911 the powers of the Lords in money matters were reduced to vanishing point and their right to reject other Commons' bills was confined to a suspensory veto. It was, therefore, arguable that thereafter the Prime Minister had to be chosen from the ranks of the Commons. The question did not arise till 1923, because the most suitable candidates were all members of the Commons. But in that year a vacancy arose because of Bonar Law's resignation on grounds of grave ill health; the most eligible candidate appeared to be Lord Curzon, but Stanley Baldwin was appointed by the King instead, ostensibly on the ground that since the Labour Party, which was by then the main Opposition party, was almost unrepresented in the Lords, the office ought to go to a commoner.[65] This appeared to be a normative precedent: the King had passed over Curzon because he thought he was *obliged* to do so, and there were good reasons for his choice. If the King had not thought himself obliged so to act – if, for example he was influenced in his choice of Baldwin by his awareness

---

65 See Sir Harold Nicolson, *King George V* (1952), pp. 375–9.

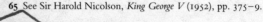

of Curzon's unpopularity among sections of the Conservative Party,[66] or if a memorandum of advice, heavily emphasizing the unsuitability of Curzon, was thought by the King to be an accurate statement of Bonar Law's views, although the memorandum was in fact composed by another and had put the case far more strongly than Bonar Law would ever have put it[67] – this could still have been cited as a persuasive precedent for the existence of such a convention, given the shift in the balance of the constitution since 1902. But there would have been more room for argument; for the establishment of a new convention would then have to be inferred mainly from propositions about what was necessary for the proper working of the constitution.[68]

2 What if there is substantial disagreement as to the existence or content of a convention? In 1940 both George VI and Neville Chamberlain would have preferred Lord Halifax to Winston Churchill as Chamberlain's successor. Here it is possible to assert that they were mistaken in thinking that such an appointment would have been constitutionally proper, even if Churchill had been compliant – and fortunately he was not. But if such a view could be seriously entertained on a point which by that time was clearly covered by convention, one must accept that divided counsel may be heard on a great many other, more controversial issues; and that personal inclination and political expediency may well be determining factors. Academic authorities on the constitution enjoy no immunity from partisan sentiment; in the Irish home rule crisis in 1913 both Dicey and Anson, active opponents of the Liberal Government, expressed manifestly unacceptable views on the conventional powers of the King to override his Ministers.[69] And even when an authority on the constitution is able to adopt a more detached attitude, the materials available to him about the precedents may be inadequate – political and royal biographies are the best sources but are not always timely or comprehensive – and opinions on what rules are necessary for the working of the contemporary constitution can reasonably differ. Differences of

---

66 As L. S. Amery indicated in his *Thoughts on the Constitution* (2nd edn, 1953), pp. 21–2. See also Kenneth Rose, *Superior Person* (1969).

67 See Robert Blake, *The Unknown Prime Minister* (1955), pp. 517–27; Thomas Jones, *Whitehall Diary* (1969), vol. 1, pp. 235–6. See further, on this difficult issue, Robert Rhodes James, *Memoirs of a Conservative* (1969), pp. 150–60; Keith Middlemas and John Barnes, *Baldwin* (1969), pp. 158–69. Probably the truth of the matter will never be known; there are discrepancies in the accounts revealed.

68 See further Marshall and Moodie, op. cit., pp. 30–34.

69 See Jennings, *Cabinet Government* (3rd edn, 1959), Appendix 3.

opinion among practising politicians as to the scope and very existence of the conventions they ought to observe are, of course, both frequent and unreasonable.

3 A convention can be created without any background of pre-existing usage. It can come into being (a) by express agreement, or (b) by a unilateral undertaking, or (c) within a limited field, by a decision imposed by the Prime Minister or adopted by the Cabinet for its own regulation. For example: (a) It was agreed at an Imperial Conference in 1930 that in future the Governor-General of a Dominion should be appointed by the Crown exclusively on the advice of the Dominion Government concerned and that the United Kingdom Government would not even have a formal part to play in such an appointment. (b) In 1949, when Eire left the Commonwealth and became the Republic of Ireland, the United Kingdom Government and Parliament undertook not to exclude Northern Ireland from the United Kingdom without the consent of the Northern Ireland Parliament. (c) Under Mrs Margaret Thatcher fewer decisions were taken by the full Cabinet and more by informal meetings of Ministers.[70] This development was designed to streamline decision-making by restricting the range of matters which individual Ministers could bring before the full Cabinet, but the main reason for it was to keep more decision-making in the Prime Minister's own hands. Ministers were obliged to accept the new procedures if they wished to remain in the Government.

4 Conventions may lose their binding force or change in content. So, of course, may rules of strict law. But conventions tend to change in different, and sometimes mysterious, ways.

A convention established by express agreement may be superseded or modified by agreement. Constitutional conventions share this characteristic with conventional rules of international law. For example, the convention relating to the appointment of Governors-General of Dominions on local advice was understood to extend, by necessary implication, to the removal of Governors-General, and to the appointment and removal of Governors-General of newly independent Commonwealth countries; but at the Mauritius Constitutional Conference in 1965 it was agreed that when Mauritius became independent, the Government of Mauritius would not advise Her Majesty to remove the Governor-General (in whom the constitution would repose a number of unusual and important personal discretionary powers)

70 See below, pp. 180–82.

except on grounds of medical incapacity upon the report of an independent tribunal appointed by the Chief Justice.[71] In this instance the general convention remained, subject to an exception.

Again, decisions by the Prime Minister or the Cabinet about the manner in which the Cabinet is to operate may be superseded by new decisions. But perhaps conventions of this sort ought to be put into a special category in that (like some of the sessional orders of the House of Commons) they are understood to be experimental, though undoubtedly binding until they are altered or discarded in the accepted manner. Judicial precedents are also binding till they are authoritatively reversed, overruled or disapproved. We do not regard them as non-binding merely because their authority may be ephemeral, unless it is clear that they are based on a wrong principle.

A convention may, alternatively, lose binding force because of a major change in circumstances. In 1961 the United Kingdom Government agreed that it would be contrary to convention for Parliament to legislate for Southern Rhodesia on any matter within the competence of the Southern Rhodesian Legislature without the consent of the Southern Rhodesian Government.[72] In 1965 the Government of Southern Rhodesia made a unilateral (and unlawful) declaration of the colony's independence. The United Kingdom Parliament immediately reasserted plenary legislative authority in relation to Southern Rhodesia.[73] This could not reasonably be construed as a breach of convention; the survival of the convention presupposed the continuance of a constitutional relationship which the Government of Southern Rhodesia had repudiated.[74] Problems of interpretation may arise where changes in circumstances are less dramatic. For example, on Harold Macmillan's resignation from the office of Prime Minister on grounds of ill health in 1963, the Queen invited Lord Home to form a Government as his successor. Home was taken to be the most acceptable candidate to the Conservative Party; but what of the convention that the Prime Minister could not be a member of the Lords?[75] A few months previously, Parliament had passed an Act under which it had

---

71 Cmnd 2797 (1965), p. 8. This convention was not written into the constitution. Mauritius became a republic in 1992. On Governors-General see Bogdanor and Marshall [1996] *Public Law* 205.

72 Cmnd 1399 (1961), p. 3.

73 Southern Rhodesia Act 1965; see also the Southern Rhodesia Constitution Order 1965 (SI 1965, No. 1952). For Northern Ireland, see pp. 50–57.

74 cf. de Smith, op. cit., p. 42.

75 See pp. 40–41.

become possible for Lord Home to disclaim his hereditary peerages.[76] He promptly disclaimed them, became Sir Alec Douglas-Home, and obtained a seat in the Commons at a by-election shortly afterwards. Presumably this change in the law was understood to have modified the convention to the extent that a peer could become Prime Minister if he agreed to disclaim his title and to try to obtain a seat in the Commons forthwith. If at the time of Home's appointment no such undertaking was offered or extracted, his appointment would probably have been unconstitutional.

Conventions have also disappeared or been varied because they have been disregarded with impunity and with general acquiescence. In this respect they differ from all rules of strict law in this country except local or mercantile customary rules. For example, before 1918 the decision when to advise the monarch to dissolve Parliament had been taken by the Cabinet as a whole. In November 1918 Lloyd George decided to advise a dissolution on his own initiative. Cabinet colleagues not merely acquiesced in this step but erroneously justified it by reference to non-existent precedents.[77] Thus arose the modern convention that the decision to advise a dissolution was for the Prime Minister alone, though it was still open to the Prime Minister to discuss the matter with his colleagues, privately or in a Cabinet meeting.[78] Doubtless all conventions are binding, but some are more binding than others. (The obvious retort is that the conventions about advice to dissolve Parliament are of major importance.) The disappearance of a convention in these circumstances might alternatively be rationalized on the ground that it had atrophied unobserved, or had dwindled to the status of a non-binding usage, compliance or deviation being equally permissible. Whether a convention retains its binding force, and if so, how much, is often demonstrable only by the empirical test of 'break it and see'. The outcome of such an experiment may still be equivocal; breach may be represented, or interpreted after the event, as a mere *ad hoc* waiver;[79] allegations of unconstitutional behaviour are frequently made in the cut and thrust of day-to-day politics and are as often shrugged off, sometimes

---

76 Peerage Act 1963, passed in consequence of the campaign waged by Lord Stansgate (Mr Tony Benn). All peers by inheritance could disclaim within a year after the Act became law; thereafter only *new* peers by inheritance (or peers who had inherited subject to infancy or another disability) could disclaim (s. 1). See further pp. 300.

77 Jennings, *Cabinet Government* (3rd edn, 1959), pp. 417–19.

78 Such discussions were certainly held by Mr Wilson, Mr Heath, Mr Callaghan and Mrs Thatcher, and probably by other post-war Prime Ministers. See Rodney Brazier, *Constitutional Practice* (1988), pp. 83–4.

79 See below, p. 198.

on the spurious ground that no binding convention on the matter had ever existed;[80] adverse pronouncements by constitutional experts and editorial writers are not endowed with the aura of prestige that surrounds the judgments of the superior courts.

We arrive at a position where there is a clear case for differentiating some conventions from most rules of strict law. When there are serious doubts as to the scope, even the very existence, of a conventional rule, and no adequate means of allaying those doubts, one cannot expect to find a widespread sense of obligation to obey that rule. Appeals to the voices of authority may evoke a Tower of Babel or the inscrutable muteness of the sphinx. Appeals to precedents may be less convincing than appeals to principle. Perhaps the most persuasive summing up is that 'the crucial questions must always be whether or not a particular class of action is likely to destroy respect for the established distribution of authority and whether or not it is likely to maintain respect for the constitutional system by changing (or sustaining) the distribution of authority'.[81] This distribution of authority implies the maintenance of limited monarchy, representative government, responsible government and efficient government; it implies also that constitutional rules must be compatible with the realities of practical politics. Given the vagueness of these criteria, it is not surprising that no attempt to list the conventions of the constitution would command universal assent. If half a dozen constitutional lawyers were separately to set down the conventions governing ministerial responsibility, it would be astonishing if six identical sets of answers were to be produced.

Replacement of conventions by statutory rules: a footnote

It has been noted that many conventions could be codified in a statutory or non-statutory form; and that Commonwealth constitutions often include provisions on matters which in this country are regulated solely by convention. It has also been observed that a loose convention about legislative relations between the Lords and the Commons was replaced in 1911 by a precise set of statutory rules. Writers occasionally misstate the effect of the Parliament Act by describing it as an enactment of constitutional conventions. On the contrary, it was a partial *supersession* of constitutional

80 cf. Dicey, op. cit., p. 441. This is the main single reason why identification of conventions is so difficult. People who ought to be *obeying* conventions deny their existence or unmake them by their disobedience.
81 Marshall and Moodie, op. cit., p. 32. See also Jennings, *Cabinet Government* (3rd edn, 1959), ch. 1.

conventions by rules of strict law. The other favourite example of the 'enactment' of constitutional conventions is the Statute of Westminster 1931. What this Act did was

1 to recite, in the *preamble*, certain conventions about Dominion status;
2 to relieve the Dominions of legal incapacities attributable to the fact that, before the Statute, they were colonies in strict law; and
3 to provide, in section 4 of the Statute, that no future Act of the United Kingdom Parliament was to extend, or be deemed to extend, to a Dominion as part of its law unless the request and consent of that Dominion were *expressly declared* in such an Act.

The exact legal effect of section 4 is still disputable.[82] But alone among the sections of the Statute of Westminster can it be compared to the enactment of a convention. The corresponding *convention* was set out in the preamble. It records 'the established constitutional position' that no law made by the United Kingdom Parliament 'shall extend to a Dominion as part of its law otherwise than at the request and with the consent of that Dominion'. Even section 4, therefore, does not precisely reproduce constitutional convention; it embodies the substance of the convention but adds something to it.

CONSTITUTIONAL REFORM

During the 1980s and into the 1990s there was much academic[83] and political[84] debate in the United Kingdom about the need for constitutional reform. A contributory spur to this debate was the long life of Mrs Thatcher's Government: some seemed to think (especially after the Conservative Government had won its fourth consecutive General Election victory in

82 See pp. 80–81. The Court of Appeal has discussed some limited questions about s. 4: in particular, it has held that provided there is an express declaration in any Act under consideration that the Dominion had so requested and consented, then the courts will not inquire into whether that request and consent had actually been given: *Manual* v. *Att.-Gen.* [1983] 1 Ch. 77 at 106.
83 See, e.g., R. Brazier, *Constitutional Reform* (2nd edn, 1998); K. Ewing and C. Gearty, *Freedom under Thatcher* (1991); J. Jowell and D. Oliver (eds.), *The Changing Constitution* (3rd edn, 1994); P. McAuslan and J. F. McEldowney (eds.), *Law, Legitimacy and the Constitution* (1985); D. Oliver, *Government in the United Kingdom* (1991).
84 Important proposals from the political parties are contained in *A New Agenda for Democracy* (Labour Party, 1993); *Here We Stand* (Liberal Democrat Federal White Paper No. 6, 1993).

1992) that parliamentary democracy was no longer working as effectively as it should, partly in that Ministers seemed to be able to obtain parliamentary approval for their policies effortlessly, without legal limits on their freedom of action. Had not the time come to reduce the unwritten British constitution to writing, and in the process to overhaul it? Only in that way could checks and balances be restored (or, according to taste, be established for the first time).[85] The Liberal Democrats, true to their radical traditions, continued to press for a new settlement, with the House of Commons elected by proportional representation, an elected (and powerful) Senate to replace the House of Lords, home rule all round for Scotland, Wales, Northern Ireland and England, and a Bill of Rights.[86] The Labour Party has embraced the most comprehensive package of constitutional reform to be set before the electorate by a major political party in modern times: it wants the incorporation into English law of the European Convention on Human Rights, the removal of hereditary peers from the House of Lords as the first stage towards an elected second chamber, devolution of power to Scotland, Wales and England, and a new system to appoint judges.[87]

The Labour Government which was elected in 1997 has begun to implement Labour's constitutional reform programme. Bills to establish a Scottish Parliament, a Welsh Assembly, and to incorporate the European Convention on Human Rights into domestic law, are currently before Parliament. Reform of the House of Lords is also promised. But the Conservative Party continues to take the view that the British constitution is basically sound, and has no reform programme to offer.

85 The Institute for Public Policy Research published the text of a draft constitution in 1991: see *The Constitution of the United Kingdom*. In the same year Tony Benn MP published a radical bill entitled the Commonwealth of Britain Bill.
86 See note 84, and *Changing Britain for Good* (Liberal Democrats, 1991).
87 See note 84.

CHAPTER 3

The United Kingdom

THE UNITED KINGDOM[1]

The United Kingdom means the United Kingdom of Great Britain and
Northern Ireland and its territorial waters. It is a unitary sovereign State.

In 1284 Wales was annexed by the Crown. Effective integration with
England was deferred till 1536, when Welshmen were placed in the same
legal position as Englishmen, Welsh constituencies were given representation in the English Parliament and the English system of local government
was extended to Wales. From 1746 till 1967 the word 'England' in an Act
of Parliament was deemed to include Wales; for Acts passed since then this
slur on the principality has been removed.[2] There is an annual debate on
Welsh affairs at Westminster. The Welsh Grand Committee is a deliberative
body and considers bills and other matters relating exclusively to Wales
which are referred to it. If it recommends that a bill should receive a second
reading the House does so without debate. Not much use is made of the
committee for legislative purposes, however, partly because few bills relate
exclusively to Wales and partly because there is a permanent anti-
Conservative majority in Wales, so that a Conservative Government's
controversial legislation might flounder in that committee.[3] Administrative
devolution is more important. In 1951 the office of Minister for Welsh Affairs
was created; at first the office was combined with another departmental

1 See D. G. T. Williams, 'The Constitution of the United Kingdom' [1972B] *Camb.
LJ* 266.
2 Welsh Language Act 1967, s. 4; Welsh Language Act 1993 (which makes Welsh
equal to English in the conduct of public business in Wales). Does Wales include
Monmouthshire? There is no all-inclusive answer to this question, but under the Local
Government Act 1972, s. 20(7), sched. 4, it does geographically, though Monmouthshire
ceased to exist as a local government unit.
3 House of Commons SO Nos. 89, 98. Since 1996 Ministers have been able to answer
questions and attend debates in the Welsh Grand Committee; and see below, pp. 293–
4, for the Select Committee on Welsh Affairs set up in 1979.

responsibility[4] but in 1964 the Welsh Office became a separate Department headed by a Secretary of State with a seat in the Cabinet. He has responsibility for primary and secondary education in Wales and a number of other local and regional services; most of the Office's work is done in Cardiff. There are also Welsh departments of some Whitehall ministries – for example the Ministry of Agriculture, Fisheries and Food. Provision has been made for the use of the Welsh language in courts sitting in Wales, and for certain official purposes.[5] Welsh nationalism, nurtured on a distinctive culture, emerged as a political force of some consequence in the late 1960s. The response to it of the Government, Parliament and of the people of Wales will be considered later in this chapter.[6]

In 1603 James VI of Scotland became James I of England; this was a *personal* union and did not make Scotland and England one. In 1707 the Acts of Union created a United Kingdom of Great Britain, merging the Scottish and English Parliaments in pursuance of negotiated Articles of Union.[7] Scotland[8] has its own Established Church,[9] judicial system, criminal and civil law[10] (rooted in Roman concepts but now substantially influenced by the common law and United Kingdom legislation), local government and educational systems. Accordingly, a substantial measure of responsibility for Scotland's internal affairs rests in Scottish hands, though by no means enough to satisfy separatists in the Scottish National Party. Most Scottish bills are considered by the Scottish Grand Committee and the Scottish Special Standing Committee; Ministers attend the Scottish Grand Committee, occasionally sitting in Edinburgh.[11] There has been a Secretary for Scotland since 1885 and a Secretary of State since 1926; he is always a member of a peacetime Cabinet. St Andrew's House, Edinburgh, is the

---

4 The first Minister for Welsh Affairs was the then Home Secretary, Sir David Maxwell Fyfe. He was known in Wales as 'Dai Bananas'.

5 Welsh Courts Act 1942; Welsh Language Act 1967; Welsh Language Act 1993.

6 See below, pp. 62–6.

7 A. V. Dicey and R. S. Rait, *Thoughts on the Union* (1920).

8 Including Rockall: Island of Rockall Act 1972.

9 The Presbyterian Church of Scotland. The Church of Ireland was severed from the Church of England in 1869 and the Church of Wales was disestablished in 1914.

10 See T. B. Smith, *Scotland: The Development of its Laws and Constitution* (1962); D. M. Walker, *The Scottish Legal System* (5th edn, 1981). There is a separate Law Commission for Scotland and a Scottish Committee of the Council on Tribunals.

11 See House of Commons SO, Nos. 86, 93–7; this procedure can, however, be blocked if ten members object, and in effect is used only if the Opposition agrees. See pp. 293–4 below for the Select Committee on Scottish Affairs established in 1979. The Scottish Grand Committee also considers the Scottish estimates. Peers of Scotland sit in the House of Lords. See also Cm 2225 (1993).

home of the five sub-departments of the Scottish Office – the Department of Agriculture and Fisheries for Scotland, the Scottish Environment Department, the Scottish Industry Department, the Scottish Education Department and the Scottish Home and Health Department. The Secretary of State also has responsibility for a number of minor Departments (for example, the General Register Office for Scotland, the Scottish Record Office), and for public corporations operating only in Scotland. He also has joint responsibility for the Forestry Commission and the Crown Estate Commissioners. A number of United Kingdom Departments have regional organizations in Scotland with Scottish directors or controllers; the Secretary of State has a miscellany of coordinating functions. There are Scottish boards, councils or committees for some of the nationalized industries and other quasi-government bodies.[12] The Lord Advocate has a unique blend of responsibilities for the Scottish legal system, particularly on the criminal side.

In the Plantagenet period Ireland was subjected to the overlordship of the Kings of England. Attempts to subdue its turbulent people were seldom sustained or efficacious. After the Reformation, Protestant settlement and discrimination against the Roman Catholic populace provoked insurrection followed by repression, more thoroughgoing in the times of Cromwell and William III than in earlier years. In 1783 the British Parliament purported to relinquish jurisdiction over Ireland; and for 'eighteen years Ireland was no more subject to England than was England to Ireland'.[13] In 1801 Ireland, which then had a separate Parliament, entered into union with Great Britain, and the Irish question entered into British politics. A hundred members of Parliament were elected for Irish constituencies.[14] Irish national-ism grew, and eventually Gladstone, at seventy-six, was converted to the cause of Irish home rule; but his party split on the issue – Dicey and Anson were among the more prominent Liberal Unionists – and his first Home Rule Bill was defeated in the Commons. The second was thrown out by the Lords. In August 1914 the Government of Ireland Act was passed under

12 See, for example, J. D. B. Mitchell, *Constitutional Law* (2nd edn, 1968); J. N. Wolfe (ed.), *Government and Nationalism in Scotland* (1969); Mitchell in Andrews (ed.), *Welsh Studies in Public Law* (1970), ch. 5; J. P. Mackintosh, *The Devolution of Power* (1968), ch. 6; Royal Commission on the Constitution, Written Evidence 2 – the Scottish Office, the Lord Advocate's Department and the Crown Office; J. G. Kellas, *The Scottish Political System* (2nd edn, 1975); M. Keating and A. Midwinter, *The Government of Scotland* (1983).
13 F. W. Maitland, *Constitutional History of England* (1908), p. 298.
14 There were also twenty-eight representative peers of Ireland in the Lords. See p. 298, note 10.

the Parliament Act procedure, providing for an internally self-governing, undivided Ireland, with its own Parliament subject to the overriding paramountcy of the United Kingdom Parliament. This measure, bitterly opposed by the Protestant majority in the province of Ulster and their sympathizers across the water, never came into effect. It was superseded by the Government of Ireland Act 1920, which provided for two separate (and subordinate) Parliaments, one for Northern Ireland and one for Southern Ireland. Because of an armed uprising in the South, only part of this Act became operative. In 1922 the Irish Free State (now the Republic of Ireland) was created and given Dominion status.[15] From then on,[16] the United Kingdom meant Great Britain and Northern Ireland.[17]

The constitution of Northern Ireland and the powers of its Government and Parliament were set out in the 1920 Act as amended by subsequent legislation of the United Kingdom Parliament.[18] Under the 1920 Act Northern Ireland had some of the trappings of an independent State – a Prime Minister, Cabinet and Privy Council, a bicameral Parliament (composed of a Senate and a House of Commons), responsible self-government, a Supreme Court with a Lord Chief Justice, and so on. The Northern Ireland Parliament had a general power to make laws for the peace, order and good government of the six counties. Appearances were not entirely deceptive. Various aspects of public law have been regulated differently in Northern Ireland. For instance, gas was never nationalized; there are no lay magistrates. In their own house the Northern Ireland authorities were, to a large extent, masters, till law and order broke down.

The United Kingdom Parliament retained plenary legislative powers in Northern Ireland (section 75 of the 1920 Act) and the powers of the United Kingdom Government were potentially unrestricted; but in relation to

15 In United Kingdom law by virtue of the Irish Free State (Agreement) Act 1922 and the Irish Free State Constitution Act 1922. For the constitutional problems arising out of the legislation, see Sir Kenneth Wheare, *The Constitutional Structure of the Commonwealth* (1960), pp. 90–94.
16 The exact date of the Free State's departure from the United Kingdom within the legal meaning of the latter term is not altogether clear. See Sir Kenneth Roberts-Wray, *Commonwealth and Colonial Law* (1966), pp. 32–5.
17 Northern Ireland comprises six of the nine counties which formerly made up the province of Ulster. The terms 'Northern Ireland' and 'Ulster' are, however, often used interchangeably.
18 The leading commentary, written from the standpoint of a moderate Unionist, is Harry Calvert's *Constitutional Law in Northern Ireland* (1968). For an informative and close critique, see Claire Palley, *The Evolution, Disintegration and Possible Reconstruction of the Northern Ireland Constitution* (1972), reprinted from (1972) 1 *Anglo-American Law Review* 368–476; and Brigid Hadfield, *The Constitution of Northern Ireland* (1989).

'transferred matters' (i.e. matters assigned to Northern Ireland competence) the practice was for the United Kingdom to intervene only at the request or with the concurrence or acquiescence of the Northern Ireland Government. Nevertheless, even before orderly civil government began to collapse, the United Kingdom was able to exert some influence over Northern Ireland's policies within the transferred field because of Stormont's financial dependence.

In the period from October 1968, when communal disturbances broke out in Londonderry, till the time of writing, more constitutional and administrative reforms in Northern Ireland have been introduced than in the preceding sixty years. The basic problem was simple to state, perhaps impossible to solve. Public life (and often private life) in Northern Ireland was dominated by sectarian faction and the problem of the border with the south. A million Protestants were overwhelmingly unionist; half a million Catholics were predominantly separatist and republican. Of the twelve MPs returned from Northern Ireland constituencies to Westminster, at least nine would be Protestant Unionists. The Unionist Party was permanently in office at Stormont; the minority had no prospect of attaining political power by constitutional means. In such circumstances the Westminster model of responsible government would not work in the manner familiar in Great Britain. By 1972 at the latest, as attitudes on both sides polarized amid mounting terrorism, repression and hatred, it had ceased to work at all.

In 1969 the main specific grievances of Catholics were found to be[19] the allegedly discriminatory allocation of public housing; discrimination in local government appointments; distortion of local government boundaries (and restriction of the franchise to ratepayers) to perpetuate local unionist dominance; failure by the Government properly to investigate complaints of unfair discrimination; resentment of the existence and conduct of the Ulster Special Constabulary (the 'B Specials'), a paramilitary force; the existence and use of the Civil Authorities (Special Powers) Act (NI) 1922, a kind of permanent Emergency Powers Act.[20] A series of reforms followed, mainly prompted by Westminster, the United Kingdom having been

19 Report of the Cameron Commission on Disturbances in Northern Ireland (Cmnd 532 (NI 1969), § 229). For a fuller study, see the Report of the Scarman Tribunal of Inquiry on Violence and Civil Disturbances in Northern Ireland in 1969 (Cmnd 566 (NI 1972)). See also the Report of the Hunt Committee on the Police in Northern Ireland (Cmnd 534 (NI 1969)).
20 For the invocation of powers under this Act before disturbances began, see *McEldowney* v. *Forde* [1971] AC 632.

obliged to send large reinforcements of troops to Northern Ireland in an attempt to restore order. Local government reforms, already under way, were expedited.[21] Universal suffrage for local electors was introduced and the 'business premises' vote for Stormont electors was abolished.[22] The 'B Specials' were stood down and the Royal Ulster Constabulary was (for the time being) disarmed; a new part-time local military force, the Ulster Defence Regiment, was formed;[23] the GOC Northern Ireland was placed in control of the RUC for security operations, with direct responsibility to United Kingdom Ministers. An interesting and important innovation was the establishment of the office of Commissioner for Complaints,[24] who has power to investigate complaints of injustice caused by maladministration by local and other public bodies lying outside the jurisdiction of the Parliamentary Commissioner for Administration. Other reforms included the establishment of an independent Community Relations Commission[25] and the vesting of responsibility for prosecutions in an independent Director of Public Prosecutions subject only to the English Attorney-General.[26]

Reform came too late to satisfy the nationalists, who had been brought increasingly under the sway of the Provisional wing of the Irish Republican Army. The situation was exacerbated by the introduction in August 1971 of the large-scale internment of security suspects under the Civil Authorities (Special Powers) Act (NI) 1922;[27] and far-reaching proposals for internal constitutional reform in Northern Ireland[28] met with little overt response among the more moderate nationalists. In March 1972 the United Kingdom imposed direct rule on Northern Ireland; the functions of the Parliament and Government of the province were vested in the Secretary of State for Northern Ireland. Westminster placed it on record that nothing done under the Act imposing direct rule (the Northern Ireland (Temporary Provisions) Act 1972) was to derogate or authorize derogation from the status of

21 In 1969, moreover, the Unionist-biased system of local government in Londonderry had been replaced by a Development Commission.

22 Electoral Law Acts (NI) 1968 and 1969.

23 Ulster Defence Regiment Act 1969; Cmnd 4188 (1969); Police Act 1969.

24 Commissioner for Complaints Act (NI) 1969. For description and evaluation, see Claire Palley, op. cit., pp. 422–5. The PCA has only a very limited jurisdiction in relation to Northern Ireland: see Parliamentary Commissioner Act 1967, s. 13.

25 Palley, op. cit., pp. 425–6.

26 SI 1972, No. 538 (agreed before direct rule was imposed).

27 For inquiries into complaints about the conduct of the security forces in connection with this operation, and in the shooting in Londonderry in January 1972, see Cmnd 4832 (1971) (the Compton Report), Cmnd 4901 (1971) (the Parker Report), and HC 220 (1971–72) (the Widgery Report).

28 See especially Cmnd 560 (NI 1971), Cmnd 568 (NI 1972).

Northern Ireland as part of the United Kingdom,[29] and a plebiscite on the border issue was held in March 1973.[30] Nearly 60 per cent of the electorate voted in favour of the province remaining a part of the United Kingdom. Troops reoccupied the Catholic 'no-go' areas in Belfast and Londonderry and Her Majesty's Government governed again. Internment by executive order, bereft of procedural safeguards,[31] had been phased out and replaced by detention in pursuance of a determination by judicial commissioners subject to appeal to a judicial tribunal.[32] Imaginative suggestions for the constitutional future of Northern Ireland were canvassed.[33]

A succession of constitutional experiments was tried subsequently. A sequel to the 1972 discussion paper was published in March 1973.[34] In order to hold the ring, direct rule under the 1972 Act was renewed for a further year. Under the Northern Ireland Assembly Act 1973 and the Northern Ireland Constitution Act 1973 the Northern Ireland Assembly and Executive, based on power-sharing between the two communities, were established, and the Stormont Parliament was abolished.[35] The paramount legislative sovereignty of the United Kingdom Parliament was retained.[36] On that basis direct rule was ended on 1 January 1974. But the implementation of the new constitution met a severe setback in May 1974 following the collapse of the Executive after two weeks of a politically motivated strike in the province by so-called 'loyalists'. Direct rule was reimposed the following day. The Assembly was prorogued and later dissolved.[37] Next came the election of a Constitutional Convention under the Northern Ireland Act 1974,[38] to deliberate for one year. As was generally anticipated it failed to agree and was, in turn dissolved.[39]

---

29 ibid., s. 2; see also Cmnd 534 (NI 1969), para. 56(1); Cmnd 4154 (1969), para 1.
30 Northern Ireland (Border Poll) Act 1972.
31 cf. (1972) 23 *NILQ* 331.
32 SI 1972, No. 1632.
33 *The Future of Northern Ireland*: a paper for discussion (Northern Ireland Office, HMSO, October 1972).
34 Northern Ireland Constitutional Proposals, Cmnd 5259 (1973).
35 Northern Ireland Constitution Act 1973, s. 31. The Act also contains anti-discrimination provisions, and established the Standing Advisory Commission on Human Rights: ibid., s. 20. The Commission reported in 1987 that 'serious and substantial' inequalities of opportunity persisted for Catholics: see Cm 237 (1987). A White Paper on fair employment (Cm 380 (1988)) preceded the Fair Employment (Northern Ireland) Act 1989.
36 ibid., s. 4(4).
37 SI 1974, No. 926; SI 1975, No. 422.
38 The Act also made continued provision for direct rule: s. 1 and sched. 1.
39 SI 1976, No. 349.

At the time of writing, therefore, Northern Ireland is still subject to direct rule by virtue of the Northern Ireland Act 1974, section 1 and schedule 1.[40] Broadly, that statute puts the Constitution Act 1973 on ice and allows Her Majesty in Council to make laws for Northern Ireland; any executive functions may be carried out by the Secretary of State for Northern Ireland. Emergency powers are exercised mainly under the Northern Ireland (Emergency Provisions) Act 1996, a statute which retains the Diplock Commission procedures to deal with terrorism.[41] The duration of the powers in that Act may be extended by Order in Council from time to time.

From 1974 to 1979 next to no overt political initiatives were forthcoming from Westminster: the maintenance of security was given priority. True, the number of Northern Irish MPs was increased from twelve to seventeen,[42] but it was not until the Conservatives regained power in May 1979 that two successive initiatives were made and two White Papers published, in 1980 and 1982.[43] On the basis of the 1982 White Paper a new Northern Ireland Assembly was elected.[44] Under the Northern Ireland Act 1982[45] a flexible approach to the ending of direct rule and to the devolution of power to the province was envisaged.[46] The Assembly was elected in 1982:[47] the mainly Catholic Social Democratic and Labour Party contested the elections and won fourteen seats, but announced that it would take no part in Assembly affairs. No real progress was made in the Assembly on devolution, but many debates on Northern Irish affairs took place.

There can be no significant improvement in the problems of Northern Ireland without some cooperation with the Republic of Ireland. For that reason a major initiative by Mrs Thatcher's Government and the Irish Government led to the conclusion of the Anglo-Irish Agreement at Hillsborough in 1985.[48] While affirming that any change in the province's status

40 Orders in Council are made at six-monthly intervals continuing the 1974 Act in force.
41 Cmnd 5185 (1972). 'Diplock courts', consisting of a judge without a jury, were set up in 1978.
42 House of Commons (Redistribution of Seats) Act 1979.
43 The Government of Northern Ireland: proposals for further discussion. Cmnd 7950 (1980); Northern Ireland: a framework for devolution, Cmnd 8541 (1982).
44 By virtue of the Northern Ireland Assembly Act 1973, s. 2 and the Northern Ireland Constitution Act 1973, s. 27(7).
45 See Gearty [1982] Public law 518.
46 Northern Ireland Act 1982, ss. 1, 2.
47 ibid., s. 3.
48 See Cmnd 9657 (1985).

can only come about with the consent of a majority of its people, the Agreement established an Inter-governmental Conference. This Conference, with representatives from Northern Ireland and the Republic, meets regularly at ministerial or civil service level as appropriate, the joint chairmen of ministerial meetings being the Secretary of State for Northern Ireland and an Irish Minister. Other Ministers, and the chief constable of Northern Ireland and the commissioner of the Irish Garda, hold separate meetings as required. Many meetings have been held at various levels and some progress has been made, but the Agreement has been bitterly resisted by Northern Irish Unionists. The Unionist majority in the Northern Ireland Assembly had formed a one-party committee to analyse the Agreement, so prompting the Alliance Party to join the Social Democratic and Labour Party in boycotting it. It having become pointless – and not inexpensive – to continue the Assembly's life, it was dissolved in 1986.[49] The Unionists launched a hopeless legal challenge to the Agreement;[50] all fifteen Unionist MPs resigned their Westminster seats to fight simultaneous by-elections to demonstrate the strength of feeling against Irish 'interference' in the affairs of the province.[51] In 1991 the four Northern Ireland constitutional parties began round-table talks under the chairmanship of the Secretary of State. These were the first talks of their kind for sixteen years. Despite progress being made, the talks were ended late in 1992. After considerable progress in talks between the two Governments and the Northern Ireland political parties, the Provisional IRA announced a ceasefire in August 1994, in which the 'loyalist' paramilitaries joined. An international body, the Mitchell Commission, was set up and reported on the decommissioning of illegally held arms and on principles which should govern further all-party talks which might include Sinn Fein. The IRA ceasefire broke in February 1996, but elections (contested by all the parties) were held to the Northern Ireland Forum under the Northern Ireland (Entry to Talks etc.) Act 1996. Sinn Fein was deemed not to have qualified to take part according to the Mitchell principles. Negotiating teams drawn from the 110-member Forum continue discussions on the possible governance of Northern Ireland, having been joined by representatives of Sinn Fein following the resumption of the ceasefire in 1997.

Any long-term constitutional change which might flow from the Anglo-

---

49 SI 1986, No. 1036.
50 See *Ex p. Molyneaux* [1986] 1 WLR 331.
51 One seat was lost to the SDLP. See Boulton [1986] *Public Law* 211.

Irish Agreement cannot be achieved in defiance of Unionist views, but equally further legal and administrative devolution to Northern Ireland remains the policy of all the main British political parties.

THE CHANNEL ISLANDS AND THE ISLE OF MAN[52]

The Channel Islands and the Isle of Man are not parts of the United Kingdom, though in some legal contexts the term 'United Kingdom' is deemed to include them. With the United Kingdom they constitute the British Islands.[53] They are dependencies of the Crown, and belong to Her Majesty's dominions. Although they fall within the definition of a 'British possession',[54] they are not colonies. Their status is unique.

The islands have other points of similarity. They have ancient institutions. Their affairs are subject to a degree of superintendence by the Home Office, acting on the recommendation of the Committees of the Privy Council for the affairs of Jersey and Guernsey and for the Isle of Man, and petitions relating to matters arising in the islands may be directed to the Privy Council. The principal channel of communication between the islands and the United Kingdom Government is the Home Office, and the Home Secretary is the dominant figure in the Privy Council Committees, which today never meet as deliberative bodies. Assent to local legislation is given by Order in Council and is not a mere formality. Modifications to measures passed by the States of Jersey and Guernsey are still sometimes made after representations by or through the Home Office. Control over Isle of Man legislation has been more freely exercised; bills have been dropped under Home Office pressure and in 1962 the royal assent was withheld from a Manx bill on wireless telegraphy. Public administration in each of the principal islands is conducted mainly through committees or boards of the legislatures; in this respect the pattern resembles that of a British local authority, and particularly in the Channel Islands there is no clear-cut separation of powers between Executive and Legislature. The customary law, on which the local law was once based, is being replaced by more modern legislation. Appeals lie from the highest courts of the islands to

52 See Report of the Royal Commission on the Constitution, Cmnd 5460 (1973), Part XI.
53 Interpretation Act 1978, s. 5 and sched. 1.
54 ibid.

the Judicial Committee of the Privy Council.[55] The United Kingdom Government is responsible for the defence and international relations of all the islands.[56]

There are also important points of dissimilarity in status and internal constitutional structure. In particular, Jersey and Guernsey have full internal self-government and financial autonomy whereas the Isle of Man has not; the Lieutenant-Governor of the Isle of Man has active executive responsibilities as an agent of the United Kingdom Government,[57] unlike the Lieutenant-Governors of Jersey and Guernsey. In 1967 the United Kingdom Parliament and Government imposed on the Isle of Man the Marine etc. Broadcasting (Offences) Act,[58] outlawing broadcasting from 'marine structures' within the British Islands and the contiguous sea area. No similar imposition has been made upon Jersey or Guernsey in recent years.

55 Appeals are infrequent. There are differences in judicial structure. In both Jersey and Guernsey there is a Royal Court, composed of the Bailiff (a lawyer and the principal insular officer) and elected jurats who can be laymen. There is a separate Court of Appeal composed of barristers from the mainland. In the Isle of Man there are Deemsters who sit as judges, and a Judge of Appeal, an English barrister, who sits with a Deemster. See further Robilliard [1979] *Crim. L. Rev.* 566; and see below, p. 384.

56 As far as practicable, the United Kingdom procures the insertion of a territorial application clause into treaties to which it becomes a party so that its obligations under the treaty shall not extend to matters lying ordinarily within the area of internal self-government of territories (including the Islands) for whose international obligations it is responsible. The treaty obligations will then only be extended to those territories with their concurrence. Today this is seldom practicable. Under international pressure and for reasons of self-interest, the United Kingdom often incurs international obligations (particularly under multilateral conventions) extending of their own force to such territories but dealing primarily with local domestic matters. The United Kingdom Government may then be impaled on the horns of a dilemma; either it becomes an international defaulter by failing to secure the *implementation* of the treaty obligations in local law; or it infringes the canons of constitutional propriety by insisting on implementation, if necessary encroaching on the field of local autonomy. The European Convention on Human Rights has recently presented problems for the enforcement of Guernsey housing laws and has also led the European Court of Human Rights to pronounce against birching on the Isle of Man. See further p. 394.

57 In the words of the Joint Evidence submitted in 1970 by the Home Office and Tynwald (the Isle of Man Parliament) to the Royal Commission on the Constitution, 'he is the head of the insular administration, his powers resemble those of an archetypal colonial governor, and he is subject only to the control of the Secretary of State' (Part B, s. 7).

58 Extended to the Isle of Man by SI 1967, No. 1276, in fulfilment of a multilateral international convention; see note 56 above.

The Channel Islands

When the Duke of Normandy became King of England in 1066, the Channel Islands were already part of the Dukedom; and when King John lost the mainland of Normandy, they remained as possessions of the Crown. These islands off the French coast now comprise the bailiwicks of Jersey and Guernsey. Within the bailiwick of Guernsey lie the only two other Channel Islands having a sizeable population, Alderney and Sark. Alderney has its own representative legislature, the States, and provides certain local services, but in 1948 responsibility for all the main services was vested in Guernsey. Sark, though nominally a dependency of Guernsey, is substantially autonomous. Owned by a feudal lord with anachronistic institutions, Sark ('where time stands still') is a survival of an age long past.[59]

The status of Guernsey[60] in relation to the United Kingdom, and its institutions of government closely resembles that of Jersey.

Jersey[61] as a Lieutenant-Governor appointed by the Crown, and insular officers (the Bailiff, who occupies a position comparable to that of the Lord Chancellor or possibly the Lord Chief Justice, the Deputy Bailiff and the Law Officers) appointed by the Crown from among Jerseymen after local consultations. Administrative decisions are made by committees of the States, the unicameral Legislature. The closest approximation to an executive branch of government is an informal meeting of the insular officers and the presidents of the principal committees. The States are composed of the Bailiff, who presides – he acts as an impartial Speaker and has a power of 'dissent' – the Law Officers and the Dean of Jersey (who may speak but not vote), twelve senators elected for six years, twenty-eight deputies elected every three years, and twelve constables elected from the parishes. (Guernsey has two separate bodies, the States of Deliberation, a legislative body, and the States of Election, which elects certain members of the States of Deliberation as well as the jurats and court officers.) There is universal suffrage. Legislation by the States falls into two main classes: Laws, which

---

59 Sark (with a population of over 600) has no motor cars (though five of its residents are reputed to own private aircraft), no income tax, no divorce law and a prison for two. The Seigneur of Sark, Michael Beaumont, continues to levy customary feudal dues from the populace and to exercise a formidable influence over local affairs.

60 *Vaudin* v. *Hamon* [1974] AC 569 is an instructive case on the sources of law in Guernsey.

61 See F. de L. Bois, *Constitutional History of Jersey* (1969) (Appx 1 to the Submission of the States of Jersey to the Royal Commission on the Constitution, 1970). See also *In re a Debtor, ex p. Viscount of the Royal Count of Jersey* [1981] Ch. 384; de L. Bois [1983] *Public Law* 385.

have effect only when assented to by Her Majesty in Council,[62] and regulations, of a more limited scope; the latter do not require the royal assent. The insular constitution is not contained in a single instrument, but much of it can be pieced together from Laws of the States.

The Crown used to legislate for Jersey by prerogative Order in Council, but as the island has acquired a Legislature with an elected majority an attempt to do so today would probably be improper.[63] Parliament retains, in strict law, plenary legislative authority for all those parts of Her Majesty's dominions which have not attained independence or over which Parliament has not renounced its sovereignty. Acts of Parliament extend to Jersey only by express words or necessary implication. The Act is accompanied by an Order in Council directing that it be registered in the Royal Court.[64] The insular authorities may suspend but not refuse registration; in any event, it would appear that such an Act is operative in the island of its own force. In practice, Parliament hardly ever legislates directly for the island; an Act intended to alter the law of the island will provide for its extension to the island by Order in Council made under the Act with such modifications of the Act as may be specified in the Order. Consultation with the insular authorities will then take place and an accommodation will be reached.

It would be contrary to constitutional practice for Parliament so to legislate for the island as to impose taxation or regulate matters of purely domestic concern or derogate from the island's constitutional autonomy without the consent of the States.

Under ancient royal grants, the island has been given immunity from United Kingdom taxation – it has its own fiscal laws – and the right to duty-free entry of its produce into the United Kingdom. Guernsey and Jersey make voluntary contributions towards United Kingdom defence.

The entry of the United Kingdom into the European Community could have posed a serious threat to the island's domestic autonomy. Under article 227(4) of the Rome Treaty, the terms of the Treaty apply to all European territories for whose external relations a Member State is responsible. Unqualified accession by the United Kingdom would have entailed the

---

62 The Lieutenant-Governor also has a power, no longer exercised, to veto a bill encroaching on the prerogative. Bills are called *projets de loi*. Transactions (including bills and regulations) passed by the States are also called 'Acts' of the States.
63 Under the rule in *Campbell* v. *Hall* (1774) 1 Cowp. 774, formulated in relation to colonies. An Order in Council establishing a Court of Appeal was made in reliance on the prerogative in 1949 but it never came into operation. Appeal courts were finally set up in 1961 after legislation had been passed in the usual way.
64 See note 58 above. A similar procedure applies in Guernsey.

economic integration of Jersey with the United Kingdom if the terms of the Treaty had been implemented in Jersey by the United Kingdom Parliament. As this would have been unacceptable, especially to Jersey, a special Protocol was negotiated by the United Kingdom Government, whereby the Channel Islands and the Isle of Man were brought within the Community for most purposes but exempted from the Treaty provisions relating to value added tax and fiscal harmonization.[65]

The Isle of Man

The island is situated in the Irish Sea. In the early 1970s the islanders, like the Jerseymen, were seeking a redefinition of their constitutional position *vis-à-vis* the United Kingdom. However, the changes they sought in the existing relationship were larger; for the Isle of Man lacked a full measure of internal self-government. Apart from legislative controls exercised through Parliament and the Privy Council,[66] the Crown asserts an ultimate responsibility through the Lieutenant-Governor for the good government of the island in respect of such matters as financial proposals, the disposition of the police, the direction of the civil service and the nomination of members of public bodies. The Lieutenant-Governor is advised by an Executive Council composed mainly of chairmen of boards of Tynwald; but he is not obliged to act on the advice tendered. Tynwald, one of the most ancient legislative bodies in the world – originally it was a court – consists of two chambers, a directly elected House of Keys, and an indirectly elected Legislative Council with a very small number of *ex officio* members. Since 1981 the Lieutenant-Governor has had the power of royal assent for bills passed by Tynwald, except for any measure which the Privy Council might reserve to itself: formerly all bills had to go for royal assent to the Queen in Council. The island has its own system of internal taxation. Even before accession to the European Community the island was in customs union with the United Kingdom under the Isle of Man Act 1958 and received a share of the duties thus collected for the island; it paid 2½ per cent of this revenue as a contribution to the United Kingdom in respect of defence

65 See Cmnd 4862-I (1972), pp. 16, 17, 82–4. The islands had to accept the common external tariff, internal free trade and common agricultural policy. Community rules on freedom of movement of persons and services extended to the islands but the islanders were not accorded reciprocal treatment in that sphere.
66 See Report of the Joint Working Party on the Constitutional Relationship between Isle of Man and the United Kingdom (Home Office, HMSO, 1969).

and common services (for example, overseas representation).[67] Insular produce was exported to the United Kingdom free of duty. The Isle of Man
Act 1979 (which repealed and re-enacted, with amendments, the 1958 Act)
continued the customs union but established, from 1980, an Isle of Man
Customs and Excise service. Officials of the United Kingdom service no
longer collect customs and excise duties or other indirect taxes in the island
on behalf of the island.

The constitutional history of the island is convoluted. Till 1266 it was
under Norse rule; then it was ceded to the King of Scotland; early in the
fourteenth century it passed, somewhat obscurely, to the King of England,
who granted it to subjects, styled Lords of Man. In 1765 it was revested in
the Crown by Act of Parliament.[68]

DEVOLUTION[69]

Labour Governments have tried since 1969 to devolve substantial legislative,
administrative and executive responsibilities to Scotland and (to a lesser
extent) to Wales.

Partly – some say largely – as a means of assuaging Scottish and Welsh
nationalist feeling in the mid-1960s the Wilson Government set up the
Royal Commission on the Constitution in 1969 (the Kilbrandon Commission). Its task was 'to examine the present functions of the central
legislature and government in relation to the several countries, nations and
regions in the United Kingdom'. The Commission reported in 1973.[70] The
Labour Government which was returned to office in 1974 introduced the
Scotland and Wales Bill.[71] It received a second reading in December 1976.
As a major constitutional measure, its committee stage was taken on the
floor of the Commons, where disaster for the Government struck. So

67 For a synopsis of the position, see references cited in notes 60 and 66 above.
68 Isle of Man Purchase Act 1765. There is no corresponding or analogous legislation
for the Channel Islands.
69 For a good short account see Colin Munro, *Studies in Constitutional Law* (1987), pp.
21–34.
70 Vol. I, Report, Cmnd 5460; Vol. II, Memorandum of Dissent, Cmnd 5460-I (1973).
71 This was partly based on the Kilbrandon Report; Devolution within the United
Kingdom; some alternatives for discussion (1974); Democracy and Devolution: proposals
for Scotland and Wales, Cmnd 5732 (1974); Our Changing Democracy: devolution to
Scotland and Wales, Cmnd 6348 (1975); Supplementary Statement, Cmnd 6585 (1976);
and on the Government's decisions subsequent to those publications: see 912 HC
Deb. 270–84 (25 May 1976); 916 HC Deb. 1455–71 (3 August 1976).

determined were the supporters and opponents of the measure fully to debate it or utterly to destroy it – or, for various motives, to achieve some intermediate result – that parliamentary progress was made agonizingly slow. In February 1977, therefore, the Government sought to introduce a 'guillotine' motion[72] to curtail debate. But this was ignominiously defeated:[73] twenty-two Labour MPs voted against it and another twenty-one abstained. The bill was, in effect, abandoned but with the promise of new proposals for the following session.

The new scheme[74] among other things involved two bills, for Scotland and Wales respectively. Fortified by the parliamentary strength which it had acquired through the Lib.-Lab. pact[75] the Government introduced the Scotland Bill and the Wales Bill, which received their second readings in November 1977 by substantial majorities.[76] Guillotine motions were speedily approved. Although several defeats were inflicted on parts of the measures, the most damaging for the devolutionists was the inclusion of a clause in the Scotland Bill against the Government's wishes which would require that if less than 40 per cent of the Scottish electorate voted 'yes' in the proposed referendum, an Order in Council would have to be laid before Parliament to allow for the repeal of the legislation.[77] (A similar clause was inserted in the Wales Bill.)[78] The Scotland Act and Wales Act of 1978 duly received royal assent. On 1 March 1979 referendums were held in Scotland and Wales. In Scotland, failure to achieve the '40 per cent requirement' meant that the implementation of the Act was not approved; in Wales, the people decisively rejected the Wales Act regardless of that requirement.[79] Following these defeats the minority Labour Government appealed for brief inter-party discussions. The Conservative Party saw this as an attempt to play for time and (not only for that reason) put down a motion of no confidence. It carried against the Government by one vote – the first successful vote of no confidence since 1924. Parliament, at the Prime

72 For the meaning of this term, see below p. 269.

73 926 HC Deb. 1234–1367 (22 February 1977).

74 For a detailed description, see 936 HC Deb. 313–28 (26 July 1977).

75 See below, p. 196.

76 See 939 HC Deb. 51–213 (14 November 1977) and 939 HC Deb. 357–512 (15 November 1977).

77 See 942 HC Deb. 1460–1548 (25 January 1978). This became s. 85 of the Scotland Act.

78 This became s. 80 of the Wales Act.

79 In Scotland, 32.5 per cent of eligible electors voted 'yes', 30.4 per cent voted 'no' and 37.1 per cent abstained. In Wales the equivalent figures were 46.5 per cent 'no', only 11.8 per cent 'yes' and 41.7 per cent abstained.

Minister's request, was dissolved, and the Conservatives won the General Election. The new Administration introduced the repeal orders, which were carried without a vote.[80]

In the late 1980s and the early 1990s, an unofficial Scottish Constitutional Convention sat in Edinburgh to try to devise a scheme of Scottish devolution. The Labour and Liberal Democrat Parties were represented, as well as non-party individuals and organizations. The Convention issued a final report in 1995.[81] It advocated a Scottish Parliament of 129 members, 73 elected by first past the post and 56 by proportional representation. The Scottish Parliament would have the power to vary the basic rate of income tax charged in Scotland by 3p, and would have legislative and executive authority over all matters save those (such as defence and foreign affairs) reserved to Westminster. There would be a Chief Minister and a Cabinet.

The Labour Government promised to legislate for devolution to Scotland and Wales in the first session of the 1997 Parliament. Indeed, the first bill to be introduced in the new Parliament by the Government was what became the Referendums (Scotland and Wales) Act 1997, giving authority to hold referendums in Scotland and Wales on the Government's devolution plans. Two White Papers were published in the summer of 1997, *Scotland's Parliament*[82] and *A Voice for Wales*.[83] The Scottish proposals closely followed the recommendations of the Scottish Constitutional Convention. In the light of the plans set out in the two White Papers the people of Scotland and Wales were asked to vote on whether they wished Parliament to give effect to legislative and executive devolution: this was to be before bills were published, in a reversal of the 1978 timetable. The referendums were held in September 1997, Scotland voting a week before Wales. Scottish voters were asked two questions; namely, whether they were in favour of a Scottish Parliament, and whether they were in favour of tax-varying powers for such a Parliament. The result was a resounding affirmative to both questions, on a turnout of 60%. Of those voting, 74.3% voted 'yes' to the first question, and 63.5% to the second. The Welsh referendum represented a much narrower victory for the Government. The voters had just one question to answer, whether they favoured the setting up of a

---

80 SI 1979, No. 928; SI 1979, No. 933.
81 See McFadden [1995] *Public Law* 215. And see the independent think-tank, the Constitution Unit, *Scotland's Parliament* (1996), *An Assembly for Wales* (1996) and *Regional Government* (1996).
82 Cm 3658 (1997).
83 Cm 3718 (1997).

Welsh Assembly. On a turnout of just 51.3%, 50.3% voted in favour of an Assembly.

Under the Scotland Bill, a Parliament will sit in Edinburgh for the first time for almost 300 years. That Parliament will be a devolved Parliament, not a legislature for an independent Scotland, and indeed the Westminster Parliament will have a reserve power to make laws for Scotland. The Queen will remain as head of State of the whole United Kingdom; the Secretary of State for Scotland will also remain in being, although with a changed role. In general, powers to be retained to the Westminster Parliament are set out in the bill, and the Scottish Parliament will have legislative powers in all other matters (subject to detailed exceptions). The main areas which will be reserved to the United Kingdom Parliament are the constitution (including the Crown, and the Parliament of the United Kingdom itself); foreign affairs and relations with the European Union; the civil service; defence; the fiscal, economic and monetary system; employment and social security legislation; and other specified matters which it is thought should remain subject to national control or operation. Disputes about the legal power of the Parliament to enact any bill would be resolved by the Judicial Committee of the Privy Council. The Scottish Parliament will receive a block grant each year from Westminster, to spend according to its wishes, and it will have the power to vary the basic rate of income tax upwards or downwards by 3p. The Scottish Parliament will be elected by the additional member system of proportional representation: one member will be elected from each of the present 73 constituencies, and a further 56 members will be allocated on the basis of votes cast for the various parties. It will be a fixed-term Parliament, being dissolved every four years, although it could also be dissolved if the Parliament so voted by a two-thirds majority or if it could not agree on whom to nominate as First Minister. There will be a First Minister and a Scottish Executive, consisting of members of the Parliament. The Parliament itself will nominate one of its members to be First Minister; its Presiding Officer will recommend his or her name to the Queen for formal appointment. The Government hopes that the Scotland Bill will be passed and all necessary preparations made so that the first elections to the Parliament can be held in 1999 with the Parliament functioning fully by the year 2000.

The Welsh Assembly will be a more modest body. Under the Government of Wales Bill it will have 60 members, elected by the additional member system every four years. It will take over most of the functions of the Secretary of State for Wales and the Welsh Office. It will have no power to enact primary legislation (which will continue to be passed for

Wales at Westminster), and so the question of what is and what is not a reserved matter should not arise. But the Assembly will have the authority to enact secondary legislation currently within the Secretary of State's remit, and it could express views on policy in the principality and exert some control over non-elected governmental bodies (quangos) there. It will have control of the annual sum which has, up to now, been made available to the Welsh Office (and which was £7 billion in 1997). Political leadership in Wales will be exercised by a First Secretary, heading an Executive Committee. That Committee will consist of the leaders of subject committees appointed by the Assembly from its membership, and the First Secretary will be elected by the Assembly from its ranks. The headquarters of the Assembly (which will be in Cardiff) will be staffed by civil servants. The Secretary of State for Wales will continue to hold office, to represent Wales in the Cabinet and in Parliament, and to promote primary legislation affecting the principality. The Government hopes that progress in establishing the Welsh Assembly will be such that the first elections to it can be held in the spring of 1999.

CHAPTER 4

Ultimate Authority in Constitutional Law

PARLIAMENTARY SOVEREIGNTY

Dicey considered the concept of parliamentary sovereignty to be the 'very keystone' of constitutional law in this country.[1] According to the orthodox view the Queen in Parliament is competent, according to United Kingdom law, to make or unmake any law whatsoever on any matter whatsoever; and no United Kingdom court is competent to question the validity of an Act of Parliament. Every other law-making body within the realm either derives its authority from Parliament or exercises it at the sufferance of Parliament; it cannot be superior to or even coordinate with, but must be subordinate to Parliament. But the world has moved on since Dicey, and the doctrine of parliamentary sovereignty has been altered by the United Kingdom's membership, since 1973, of what has become the European Union. Parliament must legislate consistently with European law, and to that important extent Parliament is no longer sovereign – at least, for as long as this country remains in the European Union. The impact of European law on parliamentary sovereignty will be considered later in this chapter.

Some writers dislike the term parliamentary 'sovereignty', and prefer to use the word 'supremacy'. 'Sovereign' and 'sovereignty' are words of many meanings.[2] We sometimes speak of the Queen as the Sovereign without attributing to her unlimited authority. We speak of sovereignty in international law when we mean independence, or freedom from external control; in this sense Australia is a sovereign State, but it does not have a 'sovereign' Parliament, because the powers of that Parliament are subject to the constitution. Is the constitution, then, 'sovereign' in Australia?

---

1 *Introduction to the Study of the Law of the Constitution* (10th edn, 1959), p. 70.
2 See F. H. Hinsley, *Sovereignty* (1966).

To John Austin, the best-known British writer on sovereignty,[3] every developed State had to have a 'sovereign', who made laws in the form of commands which were habitually obeyed, and whose legal authority was absolute, indivisible and illimitable. Obviously the location of sovereignty within a federal constitutional system is, by this token, an unrewarding pursuit.[4] Others have defined the concept of sovereignty in different ways at different periods and in different contexts. Dicey, for instance, referred to the Queen in Parliament as the legal sovereign and the electorate as the political sovereign.[5] Clearly the concepts of national sovereignty, parliamentary sovereignty and popular sovereignty have little in common with one another.[6] Hence there is a case for jettisoning the word 'sovereignty' altogether as being too ambiguous. But to discard the term in favour of the doctrine of 'supremacy' of Parliament is not particularly helpful, if only because the latter term conveys the suggestion that the House of Commons, or the Lords and Commons, as a matter of political or sociological fact, are supreme within the State; and manifestly they are not. And so the phrase 'parliamentary sovereignty' will be used, but to denote a legal concept or group of concepts which do not necessarily carry any implication about the effective seat of political power within the State.

How and when was this principle of the unlimited legislative competence of Parliament established? Was it established by Parliament itself; or by the courts; or by whom? And whence was derived the authority to lay down such a principle? Such questions about the ultimate foundations of constitutional law are not peculiar to the United Kingdom. They arise in countries where the central legislature lacks an unbounded sweep of legislative competence. What are the sources of authority for the validity of the supreme constitutions in those countries?

FOUNDATIONS OF THE CONSTITUTIONAL ORDER

A written constitution is regarded as the primary source of legal authority within a State. In it lies the explanation of the Legislature's power to make laws, the Executive's power to govern and administer, the Judiciary's power to adjudicate. But if we take one step farther, what is it that confers this

---

3 *The Province of Jurisprudence Determined* (H. L. A. Hart, ed., 1954).
4 For a subtle analysis, see Geoffrey Sawer, *Modern Federalism* (2nd edn, 1978), ch. 7.
5 Dicey, op. cit., p. 73.
6 But see pp. 83–7 on the relationship between national sovereignty and parliamentary sovereignty in the European Union context.

legitimating quality on the constitution? This question produces some convoluted answers.

Take the constitution of the Commonwealth of Australia. Here the answer seems fairly simple. The constitution is valid because it was duly enacted by the United Kingdom Parliament, which had power to enact it. Subsequent amendments to the constitution are valid because they have been made in the manner and form prescribed by the constitution. In other words, legal continuity has been preserved.

The case of Australia, however, is exceptional in the modern world. In the large majority of independent States there has been, at one time or another, a breach of legal continuity, and a constitution has been adopted or changed in a manner unauthorized by the pre-existing legal order. This happened in what was then the Soviet Union and in eastern European states when they threw over Communist rule. This is true also of a high proportion of the African states which have become independent. Since independence they have had revolutions and *coups d'état*; often the constitutional instrument has itself been abrogated and replaced, or suspended and modified, in a manner precluded by the independence constitution. And a few countries have deliberately chosen to adopt a new constitution peacefully but in a manner unauthorized by the pre-existing constitution. This is an assertion of legal nationalism, of what is called 'constitutional autochthony',[7] designed to demonstrate that the authority of the constitution is rooted in native soil, not derived from an imperial predecessor. Such a course has been followed in, for example, Eire (the Republic of Ireland), India and Sri Lanka. A constitution is adopted by a Constituent Assembly in the name of the people, or presented to the people for their approval.

Take again the constitution of the United States of America. Since its adoption in 1787 it has remained intact, apart from amendments duly made in terms of the constitution. But was the constitution valid in the first place, and if so, why? In 1776 the Thirteen Colonies had unlawfully declared their independence of Britain, and had repudiated the sovereignty of the United Kingdom Parliament.[8] 'We, the People of the United States', proceeded to 'ordain and establish a constitution'. In fact it was formulated at a convention consisting of delegates from the several states and then

7 Sir Kenneth Wheare, *Constitutional Structure of the Commonwealth* (1960), ch. 4.
8 The United Kingdom Government recognized the independence of the United States in 1783, but the American Colonies Act 1766 (the Declaratory Act), reiterating the paramount sovereignty of the United Kingdom Parliament, remained on our statute book till 1964.

ratified by the Congress. The name of the 'sovereign' People was invoked to confer upon the constitution moral authority and binding force.

The vague concept that ultimate 'sovereignty' resides in the 'people' is widely acceptable because of its political overtones. Even where a constitution has been overturned from above or below by manifestly illegitimate means, it is commonplace for the *de facto* holders of power to assert that they derive their mandate from the people, because it is awkward to be stigmatized as an undemocratic usurper. And by producing a constitution approved by or on behalf of the people, the accolade of legitimacy is achieved. Or is it?

It is one thing to say that government should rest on the consent of the governed; it is another thing to proclaim that a constitution has acquired the force of supreme law merely because it has obtained the approval of an irregularly convened Constituent Assembly or of a majority of the electorate or both. Yet to assert that all constitutions (or constitutional amendments) procured in a manner inconsistent with the pre-existing legal order are legally invalid will land one in a morass of absurd and insoluble difficulties. If the constitution of the United States is a nullity, then presumably only the United Kingdom can validate (with retroactive effect) the millions of governmental measures and judicial decisions taken in that country since independence. This is plainly ridiculous, for nobody doubts that the United States became an independent State in international law before the end of the eighteenth century. In any case, whence did the United Kingdom Parliament derive its omnicompetence? In July 1688 James II dissolved his Parliament. In December he fled the country, having dropped the Great Seal of the Realm in the Thames a few days earlier. William of Orange, having reached London, met groups of peers, former Members of Parliament and other notables; they advised him that elections should be held in the boroughs and counties. The Convention of Lords and 'Commons' met in January 1689, and next month offered the Crown to William and Mary jointly, subject to conditions set out in a Declaration of Right. The offer having been accepted, the Convention passed an Act asserting that it *was* Parliament,[9] and then enacted the Bill of Rights, incorporating the Declaration of Right. Clearly the Convention 'Parliament' had been irregularly summoned; its affirmation of its own legal authority carried the matter no farther; there had been no King from December 1688 (assuming that James II was deemed to have abdicated or to have forfeited the Crown) till February 1689; William III had no

9 Crown and Parliament Act 1689.

hereditary legal title to the throne and therefore had no authority to assent
to bills.[10] Has every purported Act of Parliament since 1688 been a nullity?
Is a Stuart still the rightful King?

Once questions such as these are asked,[11] one must acknowledge that
in certain circumstances a breach of legal continuity, be it peaceful or
accompanied by coercion and violence, may have to be treated as superseding the constitutional and legal order and replacing it by a new one. Legal
theorists have no option but to accommodate their concepts to the facts
of political life. Successful revolution sooner or later begets its own legality.
If, as Hans Kelsen has postulated, the basic norm or ultimate principle
underlying a constitutional order is that the constitution ought to be
obeyed,[12] then the disappearance of that order, followed by acquiescence
on the part of officials, judges and the general public in laws, rules and
orders issued by the new holders of power, will displace the old basic norm
or ultimate principle and give rise to a new one.[13] Thus, might becomes
right in the eye of the law.

This is a persuasive rationalization of the legal consequences of a successful
revolution, like the rebellion of the American colonists or the English
Revolution of 1688. It does not, however, answer all questions. It offers a
description, not a prescription. It does not dictate what attitude judges and
officials *ought* to adopt when the purported breach of legal continuity takes
place. However, judges in Pakistan,[14] Uganda[15] and Rhodesia (now Zim-
babwe)[16] a seem to have proceeded on the assumption that they have to accept
a successful revolution as a law-constitutive fact if they remain in office.[17]

---

10 cf. F. W. Maitland, *Constitutional History of England* (1908), pp. 283–5; T. P. Taswell-
Langmead's *English Constitutional History* (11th edn, 1960), pp. 445–59.
11 One possible answer, deducible from rationalizations of later medieval practice when
usurpations of the throne were not uncommon, is that William became King *de jure* after
he had dissolved the Convention 'Parliament' and the *new* Parliament of 1690 had
validated the legislation passed by the Convention. As a matter of State necessity (see
p. 72) a *de facto* King had been regarded as competent to summon a lawful Parliament.
12 *Pure Theory of Law* (2nd edn, transl.), p. 201; *General Theory of Law and State*, p. 115.
13 *General Theory of Law and State*, p. 118. See also H. L. A. Hart, *The Concept of Law*
(1961), pp. 114–16, 118–19, for a similar but not identical formulation.
14 *The State* v. *Dosso* PLD 1958 SC 533. But in 1972 the courts held that the case had
been wrongly decided: *Jilani* v. *State of Punjab* PLD 1972 SC 139.
15 *Uganda* v. *Prison Commissioner, ex p. Matovu* [1966] EA 514.
16 *R.* v. *Ndhlovu* 1968 (4) S.A. 515.
17 There is now a substantial body of legal literature on the problems arising from these
and similar cases. Most of the articles are referred to in Dennis Lloyd, *Introduction to
Jurisprudence* (5th edn, 1985), ch. 4; A. W. B. Simpson (ed.), *Oxford Essays in Jurisprudence*
(1973), chs. 2 (Eekelaar), 3 (Finnis); Bundu (1978) *ICLQ* 18.

The argument can be summarized in this way: sooner or later a breach of legal continuity will be treated as laying down legitimate foundations for a new constitutional order, provided that the 'revolution' is successful; there is, however, no neat rule of thumb available to judges during or immediately after the 'revolution' for the purpose of determining whether the old order survives wholly, in part or not at all. It so happened that the Revolution of 1688 gave a clear pointer to the Judiciary. There was a suspension of business in the courts, and after the throne had become vacant new judges had to be appointed because of a 'demise of the Crown'. These appointees were not at all likely to call the validity of the regime in question.[18] After a while (at the latest, after the failure of the Jacobite revolt in 1715) it would have been merely silly for a judge or commentator to deny that the Bill of Rights 1689 and other legislation passed after the Revolution were valid. Efficacy and acquiescence had established a new basis for legality. The particular circumstances in which the Revolution of 1688 took place, and its immediate practical consequences, laid a secure foundation, moreover, for judicial acceptance of the doctrine of absolute parliamentary sovereignty. The doctrine grew out of a particular state of affairs. A fundamental change of a political nature may bring about a fundamental change in legal doctrine.

The concept of necessity

One other comment must be made. In some situations where unconstitutional action has been taken by persons wielding effective political power, it is open to a judge to steer a middle course. He may find it possible to assert that the framework of the pre-existing order still survives, but that deviations from its norms can be justified on grounds of *necessity*. The principle of necessity, rendering lawful what would otherwise be unlawful,[19] is not unknown to English law; there is a defence of necessity (albeit of uncertain scope) in criminal law,[20] and in constitutional law the application

---

18 And in 1689 the Commons committed two former King's Bench judges, Pemberton and Jones JJ, to prison for a decision prior to the Revolution (see *Jay* v. *Topham* (1689) 12 St. Tr. 821), in which they had overruled a plea to the jurisdiction and given judgment against the Sergeant at Arms for an arrest carried out on the orders of the House. This was held to be a breach of the House's privileges.
19 See generally Glanville Williams (1953) 6 *Current Legal Problems* 216.
20 cf. J. C. Smith and Brian Hogan, *Criminal Law* (8th edn, 1996), pp. 251–9; Glazebrook [1972A] *Camb. LJ* 87; Law Commission, Report No. 83 (1977), which recommended that 'any defence of necessity at common law' be abolished.

of martial law is but an extended application of this concept. But the necessity must be proportionate to the evil to be averted, and acceptance of the principle does not normally imply total abdication from judicial review or acquiescence in the supersession of the legal order; it is essentially a transient phenomenon. State necessity has been judicially accepted as a legal justification for ostensibly unconstitutional action to fill a vacuum arising within the constitutional order in Pakistan,[21] Cyprus,[22] Rhodesia[23] and Nigeria.[24] To this extent it has been recognized as an implied exception to the letter of the constitution. And perhaps it can be stretched far enough to bridge the gap between the old legal order and its successor.[25]

PARLIAMENTARY SOVEREIGNTY SURVEYED

In its early days Parliament was a judicial as well as a law-making body. It was the High Court of Parliament, supreme over other courts. But it did not follow that its law-making competence was unlimited or unrivalled.

In the first place the supremacy of the Crown in Parliament was rivalled by the Crown acting outside Parliament. The Crown claimed and exercised an autonomous prerogative power to make laws by ordinance or

---

21 *Special Reference No. 1 of 1955* [1955] 1 FCR 439; Sir Ivor Jennings, *Constitutional Problems in Pakistan*. For a somewhat different approach to this principle, see *Jilani's* case (note 14, above).

22 *Att.-Gen. of the Republic* v. *Mustafa Ibrahim* (1964) Cyprus Law Reports 195; de Smith in *Annual Survey of Commonwealth Law 1965* (ed. Wade), pp. 3, 76–8.

23 *Madzimbamuto* v. *Lardner-Burke* 1968 (2) SA 284, a decision of the Rhodesian Appellate Division given before the court was prepared to recognize the success of the rebellion as fully legitimating the *de facto* Government; cf. note 16 above. On appeal the Privy Council (Lord Pearce dissenting) rejected the principle of necessity as applied by the Rhodesian judges [1969] 1 AC 645. However, it should not be inferred that the principle has no application at all in constitutional jurisprudence. Notwithstanding Lord Camden CJ's famous dictum in *Entick* v. *Carrington* (1765) 19 St. Tr. 1030 at 1073, that 'with respect to the argument of State necessity . . . the common law does not understand that kind of reasoning', such a principle was applied a few years later by Lord Mansfield in *R.* v. *Stratton* (1779) 21 St. Tr. 1045 at 1224; see also *Sabally and N'Jie* v. *Att.-Gen.* [1965] 1 QB 273 at 293, *per* Lord Denning MR.

24 *Lakanmi and Ola* v. *Att.-Gen. (West)*, 24 April 1970, where the Supreme Court of Nigeria, rejecting the Government's arguments, held that the military take-over in January 1966 had been a manifestation of necessity, not a revolutionary breach of legal continuity; and that fundamental rights under the pre-existing constitution were still in force save in so far as they were modified by the operation of necessity. This analysis of the facts may be regarded as courageous but far-fetched.

25 See, for example, note 11. Necessity here becomes a 'supra-constitutional' principle.

proclamation. Not until James I's time do we find an unequivocal pronouncement by the courts that the King could not change the general law of the land by virtue of the prerogative.[26] The King, moreover, claimed power to impose taxation incidentally to the exercise of prerogative powers (such as the power to regulate foreign affairs including external trade, and the power to take emergency measures for the defence of the realm) recognized as being vested in him; and in two great constitutional cases of the seventeenth century, the *Case of Impositions* (1606)[27] and the *Case of Ship Money* (1637)[28] – the latter decided after the *Case of Proclamations* – the courts upheld the validity of this ancillary taxing power. But the Bill of Rights 1689 laid it down that the raising of money for the use of the Crown by pretence of prerogative was unlawful. Again, the Crown had claimed – and the courts upheld the claim within certain limits in cases decided in 1674[29] and 1686[30] – a prerogative power to dispense with the operation of a statute for the benefit of an individual; but the Bill of Rights declared that in future dispensations would be invalid.[31] The Bill of Rights also declared that the 'pretended power of suspending of laws' by prerogative was unlawful; this was a reference to James II's disastrous attempt to enforce the suspension of the statutes which discriminated against Dissenters and Roman Catholics[32] – a premature experiment in religious toleration, albeit toleration with an ulterior motive, which precipitated a Glorious Revolution against royal tyranny. Thus did Parliament effectively dispose of the pretensions of the Crown to rival or subordinate its authority.

Since the Bill of Rights also changed the succession to the throne, so that title to the Crown was itself dependent on parliamentary authority, it would have been very difficult thereafter to contend that there were legal bounds to the powers of Parliament. Earlier in the seventeenth century

---

26 *Case of Proclamations* (1611) 12 Co. Rep. 74. This is perhaps the leading case in English constitutional law.

27 *Bate's case* (1606) 2 St. Tr. 371.

28 *R.* v. *Hampden* (1637) 3 St. Tr. 825.

29 *Thomas* v. *Sorrell* (1674) Vaughan 330.

30 *Godden* v. *Hales* (1686) 11 St. Tr. 1165.

31 Inland Revenue extra-statutory concessions to taxpayers may be contrary to the Bill of Rights. See *Vestey* v. *IRC* (*No. 2*) [1980] AC 1148 at 1195 *per* Lord Edmund-Davies; Dawn Oliver [1984] *Public Law* 389; but cf. Alder (1980) 130 *NLJ* 180.

32 See *Trial of the Seven Bishops* (1688) 12 St. Tr. 183. For a startling modern analogy, see *Fitzgerald* v. *Muldoon and Others* [1976] 2 NZLR 615 (New Zealand Prime Minister purported to abolish by a press notice a superannuation scheme established by statute; held invalid as being in breach of article 1 of the Bill of Rights 1689 and contrary to the undoubted principle that only Parliament has the power to make and unmake law, no other person having the ability to set aside legislation).

there had been no dearth of juristic pronouncements on the limitations on Parliament's competence, though they jostled with others proclaiming the transcendent and absolute authority of Parliament.[33] In James I's time there were dicta to the effect that Acts of Parliament contrary to common right and reason,[34] or making a man a judge in his own cause,[35] were void. That there were prerogatives inseparable from the King's person, so that no Act of Parliament could deprive him of them, was generally conceded;[36] but one of those 'inseparable' prerogatives was the dispensing power. After the Revolution of 1688 and the Bill of Rights – the product of an alliance between parliamentarians and common lawyers – these were but empty phrases. Faintly re-echoed by the words of Blackstone in 1765, paying lip-service to the primacy of natural law;[37] they had long since ceased to have legal significance; for the judges had tacitly accepted a rule of obligation to give effect to every Act of Parliament, no matter how preposterous its content.

The omnicompetence of Parliament, at least in respect of persons, matters and territory under the jurisdiction of the Crown, in the eyes of the courts can be supported by numerous dicta and some decisions squarely in point, and is illustrated by legislative practice. Attempts to impugn the validity of Acts of Parliament because of inconsistency with rules of international law have been rejected.[38] When a taxpayer challenged the validity of assessments made under a Finance Act on the ground that they were directed partly to

---

33 Dicta, extra-judicial and other, are collected together and discussed in Geoffrey Marshall's *Parliamentary Sovereignty and the Commonwealth* (1957), ch. 5.

34 *Dr Bonham's case* (1610) 8 Co. Rep. 114 at 118, *per* Coke CJ. Contrast Coke's extra-judicial comment in vol. 4 of his *Institutes*, p. 36: 'of the power and jurisdiction of Parliament, for making of laws in proceedings by Bill, it is so transcendent and absolute, as it cannot be confined either for causes or persons within any bounds'.

35 *Day* v. *Savadge* (1614) Hob. 85 at 86, 87, *per* Hobart CJ; see also the surprising dicta by Holt CJ, in *City of London* v. *Wood* (1701) 12 Mod. 669 at 686–8. The modern view of Parliament's authority to make a man a judge in his own cause is stated by Willes J, in *Lee* v. *Bude and Torrington Junction Rly* (1871) LR 6 CP 576 at 582.

36 D. L. Keir and F. H. Lawson, *Cases in Constitutional Law* (6th edn, 1979), pp. 73, 74, 83, 89, 91–2.

37 *Commentaries*, i. p. 41 (laws are invalid if contrary to the law of nature). Blackstone's words were taken seriously in the North American colonies.

38 See, for example, *Mortensen* v. *Peters* (1906) 14 SLT 227; *Cheney* v. *Conn* [1968] 1 WLR 242. Similarly, the Crown in the exercise of its prerogative power to delimit the extent of territorial water was not bound by international law: *Post Office* v. *Estuary Radio Ltd* [1968] 2 QB 740 at 757. Statute has since replaced this prerogative power: see Territorial Sea Act 1987, s1. But there is a rebuttable presumption that neither Parliament nor the Crown intended to violate a treaty or other rule of international law (ibid.). See also p. 152.

an unlawful purpose (the manufacture of nuclear weapons with a view to their possible use) it was held that even if such a purpose were contrary to international law:

What the statute itself enacts cannot be unlawful, because [it] is the highest form of law that is known to this country. It is the law which prevails over every other form of law, and it is not for the court to say that a parliamentary enactment . . . is illegal.[39]

Parliament has in fact passed retroactive penal legislation,[40] prolonged its own existence, transformed itself into a new body by the Acts of Union with Scotland and Ireland, repealed and amended provisions of those Acts which were to have permanent effect,[41] altered the procedure for making laws (under the Parliament Acts) and followed the new procedure and changed the succession to the throne (by the Bill of Rights, the Act of Settlement 1701, and His Majesty's Declaration of Abdication Act 1936). The courts will endeavour to construe Acts of Parliament so as to avoid a preposterous result, but if a statute clearly evinces an intention to achieve the preposterous, the courts are under an obligation to give effect to its plain words.[42] The safeguards against the enactment of such legislation are political and conventional, not strictly legal.

39 *Cheney* v. *Conn* [1968] I WLR 242 at 247, *per* Ungoed-Thomas J. See also *R.* v. *Jordan* [1967] *Crim. L. Rev.* 483 (an unsuccessful attack on the constitutional validity of the Race Relations Act 1965); *Madzimbamuto* v. *Lardner-Burke* [1969] I AC 645 at 723; *Blackburn* v. *Att.-Gen.* [1971] I WLR 1037 at 1041, *per* Salmon LJ.
40 An Act of 1541 enabled Lady Rocheford, an accessory to Catherine Howard's adultery, to be tried and executed for treason although she had become insane after arrest: Nigel Walker, *Crime and Insanity in England* (1973), pp. 183–4.
41 An attempt to impugn the Irish Church Act 1869, which had changed an unalterable provision of the Act of Union with Ireland by disestablishing the Church of Ireland, failed in *ex p. Canon Selwyn* (1872) 36 JP 54. This decision is criticized on the ground that the Act of Union with Ireland was a constituent Act, limiting the competence of the United Kingdom Parliament, by Harry Calvert, *Constitutional Law in Northern Ireland* (1968), pp. 27–33. cf. J. D. B. Mitchell, *Constitutional Law* (2nd edn, 1968), pp. 69–74.
42 See, however, the anomalous decision in *Green* v. *Mortimer* (1861) 3 LT 642 (private Act of Parliament treated as void because the court thought its provisions were absurd).

LEGAL LIMITATIONS ON PARLIAMENTARY SOVEREIGNTY[43]

Acts of Union

It can reasonably be argued that the Acts of Union with Scotland and Ireland were constituent Acts, establishing a new United Kingdom Parliament and setting limits to its powers.[44] The case for still regarding the Act of Union with Ireland 1800 in this light has been undermined by a series of basic legislative changes.[45] The case for so regarding the Act of Union with Scotland 1707 is not so weak. Much water has indeed flowed under the bridges since that time, but the position of the Established Church in Scotland and the Scottish system of judicature entrenched as fundamental and unalterable in the Articles of Union, remains largely intact.[46] Although the immunity of the surviving fundamental principles of the Union from legislative encroachment by the United Kingdom Parliament without Scottish consent[47] is probably to be regarded now as a matter of convention rather than of strict law, one cannot be certain that Scottish courts would take this view. In *MacCormick* v. *Lord Advocate* (1953) Lord Cooper was of the opinion that violation of fundamental terms of the Union would be unlawful but non-justiciable in a United Kingdom court.[48] No Scottish

---

43 See A. W. Bradley in J. Jowell and D. Oliver (eds), *The Changing Constitution* (3rd edn, 1994), ch. 4.

44 See p. 9, above.

45 cf. note 41; the biggest changes up to the time of writing were the establishment of the Irish Free State (now the Republic of Ireland) and a subordinate Northern Ireland Parliament (abolished by the United Kingdom Parliament in 1973). Moreover, at the time of the Union, Ireland was not unambiguously an independent State.

46 Subject to minor but significant exceptions. See the Universities (Scotland) Acts 1853 and 1932.

47 But how is Scottish consent to be signified? Through the MPs for Scottish constituencies and the Scottish peers at Westminster? Through an *ad hoc* constituent body? Through the new Scottish Parliament?

48 [1963] SC 396 at 411–13. See also MacCormick [1972] *Public Law* 176–9; T. B. Smith [1957] *Public Law* 99. In *Gibson* v. *Lord Advocate* 1975 SLT 134, Lord Keith refused an application to label s. 2(1) of the European Communities Act 1972 null and void as contrary to the Act of Union of 1707. He reserved his opinion on the situation which might be created if the United Kingdom Parliament passed an Act purporting to abolish the Court of Session or the Church of Scotland. But see also *Pringle* 1991 SLT 330: the Court of Session denied that it had jurisdiction to determine in proceedings following non-payment of poll tax whether a UK statute was invalid as contravening the Act of Union.

court has, however, held a public Act of Parliament to be void since the Union.

Substantive content of legislation: the general rule

Parliament can undoubtedly delegate its powers, setting limits to the authority of the delegate and retaining power to revoke the grant and a concurrent power to legislate. But can it effectively *deprive* itself of power to legislate on any matter or otherwise predetermine the future content of its own legislation? There is authority for the proposition that it cannot. An Act of 1919 laid down a scale of compensation for owners of compulsorily acquired slum property, and it stated that 'so far as inconsistent with that Act [other statutory] . . . provisions shall not have effect'. These provisions were held to have been impliedly repealed to the extent that they were inconsistent with other provisions in an Act of 1925, even if they were intended (which was doubtful) to have permanent effect.[49]

If there is a general rule that Parliament can do anything except bind its own future action, this may be regarded either as a limitation of parliamentary sovereignty or as a necessary characteristic of that sovereignty, since sovereignty inheres in Parliament as a continuing representative institution and not in one Parliament at a given moment of time. There is another, more mundane, explanation of the rule, divorced from ideas about sovereignty: public policy requires that no legislative body be competent to frustrate its primary purpose by creating a vacuum save where expressly authorized to do so – for example, by a written constitution. Put in this form, the principle applies to non-sovereign legislatures. Local authorities are incompetent to disable themselves from making a by-law on any matter within their allotted field.[50] And if this is an important factor sustaining the rule, then there remains the possibility that parliamentary omnicompetence can be restricted where the imposition of a fetter is consonant with the proper functions of Parliament.

Territorial competence

The orthodox view is that Parliament is competent to make any law whatsoever for any part of the world whatsoever, and that United Kingdom courts are under an obligation to give effect to any such law. Courts in

---

49 *Vauxhall Estates Ltd* v. *Liverpool Corporation* [1932] 1 KB 733; *Ellen Street Estates Ltd* v. *Minister of Health* [1934] 1 KB 590.
50 See, for example, *Cory (Willam) & Son Ltd* v. *City of London Corporation* [1951] 2 KB 475.

territories subordinate to the United Kingdom are under a like obligation, but not courts in foreign countries.[51] The obligation of courts in independent Commonwealth countries is debatable.[52]

Now, it is quite clear that Parliament can attribute legal consequences in United Kingdom law to acts done by aliens in foreign countries. It did so, for example, by the Aviation Security Act 1982.[53] And it could presumably make it an offence in United Kingdom law for a Frenchman to smoke in the streets of Paris.[54] But it is at least doubtful whether, even in terms of United Kingdom law, it has an unlimited competence to change the laws of independent countries. Since it would not, in practice, assert such authority,[55] the question is unlikely to arise before a United Kingdom court. However, untested assertions about Parliament's omnicompetence are an inadequate basis for ascribing to Parliament powers inconsistent with international comity and common sense.

Total or partial abdication by Parliament

If the United Kingdom Parliament were to proceed to liquidate itself by passing an Act transferring its functions to a new supranational European body or distributing those functions among (say) new Parliaments for England, Scotland. Wales and Northern Ireland, it would be absurd to suggest that a notional United Kingdom Parliament still existed and that it could resume its identity at any time and continue to exercise sovereign authority. Because this would be absurd, Parliament must be accepted as having the power to abdicate by extinguishing itself, thus 'committing suicide'. But what if Parliament continued to exist but purported to give away *part* of its sovereignty to another country or to new legislatures within the United Kingdom or to a supranational body?[56] Would this not be as

---

51 Or, possibly, a court in a British protected state (which was not part of Her Majesty's dominions) where the Crown had only limited jurisdiction, in respect of an Act of Parliament going beyond the Crown's jurisdiction: Sir Kenneth Roberts-Wray, *Commonwealth and Colonial Law* (1966), pp. 139–41.

52 See pp. 80–81.

53 See also *Joyce* v. *DPP* [1946] AC 337; Statute of Treasons 1351 (treason can be committed by alien in foreign country).

54 Sir Ivor Jennings, *The Law and the Constitution* (5th edn, 1959), pp. 170–71.

55 Unless one takes the view that on or soon after UDI Southern Rhodesia acquired the attributes of independent statehood; cf. Southern Rhodesia Act 1965; Southern Rhodesia Constitution Order 1965 (SI 1965, No. 1952); *Madzimbamuto* v. *Lardner-Burke* [1969] 1 AC 645; cf. *R.* v. *Ndhlovu* 1968 (4) SA 515.

56 cf. the controversy over the Irish Home Rule Bill in 1886; Marshall, op. cit., pp. 63–7; Anson (1886) 2 *LQR* 427.

ineffectual as an attempt by Parliament to preclude itself from repealing or amending a Licensing Act? This will be considered in three contexts: (1) Commonwealth affairs; (2) adoption of a written constitution; and (3) membership of the European Union.

1 – Independence in the Commonwealth

The most familiar, but not the most illuminating, questions turn on the legal effect of section 4 of the Statute of Westminster 1931,[57] ostensibly precluding Parliament from legislating for a Dominion unless the Act in question recited the Dominion's request and consent. Section 4 might be interpreted as (a) laying down a rule for the construction of statutes but (b) not imposing a fetter on the omnicompetence of Parliament because (i) it merely prescribed the insertion of a particular form of words in an Act, and Parliament could not effectively bind itself in this way[58] and (ii) in any event the power of Parliament to make any law whatsoever for any place whatsoever could not be surrendered. On this last point, there is a Privy Council dictum in a Canadian appeal supporting the view stated above;[59] an equivocal decision of the High Court of Australia;[60] and dicta in a Privy Council appeal from Ceylon,[61] and in South African cases decided while that country was still in the Commonwealth,[62] supporting a more radical interpretation – that such a provision was a renunciation of Parliament's plenary authority to make laws for those countries otherwise than in accordance with the requirement laid down by Parliament. ('Freedom once

57 See p. 46.
58 cf. Maugham LJ in *Ellen Street Estates Ltd* v. *Minister of Health* [1934] 1 KB at 597: Parliament 'cannot bind itself as to the form of subsequent legislation'. It is hard to know how much should be read into this dictum, since the question was whether Parliament could effectively prescribe that a statute should be repealable or alterable only by *express* words; held, it could not, even if it had purported to do so, which was doubtful.
59 *British Coal Corporation* v. *R.* [1935] AC 500 at 520 ('the Imperial Parliament could, as a matter of abstract law, repeal or disregard s. 4 of the Statute').
60 *Copyright Owners Reproduction Society* v. *EMI (Australia) Pty Ltd* (1958) 100 CLR 597. The decision (see p. 30, note 41) did not give a clear indication of what the attitude of Australian courts would have been had a United Kingdom statute purported unambiguously to change the law of Australia without reciting the necessary request and consent of the Commonwealth of Australia. cf. Hanks in (1968) 42 *ALJ* 286. (The power of the UK Parliament to legislate for Australia was ended by the Australia Act 1986.)
61 *Ibralebbe* v. *R.* [1964] AC 900 at 918 (on the irrevocable 'surrender' of Parliament's power by the Ceylon Independence Act 1947) and 924 (on the surrender of the Crown's prerogative legislative power).
62 *Ndlwana* v. *Hofmeyr* [1937] AD 229 at 237; *Harris* v. *Donges* [1952] 1 TLR 1245 at 1261, *sub nom. Harris* v. *Minister of the Interior* 1952 (2) SA 428.

conferred cannot be revoked.')[63] There is also an intermediate position: that United Kingdom courts would be obliged to give effect to Acts plainly intended to alter the law in Commonwealth countries despite non-compliance with the statutory conditions, but that the *local* courts, and on appeal the Privy Council (applying local law), would be entitled, or even obliged, *not* to apply such an Act.

If one looks at Independence Acts since 1960 the case for a traditionally conservative construction becomes weaker; for the United Kingdom Parliament has purported to renounce its power to legislate for those countries altogether. For example, section 1(2) of the Mauritius Independence Act 1968 provides: 'No Act of the Parliament of the United Kingdom passed on or after the appointed day [i.e., independence day] shall extend, or be deemed to extend, to Mauritius as part of its law; . . .' Is Parliament competent simply to resume its legislative sovereignty over Mauritius tomorrow?

From the point of view of the Mauritian courts, the answer is clearly not. The words of the Independence Act are unambiguous. Moreover the achievement of independence should in itself be understood as having liberated the legal order of Mauritius from its hierarchical subordination to that of the United Kingdom, so that the omnicompetence of the United Kingdom Parliament ceased to prevail in the local legal system.[64] And, looking at the matter from a common-sense point of view, English courts should adopt the same attitude. The United Kingdom Government and Parliament have renounced their authority over Mauritius, surrendering it to the competent authorities in Mauritius. One must also recognize that common sense does not always prevail in legal theory.[65]

2 – A written constitution

If the rule of judicial obedience to Acts of Parliament can be reformulated so that Parliament can effectively deprive itself of part of its sovereignty by surrendering it or transferring it to authorities *outside* the territorial limits of the United Kingdom, why can it not be reformulated by accepting that

---

63 *Ndlwana* v. *Hofmeyr*, n. 62 above. See, to like effect, Rand (1960) 38 *Can. Bar Rev.* 135 at 149; *Blackburn* v. *Att.-Gen.* [1971] 1 WLR 1037 at 1040, *per* Lord Denning MR (though his Lordship also cited, without disapproval, the dictum in the *British Coal Corporation* case, note 59).
64 See Kenneth Robinson in *Essays in Imperial Government* (ed. Robinson and A. F. Madden), p. 249. The case would have been even clearer if Mauritius had been a republic (which it became in 1992).
65 cf. pp. 78–9 .

Parliament can do exactly the same thing *within* the territorial limits of the United Kingdom? Suppose, for example, that a federal constitution were enacted, retaining a United Kingdom Parliament but purporting to restrict its legislative powers. For the courts dogmatically to insist that, so long as the United Kingdom Parliament existed, there was a mysterious rule, both fundamental and unalterable, precluding them from recognizing the efficacy of a transfer of part of its absolute sovereignty to Welsh and Scottish Parliaments, would be extremely odd, if the new federal constitution restricting parliamentary competence was known to have general public support as well as a parliamentary majority behind it. One's guess is that rather than make themselves ridiculous, the courts would fall into line and vary the 'fundamental' rule. They could vary it *ad hoc* (by declaring in a concrete case that an enactment of the reconstituted United Kingdom Parliament was inoperative) or by a general pronouncement (as when the House of Lords, acting extra-judicially, announced the abandonment of the self-imposed basic rule that it was bound by its own earlier decisions).[66] Law in the courts ought not to rest on assumptions that blithely ignore fundamental changes in constitutional structure.

One can carry this argument still farther. At present Parliament, as we have noted, is incapacitated from binding its own future action as to the substantive content of legislation where this would leave a legislative vacuum. But if Parliament adopted a written constitution under which no legislature in the United Kingdom was competent to violate certain rights and freedoms (for example, by enacting *ex post facto* penal legislation), it would be sensible for the judges to uphold the constitution against future legislative encroachments, provided at least there was a prescribed procedure for constitutional amendment. In other words, the fundamental rule of

---

66 [1966] 1 WLR 1234 (Practice Statement). Rupert Cross, *Precedent in English Law* (3rd edn, 1977), pp. 209–10, takes the view that a similar Practice Statement modifying the rule of absolute judicial obedience to Acts of Parliament would be strictly *ultra vires*, though if it were acquiesced in and acted upon it would effect a legal revolution. See also H. W. R. Wade, 'The basis of legal sovereignty' [1955] *Camb. LJ* 172 (an important and influential article), arguing that this basic rule or ultimate legal principle is alterable by judicial decision but not by statute. I have difficulty in understanding why a purported statutory modification of the present customary common-law rule should be treated either as nugatory or as less 'binding' than other statutory enactments merely because the present rule (i) is extremely important and (ii) was established neither by statute nor by judicial decision but by judicial accommodation to political facts. Nevertheless, the argument in the text above is confined to expressions of opinion as to what the judges ought to do or are likely to do if a fundamental structural change in the British constitutional system were to be adopted, and as to the present territorial scope of the rule of judicial obedience to statutes.

judicial obligation ought to be regarded as flexible, not immutable; as being susceptible to reformulation in the light of drastic innovations in legislative practice and corresponding changes in the climate of informed opinion about the limits of legislative authority.[67]

3 – Effect of membership of the European Union[68]

As was pointed out in an earlier chapter, our constitutional law must take into account legislation made by organs not subordinate to Parliament. This is the legislation of the European Union – or, as it is still correctly (and confusingly) styled, the legislation of the European Community, or Community law. In particular, the Council of Ministers and the Commission are empowered by the treaties to make regulations having direct effect in Member States and creating individual rights and duties enforceable in national courts. The concept of 'directly applicable' Community rules is recognized and implemented by section 2(1) of the European Communities Act 1972. Certain provisions of the treaties themselves are 'directly applicable' in the sense described.[69] Directives and decisions issued by the Council or the Commission normally require further implementation by the Government or other parties to whom they are addressed, but exceptionally they too may be invoked before national courts.[70]

67 The duty of the courts would probably be indicated expressly or by necessary implication by the text of such a constitution. The constitution itself might be adopted by a Constituent Assembly set up by parliamentary authority, and then be submitted for the approval of the electorate at a referendum.

68 See L. Collins, *European Community Law in the United Kingdom* (4th edn, 1990); T. C. Hartley, *The Foundations of European Community Law* (3rd edn, 1994); D. Lasok and J. Bridge, *Law and Institutions of the European Communities* (6th edn, 1994); J.-V. Louis, *The Community Legal Order* (3rd edn, 1995); A. J. Mackenzie Stuart, *The European Communities and the Rule of Law* (1977); J. A. Usher, *European Community Law and National Law: The Irreversible Transfer* (1981); de Smith (1971) 34 *Mod. L. Rev.* 597; Mitchell, Kuypers and Gall (1972) 9 *Common Market L. Rev.* 134. See also ch. 5, below.

69 For example, art. 16 of the EEC Treaty: see *Re Export Tax on Art Treasures* (*No. 1*) [1969] CML Rep. 1; ibid. (*No. 2*) [1972] CML Rep. 699. See also pp. 25–6. The first case in which the English courts had to *apply* the EEC Treaty was *Schorsch Meier GmbH* v. *Hennin* [1975] QB 416 (held, any rule at common law which required the English courts to give judgment only in sterling was incompatible with art. 106 of that Treaty): confirmed by s. 4 of the Administration of Justice Act 1977. See also *Bulmer* (*HP*) v. *J. Bollinger SA* [1974] Ch. 401 ('Parliament has decreed that the treaty is henceforward to be part of our law. It is equal in force to any statute': *per* Lord Denning MR at 418), and *Application des Gaz SA* v. *Falks Veritas Ltd* [1974] Ch. 381.

70 *Grad* v. *Finanzamt Traunstein* [1971] CML Rep. 41; *SACE* v. *Italian Ministry of Finance* [1971] CML Rep. 123.

Questions of the highest constitutional importance have arisen: English courts have acknowledged that, as a general principle, Community law prevails over English law.[71] But what if a directly applicable rule of Community law (say, a regulation) conflicts with an Act of Parliament? According to section 2(4), 'any enactment passed *or to be passed* [subject to certain exceptions] shall have effect subject to' the provisions of section 2(1). This could not be a mere rule of construction, to be displaced if the Act and the regulation cannot be harmonized. It states that Acts of Parliament shall *have effect subject to* directly applicable rules of Community law. Legislation already in existence on 1 January 1973 or (after that date) when the Community regulation is made will be impliedly repealed by the latter to the extent that the two sets of rules are irreconcilably in conflict. But what of post-accession United Kingdom legislation that is plainly inconsistent with a *prior* Community regulation? First, British courts will try to use their ingenuity to interpret the provisions such that primacy is accorded to the Community rule *and* so that no irreconcilable difference remains. That approach was approved by the House of Lords in *Garland* v. *British Rail Engineering Ltd*.[72] Second, if that method does not do the trick, our courts must apply Community law in preference even to a British statute passed after accession.[73] Now, according to the traditional British doctrine, primacy should be accorded to the subsequent statute;[74] but that doctrine has been undermined by the combined effect of the wording of section 2(4) and the political fact of Britain's membership of the European Union. According to well-settled Community doctrine, Community law (and not merely 'directly applicable' Community law) ought to prevail over *all* inconsistent national law, antecedent and subsequent. As the European Court of Justice has said, 'the Member States, albeit within limited spheres, have restricted

71 See, e.g., *Shields* v. *E. Coomes (Holdings) Ltd* [1979] 1 All ER 456; *Macarthys Ltd* v. *Smith* [1979] 3 All ER 325 and [1981] 1 All ER 111.

72 [1983] AC 751; see also *Duke* v. *GEC Reliance* [1988] 1 All E.R. 625, and below, pp. 112–14. The House also employed that technique in *Rainey* v. *Greater Glasgow Health Board* [1987] AC 224.

73 See, e.g., *Re an Absence in Ireland* [1977] 1 CMLR 5 (1971 regulation held to prevail over Social Security Act 1975, s. 82(5)(*a*)); *MacMahon* v. *Department of Education and Science* [1982] 3 CMLR 91 (1986 regulation applied in preference to inconsistent 1979 statutory instrument, SI 1979, No. 889). For the leading case, *Factortame*, see below.

74 Although in *Prince* v. *Secretary of State for Scotland* 1985 SLT. 74 Lord Cameron queried whether the European Parliament Elections Act 1978 was *ultra vires* the United Kingdom Parliament because of its apparent conflict with article 138(3) of the EEC Treaty; he did not have to decide the point as the pursuers failed on other grounds. See (1985) 101 *LQR* 149.

their sovereign rights',[75] and 'no appeal to provisions of internal law of any kind whatever can prevail' over this cession of authority.[76] By section 3(1) of the European Communities Act 1972, questions of Community law 'shall be determined' by our courts 'in accordance with the principles laid down by and any relevant decision of the European Court'.

The supremacy of Community law was unambiguously accepted by the House of Lords in the *Factortame* case.[77] Parliament had enacted the Merchant Shipping Act 1988, which had allowed the Secretary of State for Transport to make regulations under which applications could be made for permission to fish in United Kingdom territorial waters. In order to qualify under those regulations, ships had to be at least 75 per cent British-owned. Factortame Ltd, most of whose trawlers were registered in Spain, did not qualify, and its ships were denied licences. The company claimed that the 1988 Act was in breach of several articles of the EEC Treaty because it deprived the applicants of their Community law rights to trade anywhere in the Community. The company sought interim relief in the English courts, including the suspension of the Act. In the first round of litigation, the Court of Appeal and the House of Lords held that, as a matter of English law, the English courts had no power to suspend the operation of a statute, but the House of Lords sought a ruling from the European Court of Justice on the powers of national courts to grant interim relief where Community law rights were at issue.[78] The European Court ruled[79] that, in such a case, national courts must grant a temporary remedy pending a final judgment: this was thereupon done by the House of Lords, in an order suspending the operation of the 1988 Act.[80] In its final judgment in the litigation[81] the European Court ruled (not for the first time) that Member States must comply with Community law, and that, as the licensing scheme in the Merchant Shipping Act 1988 did, indeed, breach Community law in the EEC Treaty (especially by discriminating on grounds of nationality) the relevant provisions of that Act were 'ineffective'. Thus was a statute, which had been passed after United Kingdom accession to the European

75 *Costa* v. *ENEL* [1964] CML Rep. 425 at 455. See pp. 112–14.
76 *Re Export Tax on Art Treasures (No. 2)* [1972] CML Rep. 669 at 708.
77 *R.* v. *Secretary of State for Transport, ex p. Factortame (No. 2)* [1991] AC 603 (European Court of Justice and HL).
78 *Factortame Ltd* v. *Secretary of State for Transport* [1990] 2 A.C. 85.
79 *R.* v. *Secretary of State for Transport, ex p. Factortame Ltd* [1990] ECR -1 2433.
80 See reference above, note 77. The Merchant Shipping Act 1988 (Amendment) Order 1989 was made in order to suspend the relevant provisions of the statute. The common-law rule that an injunction cannot be granted against the Crown was also set aside.
81 *R.* v. *Secretary of State for Transport, ex p. Factortame Ltd* [1991] 3 All ER 769.

Community, held to be 'ineffective' by a court outside the United Kingdom; thus in the Community legal order was the orthodox doctrine that Parliament is competent to make any law whatsoever on any matter whatsoever set to one side. Within the Community legal system, the Queen in Parliament is not sovereign.[82]

The European Court gives primacy to Community law even where there is no *direct* conflict with national law. If Community (or European Union) rules have been promulgated to 'occupy the field' in a matter within Community competence, national Parliaments cannot pass *any* law on such a matter, except possibly for the ancillary purpose of implementing those rules locally on points of detail.[83] It seems, moreover, that if a competent European Union organ has made a treaty on a matter within its competence, Member States cannot legislate (or even enter into executive agreements with non-Member States) so as to detract from the operation of the Union policy, at least if that policy has been embodied in Union rules.[84]

This must all, however, be put into the full European Union political and legal context. For instance, German courts were reluctant to accept the Court's ruling that Community law prevails over inconsistent provisions of national constitutions.[85] French courts are reluctant to refer questions of Community law to the European Court. And most of the pronouncements by the Court on the primacy of Community law are made on preliminary rulings under article 177 of the EEC Treaty, under which the Court does not interpret national law but merely delivers a general interpretation of Community law in a case referred by a national court. If the national court can then apply the Community doctrine as declared by the European Court to the case before it, it should do so. If it cannot the expectation is that the national authorities will pass amending legislation as soon as possible. This has been done in the United Kingdom, and it is safe to assume that fresh legislation will be passed at Westminster in further cases of irreconcilable conflict.[86] If this action is not taken, the national authorities can be brought before the Court

---

82 On this important case, see Gravells [1991] *Public Law* 180; Magliveras (1990) 39 *ICLQ* 899; H. W. R. Wade (1991) 107 *LQR* 1.

83 See, for example, the *Hauptzollamt Hamburg* case [1972] CML Rep. 141 at 153; the *Norddeutsches Vieh* case [1971] CML Rep. 281 at 293; *Re Imported Thai Sand Flour*, ibid., 521.

84 *Re European Road Transport Agreement* [1971] CML Rep. 335 (dicta) – a difficult case.

85 See the *Internationale Handelsgesellschaft* case [1972] CML Rep. 258, 330; and further [1974] 2 CML Rep. 540.

86 For example, Equal Pay (Amendment) Regulations SI 1983, No. 1794 (passed after *Commission* v. *United Kingdom* [1982] ICR 578); Sex Discrimination Act 1986 (passed after *Commission* v. *United Kingdom* [1974] IRLR 29 and *Marshall* v. *Southampton & SW Hants. AHA* [1986] IRLR 140).

by the Commission as defaulters (articles 169–71).[87] But the Court cannot hold national legislation to be void for inconsistency with Community law. The Court is not at all like the Supreme Court of the United States.

The doctrine of parliamentary sovereignty has undoubtedly been changed, but it would fully revive in its traditional form if Parliament legislated to withdraw the United Kingdom from the European Union. For economic and political reasons it is most unlikely that Parliament would attempt to do that, but such a step probably would be effective in English law (although the European Court would probably hold that it was ineffective in Community law).

WHAT IS AN ACT OF PARLIAMENT?

Let the major issues just considered now be disregarded. How far, if at all, do the courts have jurisdiction to determine whether what purports to be an Act of Parliament is as a matter of law, an authentic statute which they are bound to apply?

The rule that judges ought to apply Acts of Parliament can be classified as a common-law rule, albeit a rule of outstanding importance. The meaning of the Queen in Parliament, and of an Act of Parliament, is governed partly by customary common law and partly by statute. The jurisdiction of the courts to examine the authenticity of purported Acts of Parliament can be considered by using inferences (in which considerations of public policy are of some consequence) drawn from common-law and statutory rules.

1 At common law, Parliament as a legislative body consists of the House of Commons, the House of Lords and the Queen. Each House must record its assent to a bill separately and the Queen has at least a formal discretion whether to assent to bills passed by them. The methods of giving and communicating the royal assent are regulated or prescribed by statute.[88] When Parliament is dissolved, its sovereignty is temporarily

---

87 This was the procedure adopted in the second *Export Tax* case, after the Italian Government and Parliament had failed to give effect to the Court's ruling under art. 177 implying that this long-standing tax was incompatible with the EEC Treaty.

88 Royal Assent Act 1967. An Act of Parliament is duly enacted if the royal assent is signified (i) by Letters Patent signed by Her Majesty under the Great Seal and pronounced in the customary manner (i.e. by Royal Commissioners in the House of Lords, the Commons also being present), or (ii) as above but announced to each House separately by the Speaker of that House (so as to avoid interruptions of the proceedings of the Commons because of the arrival of Commissioners in the Lords), or (iii) by Her Majesty in person, in the presence of both Houses. For forms of the assent, see Crown Office Rules Order 1967 (SI 1967, No. 802).

in abeyance since it is unable to legislate; there is a House of Commons, but it has no members because their seats have become vacant; there is a House of Lords, but it is incapacitated from sitting (except as a court of law) during a dissolution.

2 The customary common-law rule that each House has to pass a bill before it can be presented for the royal assent has been modified by statute. The Parliament Acts 1911 and 1949 authorize the presentation of a bill for the royal assent if certain conditions have been complied with, although the House of Lords has not passed the bill.

3 In order to express its sovereign will, Parliament must be constituted as Parliament and must function as Parliament within the meaning of existing common law and statute law. Unless these antecedent conditions for law-making have been fulfilled, the product should not be regarded as an authentic Act of Parliament.[89]

4 Nevertheless, if an official copy of what purports to be an Act of Parliament, bearing the appropriate customary words of enactment (normally[90] 'Be it enacted by the Queen's most excellent Majesty, by and with the advice and consent of the Lords Spiritual and Temporal, and Commons, in this present Parliament assembled, and by the authority of the same, as follows;') is produced, the courts will almost certainly accept this as conclusive evidence that the measure is authentic and has been duly passed. This follows from the decision of the House of Lords in *British Railways Board* v. *Pickin*.[91] In 1969 Mr Pickin had purchased part of a disused railway line and land adjoining it. But the Board subsequently claimed that it was the owner by virtue of a private statute, the British Railways Act 1968, section 18(1). Mr Pickin, however, alleged that in obtaining the passage of that Act in its favour, the Board had fraudulently concealed

89 This proposition is stated dogmatically and cannot be demonstrated to be correct, but is founded on logic. It enjoys widespread support among writers (for example, R. T. E. Latham, *The Law and the Commonwealth* (1949), pp. 523–4; Sir Ivor Jennings, *The Law and the Constitution* (5th edn, 1959), ch. 4; J. D. B. Mitchell, *Constitutional Law* (2nd edn, 1968), ch. 4; R. F. V. Heuston, Geoffrey Marshall, Hamish Gray, D. V. Cowen, B. Beinart, note 115 below).

90 Extra words are added for money bills. The usual enacting formula was evolved in the fifteenth century. By virtue of the Statute Law Revision Act 1948, s. 3(1)(a), it can be omitted altogether in a revised edition of the Statutes of the Realm. *Semble* omission of a recital that the House of Commons or (unless otherwise provided by statute) the House of Lords had consented to an Act would render the measure nugatory: *The Prince's case* (1606) 8 Co. Rep. 1a at 20a. The words of enactment have also been varied by statute for measures passed under the Parliament Acts without the consent of the House of Lords: Parliament Act 1911, s. 4(1).

91 [1974] AC 765.

certain matters from Parliament and that section 18 was therefore ineffective and did not deprive him of his proprietary rights.[92] Such an allegation,
to be tested, would require the courts to look to see what had happened
in Parliament during proceedings on the bill. The House of Lords unanimously decided that the courts had no jurisdiction to do so, either in
relation to a private or any other Act of Parliament.[93] As Lord Reid put it:

> For a century or more both Parliament and the courts have been careful not to
> act so as to cause conflict between them. Any such investigations as the respondent
> seeks could easily lead to such a conflict . . . The whole trend of authority for
> over a century is clearly against permitting any such investigation.[94]

This decision clarifies the situation which had been the subject of much
academic debate. The courts will apparently take the view that they *lack
jurisdiction* to pronounce an ostensibly authentic Act of Parliament to be a
nullity even though in fact Parliament has not functioned according to
existing law. But the point still requires further exploration.

The enrolled bill rule

Before *Pickin*'s case much had been made of the words of Lord Campbell
in *Edinburgh and Dalkeith Railway Co.* v. *Wauchope*:[95]

> All that a Court of Justice can do is to look to the Parliament Roll: if from that
> it should appear that a bill has passed both Houses and received the Royal Assent,
> no Court of Justice can inquire into the mode in which it was introduced into
> Parliament, nor into what was done previous to its introduction, or what passed in
> Parliament during its progress in its various stages through Parliament.

---

92 On the special procedure required for the passage of a private Act, see below p. 279.
93 Thus applying the dicta of, among others, Lord Campbell in *Edinburgh and Dalkeith
Railway Co.* v. *Wauchope* (1842) 8 Cl. & F. 710 at 725 and of Wilkes, J in *Lee* v. *Bude
and Torrington Railway Co.* (1871) LR 6 CP 576 at 582. When an amendment, agreed
to by both Houses, to what became the Rent (Agriculture) Act 1976 was, by an error,
omitted from the text, the Government's view was that only Parliament – and certainly
not the courts – could correct the mistake, and the Rent (Agriculture) Amendment Act
1977 was accordingly passed to put matters right. See 925 HC Deb. 1581–1622 (9
February 1977). A mistake in a bill by one House may be returned to it by the other
House for correction before royal assent. This happened with the Prosecution of Offences
Bill in 1985: see 460 HL Deb. 1438, 1449 (6 and 7 March 1985). Lord Campbell's dictum
was also applied in *Manuel* v. *Att.-Gen.* [1983] 1 Ch. 77, and in *Martin* v. *O'Sullivan*
[1984] STC 258.
94 *Pickin*'s case at 788.
95 See note 93.

Several comments can be made on this much-quoted passage.

1 The statement was a mere *obiter dictum*, a point missed by many commentators.

2 A peculiar sacrosanctity used to be attributed to the Parliament roll, the formal record of the High Court of Parliament,[96] upon which the originals of all Acts were engrossed in manuscript. Practice changed over the years.[97] From 1497 the original text was retained in the House of Lords and a *copy*, made on a Parliament roll, was sent to the Chancery. Since the middle of the nineteenth century, two copies of a bill as assented have been printed on vellum, and the Clerk of the Parliaments then adds his signature for the purpose of authentication; the 'original' is kept in the House of Lords, and the duplicate 'Parliament roll' copy now goes to the Public Record Office.[98] There was no reason of basic principle why these two official texts should have precluded all further judicial inquiry whatsoever into the procedure followed prior to enactment.

3 Copies of the Act are also printed by the Queen's Printer at Her Majesty's Stationery Office and sold to the public. Under section 3 of the Interpretation Act 1978 (which consolidated section 9 of the Interpretation Act 1889), judicial notice must be taken of all public Acts of Parliament passed since 1850; this states a rule of evidence[99] and does not specify what is an authentic Act of Parliament.

4 The courts will not encroach upon the exclusive preserves of the two Houses. Article 9 of the Bill of Rights 1689 provides that 'proceedings in Parliament ought not to be impeached or questioned in any court or place out of Parliament'. They fall within the province of parliamentary privilege. Hence the courts will refuse to inquire into such questions as whether either House was mistaken as to the facts, whether a bill had two, three or thirty-three readings, whether a quorum was present, and so on. Perhaps they would even disclaim jurisdiction to inquire whether

---

96 See Jennings, *The Law and the Constitution* (op. cit.), p. 139 and Appendix 3. But cf. R. F. V. Heuston, *Essays in Constitutional Law* (2nd edn, 1964), pp. 16–20.

97 For a historical survey, see Bond, 'Acts of Parliament' (1958) 3 *Archives* 201.

98 Erskine May, *Parliamentary Practice* (21st edn, 1989) p. 535. The Clerk of the Parliaments and the Clerk of the Records in the House of Lords kindly verified the information set out above. It must be obvious that the modern 'Parliament roll' copy of a statute need not enjoy the unique status of an original engrossed on the ancient Parliament roll, irrespective of judicial dicta suggesting that it does.

99 For the various rules of evidence relating to the proof of Acts of Parliament, see *Halsbury's Laws of England* (4th edn), vol. 17, para. 149.

a bill was in fact passed in the same form by both Houses.[100] If, however, it were to be asserted that a bill had not obtained a majority at the final reading in the House of Commons, would they, even after *Pickin*'s case, be prepared to go behind the official text of the Act and examine the Journal of the House and the notes of the official shorthand writers, on the grounds that the alleged defect was peculiarly gross and that 'a court must not decline to open its eyes to the truth'?[101] Even if they were so prepared it is doubtful whether a court would be prepared to conduct such an inspection without leave of the House, because the House has asserted the privilege not to have its internal proceedings investigated.[102]

5 What if it is alleged that procedural or formal requirements laid down by *statute* have not been complied with during the passage of a bill? Some modern statutes[103] have laid down procedural rules to be observed *before* a particular class of bill is introduced in Parliament. These rules are probably no more than directory; that is to say, non-compliance will not vitiate the end-product. One can arrive at this conclusion by two alternative assertions. The first is that the giving of the royal assent and publication with the appropriate words of enactment cure *all* prior defects. The second is that the rules in question are not of such fundamental importance to be regarded as conditions precedent to the validity of subsequent legislation.[104] Clearly these are different

---

100 Doubts on this point are expressed by Maitland, *Constitutional History of England* (1908), pp. 381−2. See also *Craies on Statute Law* (7th edn, 1971), pp. 37−40; the point is unsettled. Examples of such errors, and other irregularities in the enactment of bills, being followed by validating or amending legislation, are given by Erskine May, op. cit., pp. 535−7. The question whether the discrepancy between a bill as passed by the Commons and the bill as passed by the Lords rendered the Act invalid was actually argued before a court in *Pylkington*'s case (1455; discussed by Cowen in 16 *Mod. L. Rev.* at 275− 7) but no final decision was recorded.

101 cf. *Bribery Commissioner* v. *Ranasinghe* [1965] AC 172 at 194 (dealing with the jurisdiction of the courts, at least in Ceylon, to inquire whether a prescribed Speaker's certificate had been given in the due form on a bill before enactment). The comment in the text above is necessarily speculative. See further Beinart, loc. cit. n. 115, for a very full review of these questions.

102 Erskine May, op. cit., pp. 90−94; but see the Defamation Act 1996, s. 13 (below p. 320).

103 For example, Consolidation of Enactments (Procedure) Act 1949.

104 cf. *Clayton* v. *Heffron* (1961) 105 CLR 214, where part of the procedure prescribed for the resolution of a disagreement between the two Houses of Parliament in Victoria had not been observed in the passage of a bill; held, the requirements were only directory. This decision was followed in *Cormack* v. *Cape* (1974) 131 CLR 432 and in *Victoria* v. *Commonwealth of Australia and Connor* (1975) 134 CLR 81. Contrast *Bribery Commissioner* v. *Ranasinghe* [1965] AC at 200 (held, that the giving of a Speaker's certificate was a necessary part of the legislative process, and its omission was not cured by royal assent to a bill).

approaches, the second implying that compliance with statutory procedural rules of fundamental importance might be regarded as a condition precedent. One is not obliged to assume that fundamental rules of such a character lie within the exclusive cognizance of Parliament itself.

6 It is unlikely that a court would be prepared to issue an injunction to restrain the submission of a bill for the royal assent or otherwise intervene while the bill was before Parliament.[105] The Attorney-General could probably obtain an injunction to prevent a public body from exceeding its statutory powers by promoting a private bill before the matter came before Parliament.[106]

7 One can nevertheless imagine situations in which a measure purporting to be an Act of Parliament might be treated as nugatory by a court. For example, the Parliament Acts enable certain bills to be presented for the royal assent without the consent of the Lords, and provide that a certificate given by the Speaker of the Commons before a bill is presented for assent, and endorsed on the bill that the requirements of the Acts have been complied with, shall be conclusive for all purposes and shall not be questioned in any court.[107] But bills to prolong the duration of a Parliament beyond five years are explicitly excluded from the Parliament Act procedure.[108] If such a bill were to be passed by the Commons alone, certified by the Speaker and assented by the Queen with words of enactment stating that it had been passed in accordance with the Parliament Acts[109] a court should surely treat that 'Act' as a nullity, because it was 'bad on its face'; the body purporting to enact it would not be 'Parliament' within

---

105 The main reason being that this would be a breach of parliamentary privilege – an objection that would not apply to proceedings before a colonial legislature: *Rediffusion (Hong Kong) Ltd* v. *Att.-Gen. of Hong Kong* [1970] AC 1136.

106 *Att.-Gen.* v. *London and Home Counties Joint Electricity Authority* [1929] 1 Ch. 513 (unlawful expenditure of funds for the purpose). But the jurisdiction to award an injunction will be sparingly exercised and is unlikely to be exercised at all in proceedings between parties. See *Bilston Corpn* v. *Wolverhampton Corpn* [1942] Ch. 391 (no injunction to restrain breach of undertaking, confirmed by statute, not to oppose introduction of bill); Holdsworth (1943) 59 *LQR* 2.

107 Parliament Act 1911, ss. 2(2), 3; Parliament Act 1949. For the Speaker's certificate that a bill is a money bill within the meaning of the 1911 Act, see s. 1(3) of that Act.

108 1911 Act, s. 2(1).

109 As has already been indicated (see p. 32), an erroneous certificate that a bill was a money bill would be probably accepted as conclusive unless the error was so gross as to be indicative of bad faith. This is because the practical consequences of holding a money bill to be a nullity might be extremely grave.

the meaning of existing law. The fatal defect[110] would be apparent without any judicial intrusion into the proceedings of either House; the purported Act would be no more efficacious than a resolution of the House of Commons.[111] A broadly similar analysis might be applicable to a situation in which a Regent assented to a bill to alter the succession to the throne or the establishment of the Church in Scotland, in disregard of the prohibitions contained in the Regency Act 1937.[112] These are no doubt somewhat fanciful hypotheses, but by putting extreme examples, the limitations of an apparently rigid rule can be exposed.

Redefinition of the meaning of Parliament

Parliament is capable of redefining itself for particular purposes. It did so by the Parliament Acts, which provided a simpler, optional procedure for legislation on most topics.[113] It could make the procedure simpler still by abolishing the House of Lords. What if it were to lay down a more cumbersome procedure for legislating and prescribe it as the only procedure to be followed? Suppose, for example, that Parliament were to pass a Bill of Rights Act proclaiming the rights of the citizen, and which stated that no bill to vary that Act was to be presented for the royal assent unless it had first obtained the support of a majority of the voters at a referendum, or had been passed at its final reading with the support of two-thirds of the full membership of the House of Commons; and that no bill to amend or repeal that Act was to be presented for the royal assent unless that same

---

110 Or to use the colourful phrase used in *R.* v. *Arundel (Countess)* (1617) Hobart 109 at 111, the 'death wound'.

111 Which has no legal effect outside the walls of Parliament (*Stockdale* v. *Hansard* (1839) 9 Ad. & E. 1; *Bowles* v. *Bank of England* [1913] 1 Ch. 57), unless given such an effect by Act of Parliament: see Provisional Collection of Taxes Act 1968; and ch. 16.

112 Regency Act 1937, s. 4(2). This provision might, of course be held to be merely directory, though such an analysis seems implausible.

113 Professor H. W. R. Wade regards measures passed under this procedure as a special form of delegated legislation: see [1955] *Camb. LJ* 172 and *Constitutional Fundamentals* (1980), pp. 27–8. I respectfully prefer Dr Geoffrey Marshall's view (*Parliamentary Sovereignty and the Commonwealth* (1957), pp. 42–6) that such legislation is primary and not delegated. Professor Hood Phillips (*Constitutional and Administrative Law* (7th edn. 1987 by Hood Phillips and Paul Jackson), p. 91) goes so far as to characterize legislation passed with a Regent's assent 'as a kind of delegated legislation', and on this ground would justify a judicial decision to the effect that an 'Act' assented to by a Regent in contravention of s. 4(2) of the 1937 Act was invalid. He has also suggested (*Reform of the Constitution* (1970), pp. 18–19, 91–2) that the Parliament Act 1949 is a nullity because the 'delegate' created in 1911 enlarged its own limited powers in passing it.

procedure had been followed.[114] Could Parliament nevertheless amend or repeal the Act by ordinary legislative procedure?[115]

1 It is not enough to incant the phrase: 'A sovereign Parliament cannot bind its own future action.'[116] One of the questions to be asked is: 'What is meant by "Parliament"?' Another − essentially the same question expressed in a different way − is whether there cannot be new mandatory legal rules as to the manner and form of law-making which Parliament must observe if its enactments are to be recognized as authentic. The much-quoted dictum that 'Parliament cannot bind itself as to the form of subsequent legislation'[117] carries us nowhere, for it was uttered merely to rebut the optimistic argument that Parliament had protected an

114 Unless this last entrenching provision was present − it is absent from section 1 of the Northern Ireland Constitution Act 1973, as it was from section 1(2) of the Ireland Act 1949 − it could easily be argued that the Act imposing the special requirement could itself be amended or repealed by ordinary legislative procedure.

115 Among the main contributions are those by Cowen (1952) 15 *Mod. L. Rev.* 282, (1953) 16 *Mod. L. Rev.* 273; Beinart [1954] *Butterworth's South African Law Rev.* 135; Geoffrey Marshall, *Parliamentary Sovereignty and the Commonwealth* (1957) and *Constitutional Theory* (1971), ch. 3; R. F. V. Heuston, *Essays in Constitutional Law* (2nd edn, 1964), ch. 4; J. D. B. Mitchell, *Constitutional Law* (2nd edn, 1968), ch. 4; Gray (1953) 10 *U. of Toronto LJ* 54; Friedmann (1950) 24 *Australian LJ* 103; O. Hood Phillips, op. cit., ch. 4; Harry Calvert, *Constitutional Law in Northern Ireland* (1968), ch. 1.

116 In this context the implications of *Att.-Gen. for NSW* v. *Trethowan* (1931) 44 CLR 394; [1932] AC 526 are often misunderstood by students. Under the constitution of New South Wales as amended by local legislation passed in 1929, a bill to abolish the upper House could not be presented for the royal assent unless it had first been approved by the electorate at a referendum, and a like requirement extended to any bill to amend or repeal this procedure. Following a change of government in 1931, bills were passed by both Houses of the New South Wales Parliament to remove the referendum rule and to abolish the upper House; neither bill was submitted to a referendum. Injunctions were obtained to restrain submission of the bills for the royal assent. This may have been an inappropriate remedy (see *Hughes and Vale Pty Ltd* v. *Gair* (1954) 90 CLR 203 at 204−5), but the decision on the point of substantive law was clearly correct. Confusion has been caused by the fact that New South Wales had a non-sovereign legislature; and section 5 of the Colonial Laws Validity Act 1865, which applied to New South Wales, provided that a 'colonial' legislature could make laws relating to its constitution, powers and procedure 'in such manner and form as may . . . be required' by existing law. The applicability of section 5 furnished one reason for holding the improper procedure to be unlawful; the decision should have been the same, however, even if New South Wales had had a 'sovereign' legislature: see cases cited in notes 119 and 120, below. There is a common but wholly unfounded misconception that *because* New South Wales had a non-sovereign legislature and was held to be competent to 'bind its own future action', *it therefore follows* that a sovereign legislature like the United Kingdom Parliament is incompetent to do so.

117 See above, note 58.

ordinary enactment against implied repeal.[118] Another question, as we have already seen, is the extent to which the courts have jurisdiction to determine whether 'Parliament' has acted in conformity with the law behind Parliament.

2 Modern decisions in constitutional cases arising in South Africa[119] and Ceylon[120] show that a sovereign (i.e. omnicompetent) Parliament must function in the manner prescribed by existing law in order validly to express its legislative will. In each of the cases the constitution had laid down a special procedure (a two-thirds' majority of the two Houses in joint session, or a two-thirds' majority in the lower House, at final reading) to be followed for the enactment of legislation on certain important matters. In each of them the courts held that where bills dealing with these 'entrenched' matters had been passed by *ordinary* legislative majorities and had been duly assented to and printed, they could not be accepted as authentic Acts of Parliament. There was to be read into the constitution a necessary implication that 'Parliament' bore different meanings for different purposes.

3 These decisions, extremely interesting though they are as illustrations of basic principle, are of doubtful persuasive authority when we try to answer our hypothetical problem set in a British constitutional context. In the first place, in each of them the wording of a Speaker's certificate on the face of the Act or bill in question (or the absence of such a certificate) indicated that the specially prescribed procedure had not in

---

118 cf. *R.* v. *Drybones* [1970] SCR 282 (Can.) for the position of an extraordinary enactment (the Canadian Bill of Rights 1960) which the majority of the Supreme Court held would prevail over inconsistent legislation not expressed to be made 'notwithstanding' the Bill of Rights.

119 *Harris* v. *Donges* [1952] 1 TLR 1245, *sub nom. Harris* v. *Minister of the Interior* 1952 (2) SA 428 (two-thirds' majority of both Houses of the South African Parliament required by the South Africa Act 1909 for removal of Cape Coloured voters from the common voters' roll; held, a measure passed by both Houses sitting separately by simple majorities was not an authentic Act of Parliament, although it had been assented to); see also *Minister of the Interior* v. *Harris* 1952 (4) SA 769 (an 'Act' constituting the two Houses as the 'High Court of Parliament' with power to override the previous decision by a simple majority, also held to be a nullity). See, however, *Colins* v. *Minister of the Interior* 1957 (1) SA 552, where the desired result was achieved by a sufficiently circuitous route. For the literature on this series of legal battles, see Geoffrey Marshall, *Parliamentary Sovereignty and the Commonwealth* (1957).

120 *Bribery Commissioner* v. *Ranasinghe* [1965] AC 172 (royal assent did not cure failure to obtain a two-thirds' majority in the lower House for a measure inconsistent with the constitution). See further *R. (O'Brien)* v. *Military Governor, NDU Internment Camp* [1924] IR 32 (failure to submit a bill to a referendum held fatal to the validity of an ostensibly authentic Act; see Heuston, op. cit., pp. 11–14).

fact been followed. Although the decisions suggest that the courts can look at the original of the bill as presented for assent (and are not confined to the bare text of the published Act), they do not offer clear guidance on the proper limits of a court's scope of inquiry if there is no requirement of a Speaker's certificate, or if a Speaker's certificate or the words of enactment are notoriously false or are alleged to be false. As far as British courts are concerned, these questions remain open. In the second place, none of them deals with the legal effects of *self-imposed* procedural requirements by the Parliaments of those countries; the requirements had been imposed by the constitutional instruments from which the Parliaments derived their authority to make law.

4 None the less, there is no *logical* reason why the United Kingdom Parliament should be incompetent so to redefine itself (or redefine the procedure for enacting legislation on any given matter) as to preclude Parliament *as ordinarily constituted* from passing a law on a matter. (There are, of course, doubts as to the jurisdiction or willingness of the courts to intervene.) If Parliament can make it easier to legislate, as by passing the Parliament Acts or abolishing the House of Lords, it can also make it harder to legislate.[121]

5 Hence a two-thirds' majority rule might be analysed either as a redefinition of the meaning of 'Parliament' or a prescription of essential procedural conditions before Parliament could speak with an authentic voice; a rule imposing a duty to hold a referendum could quite persuasively be analysed as the addition of a fourth element to 'Parliament', in much the same way as the Parliament Act procedure can be analysed as involving the conditional subtraction of one of the three elements from Parliament.

6 Such an analysis can be attacked on the ground that once it is conceded that Parliament can make legislation on any topic more difficult, one must then concede that it can make legislation impossible. If it can lay down a two-thirds' majority rule it can lay down a nine-tenths' majority rule, and a similar rule for the majority to be obtained at a referendum. In this way it could, by imposing requirements as to the manner of legislating, in practice bind itself not to change the substantive content of future legislation, and this would be contrary to both established principle and public policy; a legislative vacuum must not be created;

---

121 The Parliament Acts analogy has been characterized as fallacious because the Acts only created an additional and permissive means of legislating, so that no question of limitation arises. See Colin Munro, *Studies in Constitutional Law* (1987), pp. 106–7.

consequently the courts ought not to recognize the legal efficacy of *any* such restrictive rule. The only ways of answering this point are that there exist *political* safeguards against the adoption of such restrictive rules, just as there are political safeguards against the enactment of preposterous laws by ordinary legislative procedure; and that a court could draw a common-sense line between binding rules regulating the manner of legislating and ineffectual rules which if accepted as binding would, in substance, stop Parliament from legislating at all.[122] One must, however, recognize the distinct possibility that a court might decide not to engage in such a delicate exercise.

To devote more space to this conundrum would hardly be worthwhile. We are in the realm of speculative conjecture. To dwell there longer would be justified only if there were a substantial likelihood that the hypothetical situation would assume practical importance.

PRACTICAL LIMITATIONS ON THE LEGISLATIVE POWER OF PARLIAMENT

Some of these limitations are considered more fully in chapters 10, 12 and 14. The legal effect of European Union membership has already been considered. Even if membership had not curbed the formal legal sovereignty of Parliament, the obligations entailed by membership mean that in practice Parliament will have to abstain from legislating, or legislating in particular ways, on a number of important topics; and has required that legislation (mainly under delegated authority conferred by section 2(2) of the European Communities Act 1972)[123] be passed in conformity with European Union requirements.

When one asks what are the practical limitations on the exercise of parliamentary supremacy, one is also asking what are the effective restraints operating on the Government; for the legislative programme is largely dominated by the Government. In the first place, a Government's freedom of action is inhibited by its international position, and in particular by international obligations which it has undertaken. Quite apart from the pervasive influence of European law, a Government would need to have very strong reasons for introducing legislation inconsistent with its

---

122 See Friedmann (1950) 24 *Australian LJ* at 105–6.
123 See ch. 17.

obligations under the European Convention on Human Rights, GATT, or other multilateral conventions to which this country had acceded.

Secondly, the Government would not sponsor legislation which flagrantly violated a constitutional convention restricting the territorial ambit or subject-matter of legislative competence. It would not initiate legislation intended to encroach on the autonomy of an independent Commonwealth country or, for example, to impose changes in the laws of the Channel Islands on purely domestic matters. It has often been stated that the Government must not 'exceed its electoral mandate' by introducing major constitutional changes which have not been foreshadowed by its election manifesto. One may accept that there exists a loose convention to this effect, but one must recognize that unforeseen contingencies always arise during the life of a Parliament, that the country cannot exist on a diet of dissolutions, that a party's election manifesto does not have to be comprehensive and that a vote cast at a General Election does not imply conscious support for every aspect of a party's programme.

Thirdly, the Government will not introduce legislation which it believes to be incapable of enforcement. Occasionally an Act proves subsequently to be unenforceable (for example, the Southern Rhodesia Act 1965, asserting Parliament's paramount authority over the breakaway colony and, to an extent, the legislation which introduced the ill-fated poll tax), but that is another matter. Nor will an Act be passed which requires the cooperation of the general public but which flies in the face of strong public opposition, such as one which would make it an offence to manufacture or sell all alcoholic liquor.

Fourthly, although unpopular legislation may be passed, the Government would not introduce and its normally obedient supporters in Parliament might refuse to support legislation which would court inevitable electoral disaster in the later stages of the life of a Parliament.

Fifthly, a Government's freedom of legislative initiative is circumscribed to some extent in so far as it is customary or expedient (or both) to consult in advance and pay some regard to the views of powerful organized interest groups, which are also able to exert pressure through their spokesmen in Parliament.

Sixthly, if a Government is in office without an overall majority in the House of Commons, it will obviously be at risk of losing votes on (among other things) its proposed legislation. The General Election of February 1974 resulted in the formation of a minority Labour Government, the first Government to be formed without a parliamentary majority since 1929. The October 1974 General Election gave the Government a small overall majority, but this was lost quite soon through by-election defeats. Thus the parliamentary situation was such that the Labour Government had to be careful to bring forward proposals which would carry at the least its parliamentary party. It did suffer defeats on bills, particularly relating to devolution.

Two other points must be made. First, there are still those who will solemnly affirm that Parliament ought not to legislate against the weight of public opinion; and even that the purpose of constitutional conventions is to ensure that government is conducted in accordance with public opinion. Stated in these general terms, such propositions are unacceptable. The British system of parliamentary government is above all a system of *government*. It is not a system geared to a series of opinion polls or referendums in which the garbled voice of the people is equated with deity. Among the factors which the Government and Members of Parliament have to take into account is the strength of public sentiment on particular issues. But this is one factor among many. Members of Parliament are representatives but not delegates of their constituents; nor is the Cabinet a committee of the House of Commons or of Parliament. A Government and its parliamentary supporters ought to act in the way they think best in the general interests of the country. It is open to the electorate to use criticism and ridicule, to exert pressure on their representatives by legitimate means, to voice their displeasure at by-elections and to turn the Government out at the next General Election. But there is no constitutional convention to the effect that a Government which loses the confidence of the *country* must resign or advise a dissolution of Parliament, so long as it commands a majority in the House of Commons.

The second point should be stated in order to balance this account, though its connection with the idea of the supremacy of sovereignty of Parliament is only marginal. Although Parliament, for political purposes, is not to be thought of as a collective entity, and although in the last resort a Government will normally be able to bring its supporters in the House of Commons (and its supporters and opponents in the House of Lords) reluctantly to heel, the last resort is seldom reached. Because Parliament exists, because the Opposition in the House of Commons is always probing for opportunities to discredit the Government, and because Governments prefer convincing their backbenchers to bullying them, and are anxious to avoid public recriminations within the party in front of the Opposition, a Government needs to explain and justify its position to Parliament, and through Parliament to the public at large, as persuasively as possible and with an outward show of unity. Moreover, parliamentary time is not unlimited; and draconian action to curtail debate when obstructive tactics are used in the House of Commons can prove counter-productive. These factors undoubtedly influence the content of legislation, as well as curbing a Government's general freedom of action. Prudence often dictates caution and compromise.

CHAPTER 5

The United Kingdom and the European Union[1]

THE UNION AND CONSTITUTIONAL LAW

There can be no doubt that the United Kingdom's membership of the European Union is of high importance in our constitutional law. No book on constitutional law can be considered complete if it fails to bring this fact home to the reader, and to point him to sources for wider and deeper reading than it is possible to supply in any such textbook. This chapter will not in itself, however, offer a comprehensive guide to the impact of membership, because it is best to consider certain aspects in their contexts throughout the book. Thus, for example, the question of the effect of membership on parliamentary sovereignty was considered in the preceding chapter;[2] the place of European law as a source of our domestic law was looked at in chapter 2;[3] the ability of the European Union to levy taxes directly, without reference to the United Kingdom Parliament, will be considered in chapter 14 as part of the United Kingdom's financial arrangements;[4] scrutiny by Parliament of European legislation will also be looked at in that chapter;[5] the consequences of membership on our immigration

---

1 Four very helpful short studies are J. Steiner, *Textbook on EEC Law* (4th edn, 1994); P. S. R. F. Mathijsen, *A Guide to European Community Law* (5th edn, 1990); D. Lasok and J. W. Bridge, *Introduction to the Law and Institutions of the European Communities* (6th edn, 1994) and Lawrence Collins, *European Community Law in the United Kingdom* (4th edn 1990). See also T. C. Hartley, *The Foundations of European Community Law* (3rd edn, 1994); S. Weatherill, *Cases and Materials on EEC Law* (3rd edn, 1996); S. Weatherill and P. Beaumont, *EC Law* (2nd edn, 1995). For larger reference works see B. Rudden and D. Wyatt, *Basic Community Laws* (6th edn, 1996); D. Wyatt and A. Dashwood, *European Community Law* (3rd edn, 1993).
2 See above, pp. 83–7.
3 See above, pp. 25–6.
4 See below, p. 283.
5 See below, p. 281.

law will be examined in chapter 20,[6] and there will be other, shorter, references in appropriate places.

So this chapter will concentrate on matters which are not considered elsewhere. They are (1) the political background; (2) the purposes and institutions of the European Union; and (3) Community law.

POLITICAL BACKGROUND

The European Coal and Steel Community (ECSC) was established in 1952.[7] The political will existed in continental Europe in the 1950s to take that initiative much further, and the European Economic Community (EEC)[8] together with the European Atomic Energy Community (EURATOM)[9] were born in 1958. This was followed by the merger of the institutions of the three Communities in 1965.[10] By the 1980s reference simply to the European Community had become the accepted parlance, and after the Maastricht Treaty of 1992 the nomenclature changed again to European Union. The EEC has undoubtedly been, and remains, the most important of the Communities, but the United Kingdom was not ready to join it at its inception: memories of the Empire were still relatively fresh; a considerable number of colonies remained; the 'special relationship' with the United States of America and relationships with the independent Commonwealth countries, taken together with fears about the loss of sovereignty which it was thought would be implicit in joining, kept us out. When the Leader of the Labour Party, Mr Gaitskell, said as late as 1962 that joining would mean the 'end of a thousand years of history'[11] he probably spoke for many. Accordingly the United Kingdom did not join the original six members[12] but tried instead to sit on a three-legged stool made up of the Commonwealth and colonies (with trade preference), the United States (particularly for political purposes) and a loose-knit European Free Trade Association (broadly consisting of European countries not in the EEC).

6 See below, pp. 413, 416.
7 See Cmnd 4863 (1972) (the Treaty of Paris).
8 See Cmnd 4864 (1972) (the Treaty of Rome).
9 See Cmnd 4865 (1972).
10 See Cmnd 5179 (1972).
11 At the Labour Party conference, Brighton, October 1962.
12 Belgium, the Federal Republic of Germany, France, Italy, Luxembourg and the Netherlands.

It became increasingly clear, however, that it should at least be discovered whether the United Kingdom could become associated with the European Community on acceptable terms. The EEC countries enjoyed an economic boom in the 1950s and 1960s, while the United Kingdom's economy never really recovered from the enormous costs of the Second World War. In short, the belief grew that salvation might lie in membership of the EEC. As one of the last great acts of his Administration, Harold Macmillan applied for membership in 1961. Negotiations, led for Britain by Mr Edward Heath, dragged on until 1963, when President de Gaulle vetoed the application. The Labour Party (which in the same year had elected Mr Wilson as its Leader on the death of Mr Gaitskell) underwent a change of heart and decided that when it was next in power it too would try to enter. By that time, in 1967, the President of France was quicker off the mark: the French veto came before negotiations could take place. Finally, Mr Heath's Government of 1970 made a further attempt[13] and successful negotiations led to the conclusion of the Treaty of Brussels[14] the European Communities Act 1972 and full United Kingdom membership from 1 January 1973.[15]

But a nagging doubt remained. Were we truly 'European'? The question could not be answered by a vote in the House of Commons or at a General Election, because different answers would be given by members of the same political party and of none. The Labour Government of 1974 therefore came to office pledged to put the issue to the people.[16] The Cabinet agreed upon a novel constitutional experiment: a referendum.[17] The Referendum Act 1975 allowed all those who would be entitled to vote at a local government election to participate in the referendum.[18] Public money was granted to the protagonists.[19] Under the superintendence of a Chief Counting Officer[20] the referendum was held on 5 June 1975, the majority

13 President de Gaulle had resigned in 1969, and his successor, President Pompidou, did not share his predecessor's fears of Anglo-Saxon domination of the EEC.

14 See Cmnd 4862 (1972), vols. 1 and 2.

15 Norway applied for membership at the same time, but the Norwegian electorate rejected it at a referendum. Denmark and the Republic of Ireland joined at the same time as the United Kingdom.

16 This was to be done 'through the ballot box' – a formula which left open the possibility of a referendum or another General Election.

17 See p. 197 below for the suspension of collective Cabinet responsibility on the matter – in itself a rare, but not unique constitutional device.

18 s. 1(3).

19 s. 3. Two umbrella organizations were formed, one on each side.

20 s. 2(4).

of the Cabinet being in favour of continued membership.[21] The question
on the ballot paper was 'Do you think that the United Kingdom should
stay in the European Community (the Common Market)?' Of eligible
voters, 67.2 per cent answered in the affirmative.[22]

So today the European Union comprises the following fifteen States:
Austria, Belgium, Denmark,[23] Finland, France, Germany, Greece,[24] the
Republic of Ireland,[25] Italy, Luxembourg, the Netherlands, Portugal,
Spain,[26] Sweden and the United Kingdom.[27] Membership is set to increase
under the Union's policy of enlargement: indeed the new democracies of
eastern Europe wish to move at least into close association with the Union.

PURPOSES AND INSTITUTIONS

The basic objectives of the European Union relate to economic development and to improved living standards for the people of the Member
States.[28] To those ends the Union aims to establish a customs union between
Member States and a common commercial policy towards non-members,
to achieve free movement of persons, services and capital between States
within the Union, evolve a common agricultural policy[29] and a common
transport policy, and to maintain fair competition. Although these economic
aims have been paramount in the Union, political cooperation and ultimately political union are also aspirations of the Union, and the Treaty
on European Union concluded at Maastricht in 1992 was an important

21 The Government had 'renegotiated' the terms on which the United Kingdom had
entered the Community: see Cmnd 6003 (1975).
22 On the referendum see D. Butler and U. Kitzinger, *The 1975 Referendum* (1975). The
Labour Party later campaigned at the 1983 General Election for withdrawal of the United
Kingdom, but that ceased to be Labour policy in the late 1980s. All the main political
parties are now committed to Union membership.
23 Denmark joined at the same time as the United Kingdom.
24 Greece joined in 1981. See the European Communities (Greek Accession) Act 1979.
25 Ireland joined at the same time as the United Kingdom.
26 Portugal and Spain joined in 1986. See the European Communities (Spanish and
Portuguese Accession) Act 1985.
27 Norway did not ratify its membership, following a referendum; Greenland (which
is part of Denmark although self-governing) left in 1982 after a referendum. Austria,
Finland and Sweden were the most recent adherents: see the European Union (Accessions)
Act 1994.
28 Treaty of Rome, arts. 2 and 3 (hereafter 'the EEC Treaty').
29 The common agricultural policy has been easily the most controversial of these aims.

milestone along the road to establishing such a union.[30] It will be considered in a moment. The Single European Act of 1986[31] has been of major significance in the development of the Union, especially through those of its provisions which are designed to speed up decision-making. Under the Act the Union's competence was extended to cover monetary cooperation, research and technology, environmental protection and social policy. The internal market (that area without internal frontiers against freedom of movement) was completed in 1992. A new decision-making process, cooperation procedure, increased the influence of the European Parliament, and European Political Cooperation ensures consultation about and coordination of foreign policy between Member States.

The Treaty on European Union (the Maastricht Treaty) is designed to move the European Union towards economic and monetary union. Thus the European Union embraces the Community together with areas which were previously outside its competence, so as, for example, to establish common defence, security and external relations policies. Citizenship of the Union is enjoyed by all citizens of Community states and gives them new rights. Accountability of Union institutions is strengthened under the Treaty provisions; the European Parliament's financial control is improved; an ombudsman investigates alleged maladministration. The principle of subsidiarity is recognized in the Treaty, making it clear that the Union should only be involved in decisions which cannot be taken more effectively at national levels. Economic and monetary union (EMU) would involve the creation of a single European Union currency, the euro, and a single central bank. But this would only happen when specified economic conditions had been achieved, and the United Kingdom would in any case only move to the final stage of EMU, and replace the pound with the euro, if Parliament were to pass an Act for the purpose. The virtual collapse in 1993 of the exchange rate mechanism of the European monetary system has made the timing of EMU uncertain. But the European Union still plans to introduce the euro in 1999 in those Member States who qualify to join the final stage of EMU.

The institutions of the Union are the Council of Ministers, the Commission, the Parliament, the European Court of Justice and the European Council. It is interesting to look first at the European Council. It was

30 Cm 1934 (1992); European Communities (Amendment) Act 1993; see below.
31 See Cmnd 9758 (1986). For explanations see Cmnd 9761 (1986); 479 HL Deb. 1004–9 (31 July 1986); [1987] *Camb. LJ*. 1. It was made effective in the United Kingdom by the European Communities (Amendment) Act 1986.

established in 1974 in a communiqué issued by the heads of government of the Member States meeting in Paris: it was, therefore, not mentioned in the treaties and had no further formal recognition until the Single European Act in 1986.[32] The European Council consists of heads of government, together with their Foreign Ministers, and usually meets two or three times a year. Politically the European Council is as vital as any other Union institution. For example, through three meetings of the European Council the European monetary system was agreed on and established by the Brussels resolution of December 1978, and the Maastricht Treaty was finally approved at European Council meetings. It was only at head of government level that such issues could be determined, and the European Council is a convenient forum in which such matters can be resolved. These regular meetings are high-powered gatherings which can give the Union a sense of political direction. The European Council frequently discusses international questions without being constrained by any narrow view of Union interests.

The Council of Ministers (not, of course, to be confused with the European Council) consists of one representative from each Member State.[33] They are frequently the Foreign Ministers.[34] There is an ancillary and very important Committee of Permanent Representatives, composed of national officials of ambassadorial status, which advises the Council generally and in particular on Commission proposals.[35] The Council is the principal decision-making and legislative organ of the Communities.[36] For example, it ultimately adopts Community legislation (if it agrees that it should be adopted) proposed by the Commission, adopts the budget and concludes international agreements on behalf of the Community.[37] There are usually some eighty meetings a year. Each Member State holds the Presidency of the Council for six months in rotation, and the Commission attends upon the Council at those meetings (but has no voting rights). The United Kingdom regained the Presidency in 1998.

Under the treaties, decisions by the Council of Ministers are usually taken only following a proposal by the Commission. Depending on the subject-matter, the decision is to be taken either (a) by a simple majority; or (b) by a 'qualified majority', special weight being given to the larger

---

32 Art. 1. The European Council must meet at least twice a year: art. 2.
33 EEC Treaty, art. 146.
34 But the representation varies according to the agenda. If, for example, fisheries policy is to be discussed Fisheries Ministers will attend.
35 Merger Treaty, art. 4.
36 EEC Treaty, art. 145.
37 ibid.; art. 228.

Member States;[38] or (c) unanimously – where the Council wishes to amend a Commission proposal.[39] In practice, however, where any vital interest of any Member State is at stake (what is 'vital' being determined by the Government concerned) the decision will have to be unanimous: this is to be inferred from the interpretation given to the Luxembourg Agreement of 1966.[40] Under the Single European Act qualified majority voting is extended to areas such as transport, common customs tariffs, some aspects of freedom of establishment and services, and capital movement (but not to taxation or to freedom of movement of persons).

The Commission is the executive authority which supports the Union. It has wide executive competence and a crucial role in the process of Union legislation. It consists of twenty members, one from each of the smaller States and two from each of the larger.[41] The members are appointed by agreement between the Member States. They are Union officials (though most of them have been involved in national politics)[42] and they owe their allegiance to the Union, not to the Government of any State. Indeed, the Member States undertake not to try to influence the Commissioners in their work.[43] They hold office for renewable four-year terms. A President and five Vice-Presidents are appointed by Member States from the Commissioners for renewable two-year terms.[44] Commissioners have security of tenure: only the European Court can retire a Commissioner for incapacity or misconduct, and the entire Commission could only be removed by the European Parliament – a highly unlikely prospect. The Commission is pre-eminently a supranational rather than an international body: initiating, supervising, coordinating, legislating within narrow limits,[45] drawing up the

38 For example, France, Germany, Italy and the United Kingdom have 10 votes each; Denmark and Ireland have 3 each, and Luxembourg has 2.

39 EEC Treaty, arts. 148, 149.

40 The Agreement does not record an agreement to this effect, but rather an agreement between France and the other Member States to differ on this crucial point. The Agreement seemed to be broken for the first time in 1982 when a decision on farm prices was taken by a majority, even though the minority had stated that the vote would affect their vital interests. Different interpretations of the affair are, however, tenable: see Evans [1982] Public Law 366.

41 Merger Treaty, art. 11. The United Kingdom, France, Germany, Spain and Italy each have two, the others each having one.

42 The United Kingdom Commissioners have been appointed in equal numbers from the Conservative and Labour Parties.

43 Merger Treaty, art. 10.

44 ibid., art. 14. Lord Jenkins of Hillhead, a former Deputy Leader of the Labour Party and first Leader of the Social Democratic Party, was President 1977–81.

45 See, for example, EEC Treaty, art. 48(3) (d).

budget,[46] imposing penalties on enterprises which break competition rules, instigating infringement proceedings when a Member State appears to be in breach of Community law (at the rate of up to 300 a year)[47] and conducting elaborate dialogues with the Council of Ministers. Its supranational character allows the Commission above all Union institutions to represent the Union's interests.

Each Commissioner has individual responsibility for defined aspects of the work of the European Union, although the Commission takes decisions together.[48] So, for example, there are Commissioners for External Affairs, Agriculture and so on. Under each Commissioner is a Directorate-General. The total staff of the Commission is now over 11,000. The Commission's role in the legislative process is primarily to initiate legislative proposals, which go to the Council of Ministers, who act on them usually after consulting the European Parliament. It would be wrong to assume that the Commission works in isolation in making these proposals because it consults the civil services of Member States and the staff of the Council of Ministers.[49] Where the Commission does have considerable power, however, is the treaty provision that once the Commission has made a proposal to the Council of Ministers, the Council can only amend it by a unanimous vote.[50]

The Europan Parliament was originally styled the Assembly in the treaties,[51] but in 1962 it adopted the description Parliament, a change endorsed by the Single European Act.[52] It used to consist of representatives chosen by national Parliaments from their own members. But since 1979 the electorates of each Member State elect their representatives directly, a development designed to increase the influence of the Parliament beyond its largely debating and consultative work towards greater democratic control of Community institutions. The number of members allocated to each State does not depend on population, and there are currently 624 members in total.

The United Kingdom members are elected by virtue of the European

---

46 ibid., art. 209.
47 ibid., arts. 155 and 169.
48 These can be majority decisions: Merger Treaty, art. 17.
49 EEC Treaty, art. 15.
50 ibid., art. 149.
51 ibid., art. 137.
52 The word 'Parliament' is inserted retrospectively into relevant British statutes by the European Communities (Amendment) Act 1986, s. 3.

Parliament Elections Act 1978.[53] Eighty-seven representatives are elected from the United Kingdom[54] for a five-year term.[55] The United Kingdom members are elected by the usual 'first past the post' electoral system, as used at parliamentary elections. The Government, however, is sponsoring the European Parliamentary Elections Bill under which, from the 1999 elections onwards, members would be elected by a regional list system of proportional representation. Under the European Parliament (Pay and Pensions) Act 1979, section 1, representatives receive the same salary as British MPs, charged on the Consolidated Fund. If a representative is also an MP, he receives one salary plus one-third. Expenses and other allowances are paid by the Parliament itself. Members are elected under party labels, and sit in party, not national, groupings in the Parliament chamber.

The powers of the Parliament remain primarily consultative, not legislative, the Council of Ministers seeking its views about Commission proposals.[56] The Parliament is, however, assuming greater legislative functions. Members of the Parliament can ask questions about the work of both bodies at a question time not unlike that of the House of Commons. It works largely through standing committees which cover all the main areas of Union competence. The Parliament has the ultimate power, never yet used, to dismiss the Commission if it votes to do so by a two-thirds majority, representing a majority of the total membership.[57] But in 1979 and again in 1984 the Parliament rejected the budgets proposed by the Commission – the most drastic actions of the Parliament since its inception. The Parliament may also bring enforcement proceedings in the European Court against the Commission or Council of Ministers if either fails to take action which it is obliged to take: thus in 1985 the European Court partly upheld the Parliament's complaint that the Council had failed to adopt a common transport policy.[58]

---

53 As amended by the European Parliamentary Elections Act 1993; see also Cmnd 6399 (1976); Cmnd 6768 (1977).
54 Seventy-one from England, five from Scotland, four from Wales and three from Northern Ireland: 1978 Act, s. 2. The Northern Ireland members are elected by single transferable vote. See also the European Parliament Elections Act 1981.
55 Council Decision 76/787.
56 Failure to do so would be a ground for challenging the validity of legislation: see EEC Treaty, arts. 173 and 190. See also S. A. Roquettes Frères v. Council of Ministers [1980] ECR 3333.
57 EEC Treaty, art. 144.
58 European Parliament v. Council of Ministers [1986] 1 CMLR 138. The 1986 budget was held to have been unlawfully adopted because it had not been agreed by the Council and the Parliament: Council of Ministers v. European Parliament, The Times, 4 July 1986.

The European Court of Justice[59] sits at Luxembourg and consists of fifteen judges appointed by agreement between the Member States.[60] One judge is appointed from each Member State. Judges are appointed from those who are qualified for the highest judicial office in their own State, or who are 'juriconsults of recognized competence' (a provision which allows practitioners and academics to be appointed).[61] A judge may only be removed by the unanimous vote of the other judges. The President of the Court is elected by his fellow judges. The Court is fashioned according to European models; its procedures are inquisitorial, and written submissions by counsel are more important than oral argument. Provisional conclusions are prepared by an Advocate-General, an officer who has no counterpart in the United Kingdom.[62] In interpreting legal instruments the Court may consider preparatory materials and not merely the bare text. Its judgments are frequently terse, replete with statements of general legal principle and no dissenting opinion is delivered or announced.

The Court's jurisdiction is wide-ranging. Its principal function is to see that Community law is observed. It is an 'administrative court' determining the validity of acts and decisions of Community organs broadly according to French administrative law doctrine.[63] Action may be brought by a Member State or by the Commission or the Council; there is also limited access for individuals. Luxembourg brought an action against the Parliament in 1981, claiming that a parliamentary resolution about where the Parliament should sit was invalid.[64] Actions may be brought against Member States by the Commission, or by another Member State, for failure to fulfil a Union obligation.[65] The Court also hears appeals against penalties imposed by the Commission, disputes between the Union and their officials, claims in tort and contract against the Union, and proceedings against Union organs for wrongful failure to act. In constitutional law its most important head of jurisdiction is to give preliminary rulings, under article 177 of the EEC

59 See L. Neville Brown and F. Jacobs, *The Court of Justice of the European Communities* (4th edn, 1994); K. Lasok, *The European Court of Justice: Practice and Procedure* (2nd edn, 1994); L. J. Brinkhorst and H. G. Schermers, *Judicial Remedies in the European Communities* (2nd edn, 1977); J. A. Usher, *European Court Practice* (1983). Selected judgments are reported in English in *The Common Market Law Reports* (CMLR), together with important decisions of national courts on matters of Community law, and all the Court's judgments are published in its official reports, which appear in all the official Community languages.
60 EEC Treaty, arts. 165, 167.
61 ibid., art. 167.
62 See Slynn (1984) 33 *ICLQ* 409.
63 EEC Treaty, art. 173.
64 *Grand Duchy of Luxembourg* v. *European Parliament* [1983] 2 CMLR 726.
65 EEC Treaty, art. 171. See, e.g., *Commission* v. *United Kingdom* [1984] 1 All ER 353; *France* v. *United Kingdom* [1980] 1 CMLR 6.

Treaty, on the interpretation of the treaties and the validity and interpretation of acts (including regulations and directives) of Community organs.[66] A national court or tribunal ought not to refer such a question unless an interpretation or ruling on the validity of the Community measure is necessary for its decision on the matter before it. Courts and tribunals of last instance are obliged to refer such a question unless the correct interpretation is quite clear.

Where a national court has a discretion under article 177 to refer a question to the European Court, Lord Denning MR offered guidelines, in *Bulmer (HP)* v. *J. Bollinger SA*[67] on how it should be exercised by English courts. Broadly, (*a*) the resolution of the question must be necessary to enable the English court to give judgment; (*b*) the decision must be conclusive of the case; and (*c*) even then the court must consider such matters as the difficulty and importance of the point, the delay and expense which a reference would involve, and the burden on the European Court. Rules of court prescribe the *procedure* for making references to the European Court from superior courts[68] but do not state the *principles* governing references. References ought to be made by lower courts if possible; this will reduce the costs of the parties and minimize the delay, which will in any event be of several months' duration.

The European Court makes its preliminary ruling under article 177, avoiding as far as possible any interpretation of municipal (national) law. The case then returns to the originating national court which, in deciding the case, must see how (if at all) the relevant provisions of municipal law can be reconciled with the European Court's ruling.[69]

The Court, like the Commission, has generally sought to extend the frontiers of Community law and to emphasize the concept of Community law supremacy. But no coercive sanction was provided against a defaulter,[70] except under the ECSC Treaty, until the Maastricht Treaty permitted fines to be imposed against Member States which fail to comply with the Court's judgments.[71] This lack of a general sanction was amply illustrated

66 See below, and also F. G. Jacobs and A. Durand, *References to the European Court: Practice and Procedure* (1975).

67 [1974] Ch. 401. See also above, p. 83.

68 SI 1972, Nos. 1786, 1787, 1898.

69 See above, pp. 25–6. The European Court considered the meaning of art. 177 in *CILFIT* v. *Italian Ministry of Health* [1983] 1 CMLR 472.

70 EEC Treaty, arts. 169–71. A defaulting State is obliged to comply with the Court's judgment: see *Procureur de la République* v. *Waterkyn* [1983] 2 CMLR 145.

71 Art. 88, which empowers the Commission, with the concurrence of two-thirds of the Council of Ministers, to withhold from that Member State moneys due to it and to authorize other members to subject it to fiscal sanctions.

when France ignored a ruling of the Court in 1979–80 that she should resume the import of English lamb and mutton.[72]

Under the Single European Act, a new Court of First Instance was set up to take some of the less important cases.[73] The Court of First Instance hears and determines cases in categories which have been transferred to it by the European Court. Those categories embrace disputes between Union institutions and their employees; actions by the Commission concerning levies, production, prices and restrictive agreements in the context of the ECSC Treaty; and actions against the Commission by private parties for annulment of action, or alleging failure to act, in relation to competition rules. An appeal lies to the European Court on a point of law only. The Court of First Instance has fifteen judges, appointed by the Governments of the Member States for six-year renewable terms; the judges elect their own President.

COMMUNITY LAW

It is not the intention here to consider a number of matters concerning European Community law which are dealt with elsewhere in this book. In particular the reader is referred to the discussion of the European Communities Act 1972 in chapter 4.[74] Rather, the present limited purposes are to explain what is meant by the term 'Community law', and those important effects which it has on United Kingdom law which are not explained anywhere else in these pages. The law of the European Union is still, strictly speaking, European Community law.

Community law comprises[75] the primary treaties;[76] ancillary agreements entered into by the Member States;[77] secondary legislation by Community

---

72 *Commission* v. *France* [1980] I CMLR 418. Statistics on Member States who had not complied with judgments are given at 520 HL Deb. 2090 (4 July 1990). Italy had not complied with 24, followed by Belgium (12), France (5), Germany (4) and the rest (each) (2) – except the United Kingdom, who had fully complied.

73 Arts. 4, 5, 11, 12, 26, 27; European Communities (Amendment) Act 1986, s. 2; EEC Treaty, art. 168A(1); T. Millett, *The Court of First Instance of the European Communities* (1990).

74 See above, pp. 83–7.

75 See also above, pp. 25–6.

76 These may be described as the Community's basic law: see Donner (1974) 11 CMLR 127.

77 The Union also has treaty-making competence: EEC Treaty, arts. 210, 228, 235.

organs;[78] administrative acts and decisions by those organs, and decisions and other pronouncements of the European Court of Justice. Secondary legislation[79] is made by the Council of Ministers and the Commission, and is of three types. *Regulations* are binding and directly applicable in Member States.[80] They are used to ensure a uniform application of Community policies. *Directives* are also binding, but the mode of adoption is left to each Member State, subject usually to a time-limit for that adoption.[81] *Decisions* are binding on those to whom they are addressed, sometimes to Member States, sometimes to individuals or companies.[82]

Community law is distinct from public international law and from national (municipal) law of Member States. But it is interwoven with municipal law; it is applied mainly by the courts of Member States; certain rules of Community law (notably regulations made by the Council of Ministers or the Commission) are directly applicable[83] in the sense that, of their own force, they create legal rights and duties enforceable in municipal courts. It is concerned primarily with such issues as the free movement of goods, labour, services and capital; customs duties; agriculture, and trade competition.

According to Community law doctrine, as expounded by the European Court of Justice, Community law prevails over national law (even national constitutional law) to the extent that they are inconsistent with one another. Cases of inconsistency are not confined to conflicts between directly applicable Community law and municipal law; they arise whenever municipal laws are incompatible with rights specifically conferred by rules of Community law (including provisions of the treaties, directives issued by the Council of Ministers or the Commission, and decisions of the

---

78 ibid., art. 189; see also above, pp. 83−7.

79 Such legislation must be reasoned, i.e., indicate the authority for it, the reasons for making it and state that any necessary opinions have been obtained. If it is not reasoned the European Court may annul it. Ibid., arts. 173, 174, 190.

80 ibid., arts. 189, 191. See *Leonesio* v. *Italian Ministry of Agriculture* [1973] CMLR 343; *Commission* v. *United Kingdom* [1979] 2 CMLR 48.

81 ibid., art. 189. A directive may create rights for individuals, enforceable in their national courts: see, e.g., *Van Duyn* v. *Home Office* [1975] Ch. 358; *Marshall* v. *Southampton and SW Hants. AHA* [1986] 2 All ER 584 (see above, p. 86). In *Duke* v. *GEC Reliance* [1988] 1 All ER 625 the House of Lords held that s. 2(4) does not constrain a British court to distort the meaning of a statute in order to enforce a directive against an individual when the directive has no direct effect between individuals.

82 ibid., art. 189. The Council and the Commission also make recommendations and deliver opinions. Neither is binding.

83 See Bebr (1970) 19 *ICLQ* 257, and above, pp. 25−6.

Commission), and inconsistency may exist without direct conflict if Community rules evince an intention to cover the whole field of activity in question. The European Communities Act 1972 provides that the Community treaties shall have effect in United Kingdom law,[84] that enactments 'passed or to be passed' shall be 'construed and have effect' subject to the preceding provisions,[85] and that decisions of the European Court and the principles laid down by it (including, of course the supremacy of Community law and the consequential denial of the legal doctrine of parliamentary sovereignty) shall be applied by United Kingdom courts. Attention has already been drawn, in chapter 4, to the incompatibility of some of these provisions with orthodox constitutional principles, and to the *Factortame* litigation.[86] Clearly, therefore, within the European Union's legal system, Community law prevails over domestic law.[87] This has, however, been specifically denied by some national courts.[88]

In the United Kingdom issues of Community law have arisen in courts and tribunals of all ranks, from the lowliest magistrates' courts to the judicial House of Lords. It was not easy for our courts to adapt to Community law – after all, the original Member States have shared a similar legal tradition which is largely alien here; and those States had had the chance to shape Community law from the start, whereas the United Kingdom did not join until fifteen years later. A cautious approach by our courts was therefore foreseeable and perhaps desirable. Nevertheless, Community law has had a substantial effect in several areas of our law, particularly in relation to freedom of movement of persons[89] and of goods,[90] free competition[91] and equal pay.[92]

---

84 ss. 1, 2(1).
85 s. 2(4). See *Garland* v. *British Rail Engineering Ltd* [1983] 2 AC 751 (above, p. 84); *Duke* v. *GEC Reliance* [1988] 1 All ER 625.
86 See above, pp. 83–7.
87 See, for example, *Costa* v. *ENEL* [1964] ECR 585; *Internationale Handelsgesellschaft* case [1972] CMLR 255.
88 See, for example, *Le Ski* [1972] CMLR 330 (Belgium); *Costa* v. *ENEL* [1964] CMLR 425; *Frontini* v. *Ministero delle Finanze* [1974] 2 CMLR 372 (Italy); *Directeur Général des Douanes* v. *Societé des Cafés Jacques* [1975] 2 CMLR 336 (France). These are only *examples*: there have been other instances.
89 See, e.g., *Van Duyn* v. *Home Office* [1975] Ch. 358; *R.* v. *Bouchereau* [1978] QB 732; *R.* v. *Secretary of State for the Home Department, ex p. Dannenberg* [1984] QB 766.
90 See, e.g., *Commission* v. *United Kingdom* [1979] 2 CMLR 427; *R.* v. *Henn* [1981] AC 580; *Conegate Ltd* v. *Customs and Excise Commissioners* [1987] 2 WLR 39; *R.* v. *Bow Street Metropolitan Magistrate, ex p. Noncyp* (1989) 89 Cr. App. R. 121.
91 See, e.g., *Application des Gaz SA* v. *Falks Veritas* [1974] Ch. 381.
92 See, e.g., *Commission* v. *United Kingdom* [1982] ICR 578; *Drake* v. *Chief Adjudication Officer* [1987] QB 166; *Johnston* v. *Chief Constable of the RUC* [1986] 3 All ER 135; *Pickstone and Others* v. *Freemans plc* [1988] 2 All ER 803.

PART TWO

THE EXECUTIVE

In this Part are collected the more important or interesting rules about central government. As far as is practicable they have been set against their political background. But this is not a textbook on politics or public administration, and it does not purport to give a full account of how Britain is governed.

Textbooks on constitutional law usually deal with Parliament first and the Government afterwards. Here the order is reversed (apart from the earlier treatment of parliamentary sovereignty), mainly because the Government is more important than Parliament. But Government and Parliament (Executive and Legislature) are closely interlocked, and some matters discussed in this Part of the book will reappear in Part Three.

Chapter 6 contains the rules of law about the monarchy; residual matters on which the Queen may still be entitled by constitutional convention to act in her personal discretion, and the scope of the royal prerogative, a bundle of rights, privileges and immunities belonging to the Crown and to the Crown alone. The law relating to the activities of the executive branch of government and its officers in external affairs is examined in chapter 7. The common thread running through both these chapters is the Queen, or the Crown. In British constitutional law we do not recognize 'the State' as a legal concept.

Chapter 8 deals with the Privy Council, now only a 'dignified' organ of government, and with its active committees, including the Judicial Committee. In chapter 9 the roles of the Prime Minister and his or her Cabinet colleagues in the scheme of government are analysed. Account has been taken of recent information about the use of both ministerial committees and of informal groups of Ministers in arriving at Government decisions. Chapter 10 goes on to outline the structure of central government, and the material on ministerial responsibility is considered here to emphasize that the doctrine of ministerial responsibility does not vary according to whether a Minister is or is not a member of the Cabinet. The chapter also gives an account of bodies ancillary to Departments, and some of the rules about the organization of the civil service and the legal and constitutional position of its members.

Chapter 11 deals with some aspects of the constitutional position of the armed forces of the Crown and their members.

CHAPTER 6

The Crown and the Royal Prerogative

CONSTITUTIONAL MONARCHY[1]

The Queen today remains a symbol of national identity, a focal point of national loyalty, transcending partisan rivalry and strengthening social cohesion. The national anthem is 'God Save the Queen'; British coins and postage stamps bear her image; the Queen personifies the State and the nation, their history and continuity. The Government is Her Majesty's Government; government is carried on in the Queen's name; sovereignty is attributed to the Queen in Parliament; wide legal powers are vested in Her Majesty or in Her Majesty in Council; the courts are the Queen's courts. Coronations, royal weddings and funerals, and an investiture of a Prince of Wales, are great national occasions, bringing the past into the present amid splendid pageantry and ancient ritual. The Queen is pre-eminently a 'dignified'[2] element in the British constitution. She is also a pillar of the Established Church, an exemplar of family virtue, a personage to whom deference is paid by all in public life in a society where habits of deference are diminishing. She embodies the hereditary principle. She has the misfortune to be required to live in a glare of publicity and to have reposed in her expectations which no ordinary mortal can hope to fulfil.

1 By far the best account is in Sir Ivor Jennings's *Cabinet Government* (3rd edn, 1959), especially chs. 12–14. See also Vernon Bogdanor, *The Monarchy and the Constitution* (1995). The most recent royal biographies are also instructive: see Sir Harold Nicolson, *King George V* (1952), Kenneth Rose, *King George V* (1984), Frances Donaldson, *Edward VIII* (1974), Philip Ziegler, *King Edward VIII* (1990), Sir John Wheeler-Bennett, *King George VI* (1958), Sarah Bradford, *George VI* (1989), Ben Pimlott, *The Queen* (1996) and Jonathan Dimbleby, *The Prince of Wales* (1994). There has only been one royal autobiography: The Duke of Windsor, *A King's Story* (1951). Detailed factual information is in the *Report of the Select Committee on the Civil List* (HC 29 (1971–2)). And see Rodney Brazier, *Constitutional Texts* (1990), ch. 8.
2 The term used by Walter Bagehot in his classic study, *The English Constitution* (Fontana edn, 1963), p. 61.

The smallest indiscretion or verbal lapse may be the subject of adverse comment to which she will be unable to reply on her own behalf. Perhaps in recognition of this danger the Queen does not give interviews to the media, and reporters do not put questions to her during her public engagements. She must, therefore, endeavour so to comport herself as to give offence to nobody; not only must she never do or say the wrong thing, but she must always do and say the right thing, irrespective of her private inclinations. In England at least, republican sentiment seems to be weak, although it is difficult to gauge the extent to which that sentiment has been strengthened by the adverse publicity generated by younger members of the royal family in recent years and by royal divorces.

From the late Victorian era till the middle years of the present century, the monarchy was an important factor cementing the unity of the British Empire. Local nationalist sentiment in the colonies was subdued by the well-inculcated loyalty of local peoples to the occupant of the throne. In those self-governing Dominions which were populated mainly by settlers of British stock, the growth of national self-assertion could be accommodated with the fundamental concept of common allegiance to a common and indivisible Crown. This concept broke down in the Irish Free State (Eire), and then in South Africa. In 1949 the Commonwealth Prime Ministers agreed to accept the continuance of India's membership of the Commonwealth as a republic on the understanding that India would recognize the King as head of the Commonwealth. Today, when there are fifty-four full and independent members of the Commonwealth, the Queen is head of State in only sixteen of them and is represented (except in the United Kingdom) by a Governor-General;[3] thirty-two are republics and five[4] have indigenous rulers. She remains Head of the Commonwealth, but in this symbolical capacity she exercises no constitutional function[5] For each of those Commonwealth countries of which she is still head of State she has a separate title.

It was assumed that a convention recited in the preamble to the Statute

---

3 Following a military *coup* in Fiji in 1987, Fiji was declared a republic and her Commonwealth membership automatically lapsed. Up to that moment the Queen as Queen of Fiji had publicly urged the population to remain loyal to the lawful constitution – a rare public intervention in politics by Her Majesty.

4 Malaysia, Lesotho, Swaziland, Tonga and Brunei.

5 And she does not take ministerial advice on the content of her Christmas Day and Commonwealth Day messages to the Commonwealth: see Blackburn [1985] *Public Law* 361. She does, however, show the text of her Christmas Day message to the Prime Minister for comments.

of Westminster 1931 – that the assent of the Parliament of the Dominions was required for any change in the law touching the succession to the throne or the royal style and titles – applied to all independent Commonwealth countries of which the King or Queen was head of State. The Dominion Prime Ministers were consulted in 1936 by Baldwin, the United Kingdom Prime Minister, to ascertain whether they would approve of Edward VIII's proposed marriage to Mrs Simpson; a majority of them emphatically agreed with the British Government's opposition to the idea, and Edward VIII abdicated. Appropriate legislation was then passed by the United Kingdom Parliament to give effect to the King's decision and to exclude him and his descendants from the line of succession.[6] The conventional procedures were also followed in 1948 when George VI ceased to be Emperor of India, and 1953 when Elizabeth II adopted separate titles for her several realms.[7]

Today the personal characteristics of a monarch's proposed consort would be unlikely to arouse strong emotions outside the United Kingdom – although the possibility that the Prince of Wales might one day remarry continues to attract interest within the United Kingdom. Since, moreover, the number of independent Commonwealth countries continuing to owe allegiance to Her Majesty will continue to diminish as a result of republican trends, the constitutional niceties relating to the law touching the succession to the throne and the royal style and titles will probably be reduced to matters of small practical consequence.[8]

The principal convention of the British constitution is that the Queen shall exercise her formal legal powers only upon and in accordance with the advice of her Ministers, save in a few exceptional situations. In independent

6 His Majesty's Declaration of Abdication Act 1936. Only the 'Dominions' (listed in s. 1 of the Statute of Westminster 1931) are covered by this convention; today only Canada and Australia remain in that list.
7 The Royal Titles Act 1953 recognized the authority of the Queen to adopt a new title for the United Kingdom and for the other territories for whose foreign relations the United Kingdom Government was responsible. The style and title proclaimed for the United Kingdom and its dependencies was 'Elizabeth II, by the Grace of God of the United Kingdom of Great Britain and Northern Ireland and of her other Realms and Territories Queen, Head of the Commonwealth, Defender of the Faith'. See further de Smith (1953) 2 *ICLQ* 263. The validity of this measure in relation to Scotland (she was the first Elizabeth to be Queen of Scotland) was unsuccessfully challenged in *MacCormick* v. *Lord Advocate* 1953 SC 396, partly on the grounds of lack of *locus standi*.
8 The adoption of a separate royal title for a newly independent Commonwealth country of which Her Majesty remains Queen has not recently been accompanied by the assent of the Parliaments of other independent Commonwealth countries. To this extent the convention recited in 1931 has partly lapsed.

Commonwealth countries the powers of the Governor-General, her personal representative, are similarly restricted, except in so far as they may have been enlarged or attenuated by the text of the constitution.[9]

This is not to say that the monarch must be a mere cipher. As Bagehot wrote,[10] she has 'the right to be consulted, the right to encourage, the right to warn'. He could have added that she also has the right to offer, on her own initiative, suggestions and advice to her Ministers even where she is obliged in the last resort to accept the formal advice tendered to her.

To be more explicit, she has the conventional rights to receive Cabinet papers and minutes, to be kept adequately informed by the Prime Minister (with whom she has regular weekly audiences) on matters of national policy, to receive Foreign Office dispatches and telegrams and other State papers,[11] and to be notified of proposed appointments and awards to be made in her name so that she can express her views informally. She can make such private comments as she thinks fit; she can remonstrate and offer strong objections to a proposed course of action. How much attention is paid to her views will depend upon the context. Any objection that she may raise to the introduction of politically controversial legislation to which the Cabinet is committed is unlikely to be pressed or taken seriously, particularly if the Government is not of a conservative complexion; the monarch, aware of the monarchy's conservative image, is obliged to use extreme tact. More generally, the length and range of her experience of public affairs (the Queen has been on the throne since 1952), and her personal acquaintance with a large number of overseas dignitaries, may lend weight to suggestions she chooses to offer. George VI was never a political sage; but there are some grounds for believing that his comments in 1945 may have been instrumental in persuading Attlee to reconsider and then change his original intention of placing Bevin in the Treasury and Dalton in the Foreign Office;[12] in 1940 he urged Churchill not to recommend Beaverbrook as Minister of Aircraft Production

9 See generally S. de Smith, *The New Commonwealth and its Constitutions* (1964), ch. 3. See also pp. 32–3.

10 Bagehot, op. cit., p. 111.

11 Which take her two or three hours a day to read. Memorandum of the Queen's Private Secretary to the Select Committee on the Civil List (HC 29 (1971–72)), Minutes of Evidence, App. 13, § 3.

12 Wheeler-Bennett, op. cit., p. 638; Ben Pimlott, *Hugh Dalton* (1985), ch. XXIV ('. . . it is reasonable to suppose that the King's advice was an important factor' in switching Dalton and Bevin: p. 415). Earl Attlee denied this in the *Observer*, 23 August 1959, but the accuracy of his recollection of the matter is not beyond question; see Driberg (1969) 50 *The Parliamentarian* at 165; Pimlott, ibid.

(although fortunately the Prime Minister was able to convince the King to acquiesce);[13] and we know that in 1944 he took it upon himself in effect to direct Churchill not to accompany the invasion force to Normandy.[14] George V had a mind of his own, as well as a high place in popular esteem, and his habits of gruff and forthright expression doubtless influenced not only the manner in which advice was presented to him but also, on occasion, the substance of that advice. He appears to have exercised some influence over senior military appointments; his expostulations addressed to the Prime Minister over the forcible feeding of militant suffragettes probably conduced to a change of policy; he did his best, though with scant success, to lower the political temperature during the recurrent Irish troubles in the first half of his reign.[15]

Any *public* disclosure of disagreement between the Queen and the Prime Minister of the day could be damaging. In 1986 a senior source within Buckingham Palace confirmed in a response to a newspaper's inquiries that the Queen was 'dismayed' by 'an uncaring Mrs Thatcher' and that the Queen disapproved of several major Government policies. The Queen's Private Secretary intervened, however, in a rare letter to the press to deny the published account.[16]

In times of national crisis the role of a non-partisan head of State as a bridge-builder is potentially significant. When the possibility of civil war in Ireland over the home-rule issue became imminent in 1914, George V took the initiative in convening an inter-party conference, with the Prime Minister's agreement, and addressed its opening session. In 1931, after the collapse of Ramsay MacDonald's Labour Government, he encouraged the formation of a National Government under MacDonald's leadership, but did not exert any improper pressure. If the normal machinery of democratic government breaks down, the monarch's ill-defined residuary discretionary powers may have to be exercised in novel or highly unusual circumstances. Obviously personal interventions of this kind may imperil the status of the monarchy; they are therefore justifiable only as the least of evils. If only because one cannot readily envisage all these hypothetical situations, it is impracticable to state exhaustively the scope of the residual powers. However, the main situations in which the Queen has, or may possibly

13 See Martin Gilbert, *Finest Hour* (1983), p. 328; Sir John Colville, *The Fringes of Power* (1985), p. 211.
14 W. S. Churchill, *The Second World War*, vol. 5 (1951), *Closing the Ring*, pp. 547–50.
15 Nicolson, op. cit., and Rose, op. cit., *passim*.
16 See the *Sunday Times*, 20 July 1986; *The Times*, 29 July 1986; Marshall [1986] *Public Law* 505.

have, a conventional right to exercise her prerogative powers[17] without or against ministerial advice can be briefly listed.[18]

Appointment of a Prime Minister

On several occasions since 1923 the choice of a new Prime Minister upon the resignation of the incumbent has not been predetermined by constitutional rules, and the monarch has had to exercise a judicious discretion. For reasons to be explained in a later chapter,[19] the Queen has now been relieved of this responsibility save where no party leader commands a majority in the House of Commons.

Dismissal of a Government

If a Government, having lost a vote of confidence in the House of Commons, were to insist on remaining in office instead of offering its resignation or advising a dissolution, the Queen would be justified, after the lapse of a reasonable period of time, in requesting the Prime Minister to advise her to dissolve Parliament and, if he were to refuse, in dismissing him and his Ministers. She would also, it is submitted, be justified in dismissing her Ministers if they were purporting to subvert the democratic basis of the constitution – for example, by prolonging the life of a Parliament in order to avoid defeat at a General Election, or by obtaining an electoral majority through duress or fraudulent manipulation of the poll. Expediency would be the only factor restricting her discretion. Since such an intervention on her part would tend, in Asquith's phrase,[20] to make the Crown 'the football of contending factions' at an ensuing General Election, and since no Government has been unambiguously dismissed since 1783,[21] this, the most dramatic form of royal initiative, must be a recourse of last resort, an ultimate weapon which is liable to destroy its user.

A drama in Australia is instructive. The Queen's representative, the Governor-General Sir John Kerr, was emphatically of the opinion that he had the power and indeed the duty under the prerogative to dismiss Mr Whitlam and his Government in November 1975. The majority opposition

17 For the definition of prerogative, see pp. 134–7.
18 See further Rodney Brazier, *Constitutional Practice* (2nd edn, 1994), ch. 9.
19 See pp. 168–71.
20 Quoted in Jennings, op. cit., p. 408.
21 For the equivocal precedent of 1834, see ibid., pp. 403–5.

in the Senate refused to pass appropriation bills because of alleged ministerial improprieties in obtaining overseas loans; Mr Whitlam, who had a majority in the House of Representatives, would only recommend a Senate not a General Election; Sir John was given an undertaking by the Leader of the Opposition, Mr Fraser, that, as Prime Minister, he would recommend a General Election; Sir John then dismissed Mr Whitlam. Mr Fraser formed a minority government; the Senate passed the bills, and Mr Fraser's party won the promised General Election (in which Asquith's fears about footballs were amply justified). Both the Governor-General and the Chief Justice of Australia were of the view that a British Government which could not procure the passage of legislation to raise revenue and which refused to recommend a General Election or to resign could be properly dismissed by the Queen.[22]

Insistence on a dissolution

Much the same considerations apply as those applicable to the dismissal of a Government. It is true that the Queen might urge upon the Prime Minister that a dissolution would be in the best interests of the country, and he might reluctantly agree to advise her to dissolve. But if he did not agree and the Queen were to insist on a dissolution, then she would have to remove the Prime Minister and find a new one; the procedure upon a dissolution of Parliament entails the making of an Order in Council and the issue of royal proclamation under the Great Seal, and this requires the cooperation of Ministers. Unless, therefore, the Prime Minister's own colleagues were prepared to form a new Government, the Queen would have to send for the Leader of the Opposition and ask him to form a Government for the purpose of an immediate dissolution. She would then become a 'football of contending factions'.

To this general analysis, one qualification must be added; she may *possibly* have a right to insist on a dissolution before agreeing to exercise her prerogative to create new peers in order to swamp opposition to the Government in the House of Lords.[23]

---

22 On this affair, see Polyviou, 1976 *Annual Survey of Commonwealth Law* 16; Sir John Kerr, *Matters for Judgment* (1978) and Gough Whitlam, *The Truth of the Matter* (1979). An excellent collection of essays on the many events during the Whitlam years of constitutional importance to Australia and, by analogy, to the United Kingdom is in Gareth Evans, *Labour and the Constitution 1972–1975* (1977).
23 See pp. 126–7.

Refusal of a dissolution

If a Prime Minister were improperly to request a dissolution, the Queen would at least be entitled, and might perhaps be obliged, to reject it. For example, if a Prime Minister whose party had been defeated by the Opposition party at a General Election were to request an immediate second dissolution on the ground that the victory of his opponents had been obtained by misrepresentation of the electorate, or if Neville Chamberlain in 1940 had, instead of resigning, requested a dissolution at a time when the country was threatened with military defeat, the monarch could justifiably refuse, since resignation would be the only proper course for the Prime Minister to adopt. Undoubtedly there are other situations in which a request for dissolution could be refused; cogent arguments to this effect have been advanced over the years by monarchs, their advisers, and writers of authority. Confident identification of those situations is not easy. In the first place, in the United Kingdom there has been no unequivocal instance of an absolute rejection of a request for a dissolution in modern times,[24] though on several occasions requests have been granted with reluctance. Secondly, the absence of precedents for a refusal means that the scope of the power to refuse has to be inferred from general constitutional principles; and opinions will differ on both the definition of those principles and the inferences to be drawn from them. Hence, such a refusal would now be highly controversial, unless the request itself was manifestly improper; and this fact alone must make any attempt at definition highly tentative.

Perhaps the following proposition would command a wide measure of support: the Queen may properly refuse a Prime Minister's request for a dissolution if she has substantial grounds for believing (i) that an alternative Government, enjoying the confidence of a majority of the House of Commons, can be formed without a General Election, and (ii) that a General Election held at that time would be clearly prejudicial to the national interest.

---

24 In November 1910 George V was thought to have refused a request for dissolution but to have changed his mind after discussing the matter with senior Ministers: Jennings, op. cit., p. 424. See, however, the more equivocal account of this episode given by Sir Harold Nicolson in his official biography, *King George V* (1952), pp. 125–39 and 150; Rose, op. cit., pp. 115–25.

For extensive examinations of refusals of requests for dissolution by Governors-General and Governors in self-governing Commonwealth countries, see Eugene Forsey, *The Royal Power of Dissolution of Parliament in the British Commonwealth* (1943); H. V. Evatt, *The King and his Dominion Governors* (2nd edn, 1967). See also B. S. Markesinis, *The Theory and Practice of Dissolution of Parliament* (1972).

As thus formulated, her power could seldom be appropriately exercised except where no party leader in the House of Commons enjoyed an overall majority.[25] Even then it might prove impolitic for her to exercise the power. The minority Prime Minister might resign at once, protesting volubly, instead of acquiescing quietly in her decision; and she might be mistaken in her belief that a stable alternative Government could be formed without an election, in which case she would be obliged to grant the new Prime Minister what she had refused to his predecessor, thus conveying in some quarters an impression of partisanship.[26] Protests notwithstanding, a refusal would probably be justified and broadly acceptable if a Prime Minister, placed in a minority within his own Cabinet and threatened with repudiation by his parliamentary party, suddenly asked for a dissolution in order to forestall the prospect of his imminent supersession.[27] Refusal might be still more readily justifiable if the rebels were known to be prepared to form a coalition Government with an opposition party, or if the country were in the throes of a serious economic crisis or widespread civil strife. *A fortiori*, a Prime Minister who has actually been repudiated by his own parliamentary party in favour of one of his colleagues can claim no constitutional right at all to demand a dissolution. It is also possible to imagine a marginal situation in which the fact that a General Election had been held only a short while previously might tip the balance against granting a request for a dissolution.

Support for the view that the Queen might properly refuse a requested dissolution in some circumstances may be extrapolated from events in

---

25 Though Neville Chamberlain (in the hypothetical case mentioned above) still enjoyed the support of his Cabinet and a majority of the House. Refusal of a request for a dissolution in these circumstances would have been justified, however, by reason of extreme national danger.

26 This was the embarrassing situation in which Lord Byng, the Governor-General of Canada, found himself in 1926. It does not follow that in refusing a dissolution to Mackenzie King and then granting one to Meighen, the former Opposition leader (who lost the ensuing General Election), Lord Byng had acted unconstitutionally; but Mackenzie King insisted that he had in fact so acted. See Forsey, op. cit., and pp. 122–3 for the Whitlam affair.

27 This was broadly the position in South Africa in September 1939, when the Governor-General, Sir Patrick Duncan, refused a dissolution to General Hertzog, who favoured a policy of neutrality against the views of a majority of his colleagues and his party, and had been placed in a minority on this issue in the House. Hertzog resigned and Smuts, having accepted office as Prime Minister, was able to form a Government with a stable majority. cf. Markesinis, op. cit., chs. 5, 7, arguing that royal discretion is narrower than is suggested in the main text above, and rejecting the still broader view adopted by Forsey.

Ontario in 1985.[28] A minority Conservative Government had been formed after a General Election, but two opposition parties (who together had a majority in the Legislative Assembly) published an agreed parliamentary pact, including a resolution that any Government formed by them would not recommend a dissolution for at least two years. The minority Government was then defeated on a vote of confidence. The Lieutenant-Governor had made it known informally that any request for a second dissolution would, in view of the published pact, be refused. Not surprisingly, the Conservative Premier did not recommend a further dissolution, but resigned, and the two opposition parties formed a coalition Government.

Coercion of the Lords[29]

In 1712, Queen Anne created twelve new hereditary peers in order to secure the approval of the House of Lords for a peace policy. In 1832, William IV reluctantly accepted (after having initially rejected) his Government's advice to create a sufficient number of Whig peers to carry the Reform Bill (substantially enlarging the franchise and reforming the electoral constituencies) through the House of Lords, which had rejected three similar bills in rapid succession. The creation of the new peerages became unnecessary because some Tory peers, apprised of the threat, abstained from voting against the bill, which duly passed. A broadly similar situation arose in 1910–11. The Lords had rejected the Liberal Finance Bill in 1909. They agreed to pass it only after the Government had gone to the country and had been returned to power (though the Liberal Party lost its absolute majority in the House of Commons) in January 1910.[30] The Government had decided to introduce legislation to reduce to a suspensory veto the power of the Lords to reject a bill outright. Edward VII expressed the view that it would not be justifiable to ask him to exercise his prerogative to swamp the Lords with new hereditary peers in order to pass such legislation unless the electorate had shown themselves to be in favour of it. In May 1910 he died, shortly after the introduction of the Parliament Bill. Asquith, the Prime Minister, agreed to advise the new King, George V, to dissolve Parliament so that the electorate could pronounce its verdict on the bill.

---

28 See Brazier, op. cit., pp. 45–6.
29 See Jennings, op. cit., pp. 428–48, for an analysis of the cited precedents.
30 The balance between the Liberals and the Conservatives was held by the Irish Nationalists and the Labour Party, who generally supported the Liberal Government. See Roy Jenkins, *Mr Balfour's Poodle* (1954), and ch. 15.

The King reluctantly agreed to the creation of the requisite number of peers if the Government were returned and the Lords refused to pass the bill. This contingent promise was not disclosed till after the Government had been returned to power at the second General Election of 1910 – the results were almost identical to those in the January election – and the Lords, in July 1911, had passed wrecking amendments to the bill. In August 1911 the Lords accepted the rejection of most of their amendments by the Commons, and passed the bill by a small majority.

Neither in 1831–2 nor in 1910–11 was it accepted that the Government had an absolute right to require the monarch to exercise his prerogative for such a purpose. Jennings, commenting on the present conventional rules, wrote that it was 'clear that the power to refuse is extant'.[31] However, an outright refusal might compromise the political neutrality of the monarchy. The imposition of a requirement that approval of the electorate for the measure for which the exercise of the prerogative[32] was so sought should first be obtained might well be justifiable.[33] In practice the situation is unlikely to arise, now that the Parliament Acts have reduced the suspensory veto of the Lords to one month for money bills and just over a year for other public bills.[34]

Refusal of the royal assent

In 1913 and 1914, George V appears to have thought that he retained a residual power to refuse his assent to the Irish Home Rule Bill[35] though he did in fact assent to it. Refusal of the royal assent on the ground that the monarch strongly disapproved of a bill or that it was intensely controversial would nevertheless be unconstitutional. The only circumstances in which the withholding of the royal assent might be justifiable would be if the Government itself were to advise such a course – a highly improbable contingency[36] – or possibly if it was notorious that a bill had been passed in disregard of mandatory procedural requirements; but since the Government

31 Jennings, op. cit., p. 447. Any reasoned opinion expressed by Sir Ivor Jennings is entitled to the greatest respect.
32 On the statutory power to create life peerages, see pp. 298–9.
33 See p. 123, on insistence upon a dissolution.
34 See below, pp. 304–8. Procedural rules of the House of Lords could also delay the introduction of 'swamping' peers: see Brazier, op. cit., pp. 152–3.
35 Jennings, op. cit., pp. 395–400.
36 It could hardly arise unless a change of Government occurred without a General Election within the brief interval between the passage of the bill and its presentation for assent.

in the latter situation would be of the opinion that the deviation would not affect the validity of the measure once it had been assented to, prudence would suggest the giving of assent.

Appointments and honours[37]

The Queen personally appoints members of her own private household; by far the most important member of her staff is her Private Secretary, who maintains contact with the Prime Minister and overseas dignitaries on her behalf, offers her and others informal counsel on matters of constitutional propriety and ceremonial decorum, and has been known to occupy a key position, as a liaison officer, in delicate constitutional situations.

When other appointments are made in her name, and when titles, honours and dignities are bestowed, she must act on the Prime Minister's advice (or, in the case of Commonwealth countries of which she is Queen, on the advice of the relevant Prime Minister) except on the appointment of a new Prime Minister and in the award of certain honours. Membership of the Royal Victorian Order is granted for personal services to the monarchy; normally no political implication is to be read into such an award, but in November 1965, after the unlawful unilateral declaration of independence by the Ministers in Southern Rhodesia, she created Sir Humphrey Gibbs, the loyalist Governor, a KCVO, acting in her personal discretion. When he retired in July 1969 she awarded him the GCVO. She is also entitled to make appointments to the Order of Merit and the Orders of the Garter and the Thistle in her discretion. Suggestions may, of course, emanate from the Prime Minister, just as she may herself initiate suggestions for the bestowal of titles, honours and dignities in respect of which she must act on the Prime Minister's advice.

The Queen also has numerous social and ceremonial functions to perform in her capacity as head of State. Among them are State visits to foreign and Commonwealth countries and the reception of heads of State from overseas. In the constitutional law of the United Kingdom a great many formal acts have to be done by her in the traditional manner, and require her personal signature or approval. She also presides in person at meetings of the Privy Council, and reads the Queen's speech at the opening of a new Parliament or a parliamentary session. She receives letters of credence from newly appointed foreign ambassadors, receives homage from new bishops, and holds some two hundred formal audiences of one sort or another

37 See generally Jennings, op. cit., ch. 14.

in the course of a year, apart from dispensing a great deal of informal entertainment.

LEGAL RULES AFFECTING THE MONARCHY

Title to the Crown is hereditary; the line of succession depends partly on statute and partly on customary common-law rules. Upon the death or abdication of a monarch, the throne and the prerogatives of the Crown pass at once – there is no interregnum:[38] 'the king never dies' – to the person next in succession. Lineal Protestant descendants of Sophia, Electress of Hanover, are alone eligible to succeed.[39] If the reigning monarch has children, sons succeed before daughters, and in accordance with primogeniture. When George VI died leaving two daughters and no son, it was assumed that the elder daughter was entitled to succeed as Elizabeth II, and did not inherit the throne jointly with her sister as a coparcener in accordance with the feudal law of succession to real property.

Roman Catholics and persons marrying Roman Catholics are excluded by statute from the throne; and the monarch must be in communion with the Church of England, declare himself to be a Protestant, swear to maintain the Established Churches in England and Scotland, and take the Coronation Oath.[40] Until the attitude of the Church of England towards divorce is changed, it is possible that the monarch would be advised not to take a divorced person as consort, or, indeed, to remarry if the Sovereign were to be divorced.[41]

38 The last interregnum in British history occurred in 1688–9. James II was deemed to have abdicated on 11 December 1688 (the day he first tried to flee the country and dropped the Great Seal into the Thames). 'From that day until the day when William and Mary accepted the crown, 13 February 1689, there was no king of England' (F. W. Maitland, *Constitutional History of England* (1908), p. 284).

39 Act of Settlement 1701. Edward VIII and his issue were excluded by His Majesty's Declaration of Abdication Act 1936.

40 Provisions to this effect are contained *inter alia* in the Bill of Rights 1689, the Act of Settlement 1701 and the Succession to the Crown Act 1707. The Coronation Oath, prescribed by statute immediately after the Revolution of 1688, and subsequently modified by statute, has since been modified without statutory authority. Elizabeth II swore to govern the peoples of her realms and territories according to their respective laws and customs, and to maintain the established Protestant religion in the United Kingdom.

41 This is to be inferred from the circumstances surrounding Edward VIII's decision in 1936 to abdicate, the King having been advised by the Cabinet that they and the Dominion Governments could not approve of his proposed marriage to Mrs Simpson. Today, however, ministerial advice would take account of public opinion which might not be opposed to such a marriage.

The law relating to the succession to the throne is uniform throughout Her Majesty's dominions. The diversification of the royal titles in 1953 implied that the Crown was no longer indivisible or undivided;[42] but although the Queen of Jamaica, for example, is probably to be regarded as a different legal person from (though the same natural person as) the Queen of the United Kingdom and its dependent territories, the Queen of some of the older Commonwealth countries is perhaps still regarded as the same legal person as the Queen in the United Kingdom even though she bears a different title. However, in so far as the Crown is still undivided, it may be unwise to read implications into the concept. There is no doubt that legal proceedings can be brought by one of Her Majesty's realms against another, or by one Australian state against another, or that the prerogatives of the Crown in right of Canada may be at variance with her corresponding prerogatives in right of a province of Canada.

Immediately upon a demise of the Crown, it is customary to convene an Accession Council, composed of Privy Counsellors and other leading citizens – in 1952, Commonwealth High Commissioners in London were also present – by whom the Queen is formally proclaimed. The Coronation Service will take place some months later; it is attended by picturesque ceremonial, but has no significance in relation to the legal attributes or powers of the monarch. Edward VIII was never crowned.

For most legal purposes no distinction is drawn between the Crown and the monarch; the references to the Sovereign for the time being are to be construed as references to the Crown.[43] In some contexts a distinction must necessarily be drawn. Thus, a conspiracy to cause death, or an attempt on the life, of the Queen Regnant is treason, which is still punishable by death.[44] A conspiracy or attempt to depose the Queen is treason felony.[45] Ordinary civil proceedings can be brought against the Crown but not against the Queen.[46] The general concept of allegiance, however, imports duties owed to the Queen which can equally be expressed in the form of duties owed to the Crown.

---

42 See p. 119. The correctness of this view was confirmed in *R.* v. *Secretary of State for Foreign and Commonwealth Affairs, ex p. Indian Association of Alberta* [1982] 1 QB 892 (CA).

43 Interpretation Act 1978, ss. 10, 21(2). See further, p. 134.

44 Statute of Treasons 1351. It is also treason to commit these offences in respect of the King's consort, but not in respect of the consort of a Queen Regnant.

45 Treason Felony Act 1848, which carries a maximum penalty of life imprisonment.

46 See further, ch. 29.

The royal family

Miscellaneous rules of law and custom affect members of the royal family. Under the archaic Royal Marriages Act 1772, the marriage of a descendant of George II (other than the issue of princesses who have married into foreign families) is void unless the Queen has signified her formal consent.[47] Such a person may marry without her consent if he is over twenty-five, provided that he gives twelve months' notice to the Privy Council and the two Houses of Parliament do not register objection during that period. The monarch's consort does not in general occupy a special position in the eyes of the law, though violation of the chastity of a female consort is treason.[48] Prince Albert was designated as Prince Consort, and he exercised a substantial and beneficent influence over Queen Victoria in constitutional matters till his death in 1861. Prince Philip has not been so designated, but has been accorded official precedence immediately after the Queen. The monarch's eldest son becomes Duke of Cornwall at birth; he will later be created Prince of Wales.[49] His life, the life and chastity of the Princess of Wales during marriage, and the chastity of the monarch's eldest daughter being unmarried are protected by the law of treason.[50] In accordance with precedent, Princess Anne has been created Princess Royal. The title of 'Royal Highness' is conferred upon the sons and daughters of the monarch and on the sons' wives and on the children of the monarch's sons. The Queen decided in 1996 that a person who becomes a Royal Highness on marrying into the royal family would lose that title on divorce.

Regency and Counsellors of State

No general statutory provision existed until 1937 for the exercise of the royal functions if the monarch were a minor, or were incapacitated or absent from the realm. The Regency Act 1937 dealt with these matters; it was amended by Acts of 1943 and 1953.

(i) There will be a regency if the Sovereign is under eighteen years of age, or if the Sovereign is incapacitated by infirmity of mind or body or is 'for

---

47 For a persuasive argument to the effect that the Act of 1772 does not apply to any of Queen Victoria's descendants, see C. d'Olivier Farran (1951) 14 *Mod. L. Rev.* 53.
48 Statute of Treasons 1351: See also note 44.
49 On the Prince of Wales's constitutional position see Brazier [1995] *Public Law* 401.
50 Statute of Treasons 1351. The separation of the Prince and Princess of Wales in 1992 did not affect their constitutional positions. See also 215 HC Deb. 845 (9 December 1992).

some definite cause not available' (for example through being a prisoner of war) for performing the royal functions. A declaration as to the Sovereign's incapacity or unavailability is to be made by the Sovereign's spouse, the Lord Chancellor, the Speaker of the House of Commons, the Lord Chief Justice and the Master of the Rolls, or any three or more of them; and a regency will continue till a declaration as to the removal of the incapacity is similarly made. The Regent is to be that person of full age who is next in the line of succession to the throne, provided that he is a British citizen resident in the United Kingdom and is not disqualified on religious grounds. He may exercise all royal functions except that he is precluded from assenting to a bill to alter the succession to the throne or to repeal the Acts securing the Scottish religion and Church.[51]

(ii) If the Sovereign is suffering from a lesser degree of incapacity than would justify the establishment of a regency, or if she is or intends to be temporarily absent from the realm, she may appoint Counsellors of State (not a Council of State) by letters patent and delegate to them such royal functions as may be specified. They may not, however, dissolve Parliament except on her express instructions,[52] or grant any title or dignity of the peerage. The Counsellors of State are to be the spouse of the Sovereign, the four persons next in succession to the throne (unless disqualified for being Regent or absent from the realm), and Queen Elizabeth the Queen Mother.

Crown revenues[53]

For many centuries no distinction was drawn in financial matters between the King in his public capacity (the Crown) and the King in his private capacity. The King was expected to live from his own means, and only for special purposes was he to have recourse to Parliament in order to obtain extra money by the levying of taxation. When he did come to Parliament, the Commons (especially under the early Stuarts) were apt to demand redress of grievances before agreeing to grant taxes or to appropriate supplies. Gradually this system broke down and parliamentary grants were made to

51 For the possible effect of disregard of this prohibition (Regency Act 1937, s. 4(2)), see p. 93.
52 When the Queen was on a Caribbean tour in 1966 leaving Counsellors of State, the request and assent for a dissolution were communicated in letters exchanged between the Prime Minister and Her Majesty: Harold Wilson, *The Labour Government 1964–1970, A Personal Record* (1971), p. 215.
53 For the substantial body of law on this matter, see *Halsbury's Laws of England*, 4th edn, vol. 8, 'Constitutional Law', paras. 1411–1636.

the Sovereign for the time being for his private purposes during his lifetime. In exchange the Sovereign surrendered to the Exchequer most of the time-honoured hereditary revenues of the Crown.

In 1800 the Sovereign was enabled by statute to hold land in a *private* capacity; this is alienable and is taxable. It seems that the Sovereign paid tax on private wealth until 1937, when George VI persuaded the Chancellor of the Exchequer that such taxes should not be paid. He and his successor paid no personal taxes until 1900, when the present Queen (following some public debate about the issue) offered to pay income, capital gains and inheritance taxes.[54] She now pays those taxes on her personal income. As part of the same arrangement, the Queen reimburses Civil List payments (on which see below) made to her for all members of the royal family other than the Queen Mother and Prince Philip. Prince Charles (who was already paying tax on his personal income), also agreed to pay tax on his Duchy of Cornwall income, which had previously been exempt. Today the Queen's private estates are managed separately from the Crown lands, which are exempt from fiscal burdens and are administered by Crown Estate Commissioners.

A Civil List Act is passed at the beginning of each reign, providing for annual sums of money[55] for the Sovereign's privy purse, salaries and expenses of her household, and miscellaneous matters including annuities and expenses of some other members of the royal family. The Civil List Act 1972, amending the Civil List Act 1952, allows the annual sums to be increased by the Treasury at any time by statutory instrument, subject only to the power of the House of Commons to annul it. The Civil List Act 1975 enacted that the Civil List may be supplemented by the Treasury out of money provided by Parliament[56] An annual rate of £8 million was set in 1990, and will remain at that rate until 2000.

Signification of the royal pleasure

Fortunately, not every act of government done in the Queen's name requires her personal participation. Nevertheless, either by custom or by statute, she has to take part in a great number of such acts. For example,

---

54 See Prime Minister's statements at 177 HC Deb. 299–300 (24 July 1990), 218 HC Deb. 1111–12 (11 February 1993), and see Pearce-Crump [1994] *British Tax Review* 635.
55 The Civil List is charged on the Consolidated Fund and does not, therefore, require annual authorization by Parliament.
56 But see above, and note 54. Some royal expenses are borne on departmental votes. The Queen has not drawn the sums allocated to her privy purse.

when an Order in Council has to be made, or when any other transaction has to take place in Council, she must preside at a formal meeting of the Privy Council. About ten meetings are held annually. Some royal appointments (for example, ambassadors) are made under the royal sign manual (the Queen's personal signature); some (for example, appointments of most Cabinet Ministers) are made by personal delivery of the seal of office. Many classes of acts (for example, the issue of royal proclamations, writs for the holding of elections, letters patent for the conferment of peerages, the appointment of royal commissions, and charters of incorporation for boroughs and universities, and the ratification of certain treaties) involve the affixing of the Great Seal of the Realm, of which the Lord Chancellor is custodian; this can normally be brought into use only by virtue of a warrant under the royal sign manual.

THE ROYAL PREROGATIVE[57]

The royal prerogative, 'in its nature singular and eccentrical',[58] can be roughly described as those inherent legal attributes which are unique to the Crown. For 'the Crown' we can substitute 'the Queen'. Prerogative powers belong to the Queen as a person as well as to the institution called the Crown; in law the Queen is the Crown, or Her Majesty's Government,[59] or the State, except where an Act of Parliament or common sense differentiates them expressly or by necessary implication.[60] Powers and duties are often vested by statute directly in named Ministers. But prerogatives are non-statutory attributes of the Crown, not statutory attributes of its servants.

Prerogatives are *inherent* in so far as they are derived from customary common law. They are *legal* in so far as they are recognized and enforced by courts; and, as the *Case of Proclamations* (1611)[61] made abundantly plain,

57 For an excellent survey of history and the prerogative, see D. L. Keir and F. H. Lawson, *Cases in Constitutional Law* (6th edn, 1979), ch. II. See also R. Brazier in M. Sunkin and S. Payne (eds.), *The Nature of the Crown* (1998).

58 Blackstone, *Commentaries*, vol. 1, p. 238.

59 Or 'Her Majesty's Government in the United Kingdom'. See, for example, Jamaica Independence Act 1962, s. 1(1), and other statutes dealing with external relations.

60 See pp. 129, 132. For a skilful critique, see Geoffrey Marshall, *Constitutional Theory* (1971), pp. 17–34.

61 12 Co. Rep. 74. A proclamation forbidding under penalty new building in and around London was held to be unlawful. Similar proclamations had been issued and enforced under Elizabeth I – for example, a proclamation of July 1580 made at Nonsuch.

their ambit is determinable by the courts. When Blackstone described the prerogative as 'that special pre-eminence which the King hath, over and above all other persons, and *out of the ordinary course of the common law*, in right of his regal dignity,'[62] he was not asserting that the Crown could conclusively determine the limits of its own prerogative; he was merely emphasizing the *uniqueness* of the prerogative. Prerogative attributes are not shared with subjects, though there may be close similarities; the royal prerogative in time of real or apprehended war differs in degree rather than kind from the general common-law doctrine of necessity. The courts have stopped using the term 'Crown privilege' and employ the phrase 'public interest privilege' instead to describe the power to procure the exclusion of evidence from judicial proceedings on grounds of public interest, and it must be doubted whether this is to be regarded as a prerogative at all, because it is not a power peculiar to the Crown.[63]

The prerogative consists mainly of executive governmental powers – powers to conduct foreign relations, to make war and peace, to regulate the disposition of the armed forces, to appoint and dismiss Ministers, to dissolve Parliament, to assent to bills, and so on. The exercise of these powers is controlled by constitutional convention. It also includes immunities (for example, the Queen's personal immunity from suit or prosecution), privileges (for example, proprietary rights over royal fish, the status of the Crown as a preferred creditor) and miscellaneous attributes, such as the prerogative of protection which is in some aspects a legal duty.

Other definitions can be considered. To Dicey,[64] the royal prerogative was 'the residue of discretionary or arbitrary authority, which at any given time is legally left in the hands of the Crown'. This definition is incomplete because it is restricted to powers. However, it includes some important features. It stresses the *residual* features of the prerogative within the realm. The prerogative is traceable to the days before Parliament ever existed, but cannot be enlarged by the Crown except in certain dependent territories. 'It is 350 years and a civil war too late for the Queen's courts to broaden the prerogative.'[65] Prerogatives can be and have been abrogated or diminished by

---

62 loc. cit. (italics supplied).

63 See especially *R.* v. *Lewes JJ, ex p. Home Secretary* [1973] AC 388 (HL). Another reason may be that such claims, even if made by Ministers, are reviewable by the courts: see *Conway* v. *Rimmer* [1968] AC 910, and ch. 32.

64 *Introduction to the Study of the Law of the Constitution* (10th edn, 1959), p. 424. His definition has been cited in a number of judgments.

65 *British Broadcasting Corporation* v. *Johns* [1965] Ch. 32 at 79, *per* Diplock LJ. See also *The Zamora* [1916] 2 AC 77 (the Crown may mitigate but not extend its own prerogative in prize law).

statute; the Crown Proceedings Act 1947 deprived the Crown (but not the monarch in her private capacity) of various immunities in civil litigation. They have also been lost by other means. For certain colonies the Crown could lose its plenary legislative powers under the prerogative by granting a representative legislature.[66] Prerogative powers in the administration of justice passed into the hands of Her Majesty's judges.[67] Other prerogatives came to be shared by subjects and lost their original character and function.[68] Some appear to have quietly withered away.[69] Yet a vanishing prerogative is a strange creature, for there is no generally accepted principle of law that a prerogative may be lost merely by desuetude.[70]

It used to be said that prerogative discretionary powers are also absolute (which is what Dicey meant by 'arbitrary') in the eyes of the courts, in the sense that once the existence, scope and form of a prerogative power were established to their satisfaction, the courts would disclaim jurisdiction to review the propriety or adequacy of the grounds upon which that power had been exercised.[71] As a result, however, of the modern development of judicial review of executive action, and in particular in the light of the opinions of the majority in *Council of Civil Service Unions* v. *Minister for the Civil Service*[72] (the GCHQ case), the last part of that proposition no longer stands. In that case the Prime Minister, as Minister for the Civil Service, gave instructions under a prerogative Order in Council forbidding staff at the Government Communications Headquarters at

---

66 *Campbell* v. *Hall* (1774) 1 Cowp. 204.

67 See especially *Prohibitions del Roy* (1607) 12 Co. Rep. 63 (King could not administer justice in person). For criticisms of the casuistic reasoning adopted by the judges, see Dicey, op. cit., p. 18.

68 For example, the prerogative writ *ne exeat regno* by which the monarch could (and possibly still can) (see Bridge (1972) 88 *LQR* 83; Anderson (1987) 104 *LQR* 246) command a subject not to leave the realm, at least in time of emergency; cf. *Felton* v. *Callis* [1969] 1 QB 200 showing the strict limitations of the scope of the writ in proceedings between subjects, and see *Lipkin Gorman* v. *Cass*, *The Times*, 29 May 1985; *Al Nahkel for Contracting and Trading Ltd* v. *Lowe* [1986] 2 WLR 317.

69 For example, the power to impress men into the navy.

70 F. W. Maitland, *Constitutional History of England* (1908), p. 418. For a definition of the royal prerogative given by the Government in 1994 see 559 HL Deb. 49 (written answers 1 December 1994).

71 See, for example, *R.* v. *Allen* (1862) 1 B. & S. 850 (grounds for entering a *nolle prosequi*); *Engelke* v. *Musmann* [1928] AC 433 (recognition of diplomatic representative for purpose of according diplomatic immunity – a matter now regulated by statute); *Chandler* v. *DPP* [1964] AC 763 (disposition of armed forces; though cf. the reservation entered by Lord Devlin at 809–10) and see p. 152.

72 [1985] AC 374.

Cheltenham from belonging to trade unions. The House of Lords held that regardless of the source (whether statutory or prerogative) of a Minister's power, its exercise was potentially reviewable, although not all prerogative acts are justiciable.[73] So today the grounds upon which executive action is carried out in pursuance of a prerogative power are in general, open to judicial scrutiny,[74] although the propriety of the exercise of some prerogative powers is unsuitable to and remains immune from judicial review, such as, for example, certain action taken on the grounds of national security (as in the GCHQ case itself), the conclusion of treaties,[75] the dissemination of information,[76] the dissolution of Parliament, the appointment of Ministers or the granting of honours. A court might conclude that a power claimed by the Crown (for example, to take property for defence purposes) existed in law but imported a duty to pay compensation to the persons whose interests were encroached upon.[77] The refusal of a passport is now reviewable,[78] as is the exercise of the prerogative of mercy[79].

Some general problems

If one were to devote a whole book to examining the scope of the royal prerogative today,[80] one would still leave a number of questions unanswered. Writing in 1888, Maitland observed that there was 'often great uncertainty as to the exact limits' of the prerogative; and he concluded his short but masterly survey with these words: 'Thus our course is set about with difficulties, with prerogatives disused, with prerogatives of doubtful existence, with prerogatives which exist by sufferance, merely because no one

---

73 The trade unionists' action failed in the face of the Government's assertion of national security considerations: see below, p. 534. The new Labour Government ended the ban on union membership in 1997.

74 Such as, in limited circumstances, whether a civil servant has been dismissed fairly; R. v. *Civil Service Appeal Board, ex p. Bruce* [1989] 2 All ER 907.

75 *Blackburn* v. *Att.-Gen.* [1971] 1 WLR 1037; *McWhirter* v. *Att.-Gen.* [1972] CMLR 882.

76 *Jenkins* v. *Att.-Gen., The Times*, 13 August 1971.

77 For example, *Burmah Oil Co.* v. *Lord Advocate* [1965] AC 75.

78 R. v. *Secretary of State for Foreign and Commonwealth Affairs, ex p. Everett* [1989] 1 All ER 655; see below, p. 422.

79 R. v. *Secretary of State for the Home Department, ex. p. Bentley* [1993] 4 All ER 442.

80 cf. Joseph Chitty, *The Prerogatives of the Crown* (1820) (the best-known monograph); A. B. Keith, *The King and the Imperial Crown* (1936); G. S. Robertson, *Civil Proceedings by and against the Crown* (1908).

has thought it worthwhile to abolish them.'[81] The problem of identification, then, is very real. No comprehensive authoritative statement was offered in medieval times; and in the seventeenth century the scope of the prerogative was hotly disputed. We can identify, as a matter of historical interest, some of the disputed and undisputed prerogatives of which the Crown has been explicitly deprived by statute. But the concept of the prerogative as a bundle of inherent and residuary attributes is intrinsically vague. In 1957 a Committee of Privy Counsellors thought that telephone-tapping authorized by a Minister might possibly be justified as a manifestation of an ancient prerogative power to intercept communications between subjects;[82] yet it is more than doubtful whether such a prerogative ever existed. That the Crown still has certain prerogative powers in time of grave national emergency to enter upon, take and destroy private property seems clear. The conditions under which these powers are exercisable are far from clear, partly because the powers were never precisely defined, partly because the scope of the war prerogative was not considered in general terms by the courts for nearly three hundred years, and partly because in modern times various statutory provisions have been made for these matters.[83] Again, it is not clear how far the royal prerogative in foreign affairs and the concept of an 'act of State' are coterminous.[84]

Archaic prerogatives: a suggestion

In a Scottish appeal to the House of Lords. Lord Simon of Glaisdale said that 'a rule of the English common law, once clearly established, does not become extinct merely by disuse'; it may 'go into a cataleptic trance', but, like Sleeping Beauty, it can be revived 'in propitious circumstances'. It cannot, however, revive if it is 'grossly anomalous and anachronistic'.[85] Probably this proposition offers the best available explanation of the fate of obsolescent prerogatives like the powers to forbid a subject to leave the realm, and to impress him into naval service.[86] Conceivably the former

---

81 *Constitutional History of England*, pp. 418, 421.

82 Cmnd 283 (1957), pt 1. See also *Malone* v. *Metropolitan Police Commissioner* [1979] Ch. 344. cf. R. F. V. Heuston, *Essays in Constitutional Law* (2nd edn, 1964), pp. 50–52, and below, p. 445, for the Interception of Communications Act 1985.

83 See *Att.-Gen.* v. *De Keyser's Royal Hotel Ltd* [1920] AC 508; *Burmah Oil Co.* v. *Lord Advocate* [1965] AC 75; *Nissan* v. *Att.-Gen.* [1970] AC 179.

84 *Nissan's* case (see note 83).

85 *McKendrick* v. *Sinclair* 1972 SLT (HL) 110 at 116, 117.

86 See p. 136, notes 68, 69.

power might revive in circumstances which are, admittedly, hard to envisage; but the latter power must surely be unresponsive to any Prince Charming.

Statute and prerogative powers

The relationship between statute and prerogative remains strangely abstruse. Statutes can bind the Crown;[87] and a prerogative can be abolished by express words. Alternatively the wording of a statute may leave no room for doubt that Parliament, when conferring powers on the Crown, intended to leave the prerogative intact;[88] or to maintain the prerogative but regulate the way in which it can be exercised.[89] Puzzles arise where Parliament neither extinguishes nor saves a prerogative but simply confers powers on the Crown in an area hitherto occupied only by prerogative. In such a situation, the Crown must indeed abide by any statutory restrictions imposed on the exercise of its powers (for example, procedural requirements, or a duty to pay compensation) and cannot fall back on its original absolute prerogative. To the extent of *this* inconsistency the prerogative is abrogated.[90] But suppose a statute merely covers the same ground as prerogative without expressly restricting the Crown's competence. Do statute and prerogative then coexist, or is the prerogative swallowed up and superseded?[91] If superseded, does it revive when the statute is repealed?[92]

Answers to these questions must be tentative. Because the prerogative is tenacious and the Crown is not readily held to be bound by mere implication,[93] the courts are unlikely to hold that a prerogative has been

---

87 See generally, pp. 141–3.
88 For example, Emergency Powers (Defence) Act 1939, s. 9; Crown Proceedings Act 1947, ss. 11(1), 40(1).
89 See Royal Assent Act 1967.
90 *Att.-Gen.* v. *De Keyser's Royal Hotel Ltd* [1920] AC 508 (requisitioning).
91 See the differences of opinion on this point expressed by Lord Denning MR and Russell LJ in *Sabally and N'Jie* v. *Att.-Gen.* [1965] 1 QB 273. See also Sir Kenneth Roberts-Wray, *Commonwealth and Colonial Law* (1966), pp. 164–6, 169–72, 190–97. The prerogative power to maintain the peace was not abridged or placed in abeyance by the Police Act 1964, s. 41; so the Home Secretary may use that power to issue plastic bullets to chief constables even if their police authorities object. See *R.* v. *Secretary of State for the Home Department, ex p. Northumbria Police Authority* [1988] 1 All ER 556.
92 For an answer derived from *Att.-Gen.* v. *De Keyser's Royal Hotel Ltd* [1920] AC 508 at 539, see Colin Munro, *Studies in Constitutional Law* (1987), pp. 171–2.
93 See p. 141.

excluded by implication unless legislation evinces a very clear intention to cover the field in question exhaustively.[94]

Assuming that a prerogative is superseded by a statute and the statute is later repealed, it is submitted that the prerogative ought not to be held to revive unless it is a major governmental attribute[95] or is otherwise consonant with contemporary conditions.[96] Hence archaic Crown privileges or immunities expressly abolished by the Crown Proceedings Act 1947 should not be construed as having been restored merely by a repeal of the relevant parts of the Act. It has been held that the Home Secretary could not create a fresh criminal injuries compensation scheme under the prerogative while a different scheme remained on the statute book, albeit not in force.[97]

The prerogative today: domestic affairs

Prerogative powers in an emergency will be considered in chapter 25. The other surviving prerogatives in domestic affairs are a mixed bag of residual loose ends; some linger on as reminders of feudal days, some are of major importance in the conduct of public affairs. Most of the prerogatives are rights and powers, but it may be convenient to touch first on the main prerogative attributes which are in the nature of privileges, immunities and duties.

The King (or Queen Regnant) can do no wrong. Over the years the prerogative of perfection has borne a variety of meanings, ranging from the total unaccountability of the monarch to any human agency, to the simple rule

---

94 Thus the prerogative power to declare the extent of United Kingdom territorial waters has clearly been replaced by the Territorial Sea Act 1987. It declares that the territorial sea extends to twelve nautical miles (s. $1(1)(a)$), and that the baselines are to be established by Orders in Council made under the Act: the Territorial Waters Order in Council 1964 and the Territorial Waters (Amendment) Order in Council 1979 are deemed to have been made the Act. (s. $1(1)(b)$). For the earlier position under the prerogative, see *R.* v. *Kent JJ, ex p. Lye* [1967] 2 QB 173; *Post Office* v. *Estuary Radio Ltd* [1968] 2 QB 740; *The Fagernes* [1927] P. 311; Edeson (1973) 89 *LQR* 364.

95 As in the *De Keyser* case (see above; power to requisition for defence purposes in wartime), in which event the prerogative may reasonably be held to lie in suspense; see [1920] AC at 539–40. See also ibid., 554, 561.

96 cf. *New Windsor Corporation* v. *Taylor* [1899] AC 41 (local customary franchise of tollage superseded by statutory right; statute later repealed; held, old franchise was not thereby revived). The terms of sections 15 and 16(1) of the Interpretation Act 1978 may not be irrelevant in this general context.

97 R. v. *Secretary of State for the Home Department, ex p. Fire Brigades Union* [1995] 2 All ER 244.

that the monarch in person cannot be prosecuted or sued for a wrongful act in the courts. The latter rule still prevails, though it is possible to bring a petition of right against the monarch in the High Court for alleged breaches of contract and a few other legal wrongs, thus obtaining a judicial remedy unaccompanied by coercive relief. Before the Crown Proceedings Act 1947 it was therefore impossible (subject to a small number of exceptions) to sue the Crown as a matter of strict law for tortious acts or omissions, or to sue the Crown vicariously for the torts of its employees. Fortunately this absurd anachronism has been substantially removed from our law.[98]

Since the days of Elizabeth I it has been acknowledged that acts done by the Crown purportedly under the prerogative may be held by the courts to be *ultra vires*[99] – a proposition challenged only by the most extreme Stuart theoreticians.

Because it may be unseemly to hold the monarch personally to account for an invalid or potentially controversial act performed by her in her public capacity, custom requires the participation of Ministers in most of such acts – for example, by countersignature, or by presence at a Privy Council meeting where formal business is transacted. Thus, it is the Ministers who attract responsibility.

The King is a preferred creditor. If a debtor is insolvent, the Crown has priority as a creditor at common law. This matter is now largely regulated by statute. But in the levying of execution or distress against the property of a subject, the Crown still enjoys priority under the prerogative.

Time does not run against the King. The normal periods of limitation did not apply to the Crown in criminal proceedings and as a plaintiff in civil litigation. In most forms of civil proceedings, and to a lesser extent in criminal proceedings, this immunity has been abrogated by statute.

The Crown is not bound by statute save by express words or necessary implication. In its origin a prerogative immunity, this proposition can also be formulated as a particular rule of statutory interpretation. It covers the imposition of obligations, restraints and other burdens. General words directed to such

---

98 See ch. 29, where the state of the law is considered in more detail.
99 See, for example, *Willion* v. *Berkley* (1561) Plow. 223; *Case of Monopolies* (1602) 11 Co. Rep. 84b.

ends will normally be construed as excluding the Crown.[100] That principle has, on the whole, been rigidly applied; and Crown immunity has been understood to mean that Crown tenants, and tenants of a body ancillary to the regular armed forces, do not enjoy the protection of the Rent Acts,[101] that government Departments do not have to obtain planning permission in order to effect a material change in the use of land occupied by them,[102] that land occupied for Crown purposes (for example, for use as county courts)[103] is immune from local taxes,[104] that a court cannot make an order for the abatement of a nuisance committed in a hospital administered under the National Health Service,[105] and even (till the Road Traffic Acts were expressed to bind the Crown) that a Crown servant on duty driving a vehicle for Crown purposes and under superior orders to deliver a load quickly, could not be convicted of exceeding a statutory speed limit.[106]

The narrower principle, also founded on the prerogative, that the Crown is immune from central government taxation in the absence of express words or necessary intendment, has a more secure and rational basis. Why should an intention be imputed to Parliament to raise money *from* the Government? Government Departments are exempt from income tax; so is the Queen in her personal capacity (at least as a matter of practice);[107] civil servants in their private capacities are not, of course, exempt. However, difficult marginal cases arise. Public bodies which are servants or agents of

---

100 See *Lord Advocate* v. *Dumbarton District Council* [1990] 2 AC 580; and see *Bombay Province* v. *Bombay Municipal Council* [1947] AC 88, and *The Queen in Right of Alberta* v. *Canadian Transport Commission* (1977) 75 DLR (3d) 257, *Department of Transport* v. *Egoroff* (1986) 278 EG 1361; though cf. *Madras Electric Supply Corpn Ltd* v. *Boarland* [1955] AC 667 (where the word 'person' in a special rule in an Income Tax Act was held to include the Crown). The prerogative immunity in Scots law is possibly less far-reaching: Mitchell [1957]. *Public Law* 304.

101 *Territorial Forces Association* v. *Nichols* [1949] 1 KB 35; *Tamlin* v. *Hannaford* [1950] 1 KB 18 (dicta). This rule has since been modified by statute.

102 *Ministry of Agriculture* v. *Jenkins* [1963] 2 QB 317.

103 *R.* v. *Manchester Overseers* (1954) 3 E. & B. 336.

104 See generally *Mersey Docks and Harbour Board Trustees* v. *Cameron* (1964) 11 HLC at 464–5. In practice the Crown has paid contributions in lieu of local taxes, and the legal exemption is to be ended under the Local Government and Rating Act 1997, s. 3.

105 *Nottingham Area No.1 Hospital Management Committee* v. *Owen* [1958] 1 QB 50. Crown immunity has been removed from health service bodies for most purposes: National Health Service and Community Care Act 1990, s. 60. For another aspect of Crown immunity (in respect of patented drugs) in connection with the National Health Service, see *Pfizer Corporation Ltd* v. *Ministry of Health* [1965] AC 512.

106 *Cooper* v. *Hawkins* [1904] 2 KB 164. See now Road Traffic Regulation Act 1984, s. 130, Road Traffic Act 1988, s. 183, Road Traffic Offenders Act 1988, s. 92, binding the Crown.

107 See p. 132 above.

the Crown, or which act as instruments of the Crown, are exempt. But how and where is a court to draw the line? The general functions of local authorities, and public corporations conducting the affairs of the remaining nationalized industries, are not performed as servants or agents of the Crown; they enjoy a substantial degree of independence from the Crown, and their functions are not unambiguously within the province of central government,[108] they do not, therefore, attract the immunities and privileges of the Crown.[109] For similar reasons the BBC has been held to be subject to income tax.[110] The Custodian of Enemy Property was held to be a Crown servant, mainly because of the degree of control that Ministers were entitled to exercise over him, and tax was therefore not payable on the income from property disposed of by him while acting in that capacity.[111] Hair-splitting distinctions may still have to be drawn where it is doubtful whether a body is a Crown agent, or where a body is clearly not a Crown agent but performs functions associated with the business of central government.

The prerogative of protection. This prerogative does not fit neatly into any analytical category. In some aspects it is a duty, in others a power.[112] The Crown has a duty to 'protect' its own subjects by granting them diplomatic protection in foreign countries; but this duty is not directly enforceable in a court of law[113] and in any event the 'duty' is now probably limited to British citizens, British Dependent Territories citizens, British Overseas citizens and British protected persons. It is under no legal duty to grant them passports. Nor is it under any legal duty to offer armed protection to such of its intrepid subjects as engage in hazardous ventures on the high seas or in foreign countries; if it decides in its discretion to offer this form of protection, it can impose a condition that the subject shall pay for the protection offered.[114] The Crown does owe limited duties of protection to

---

108 See *Mersey Docks and Harbour Board Trustees* v. *Gibbs* (1866) LR 1 HL 93 on the separate legal status of autonomous and semi-autonomous public authorities.

109 See *Tamlin* v. *Hannaford* (note 101), on nationalized industries; and generally J. A. G. Griffith (1952) 9 *U. of Toronto LJ* 169. The now defunct Central Land Board was held to be a Crown servant: *Glasgow Corporation* v. *Central Land Board* 1956 SC (HL) 1. That nationalized industries do not enjoy Crown immunities is now usually made clear by statute. See, for example, Post Office Act 1969, s. 6(5).

110 *British Broadcasting Corporation* v. *Johns* [1965] AC 32.

111 *Bank voor Handel en Scheepvaart* v. *Administrator of Hungarian Property* [1954] AC 584.

112 See two thought-provoking articles by H. Lauterpacht (1947) 9 *Camb. LJ* 330, and Glanville Williams (1948) 10 *Camb. LJ* 54. See also Clive Parry (ed.), *A British Digest of International Law*, vol. 5, s. 3.

113 See *Mutasa* v. *Att.-Gen.* [1980] QB 114.

114 *China Navigation Co.* v. *Att.-Gen.* [1932] 2 KB 197.

persons owing allegiance, including aliens owing local allegiance; the extent and implications of these duties will be considered later.[115]

The capacity of the Crown as *parens patriae* implied a prerogative to protect the welfare of infants. This power or duty has long been exercised only through the Queen's courts by judges; in other words, it has become an 'ordinary' prerogative as distinct from an 'absolute' prerogative. But an alien infant owing allegiance is within the scope of the prerogative of protection, so that the Chancery Division has jurisdiction to exercise its discretion whether to make him a ward of court.[116] In so far as the prerogative of protection encompasses the superintendence of charities and the welfare of persons of unsound mind, it appears to have been almost entirely engulfed by statute.

Miscellaneous domestic prerogatives

Power to appoint and dismiss Ministers, to dissolve and prorogue Parliament, and to assent to legislation is derived from the prerogative. As the fountain of honour the Queen creates hereditary peerages and confers other titles and dignities. As head of the established Church, she appoints archbishops and diocesan bishops, and assents to measures of the General Synod approved by both Houses of Parliament. As head of the armed forces, she directs their disposition and commissions officers. War is declared and a state of war terminated by virtue of the prerogative.

The diffusion of government information[117] and the regulation of the civil service[118] fall partly or wholly within the scope of the prerogative. Enemy aliens can be interned or expelled. The issue and revocation of a United Kingdom passport fall within the prerogative.

The Queen is the fountain of justice, and in relation to the administration of justice several prerogatives remain vested in the Crown. There is a prerogative power to create new courts, but only courts to administer the common law.[119] Prosecutions for indictable offences are conducted in her name. The power to enter a *nolle prosequi*, to stop or discontinue a prosecution or indictment, is exercised by the Attorney-General[120] on behalf of Her Majesty; this power is occasionally used to secure the discontinuance

---

115 See pp. 420–23.
116 *Re P.* (*G.E.*) (*an Infant*) [1965] Ch. 568.
117 See note 76.
118 See ch. 10.
119 *Re Lord Bishop of Natal* (1864) 3 Moo. PCC (NS) 115.
120 See below, p. 385.

of a private prosecution. The prerogative of pardon (exercisable only on the advice of a Secretary of State) is used to grant absolute or conditional pardons to persons convicted of criminal offences[121] or to remit part of the sentence of imprisonment or the fine imposed. A conditional pardon substitutes, by commutation, a different penalty for that imposed by the court; whether the person convicted could reject the condition is a nice question;[122] in the last resort the Crown could, if it saw fit, grant a free pardon. Statutory authority exists for the early release of prisoners.[123]

The Crown also has prerogative rights and powers in respect of *bona vacantia*, sturgeon and certain swans and whales,[124] coinage, the granting of charters of incorporation, the award of franchises (including the right to hold markets and fairs, and to collect tolls[125] from bridges or ferries), the construction and supervision of harbours, and the printing and publication of statutes and other legislative instruments, the authorized version of the Bible and the Book of Common Prayer.[126]

---

121 It would seem that a pardon may be granted *before* conviction; but this power is not exercised. The line between pardon before conviction and the unlawful exercise of dispensing power is thin. A pardon removes all the 'pains, penalties and punishments' flowing from a conviction, but in no sense eliminates the conviction itself, according to the Court of Appeal: *R.* v. *Foster* [1985] QB 115; see also *R* v. *Secretary of State for the Home Department, ex p. Bentley* [1993] 4 All ER 442. A statutory right to compensation for those wrongly convicted and sentenced was provided for the first time in 1988.

122 See Brett (1957) 20 *Mod. L. Rev.* 131.

123 Criminal Justice Act 1991, Part II (formerly parole).

124 Other archaic prerogative proprietary rights were abolished by the Wild Creatures and Forest Laws Act 1971.

125 See *Nyali Ltd* v. *Att.-Gen.* [1956] 1 QB 1.

126 And may license their printing and publication by others, but not so as to authorize a breach of copyright: *Oxford and Cambridge Universities* v. *Eyre and Spottiswoode Ltd* [1964] Ch. 736.

CHAPTER 7

The Royal Prerogative in
External Affairs

GENERAL

External relations are conducted pre-eminently under prerogative powers.[1] Not only the declaration of war, the dispatch of armed forces and the annexation of territory, but also the conclusion of treaties, the accrediting and reception of diplomats, the recognition of new states and revolutionary governments fall within the scope of the prerogative. Such acts are sometimes called acts of State – assertions of State sovereignty in international relations. The term 'acts of State' is also used in other specialized senses; and it does not invariably connote an act done in pursuance of the royal prerogative.[2]

As has been indicated already, prerogative powers in relation to dependent territories are not merely a residue.[3] For colonies acquired by conquest or cession they are plenary in the absence of special circumstances; and they may be lost but later resumed.[4] For colonies acquired by settlement, its prerogative legislative power is more limited and has been largely superseded by statue. In those dependent territories which are not British possessions the prerogative is again more than a residue. In colonial-type protectorates (of which no specimens survive today) the legislative powers of the Crown, though regulated by the Foreign Jurisdiction Acts, were derived from the prerogative; and the Crown could have extended its own jurisdiction even though it may have originally been limited.[5] In British protected states (of which, again, none survives today) which had indigenous rulers and enjoyed a degree of autonomy, the Crown did not claim unlimited jurisdiction;

1 On the prerogative generally, see ch. 6.
2 See pp. 153–5.
3 p. 135.
4 *Campbell* v. *Hall* (1774) 1 Cowp. 204; *Sammut* v. *Strickland* [1938] AC 678.
5 *Sobhuza II* v. *Miller* [1926] AC 518; *Nyali* v. *Att.-Gen.* [1956] 1 QB1 (affd. [1957] AC 253); Sir Kenneth Roberts-Wray, *Commonwealth and Colonial Law* (1966), pp. 187–97.

but it acquired such jurisdiction as it possessed by virtue of the prerogative,[6] and we must assume that in terms of British constitutional law the Crown was competent to enlarge as well as diminish it by prerogative.

TREATIES AND TREATY IMPLEMENTATION

Treaties[7] are international agreements. Such agreements may be called treaties, conventions, covenants, pacts, charters, agreements, protocols, even statutes, declarations or exchanges of notes. They may be bilateral or multilateral; they may be concluded between heads of State, or between governments, or between governments and international organizations. They may deal with political, defence, economic, legal, social or cultural matters. Any such international instrument to which the United Kingdom is a party binds the United Kingdom in international law. Normally it becomes binding only when ratified by the Executive, though some agreements have effect upon signature, and a few have effect only when approved by Act of Parliament. The treaty itself may specify when and in what circumstances it shall come into effect. It is a constitutional usage, and possibly a binding convention, to lay the texts of international agreements before both Houses of Parliament for twenty-one days before ratification, if ratification is required.[8]

The conclusion of a treaty is an act of State and an exercise of the royal prerogative, even though the Queen has not played a formal role in the matter (for example, by granting full powers to plenipotentiaries to negotiate and sign on her behalf, and by ratifying the treaty under the Great Seal); the prerogative, or part of it, may be exercised by the Secretary of State for Foreign and Commonwealth Affairs as her delegate. It is unnecessary to go into the details of this complex branch of the law. But one point stands out. Whereas in a number of legal systems (for example, the United States of America, Germany), a treaty is self-executing – i.e. it becomes part of the municipal law of the land, as soon as it is finally concluded[9] – this is

6 Roberts-Wray, op. cit., p. 116.
7 See Lord McNair, *Law of Treaties* (2nd edn, 1961); D. L. Mendis [1992] *Statute Law Review* 216.
8 171 HC Deb. 2001 (1 April 1921). This is commonly called the 'Ponsonby' rule. For an explanation of the rule by the Government in 1995 see 566 HL Deb. *159–60* (written answers 11 November 1995) and 567 HL Deb. *38* (written answers 28 November 1995).
9 In the United States, however, treaties require the sanction of a two-thirds' majority in the Senate; instruments known as executive agreements do not.

not the rule in United Kingdom law. With few exceptions, internationally binding obligations still need to be given legislative effect if they are to be enforced as law by the courts of this country.[10] They may be given such effect if their provisions (or some of them) are incorporated in or scheduled to an Act of Parliament, or in a statutory instrument (for example, an Order in Council) made under the authority of an Act of Parliament.[11]

There are exceptions to the rule that the Executive cannot alter the law applied in United Kingdom courts merely by incurring international obligations. European Union treaties are cases in point, for according to Community law certain provisions of such treaties may be directly applicable in the laws of Member States.[12] There may be another exception. In a flight of fancy, Walter Bagehot asserted that the Crown has a prerogative power to cede Cornwall.[13] It is very doubtful whether the Crown has a prerogative to cede any part of the United Kingdom. But there have been past examples of the cession of parts of Her Majesty's dominions beyond the seas by prerogative acts[14] (for example, the recognition of American independence in 1783), especially in treaties of peace. If this prerogative has disappeared, it is not clear how, though in modern practice the transfer of British territory and the implementation of a peace treaty are always effected by statute.

10 This rule is clearly settled; the leading authority is *The Parlement Belge* (1879) 4 PD 129 at 154; *Littrell* v. *United States of America (No. 2)* [1994] 4 All ER 203. See also *Maclaine Watson & Co. Ltd* v. *Department of Trade and Industry* [1989] 3 All ER 523; *R.* v. *Secretary of State for Foreign and Commonwealth Affairs, ex p. Rees-Mogg* [1994] 1 All ER 457.

11 For example, extradition treaties, under the Extradition Acts. If a treaty needs legislative implementation, it is unlikely to be ratified by the Crown until the necessary legislation is passed. If there is ambiguity in a statute which incorporates a treaty into United Kingdom law the courts will examine the treaty itself as an aid to interpretation of the statute: *Fothergill* v. *Monarch Airlines* [1981] AC 251.

12 This is a complex point. Article 95(1) of the EEC Treaty (prohibiting various discriminatory trade practices) is directly applicable, without further enactment, in the laws of Member States. But the United Kingdom has incorporated this rule into municipal law by implication in enacting the European Communities Act 1972; see ss. 1, 2(1), 3, sched. 1. Under the Act, future Union treaties (which *may* contain directly applicable provisions) are to be authenticated by Order in Council (s. 1(3) – will this be *giving statutory effect* to such a treaty?), and the Order in Council will have to be approved in draft by resolutions of both Houses if the United Kingdom is itself a party to it (ibid.). For an unsuccessful challenge to a draft Order in Council made under s. 1(3), see *R.* v. *HM Treasury, ex p. Smedley* [1985] QB 657 (and see below, p. 351). See also *R.* v. *Secretary of State for Foreign and Commonwealth Affairs, ex p. World Development Movement Ltd* [1995] 1 All ER 611.

13 *The English Constitution*, Introduction to the 2nd edn (Fontana edn), p. 287.

14 See generally Roberts-Wray, op. cit., ch. 4. See also *Damodhar Gordhan* v. *Deoram Kanji* (1876) 1 App. Cas. 332.

The general rule is that a treaty is not a source of legal rights directly enforceable against the Crown in United Kingdom courts, even though it may be intended to benefit particular individuals (for example, where the Crown receives money from a foreign government by way of compensation for injuries done to them);[15] it is an act of State, not a transaction in the nature of a contract or a declaration of trust.[16] Under the Foreign Compensation Acts 1950 and 1969, the allocation of sums received from foreign governments under treaty as compensation for the confiscation or destruction of British-owned property is made on a discretionary basis by an independent statutory body, the Foreign Compensation Commission. A claimant before the Commission may impugn in the courts a determination that he did not comply with the *statutory* conditions necessary to establish a claim, or a determination reached in disregard of minimum procedural standards,[17] but he cannot obtain a judicial declaration that he is entitled to any particular sum. European Union treaties stand in a special position; they are capable in Community law (adopted in this country by the European Communities Act 1972) of conferring or imposing judicially enforceable legal rights and obligations on individuals.

CONCLUSIVE CROWN CERTIFICATES

In the late Victorian era a Miss Mighell issued a writ for breach of promise of marriage against a Mr Albert Baker; whereupon Mr Baker revealed to the court that he was none other than the Sultan of Johore (who had been living for a time in England under a pseudonym), and pleaded sovereign immunity from the jurisdiction of the court. On behalf of the Crown, the Colonial Office obligingly certified that he was the sovereign ruler of an independent State. The court accepted this certificate as conclusive evidence

---

15 *Rustomjee* v. *R.* (1876) 2 QBD 69. The position is the same where the provisions of the treaty have been implemented by statute: *Civilian War Claimants' Association Ltd* v. *R.* [1932] AC 14. But see below on Community treaties.

16 Though in the *Civilian War Claimants' Association* case, Lord Atkin indicated (at 26–7) that the position might be different if the Crown purported expressly to act as trustee or agent for a subject.

17 *Anisminic Ltd* v. *Foreign Compensation Commission* [1969] 2 AC 147; cf. Foreign Compensation Act 1950, s. 4(4); Tribunals and Inquiries Act 1992, s. 9. See now Foreign Compensation Act 1969, s. 3, superseding s. 4(4) of the 1950 Act, and providing for an appeal on points of law from determinations of the Commission to the Court of Appeal. See p. 524, below.

of the facts stated (although the claim of Johore, a British protected state in Malaya, to be an independent international person was tenuous in the extreme), and the defendant having thus established his immunity from suit, Miss Mighell's action could proceed no further.

This somewhat bizarre case[18] illustrates the disinclination of the courts to make an independent determination of certain questions of law and fact in politically sensitive areas; they indeed abdicated in favour of the Executive. Parliament has since asserted itself by passing the State Immunity Act 1978, which considerably extended the circumstances in which a State will not be immune from suit in the English courts. The Act was designed to bring United Kingdom law into closer harmony with the more restrictive rules of other States. Accordingly, among other things, immunity was removed in relation to commercial transactions,[19] contracts to be performed in the United Kingdom, certain torts and actions over immovable property in the United Kingdom. A head of State, his family and personal servants, continue to enjoy sovereign immunity (section 20), but a government of an independent State and its public property,[20] although in general immune from the jurisdiction of the courts (section 1), must now submit to that jurisdiction in the circumstances set out in sections 2 to 11 of that Act.[21] Persons having diplomatic or consular status enjoy immunities of various kinds, depending on their position in the diplomatic mission or consulate. Diplomatic and consular immunities have been restated by statutes giving effect to the terms of multilateral international conventions,[22] and nothing in the State Immunity Act 1978 limits any diplomatic privileges in those statutes (section 16). Whether a person is entitled to diplomatic or consular status and, if so, to what category he belongs is conclusively determined

18 *Mighell* v. *Sultan of Johore* [1894] 1 QB 149.
19 See, e.g., *Alcom Ltd* v. *Republic of Colombia* [1984] AC 580; *Kuwait Airways Corporation* v. *Iraqi Airways Co.* [1995] 3 All ER 694.
20 Difficult questions as to the immunity of vessels owned by independent States are settled by reference to s. 10 of the 1978 Act, which enacts that ships owned by a State (or in which it has an interest) and which are used for commercial purposes will enjoy no immunity.
21 So, e.g., a landlord successfully pleaded the Act against the French Government which had leased his property as a private dwelling: *Intpro Properties (UK) Ltd* v. *Sauvel* [1983] QB 1019.
22 Diplomatic Privileges Act 1964; Consular Relations Act 1968. See also the International Organizations Act 1968 and 1981; Diplomatic and other Privileges Act 1971; Diplomatic and Consular Premises Act 1987; Arms Control and Disarmament (Privileges and Immunities) Act 1988.

by a certificate entered by a Secretary of State,[23] these certificates are now given under statutory authority, but the conclusiveness of certificates on questions of sovereign and state immunity entails an exercise of the prerogative. Immunities from suit may be waived in the appropriate form. Members of many diplomatic missions in London have taken full advantage of their immunity by refusing to pay penalties for car parking offences.

By virtue of the prerogative, the Crown is also entitled to determine conclusively a range of other matters. These may be summarized as follows:

1 Whether a state of war exists between Her Majesty and a foreign country. Thus, in one case, soon after the end of armed hostilities in the Second World War, the Crown was still detaining and wished to deport a German national as an enemy alien; he brought an application for a writ of habeas corpus, contending that the state of war was at an end and that in any case Germany no longer existed as a State; the court accepted as conclusive a certificate entered by a Secretary of State contradicting these contents.[24]

2 Whether a State is recognized by Her Majesty as an independent State.[25]

3 What dealings (if any) should take place between Her Majesty's Government and a regime which comes to power unconstitutionally in a State.[26]

These issues usually arise in connection with claims to jurisdictional immunity, but they may also arise in other contexts – for example, what

23 Broadly speaking, under the 1964 Act (i) the head of the mission and the principal members of the staff and their families are immune not only from criminal liability but also from most forms of civil liability; (ii) members of the administrative and technical staff are immune from criminal liability but not from civil liability save in respect of acts performed in the course of their official duties; (iii) members of the domestic staff are immune neither from criminal nor from civil liability for acts outside the course of their duties. Although a certificate tendered by the Secretary of State is conclusive as to the matters specified in the text above, the courts retain jurisdiction to ascertain whether, for categories (ii) and (iii), the conduct in question took place in the course of official duties: see *Empson* v. *Smith* [1966] 1 QB 426. They are also entitled to decide questions of waiver and submission to the jurisdiction. See also *Agbor* v. *Metropolitan Police Commissioner* [1969] 1 WLR 703 for independent judicial determination of a question (whether premises were the 'private residence of a diplomatic agent') arising under the 1964 Act.
24 *R.* v. *Bottrill, ex p. Kuechenmeister* [1947] KB 41.
25 For an example, see *Gur Corporation* v. *Trust Bank of Africa* [1987] QB 599.
26 The former practice of recognizing a regime as the *de jure* or *de facto* government was abandoned in 1980, mainly because 'recognition' could imply an *approval* of the new regime, which does not necessarily follow: see 984 HC Deb. 277–9 (written answers 25 April 1980), and Symmons [1981] *Public Law* 249. See also *Republic of Somalia* v. *Woodhouse Drake and Carey (Suisse) SA* [1993] 1 All ER 371.

effect, if any, is to be accorded in English law to the enactments, orders, or judgments of organs of such a political body.[27]

We must not suppose that rules such as these are eccentricities peculiar to British constitutional law. In a number of legal systems the courts look to the Executive for authoritative guidance on matters lying especially within the domain of external affairs; and some systems have developed a coherent concept of non-justiciable 'political questions'. In this country there is no coherent concept; moreover, some questions with marked political overtones are decided by the courts on the basis of the evidence and legal submissions where there is no provision for a conclusive executive certificate or where no such certificate is tendered.[28]

It is also true that in some systems the rules of international law form part of municipal (or domestic) law, and the courts will make an independent determination of the content and applicability of those rules. In Britain the courts adopt a rebuttable presumption that Parliament has not intended to legislate inconsistently with rules of public international law, and common-law rules will, as far as practicable, be so stated as to conform with corresponding international rules[29] but if there is a plain inconsistency, the international

---

27 See, for example, *Carl Zeiss Stiftung* v. *Rayner and Keeler Ltd* [*No. 2*] [1967] I AC 853 (Foreign Secretary certified that Her Majesty's Government did not recognize the German Democratic Republic (East Germany) *de facto* or *de jure*, but that the USSR was recognized as being entitled to exercise *de jure* authority there; House of Lords accepted this declaration as conclusive, but nevertheless attributed legal effect to a decree of the unrecognized government since it was to be regarded as a subordinate organ of a recognized government). *Semble*, such a certificate is not absolutely conclusive where the question is one of usurpation of sovereignty in a British dependency: *Adams* v. *Adams* [1971] P. 188 (Rhodesia). The courts will not challenge the validity of a certificate unless it (i) is not genuine, or (ii) appears on its face to have been made *ultra vires*: *R.* v. *Secretary of State for Foreign and Commonwealth Affairs, ex p. Trawnik, The Times*, 21 February 1986.
28 The State Immunity Act 1978, s. 21, has improved the situation somewhat: a Secretary of State's certificate, if entered, will be conclusive, among other things, as to whether any country is a State, and who must be regarded as the head or Government of a State. But problems remain: see *Agbor*'s case (note 23 above; question of entitlement to occupation of diplomatic premises in London arising out of the civil war in Nigeria). Contrast *Buck* v. *Att.-Gen.* [1965] Ch. 745, where the English Court of Appeal would have disclaimed jurisdiction, as a matter of comity, to declare the constitution of a former colony (Sierra Leone) invalid following the grant of independence; and cases where ulterior motives are attributed by prisoners to governments seeking their surrender as fugitive offenders.
29 See, for example, *Salomon* v. *Customs and Excise Commissioners* [1967] 2 QB 116. If the United Kingdom legislation purports to give effect to an international convention, the wording of the convention can be considered as an aid to interpretation: *Post Office* v. *Estuary Radio Ltd* [1968] 2 QB 740.

law rules will have to give way.[30] Only the Prize Court in wartime purports to apply international law as such, and even this court must, of course, enforce statutes conflicting with international law. Rules of Community law again stand in a special position; for United Kingdom law has effect subject to any relevant Community law rules.[31]

ACTS OF STATE AND LEGAL PROCEEDINGS[32]

Acts of State are primarily prerogative acts of policy in the field of external affairs – for example, the declaration of war, the conclusion of a treaty, an annexation of territory, the recognition of a foreign sovereign, state or government. However, there can be no all-inclusive short definition, covering the different senses in which the term 'act of State' has been used. In one aspect an act of State is a manifestation of national sovereignty by the executive branch of government. When the courts say that an act of State is not cognizable by municipal courts (i.e. United Kingdom courts, and for most purposes, the Judicial Committee of the Privy Council), they usually mean that once it is established to their satisfaction that an act performed by or with the authority of the Crown or a foreign government falls within the legal concept of an act of State, they are not concerned with the propriety of the grounds on which it has been exercised; they do not mean that the Crown can remove a matter from their jurisdiction by the bare assertion that it is an act of State.[33]

There are certain differences of substance or terminology between some acts of State and some prerogative acts.

1 Not every prerogative act is called an act of State; the latter term is reserved for executive acts having an effect in external affairs or performed in relation to persons not fully within the protection of the Crown. The granting of a new charter to an English university is a prerogative act but is not called an act of State.

2 A cause of action against the Crown can seldom be founded on a valid

---

30 See, for example, *Cheney* v. *Conn* [1968] 1 WLR 242.
31 European Communities Act 1972, ss. 2(4), 3(1).
32 For a typically illuminating short survey, see D. L. Keir and F. H. Lawson, *Cases in Constitutional Law* (6th edn, 1979), pp. 144–73. For full studies, see E. C. S. Wade (1934) 15 *BYIL* 98; Holdsworth (1941) 41 *Columbia L. Rev.* 1313; Collier [1968] *Camb. LJ* 102; Cane (1980) 29 *ICLQ* 680.
33 *Entick* v. *Carrington* (1765) 19 St Tr. 1030; *Musgrave* v. *Pulido* (1879) 5 App. Cas. 102.

act of State (for example, the conclusion of a treaty).[34] On the other hand, a lawful exercise of the prerogative (for example, the taking of property for defence purposes) may give rise to a justiciable claim against the Crown for compensation.[35]

3   It is sometimes said that the term 'act of State' refers only to acts performed outside Her Majesty's dominions. This cannot be correct. Although acts of State can be performed outside her dominions, certain acts of State (for example, the making of a treaty) may also be performed inside them. The detention of an enemy alien in wartime[36] or the deportation of such a person[37] can be classified either as a prerogative act or as an act of State; this is merely a matter of terminology.

4   It is also sometimes said that an act of State cannot, whereas the royal prerogative can, be pleaded by way of justification in proceedings instituted by a British citizen.[38] This suggestion will be considered below.

5   In certain situations a British citizen may successfully plead that an ostensibly unlawful act is lawful because it was carried out in pursuance of an act of State of a foreign government, the validity of which will be recognized by an English court.[39] Such acts would not generally be called prerogative acts.

6   There are doubts as to the operation of the royal prerogative outside Her Majesty's dominions,[40] doubts which do not apply with equal force to acts of State. That certain prerogative powers (for example, in relation

34 See p. 147; or on an annexation (*Secretary of State for India* v. *Kamachee Boye Sahaba* (1859) 12 Moo. PCC 22); Collier, loc. cit., at 105–9.

35 See *Nissan* v. *Att.-Gen.* [1968] 1 QB 286 (CA); *Att.-Gen.* v. *De Keyser's Royal Hotel Ltd* [1920] AC 508. Note also the distinction between prerogative powers and acts of State drawn in *Commercial and Estates Co. of Egypt* v. *Board of Trade* [1925] 1 KB 271 (prerogative power of angary; wartime requisitioning of goods within the realm belonging to absent neutral; compensation payable). In that case Scrutton LJ (at 290) and Bankes LJ (at 297) said *obiter* that act of State could never be pleaded as a defence to an action in tort arising out of an act done in the realm. But the plaintiff was non-resident and apparently did not owe local allegiance. On principle, therefore, it is arguable that act of State could have been successfully pleaded, but for the fact that the situation fell within the rules governing angary.

36 *R.* v. *Vine Street Police Station Superintendent, ex p. Liebmann* [1916] 1 KB 268.

37 *Netz* v. *Chuter Ede* [1946] Ch. 224; *R.* v. *Bottrill, ex p. Kuechenmeister* [1947] KB 41.

38 The phrase 'British citizen' for the purposes only of the rest of this chapter should be read as also including British Dependent Territories and British Overseas citizens, and British protected persons.

39 *Dobree* v. *Napier* (1836) 2 Bing NC 781; *Carr* v. *Fracis Times and Co.* [1902] AC 176; Zander (1959) 53 *Am. JIL* 826. The act must be within the foreign government's own jurisdiction.

40 See *Nissan* v. *Att.-Gen.* [1970] AC 179; note 45, below.

to the disposition of the armed forces, and in relation to protected states) are exercisable on foreign soil is reasonably clear; what is not clear is where the line is to be drawn.

7 The term 'act of State' is sometimes loosely used to include acts done in pursuance of statutory authority which has superseded prerogative (for example, the conclusiveness of a certificate as to diplomatic immunity).

ACTS OF STATE AND INDIVIDUAL RIGHTS

An act of State has been described as 'an act of the executive as a matter of policy',[41] and as 'an exercise of sovereign power'.[42] Those descriptions fit most of the situations in which conduct has been held in judicial proceedings to constitute an act of State. But there have been cases in which the quality of an act of State has been attributed to the individual initiative of a not very senior Crown servant ratified by the Crown.[43] On the other hand, the requisitioning and use of a hotel in Cyprus by British troops engaged in a peace-keeping operation was held not to fall within the description of an act of State.[44] Since the Law Lords gave a number of different reasons for their conclusion on this point, the case is not helpful except in so far as it suggests that nowadays only acts which are part of or necessarily incidental to a high-level policy decision (and possibly other acts expressly ratified by the Crown) will be treated as acts of State.

Many of the decisions on act of State have an archaic flavour. They deal with the annexation of territory in India and Southern Africa in the heyday of imperial expansion, when judges often seemed to be as executive-minded as the Executive. It is not certain how much weight should be attached to some of these decisions; sometimes it is not even clear what were the material facts. But the principles laid down in them may still have to be taken into account in connection with claims arising from acts done by British peace-keeping forces overseas; the age of military intervention is not over, though one can optimistically assume that nowadays intervention will seldom take place except at the request or with the concurrence of the government of the territory or country concerned or as part of a United Nations or other international force. Unfortunately the only modern case

41 E. C. S. Wade (1934) 15 *BYIL* at 103.
42 *Salaman* v. *Secretary of State for India* [1906] 1 KB 613 at 639.
43 For example, *Buron* v. *Denman* (1848) 2 Ex. 167 (see below).
44 *Nissan* v. *Att.-Gen.* [1970] AC 179.

in which the Crown pleaded act of State as a defence in legal proceedings (*Nissan* v. *Att.-Gen.*) was a disaster for students of the law. The decision of the House of Lords lacks any clear *ratio decidendi* on any point now under consideration. Important questions of law were raised but left half-answered or unanswered, and points that once seemed clear were left shrouded in obscurity.[45]

The following observations about the state of the law must therefore be regarded as very tentative.

1 Act of State can successfully be pleaded by way of defence to an action in tort brought by an alien in respect of an ostensibly wrongful act committed against him outside Her Majesty's dominions by the Crown or with the authority, antecedent or subsequent, of the Crown: *Buron* v. *Denman* (1848), an action for trespass.[46] The rationale of this rule is twofold: an alien in a foreign country or on the high seas does not ordinarily owe allegiance to the Crown[47] and is therefore not entitled to the protection of the Crown or indeed protection against the Crown; and he can look to his own government for diplomatic redress and, if any appropriate forum exists, the institution of proceedings for a breach of international law. Whether these are adequate reasons for treating a

---

45 [1970] AC 179. For critiques, see Gilmour [1970] *Public Law* 120; Bridge (1971) 34 *Mod. L. Rev.* 121; Collier [1969] *Camb. LJ* 166; see also H. W. R. Wade and C. F. Forsyth, *Administrative Law* (7th edn, 1994), p. 843; de Smith (1969) 32 *Mod. L. Rev.* 427. N, a British subject in Cyprus, was claiming that he was entitled to (i) *compensation* for the requisitioning of his hotel, and the use of the contents, under the royal prerogative; or (ii) declarations as to a breach of contract; or (iii) a declaration that he was entitled to damages in tort for trespass to his chattels. The Crown denied the allegations and also pleaded act of State; it then withdrew the defence of act of State in respect of claim (iii). The case was not fully disposed of but determined on preliminary points of law. No majority view emerged in the Lords as to the definition of an act of State; the scope of the *defence* of act of State (for instance, when, if at all, it was available against British subjects; whether it was available against claims not sounding in tort); or whether acts of State and prerogative acts were materially distinguishable; or whether the royal prerogative to take or destroy property subject to compensation applied outside Her Majesty's dominions.

46 (1848) 2 Ex. 167. A British naval officer, with general instructions to suppress the slave trade, exceeded them by landing in West Africa, destroying a barracoon (shed) and liberating slaves belonging to a Spaniard; his conduct was ratified by the Crown and he was awarded a large gratuity. The Spaniard's action for trespass failed. Today no action for trespass to land (as distinct from goods) situate abroad would be entertained by the High Court. This point was relevant to the statement of claim in *Nissan*'s case.

47 Unless he is an alien who has left family, goods or effects here, evincing an intention to return, or possibly if he holds a British passport.

deliberate wrong perpetrated at the instance of the Crown as being a non-justiciable matter is questionable.

2 A person who is a friendly alien (even though he is engaging in unfriendly conduct) within Her Majesty's dominions owes local allegiance and is therefore entitled to protection, so that act of State cannot be pleaded in respect of a tortious act done to him with the authority of the Crown: *Johnstone* v. *Pedlar*.[48]

3 *A fortiori*, act of State is not a defence to an action arising out of such an act done to a British citizen within Her Majesty's dominions: *Walker* v. *Baird* (1892).[49]

4 Nor, so it would seem, is act of State available as a defence to a tort committed against a British citizen outside Her Majesty's dominions (for example, Cyprus).[50]

5 The term 'British citizen' in propositions 3 and 4 does not include citizens of independent Commonwealth countries, since they have the status of 'Commonwealth citizen' in United Kingdom law only by virtue of their citizenship of those countries,[51] owe allegiance primarily or solely to their own states or governments,[52] and are entitled to international protection by them.

6 It is doubtful how far, if at all, aliens owing local allegiance to the Crown but temporarily absent from the realm are entitled to immunity from a plea of act of State.[53]

7 All persons, including British citizens, may become the *indirect* victims of an act of State by the Crown. Act of State in this context does mean an act of high policy. Thus, a declaration of war may frustrate contracts. Upon the acquisition of territory the Crown does not succeed to the

---

48 [1921] 2 AC 262 (seizure of money belonging to American arrested for subversive activities in Dublin, then a part of Her Majesty's dominions, not defensible as act of State). Possibly the decision would now be different if the act complained of were done in an independent Commonwealth country.

49 [1892] AC 491 (seizure of lobster factory in Newfoundland, in purported implementation of a treaty with France).

50 This defence having been abandoned in *Nissan*'s case (note 44, above). Cyprus, although within the Commonwealth, is a republic and therefore not within Her Majesty's dominions.

51 British Nationality Act 1981, s. 37(1).

52 For example, they cannot be convicted of treason in United Kingdom law unless the conduct in question was treasonable if done by an alien in a foreign country (ibid., s. 3(1)).

53 See pp. 420–33, below. *Semble* in any event act of State is pleadable in respect of seizure of property within the realm belonging to a non-resident alien who does *not* owe local allegiance; though cf. note 35, above.

obligations of the predecessor government, but has a free discretion whether or not to accept them: *Cook* v. *Sprigg* (1899);[54] *West Rand Central Gold Mining Co.* v. *R.* (1905).[55]

8   There is also some authority for the proposition that in certain ill-defined circumstances direct injury inflicted on British citizens may be justified under the plea of act of State. For example, it has been suggested that damage done by the armed forces in the course of a military operation falling short of war to the property of citizens on foreign soil may be an act of State and therefore non-compensable.[56] (If it were attributed to an exercise of the royal prerogative, compensation might be payable by the Crown as a matter of obligation.)[57] In this sense the defence of act of State would be a by-product of an 'act of policy'. Again, the seizure of British-owned property on behalf of the Crown may possibly be so connected, causally and in point of time, with an act of State (for example, a treaty or an annexation) as to be regarded as part of it or necessarily incidental to it;[58] but it is very doubtful whether a court ought ever to accept such an argument today.

54 [1899] AC 572 (refusal to recognize railway concession granted by former government to one who was apparently a British subject).

55 [1905] 2 KB 391 (refusal to accept responsibility for allegedly wrongful seizure of gold bars by former South African Republic).

56 There are dicta to this effect in *Nissan's* case [1970] AC 179 at 221 (Lord Morris), 235 (Lord Wilberforce) and 240 (Lord Pearson); Lord Pearce (at 227) left the point open and only Lord Reid (at 213) rejected this view.

57 *Burmah Oil Co.* v. *Lord Advocate* [1965] AC 75; but no compensation would be claimable as of right during a state of war or apprehended war for battle damage or denial damage, even in Her Majesty's dominions: War Damage Act 1965. In *Nissan's* case Lord Reid (at 213) and Lord Wilberforce (at 236) doubted whether the *Burmah Oil* rule about the prerogative applied to foreign soil. (The *Burmah Oil* case arose within Her Majesty's dominions.) Lord Denning MR in the Court of Appeal ([1968] 1 QB 286 at 340) and Lord Pearce ([1970] AC at 229) took the broader view of the applicability of the prerogative.

58 See, for example, *Secretary of State for India* v. *Kamachee Boye Sahaba* (1859) 12 Moo. PCC 22; *Salaman* v. *Secretary of State for India* [1906] 1 KB 613 (seizures of property of former rulers upon annexation of their territory; presumably they became British subjects on annexation). In *Cook* v. *Sprigg* [1899] AC 572, see note 54 above – 'a case of doubtful authority' (*per* Lord Wilberforce in *Nissan's* case [1970] AC at 232) – it is not clear whether the plaintiff's property was in fact seized.

CHAPTER 8

The Privy Council

I

The Privy Council, like the monarchy, is an ancient and dignified institution of government. Unlike the monarchy, it is not an important feature of the British constitutional system. If the monarchy were to be abolished, a new personage or institution would have to be endowed with the functions which only a head of State can exercise. The functions now performed by the Privy Council and its committees could be distributed tomorrow among other existing organs of government, and few people in the United Kingdom would notice any difference. Only the Judicial Committee of the Privy Council, which is in fact a court, almost entirely concerned with the hearing of appeals from Commonwealth countries overseas, would obviously need to be replaced by a separate new institution.

The Privy Council today[1] has over 400 members. All are entitled to be addressed as 'The Right Honourable . . .' Members must be British citizens in United Kingdom law, or citizens of the Republic of Ireland. Appointments are made by letters patent on the Prime Minister's advice, and are for life, though a Privy Counsellor may be removed on advice or at his own request.[2] By convention, all Cabinet Ministers must be sworn as Privy Counsellors.[3] It is also conventional or customary to appoint the Archbishops of Canterbury and York, the Speaker of the House of

1 The Scottish Privy Council was merged with the English Privy Council in 1708, after the Act of Union. There is a separate Privy Council for Northern Ireland but no new appointment to it has been possible since 1973; Northern Ireland Constitution Act 1973, s. 32(3).
2 Sir Edgar Speyer was removed for his pro-German sympathies after the First World War, and Mr John Profumo, Mr John Stonehouse and Mr Jonathan Aitken were removed at their own requests in 1963, 1976, and 1997 respectively.
3 For an amusing account of the swearing ceremony, see R. H. S. Crossman, *Diaries of a Cabinet Minister*, vol. 1 (1975), p. 29.

Commons, the Lords of Appeal in Ordinary (the Law Lords), the Master of the Rolls, the Lords Justices of Appeal, the Lord Chief Justice and the President of the Family Division. Senior non-Cabinet Ministers, dignitaries and eminent judges from Commonwealth countries and a small number of other persons upon whom it is appropriate to confer a special honour for public or political service (for example, leadership of the small political parties) may also be appointed.[4]

Upon admission, a new Privy Counsellor must swear an oath or make an affirmation not to divulge any matter disclosed to him confidentially in the Council. The general understanding used to be that the secrecy of Cabinet proceedings is preserved by the undertaking thus given; but this view cannot be sustained either by a literal interpretation of the oath (because the Cabinet is neither the Privy Council nor a committee of the Privy Council) or after the decision in *Attorney-General* v. *Jonathan Cape Ltd* (the Crossman Diaries case).[5]

Meetings of the Privy Council are held in the presence of the Queen (or Counsellors of State if she is absent from the realm or indisposed), normally at Buckingham Palace. The business transacted is purely formal, approving and recording decisions already taken elsewhere. The Lord President of the Council, a senior Minister (who need not be a peer), is responsible for the summoning of members and the preparation of the list of business; usually only three or four members are called, and they will be Ministers concerned with the matters to be transacted; meetings of the Council are very brief; indeed, the members remain standing. On rare ceremonial occasions a larger meeting, including persons other than Ministers, is convened – for example, to proclaim a new monarch, or to hear the monarch give consent to a royal marriage.

The dissolution, summoning and prorogation[6] of Parliament are effected by royal proclamations in Council; so are the declaration and termination of a state of war, and the declaration of a statutory state of emergency. *Projets de loi* (bills) passed by the States of Jersey and Guernsey are assented to by Order in Council; and it is by Order in Council that the Royal Courts of the islands are directed to register Acts of the United Kingdom Parliament having effect in the islands.

Some Orders in Council are of a judicial character, formally promulgating

---

4 The current annual volume of *Whitaker's Almanack* gives a list of the membership.
5 [1976] QB 752, and below, p. 199.
6 See ch. 12.

the report (or judgment) of the Judicial Committee.[7] The great majority are legislative Orders in Council. Apart from those few Orders in Council which are still made under prerogative powers (for example, for altering the constitutions of the diminishing group of colonies,[8] for altering rates of pensions for the armed services, or for dealing with recruitment to the civil service, coinage),[9] legislative Orders in Council are made in pursuance of powers delegated to Her Majesty in Council by statute. These have exactly the same status as regulations made by individual Ministers under delegated legislative powers; they fall within the definition of 'statutory instruments',[10] are numbered and published in the annual volumes of Statutory Instruments, and differ from departmental regulations only in their formal source. Unless they are of exceptional importance (in which case parliamentary draftsmen may be enlisted) they are drafted by the legal advisers to the Department with whose business they deal. The reasons for giving Her Majesty power to make Orders in Council on certain matters instead of vesting a Minister with power to make regulations are partly traditional and partly psychological. It is more dignified and impressive for an independence constitution, or an instrument giving effect to an extradition treaty or creating new parliamentary constituencies or altering electoral boundaries, to be made by Her Majesty in Council. Or so it seems to some people; and appearance is occasionally more important than reality, even if hardly anyone is misled by the ceremonial trappings. The draft Orders are not discussed at the meeting of the Council; the Lord President reads out their titles, the Queen (who has been fully informed in advance of the business to be transacted) approves them orally, and they are then authenticated by the signature of the Clerk of the Council and the affixing of the seal of the Council.

7 The distinction between a judicial and a legislative Order in Council was clearly emphasized in *Ibralebbe* v. *R.* [1964] AC 900.

8 For example, colonies originally acquired by conquest or cession, such as Gibraltar.

9 Prerogative Orders in Council of a legislative character are published as an Appendix to the annual volumes of Statutory Instruments. They are not numbered and are not, of course, *statutory* instruments.

10 Statutory Instruments Act 1946, s. 1, and the regulations made thereunder. See ch. 17.

II

Various committees of the Privy Council have been formed at different times and for a range of purposes. Today the Privy Council has a miscellany of standing committees, none of recent origin, and most resting on a statutory basis – the Universities Committee, reporting on petitions concerning Statutes of the Universities of Oxford and Cambridge and their colleges; a somewhat similar Scottish Universities Committee; a Baronetage Committee to report on claims to baronetcies; the Political Honours Scrutiny Committee (a committee of three persons, not being members of the Government, reporting in the first instance to the Prime Minister on the suitability of persons to be recommended by him for the award of titles and dignities at CBE level and above for political or any other services);[11] and committees on the Channel Islands and the Isle of Man, to which bills passed locally are referred for report. The Honours Committee (composed of elder statesmen, one from each of the main parties) and the Universities Committees are fairly active, non-political, advisory bodies. The Committees on the Channel Islands and the Isle of Man are composed of the Lord President, the Home Secretary and other Ministers; they are political organs of the United Kingdom Government, but seldom do they meet and deliberate as committees. There are *ad hoc* committees – for example, to consider applications by other institutions for charters and Statutes; and committees of the Council, or consisting of Privy Counsellors, to consider special problems appropriate for investigation by an eminent non-partisan body, for instance the use of questionable interrogation techniques by security forces or the recruitment in this country of mercenaries to fight abroad, or the lessons of the Falklands conflict of 1982. And then there is the Judicial Committee. Hence the Privy Council is not entirely superfluous. Although all its non-judicial functions could be transferred to the Cabinet or Departments of State, and its committees could be detached as autonomous statutory bodies or as advisory bodies to Departments, such a redistribution

---

11 Members are appointed on the Prime Minister's recommendation following consultations with the Leader of the Opposition and the Leader of the Liberal Democrats: 260 HC Deb. *141* (written answers 23 January 1996). The Prime Minister widened the function of the Committee to include examination of recommendations based on *non*-political services, but, misleadingly, the Committee's title was left unchanged: see 974 HC Deb. 880 (26 November 1979). It has always been the case that if the Committee reports adversely and the Prime Minister proceeds with his recommendation, the Queen is to be informed of the Committee's view.

would not in every instance be as convenient as the present arrangements, and in some cases the retention of ancient forms is of political value.

III

The Judicial Committee of the Privy Council[12] can be mentioned at this point. After the abolition of the conciliar courts, the Council was still able to entertain appeals from the overseas dominions of the Crown. With the expansion of the colonial empire, it became essential to make adequate provision for the determination of appeals, and in 1833 Parliament constituted a Judicial Committee of the Privy Council; its composition and jurisdiction have been modified many times since.

Today the Judicial Committee consists of the Lord President (who never sits), persons who hold or have held high judicial office in the United Kingdom and are Privy Counsellors, and leading members of the Judiciary from certain Commonwealth countries (notably New Zealand) from which appeals still lie to the Privy Council. The quorum of the Judicial Committee is three; normally five members sit to hear an appeal,[13] more often than not, they are the Law Lords. The Judicial Committee is sometimes referred to as the Board; its reports are in the form of advice and are promulgated, as we have seen, by Order in Council. It is not strictly bound by its own decisions. Before 1966 no dissenting opinion could be delivered, because advice to the Crown should not be divided, but this anachronistic rule has been abandoned.[14]

The Judicial Committee's jurisdiction is regulated by statute, subordinate legislative instruments, and local constitutions and legislation. It hears appeals from the superior courts of the Channel Islands, the Isle of Man, colonies and such independent Commonwealth countries as have retained the appeal from their own courts. It receives about fifty appeals each year from courts overseas. Appeals may lie as of right, with leave of the court below, or by special leave of the Judicial Committee. The power to grant special leave to appeal is a prerogative power placed on a statutory basis,

12 Sir Kenneth Roberts-Wray, *Commonwealth and Colonial Law* (1966), pp. 433–63; Beth [1975] *Public Law* 219.
13 In the *Australian Banks Nationalisation* case (*Commonwealth of Australia* v. *Bank of NSW* [1950] AC 235), a Board of seven members was convened. Two members died during the hearing, which was of unprecedented length.
14 Judicial Committee (Dissenting Opinions) Order 1966 (SI 1966, No. 1100); Lock [1985] *Public Law* 64.

and cannot be abrogated by a colony.[15] Appeals in criminal matters lie only by special leave, save in matters concerning the guarantees of fundamental rights and freedoms embodied in constitutions since 1959; generally the appeal will lie as of right in the latter class of case. Petitions for special leave to appeal are granted sparingly; and the Judicial Committee declines to act as a general Court of Criminal Appeal.

By virtue of the Statute of Westminster 1931, and subsequent independence Acts, independent Commonwealth countries have acquired power (subject to any restriction imposed by their own constitutions) to terminate the appeal, and a number have done so. Among Commonwealth countries which achieved independence before 1950, Canada, India, Sri Lanka and Australia[16] have abolished all appeals; appeals still lie on a wide range of matters from New Zealand but are infrequent. If a Commonwealth country which becomes a republic or comes under a separate monarchy on or after the attainment of independence still wishes to retain the appeal, this may be done by one of two methods: by providing either (i) that appeals shall be referred by the local head of State to the Judicial Committee, which will submit its report to him (as in Malaysia), or (ii) that appeal shall lie not to 'Her Majesty in Council' – the form used in the constitutions of those countries of which the Queen is still head of State – but simply to the 'Judicial Committee'.[17]

Under the constitutions of some Commonwealth countries, a superior judge cannot be removed except for inability or misbehaviour established to the satisfaction of the Judicial Committee following an adverse report by a local judicial tribunal of inquiry.

The Judicial Committee of the Privy Council is essentially a Commonwealth court, but it also has a place in the legal system of the United Kingdom. Here its jurisdiction is exclusively statutory and, like the powers of the Privy Council itself, comprises a mixed assortment.

15 Southern Rhodesia remained a colony despite the unilateral declaration of independence (UDI) by its government in November 1965, and the purported abolition of the appeal to the Privy Council by the Smith Constitution was therefore ineffective in law; see *Madzimbamuto* v. *Lardner-Burke* [1969] 1 AC 645. The Appellate Division of the High Court of Southern Rhodesia refused to follow this Privy Council decision and accepted the Smith Constitution as binding: *R.* v. *Ndhlovu* 1968 (4) SA 515.
16 Australia Act 1986, s. 11.
17 Appeals still lie from Antigua and Barbuda, Bahamas, Barbados, Belize, Dominica, Gambia, Jamaica, Kiribati, Malaysia, Mauritius, New Zealand, St Kitts–Nevis, St Lucia, St Vincent, Singapore, Trinidad and Tobago, Tuvalu. The Judicial Committee may also hear appeals from the Supreme Court of Brunei: Brunei (Appeals) Act 1989.

1 It hears appeals from the decisions of certain professional disciplinary bodies, medical, dental, optical and in respect of professions ancillary to medicine. It also has a limited appellate jurisdiction from higher ecclesiastical courts, and in wartime it hears appeals from the Prize Court.

2 Under section 7 of the House of Commons Disqualification Act 1975, a member of the public may apply to the Judicial Committee for a declaration that a member of the House is subject to a statutory disqualification under that Act.

3 The Crown may, under section 4 of the Judicial Committee Act 1833, refer any matter to it for an advisory opinion. Unlike its appellate determinations, which are advisory only in form, such opinions are truly advisory, though they will almost invariably be treated as authoritative. It would be possible so to refer a matter that was not characteristically justiciable, though in practice its advice has been sought only on legal questions.[18] The last special reference was made in 1957, at the request of the House of Commons and upon the initiative of the Committee of Privileges, in order to obtain an authoritative interpretation of the effect of an obscure eighteenth-century statute on the article of the Bill of Rights, which guarantees freedom of speech and proceedings in Parliament.[19]

18 See Roberts-Wray, op cit., p. 449, for a synopsis of the matters specially referred. In the past, mixed questions of law and policy were occasionally referred for an advisory opinion to a mixed *ad hoc* committee of the Privy Council, composed of judicial and other members of the Council: see, for example *Re States of Jersey* (1853) 9 Moo. PCC 185.

19 *Re Parliamentary Privilege Act 1770* [1958] AC 331. This was one stage in the controversy in the *Strauss* case; see p. 319 below.

CHAPTER 9

The Prime Minister and the Cabinet[1]

IN GENERAL

No series of terse comments on existing practice can be free from dogmatic assertion, or be based on sufficient or reliable information on matters which are still to a large extent confidential; nor can a brief description pay proper regard to the work of constitutional and political historians or students of politics and political sociology. Investigations into the processes by which major policy decisions have been made, the organization and behaviour of the two main political parties in and out of Parliament, the selection of parliamentary candidates by constituency parties, the impact of the media of information on public opinion, the realities behind voting behaviour, and so on, have contributed much to an understanding of how the British constitutional and political system works in practice. This book is concerned less with evaluation than with rules and institutions.

The rules about the principal institutions of executive government are not, of course, mainly rules of strict law. The monarchy and the Privy Council are encrusted with rules of strict law in abundance; but they are not principal institutions of executive government. The Cabinet and the Prime Minister, on the other hand, are hardly recognized in the statute book and they are almost invisible in the law reports. The Prime Minister is the keystone of the Cabinet arch, a sun around which planets revolve, an elected monarch, a President, or what you will; yet he was not mentioned in an Act of Parliament till 1917, and the main statutes relating to his office are those providing for his salary and pension.[2] His powers and duties are

1 See Rodney Brazier, *Constitutional Practice* (2nd edn, 1994), chs. 5, 6, and *Constitutional Texts* (1990), chs. 1–4.
2 The main one is the Ministerial and other Salaries Act 1975. The maximum annual salary is £143,000. A Prime Minister resigning after 1991 will receive a pension equivalent to half his annual salary: Ministerial and other Pensions and Salaries Act 1991, s. 3. There are a few other random statutory references to the Prime Minister: see, for example, the

determined almost exclusively by convention and usage. The Cabinet has been virtually ostracized by the parliamentary draftsman. It appeared in 1937 (also in the context of ministerial salaries) but has made little further progress towards statutory recognition.[3] Its composition, mode of selection, powers and procedures have to be elicited from political announcements, inference, breaches of confidence, and optimistic speculation. The strict law of the constitution tells us as much and as little about political parties and the Leader of the Opposition.[4]

It is nevertheless possible to list a number of conventional rules about the Prime Minister and the Cabinet. The authenticity of some of the rules is dubious, since their binding force is sometimes questionable and they are apt to change with a disconcerting frequency. Again, it is possible to place a variety of reasonable interpretations on the relationship between the Prime Minister and his Cabinet at any given moment (although no one would dispute the dominance of Margaret Thatcher over *her* Cabinet)[5] and nearly all commentators regard any Cabinet as being in some degree subordinate to the Prime Minister. Hardly anyone today will make out a case for the proposition that the Prime Minister is merely *primus inter pares*,

---

Chevening Estate Acts 1959 and 1987; Parliamentary Commissioner Act 1967, s. 8(4); House of Commons (Administration) Act 1978, s. 1(4); National Heritage Act 1980, s. 1(2); Police Negotiating Board Act 1980, s. 1(2); National Audit Act 1983, s. 1(1); Interception of Communications Act 1985, ss. 7, 8; National Lottery etc. Act 1993, s. 40.

3 Under the First Schedule to the Ministerial and other Salaries Act 1975 the salaries of specified Ministers are fixed according as to whether they are or are not members of the Cabinet. Cabinet papers and proceedings (certified as such by the Secretary of the Cabinet with the approval of the Prime Minister) are not to be divulged to the Parliamentary Commissioner for Administration (the 'Ombudsman') in the course of his investigations: Parliamentary Commissioner Act 1967, s. 8(4). The Cabinet Office lies outside the Commissioner's field of inquiry: ibid., sched. 2, note 6.

4 See Ministerial and other Salaries Act 1975, s. 2(1) (definition of the meaning of Leader of the Opposition by reference to the largest opposition party); Companies Act 1985; s. 235 (directors' reports to disclose contributions by companies to political parties). See also *John* v. *Rees* [1970] Ch. 345 (natural justice to be observed by party's national executive before disaffiliating or suspending activities of a constituency party); *Conservative and Unionist Central Office* v. *Burrell* [1982] 1 WLR 522 (funds and income held by Central Office for the Conservative Party not subject to corporation tax); *R.* v. *Broadcasting Complaints Commission, ex p. Owen* [1985] QB 1153 (challenge to fairness of treatment on television of SDP/Liberal Alliance).

5 For testimony to this of former Cabinet colleagues, see, e.g., James Prior, *A Balance of Power* (1986), especially pp. 114–19 and ch. 8; Francis Pym, *The Politics of Consent* (1984), ch. 1; Nigel Lawson, *The View from No. 11* (1992), and Geoffrey Howe, *Conflict of Loyalty* (1994).

the first among equals, except in the formal sense that all are servants of the Crown. The central feature of recent controversies is the question how far it is justifiable to speak of prime ministerial government rather than Cabinet government.[6] For two centuries the Cabinet has been regarded as the primary executive organ of government, discussing and deciding the main issues of national policy and coordinating the work of the Departments; but since 1945 at the latest some Prime Ministers with sufficient political authority and enjoying strong personalities have been able to dominate it.

CHOICE OF PRIME MINISTER[7]

The general rule is that in appointing a Prime Minister, the Queen should commission that person who appears best able to command the support of a stable majority in the House of Commons.

A change of Prime Minister may be necessary because of the resignation, death or dismissal of the incumbent. The last possibility, dismissal, would arise only in highly exceptional circumstances and, one would suppose, in a near-revolutionary situation;[8] in such a context the Queen would have to find somebody to form an emergency Government, perhaps without a majority in the House but prepared to advise a dissolution of Parliament at the earliest practicable moment. All vacancies in the office since Victoria came to the throne have arisen through resignation or death. Resignation may occur because the Government has been defeated at a General Election (as in 1945, 1951, 1964, 1970, February 1974 and 1979) or has collapsed through internal dissension (as in 1931) or has been defeated on a vote of

---

6 The prime ministerial thesis has been argued by R. H. S. Crossman, Introduction to Walter Bagehot's *The English Constitution* (1963 edn) – but later, having held Cabinet office, he became more ambivalent: see *The Diaries of a Cabinet Minister*, vols. 1 (1975), 2 (1976) and 3 (1977), *passim*; John Mackintosh, *The British Cabinet* (3rd edn, 1977) – although he, too, became more guarded in each edition; and Humphrey Berkeley, *The Power of the Prime Minister* (1968). The thesis has been vigorously opposed by Herbert Morrison, *Government and Parliament* (3rd edn, 1964); Patrick Gordon Walker, *The Cabinet* (revised edn, 1972) (both of whom had sat in Cabinets); and by a former Prime Minister: Harold Wilson, *The Governance of Britain* (1976), *passim*. See also Ian Gilmour, *The Body Politic* (1969), and for a particularly well argued appraisal, A. H. Brown [1968] *Public Law* 28, 96.
7 See Brazier, *Constitutional Practice*, chs. 2, 3, and Brazier, *Constitutional Texts*, ch. 1.
8 See pp. 122–3.

confidence in the House of Commons (as in 1895,[9] 1923[10] and 1979[11]). In such cases it is the duty of the Government as a whole to resign (unless, in the event of a defeat in the House, the Prime Minister elects to request a dissolution)[12] and of the Queen to send for the Leader of the Opposition or, when a Government resigns as soon as the results of a General Election are known and Parliament still stands dissolved, the person who was Leader of the Opposition in the House of Commons before the dissolution;[13] he will normally accept office as Prime Minister, but in an exceptional situation may prefer to advise (as Baldwin advised in 1931) that a coalition Government under another person[14] be formed. The resignation of a Prime Minister may take place for other reasons – because of ill health or old age, or because he feels or is persuaded to feel that he has become a liability to his party, or loses (or withdraws from) his party's leadership election, or is an obstacle to the formation of a coalition in wartime. In these situations, which have often arisen – in 1923 (Bonar Law), 1935 (MacDonald), 1940 (Neville Chamberlain), 1955 (Churchill), 1957 (Eden), 1963 (Macmillan) and 1990 (Thatcher) – the party in office still retains a majority in the House and the Prime Minister's resignation is personal, almost as if he had died in office; the Ministers place their offices at his successor's disposal, but the Government as a whole does not vacate office. His successor may decide to make few changes, and those Ministers who continue in their posts do not have to be reappointed. But how is his successor chosen? The Queen will wait until the Government party has elected its new leader, and then send for him. This happened in 1976 when Mr Wilson announced

9 When Lord Rosebery's Government was defeated on the 'cordite vote'.
10 When Baldwin's Conservative Government was defeated on an amendment to the address in reply to the King's speech. See also the 1924 case (below).
11 When Mr Callaghan's minority Labour Government was defeated on an Opposition motion of no confidence: see 965 HC Deb. 461–590 (28 March 1979). Mr Callaghan forthwith requested and obtained a dissolution. The Conservative Party under Mrs Thatcher won the ensuing General Election with a forty-three-seat majority. A defeat on a vote of confidence has been very rare. See further Norton [1978] *Public Law* 360.
12 Ramsay MacDonald so advised in 1924, and George V accepted his advice though he was not obliged to do so.
13 Assuming, of course, that his party has won a majority at the General Election and he has himself been re-elected in a constituency. When an Opposition party has won an overall majority in the House at the General Election, it is conventional for the Government to resign before the new Parliament meets.
14 In this instance, MacDonald, the outgoing Prime Minister, who cut himself adrift of the majority of his Labour colleages. In a multi-party situation, where the Government has lost its majority but the Opposition cannot command one, the Leader of the Opposition may alternatively agree to form a minority Government. This situation arose after the February 1974 General Election. See note 18.

that he would resign as soon as the Parliamentary Labour Party had elected a new leader. Mr Callaghan was elected three weeks after that announcement; Mr Wilson resigned and the Queen appointed the new Leader of the Labour Party as Prime Minister.[15] With a change of Conservative Prime Minister the monarch had a personal discretion till February 1965, when the Conservative and Unionist Party adopted a new procedure for electing a party leader by ballot among Conservative MPs.[16] That procedure was used with a vengeance in 1990 when Margaret Thatcher was ousted from office after more than eleven years as Prime Minister. A perception had developed in the Conservative Party that her determination to veto any changes to the deeply and widely unpopular poll tax (which her Government had introduced), together with her negative attitude towards the development of the European Community, invited defeat at the following General Election. Mr Michael Heseltine, then a backbench MP, forced a leadership election. Although Mrs Thatcher beat him in the first round, she failed to obtain the required majority. Members of the Cabinet, and others, persuaded her not to fight the second round, and she informed the Queen that she would resign as Prime Minister as soon as the party election procedures had been completed. On Mr John Major's election, Mrs Thatcher resigned and Mr Major was appointed Prime Minister by the Queen.[17] It can, therefore, be assumed that the Queen will not now have to exercise personal discretion on a change of Prime Minister resigning for personal reasons, as she had to do in 1955, 1957 and 1963. In 1955, however, Sir Anthony Eden (later the Earl of Avon) was the obvious successor to Churchill. On the resignations of Eden in 1957 and Macmillan in 1963 the successor was not obvious. In 1957 she consulted Sir Winston Churchill and Lord Salisbury, two elder statesmen of the party; neither of them was

15 Mr Callaghan was elected by the Parliamentary Labour Party under the then current party election rules. See now below, p. 265, for the 1981 changes in electing a Leader of the Labour Party.

16 In July 1965 Mr Edward Heath was elected leader by this new procedure in succession to Sir Alec Douglas-Home (formerly Lord Home) who resigned the leadership; the party was then in opposition. The Conservatives' rules have since been amended to require annual re-election: Mr Heath so offered himself in 1975 and lost to Mrs Thatcher. Leaders of the Labour Party had always been elected annually when in opposition, but see below, p. 265.

17 On this episode, and for Margaret Thatcher's effect on the constitution, see Brazier (1991) 54 *MLR* 471; Alan Watkins, *A Conservative Coup* (1991). Five years later, to meet criticisms of him within his party, Mr Major took the unprecedented step of resigning the leadership and seeking re-election. Mr John Redwood resigned from the Cabinet to contest the election: the Prime Minister beat him by 218 votes to 89 with 22 abstentions. See Brazier [1995] *Public Law* 513.

any longer a candidate for the office; both recommended Harold Macmillan in preference to R. A. Butler, the alternative choice, and she commissioned Macmillan to form a Government. In 1963 the position was more difficult. Macmillan, having decided to resign on grounds of illness, arranged for soundings to be taken among the Cabinet, the Parliamentary Party, the Conservative peers and the constituency parties; the collective weight of opinion appeared to favour Lord Home, and Macmillan advised the Queen accordingly. Although the monarch was not obliged to seek or follow the outgoing Prime Minister's advice, she could hardly have acted otherwise in those circumstances. The procedure and its outcome gave rise to some dissatisfaction within the party, which decided to alter its practice soon afterwards.

Hence the Queen is unlikely to have to exercise a personal discretion again unless no party has an overall majority in the House, or the formation of a coalition is advised, or a coalition, having been formed, disintegrates. In such situations her duty will be to take such counsel as is proper and expedient to assist her in deciding who is the most appropriate person to invite to form a Government with a reasonable prospect of maintaining itself in office. That person will normally, but not invariably, be the leader of the largest party in the House of Commons.[18] In any event, the procedures now adopted by all the major political parties for electing their own leaders seem to carry a necessary implication that the Prime Minister, when appointed, shall be a member of, or shall be about to occupy his seat[19] in, the House of Commons.

THE PRIME MINISTER'S POWERS

The following are the principal conventions concerning the Prime Minister.

1 The Prime Minister invariably holds the office of First Lord of the Treasury. The legislation providing for his salary and pension presupposes that he will fulfil this dual role.

18 As he was after the first 1974 General Election. Mr Heath (who had lost the Election and had failed to negotiate a coalition with the Liberals) was succeeded as Prime Minister by Mr Wilson, who led the largest party, there being no majority party in the new House. Hence the Queen's part may in such circumstances be largely formal.

From 1931 to 1935 MacDonald held office as Prime Minister of the 'National' Government although he was the leader of a small minority party. He was dependent on the favour of the Conservatives, the majority party and the dominant partner in the coalition; his personal position was conspicuously weak.

19 Where a change of Prime Minister is necessary after an election while Parliament stands dissolved.

2 Although his Treasury duties may be nominal – the Minister effectively
   in charge of the Treasury is the Chancellor of the Exchequer – it seems
   to follow that the Prime Minister must be (or must become immediately
   after his appointment) a member of the House of Commons, if only
   because the House of Lords no longer has any control over finance.
   There are other, more obvious reasons why he must be in the Commons:
   the unrepresentative character of the Lords, its diminished status in the
   constitution since 1911, the role of the House of Commons as the
   political cockpit and the fact that a Government has to retain a majority
   in the Commons to remain in office but can flout a hostile House of
   Lords. Apart from Lord Home, who swiftly transmuted himself into a
   member of the Commons,[20] no Prime Minister has been a member of
   the Lords since 1902.

3 Since 1968 the Prime Minister has been designated Minister for the Civil
   Service. In that role and as First Lord of the Treasury he has responsibility
   for civil service affairs and his approval is required for proposals for the
   appointment of permanent heads of departments.[21]

4 The Prime Minister presents a list of his proposed ministerial colleagues
   for the Queen's approval. She may make observations, suggestions and
   objections, but the Prime Minister is entitled to insist on his own choice.
   The appointment of junior Ministers takes effect when the Queen
   approves the Prime Minister's submission to her of their names.

5 The Prime Minister decides which Ministers are to be members of the
   Cabinet. His selection will be determined mainly by personal inclination
   and political expediency, although a Labour Prime Minister is required
   by the party's standing orders to include the elected members of the
   Shadow Cabinet in his first Cabinet (a rule broken, however, by Mr
   Harold Wilson in 1964 and by Mr Tony Blair in 1997 when forming
   their first Cabinets). By convention or custom, certain Ministers – the
   Chancellor of the Exchequer, the Secretary of State for Foreign and
   Commonwealth Affairs, the Home Secretary, the Lord Chancellor, the
   Secretary of State for Scotland, the Secretary of State for Defence and
   that Minister whom the Prime Minister designates as Leader of the House
   of Commons – must always be in a peacetime Cabinet; and it would be
   odd if Ministers in charge of the other main Departments (for example,
   education and employment, health, social security, agriculture) were to

20 See p. 43.
21 See pp. 206–11.

be excluded. All Cabinet Ministers must be sworn as members of the Privy Council.

6 In assigning Ministers to Departments the Prime Minister must have regard to certain well-established conventions. All Ministers[22] must be or become members of one or other House of Parliament; if a Minister is not a member of either House at the time of his appointment, he must obtain a seat at the earliest opportunity or resign. Hence although it was proper to appoint Mr Patrick Gordon Walker as Foreign Secretary in 1964 in spite of his defeat in his constituency at the General Election, it was necessary for him to resign from office when he failed to win a seat at a by-election shortly afterwards.[23] Each Department must have a ministerial spokesman in the House of Commons; no corresponding rule applies to the Lords. The Chancellor of the Exchequer must be a member of the House of Commons.

7 The Prime Minister may require a Minister to resign at any time and for any reason he thinks fit. So, for example, by 1981 Mrs Thatcher had shuffled out almost all Cabinet Ministers (popularly known as 'wets') who did not share her economic philosophy. If the Minister refuses to comply, the Prime Minister may in the last resort advise the Queen to dismiss him.[24] Whether there are any circumstances in which the Queen could properly refuse a Prime Minister's advice to dismiss his colleagues is debatable.[25]

8 The Prime Minister may decide to advise a dissolution without prior reference to the Cabinet. In some situations, as we have already noted,[26] it would be constitutionally proper for the Queen to refuse such a

---

22 Except the Lord Advocate and the Solicitor-General for Scotland, one or both of whom have not infrequently been outside Parliament.

23 Mr Hamish Gray lost his seat at the 1983 General Election but was created a life peer and retained ministerial office. This also happened to Mrs Lynda Chalker after the 1992 General Election.

24 In 1975 Mr Heffer, Minister of State for Industry, was dismissed on the Prime Minister's advice for breaking the Cabinet guidelines agreed for the suspension of collective responsibility during the EEC referendum campaign (see below, p. 198). In 1981 Mr Speed, Under-Secretary of State for Defence, was dismissed for making a speech which contradicted the Cabinet's agreed but not then announced cuts in naval spending.

25 Sir Ivor Jennings has asserted (*Cabinet Government* (3rd edn, 1959), p. 86) that: 'The Queen must not intervene in party politics. She must not, *therefore* [my italics], support a Prime Minister against his colleagues. Accordingly, it would be unconstitutional for the Queen to agree with the Prime Minister for the dissolution of a Government in order to allow the Prime Minister to override his colleagues.' This view is sustainable if the Prime Minister is known to have been placed, or is believed to be on the point of being placed, in a minority in his own Cabinet, but not otherwise.

26 See pp. 124–6.

request, absolutely, temporarily or conditionally, and one of those situations may be the case of a Prime Minister, placed in a minority in his own Cabinet, seeking to appeal to the electorate against his colleagues instead of following the more appropriate course of resigning. Nevertheless, the widespread assumption that it is within the Prime Minister's sole authority to fix the date of the next General Election enhances his personal power in relation to his ministerial colleagues and his party, and in the country as a whole. All recent Prime Ministers have, however, consulted senior colleagues about the timing so as (among other things) to implicate them in it if the Election is lost.[27]

9   When Parliament is dissolved the Government continues in office; it vacates office only if the election results show that it has lost its majority in the House, in which case it must resign.

10 The Prime Minister has substantial control over the organization as well as the personnel of central government. Not only does he choose, switch, promote, demote and discard his colleagues; he places them in an informal order of seniority;[28] he may nominate one to be Deputy Prime Minister;[29] he can take the initiative in creating a new Department or ministerial office, winding up a Department, and transferring functions from one Minister to another (though in some instances the change can only be effected by legislation); he can decide to create a new Ministerial Committee of the Cabinet, prescribe its terms of reference and give it decision-making powers; he can determine when the Cabinet shall meet; and in the last resort he can decide what shall or shall not be discussed at Cabinet meetings. He can thus control the allocation of functions between Cabinet, Ministerial Committees and individual Departments. He can also decide which non-Cabinet Ministers shall be appointed to membership of Ministerial Committees. Through his control over the Cabinet Office – a Cabinet Secretariat was created by Lloyd George in 1916 – he is in a position to see that the decisions of the Cabinet and its committees are implemented.[30]

11 He is entitled to say what issues shall be referred to him personally for decision outside the Cabinet. Interdepartmental disputes or deadlocks

---

27 See Brazier, *Constitutional Practice*, p. 91.
28 A 'pecking order' emerges in the list of Ministers, published regularly in *Hansard*. The order in which the names of Cabinet Ministers appear is generally attributed to the Prime Minister's personal decision. It does not follow, however, that the Prime Minister is impliedly indicating that the second name in the list is that of his most appropriate successor.
29 See Brazier [1988] *Public Law* 176.
30 On the Cabinet Office, see p. 179.

in Ministerial Committees may be resolved by his informal rulings. And he may simply, by an uninvited personal initiative or pronouncement confront his colleagues with a *fait accompli*.

12 The Prime Minister personally presides not only in the Cabinet but also in some of the more important standing Ministerial Committees – for example, the Defence and Overseas Policy Committee, the committee on economic strategy, and on the supervision of the Security Service (MI5) and the Secret Intelligence Service (MI6). The Prime Minister, as the country's principal spokesman on the international scene, must inevitably concern himself closely with foreign and Commonwealth affairs, matters of defence and security, and economic policy.

13 Since the Prime Minister is an international figure and a national leader, he is potentially capable of dominating his colleagues. His visits overseas to discuss matters of high policy, his speeches, answers to questions (which are regularly broadcast on television) and interventions in the House of Commons, his performances on television and his other public addresses attract a degree of attention which no other politician in the country is likely to emulate. Moreover, he controls the Government's information services. As leader of his party he has another powerful organization behind him to project his image in its most favourable light; for if the public reputation of the Prime Minister sags, the prospects of the party remaining in office after the next General Election will dwindle; and it is not easy to remove a party leader tenacious of office and of the authority and deference that go with it – although as Margaret Thatcher learned, this is not impossible.

14 At a General Election, the voters know that they are choosing a Government. To many of them, the choice is not so much between party programmes or party images as between the personal qualities of the Prime Minister and the Leader of the Opposition. If a Prime Minister and his advisers on public relations see this as the dominant factor in voting behaviour, the consequence will be the devotion of a dispro- portionate amount of publicity to the Prime Minister at the expense of his colleagues. This has been seen in all recent General Elections, which to an ever-increasing extent have been fought through the medium of television. The electorate's perception of Mrs Thatcher's qualities was a major factor in her success in winning three consecutive General Elections – a record this century – and in becoming the longest-serving Prime Minister in one continuous period since Lord Liverpool.

15 The Prime Minister enjoys, by convention, substantial powers of patronage. Some of these powers are apt to be a nuisance – 'Damn!

another bishop dead,' as Lord Melbourne remarked[31] – and others, such as the power to advise on appointments to the highest judicial and military offices, are of no political advantage to him because of expectations that appointments shall be non-partisan. But there are others which enhance his personal authority, if only because the hope of preferment tends to muffle the voices of carping critics. One who attracts the favourable notice of the Prime Minister or those closest to him may cherish the prospect, if not of political office, at least of a place in the honours list, even a peerage, or perhaps the chairmanship of one of the multifarious statutory corporations, advisory and consultative bodies, royal commissions or committees of inquiry by virtue of the Prime Minister's nomination. The increase in the peripheral adjuncts of government, as the reach of central government has expanded and its workings have become more complex, has undoubtedly enlarged the area of ministerial patronage.

16 The Prime Minister is the channel of communication between the Cabinet and the Queen. It is his duty to keep her adequately informed on matters of State, and she holds a private audience with him weekly during the parliamentary session. These contacts tend to enhance the prestige of his office.

PRIME MINISTERIAL POWER: SOME CORRECTIVES

A good deal has been said about the Prime Minister but precious little about the Cabinet. Because the Prime Minister's conventional powers and general authority in the scheme of the constitution are very great, and because one can point to examples of dramatic prime ministerial decisions (such as Eden's decision to engage in the Suez venture, or Macmillan's decision to dismiss a third of his Cabinet) taken outside the Cabinet, one can easily be led to the conclusion that the Cabinet is no more than a Prime Minister's instrument at any given time. For reasons which must already be fairly obvious, it is too early to draw such a conclusion.

Disquisitions on the sovereignty of the Prime Minister bear some resem-

---

31 Lord Melbourne would have welcomed the setting up of the Church Commission on Crown Appointments in 1978. It gives the Prime Minister two names for any vacant archbishopric or bishopric, stating a preference for one. The Prime Minister then passes on this advice to the Queen. Mr Blair unprecedentedly declined to pass on either name suggested in 1997 for the bishopric of Liverpool. For a list of public appointments in the Prime Minister's gift see 236 HC Deb. *359–60* (written answers 27 January 1994).

blance to discussions of the sovereignty of Parliament. Parliament in its wisdom might pass any number of appalling Acts without stepping beyond the limits of its constitutional authority, but somehow it does not regularly perpetrate gross abuses of its formal omnipotence. If a Prime Minister were to behave in a preposterous manner he would lose credit among his senior colleagues (who would resign if he had not already dismissed them), in the country and in his party; such a combination will be fatal to anyone but the most reckless autocrat, and a reckless autocrat who will neither resign nor mend his ways may have to be dealt with by unconventional and even extra-legal means. No modern Prime Minister has been a reckless autocrat. Illustrations of high-handed behaviour indicate not so much what a Prime Minister can do as the extent to which he may place his own position at risk. The misfortunes of Suez undermined Eden's health and personal prestige, and his resignation soon followed; Macmillan's standing in the Conservative Party and among the electorate, so strong in 1960, was not restored and may have suffered irretrievable damage by the dismissals of 1962; Margaret Thatcher's intransigence led directly to her downfall in 1990.

The personification of a Government by the Prime Minister is also an uncertain asset. In March 1966 the size of the Labour Party's electoral victory could be attributed mainly to admiration of Harold Wilson's capacity to inspire confidence in his ability. The financial and economic crisis in the autumn of 1967 impaired the Prime Minister's personal credibility as an astute leader; his Government and his party might have suffered less in popular support if they had not been so closely identified with the qualities of their leader.

And so one soon arrives at the conclusion that few conclusions except the banal and platitudinous can be drawn from recent experience. The authority of a Prime Minister will depend mainly on such variables as the confidence and popularity he commands as a leader, his intellectual grasp of the problems of government, his tactical acumen, his performances as an orator and on the floor of the House of Commons, his ability to make quick and acceptable decisions and to carry his senior colleagues and his party with him, the stature of those colleagues (particularly as potential alternative Prime Ministers), the international climate, the state of the country's economy, sheer luck,[32] and the often fickle moods of public

---

32 Thus Macmillan's luck seemed to desert him from 1962, with security lapses, by-election reverses, his dismissal of seven Cabinet colleagues in a drastic purge (which was seen as a panic measure), the Profumo scandal (see p. 192) and his illness and resignation. Mr Callaghan's sureness of touch in dealing with the trade unions left him by the time of the 'winter of discontent' in 1978–9 – which cost Labour the 1979 General Election.

opinion ('It's time for a change'). In wartime the personal authority of a Prime Minister may be overwhelming, as it was under Lloyd George from 1916 to 1918 and under Churchill from 1940 to 1945; it was by no means overwhelming under Asquith from 1914 to 1916 or under Chamberlain from 1939 to 1940. One is tempted to assert that all generalizations are false, including, of course, the one just offered.

The effective power of the Prime Minister in relation to that of his ministerial colleagues has been greater in the period since 1945 than during the inter-war years. But this must not be exaggerated. The office of Prime Minister is largely what an incumbent wishes and is able to make of it. While Mrs Thatcher seemed to be the personification of prime ministerial government, her successor preferred to revert to more traditional under-standings of collegiate Cabinet government. And no matter how versatile, energetic and able a Prime Minister may be, he can never be in a position to exercise close supervision over all the increasingly complex activities of the Departments, or indeed keep fully abreast of the technological and scientific developments with which their expert officials and advisers must be familiar. Coordination, supervision and the resolution of disagreements are achieved through interdepartmental committees, Ministerial Commit-tees and the Cabinet as a whole, as well as by the Prime Minister's informal rulings and by the machinery of the Cabinet Office.

Some of the propositions set out in the preceding sections must also be amplified or qualified. The Prime Minister does indeed control the Cabinet's agenda, but in practice he will often find it imprudent and will sometimes find it impracticable to exclude discussion of a question which other Ministers regard as important. He decides when the Cabinet is to meet; he presides at meetings; he is not bound to defer to the opinion of a majority of the Cabinet on any given issue, but if he persists in bypassing or attempting to override a majority of his colleagues the Government will soon disintegrate through resignations,[33] and it is therefore in his interest to attempt by persuasion to establish a consensus in favour of his own views (if he has already formed a firm view) but not to press his colleagues too hard. The fact that by the act of resignation an individual Minister may consign himself to years in the political wilderness is not enough to encour-age a Prime Minister to court mass resignations or a major revolt.

Again, it is sometimes said that the power of the Prime Minister (acquired since the First World War) to advise a dissolution of Parliament without

---

33 On ministerial threats of resignation as a tactical weapon to influence government policy, see R. K. Alderman and J. A. Cross, *The Tactics of Resignation* (1967), ch. 2.

the prior concurrence of his colleagues places in his hands an enormously potent weapon to subdue restiveness or crush rebellion within the ranks. Here analogies with nuclear weapons are relevant. They can be used, but the result is likely to be suicidal; hence threats to use them may not always be taken seriously. If the threat is carried out, the electorate may well turn away from a party in disarray and put the Opposition in office; a penal dissolution is apt to prove a boomerang and everybody knows this. This is not to say that an open threat by the Prime Minister to advise a dissolution will have no positive political impact whatsoever; but it does imply that the fairest comparison is with a threat by the Prime Minister to tender his Government's resignation. Mr Major did, however, openly and successfully use such a threat in 1993 to coerce rebel Conservative MPs to support him on a vote of no confidence in his administration. Dissent is better dealt with by bold leadership, or by accommodation and compromise, or, if necessary, by the dismissal of malcontents from the Government, or withdrawal of the party whip from backbench rebels, or simply by non-endorsement of a candidate at a General Election to be held at an indeterminate date; again, everybody knows this, and facts which everybody knows tend to condition political behaviour.

When one says that the Prime Minister controls the Cabinet Office, one is not asserting that this Office is merely his pliant instrument. The main constitutional function of the Office[34] is to provide a Secretariat for the Cabinet and its committees, distributing memoranda and agenda papers, recording proceedings and compiling and circulating minutes. Documents issued by the Secretariat go to departmental Ministers who are not members of the Cabinet. The work of the Secretariat therefore enables all Ministers to become better informed about major decisions and their factual background. This makes a Government more efficient, and incidentally justifies a reduction in the size of a Cabinet; it does not necessarily elevate the Prime Minister still higher above his colleagues, though it provides special briefs for the Prime Minister and helps him to follow up action taken in pursuance of decisions. The Cabinet Office, moreover, is not the Prime Minister's private office. It is staffed mainly by permanent civil servants, of whom a substantial proportion are officers of high seniority and standing; and the Secretary of the Cabinet, the head of this Office and just as independent as his colleagues, is possibly the most important member of the public service. Nevertheless, a Prime Minister's close personal relations with the

---

34 See generally, R. K. Mosley, *The Story of the Cabinet Office* (1969); Mackintosh, op. cit., pp. 517–21; Gordon Walker, op. cit., pp. 47–55.

Secretary of the Cabinet[35] will place him at an advantage in controlling the machinery of central government, and successive Prime Ministers have felt so well served by the Cabinet Office that they have seen no need to set up a Prime Minister's Department.[36] He will also have close relations with the head of the Policy Unit, which concentrates on various policy issues.[37]

The Prime Minister also has a small separate Private Office: this is also composed mainly of established civil servants, but it will naturally include persons whom the Prime Minister finds particularly congenial. There is also a separate Political Office, designed to keep him abreast of party feeling in the country as a whole; it is staffed by party workers.[38]

MINISTERIAL COMMITTEES AND MINISTERIAL MEETINGS

The Cabinet committee system is clearly of first-class importance in the machinery of central government. But the secrecy enveloping this system has been even harder to penetrate than the working of the Cabinet itself. Until 1992, in no official publication was there so much as a full list of these committees, let alone the names of their chairmen and members, a statement of their functions, or their relationships with the Cabinet as a whole.[39] When a Government departed from the political scene, a fuller account of its committee system often became available,[40] contemporary

---

35 Patrick Gordon Walker (*The Cabinet*, p. 55) comments that 'the Cabinet Secretary has become something like a Permanent Secretary to the Prime Minister'. Since 1981 he has also been Head of the Home Civil Service. Sir Robert Armstrong (1979–87) brought unprecedented publicity to the office during his evidence to the Defence Select Committee on the Westland affair in 1986 (on which see below, p. 295), and during his evidence before the Australian courts during the British Government's unsuccessful attempt to prevent the publication there of Peter Wright's *Spycatcher*.
36 See, e.g., James Callaghan, *Time and Chance* (1987), p. 408.
37 See Bernard Donoghue, *Prime Minister* (1987), pp. 19–25.
38 For the roles of the Cabinet Office, Policy Unit, Private Office and Political Office in the 1974–9 Labour Government, see Bernard Donoghue, op. cit., pp. 16–37, James Callaghan, op. cit., pp. 403–8.
39 The need for complete secrecy was justified by Sir Burke Trend, the Secretary of the Cabinet, giving evidence before the Franks Committee on Section 2 of the Official Secrets Act 1911 (Cmnd 5104 (1972), Minutes of Evidence, vol. 3, pp. 324–6) as being essential for the maintenance of collective responsibility for Cabinet decisions – a most unconvincing reason – and the prevention of leakages.
40 See Harold Wilson, *The Governance of Britain* (1976), pp. 62–8.

details were rarely divulged. There have been a number of modern exceptions. It was made known at the time of the Falklands conflict in 1982 that military operations were being overseen by a Cabinet committee chaired by Mrs Thatcher and made up of four other Cabinet Ministers; it was popularly known as the War Cabinet. A similar committee was convened to oversee British involvement in the Gulf conflict in 1990–91. And in 1983 Mrs Thatcher confirmed the existence of four standing committees: the Defence and Overseas Policy Committee; the Economic Strategy Committee; the Home and Social Affairs Committee, and the Legislation Committee.[41]

After the 1992 General Election, Mr Major accepted that this secrecy was unjustified. He therefore authorized the publication of the titles, membership and terms of reference of sixteen Cabinet committees, which are known as Ministerial Committees, and of ten 'ministerial subcommittees'.[42] The first category comprised committees on Economic and Domestic Policy, Defence and Overseas Policy, the Gulf, Nuclear Defence Policy, European Security, Hong Kong and the Dependent Territories, Northern Ireland, Science and Technology, and the Intelligence Services – all chaired by the Prime Minister; and also committees on Industrial and Commercial Affairs, Environment, Home and Social Affairs, Local Government, Queen's Speeches and Future Legislation, Legislation[43] and on Civil Service Pay – all chaired by the Leader of the House of Commons. The ministerial subcommittee group included subcommittees on Health Strategy, Public Sector Pay, European Questions, Eastern Europe, Terrorism, Drug Misuse, and Women's Issues. The subcommittees were to report, as necessary, to specified Ministerial Committees. This published list was incomplete: it did not include committees which were set up *ad hoc* and were then disbanded when they had served their purpose, and periodic changes in

41 See 45 HC Deb. *7–8* (written answers 4 July 1983). The existence of a Cabinet committee on the environment was later confirmed in a White Paper: Cm 1200 (1990). On Mrs Thatcher's Cabinet committees see Peter Hennessy, *Cabinet* (1986), pp. 100–103. For the Cabinet committee structure under Mr Callaghan see Bruce Page, *New Statesman*, 21 July 1978.

42 *Ministerial Committees of the Cabinet: Membership and Terms of Reference* (Cabinet Office, 1992). It was revised and republished by Mr Tony Blair as the *Ministerial Code* (Cabinet Office, 1997). Mr John Major also published, for the first time, the ministerial 'rule book', *Questions of Procedure for Ministers* (Cabinet Office, 1992). The list of Ministerial Committees was updated in 1995: see 263 HC Deb. *1005–12* (written answers 18 July 1995). Several were chaired by the Deputy Prime Minister. Mr Blair published similar details about his committees: see 295 HC Deb. *302–10* (written answers 9 June 1997).

43 See below, p. 270.

the committees were not to be published. The terms of reference were expressed in very bland terms.[44]

A Cabinet, or Ministerial Committee properly so called is a committee of Ministers (and may include non-Cabinet Ministers), established by the Prime Minister and which has formal procedures and is serviced by the Cabinet Secretariat (but not having civil service members). Ministerial Committees may be standing or *ad hoc*: the latter are set up to consider specific problems and are then dissolved. Mrs Thatcher, it has been estimated, had between thirty and thirty-five standing committees and, at any one time, some 120 *ad hoc* committees.[45] Many Ministerial Committees are supported by a parallel official committee of senior civil servants belonging to the Departments most closely concerned. Some Prime Ministers (such as Mr Heath and Mr Callaghan) have also used on occasion mixed committees of Ministers and civil servants, in Mr Callaghan's case the main one being dubbed 'the seminar' on central economic questions.[46]

The use of Ministerial Committees undoubtedly increases a Prime Minister's power over his colleagues. He chooses whether to establish a particular committee, what its terms of reference and membership are to be, who will be its chairman, whether any 'appeal' may be taken to the Cabinet against its decisions[47] and when to disband it. Moreover, the increased use of such committees has allowed the Prime Minister to summon the Cabinet to meet usually only once a week (compared with regular twice-weekly meetings up to the 1960s): there are thus fewer opportunities for Cabinet Ministers as a whole to raise and debate issues which the Prime Minister might prefer not to be raised. Mrs Thatcher went further and sometimes arrived at decisions through informal meetings of Ministers, outside the formal Cabinet committee structure, made up of selected colleagues who were likely to further her preferred solutions.[48]

---

44 Thus, e.g., the Environment Committee 'considers questions of environmental policy'; the Science and Technology Committee 'reviews science and technology policy', and so on.

45 Hennessy, op. cit.

46 See Donoghue, op. cit., pp. 101–2. A standing mixed committee is the Civil Contingencies Unit: see David Bonner, *Emergency Powers in Peacetime* (1985), pp. 28–32.

47 Mr Wilson gave Cabinet committees executive authority and only allowed 'appeals' with the consent of their chairmen: see Harold Wilson, op. cit., pp. 65–6.

48 See Lord Hailsham (1987) 1 *Contemporary Record* 58; James Prior, op. cit., pp. 133–4.

CONFIDENTIALITY OF PROCEEDINGS AND PAPERS

The Cabinet and its committees must be able to deliberate in private and with some certainty that neither their proceedings nor their papers will subsequently be made public without their consent. The conventional reasons which ensure that Ministers themselves do not make unauthorized disclosures[49] stem from the tradition of secrecy in Westminster and Whitehall, loyalty to colleagues, a desire not to inhibit future discussion and the ultimate political threat – dismissal. There are also guidelines recommended by the Radcliffe Committee on Ministerial Memoirs[50] which require fifteen years to elapse before certain types of Cabinet material may be disclosed by former Ministers; not all ex-Ministers have, however, abided by them.[51] Now, Ministers still in office do not maintain a stony silence when they are not making official utterances: they leak information to journalists when it is in their interests to do so – for example, to distance themselves from an unpopular Government decision and to let their supporters know their views.[52] Leaks by or on behalf of Ministers can make a nonsense of the confidentiality of Cabinet discussions, but at least the public is better informed than it would otherwise be.

Cabinet papers are Crown property, and so improper publication of them could be actionable as in breach of the Crown's copyright.[53] Former Ministers who wish to refresh their memories from papers which they saw while in office may see them in the Cabinet Office where, on resignation, their papers are deposited.[54] Access to one Government's papers by a

---

49 For the power of the courts to ensure confidentiality see *Att.-Gen.* v. *Jonathan Cape Ltd* [1976] QB 752: see below, p. 200. Ministers could not, it seems, be prosecuted under the Official Secrets Act 1911, s. 2 (on which see below, note 51) because they could authorize themselves to disclose information: see Report of the Franks Committee on Section 2 of the Official Secrets Act 1911, Cmnd 5104 (1972), pp. 14–15.
50 Cmnd 6386 (1976).
51 Notably Richard Crossman's literary executors in publishing his three-volume *Diaries of a Cabinet Minister*, Barbara Castle, in *The Castle Diaries 1974–1976* (1980), and Hugh Jenkins, in *The Culture Gap* (1979). A former Minister could now face prosecution under the Official Secrets Act 1989 (which replaced s. 2 of the 1911 Act) if, e.g., he were to make a 'damaging disclosure' on defence or international relations: see Brazier [1990] *Public Law* 300.
52 See below, p. 199.
53 See generally Brazier [1996] 55 *Camb. LJ* 65.
54 Sir Edward Heath was allowed (seemingly on medical grounds) to have photocopies made of his Government's papers and to use the photocopies at his home while working on his autobiography.

successor Administration is governed by a number of understandings.[55] So, Ministers may not see the papers of a previous Government of a different party (because they might want to make party-political capital out of them) unless the former Prime Minister of that Government agrees (or, if he is not available, the current Leader of the relevant party); they may see the papers of previous Administrations of their own party. Some papers deemed to be in the public domain, such as Ministers' letters to MPs, are freely available to former Ministers. These are sensible, workmanlike arrangements.

[55] See Lord Hunt of Tanworth [1982] *Public Law* 514.

CHAPTER 10

Ministers, Departments and Civil Servants

CENTRAL GOVERNMENT

Ministers and Departments[1]

There are usually between twenty-two and twenty-four Ministers in the Cabinet. In addition there are over eighty junior Ministers and other members of the Government – Ministers of State, the four Law Officers, parliamentary under-secretaries of state,[2] parliamentary secretaries, financial secretaries, Government whips,[3] and the like. In short, the Government numbers over one hundred. A large majority of the Ministers who sit in the Commons have unpaid backbench MPs as their parliamentary private secretaries. All but a dozen or so of the senior Ministers are members of the Commons. About a fifth of the membership of the House of Commons consists of members of the Government or MPs closely associated with the work of Ministers, though the maximum number of holders of paid ministerial offices, who may sit and vote in the House, is fixed by statute at ninety-five.[4] Yet in 1914 when the Government had already begun to assume responsibility for providing minimum standards of social welfare, the number of senior ministerial offices, excluding the Law Officers, was

---

1 See Rodney Brazier, *Constitutional Practice* (2nd edn, 1994), ch. 7, *Ministers of the Crown* (1997), chs. 1, 2 and *Constitutional Texts* (1990), chs. 5, 6.
2 If the Minister in charge of a Department is a Secretary of State.
3 Government whips have various designations. The Government Chief Whip in the House of Commons is the Parliamentary Secretary to the Treasury. Other Government whips in the Commons hold nominal offices in the Royal Household or are styled Junior Lords of the Treasury or merely Assistant Whips. In the Lords all Government whips hold nominal offices connected with the Royal Household.
4 House of Commons Disqualification Act 1975, s. 2(1). The maximum numbers of holders of various classes of political offices to whom salaries may be paid are also fixed by statute: Ministerial and other Salaries Act 1975, s. 1 and sched. 1.

only twenty-one. The big increase since that time is attributable to a large expansion in the function and activity of central government.

It cannot be said that there have been changes of high constitutional importance in the machinery of central government during the last few years. The most interesting development has probably been the evolution of five very large Departments – the Ministry of Defence; the Foreign and Commonwealth Office; the Department of Health and Social Security; the Department of the Environment; and the Department of Trade and Industry. In 1970 the powers formerly exercised by three separate Ministers (Housing and Local Government; Transport; Public Building and Works) were vested in a Secretary of State for the Environment. The Ministry of Technology and the Board of Trade were absorbed by a Department of Trade and Industry. In 1976 the Department of the Environment was considered to be too cumbersome and a Department of Transport was created, removing transport responsibilities from Environment. Mr Blair re-merged the two Departments in 1997 into a new Department of the Environment, Transport and the Regions. Mrs Thatcher split the Department of Health and Social Security into a Department of Health and a Department of Social Security in 1988.

A second feature, of longer standing, is the large number of Ministers of State who are not in charge of Departments. This is attributable partly to the extensive involvement of central government in economic and social affairs, and partly to the need for having Ministers available for the conduct of discussions and negotiations outside the United Kingdom or with national interest groups.

Departments and other agencies

Under the British system of government it is expected that there shall be a Minister politically accountable for the more controversial acts of central government agencies. Political accountability cannot readily be achieved unless the activity is carried on by a Department or Office directly headed by a Minister.[5]

This general proposition needs to be qualified. Although the prospects for taking major government activities 'out of politics' are limited, the allocation of government functions to largely autonomous bodies has become an important feature of public administration in Britain today.

---

5 Such functions may be carried out by an executive agency at arm's length from the responsible Minister. See p. 208.

There are miscellaneous other bodies performing what can broadly be described as functions of central government but lying outside the reach of detailed ministerial control. Most of them are statutory creations, but a few are non-statutory; some are incorporated, some are not; their sources of revenue are various; none is headed by civil servants, but some are staffed by them; some have executive powers, some are merely advisory, some are both; there is no common pattern. Their powers may involve the provision of a public service (for example, the British Broadcasting Corporation, the Commonwealth War Graves Commission, the Forestry Commission the National Museums and Art Galleries), the regulation or management of a public service (for example, the Independent Television Commission, the Radio Authority, the Countryside Commission), or the regulation or promotion of private and public activity (for example, the Civil Aviation Authority, the Commission for Racial Equality, the Arts Council, the Advisory, Conciliation and Arbitration Service, the British Tourist Authority). The functions of the British Council, which is not a Government Department – its officers and servants are not civil servants – range over all these fields and are also advisory.

Then there is an assortment of bodies staffed mainly or entirely by civil servants but without any ministerial head, though a Minister is answerable in Parliament for some or all of their activities.[6] They have been kept at arm's length from the principal Departments for a variety of reasons: because they perform specialized functions which are not likely to be politically controversial; because some of these functions ought not to be the subject of political controversy (for example, because they are judicial or analogous to the judicial); or because the organ was originally created outside the framework of a political Department and there has never been a sufficiently strong reason for bringing it within one. Some are so closely associated with a political Department that they are in effect sub-departments, for example, the Board of Inland Revenue, the Board of Customs and Excise, the Export Credits Guarantee Department, and the Intervention Board for Agricultural Produce, the Government Actuary's Department, the Royal

---

6 Thus, the Chancellor of the Exchequer answers a question in the House of Commons in connection with the Office of National Statistics, the Department of the Government Actuary, the Royal Mint and the National Debt Office; the Meteorological Office is answered for by the Secretary of State for Defence; the Secretary of State for the Environment answers for the Ordanance Survey. The Lord Chancellor answers in the Lords for the Land Registry and the Public Record Office, and the Chancellor of the Duchy of Lancaster (as Minister for Public Service) answers for the Central Office of Information.

Mint. Others, to which a separate Supply vote may be allocated in the Civil Estimates,[7] are more loosely associated with political Departments – for example, the Central Office of Information, Her Majesty's Stationery Office, the Charity Commission, the Crown Estate Office, the Registry of Friendly Societies, the National Investment and Loans Office, the Land Registry, the Ordnance Survey, the Meteorological Office, the Public Record Office, the Registrar General's Office.

Whether every one of the bodies listed in the latter group is properly to be described as a Government Department is questionable. Indeed, several now have executive agency status.[8] There is no recognized definition of a Government Department; normally it is understood to mean a central government body staffed by civil servants and receiving its funds directly out of moneys provided by Parliament,[9] but anomalies abound; the 'rich Byzantine structure'[10] of British central government is nowhere more apparent than in these twilight zones.

The Law Commissions owe their existence to an act of policy; but their chairmen are superior judges and their members, though salaried, are entirely independent of the Government, and their functions are also advisory; they should no more be regarded as Government Departments than the Council on Tribunals.

Government Departments dealing with domestic affairs make use of a great number of standing advisory committees and councils composed of outside experts or representatives of interest groups. Occasionally, the functions of such a committee (for example, the Social Security Advisory Committee) are prescribed by statute; usually the committee rests on a less formal basis. At a more exalted level, there are the advisory research councils concerned with government-sponsored research. A full description of the machinery of central government would require an account of the functions exercised by these multifarious ancillary bodies.

---

7 This feature is, however, inconclusive of status. For example, there is a separate vote for the British Council.
8 See p. 208.
9 W. J. M. Mackenzie and J. W. Grove, *Central Administration in Britain* (1957), pp. 183–4; see also Sir Ivor Jennings, *Cabinet Government* (3rd edn, 1959), ch. 4. Schedule 2 to the Parliamentary Commissioner Act 1967 lists Government Departments and other authorities subject to investigation, without distinguishing the one group from the other.
10 Brian Chapman, *British Government Observed* (1963), p. 18.

MATTERS HISTORICAL AND LEGAL[11]

Of the modern ministerial offices, a few, such as those of Lord Chancellor, Lord President of the Council, Chancellor of the Duchy of Lancaster and Lord Privy Seal, are traceable to the Tudor period and even earlier. The office of Secretary of State developed from a secretarial office in the royal household and became, in the seventeenth century, an important ministerial post. In Charles II's time there were two Secretaries of State; by 1784 there were three; the numbers increased as the functions of government extended and became more complex, and today there are fourteen.[12] Their individual responsibilities are seldom prescribed by statute, and indeed where powers and duties are conferred by legislation on 'a' or 'the' Secretary of State, the function could, as a matter of strict law, be exercised by any of the Secretaries of State unless one is specifically designated by the Act or Order.

The office of Chancellor of the Exchequer is less ancient; the Lord High Treasurer[13] was a high officer of State in Tudor times and before, but the office was put into commission and discharged by a board composed of Lords Commissioners of the Treasury in 1714. The Board never meets, but the First Lord of the Treasury is now invariably the Prime Minister, and the second Lord, in charge of the Treasury, the principal Department of State, is the Chancellor of the Exchequer; the Junior Lords sign formal Treasury warrants, but their main function is to act as Government whips in the Commons. Several of the surviving medieval offices of the Royal Household are occupied by Government whips in the Lords.

The existence of some ministerial offices (for example, Lord Chancellor, Secretary of State) is derived from the prerogative, but statutory functions can be assigned to a prerogative office-holder. The majority of ministerial offices have been established by legislation. The Minister is created a corporation sole, given a seal of office and entrusted with a loosely defined range of functions which can be supplemented by other statutes and statutory instruments. In general, legislation recognizes the Minister, not his Department; and acts done by departmental officials will be performed in the Minister's name. Under the Ministers of the Crown Act 1975, functions may be transferred by Order in Council from one Minister to

11 See Brazier, *Constitutional Practice*, 2nd edn, 1994, ch. 7, and *Ministers of the Crown* (1997), ch. 2.
12 The maximum number cannot, in practice, exceed twenty-one: Ministerial and other Salaries Act 1975, sched. 1, part V.
13 Mackenzie and Grove, op. cit., pp. 167–70.

another, the designations of Ministers may be altered, and Ministers and their Departments may be similarly wound up. In order to create a ministerial office with entirely new executive functions, an Act of Parliament is required unless the office is that of a Secretary of State. All Ministers hold office during Her Majesty's pleasure and are removable, by convention, on the advice of the Prime Minister.

Within the general framework of the principle that a Minister must not allow a conflict to develop between his public responsibilities and his private interests, detailed rules and criteria have been laid down by Prime Ministers limiting the permissible range of private activities of members of a Government.[14] For example, Ministers must not hold directorships in public companies or engage in speculative investments in respect of which information acquired in their official capacities might be beneficial; though they are not required to dispose of all private shareholdings. Association with non-profit-making organizations may also be incompatible with the discharge of ministerial duties. The principles are flexible enough to accommodate special cases when it appears to the Prime Minister expedient to do so. When Mr Frank Cousins became Minister of Technology in 1964 he was allowed to retain the office of General Secretary of the Transport and General Workers' Union on indefinite leave; on his resignation from ministerial office in 1966 he resumed his activities as union secretary.

MINISTERIAL RESPONSIBILITY[15]

That Ministers are 'collectively responsible' is an undoubted constitutional convention. But what does collective responsibility signify? In many of the newly independent Commonwealth countries British conventions have been spelt out in some detail, often with modifications, in the texts of the constitutions. On Cabinet responsibility, Barbados is nevertheless laconic. 'The Cabinet shall be the principal instrument of policy and shall be charged with the general direction and control of the government of Barbados and shall be collectively responsible therefor to Parliament.'[16] It is wise not to attempt to define in a constitutional document what exactly collective

---

14 The rules are set out in the *Ministerial Code* (Cabinet Office, 1997), paras. 111–29. See also Brazier, *Constitutional Practice*, pp. 140–54, *Ministers of the Crown*, ch. 15.

15 See Brazier, *Ministers of the Crown*, ch. 7; First Report of the Committee on Standards in Public Life, Cm 2850 (1995) and J. A. G. Griffith and M. Ryle, *Parliament: Functions, Practices and Procedures* (1989), pp. 23–40.

16 Barbados Independence Order 1966 (SI 1966, No. 1455), Schedule, s. 64(2).

responsibility means, because the outlines of the concept are so vague and blurred. It can be described at a high level of generality; it can be illustrated by specific examples; a neat but comprehensive set of propositions cannot be devised, if only because the gulf between traditional constitutional theory (to which lip-service may still be paid) and political practice yawns so widely.

Responsible for what and to whom? And what exactly do we mean by 'responsible'? Does the substitution of words like 'accountable' or 'answerable' clarify the issues at all?[17] Perhaps it is more helpful to begin with the concept of the *individual responsibility* of Ministers, which raises some of the questions in a still more difficult way. Historically, moreover, the principle of individual ministerial responsibility preceded the doctrine of collective responsibility.

All Ministers, whether they be in or outside the Cabinet, are responsible for their personal acts, the general conduct of their Departments and acts done (or left undone) in their name by their departmental officials. Responsibility may be political, legal, or both political and legal; and the meaning of responsibility, and the persons or bodies to whom it is owed, will vary according to the context.

Ministers are legally responsible in their private capacities for acts which they order or authorize to be done, or in which they actively participate. If, for example, such an act proves to be a trespass, the Minister can be sued personally for damages as a tortfeasor. To Dicey, the personal liability of Ministers and officials for civil wrongs before the ordinary courts applying the ordinary law of the land, subject to any special statutory powers that might be vested in them to encroach on private rights, was a cardinal feature of the rule of law in Britain. Today this aspect of ministerial responsibility is of little practical importance, for since 1947 it has been possible to sue the Crown as the Minister's employer for torts committed in the purported exercise of legal powers and duties.

Ministers are legally and politically responsible for formal acts done by the monarch, under prerogative or statutory powers, in which they have participated by virtue of their attendance at a meeting of the Privy Council, or their countersignature of the royal sign manual or their custody of a

17 cf. Geoffrey Marshall and G. C. Moodie, *Some Problems of the Constitution* (5th edn, 1971), ch. 4; Geoffrey Marshall (ed.), *Ministerial Responsibility* (1989); Henry Parris, *Constitutional Bureaucracy* (1969), chs. 3, 4, 10. Issues of ministerial responsibility and accountability were considered by the House of Commons Public Service Committee in HC 313 (1995–6), and by Sir Richard Scott in his report on the export of defence equipment to Iraq, HC 115 (1995–6).

royal seal.[18] The strictly legal rationale of these customary procedures has now disappeared.

Ministers are politically answerable in respect of matters lying within their statutory or conventional fields of responsibility. They are responsible not only for their personal acts but for the conduct of their Departments. The area of statutory responsibility is determined by the legislation (if any) establishing their offices and particular Acts and subordinate legislative instruments endowing them with powers and duties. If a Minister has no power or duty to take any action with regard to a matter, he cannot properly be left accountable to Parliament for what is done or left undone; hence, a Minister is not expected to answer parliamentary questions about public corporations, or most of the activities of local government authorities or the police.[19] To some Ministers powers and duties are assigned by convention – for example, to the Secretary of State for Foreign and Commonwealth Affairs, most of whose functions are non-statutory; to the Home Secretary in respect of advice on the exercise of the prerogative of pardon; to the Attorney-General in respect of decisions whether to enter a *nolle prosequi* to stop a trial on indictment. The conventions may, like those just referred to, be well established, surviving changes of government; or they may be the product of an informal re-allocation by the Prime Minister of responsibilities among his Ministers, especially Ministers such as the Lord President of the Council, the Lord Privy Seal, the Chancellor of the Duchy of Lancaster and the Paymaster-General, whose formal departmental functions are small or nominal.

The meaning of political responsibility cannot be precisely defined. If a Minister is personally blameworthy, he ought to make a public admission of his responsibility. Personal culpability may be attributable to private or public conduct unbecoming to a Minister of the Crown, in which case there will be an expectation that he will resign;[20] or to bad judgement or

---

18 See ch. 8.

19 See p. 292.

20 Mr Parkinson resigned in 1983 when it became known that a woman who was not his wife was expecting his child. He was reappointed to the Cabinet in 1987. Mr David Mellor resigned in 1992 after revelations about an extramarital affair and after allegations that he had not properly accounted for personal gifts. The Prime Minister exonerated him over the gifts, but (as in Mr Parkinson's case) media obsession with the story made it impossible for him to function efficiently as a Minister. Earl Jellicoe and Mr Lambton resigned in 1973 following revelations that they had been associating with prostitutes. Mr John Profumo resigned in 1963 after it was revealed that he had made a false statement to the House of Commons in rebuttal of allegations about his private life. For a list of resignations this century and notes on the reasons, see David Butler and Gareth Butler, *British Political Facts 1900–1985* (6th edn, 1986), pp. 85–7. See also Brazier [1994] *Public Law* 431.

departmental maladministration, in which case there cannot be said to be any clear-cut convention about a duty to offer resignation.[21] Unless the Prime Minister is unwilling to stand by the Minister under attack – and in this context the personal authority of a Prime Minister is of great importance – a Minister may choose, and has not infrequently chosen in recent years, to brazen out appalling indiscretions, gross errors and omissions, plans gone awry and revelations of disastrous mismanagement within his Department. If the Opposition is allowed time to move a vote of censure, or if an Opposition Day is selected for the purpose of moving a motion to reduce the Minister's salary, the Minister can confidently expect to emerge triumphant in the division lobbies, with members voting strictly along party lines. Yet his victory may prove to be Pyrrhic and ephemeral. The Prime Minister may shift him to another office carrying less prestige in the next ministerial reshuffle; he may 'kick him upstairs' to the Lords; he may quietly call for the Minister's resignation at a moment less embarrassing for the Government, or gratefully accept a half-hearted offer of resignation if it comes. A Minister who is incapable of explaining and justifying his conduct of affairs persuasively in the face of a hostile Opposition, or to the satisfaction of his own backbenchers, is a liability to the Government and the party. So Mr Leon Brittan had to resign in 1986 following the improper leaking of a Law Officer's letter with Mr Brittan's approval by a civil servant in his Department during the Westland affair.[22] And Mr Nicholas Ridley resigned in 1990 after his views about Germany, expressed in trenchant and occasionally offensive terms, were published in a magazine interview.

Given that the idea of ministerial culpability for personal failings is so shapeless, a detailed analysis of *degrees* of ministerial responsibility for the conduct of departmental affairs and officials would not be very helpful. A Minister is expected to answer questions about these matters in Parliament unless the question must be disallowed by parliamentary practice (for example, because it deals with an issue *sub judice*) or unless the Minister feels bound to refuse an answer or a full answer on grounds of national security, in which case he will have to face the prospect of personal

21 The Foreign Secretary, Lord Carrington, and two other Foreign and Commonwealth Office Ministers felt compelled to leave office in 1982 after the Argentinian invasion of the Falkland Islands because they believed that their Department had not adequately assessed Argentina's intentions. See also Finer (1956) 34 *Public Administration* 377; Madgwick (1966–7) 20 *Parliamentary Affairs* 59; R. K. Alderman and J. A. Cross, *The Tactics of Resignation* (1967).
22 On Westland, see below, p. 197.

criticism.[23] In answering questions or in replying to a debate, he cannot be expected to accept that he is himself culpable whenever a departmental official has committed a dishonest act or has disobeyed instructions or exceeded his authority. He is entitled to explain in public what has occurred; but he cannot totally absolve himself of responsibility. To use a colloquialism which, eluding exact definition, is still well understood, he must, in the last resort, 'carry the can'.[24] If maladministration within his Department is attributable to bad organization or procedures or defective supervision, or exists on such a large scale or at so high a level that he ought to have been able to prevent it, then he is in some degree blameworthy.[25] But Sir Thomas Dugdale's personal decision to resign as Minister of Agriculture in 1954 because of the exposure of maladministration by senior officials in the over-celebrated Crichel Down affair[26] was not demanded by convention; certainly other Ministers (particularly in the 1979 Conservative Government) have not sought to emulate him by exacting the supreme political penalty on themselves, and it would be unrealistic to expect them to do so, particularly if wide decision-making powers have been delegated to the official concerned.[27] The further the Minister was, geographically or hierarchically, from the events complained of, the less he will generally be expected to take the blame for them and resign. So Mr Lennox-Boyd did not resign as Colonial Secretary in 1959 after fifty-two people had been killed by the security forces in Nyasaland,[28] nor did Mr Whitelaw as Home Secretary in 1982 after an intruder had confronted the Queen in her bedroom, nor did Mr Prior as Northern Ireland Secretary after a mass prison escape in Northern Ireland.[29] Both Mr Kenneth Baker and Mr

23 For a list of matters on which successive Ministers have refused to answer questions, either for reasons of public interest or because they lie outside the field of ministerial responsibility, see *Report of the Select Committee on Parliamentary Questions* (HC 393 (1971 – 2), pp. 114–17). See also the Scott Report (note 17 above), paras. K8.1–K8.16.

24 cf. the Report of the Parker Committee on the Use of Authorized Procedures for Interrogation of Persons Suspected of Terrorism in Northern Ireland (Cmnd 4901 (1972)), indicating that the unlawful practices adopted had never in fact been authorized by a Minister and may not have even been known to Ministers. They were nevertheless politically answerable for the conduct of the security forces.

25 cf. the slightly different formulation by the then Home Secretary, Sir David Maxwell Fyfe, in 530 HC Deb. 1285–8 (20 July 1954).

26 Cmd 9176 (1953); Cmd 9220 (1954); Geoffrey Marshall, *Constitutional Conventions* (1984), p. 66; J. A. G. Griffith (1955) 18 *Mod. L. Rev.* 557, (1987) 1 *Contemporary Record* 35. Dugdale was later elevated to the peerage as Lord Crathorne.

27 As in the Vehicle and General affair; note 34.

28 See Harold Macmillan, *Riding the Storm* (1971), pp. 733–8.

29 Mr Prior's offered resignation was refused by Mrs Thatcher: see James Prior, *A Balance of Power* (1986), p. 232.

Michael Howard showed great tenacity of the office of Home Secretary despite many criticisms of their tenure of it.

The political answerability of Ministers has helped to preserve the impartiality and anonymity of civil servants; they have been reasonably secure from public censure and, therefore, find it easier to give unstinted loyalty to a succession of political masters. But official anonymity has not been an unmixed blessing; and, as the Fulton Committee on the civil service pointed out,[30] it has been eroded. This is the result, in particular, of the activities of departmental select committees of the House of Commons[31] and the Parliamentary Commissioner for Administration[32] (the Ombudsman). The Parliamentary Commissioner not only scrutinizes departmental procedures but has, on rare occasions, singled out identifiable civil servants for criticism.[33] He has yet to go as far as the judicial tribunal of inquiry on the collapse of the Vehicle and General Insurance Co. (1972), which affixed blame on a named senior civil servant in the Department of Trade and Industry for failing to set in motion an investigation of the Company's affairs, but exonerated the responsible Ministers.[34] If this type of inquisition became frequent, it would be impossible to expect civil servants not to answer back. Nevertheless, ministerial responsibility remains as a protective, if slightly tattered, cloak for the civil service, and at least no serious complaint of political partisanship against senior civil servants has yet been substantiated.

The *collective responsibility* of Ministers to the House of Commons is still sometimes spoken of as a democratic bulwark of the British constitution. After all, did not five Governments resign between the years 1852 and 1859 as a result of being defeated on votes of confidence in the House?[35] Rather more to the point is that only two Governments, both in a minority in the Commons, have lost the confidence of that House since 1924. In that year Ramsay MacDonald's first Labour Government found itself deserted by its Liberal allies. And Mr Callaghan, who took over a tiny Labour majority on Mr Wilson's retirement in 1976, lost his majority through by-election

30 Cmnd 3638 (1968), vol. 1, p. 33.
31 See ch. 14.
32 See ch. 30.
33 See, for example, HC 316 (1968–9).
34 HC 133 (1971–2); the report was debated in 835 HC Deb. 33–161 (1 May 1972). There was much criticism that the civil servant concerned had not been granted adequate facilities to defend himself before the tribunal of inquiry.
35 Particulars are supplied by Jennings, *Cabinet Government* (3rd edn, 1959), pp. 512–15.

defeats and defections; and his Government was defeated on a Conservative motion of no confidence in 1979.[36] But the very unusual parliamentary background to these defeats must be stressed: both were *minority* Governments – an extremely rare phenomenon in modern British constitutional history. On several occasions since 1945, Governments have been defeated in the House on particular issues because their whips have been out-manoeuvred by the Opposition or because of absenteeism. The Government has then usually mustered in its full resources and procured a reversal of the vote. There has been no other defeat on an unequivocal issue of confidence,[37] such as the budget resolutions or the address in reply to the Queen's speech at the opening of a session. Mr Harold Wilson was able to sustain himself in office from 1964 to 1966 with a majority of less than six; and he then won a handsome victory at a General Election held at the most advantageous moment for his party. And again the Labour Government of March to October 1974 survived without a majority, and, after the October 1974 Election, continued at first with a tiny, then without, a majority – although a number of defeats were sustained. That Government's success in the Commons until it was driven to the country in 1979 was partly the result of the pact which it concluded with the Liberals in March 1977 and which continued until the end of the 1977–8 parliamentary session. In return for Liberal votes 'in the pursuit of economic recovery' the Government gave various undertakings about Government policy to Liberal MPs.[38] Mr John Major, too, managed to stay in office despite losing his majority in 1995 after successive by-election defeats. To go further back, Neville Chamberlain, on the other hand, decided to resign after a vote in the House on a motion of censure in May 1940; but the motion was defeated by eighty-one votes. It is a nice question which was the more significant fact – that he retained a substantial parliamentary majority after having forfeited the confidence of the general public, or that thirty-three Conservatives voted against their own leader and eighty others abstained.

Because a Government must maintain a majority in the House of Commons as a condition of survival – it can ignore defeats in the Lords –

36 See above, pp. 62–6.
37 There is no formal definition of a matter of confidence. If a Government explicitly states that it regards a vote as one of confidence, or if the Opposition has moved a motion of no confidence, the Government must, of course, stand or fall by the result. The Conservative Government did that over what became the European Communities (Finance) Act 1995.
38 See Alistair Michie and Simon Hoggart, *The Pact* (1978), and David Steel, *A House Divided* (1980).

it has to ensure party solidarity. Doubtless this reduces the results of most of the contentious debates in the House to foregone conclusions; but a Government which is driven to rely on disciplinary sanctions and threats of sanctions, and an autocratic disregard of the interests of the Opposition and private members generally in the allocation of parliamentary time, is not going to endear itself to the electorate. The fact that the executive branch is parliamentary has an influence, which cannot be quantified, on the style of British politics.

Collective responsibility also implies that all Cabinet Ministers assume responsibility for Cabinet decisions and action taken to implement those decisions. A Minister may disagree with a decision[39] or with the manner of its implementation, but if he wishes to express dissent in public he should first resign. The Westland affair[40] is instructive. The Westland company supplied helicopters to the Ministry of Defence, and by 1985 urgently needed financial reconstruction. Two rival packages were on offer, one emanating from the United States, the other from a European consortium. Mr Michael Heseltine (the Defence Secretary) preferred the European option, while Mr Leon Brittan (the Trade and Industry Secretary) and perhaps the Prime Minister as well favoured the other. The Cabinet as a whole was supposed to be neutral as between the competing offers. At a Cabinet meeting in January 1986 it was agreed that, to prevent Ministers from speaking with different voices on the issue, all further ministerial statements on Westland would be cleared by the Cabinet Office. Mr Heseltine considered this to be an attempt at censorship by the Prime Minister which he could not accept; he also thought that Mrs Thatcher had unilaterally cancelled an arranged Cabinet committee meeting on Westland, and that both these events showed that the Cabinet government system was breaking down.[41] He therefore resigned. Sir Geoffrey Howe's resignation in 1992 over Mrs Thatcher's attitude towards Europe provided another example of a Cabinet Minister leaving the Government over a policy (and personality) clash with the Prime Minister.

A number of points need to be added to explain and qualify the obligation of public unanimity which flows from the doctrine of collective responsibility.

39 But the practice of having his dissent recorded in the minutes was ended in 1964: see Harold Wilson, *The Governance of Britain* (1976), pp. 58–9.
40 On which see Marshall [1986] *Public Law* 184; M. Linklater and D. Leigh, *Not With Honour* (1986); Defence Select Committee, HC 519 (1985–6); HC 92 (1985–6); Cmnd 9841 (1986).
41 See his account in the *Observer*, 12 January 1986.

1 The convention of public unanimity is settled, at least to the extent that it will be regarded as constitutionally improper for a Minister to remain in office if he has overtly dissociated himself from Cabinet policy. It is open to the Prime Minister to condone a verbal indiscretion by a colleague, and even to overlook a studied refusal by a colleague to offer positive commendation of a policy which he dislikes, though the line between half-hearted formal acquiescence and hints of real disagreement may wear thin. Mr Peter Walker made some extra-parliamentary speeches in such a way as to make clear his lukewarm approval of Mrs Thatcher's economic policies, despite being a member of her Cabinet. During the 1974–9 Labour Governments some Cabinet Ministers, notably but not only Mr Tony Benn, came very close to public dissociation from Government policy. Mr Wilson had to issue a not wholly successful minute to Ministers reminding them of the doctrine of collective Cabinet responsibility. In this century the convention has been expressly waived three times. In 1975 that convention, in so far as it required Ministers not to disagree with Cabinet decisions in public, was waived by the Cabinet to allow those Ministers who disagreed to say in public, but outside Parliament, that they dissented from the Cabinet's recommendation that the electorate should vote to remain in the EEC in the referendum held under the Referendum Act of that year. Once the referendum result was announced, full collective responsibility was restored. Secondly, the doctrine was waived on an *ad hoc* basis, for the purposes of what became the European Parliament Elections Act 1978, because of the deep divisions in the Labour Cabinet and parliamentary party over direct elections to the European Parliament. Indeed, the Prime Minister, Mr Callaghan, was moved to remark that '. . . I certainly think that the doctrine should apply, except in cases where I announce that it does not.'[42] Both of those suspensions were a success for the Prime Ministers concerned. But the third, and earlier, experiment adopted by the 'National' Government in 1932 over its protectionist policies, and which was intended to allow the coalition parties to 'agree to differ' indefinitely, failed after only a few months.[43] Such experiments are obviously rare and, despite occasional deviations from the norm, the general principle stated above is clear.

2 Public unanimity conforms to expectations of the electorate (which frowns upon a Government in disarray) and strengthens the hands of a

42 933 HC Deb. 552 (16 June 1977).
43 See David Marquand, *Ramsay MacDonald* (1977), ch. 28.

Government in relation to its own backbench dissenters, the Opposition and political commentators, all of whom are alert to any suspicion of discord within the Cabinet. But from time to time, when a Minister finds the strains of maintaining a tight-lipped silence insupportable, he will deliberately 'leak' his 'unattributable' private views to a journalist. Leaking is resorted to by Ministers – and the Prime Minister – to fortify or explain their positions. Unprecedented leaking took place during the Westland affair. Political correspondents at Westminster receive daily 'briefings on Lobby terms' from the Prime Minister's Press Secretary; in return for the information divulged those terms require that the exact source not be identified.[44] Such 'briefing' is said to involve the authorized disclosure of information, but the distinction between such 'briefing' and 'leaking' may be too subtle for most of us.[45] Leaking and briefing remain essential to the maintenance of collective responsibility, and are underpinned by the symbiotic relationship between leaker and journalist.

3 The obligation to preserve an outward show of unanimity about past decisions is supposed to continue after the Government, or the Minister who had been placed in a minority, has left office. But the force of this obligation is very weak.

(a) If a Minister has decided to resign because of disagreement on a policy issue.[46] He is customarily allowed to publish the nature of the disagreement in his letter of resignation and to make a resignation speech in Parliament if he so wishes.

The general principle is that disclosures of Cabinet discussions or decisions by former Ministers are permissible only with the Sovereign's consent, communicated by the Prime Minister of the day through the medium of the Cabinet Office.[47] The national interest, and the interest in encouraging the utmost frankness in Cabinet discussions leading up to a policy decision, will sometimes be prejudiced if it is thought that Ministers will be at liberty to rush into print or be propelled on to the television screen with their memoirs and reminiscences as soon as they

---

44 Now well documented. See Jeremy Tunstall, *The Westminster Lobby Correspondents* (1970); Michael Cockerell *et al.*, *Sources Close to the Prime Minister* (1984).

45 cf. Mr James Callaghan, giving evidence to the Franks Committee on Official Secrecy: 'You know the difference between leaking and briefing. Briefing is what I do and leaking is what you do' (Cmnd 5104 (1972), vol. 4, p. 187).

46 See Alderman and Cross, op. cit., Appendix. For examples, see Butler and Butler, ibid.

47 It may be doubted whether ex-Ministers still obtain such clearance for their resignation statements: see Brazier, *Constitutional Practice* (2nd edn, 1994), p. 81.

leave office. Yet over the years, and particularly since 1970, ex-Ministers have disclosed with impunity Cabinet discussions and disagreements; the general principle has been tested in the courts and found wanting. Mr Richard Crossman held various Cabinet posts in the Labour Governments of 1964–70. He kept detailed diaries of his life and work as a Minister. After he left office the *Sunday Times* wanted to serialize them, and after his death in 1974 his literary executors wished to publish them in book form. The Secretary of the Cabinet was not satisfied by the cuts which they were prepared to make, so the Attorney-General brought an action against the newspaper, the executors and the book publishers seeking a permanent injunction to prevent such publication. He relied on both the confidential nature of the materials, which flowed from the convention of collective Cabinet responsibility, and also on the argument that free discussion in future Cabinets would be inhibited if the materials were published in a way which disclosed the attitudes and views of individual Ministers – and civil servants. The Attorney-General did *not* rely on Mr Crossman's oath as a Privy Counsellor or on the Official Secrets Acts (both of which had previously been assumed to buttress the secrecy of Cabinet discussions and to form the bases of the vetting procedure). The injunctions were refused.[48]

The Lord Chief Justice held that the courts indeed have the power to prevent publication of Cabinet material if such publication (i) would be a breach of confidence and (ii) would be against the public interest in prejudicing the maintenance of the doctrine of collective responsibility. However, there would, in his Lordship's view, come a time when the confidential nature of the material ceased to exist, such time depending on the circumstances of each case; as nearly ten years had elapsed since the events contained in the first volume of the diaries, publication could not prejudice the doctrine of collective responsibility in the 1975 Cabinet – despite the fact that many of its members had sat in the Cabinet with Mr Crossman.[49]

48 *Att.-Gen.* v. *Jonathan Cape Ltd and others, Att.-General* v. *Times Newspapers Ltd* [1976] QB 752. The report of the case also provides fascinating details about the vetting procedure and the role of the Secretary of the Cabinet in it, on which also see Cmnd 5104 (1972), vol. 3, pp. 330–32.

49 For the sequel see the Radcliffe Report on Ministerial Memoirs, Cmnd 6386 (1976), which, among other things, recommended that fifteen years should elapse before certain types of material should be published by former Ministers. The Report was accepted by the Prime Minister. See further, Wright (1977) 30 *Parliamentary Affairs* 293; Hugo Young, *The Crossman Affair* (1976); Barbara Castle, *The Castle Diaries 1974–1976* (1980); Brazier, *Ministers of the Crown*, ch. 17.

(b) The convention (such as it is) extends to decisions of which a Minister was not aware at the time but to which he subsequently gave his tacit approval by continuing in office with full knowledge of the facts. But here the force of the convention is even weaker. One can hardly expect a Minister to accept the same degree of responsibility for a decision in which he had no opportunity to participate as for a decision where he had such an opportunity.

(c) For this reason the *ex post facto* responsibility of non-Cabinet Ministers for Cabinet decisions is not at all clear-cut, unless the Minister concerned was a member of a Ministerial Committee which took or recommended the actual decision. Criticism of a Cabinet decision by the Minister after his departure from office may be condoned, if he learned of it only when Cabinet minutes were circulated to him; it ought to be excused if the decision was never brought to his notice at all.

4 Nevertheless, a non-Cabinet Minister will not be allowed to express public disagreement with government policy and remain in office, unless it is expedient for the Prime Minister to overlook the transgression; for a transgression it is. The practice followed in Attlee's Government after 1945 was instructive. The Government Chief Whip in the House of Lords described the Government handling of a dock labour dispute as 'absolutely crazy'; out he went. The Parliamentary Secretary to the Ministry of Agriculture did not survive his public criticism of the Government's 'feather-bedding' of farmers. And out went a group of parliamentary private secretaries (not even Ministers, but unpaid aides to individual Ministers) who failed to support the Government in an important division on the Ireland Bill which recognized (*inter alia*) the continued partition of Ireland.[50] Such an involvement of non-Cabinet Ministers in the consequences of the doctrine of collective responsibility has been followed by all Prime Ministers since Attlee.

5 Just as Ministers are expected to be loyal to their colleagues, so they can reasonably claim to be entitled to the loyalty of their colleagues. Mr Nigel Lawson, who resigned as Chancellor of the Exchequer in 1989, might say that Mrs Thatcher's refusal to dismiss Alan Walters (her part-time economic adviser) was disloyal. Sir Alan's advice conflicted with Mr Lawson's, who ultimately resigned. If Ministers implement Cabinet policies badly, or if they incur criticism as a result of purely departmental failings or indications of personal ineptitude, they will not have any corresponding claim to corporate solidarity. In 1935, the Foreign

50 On parliamentary private secretaries, see Norton [1989] *Public Law* 233.

Secretary, Sir Samuel Hoare, exceeded his mandate by concurring in an agreement that would have given the Italian invaders of Abyssinia a slice of that country. The Cabinet could have repudiated Hoare but decided to stand by him. When the terms of the agreement were published, a national outcry arose. In an attempt to retrieve its reputation, the Cabinet then insisted on Hoare's resignation. In the circumstances this was a clear breach of convention. Hoare was duly rewarded for allowing himself to be sacrificed for the national good; he was given another, not quite so exalted, Cabinet post a few months later.

THE CIVIL SERVICE

A civil servant is a Crown servant (other than the holder of a political or judicial office or a member of the armed forces) appointed directly or indirectly by the Crown, and paid wholly out of funds provided by Parliament and employed in a Department of Government. The definition of a civil servant has not yet given rise to serious legal problems; the meaning of the term 'Crown Servant' (which may include bodies corporate) has posed bigger difficulties.[51]

It is not, of course, realistic to think of the civil service only as a body of advisers to Ministers. First, a great number of decisions, the responsibility for taking which is committed by law to Ministers, are in fact taken by civil servants in the Minister's name without reference to the Minister personally.[52] Unless the class of decision is so important that nothing less than the Minister's personal attention is appropriate, the courts will accept the propriety of such a procedure even though the Minister has not explicitly authorized the civil servant to make the decisions.[53] However, in immigration law special legal consequences are attached to decisions taken by the Secretary of State in person.[54] Secondly, some statutes vest powers of decision directly in named classes of civil servants (for example, customs and excise officers, inspectors at town planning inquiries). Thirdly, in some Departments large questions of policy will in practice be decided by civil servants with the Minister's formal concurrence. A combination of thrustful

---

51 See pp. 142–3, 599–601.
52 A point made spectacularly but perhaps over-emphatically by the judicial tribunal of inquiry into the *Vehicle & General Insurance Co.* affair: HC 133 (1971–2).
53 *Carltona Ltd.* v. *Commissioners of Works* [1943] 2 All ER 560; *Lewisham Borough* v. *Roberts* [1949] 2 KB 608 at 629; *R.* v. *Skinner* [1968] 2 QB 700.
54 Immigration Act 1971, ss. 13(5), 14(3), 15(4); see ch. 20.

and strong-minded senior civil servants, complex issues demanding both a substantial body of factual knowledge and an appreciation of the personal qualities of persons with whom the Department has to deal, and an inexperienced, indolent, ill-endowed or indecisive Minister, will sometimes lead to a situation in which a Minister is heavily reliant on advice from his civil servants. Civil servants may seek to influence a ministerial decision in a particular direction by their methods of selecting and summarizing facts, stating the problems and presenting alternative courses of action to the Minister, and they are usually expert in putting to a Minister the objections against a decision that he may wish to take; but they are aware of the need for preserving political neutrality by conscious self-restraint, and the constitutional importance of having an effective political head of their Department.[55] Ministers, if only for reasons of self-respect and personal ambition, know that they must be able to present departmental decisions persuasively to their colleagues, to Parliament, to the public at large and to any groups with whom they have been negotiating.

Following the Westland affair the Treasury and Civil Service Select Committee made many recommendations for the reform of the duties and responsibilities of civil servants in relation to Ministers.[56] The Government in effect rejected all of them, including a proposal that civil servants should be free to give evidence to select committees about alleged misconduct in Government Departments (rather than passing it to more senior members of the service).[57] But the Government was later persuaded to promulgate the Civil Service Code, in part spurred by the First Report of the Committee on Standards in Public Life.[58] The Civil Service Code sets out the constitutional duties of civil servants, the proper relationship between Ministers and their officials, as well as their obligations and rights.

Political activities of civil servants

Overt political partisanship cannot be reconciled with the principle of official impartiality. Civil servants are disqualified by statute for membership of the House of Commons; and a civil servant who wishes to stand at a parliamentary election is obliged by regulations of the service to resign his

55 See R. H. S. Crossman, *Diaries of a Cabinet Minister*, vols. 1–3 (1975–7), *passim*.
56 See HC 92 (1985–6).
57 See Cmnd 9841 (1986).
58 See respectively Civil Service Order 1995; Cm 2850 (1995). And see Brazier, *Ministers of the Crown*, ch. 8. Rules about civil servants' conduct are spelled out in the Civil Service Code and the Civil Service Management Code.

post before announcing himself as a candidate or prospective candidate, though in certain cases[59] he will be entitled to reinstatement if he is not elected or after he has ceased to be a member of the House. By pursuing logic to a facile conclusion, one will rapidly decide that all civil servants ought to be denied every form of political activity except that of casting a vote at an election. But the reasons of public policy that impose the utmost discretion on civil servants closely associated with the work of their Minister are largely irrelevant to the van driver, the porter and the junior clerk. In order to allow civil servants a reasonable measure of freedom of political expression, they are divided into three main groups.[60] The 'politically restricted' are senior members of the service; they are debarred from national political activities (including the public expression of views on matters of national political policy), but are entitled to take part, with the permission of their Department, in local political activities, provided that they act 'with moderation and discretion, particularly in matters affecting their own Department'. Some fifty politically restricted civil servants currently have permission to engage in local political activity. Secondly, there is a large 'intermediate' group, consisting of clerical officers, typists and persons charged with technical and specialized responsibilities not involving questions of political policy. Members of this group may be given (and many tens of thousands have been given) permission by their Department to take part in both national and local political activities; permission is likely to be refused, however, to officers who come into direct contact with members of the public in the course of participating in discretionary decisions (for example, at jobcentres or tax offices) or who are closely associated, though in a subordinate capacity, with Ministers and senior policy-makers. Following the Armitage Committee Report,[61] the 'intermediate group' was increased by some 175,000 civil servants in the executive officer grade who were transferred to that group from the 'restricted category'. The remainder of the civil service, and much the largest group, is politically unrestricted (subject to the rules about parliamentary candidature), except in so far as they have to observe the Official Secrets Acts, may not engage in political activity while on duty or in uniform or on official premises, and have to observe a due measure of restraint so as to avoid embarrassing their Ministers and Departments.

---

59 Those civil servants who are not in the 'restricted' or 'intermediate' groups: see below.
60 The rules are stated in the Civil Service Management Code.
61 Cmnd 7057 (1978).

Private interests of civil servants[62]

There is no precisely formulated code of conduct governing the private economic activities of civil servants, but they must not allow a conflict to develop between their public responsibilities and their private interests as shareholders and investors. Fortunately, cases of corruption among senior civil servants are exceedingly rare.[63] A certain amount of disquiet has been caused by the frequency with which senior officers, upon their retirement, are appointed to executive or advisory posts in commercial and industrial firms with which they have conducted direct negotiations while they were officials; but under rules of the service such offers of appointment cannot be accepted within two years of retirement except with the consent of the Government.[64]

Anonymity and secrecy

Government Departments have often been criticized for their disinclination to divulge interesting and useful information to members of the public.[65] The fiction that all departmental decisions were taken by the Minister (who is alone politically answerable for them), coupled with a deep-seated belief that any exposure of the processes of departmental decision-making would tend to cause trouble and reduce administrative efficiency, brought about a state of affairs in which secretiveness was sometimes carried to absurd lengths. Inspectors' reports to Ministers on housing and town planning inquiries were not disclosed – and the courts upheld the departmental view that natural justice did not require their disclosure[66] – till 1958.[67] The Franks Committee's emphasis on the need for openness in the procedures for taking decisions on matters directly impinging on individual rights led to a healthy ventilation of the corridors of Whitehall which has enhanced

---

62 See Chester and Wilson, *Organization of British Central Government*, pp. 117–19.

63 But not unknown. In the wake of the 'Poulson affair' a Royal Commission on Standards of Conduct in Public Life was set up in 1974. In its report, Cmnd 6524 (1976), sweeping changes in the law were recommended, including new statutory rules which would affect civil servants. The Commission recorded that from 1966 to 1976 seventeen civil servants had been convicted on corruption charges.

64 The Advisory Committee on Business Appointments advises Ministers on this, operating procedures suggested by the Committee on Standards in Public Life in its First Report (see note 58 above); see also 273 HC Deb. 5 (written answers 4 March 1996).

65 For measured criticisms, see D. G. T. Williams, *Not in the Public Interest* (1965).

66 *Local Government Board* v. *Arlidge* [1915] AC 120.

67 See further, ch. 28.

public confidence in the processes followed. The prevailing image of central administration is less monolithic. And it is fair to say that, for many years past, senior civil servants have been more accessible for informal interviews than their bureaucratic counterparts in a number of other countries (provided, at least, that the interviewer was not proposing to publish 'confidential' information); and that formal and informal consultations between officials and representatives of organized interest groups have long been a feature of central administration in Britain.

In 1977 the then Government agreed to make publicly available as far as possible the information used as the background to major policy studies, and heads of departments were actually encouraged in a letter to them from the then Head of the Home Civil Service, Sir Douglas Allen, to cooperate fully in this sortie into open government.[68] The 1979 Conservative Government adopted a more general policy of seeking to promote open government, underpinned by a code of practice on the matter.[69]

Regulation, organization and structure

The civil service is regulated primarily under the royal prerogative. Formal prerogative Orders in Council relating to the civil service are, however, few: the main one was promulgated in 1995. Regulations, minutes and circulars issued formerly by the Treasury, between 1968 and 1981 by the Civil Service Department, and since then by the Office of the Minister for the Civil Service, have been the main substance of the law and custom of the civil service; they are supplemented by a few statutes (for example, the Superannuation Acts) and judicial decisions (for example, on civil liability, tenure of office). The Secretary of the Cabinet is also Head of the Home Civil Service. There is a separate Head of the Diplomatic Service (the Permanent Under-Secretary of State to the Foreign and Commonwealth Office). The Civil Service Commissioners are mainly responsible for the recruitment and selection of civil servants by competitive examination and interview. Departments also recruit their own specialist and temporary staff by other methods; promotions within the service, except at the very highest levels, are matters reserved for individual Departments.[70] Top appointments

---

68 Sir Douglas was raised to the peerage as Lord Croham on his retirement: his epistle is immortalized under the name of the 'Croham Directive'. For the text, see 942 HC Deb. *691–4* (written answers 26 January 1978).

69 See Cm 2290 (1993).

70 An executive agency, Recruitment and Assessment Services, administers recruitment and selection of civil servants for the Civil Service Commissioners.

to Permanent Under-Secretary and Deputy Under-Secretary are made by the Prime Minister on the recommendation of the Head of the Home Civil Service, who is assisted by the Senior Appointments Selection Committee, composed of senior Permanent Under-Secretaries and a few senior professional officers.

The elaborate procedural and substantive rules relating to conditions of service, promotions and tenure have been evolved to a large extent by means of collective agreements reached between senior officials and trade-union representatives. If agreement cannot be reached, the matter may be committed to an arbitral body or the Government may take a unilateral decision. In any event, the system is technically only advisory.[71] The rules governing 'established' (or permanent) civil servants are published in the Civil Service Management Code.

The recommendations of the Fulton Committee on the Civil Service[72] gave impetus to change. The Civil Service Department was created soon afterwards. It was abolished in 1981, responsibility for civil service manpower, pay and superannuation returning to the Treasury, while responsibility for organization, management, recruitment policy, training, personnel matters and for overall efficiency was transferred to a new Management and Personnel Office within the Cabinet Office. In 1987 the functions of the Management and Personnel Office were divided between the Treasury and a new Office of the Minister for the Civil Service, the Management and Personnel Office being abolished.[73] The Office of Public Service within the Cabinet Office carries out routine tasks under a separate Minister on behalf of the Minister for the Civil Service. In 1970 a Civil Service College for advanced training was opened. Within the service, separate grades have been merged or grouped together; stratification has diminished, promotions and transfers have been facilitated. Special arrangements have been made for the compulsory retirement of the inefficient. Modern methods of job analysis, personnel management, planning and budgetary accounting, bandied around by their abstruse initials, are all the rage. Fixed-term contracts have been introduced for some civil servants.[74]

The Heath Government also introduced a small top-level Central Policy Review Staff, headed by a Labour peer and industrialist, to advise Ministers on forward planning, the allocation of priorities and issues cutting across

71 Some matters are dealt with by direct negotiation with the various staff associations.
72 Cmnd 3638 (1968).
73 SI 1987, No. 2039. The Office of the Minister for the Civil Service is a sub-department of the Cabinet Office.
74 See Cm 2627 (1994).

departmental boundaries, such as the Concorde project, sponsored research, the role of the City of London, and policy on energy, population and the regions. Mrs Thatcher abolished the CPRS in 1983.

A major initiative on the management of the civil service was started in 1988 – the 'Next Steps' initiative.[75] The main aim is to ensure that to the greatest practicable extent executive functions of government (as distinct from policy formulation) are carried out by 'Next Steps' or executive agencies within Government Departments. Responsibility for day-to-day operations of each of these agencies is delegated to a chief executive, who is responsible for management within a framework of policy objectives and resources set by the relevant Minister, in consultation with the Treasury. Each agency is accountable to Parliament through its Minister, who is, however, expected to let the chief executive manage. The agencies' staff remain civil servants. The first agencies included unemployment offices and jobcentres, the Driver and Vehicle Licensing Centre at Swansea, the Passport Office, Her Majesty's Stationery Office, and the Meteorological Office. About three-quarters of all civil servants are working in executive agencies; it is envisaged that eventually the number of policy-makers in the civil service could be as few as 20,000. There are over a hundred executive agencies. Ministers who are responsible for the management of the home civil service may delegate personnel matters to others under the Civil Service (Management Functions) Act 1992.

The remarkably high degree of security enjoyed by established civil servants, surpassed only by the Judiciary, was not recognized by rules applied in the courts. In the eyes of the common law, civil servants held their offices at the pleasure of the Crown. Their offices would be vacated summarily at any time for any reason that Her Majesty thought fit.

The common-law rule that a civil servant has no right of recourse to the courts for wrongful dismissal is reasonably clear.[76] But what is the basis of the rule; and are there any exceptions to it? It has sometimes been said that a civil servant enjoys a legal status but is not employed under a contract.[77] Even if this is so, it would not preclude the officer from recovering damages for wrongful dismissal, or, indeed, a declaration that he was entitled to

---

75 See the Prime Minister's statement at 127 HC Deb. 1149 (18 February 1988); and see 187 HC Deb. 734–6 (written answers 13 March 1992); *The Next Steps: Review 1995* (Cm 3164 (1996)). See also Drewry [1989] *Public Law* 505, [1990] *Public Law* 322.
76 See, for example, *Shenton* v. *Smith* [1895] AC 229 (PC); *Terrell* v. *Secretary of State for the Colonies* [1953] 2 QB 482. But see below on the statutory position.
77 See Blair (1958) 21 *Mod. L. Rev.* 265, [1958] *Public Law* 32.

reinstatement.[78] And at least one decision of the House of Lords has rested ambiguously on the presupposition that the relationship between civil servants and the Crown is contractual.[79]

Again, the fact that the power to appoint and regulate the conduct of civil servants is derived from the royal prerogative is not inconsistent with the existence of a contract of employment. The Crown can enter into binding contracts (for example, for the supply of food) in the exercise of its prerogative functions.

Yet, assuming that the relationship is contractual, it appears that the right to dismiss at pleasure cannot be displaced by engagement for a fixed period,[80] or by official circulars[81] or non-statutory regulations[82] laying down a regular procedure to be followed before dismissal. It is indeed doubtful whether any ostensibly contractual term inconsistent with the power of the Crown to dismiss at pleasure (for example, a statement that a Crown servant would be dismissible only 'for cause',[83] or for inability or misbehaviour) would be endorsed by a court, unless, of course, the restriction on the Crown's freedom to dispense with a servant at will had been imposed by statute.[84] Now, if the power to dismiss at pleasure were to be construed as an ordinary implied term of contract, it could be displaced by an express term of a contractual engagement incompatible with it.[85] If it cannot be so displaced, this must be either because the Crown is incapacitated from fettering its future executive discretion in this way[86] (so that an incompatible undertaking would simply be *ultra vires* and void)[87] or because it is a special kind of implied term, imported by precedent and for reasons of public policy into all engagements with the Crown irrespective of their wording. These rationalizations of the rule are unconvincing and cast doubt on the content of the rule. Public policy

---

78 cf. *Vine* v. *National Dock Labour Board* [1957] AC 488 (dock labourers); *Ridge* v. *Baldwin* [1964] AC 40 (chief constables).

79 *Sutton* v. *Att.-Gen.* (1923) 39 TLR 294. The point was not argued and the precedent is therefore *sub silentio*; but all the Law Lords assumed that the engagement in question was contractual. See now *Kodeeswaran* v. *Att.-Gen. of Ceylon* [1970] AC 1111 (PC) supporting this view.

80 *Dunn* v. *R.* [1896] 1 QB 116.

81 *Rodwell* v. *Thomas* [1944] KB 596. But see *Sutton* v. *Att.-Gen.* (note 79); and Blair [1958] *Public Law* at 43–6.

82 *Riordan* v. *War Office* [1959] 1 WLR 1046.

83 Though cf. *Reilly* v. *R.* [1934] AC 176 at 179–80 (dicta); *Robertson* v. *Minister of Pensions* [1949] 1 KB 227 at 231 (dictum).

84 As in *Gould* v. *Stuart* [1896] AC 575 (PC). See also below.

85 See dicta cited in note 83, above; and see *Sutton* v. *Att.-Gen.* (1923) 39 TLR 294.

86 cf. *Rederiaktiebolaget Amphitrite* v. *R.* [1921] 3 KB 500; pp. 600–601, below.

87 See *Riordan's* case [1959] 1 WLR at 1053; *Rodwell* v. *Thomas* [1944] KB at 602.

may indeed suggest that an unsuitable or redundant civil servant should be dispensable at any time when the interests of the State so demand; but this merely means that a court of law ought not to award a declaration that a dismissed civil servant is entitled to reinstatement; it does not imply that he should be denied monetary compensation for wrongful dismissal.

The Industrial Relations Act 1971 made an important addition to the law, which was subsequently strengthened and is now contained in the Employment Rights Act 1996. If a civil servant is unfairly dismissed an industrial tribunal may order that he be reinstated or re-engaged, and that he receive compensation.[88]

The Court of Appeal has held[89] that a decision of the Civil Service Appeal Board (which had confirmed that a former civil servant in the Inland Revenue had been fairly dismissed) was susceptible to judicial review by the courts. The court accepted that the applicant held his post at the Crown's pleasure, having no contract of employment with it, and decided that the usual remedy for a civil servant who believed that he had been unfairly dismissed was to go to an industrial tribunal. That decision was not followed, however, by the Divisional Court in a subsequent case[90] on the ground that a civil servant, employed in the Lord Chancellor's Department, *was* so employed under a contract of service. The essential ingredients of a contract (offer, acceptance, intention to create legal relations) existed, and that displaced the statement in the Civil Service Pay and Conditions Code (now the Civil Service Management Code) that the relationship was not contractual. He could therefore pursue private law remedies (and could not seek judicial review) to challenge disciplinary proceedings which had been taken against him.

The salaries of civil servants are determined by references to arbitral bodies. There have been judicial dicta to the effect that a civil servant has no legally enforceable right to his pay.[91] Even if this is a correct statement

---

88 Employment Rights Act 1996 ss. 111–32, 191. The concept of 'unfair' dismissal is related to non-observance of the principles laid down in the Code of Practice prepared by the Advisory, Conciliation and Arbitration Service. A Minister may exclude a Crown employee from the protection of the Act on grounds of national security: s. 193. The Foreign and Commonwealth Secretary did so in relation to employees at the Government Communication Headquarters at Cheltenham in 1984; see *Council of Civil Service Unions* v. *Minister for the Civil Service* [1985] AC 374.

89 R. v. *Civil Service Appeal Board, ex p. Bruce* [1989] 2 All ER 907.

90 R. v. *Lord Chancellor's Department, ex p. Nagle* [1992] 1 All ER 897. See also Fredman and Morris [1991] *Public Law* 485.

91 *Mulvenna* v. *Admiralty* 1926 SC 842 at 859; *Lucas* v. *Lucas* [1943] P. 68 at 78 (criticized by Logan (1945) *LQR* 240).

of the common-law rule regarding future payments, it is now clear that at common law a civil servant is entitled to recover any part of his salary withheld from him in respect of the work he has already done.[92]

The superannuation of civil servants is regulated by statute, but before 1972 the wording of the legislation presupposed a lack of judicially enforceable entitlement to the rates of superannuation prescribed or indeed to any pension at all.[93] Questions of law arising out of civil service superannuation schemes are now potentially justiciable.[94]

Security procedures[95]

The growth of peacetime espionage, particularly in connection with nuclear research and technology, led to the adoption of special security measures within the civil service in 1948. Following the defection of two senior Foreign Service officials, Burgess and Maclean, to the Soviet Union, and the conviction of some Crown servants, including George Blake, an important controller of British agents,[96] for espionage, committees were appointed to investigate and report on security procedures. Their recommendations[97] resulted in the introduction of new procedures. Typically, all the rules rest on a non-statutory basis.

The procedures have been applied to only a small proportion of civil servants, holding positions where personal unreliability might give rise to serious risks to national security. They have been more selective (though not necessarily more efficacious) than those adopted in the United States.

In 1948 it was decided that civil servants with Communist or Fascist affiliations should not be employed in work vital to the security of the State. Where practicable they would be transferred to non-secret work. From a provisional decision by a Minister that an official ought to be transferred or removed on security grounds, an appeal would lie to an

92 *Kodeeswaran* v. *Att.-Gen. of Ceylon* [1970] AC 1111, disapproving dicta to the contrary effect and applying general principles.
93 Superannuation Act 1965, s. 79. See *Nixon* v. *Att.-Gen.* [1931] AC 184.
94 Superannuation Act 1972, s. 2(6).
95 See Harry Street, *Freedom, the Individual and the Law* (5th edn, 1982), pp. 236–47; D. G. T. Williams, *Not in the Public Interest* (1965), chs. 3, 7, 9; Geoffrey Wilson, *Cases and Materials on Constitutional and Administrative Law* (2nd edn, 1976), pp. 89–98.
96 *R.* v. *Blake* [1962] 2 QB 377. For his activities he was sentenced to three consecutive terms of imprisonment of fourteen years each. He escaped from prison to eastern Europe in 1967, and was subsequently awarded the Order of Lenin.
97 Cmd 9715 (1955) (the Privy Counsellors' Report); Cmnd 1681 (1962) (the Radcliffe Report).

advisory tribunal, the 'Three Advisers', who would meet in private. In 1952 civil servants employed on top secret work became subject to a more rigorous form of scrutiny, known as 'positive vetting', extending to general character defects; no reference to the Three Advisers would lie from an executive decision in this context. High-level reports on security measures, published in 1955 and 1962,[98] emphasized that personality or behavioural defects or disorders, such as homosexual conduct, alcoholism and drug addiction (which might render an official vulnerable to blackmail or subject to financial temptation), as well as known political affiliations or sympathies, were indicators of security risks; but precautionary measures in such cases were left to departmental action. Security procedures were modified in 1957; and in 1964 a new, and almost inevitably non-statutory, organ, the Security Commission, under the chairmanship of a superior judge, was set up to investigate, at the Prime Minister's request, breaches of security in the public service, and to report and advise generally on security arrangements.[99]

Mrs Thatcher announced a further extension of security measures in 1985.[100] They applied to all those employed on work the nature of which is vital to the security of the State, whether they be civil servants or employees of private companies. Moreover, Ministers could bar trade-union officials from any Government establishment or refuse to negotiate with them because they might need access to classified information during the course of those negotiations.

With the collapse of Communism in the Soviet Union and eastern Europe, and given the continued threat posed by terrorism, a further revision of procedures was implemented in 1990.[101] The three tiers of vetting have become five: (a) reliability checks (for civil servants with, for example, unescorted access to buildings containing highly classified material), (b) counter-terrorist checks (for use, for example, where the civil servant is employed in proximity to public figures), (c) 'positive vetting (S)' and (d) 'positive vetting (TS)' (to be used, respectively, with those having access to secret information, and to top secret information), and (e) extended positive vetting (for members of the Security Services). In 1994 positive vetting (S) was replaced by a security check which includes a financial investigation; and positive vetting (TS) together with extended positive

---

98 See above, note 97.
99 The other members of this standing commission are judges and very senior ex-members of the civil service and the armed forces. See Leigh and Lustgarten [1991] *Public Law* 215.
100 76 HC Deb. *621* (written answers 3 April 1985); 78 HC Deb. 895–902 (9 May 1985).
101 See the Prime Minister's statement at 177 HC Deb. *159–161* (written answers 24 July 1990).

vetting were merged and restyled as developed vetting.[102] People subject to levels (c) to (e) are told that they are being vetted. The guiding principle now is that no one will be employed in connection with work which is vital to the security of the State who (i) is, or has been, involved in any way with espionage, terrorism, sabotage, or actions intended to overthrow or undermine parliamentary democracy by political, industrial or violent means or (ii) is, or has recently been, a member of or associated with any organization which has advocated those activities, or (iii) is susceptible to pressure from any such organization, or from a foreign intelligence service or hostile power, or (iv) suffers from any character defect which might expose him to blackmail from such sources. Out go the Communist and Fascist demons of the cold war and earlier; a much sharper emphasis is placed on the terrorist menace.

Proceedings before the Three Advisers (two of whom are normally retired civil servants with a High Court judge as chairman, and whose findings are not binding on the Minister) do not conform to the standards of natural justice imposed on a judicial tribunal. After the Minister has decided that a *prima facie* case has been made out – there is no preliminary hearing – particulars of the allegations are disclosed to the Advisers, but the civil servant will not be supplied with details which would reveal the sources of the information against him. The civil servant may appear in person, but he cannot be represented by a lawyer or anybody else; he is merely entitled to be accompanied by a friend when he is presenting his opening statement. He may call witnesses to testify to his character and record, but he is unable to cross-examine the anonymous and invisible informants. The advice tendered by the tribunal to the Minister is not revealed.

This procedure may well be 'a travesty of justice as Englishmen are accustomed to it'.[103] The Franks Committee had insisted[104] that the proceedings of statutory administrative tribunals should be characterized by 'openness, fairness and impartiality'; it is questionable whether any of these criteria is met by the machinery outlined above, though it can be assumed that Ministers and the Advisers do their best to act fairly. But to speak of a travesty belittles the fact that even the most lenient security programme must rest on a harsh assumption: that measures injurious to

---

102 See the Prime Minister's statement at 251 HC Deb. *764–6* (written answers 15 December 1994).
103 Street, op. cit., p. 244.
104 Cmnd 218 (1957), p. 5.

possibly innocent persons will have to be taken on the basis of reasonable suspicions, suspicions insufficient to justify a prosecution. The balance will inevitably be delicate. We have no means of evaluating the soundness of the decisions that have in fact been taken, or how much harm might be done if the 'defendant' or the representative he would prefer to choose were to be supplied with full particulars of the case against him and were to be given the right to confront informants. It is worth mentioning that in the first thirteen years of the special security programme, only twenty-four civil servants were dismissed and twenty-four others were induced to resign on security grounds, and eighty-three were transferred to non-secret work.[105] During the two world wars, thousands of innocent and innocuous persons were placed in preventive detention as a result of policy decisions and excesses of executive zeal.

Security precautions extend beyond the civil service and the Atomic Energy Authority.[106] Government contracts placed with private firms for secret work include terms which have the effect of barring any employee of the firm who is designated by the Minister as a security risk from having access to secret matters. In 1955 ICI dismissed their assistant solicitor because the Government, on ostensibly flimsy grounds, refused to place with them any further secret contract to which he would have access. Such an employee is now able to have his case referred to the Three Advisers.[107]

Special advisers

In the 1970s individual Ministers started the practice of appointing one or two personal advisers.[108] They are now in two groups.[109] 'Political advisers' are not civil servants and are paid from party, not public, funds. Their functions are to give Ministers advice on implementing their party manifesto, and information about party opinion. 'Special advisers' are civil servants with terms of appointment similar to those of other civil servants, who give independent, non-party political advice. All advisers leave office

---

105 Joelson [1963] *Public Law* 51, at 56–7.

106 Under the First Schedule to the Atomic Energy Authority Act 1954, the Authority may not terminate the employment of any of its employees on security grounds without the consent of the Minister (now the Secretary of State for Energy).

107 For non-statutory references of politically sensitive immigration 'appeals' to the Three Advisers, see ch. 20.

108 See Mitchell (1978) 56 *Public Administration* 87; Hoskyns (1983) 36 *Parliamentary Affairs* 137 at 146; Harold Wilson, *The Governance of Britain* (1976), Appendix V.

109 See Mrs Thatcher's explanation in 58 HC Deb. *155–6* (written answers 10 April 1984).

with the Minister. The aim is to provide a Minister with mainly political advice about his responsibilities, especially in the carrying out of his party's manifesto programme. The Treasury and Civil Service Select Committee has recommended an extension of this idea, so that all Ministers would have policy units staffed by non-civil servants.[110]

110 See HC 92 (1985–6), para. 5.

CHAPTER 11

Constitutional Position of the Armed Forces

STRUCTURE AND STATUS[1]

The armed forces are instruments of the central government, equipped, disciplined and trained for the exercise of physical force in the interests of the State. In a number of states the military servants of the State have become masters. No constitutional or legal device can afford a guarantee against a military take-over when the political structure is in a condition of decadence or collapse. The British rules relating to the status of the armed forces presuppose a set of public attitudes and assumptions towards the roles of the civil and military powers within the State. The primacy of the civil power is a sociological as well as a constitutional fact. No British Government has been overthrown by military force since 1688. No senior officer of the regular armed forces has ever been Prime Minister except the Duke of Wellington (1828–30, 1834), and he had long since retired from active service.

The feudal levy, supplied by military tenants of the Crown, was abolished in 1660. The pre-Norman *fyrd*, a national levy, had been transformed into the militia, and it was regulated by statute in 1661. But such was the rancour aroused by James II's use of troops that the Bill of Rights 1689 prohibited the raising or maintenance of a standing army within the realm in time of peace without the consent of Parliament. Since a regular armed force was necessary at that time, a Mutiny Act, giving a requisite parliamentary authority, was passed but was limited to a year's duration. Annual Mutiny Acts were passed for nearly two hundred years. In 1881 an Army Act was passed, embodying rules of military law which had previously been embodied in the Mutiny Acts and articles of war.[2] When a separate air

---

1 This chapter will not deal with the reserve forces (see Reserve Forces Act 1996) or the auxiliary, territorial or women's services.
2 Till the eighteenth century, articles of war for the governance of soldiers had been issued only in time of war.

force was created in 1917, a similar Act was passed. These were kept alive for periods of twelve months by Army and Air Force (Annual) Acts. In 1955 the Army and Air Force Acts were revised and consolidated, and the system of annual renewal was modified; instead of an annual Act of Parliament (the debates on which provided the Opposition with a useful opportunity for consuming legislative time) they would be renewed from year to year by Orders in Council, which would be subject to approval in draft by both Houses of Parliament. After five years of renewal, however, a fresh Act of Parliament is required. The current enabling statute is the Armed Forces Act 1996; it will expire in 2001 before which a new Act will, no doubt, be passed.

The maintenance of a navy, which was seldom, if ever, regarded as an instrument of royal oppression, has never needed parliamentary approval. The navy exists by virtue of the royal prerogative; indeed, the prerogative power to impress seafaring men into the navy has never been expressly abrogated. But naval discipline is dependent on an Act of Parliament (the Navy Discipline Act 1957, as amended), and the money needed for the navy, as for the other armed services, has to be determined by the Government and authorized by Parliament. Parliamentary debate on any of the armed services may take place on the presentation of the annual estimates, the introduction of supply legislation, and any other legislative measures relating to them. Since 1971 the Naval Discipline Act has been renewable in the same way as the Armed Forces Act.

How far the army and the air force are regulated by prerogative is an interesting but obscure question. The disposition of the forces[3] and the commissioning of officers certainly fall within the scope of the prerogative. The enforcement of military discipline and the trial of offences under military law are regulated by statute; and statutory regulations made by the Defence Council may prescribe terms and conditions of service.[4] Pay and pensions are determined by royal warrants under the prerogative. Although the relationship between a member of the forces and his employer, the Crown, has a distinct statutory flavour, there is ample judicial authority for the proposition that, save where a sentence has been imposed by a court martial or other statutory disciplinary authority, the relations between the soldier and the Crown are not cognizable by the courts. Not only is he

3 *Chandler* v. *DPP* [1964] AC 763. It is most unlikely to be justiciable even after *Council of Civil Service Unions* v. *Minister for the Civil Service* [1985] AC 374 (see above, p. 136).
4 Armed Forces Act 1966, s. 2.

disabled from suing for wrongful reduction of pay[5] or arrears of pay,[6] but he cannot sue for wrongful dismissal[7] even, it seems, in the face of inconsistent statutory or contractual provisions; nor can an officer resign his commission without leave.[8] An ex-member of the forces cannot sue for his pension. The rules are based partly on the prerogative and partly on an overriding judge-made concept of public policy which frowns upon litigation between the soldier and his employer. On the other hand, the Crown can hold the soldier to the terms of his enlistment to serve for a term of years unless he purchases his discharge, and it exercises this power.

Central government organization for defence is now based partly on prerogative but mainly on statute.[9] There are a Secretary of State and two Ministers of State, one for the Armed Forces, the other for Defence Procurement, each having a parliamentary under-secretary of state. Within the Ministry of Defence there is located a Procurement Executive, using up-to-date managerial and accounting techniques.[10]

There is a chiefs of staff committee, composed of the Chief of Defence Staff and the chiefs of staff of the three services; they have a right of direct access to the Prime Minister and are occasionally asked to attend Cabinet meetings. The detailed regulation of the services is entrusted to a statutory Defence Council consisting of the Secretary of State and the Ministers of State, the chiefs of staff, the Permanent Under-Secretary of State to the Ministry of Defence and the Chief Executive for Procurement. For each of the three services there is a separate Defence Board. At Cabinet level there is a Defence and Overseas Policy Committee, presided over by the Prime Minister; the Secretary of State for Foreign and Commonwealth Affairs, the Chancellor of the Exchequer and the Home Secretary are among its members; the service chiefs of staff are frequently invited to attend. The Security Service (MI5, which is responsible for internal security) and the Secret Intelligence Service (MI6, which gathers intelligence from

---

5 *Worthington* v. *Robinson* (1897) 75 LT (NS) 446 (an action against a superior officer); *Leaman* v. *R.* [1920] 3 KB 663; cf. Logan (1945) 61 *LQR* at 260.

6 *Ex p. Napier* (1852) 21 LJQB 332; cf. Glanville Williams, *Crown Proceedings*, p. 69.

7 *Re Poe* (1833) 5 B. & Ad. 681; *Grant* v. *Secretary of State for India* (1877) 2 CPD 445; *De Dohse* v. *R.* (1886) 3 TLR 114. The Employment Rights Act 1996, ss. 192, 193 apply employment law generally to the armed forces of the Crown, but it may be denied to them by ministerial certificate on grounds of national security.

8 *Marks* v. *Commonwealth of Australia* (1964) 111 CLR 549; *O'Day* v. *Commonwealth*, ibid., 599.

9 See Cmnd 2097 (1963); Defence (Transfer of Functions) Act 1964 and statutory Orders in Council made thereunder.

10 Cmnd 4641 (1971); Colin Turpin, *Government Contracts* (1972), pp. 122–3.

outside the country) have intimate links with the Prime Minister, the Secretary to the Cabinet, the Ministry of Defence, the Foreign Office, the Home Office and the Special Branch of the Metropolitan Police.[11]

In Britain, as in a large number of other countries, there is a tendency for regular officers in the armed services to show a profound distaste for party politics or to hold views sympathetic to the far right wing in politics; or to entertain both attitudes simultaneously, if sometimes unwittingly. But it is part of the service tradition to accept a position of subordination to the civil power – a tradition rudely interrupted by the Curragh incident in Ireland early in 1914,[12] but unbroken since then[13] – and although the British public has often been disenchanted with its political leaders, it is averse from turning to the regular armed forces for salvation. Even in times of civil disorder within the realm, the forces must normally (as we shall see in a later chapter)[14] act only under the direction of the civil authorities.

MILITARY LAW AND THE CIVIL LAW

As Dicey emphasized, a soldier[15] is, for most purposes, a civilian in uniform. Although he is subject to certain special rules of law, he is not exempt from the general law of the land.[16]

Those rules which differentiate soldiers from other sections of the community are a consequence of their special responsibilities. Regular soldiers, like civil servants, are disqualified from membership of the House of Commons.[17] The regulations of the service restricting the political activities of members of the forces are stricter than the corresponding rules for civil

11 See below, p. 449.
12 cf. Kenneth Rose, *King George V* (1984), pp. 153–7 (when fifty-eight officers in Dublin, including a General, purported to resign their commissions rather than take part in coercing Ulster into an undivided self-governing Ireland).
13 It is possible, however, that the Wilson Government's decision not to attempt to crush by force the rebellion in Southern Rhodesia in or after November 1965 was partly influenced by doubts as to the morale of the troops. The Defence Secretary of the day gave the Chief of the General Staff 'a severe warning' about 'some mutinous mutterings among senior army officers about British policy towards Rhodesia': Denis Healey, *The Time of My Life* (1989), p. 332.
14 See ch. 24.
15 'Soldier' is here used to include members of the navy, the air force and the marines, as well as the army, subject to verbal modifications.
16 *Introduction to the Study of the Law of the Constitution* (10th edn), ch. 9. See also *Lynch v. Fitzgerald* [1938] IR 382.
17 House of Commons Disqualification Act 1975, s. 1(1).

servants. A regular soldier is absolutely prohibited from standing as a parliamentary candidate. In practice a serviceman who applied for nomination papers as a parliamentary candidate would be given his discharge by the service authorities: he must, however, first satisfy a special advisory committee as to his *bona fides*.[18]

Serving members of the forces are entitled to vote by post or proxy at elections; they are exempt from jury service; they may make informal wills while on actual military service.

Serving members of the armed forces are subject to military law as well as the ordinary law of the land. Military law is a readily ascertainable body of rules, collected in the official *Manual of Military Law*.[19] It is primarily a body of criminal law, contained in statutes and subordinate legislative instruments. It must be sharply distinguished from martial law, which is not a crystallized code of rules at all but a state of affairs in which there has been a complete breakdown of civil authority and the governance of the populace is handed over to or assumed by a military commander.[20]

In the United Kingdom, certain very serious criminal offences committed by members of the forces are triable only by the civil (i.e. ordinary criminal) courts. Other offences are triable by court martial. A court martial is composed of military officers sitting without a jury; they are assisted by a judge advocate, a barrister who sums up the evidence and advises the court on questions of law. Minor offences are triable summarily by commanding officers. A number of offences under military law have no equivalent in the ordinary criminal law – for example, conduct to the prejudice of good order and military discipline.

Till 1951 the enforcement of military discipline and the criminal law by courts-martial was largely a self-contained system; only superior officers and, in the last resort, the Army Council (as it then was) could review a conviction of a person subject to military law or the sentence imposed on him, with an ultimate right of recourse to the royal prerogative of mercy. True, the High Court would issue habeas corpus to direct the release of a person detained by the military authorities if he was not subject to military law, or certiorari to quash a decision if jurisdiction had been manifestly exceeded.[21] But although the High Court was capable of exercising the same supervisory jurisdiction (by orders of certiorari, prohibition and

18 R. Blackburn, *The Electoral System in Britain* (1995), p. 172.
19 See also Stuart-Smith (1969) 85 *LQR* 478.
20 See ch. 24.
21 As in *R v. Wormwood Scrubs Prison Governor, ex p. Boydell* [1948] 2 KB 193.

mandamus) over courts martial as over other inferior statutory tribunals, in practice it was extremely reluctant to intervene even when grave procedural irregularities had been established;[22] the judges affirmed that they would interfere if the 'civil rights' of an individual had been infringed, but were conspicuously vague in explaining what they meant by the civil rights of a soldier.[23] A similar reluctance to appear to prejudice the administration of military discipline in any way whatsoever was exhibited by the courts in other contexts: in the decisions on dismissal and pay; in decisions that no action would lie against members of a court martial or a commanding officer for false imprisonment or malicious prosecution while acting within their jurisdiction even if actuated by improper motives and lacking reasonable cause,[24] and that reports written by a superior officer upon another officer in the course of duty[25] and the proceedings of a military court of inquiry enjoyed absolute privilege in the law of defamation.[26] Military discipline and justice in the courts seemed to be uneasy bedfellows.

Some of the older decisions on immunity from civil liability may still be good law. But the administration of military discipline is no longer a self-contained system. In 1951 a Courts-Martial Appeal Court, composed of High Court judges and Scottish and Northern Ireland judges of like status, was constituted and given jurisdiction to hear appeals from courts martial after internal review procedures had been exhausted. Thus was reasserted the primacy of the civil power. Recourse to the common-law supervisory remedies (other than habeas corpus) became largely superfluous; in any event these remedies have territorial limitations, whereas the jurisdiction of the new court extends to courts martial held in any part of the world.

Under the present law[27] appeal will lie to the court, after military remedies have been exhausted, against a conviction by a court martial. Leave of the Appeal Court must be obtained. A further appeal will lie to the House of Lords at the instance of the accused or the Defence Council (the respondent) if the Appeal Court or the Lords give leave and the Appeal Court certifies

22 As in *R* v. *Army Council, ex p. Ravenscroft* [1917] 2 KB 504; *R* v. *Secretary of State for War, ex p. Martyn* [1949] 2 All ER 242; *R.* v. *OC Depot Battalion, RASC Colchester, ex p. Elliott,* ibid. 373.

23 See *Re Mansergh* (1861) 1 B. & S. 400, and *Martyn*'s and *Elliott*'s cases, above.

24 *Heddon* v. *Evans* (1919) 35 TLR 642. See also *Johnstone* v. *Sutton* (1786) 1 TR 493, 510, 784; *Fraser* v. *Balfour* (1918) 34 TLR 502.

25 *Dawkins* v. *Paulet* (1869) LR 5 QB 94.

26 *Dawkins* v. *Rokeby* (1875) LR 7 HL 744.

27 Consolidated in the Courts-Martial (Appeals) Act 1968.

int of law of general public importance is involved. The royal
_ative of mercy is preserved.

SUPERIOR ORDERS

Before 1966 a member of the forces might incur double jeopardy. If he
were convicted of an offence under military law, he could still be charged
with and convicted of the same offence in a civil court, though the latter
was to take into account any sentence imposed by the military authorities.
(Conviction by a civil court precluded trial for the same offence by court
martial, though the facts constituting the civil offence might give rise to a
separate *disciplinary* charge under military law.) Since 1966 the anomaly has
been largely removed. Conviction by a court martial precludes trial by a
civil court for any offence that is substantially the same.[28]

A member of the forces may nevertheless stand in double jeopardy in a
different context. If, in obedience to superior orders, he commits a criminal
offence or a civil wrong (for example, wounding a rioter in circumstances
where this is not reasonably justifiable) he may incur legal liability before
the ordinary courts. If, on the other hand, he refuses to obey an order
because he believes it to be unlawful, he may be court-martialled. It may
be said that the dilemma is unreal because it is not an offence under military
law to disobey an unlawful command; a soldier cannot be convicted for
disobedience unless the command was lawful. But since a soldier is a
member of a disciplined force conditioned to the habit of obedience, and
since, moreover, a court martial may well hold the command to be lawful,
the dilemma and the risk can be very real. Is it reasonable, then, to assert
that obedience to superior orders can never be a defence to an unlawful
act in proceedings before the courts? The Nuremberg War Crimes trials
proceeded on the footing that superior orders were no defence, though
they might be pleaded in mitigation of punishment. This general proposition
is adopted in modern editions of the *Manual of Military Law*, though it is
conceded that obedience to superior orders may afford a defence to particular
offences, for instance, negativing the existence of criminal intent where
this is relevant. Doubts as to the content of the rule still persist. In a
much-quoted South African case, decided during the Boer War,[29] it was

---

28 See Armed Forces Act 1966, ss. 25, 26, 35.
29 *R* v. *Smith* (1900) Cape of Good Hope SC 561. See also *Keighley* v. *Bell* (1886) 4 F.
& F. 763 at 790, *per* Willes J.

held that an honest belief in the lawfulness of an order to shoot an African civilian was a good defence to a charge of murder, the order not being manifestly illegal. The dangers of such a principle are illustrated by the facts of the case; and there is no general rule of criminal law that a reasonable mistake of law is a defence.[30] Yet a reasonable mistake induced by an order given by a military superior to do an act which, in the circumstances, is not manifestly illegal may in some situations be akin to the operation of duress on a soldier, and can fairly be analysed in that fashion. The civil liability of the soldier will not necessarily be governed by the same considerations, particularly where vicarious liability can be affixed to the Crown.

CIVILIANS AND COURTS MARTIAL

Courts martial outside the United Kingdom have jurisdiction over a wide range of civilian dependants and employees of the forces. Their jurisdiction extends not only to all criminal offences under English law but also to certain offences of a disciplinary nature (for example, breach of a local curfew). The jurisdiction embraces criminal offences in respect of which United Kingdom courts have no extraterritorial jurisdiction, and others which, if committed in the United Kingdom, would be triable only in a civil court.

This is not an entirely satisfactory state of affairs: pre-trial safeguards are not as efficacious as in a civil court; guilt and sentence are determined by a simple majority of a panel of military officers who will hardly ever have legal qualifications; the accused will often lack the services of a lawyer to defend him.[31] The existence of the Courts-Martial Appeal Court is an ameliorating factor but cannot cure every defect.[32] The Armed Forces Act 1976, sections 6 to 9 and schedules 3 and 4, meet these objections to some extent. Standing Civilian Courts have been established, consisting of a 'magistrate' – an assistant to the Judge Advocate General who will have knowledge of the law – and not more than two assessors drawn from a panel of civilians and military officers. An accused has the right of appeal to a court martial, or to elect to be tried by court martial instead of by the

---

30 See J. C. Smith and Brian Hogan, *Criminal Law* (8th edn, 1996), pp. 222–4. cf. Ashworth [1974] *Crim. LR* 562.
31 The accused is, however, entitled to be represented by a defending officer.
32 cf. the position under American constitutional law as interpreted by the Supreme Court of the United States: *Reid* v. *Covert* 354 US 1 (1957), and subsequent cases holding that trial of civilian dependants and employees by court martial was unconstitutional.

Standing Civilian Court. Regulations have been made by the Secretary of State which deal with the procedure of the Court, including the question of the representation of an accused person before it.[33]

Under the Visiting Forces Act 1952, members of visiting Commonwealth forces, and of such other countries as may be designated by Order in Council (in pursuance of an international agreement for common defence), stationed in the United Kingdom, and their civilian components, are exempt from the jurisdiction of the ordinary criminal courts in respect of offences.[34] committed on duty or against the persons of forces personnel or the property of the forces and their personnel; the operation of the Act has been extended to certain British dependencies. In addition, tort claims are settled by special arrangements and are not determinable by the ordinary courts unless the claimant is denied satisfaction through administrative channels.

33 See generally Rowe and Jetha (1977) 40 *Mod. L. Rev.* 444.
34 See note 32 on constitutional limitation of the jurisdiction of American courts martial over civilians – a point not yet established in 1952, when the agreement was made and the Act was passed. American courts martial try American servicemen for those criminal offences excluded from the jurisdiction of the local courts.

PART THREE

PARLIAMENT AND LEGISLATION

Chapter 12 deals first with some of the basic rules about the working of Parliament (for example, adjournment, prorogation and dissolution), and then with the general functions of parliamentary institutions within the scheme of the British constitution. Once again we observe the close interrelationship of the Executive and the Legislature. But although the Government is the dominant force in Parliament and although legislation is primarily a function of the Government in office, it is an over-simplification to speak of Cabinet or prime ministerial dictatorship.

The next two chapters are about the House of Commons. First, in chapter 13 there are the rules relating to the right to vote, the delimitation of constituencies, the conduct of electoral campaigns and the system of voting (a very controversial topic: a comment is offered on some alternative systems), legal disqualifications for membership, the selection of candidates, and ways of disputing the validity of elections. Chapter 13 also examines electoral law. Chapter 14 considers the functions and procedure of the House of Commons, including the process of legislation, discussion of financial matters, scrutiny of policy and administration, and the roles of backbenchers. The machinery for determining the levels of MPs' pay and allowances is noted. In these two chapters the roles of national political parties are far from ignored. Chapter 14 includes comments on European Union legislation, and the effects of European Union membership on financial legislation.

There follows a chapter on the House of Lords and the means of resolving conflicts between the two Houses; this includes a review of the changes which have been made in the membership and functions of the upper House, and comments on possible reforms of it.

In chapter 16 we are on well-trodden ground – the privileges and immunities of the Houses of Parliament and of their members acting in their capacity as members. Select committees of the House of Commons have recommended some reforms in the law of parliamentary privilege, and the House has implemented some of them.

Part Three concludes with a chapter on subordinate legislation (mainly legislation by Ministers under powers delegated by Act of Parliament). Delegated legislation could alternatively have been discussed in Part Five of the book ('Administrative Law'), but it has been placed here because it is legislation and, like most of Parliament's own general legislative output, it is initiated by Ministers. Particular attention is paid to the special safeguards against the abuse of delegated powers. Attitudes towards the dangers inherent in delegated legislation have often been excessively alarmist – a point underlined in the course of this chapter. But some recent developments, and in particular membership of the European Union, have brought the need for adequate safeguards into the foreground once again.

CHAPTER 12

Parliament: Background and Framework

SOME BASIC RULES[1]

Frequency of Parliaments

The Bill of Rights 1689 provided that Parliament 'ought to be held frequently'. By virtue of the Meeting of Parliament Act 1694 (which is still in force) not more than three years must elapse between the dissolution of one Parliament and the meeting of its successor. In practice, and by convention, Parliament must be summoned to meet each year. The most remunerative taxes and grants of supply to the Crown are provided by Act of Parliament annually; and authority for the maintenance of the army and its discipline requires annual renewal by the authority of both Houses.[2]

The two Houses. The House of Commons is a wholly elected body; the House of Lords is wholly non-elected. Since the late Middle Ages it has been an accepted rule that the two Houses meet, deliberate and vote separately. There is no statutory or other provision for joint sessions, though for certain purposes there can be joint select committees. A bill may be introduced in either House unless it is a Finance Bill (authorizing taxation) or a Consolidated Fund or Appropriation Bill (authorizing national expenditure), in which case convention and the privileges of the Commons require that it be introduced in that House and by a Minister. Other money bills may be introduced in the Lords.[3] But it is a constitutional convention, and one of fundamental importance, that every amendment or motion to authorize central government expenditure, or to increase or impose a tax,

---

[1] See Robert Blackburn, *The Meeting of Parliament* (1990).
[2] See above, pp. 216–17.
[3] House of Commons SO No. 78.

must have the Queen's recommendation[4] – that is to say, it must be introduced or moved by a Minister. This necessarily implies that the power of the purse belongs to the Government and not to private members. Hence, if a bill introduced by a private member requires the expenditure of public money for the fulfilment of its purposes – and it does so require more often than not – the member must be able to persuade a Minister to move a financial resolution in the House; otherwise the bill cannot be passed. No such restriction applies in the United States Congress or in a number of other foreign legislatures.

The customary common-law rule is that a bill cannot become law unless it has been passed by both Houses and assented to by the Queen. Under the Parliament Acts 1911 and 1949 most classes of bills may, after a period of delay, be presented for the royal assent, although they have not been passed by the Lords.[5]

Duration of a Parliament

In 1694 it was enacted that no Parliament was to last more than three years. This provision was repealed by the Septennial Act 1715 (passed in the state of alarm engendered by the first Jacobite revolt) which extended the maximum duration of a Parliament to seven years. The Parliament Act 1911 reduced this period to five years (s. 7), and laid it down that the new procedure whereby a bill could be presented for assent without the Lords' consent was not to apply to bills to prolong the life of Parliament (s. 2(1)); these rules are still in force. Parliament may, however, prolong its own life by an Act passed in the normal manner. Thus, the Parliament elected in 1910 was prolonged by annual Acts during the First World War, and was not dissolved till November 1918; the Parliament elected in 1935 was similarly prolonged during the Second World War and was dissolved in June 1945. An attempt by a Government to procure the deferment of a General Election in any situation other than one of armed conflict would provoke a serious constitutional crisis.

Parliament may be, and nearly always is, dissolved by the exercise of the royal prerogative before its five-year term comes to an end. The constitutional conventions regulating the exercise of this prerogative have

---

4 These rules are partly embodied in standing orders of the House (SO Nos. 46–8, 77–8).
5 See pp. 304–8.

already been considered.[6] The main practical effect of these conventions (save in those circumstances in which the Queen is entitled to refuse a request for dissolution) is to enable the Prime Minister to choose the most advantageous, or least disadvantageous, date for a General Election. The fact that this power lies in his hands tends both to enhance his stature within the Government and to rally the ranks of party waverers once it is suspected that a dissolution may be imminent. If the power to dissolve were to be eliminated (so that we had Parliaments of fixed duration) or narrowly restricted, one could expect party discipline within the House of Commons to be more difficult to enforce.

The modern practice is for the Prime Minister to announce the date of the dissolution and election (after he has tendered the necessary request to Her Majesty) about ten days before the actual dissolution. Dissolution is effected by a royal proclamation in Council, which also names the date for the summoning of the new Parliament. In practice polling day will be about a month after the announcement of the intended dissolution,[7] and a couple of weeks will elapse thereafter before the new Parliament meets.

The proclamation is followed immediately by an Order in Council, directing the Lord Chancellor to issue writs to the returning officer (who will be the mayor or chairman of a local authority or the sheriff of a county) in each constituency to cause an election to be held on the day named, and writs of summons to individual peers and bishops to attend the meeting of the new Parliament.

The commencement of a Parliament is accompanied by picturesque ceremonial. Parliament is formally opened by Lords Commissioners in the House of Lords. The Commons repair to their own chamber to elect a Speaker and swear in members. The following day or shortly afterwards, Her Majesty attends in person to read the Queen's speech in the House of Lords;[8] this speech is prepared for her under the direction of the Prime Minister, and outlines the Government's legislative programme for the session and its broad policies. The Commons are present at the bar of the House of Lords. The main substantive business of the new Parliament begins with a general debate in each House on the address in reply to the Queen's speech.

At common law, Parliament was dissolved automatically by a demise of the Crown (the death or abdication of the monarch). This rule was abrogated

---

6 See pp. 124–6.
7 See Blackburn, op. cit., pp. 8–9.
8 If she is unable to attend personally, the Lord Chancellor reads it on her behalf.

by statute in 1707. Under the present law[9] the effects of a demise of the Crown are: (i) the two Houses are to meet immediately if prorogued or adjourned; and (ii) if the demise of the Crown occurs while Parliament is dissolved and before polling day, the meeting of Parliament after the election is to be delayed for fourteen days.

Sessions: prorogation and adjournment. It is the invariable custom for the life of a Parliament to be divided up into a number of sessions. These are usually of about one year's duration, though there is no fixed practice. If Parliament were not to sit at all for a full year, some vital Acts which have to be renewed or passed annually would lapse. A speech from the throne is read by the Queen in the Lords, with the Commons in attendance, at the opening of each session. Typically, a session will begin and end in October and will be interspersed with adjournments each night, at week-ends, at Christmas, Easter and Whitsun, and during the long summer recess beginning late in July. It is possible for the Commons to be sitting while the Lords are adjourned. Nowadays the Commons sit for about 180 days altogether during a calendar year. Each House determines, on the Government's initiative, on which dates it will adjourn and reassemble.

A session of Parliament is terminated by prorogation, a prerogative act; a short formal speech is made on behalf of the Queen, summarizing the work done during the session, and the Parliament stands prorogued till a named date, which (unless prorogation precedes a dissolution) will be only a few days later, when a new session will be opened by the reading of the Queen's speech. These dates are decided on the Government's advice. Prorogation has the effect of causing all public bills that have not yet passed into law to lapse; if they are to be reintroduced in the new session they must go through all their stages again. Private bills (i.e. bills of a local or personal character) are carried forward into the new session by resolution of each House, so that they can be continued at the stage they have already reached. The main casualties of a prorogation will be public bills introduced by private members (private members' bills) but occasionally bills introduced by Ministers (Government bills) will lapse too. Prorogation therefore induces the Government to manage its legislative programme efficiently.

The reason why Parliament is adjourned, instead of standing prorogued, in midsummer is strictly practical. In the first place, if it becomes necessary

9 Succession to the Crown Act 1707; Representation of the People Act 1867; Representation of the People Act 1985, s. 20.

to recall a prorogued Parliament to deal with a matter of unexpected urgency, a royal proclamation has to be issued. It is simpler and may be more expeditious to reassemble an adjourned Parliament; this can be done by the Speaker and the Lord Chancellor acting on the Prime Minister's request.[10] Secondly, at the end of a summer recess it is often desirable to spend a few days dealing with unfinished legislative business (for example, considering late Lords' amendments to Government bills), debating an important issue that has arisen during the recess or making policy announcements before the session terminates.

THE ROLE OF PARLIAMENT

It has often been said that Parliament has three main constitutional functions: making laws; controlling national expenditure and taxation; and a third class of function, comprising criticism of national policy, scrutiny of central administration, and procuring the redress of individual grievances.

A preliminary difficulty with this classification is that the word 'Parliament' is being used in different senses. There are more serious difficulties inherent in any classification by reference to function when expressed in legal or institutional terms. The familiar classification is too much at variance with the facts. Legislation is primarily a function of Government. Even if one ignores the mass of non-parliamentary or subordinate legislation made by the Queen in Council or Ministers, a very large majority of Government bills, introduced into Parliament by Ministers, are passed into law substantially in their original form. In the 1995–96 session, all forty-three Government bills which were introduced were passed; seventeen private members' bills reached the statute book (out of eighty-nine which were introduced). Again Parliament 'controls' national finance in the formal sense that its sanction is needed for the imposition of taxation and the authorization of expenditure; but bills authorizing public expenditure are dominated even more than the content of ordinary legislation by the will of the Government, and in particular the views of the Treasury. A lot of time in the House of

---

10 This practice is provided for in standing orders of the House of Commons (SO No. 12) and sessional orders of the House of Lords. The Speaker and the Lord Chancellor are not obliged to comply with the Prime Minister's request, but it would be remarkable if they were to refuse unless no substantial reason for the request was supplied.

Parliament must also be summoned to meet within five days if a royal proclamation of a state of emergency is made under the Emergency Powers Acts 1920 and 1964. See ch. 24.

Commons is spent on debating what are in form financial matters; but the House has largely given up the pretence that it has real authority over these measures, and most debates on public expenditure concentrate on aspects of policy and administration to which questions of expenditure may be only peripheral.

The deeper one digs, the bigger yawns the gulf between appearance and reality. Neither Parliament nor the House of Commons acts as a collective entity save on special and rare occasions. In recent years political scientists, though prone to disparage or be ignorant of legal rules, have rightly concentrated their attention on party organization and activity in and out of Parliament; the role of pressure groups operating on Ministers, civil servants, parties and MPs; the potential expansion of scrutinizing select committees; the meaning of public opinion; and the nature of General Elections to the House of Commons. In other words, parliamentary institutions cannot meaningfully be considered in isolation from the forces which influence decisions; and some of those decisions may not even require to be formally registered by Parliament. Having made this point, it must be reiterated that this is a book about constitutional law and not a general work on British government. The main emphasis must, therefore, be placed on aspects of parliamentary institutions which are not necessarily the most important.

Against this complex background, the question: What is the constitutional role (or what are the functions) of Parliament? becomes altogether too ambiguous. Answers will depend on whether one is thinking of the Queen in Parliament, the two Houses, or the House of Commons alone; on whether one is thinking of all the members on the Government side, or of those members on the Government side who are not Ministers, or of members on the Opposition side; on whether one is thinking of the political activities of members outside as well as inside Parliament. One can set out the following general propositions.

1 The House of Commons gives the Government a legitimate foundation. The Prime Minister must be that person who is best able to command the support of a majority of members of the House; he is normally the leader of the majority party; the majority party in the House is identified by the party affiliations of the successful candidates in individual constituencies at a General Election. The Prime Minister forms a Government;[11]

---

11 The Government, when formed, does not (as in some countries) have to obtain a formal parliamentary vote of confidence.

the members of the Government must be or become members of one or other House. Thereafter supporters of the Government in the House of Commons sustain it in office by thwarting the Opposition's motions of censure and enabling the Government to enact its legislative programme.

2 The role of the Opposition in the House of Commons[12] must be conditioned by the constant need to present itself to the electorate as the alternative Government. This objective can be frustrating when the next General Election may be four years distant. Mrs Thatcher's hat trick of General Elections of course dismayed the Opposition, and when the Conservative Government won a fourth consecutive victory in 1992 – a feat unprecedented since the early nineteenth century – they must, again, have sustained themselves with the thought that the Conservatives' good fortune could not hold indefinitely ('One more heave'). Victory will not be thought of as unattainable, for the main political parties are broadly based; they are not reflections of a permanent majority or minority group (the situation in Northern Ireland is essentially different); there is a sizeable floating vote; we have free elections; only three times this century has the same party won three consecutive General Elections.[13] To say that the function of the Opposition is to oppose would be an oversimplification; a substantial majority of Government bills are passed without any move to reject them, and there is a large area of common ground between the two main parties on matters of national policy. The Prime Minister often gives the Leader of the Opposition confidential information and consults with him privately on non-party matters of national concern. But in fulfilling its role the Opposition will frequently attack the Government in debate and at question time on issues of principle and detail. Parliament is the only public forum in which Ministers are obliged to present reasoned (and sometimes unprepared) answers to these criticisms.

3 Irrespective of the political complexion of the Government in office, the Conservative Party remains the largest single group in the House of Lords. But because of the peculiar composition and limited powers of the upper House, the roles of Government and Opposition in the Lords cannot be considered in the same terms as in the Commons. Perhaps

12 On which see Brazier, *Constitutional Practice* (2nd edn, 1994), ch. 8.
13 The Liberals in 1906 and 1910 (twice), though in the 1910 elections they failed to obtain an overall majority of seats in the Commons and retained office only with the support of minority parties; and the Conservatives in 1951, 1955 and 1959; and again in 1979, 1983 and 1987 – and a fourth in 1992.

incongruously, it is possible to review the constitutional functions of the House of Lords more coherently than those of the House of Commons.[14]

4 In both Houses, and particularly in the Commons, the Government's policies and its conduct of administration are subjected to open scrutiny; and adverse criticism does not come only from members on the Opposition side. To this extent Parliament is a 'grand inquest of the nation'. Voting figures in the division lobbies tell only part of the story. Criticism often takes the form of putting down detailed amendments to Government bills; these amendments are not necessarily, or indeed usually, prompted by considerations of party politics and Ministers will seldom be able to afford merely to brush them aside. Fuller investigation of aspects of policy and administration will be a matter for scrutinizing select committees.

5 The House of Commons provides a forum for ventilating the grievances of individuals, localities and organized groups. An MP may raise such an issue by asking a parliamentary question, putting down an 'early-day' motion, raising the matter in debate (especially the debate on the daily adjournment of the House), putting down amendments to bills, or seeking to introduce a private member's bill himself. However, effective *redress* for injustices suffered by individuals at the hands of the Administration is more likely to be achieved outside Parliament, by members' letters and other representations to Ministers, by attracting the attention of the media, or through an inquiry by the Parliamentary Commissioner for Administration into a complaint of maladministration referred to him by an MP, through a more formal committee or tribunal of inquiry or by statutory machinery for appeal or by judicial review.

6 The publicity given to its proceedings, moreover, tends to enhance public interest in public affairs, and to educate and inform by the wider diffusion of facts, arguments and statements of policy. This tendency must not be exaggerated. Few people read *Hansard*; in England only four daily newspapers, with a total circulation of barely three millions, offer even a cursory coverage of parliamentary proceedings; most of the electorate now obtains its information about current affairs mainly from television programmes, and party political broadcasts are not popular with viewers except during an election campaign; only important set-piece debates and Prime Minister's Questions are broadcast live on television; professions of intent by politicians are regarded

14 See ch. 15.

with widespread scepticism; because the outcome of divisions in the House of Commons is normally a foregone conclusion, parliamentary debates fail to attract the attention given to contests where the result is in doubt.

CHAPTER 13

The House of Commons:
Elections and Members

THE ELECTORAL SYSTEM

The franchise

In order to exercise the franchise in a parliamentary constituency, a person must be included in the electoral register for that constituency. The register is compiled annually, on the basis of information provided by householders, by the registration officer, who is the chief executive of a local authority. A person, though legally qualified to vote in every other respect, will not be permitted to vote if his name is not on the register.

To be included in the register, a person must[1] 1. be eighteen years of age, or be due to attain his eighteenth birthday within twelve months of the publication of the register, thus becoming eligible to vote in an election held after his birthday; 2. be a Commonwealth citizen or a citizen of the Republic of Ireland; 3. not be subject to any legal incapacity;[2] and 4. be resident in the constituency on the qualifying date (10 October in Great Britain)[3] for compiling the register.

The following points should be noted.

(*a*) It is a criminal offence for a person to vote in more than one constituency even though his name appears on the electoral register for each constituency. Again, it is an offence to vote if one knows or has reasonable grounds for believing that, notwithstanding one's appearance on the electoral register,

---

[1] Representation of the People Act 1983, S. 1; hereafter 'the 1983 Act'. On electoral law generally, see Erskine May, *Parliamentary Practice* (21st edn, 1989) chs. 2, 3; H. F. Rawlings, *Law and the Electoral Process* (1988); J. A. G. Griffith and M. Ryle, *Parliament: Functions, Practice and Procedure* (1989), pp. 44–55; R. Blackburn, *The Electoral System in Britain* (1995).

[2] See p. 238.

[3] 1983 Act, s. 4(1).

one is subject to a legal disqualification. Hence although absence from the register is conclusive of inability to vote, presence on the register is not conclusive of entitlement to vote.

(b) The term 'Commonwealth citizen' includes, as well as British citizens, British Dependent Territories citizens and British Overseas citizens,[4] together with citizens of independent Commonwealth countries.[5] Citizens of the Republic of Ireland (which of course is not a Commonwealth country) are not British citizens in United Kingdom law, but they are excluded from the definition of aliens[6] and are accorded much the same rights and privileges in the United Kingdom as citizens of Commonwealth countries.[7]

(c) To be included in the register, a person who is otherwise qualified needs to be 'resident' at an address in the constituency only on the qualifying date.[8] No period of residence is necessary, except in Northern Ireland where three months' continuous residence is required. A person ought not to be put on the register unless his ordinary place of residence[9] is in the constituency. However, it is irrelevant that his place of residence is, for example, merely a tent: if, as a matter of fact, that is the person's residence, he is entitled to be registered there.[10] And university students pursuing their courses of study are entitled to be registered in the constituency where they are residing for that purpose.[11]

(d) Persons with service qualifications (members of the armed forces, Crown servants and British Council officials overseas, and their spouses living overseas with them), and merchant seamen, are entitled to be treated as if they were resident in a constituency on the qualifying date, provided

4 British Nationality Act 1981, s. 37(1)(a).

5 ibid., s. 37(1)(b).

6 ibid., s. 50(1).

7 See generally the Ireland Act 1949, s. 2 and the Representation of the People Act 1983, s. 1.

8 1983 Act s. 5. If he moves house to another constituency, he can apply for a postal or proxy vote pending the next annual registration: Representation of the People Act 1990, s. 1.

9 A prison will not be accepted as an address for the registration of a person incarcerated there: 1983 Act. s. 5(3). A mentally disordered person is not resident at the place where he is detained: ibid., s. 7(1); whether he is able to register elsewhere is a question of fact. A voluntary mental patient may register at a place outside his psychiatric hospital and obtain a postal vote: ibid., ss. 7, 19.

10 Hipperson v. Electoral Registration Officer for Newbury [1985] QB 1060 (women protesting at Greenham Common).

11 Fox v. Stirk [1970] 2 QB 463. If they have a home in another constituency, they can be registered there as well.

that they would have been so resident but for their assignment elsewhere.[12]
(e) A British citizen resident outside the United Kingdom may vote as an
overseas elector.[13] To do so he must be qualified but for that absence, and
have been included on a register in a constituency not more than twenty
years before the date on which he wishes to qualify as an overseas elector.
He must make an overseas elector's declaration, and may vote by post or
proxy.[14] Some 30,000 people were qualified to vote in the 1992 General
Election in this way.[15]

Disqualification. The following classes of persons are not entitled to exercise
the franchise even if their names appear on the electoral register.

(i) Aliens.[16]

(ii) Minors (persons under eighteen years of age).

(iii) Peers, other than peers of Ireland.[17]

(iv) Persons serving sentences of imprisonment, or who are unlawfully at
large having escaped.[18]

(v) Persons convicted of corrupt practices at elections (who are disfranchised for five years); and persons convicted of illegal practices at
elections (election offences of a lesser order), who are also disfranchised
for five years but only in respect of the constituency in question. The
line drawn between corrupt and illegal practices is not altogether
logical. To incur unauthorized expenditure to promote the election
of a candidate is a corrupt practice; to publish a false statement that a
candidate has withdrawn from the contest is an illegal practice.

---

12 See 1983 Act. ss. 14–17.

13 Representation of the People Act 1985, ss. 1–4. He may also vote in elections to the
European Parliament.

14 Representation of the People Act 1989, s. 1. See below, p. 245.

15 See 204 HC Deb. *102–113* (written answers 3 March 1992).

16 This term excludes citizens of the Republic of Ireland (see above).

17 By custom the Lords Spiritual (see p. 297) do not vote, although the courts have
never ruled on the matter. The Archbishop of Canterbury voted in the 1983 General
Election, but the Anglican bishops subsequently declared that they would in future abide
by the custom. See 443 HL Deb. 242–5 (29 June 1983).

18 Representation of the People Act 1983, s. 3, as amended by the Representation of
the People Act 1985, sched. 4. Such a person may, of course, have been correctly included
in the electoral register before his term of detention began.

The register[19]

The registration officer[20] must issue a provisional electoral register for the constituency on 28 November; this is to be exhibited in public libraries and other public buildings. He must also keep lists of voters entitled to vote by post or proxy.[21] If he realizes that he has made a mistake in compiling the register, then (subject to any appeal from a decision on a claim or objection) he must correct it.[22] Any person may object to the inclusion or exclusion of any name by 16 December; the registration officer must hear and determine any objection and may rectify the register accordingly. An appeal lies from his determinations to the county court and thence, on a point of law, to the Court of Appeal; alternatively his determination, or that of the Circuit judge, may be impeached before a Divisional Court of the Queen's Bench Division.[23] The register for the constituency comes into force on 16 February and is operative for any election held there during the following twelve months.

Delimitation of constituencies

In the American Constitution it is laid down[24] that no state shall deny any person within its jurisdiction 'the equal protection of the laws'. In *Baker* v. *Carr* (1962)[25] one of the most remarkable and influential decisions ever given by the United States Supreme Court, it was held that the equal protection clause implied the doctrine of 'one man, one vote, one value', so that electoral districts (constituencies) established under state law for the federal House of Representatives had to have approximately equal numbers of electors. This decision, and others that followed[26] led to a massive legislative reapportionment of electoral districts not only for congressional

19 1983 Act, ss. 9–13.
20 The sheriffs of counties, chairmen of district councils and mayors of London boroughs are returning officers, but their duties are delegated to registration officers: Local Government Act 1972, ss. 39, 40.
21 1985 Act, ss. 6–7. On postal and proxy voting, see below, p. 244.
22 1983 Act, s. 11.
23 By an application, made by a party aggrieved, for an order of certiorari to quash the determination (for example, for excess of jurisdiction) or for an order of mandamus to compel him to perform his public duty.
24 Fourteenth Amendment, s. 1.
25 369 US 186 (1962).
26 See, for example, *Reynolds* v. *Sims* 377 US 533 (1964) (principle of broadly equal electoral districts held to govern representation in *both* houses of a state legislature; contrast the position in the United States Senate).

elections but also at the state and local levels so as to modify the prevailing over-representation of sparsely populated rural areas.

No decision of a United Kingdom court could propel Parliament into radical reform. The present machinery for constituency delimitation, based on a scheme introduced in 1944,[27] is designed to work impartially and to promote approximately equal electorates; but the last word rests with Parliament, and politics tends to keep creeping in.

Under the Parliamentary Constituencies Act 1986 (which consolidated the House of Commons (Redistribution of Seats) Acts 1949 to 1979), four Boundary Commissions, one each for England, Scotland, Wales and Northern Ireland, are charged with the duties of reviewing representation in the House of Commons, and submitting to the Secretary of State reports recommending such redistribution of seats as may be necessary at intervals of not less than ten or more than fifteen years. As soon as may be after they have reported, the Home Secretary must lay their reports before Parliament, *together with* drafts of Orders in Council giving effect, with or without modifications, to their recommendations for boundary changes. The Act thus permits the Home Secretary to vary but not to ignore or reject the recommendations. If the draft Orders are approved by resolutions of each House, Orders in Council will then be made, and will have effect at the next General Election.

The chairman of each Commission is the Speaker of the House of Commons; the deputy chairman must be a superior judge; each Commission has two other members who are not to be MPs, and is advised by senior public officials – in England the Registrar-General and the Director-General of Ordnance Survey. The Commissions are guided by a number of rules laid down in the Act. When a Commission has provisionally decided to recommend changes, it must give public notice of its proposals in the constituencies concerned and invite representations to be made to it; it may conduct local inquiries. The total number of constituencies (all of which are to be represented by a single member) for Great Britain is not to be substantially greater or less than 613; this number is to include at least seventy-one Scottish and thirty-five Welsh constituencies; there are also to be seventeen constituencies in Northern Ireland.[28] The electorate of a

27 See generally Blackburn, op. cit., ch. 4. The original Act was the House of Commons (Redistribution of Seats) Act 1944. There had been no general redistribution since 1918 despite the movement of population from city centres to suburbs. The movement was accelerated during and after the Second World War; and new towns to siphon off population from the big cities were deliberately created and expanded as an act of policy. 28 An increase from twelve made by virtue of the House of Commons (Redistribution of Seats) Act 1979.

constituency is to be as near as practicable to a quota ascertained by dividing the total electorate within the region covered by a Commission by the number of constituencies in that region; deviations from the quota are permissible in order to respect local government boundaries or for reasons of geographical dispersal. The total number of United Kingdom constituencies is not fixed by Act of Parliament; it is currently 651.

Each set of proposals by the Commissions has proved controversial. The first reports of the Commissioners, in 1948, recommended very extensive boundary changes in the light of shifts in the distribution of population since 1918; the Commission for England also deviated from the rules to give an advantageous weighting to rural areas, which happened to be mainly Conservative; the Labour Government redressed the balance by introducing amending legislation to add seventeen urban seats, eight of which were in fact won in 1950 by Conservative candidates. The 1954 reports of the Commissions were implemented in full but aroused a good deal of local resentment. Two unsuccessful attempts were made to impugn the validity of recommendations or draft Orders in Council in the courts.[29] For technical reasons it was not easy to see how in practice the courts could be persuaded to go into the question of *vires*.[30] The 1969 recommendation[31] precipitated a crisis. If they had been fully implemented, the Labour Party might possibly have lost about ten seats at the next election, mainly through the disappearance of depopulated urban constituencies. Some weeks after they had been received the Home Secretary presented them

---

29 *Hammersmith BC* v. *Boundary Commission of England. The Times*, 15 December 1954 (attempt to obtain mandatory injunction to direct the Commission to withdraw its recommendations *after* it had reported; held, the Commission had no power to do this); *Harper* v. *Home Secretary* [1955] Ch. 238 (attempt to prevent draft Order in Council, already approved by both Houses, from being presented to Her Majesty in Council). See generally Craig [1959] *Public Law* 23.

30 Among the difficulties are the unavailability of injunctions against Crown servants acting as such (Crown Proceedings Act 1947, s. 21), the fact that the courts are fearful of encroaching on parliamentary privilege by interfering with a 'proceeding in Parliament' (though this objection would not arise if there were a reasonable interval between publication of the report and laying before Parliament) and the provision of the 1949 Act (unaffected by the 1958 Act or by the Parliamentary Constituencies Act 1986) that the validity of an Order in Council thus made cannot be called in question in any legal proceedings whatsoever (1986 Act, s. 4(7)). In an extreme case a court might nevertheless be persuaded to intervene; and in any event it might be possible to obtain an order of mandamus to compel the Home Secretary to comply with his express statutory duties (see p. 242).

31 The period between reviews had been extended to a maximum of fifteen years by the 1958 Act.

to Parliament[32] but did not produce draft Orders in Council to give effect to them, either with or without amendment. Instead the Government decided to implement them only in part, explaining that local government areas were being subjected to a comprehensive review, that there ought not to be too big a discrepancy between local government and parliamentary constituency boundaries, and that it would be undesirable to have two major delimitations within the course of a few years. The Home Secretary introduced a new House of Commons (Redistribution of Seats) Bill, implementing the recommendations for Greater London and a few very large constituencies but absolving him from performance of his existing statutory duty to give effect to the Commissions' recommendations. The Opposition and some independent critics maintained that the bill involved gerrymandering. The Conservative majority in the Lords passed the bill but only subject to wrecking amendments. The two Houses adjourned for the summer recess in in a state of deadlock, with the Home Secretary facing the prospect of an application to the High Court for an order of mandamus to compel him to carry out his legal duties. When Parliament reassembled, the Home Secretary moved compromise amendments and warned that if the Lords rejected them, he would lay all the recommendations for constituency changes together with draft Orders giving effect to them, but would ask Government supporters not to approve any of them. The Lords rejected the Commons' amendments to the bill. The application for mandamus was withdrawn,[33] the Home Secretary having declared that he would comply with his statutory duty. The bill lapsed on prorogation, and no attempt was made the following session to override the Lords under the Parliament Acts procedure. Instead, the reports and draft Orders giving effect to them were laid before the Commons by the Home Secretary; and

---

32 The reports were published as Command Papers, and presented to the House of Commons (see SO No. 137) by being placed in the Votes and Proceedings Office. It was at first claimed on behalf of the Home Secretary that they had not been 'laid' before Parliament within the meaning of the parent Act; hence the duty to lay draft Orders in Council at the same time did not arise. When the reports were presented to the House a second time, accompanied by draft Orders (see below), they were expressed to have been laid in pursuance of the Act; again they were deposited in the Votes and Proceedings Office. It seems artificial in the extreme to contend that the first laying was not a performance of a statutory duty but an act of obedience to Her Majesty's command. cf. *Att.-Gen.* v. *De Keyser's Royal Hotel Ltd* [1920] AC 508; p. 139 above. And see *R.* v. *Immigration Appeal Tribunal, ex p. Joyles* [1972] I WLR 1390, showing that presenting a Command Paper to the House is laying within the meaning of the Act.

33 *R.* v. *Home Secretary, ex p. McWhirter, The Times,* 21 October 1969. The several interesting issues raised by the application (for example, whether it constituted an impeachment of 'proceedings in Parliament'; see ch. 16) were not determined.

the draft Orders were duly voted down by the House.[34] The subsequent General Election in 1970 was therefore conducted on the basis of the 1954 delimitation. In November 1970 the new Conservative Home Secretary reintroduced the draft Orders and they were given parliamentary approval.

In 1983 the Labour Party again objected to the effects of the recommendations of the Boundary Commission for England, as it believed that once more they would cost the Party seats at the General Election. The Leader and other senior members of the Labour Party sought orders of prohibition and injunctions to restrain the Commission from submitting its proposals to the Home Secretary on the ground that the Commission had misdirected itself in law. The Court of Appeal rejected the challenge, broadly because the Commission had in its view properly interpreted the rules in and under the House of Commons (Redistribution of Seats) Acts of 1949 and 1958 and had exercised its discretion on all points reasonably.[35] The changes were implemented in the ordinary way. The Boundary Commissions Act 1992 brought forward the deadline for the completion of the Commissioners' next review to the end of 1994.

Method of voting[36]

The general rule is that on election day voters must go in person to the appropriate polling station in their constituency, where they will be handed a ballot paper listing the names of the candidates. The voter enters a polling booth and makes a cross in a space alongside the name of one candidate; the voter folds the ballot paper and drops it into a sealed ballot box. The fiction that a voter chooses the most suitable candidate irrespective of his party affiliations was maintained by a rule precluding the incorporation in the ballot paper of words indicating the political attitudes of candidates till 1969, when a statute permitted the insertion of up to six words descriptive of the candidate's political associations.[37] A candidate cannot be stopped from using a party label on the ballot paper which will confuse voters or spoil another candidate's chances of winning – for example, by calling himself a Literal Democrat.[38]

---

34 791 HC Deb. 428–571 (12 November 1969).
35 R. v. *Boundary Commission for England, ex p. Foot and others* [1983] QB 600. In appropriate cases relief would be granted by a declaration, not prohibition, as the latter would wholly preclude Parliament from considering the Commission's proposals: ibid. pp. 567–9.
36 See Representation of the People Act 1985, s. 5.
37 See now 1983 Act, s. 23 and sched. 1, rule 6(2), (3).
38 *Sanders* v. *Chichester*, the *Guardian*, 14 November 1994.

In the celebrated case of *Ashby* v. *White* (1703)[39] it was held that the right to vote was in the nature of a proprietary right, and that a returning officer refusing for improper motives to allow a qualified elector to cast his vote was liable in damages. Under section 63 of the Representation of the People Act 1983,[40] no civil liability is incurred by an election officer in respect of a breach of his official duties, though he may be criminally liable. No election officer may refuse to give a ballot paper to a person whose name appears on the register – save in Northern Ireland:[41] there, voters must first furnish a specified identity document,[42] and if there is reasonable doubt whether the voter is who he claims to be he may be refused a ballot paper.[43] In England, Wales and Scotland, if the election officer has grounds for believing that any such person is legally disqualified (for example, by reason of minority, or because he has already voted) it is his duty so to warn him; if that person nevertheless proceeds to vote though disqualified, he may be prosecuted for an election offence.

Special arrangements are made for casting of votes by persons with service qualifications and by persons who have applied to be registered as absent voters.[44] As a general rule, service and absent voters may vote by post or by proxy. To qualify as an absent voter an elector may be registered as such either for an indefinite period (because, for example, of the nature of his employment, or his illness or infirmity), or for a particular election (because, for instance, he will be away on holiday on the day of the poll).

At the close of the polls (10 p.m.) the ballot boxes are transported to a central counting station in the constituency and emptied, and the ballot papers are counted together with postal and proxy votes. The candidate with the largest number of votes is declared by the returning officer to be elected. There is no requirement that a candidate obtain a minimum percentage of the total vote to be elected.

By-elections to fill vacancies caused by death, resignation or other cause are conducted in essentially the same manner.

The British system of election is often called 'first past the post'. It has been criticized as unfair to parties other than Conservative or Labour. For

39 2 Ld. Raym. 938.
40 As amended by the Representation of the People Act 1985, sched. 4.
41 Elections (Northern Ireland) Act 1985, s. 1(2).
42 i.e. a driving licence, Social Security payment or order book, NHS card or marriage certificate: ibid.
43 A refusal is subject to an election petition (see below, p. 257), but is otherwise final: ibid., s. 2.
44 See 1985 Act, ss. 6–9.

example, at the General Election of 1987, Social Democratic and Liberal Alliance candidates obtained 22.6 per cent of the national vote, but only 3 per cent of the seats in the House; Labour achieved only rather more of the popular votes (30.8 per cent), but the system awarded it 36 per cent of the seats. At the 1997 General Election the Liberal Democrats polled 17 per cent of the vote, but again received only 7 per cent of the seats. Moreover, the Labour Party's landslide election victory was achieved on only 44 per cent of the votes cast. These figures above speak of injustice.[45] But the first-past-the-post system is traditionally defended by arguing that a General Election is, in effect, the choice of a Government. A party winning 42 per cent of the national vote is almost certain to have an overall majority of seats in the House.[46] Many people who might otherwise be inclined to vote for non-Conservative and non-Labour candidates traditionally have either abstained from voting or have voted for a candidate of one of the two major parties in order not to 'waste' their vote; they have believed that the election of a few more members from the smaller parties will not affect the formation of the next Government.

There is obviously a case for reforming the electoral system with a view to reducing the discrepancy between votes cast for and seats won by a party campaigning on a national scale. That case has been argued for years by the Liberal Party and subsequently by the Liberal Democrats,[47] and proportional representation has been introduced in part of the United Kingdom – Northern Ireland (for the Northern Ireland Assembly in 1973, and for Northern Ireland elections to the European Parliament in 1978). The most favoured systems[48] are the alternative vote and proportional

45 For a powerful criticism, see H. W. R. Wade, *Constitutional Fundamentals* (1980), ch. 2, in which the author calls for a redistribution of seats on a more representative basis, election to the Commons by proportional representation and a fair system for the selection of candidates.

46 Only in 1900, 1918, 1931 and 1935 has a party achieved over 50 per cent of the vote. Even Mrs Thatcher's landslide majority of 144 seats in 1983 was obtained with only 42.4 per cent of the votes cast; her 101-seat majority in 1987 resulted from a slightly smaller percentage.

47 See above, p. 46. But the Liberal Party claim that the present electoral system is in breach of a provision of the European Convention on Human Rights which guarantees the free expression of the people's will was rejected by the European Commission on Human Rights in *Liberal Party* v. *United Kingdom* (1980) 4 EHRR 106.

48 For fuller details see, for example, The Plant Report: Report of a Working Party on Electoral Reform (Labour Party, 1993); Enid Lakeman, *How Democracies Vote* (3rd edn, 1970) and *Power to Elect* (1982); V. Bogdanor and D. Butler, *Democracy and Elections* (1983); Blake Report of the Hansard Commission (1976); Oliver [1983] *Public Law* 108; Liberal Democrats, *Here We Stand* (1993).

representation. The *alternative vote* is used in single-member constituencies at elections to the Australian House of Representatives when there are more than two candidates. The voter must place the candidates in order of preference by marking his ballot-paper 1, 2, 3 . . . If no candidate obtains an absolute majority by counting first preferences, the candidate at the bottom of the poll is eliminated, and his second preference votes are distributed among the other candidates, and so on (if necessary) till one candidate has more than 50 per cent of the vote. The result may be that the candidate placed second on the first count wins the seat. A closer correspondence between votes cast and seats won can be achieved by a system of *proportional representation*. The best-known proportional systems are the single transferable vote (STV) and the party list system; there are numerous variants, including mixed systems. Proportional systems require multi-member constituencies. Under STV (which is used in elections in Ireland and Malta and for the Australian Senate) the voter marks his preferences numerically against the names of candidates; where a candidate has obtained a large enough percentage of the total poll to ensure that he must be elected,[49] his second preferences are redistributed among the other candidates, and so on till all the seats are filled. The larger the number of seats to be filled in a constituency, the more closely will their allocation reflect the electoral support enjoyed by the various candidates. Under the party list system in its simplest form, each party puts up a national list of candidates in ranking order; each voter casts a single vote for one party list; a party obtaining 40 per cent of the national vote will fill 40 per cent of the seats with the candidates ranked highest in its list.

Various western European countries use proportional electoral systems. More often than not they bring about coalition or minority governments because no party wins an overall majority. But plans for basic changes in the electoral system in the United Kingdom founder on the combined hostility of the two main parties. Each party believes that under the first-past-the-post system it has a good chance of winning the next (or next but one) General Election with an outright majority; and to win an election is to win power for four or five years. Why, then, meddle with our ancient institutions which have served us so well for so long? At least in this context, 'consensus politics' is not a figment of the imagination. And yet both the

---

49 If, for example, four seats are to be filled in a constituency where 100,000 persons vote, a candidate obtaining $[100,000/(4 + 1)] + 1$ (i.e. 20,001) votes from first preferences will be declared elected, because it is impossible for any four other candidates to beat him.

Labour Party and the Liberal Democrats committed themselves at the 1997 General Election to set up a commission to recommend one proportional alternative to the first-past-the-post system, and to a national referendum offering a choice between the status quo and the selected proportional alternative. That commission is now at work.

MEMBERS

Before touching upon the conduct of an election campaign, we need to say something of the qualifications for membership of the House of Commons and the ways in which a candidate may be selected.

Disqualification for membership of the House

There are three preliminary points. First, there is no list of basic qualifications; there is simply a list of disqualifications. The former property and residential qualifications for candidates were abolished long ago; it is indeed fairly unusual for a candidate from one of the two main national parties to be a local man, though he is usually expected by his constituency party to take up local residence when he becomes their prospective candidate. Secondly, some disqualifications, significant in their day, have been removed by statute as being obnoxious or unnecessary. All religious disqualifications had been removed by 1888; the disqualification (or lack of qualification) of women was removed in 1918; the remaining disqualifications attached to Government contractors and Crown pensioners were abolished in 1957. Thirdly, if a candidate is subject to a legal disqualification, the returning officer is not allowed to reject his nomination papers if they are otherwise in order; his rights to be elected and to sit in the Commons are determinable (as we shall see) by other means if he is elected to the seat.

The following are disqualified.[50]

1 Aliens. These are persons who are neither British citizens nor Commonwealth citizens nor citizens of the Republic of Ireland.[51]

---

50 See Sir Thomas Erskine May, *Parliamentary Practice* (21st edn, 1989), ch. 3; *Halsbury's Laws of England* (4th edn), vol. 34, *Parliament*, with Cumulative Supplement. Some disqualifications do not automatically cause vacation of the seat but debar a member from sitting and voting while subject to the disability. In practice it is impossible to *sit* without participating in a vote; the recurrent formal resolutions passed every day without a division will entail a unanimous vote.

51 For definitions of these terms see above, p. 237.

2 Persons under twenty-one years of age.[52]

3 Persons suffering from severe mental illness. They were disqualified at common law; the non-statutory disqualification has been supplemented by section 141 of the Mental Health Act 1983 under which the Speaker must be notified if a member is detained as a mental patient; if the member is still detained as a mental patient six months later, his seat will be vacated.

4 Peers and peeresses in their own right[53] other than peers of Ireland (who are not qualified to sit in the House of Lords.[54]

5 Persons who receive a prison sentence of more than one year, or an indefinite sentence, are disqualified from membership of the House while detained.[55] If a person so disqualified is elected to the House, then that election is void, and if a sitting member is so disqualified his seat is vacated.[56] A member who is imprisoned for any other lesser period for an offence other than treason is merely prevented from sitting and voting while serving his sentence,[57] but the House could vote to expel him. A person serving a definite prison sentence of less than one year for a non-treasonable crime is not disqualified from election. Persons serving sentences for treason are disqualified.[58]

6 Bankrupts. Persons adjudged bankrupt by a court are disqualified from being elected to, or sitting or voting in, the House. The disqualification ceases on discharge from bankruptcy. The court must inform the Speaker forthwith of a member's declaration of bankruptcy and, if that bankruptcy lasts for six months or more, his seat is vacated.[59]

---

52 This provision was preserved by the Family Law Reform Act 1969 which for most legal purposes reduced the age of majority to eighteen; see s. 1(4) of that Act and para. 2 of sched. 2. Before 1832 several infants (including Charles James Fox) nevertheless sat as members.

53 For the meaning of this concept, see p. 298.

54 See *Re Earl of Antrim's Petition* [1967] 1 AC 691.

55 Representation of the People Act 1981, s. 1. The Act is also retrospective to include such sentences passed before 1981, a provision which has rightly been criticized: see Walker [1982] *Public Law* 389.

56 ibid., s. 2.

57 This appears to be the result of the amendment of s. 2 of the Forfeiture Act 1870 by s. 10 of and Part III of the Third Schedule to the Criminal Law Act 1967.

58 Forfeiture Act 1870 (as amended by the Criminal Law Act 1967, sched. 3). The Speaker reports the imprisonment of any member to the House: see, e.g., 195 HC Deb. 1 (15 July 1991) – Mr Terry Fields, sentenced to sixty days' imprisonment for refusal to pay his poll tax.

59 Insolvency Act 1986, s. 427. The old rule which continued a member's disqualification for five years after discharge was repealed by the 1986 Act.

7 Persons convicted of corrupt and illegal practices at elections. These disqualifications are rather more extensive than those affecting the exercise of the franchise by persons so convicted.[60]

8 Clergy. A motley collection of statutory provisions, enacted at different times to meet particular problems, disqualify some ministers of religion but not others. Ministers of the Church of England, the Episcopalian Church of Scotland and all other Protestant clergymen (including ministers of the Church of Ireland)[61] ordained by bishops, except ministers of the disestablished Church of Wales, are disqualified; so are Roman Catholic priests, and ministers of the Established (Presbyterian) Church of Scotland; but nonconformist ministers, and ministers of non-Christian denominations, are not disqualified. To say that the law is a mass of archaic anomalies is one thing; to rationalize it, given the discordant sentiments expressed by the religious bodies themselves, is another. A select committee of the House which investigated the whole matter in the early 1950s recommended[62] that no change be then made, and the same view was taken by another select committee a few years later.[63] This strange tangle is likely to be with us for some time.[64]

9 Ministers of the Crown. Not more than ninety-five holders of specified ministerial offices may sit and vote at any one time in the House of Commons (House of Commons Disqualification Act 1975, s. 2(1) and Schedule 2). Since by convention a Minister must have or obtain a seat in one or other House, the appointment of a person to ministerial office when the maximum number has already been reached implies that he must be a peer or be granted a peerage; or that a sitting member be granted a peerage to make room for him; or that legislation be passed rapidly to regularize the position; or (possibly) that the new Minister be given an office not hitherto recognized by statute; though amending legislation would again be needed to provide him with a salary and legal powers.[65] The maximum number of persons to whom salaries may be

---

60 Representation of the People Act 1983, ss. 159, 160, 173, 174.

61 *Re MacManaway* [1951] AC 161.

62 HC 200 (1952–3).

63 Select Committee on the House of Commons Disqualification Bill (HC 349 (1955–6)).

64 Though informed opinion in the Church of England now seems to favour repeal of the disqualifications: see *Church and State* (1970), pp. 57–8 (The Report of the Archbishops' Commission).

65 The last two expedients were resorted to in 1964 when Mr Wilson appointed a number of Ministers in excess of the maximum then authorized: see Park (1965) 28 *Mod. L. Rev.* 338.

paid as holders of certain ministerial offices is prescribed by statute.[66] In 1937 the Ministers of the Crown Act rationalized the law by grouping ministerial offices and specifying how many holders of offices in each group could sit and vote in (i.e. be members of) the House of Commons at any one time. The permissible number was enlarged by individual Acts creating new Ministers, and again, in more general terms, by statutes passed in 1957 and in 1964. The governing statute is now the House of Commons Disqualification Act 1975.[67] The modern policy is to strike a balance between the principle that every major Department ought to have a ministerial spokesman in the Commons and the undesirability of having the Government side of the House over-weighted by Ministers at the expense of backbenchers.

10 Holders of public offices. The meaning of an office or place of profit which disqualified or rendered its holder liable to vacate his seat and stand for re-election was obscure. The only remedy was to enact an explicit list of offices, tenure of which ought to disqualify because they required a degree of political impartiality or a burden of continuing responsibility incompatible with membership of the House of Commons. A bill to this effect was introduced in 1955, amended after detailed examination by a select committee of the House,[68] and passed into law as the House of Commons Disqualification Act 1957 (now the House of Commons Disqualification Act 1975).

The main classes of persons thus disqualified for membership are as follows.[69]

(a) Professional full-time judges.

(b) Civil servants.

(c) Members of the regular armed forces.

(d) Full-time members of a police force.

(e) Members of the legislatures of non-Commonwealth countries (which also excludes members of the Irish Parliament).

(f) Members of independent public boards and commissions, the chairman and sometimes the members of 'administrative' tribunals, and other persons occupying offices requiring political neutrality, judicial

---

66 Ministerial and other Salaries Act 1975.

67 Section 2(1) and sched. 2.

68 For the report of the Select Committee, see HC 349 (1955–6). For the report of an earlier committee, reviewing more fully the history of the problem, see HC 120 (1940–41).

69 In 1995 about a million people were disqualified under the 1975 Act: see 263 HC Deb. 31–2 (written answers 3 July 1995).

detachment or other characteristics inconsistent with membership of the House. These disqualifying posts are listed in full in the First Schedule to the 1975 Act; the list may be varied by statute, or by Order in Council made in pursuance of a resolution of the House. The 1975 Act may be reprinted in an amended and up-to-date form so that candidates and members may know how they stand.

11 Acceptance of the offices of bailiff or steward of the Chiltern Hundreds or the Manor of Northstead. This is the traditional manner of resigning membership; these offices are sinecures and nominal offices of profit under the Crown, and acceptance of any of them is expressly preserved as a ground of disqualification by section 4 of the 1975 Act.

12 Expulsion by resolution of the House. The House may declare a member's seat vacant, either because he has incurred a legal disqualification or for any other reason whatsoever; this is one of its privileges. It cannot, however, prevent that person from standing as a candidate at a by-election.[70]

Effect of disqualification. (1) If a person already subject to a legal incapacity (for example, peerage) is elected to membership then (*a*) the House may declare his seat vacant, or (*b*) a petition may be lodged to have him unseated in pursuance of the finding by an election court that his election was void.[71] (2) If a sitting member incurs a disqualification, then (*a*) the House may declare his seat vacant, if it is not automatically vacated by the nature of the disqualification; or (*b*) any member of the public may apply to the Privy Council for a declaration that a member is disqualified under the 1975 Act; the matter is to be referred to the Judicial Committee;[72] or (*c*) the House itself may petition the Crown to have the matter referred to the Judicial Committee for an advisory opinion;[73] or (*d*) the House may, if it thinks fit,

---

70 See p. 325.

71 For election petitions, see pp. 257–8. When Mr Tony Benn succeeded to his father's peerage as Viscount Stansgate, he argued that he was entitled to retain his seat in the Commons because he had not applied for a writ of summons to the Lords. The House referred the matter to the Committee of Privileges; the Committee found against Mr Benn and the House adopted its report and declared his seat vacant. He stood as a candidate at the ensuing by-election, which he won, but was unseated on an election petition by his defeated opponent: *Re Parliamentary Election for Bristol South-East* (1961), reported [1964] 2 QB 257. When the Peerage Act 1963 was passed he immediately disclaimed his peerage and was able to regain his seat.

72 House of Commons Disqualification Act 1975, s. 7. The applicant must furnish security for costs. No such proceeding has been brought; this is hardly surprising.

73 Under section 4 of the Judicial Committee Act 1833. This procedure was adopted in *Re MacManaway* [1951] AC 161.

waive the effect of a disqualification under the 1975 Act if it has already been removed[74] or (e) a common informer may still pursue his action for penalties against an episcopally ordained clergyman who sits and votes while subject to the disqualification.[75]

Selection of candidates

Under our present system of two alternately dominant parties, a large majority of seats will be 'safe' for either the Conservative or the Labour candidate at a General Election,[76] unless there is a substantial swing in public support away from one of the parties, in which case safe seats may become marginal. Hence the selection of the official candidate for the Conservative or Labour Party, as the case may be, will as a rule effectively determine who will win the seat. For most of those who vote, a General Election is a ritualistic affirmation of support for (or hostility to) one of the two main national parties and a means of choosing a Government; and an unattractive candidate will seldom cause his party to lose the seat. In England, it is rare, but not impossible,[77] for an Independent MP to be elected even at a by-election.[78] In both Scotland and Wales the pattern is nowadays far from the same as in England. Nationalists and Liberal Democrats may win a fair proportion of the seats, and the personal attributes of candidates will sometimes count for more than the blessing of a mass party organization. Northern Ireland, too, may provide a number of Independent MPs in the Commons.

The role of political parties in the British system of government is too big a topic to be considered adequately in a primarily legal work.[79] The part played by the parties in the House of Commons will be briefly touched on in the next chapter. In the selection of candidates, party choice is wholly unregulated by rules of strict law, and depends on extra-legal[80] party rules

74 As by resignation from the disqualifying office: 1975 Act, s. 6.
75 Under the House of Commons (Clergy Disqualification) Act 1801.
76 The position may be more fluid at a by-election, where candidates from smaller national or regional parties, or even independents, may benefit from a big 'protest' vote or large-scale abstentions. At by-elections the voters know that they are not participating in the choice of a Government.
77 See p. 253.
78 For the figures from 1900 to 1979, see David Butler and Gareth Butler, *British Political Facts 1900–1994* (7th edn, 1994), pp. 167–8.
79 A still-useful work is R. T. McKenzie, *British Political Parties* (2nd edn, 1970).
80 Though cf. *John v. Rees* [1970] Ch. 345 (natural justice to be observed in disaffiliation or suspension of local party organization).

and practices. In many states in the United States of America, and in a few other countries, statutory provision is made for primary elections to select official party candidates. This democratic safeguard is absent in Britain (though the Liberal Democrats always conduct ballots to select prospective party candidates), and party choice is sometimes still determined by an inner group of party activists and national office-holders.

Selection[81] is mainly a matter for local constituency parties. In the Labour Party, nominations of prospective candidates come from ward branches and affiliated organizations (normally trade unions). Labour Party head-quarters has lists of officially approved candidates. The executive committee of the constituency party draws up a short list, and the candidate is then chosen, subject to the approval of the National Executive Committee of the party, by a selection conference of the constituency party's general management committee. Constituency parties choose their candidate using a system which gives every constituency party member one vote, which must be exercised in person. Occasionally a prospective candidate, or a sitting member, is vetoed as an official candidate by the National Executive Committee; this will lead to the nomination of another candidate with official backing at the national level, and may entail disaffiliation of the constituency party. A Labour candidate lacking official backing will nor-mally have no chance at all of being elected. Many Labour MPs are sponsored by trade unions.[82]

The Conservative Party requires ratification of the final choice to be made by a general meeting of the whole constituency association (and occasionally by postal ballot of members). The Conservative Central Office also has its approved list, but it hardly ever refuses to endorse a local choice. Conservative candidates and MPs are not allowed to make more than a nominal contribution to their constituency association's funds. In practice Conservative MPs come from a smaller range of social groups than Labour MPs, more having been to public schools and Oxbridge, and very few manual workers occupy Conservative seats. Nevertheless, the differences between the social complexions of the front benches of the two parlia-

---

81 See Blackburn, op. cit., ch. 5, and Michael Rush, *The Selection of Parliamentary Candidates* (1969) for a very full study.
82 See K. Ewing, *The Funding of Political Parties in Britain* (1987). Companies contributing to national party funds must now disclose the fact in their accounts: Companies Act 1985, s. 235. As was to be expected, the contributions go overwhelmingly to the Conservative Party. A large part of the Labour Party's income has been derived from trade unions and the political levy imposed on their members, but more is being obtained from individual subscriptions and donations.

mentary parties are now less striking than their similarities. The number of women MPs has risen steadily, sixty being returned in 1992 and 120 in 1997. This is partly attributable to a deliberate attempt in the Labour Party to encourage more women to be adopted as parliamentary candidates.

There is no constitutional procedure whereby an MP can be compelled by his constituents to vacate his seat, but it is open to the constituency party or association to adopt a different candidate at the next General Election if they are dissatisfied with their member's conduct or political stance. This can be a very real threat to a member's independence. Since 1980 the Labour Party has had a reselection process: each MP must undergo reselection (or, if he is unlucky, deselection) once in every Parliament, provided that the constituency party decides (by one member, one vote) that he should. Several Labour MPs have thereby indirectly lost their seats. A member may, of course, be refused official backing by party headquarters at an election. It is also open to the national party headquarters to seek to protect the member; but their practical freedom of action is restricted, especially in the Conservative Party, although a constituency association can deselect its candidate.[83]

ELECTORAL CAMPAIGNS[84]

Following a dissolution, candidates wishing to stand for election must submit nomination papers (signed by a proposer, a seconder and eight other voters) to the returning officer within eight clear days; polling day will be nine clear days afterwards – in practice on a Thursday. The rules governing by-elections are basically the same except that the issue of the writ for holding an election will be made by the Speaker on the resolution of the House of Commons. By custom the necessary motion is moved by a whip from the party which held the seat before the vacancy arose.[85] A party fearing loss of such a seat sometimes refrains from moving the motion for up to three months, leaving the constituency unrepresented.[86] The Recess

---

83 Sir Anthony Meyer was deselected by his constituency association in 1989 after he had challenged Margaret Thatcher for the Conservative leadership, one year before the challenge which unseated her.

84 See Blackburn, op. cit., ch. 6.

85 A custom confirmed by the House in 1983 when an Opposition party sought to move for a by-election writ against the wishes of the Government which had held the seat in question: 11 HC Deb. 164–71 (19 April 1983).

86 A Speaker's Conference on Electoral Law has recommended that normally a writ should be sought within three months of a vacancy: see Cmnd 5000 (1973); by custom, that period is not now exceeded.

Elections Act 1975, which replaced earlier statutory provisions, puts the Speaker under a duty to issue writs for by-elections at the request of any two members during a parliamentary recess; it would be interesting to see this procedure invoked against the wishes of the party that held the seat.

Before party candidates are nominated, it is usual for them to be formally adopted at a special constituency members' meeting, though that is not required by law. But every candidate must appoint an election agent (who may be himself), and the agent will be accountable to the returning officer after the polls for election expenditure. Some frivolous candidatures may still be discouraged by the rule that upon nomination a candidate must deposit the sum of £500 which will be forfeited if he fails to obtain more than one-twentieth of the votes cast.[87]

Attempts have been made by legal regulation to ensure as far as possible that election campaigns are fairly conducted.[88] Bribery, treating and undue influence in the nature of duress are corrupt practices. Candidates are allowed to send an election address to each voter free of postage, and are not to be refused permission to hire schools maintained by the local education authority for election meetings. Under non-statutory agreements between the main parties, the broadcasting authorities allocate time for party election programmes in a reasonably equitable manner on a national basis.[89] And expenditure on elections is limited by law so that not too much weight shall be given to the power of the purse. The law relating to election expenses is in some respects intricate, obscure and unsatisfactory – characteristics reflecting not merely the intrinsic difficulty of detailed regulation but also the influence of vested interests in the main parties which would prefer the law to be vague on certain points. The main general rules are as follows.

1 That no expenditure may be incurred with a view to promoting or procuring the election of a candidate at an election by any person other than the candidate himself or his agent or a person authorized by the agent.[90]

---

87 Representation of the People Act 1985, s. 13. Before that Act the deposit had been £150 and a poll of one-eighth of the votes cast saved it. Despite the increased deposit, the 1992 General Election attracted 25 per cent more candidates than the 1987 poll.
88 Probably the best account of the details of electoral law is in *Halsbury's Laws of England* (4th edn), vol. 15, *Elections*, with Cumulative Supplement.
89 See Boyle [1986] *Public Law* 562; (1990) 61 *Political Quarterly* 200.
90 Representation of the People Act 1983, s. 75. Criticism of an opponent is capable of promoting the election of a candidate who might incur an unauthorized expense in so doing: *DPP* v. *Luft* [1977] AC 962.

2 That the maximum expenditure to be incurred at an election shall be restricted to an amount calculated by adding a prescribed lump sum per constituency to a prescribed sum for each voter in a constituency (the latter amount being higher in county constituencies).[91]

3 That certain kinds of expenditure (notably on broadcasting from outside the United Kingdom except by arrangement with the BBC and the IBA)[92] which might give a wealthy party an unfair advantage shall be absolutely prohibited. The cost of national party election broadcasts and of postage for candidates' election addresses is, however, met by the State.

The difficulties are mostly concerned with the first of these rules, taken in conjunction with the second. What is the relevant period for the purpose of election expenditure? Does it begin with the announcement of a forth-coming dissolution, the proclamation of dissolution, the adoption of candidates, the presentation of nomination papers?[93] Probably the earliest of these dates is the relevant one,[94] though in a sense the party organizations are waging a continuous electoral campaign throughout the life of a Parliament. Again, does expenditure at the national level during the election period have to be apportioned between all constituencies in which the party's candidates are standing, or is it only relevant to consider propaganda distributed or otherwise used in the particular constituency? British electoral law places its emphasis, with a disarming lack of conviction, on the individual constituency and the individual candidate; and the general interpretation, supported directly or indirectly by two modern judicial decisions, is that only expenditure for the purpose of promoting the election of an individual candidate in his constituency (as distinct from expenditure directed to

91 1983 Act, s. 76(1), (2), (3) and 76A (added by the Representation of the People Act 1985, s. 14) allows the Secretary of State to raise these amounts by statutory instrument 'where in his opinion there has been a change in the value of money' since the previous increase – the phenomenon of inflation thus being recognized in the statute book. This is done regularly.

92 1983 Act, s. 92. Broadcasts within this country about a constituency during an election period cannot include a candidate without that candidate's consent: a veto is given to a candidate who would actively participate in a broadcast (as in an interview), but not to a candidate who would merely be shown in it (for example, on film canvassing: *Marshall* v. *BBC* [1979] 1 WLR 1071).

93 Authorities are considered in *Halsbury's Laws of England* (4th edn), vol. 15, paras. 707–12.

94 See s. 93 of the 1983 Act, adopting the announcement of dissolution for the purpose of rules concerning broadcasts 'during' elections.

procuring the election or defeat of candidates of a particular party in general) has to be counted as an election expense.[95] The Labour Government has ordered an independent inquiry into the system of party funding, and as a result legislation may limit the amount of expenditure that parties may incur in their national campaigns. In any event, newspaper articles and comments and political broadcasting programmes (as distinct from advertisements) are expressly excluded from the definition of election expenses, even if the money is spent with a view to promoting the election of a particular candidate.[96]

References in this chapter to the role of the returning officer must not obscure the fact that the burden of organizing the machinery of an election, and particularly the poll and the count, rest mainly on the registration officer.

ELECTION PETITIONS

A voter or a defeated candidate may lodge a petition against the validity of an election.[97] Petitions are heard by an election court, consisting in England of two judges of the Queen's Bench Division, who may sit in the constituency in question.

Petitions based on illegal or corrupt practices or other irregularities at parliamentary elections are now extremely rare; this is partly because very close contests are uncommon and even if the court finds that irregularities were present it may determine that the result ought to stand since they were unlikely to have affected the result.[98] A petition may also be lodged on the ground that the successful candidate was subject to a legal incapacity

95 See *R. v. Tronoh Mines Ltd* [1952] 1 All ER 697 (newspaper advertisement by company advocating defeat of the Labour Government at the impending General Election of 1951, held not an election expense within the meaning of s. 63 of the 1949 Act: now s. 75 of the 1983 Act); see also *Grieve v. Douglas-Home* [1965] SC 313 (party political broadcast featuring the then Prime Minister held not to be expenditure 'with a view to' procuring his election in his constituency).
96 1983 Act, s. 75(1); this amendment resolved any doubt that survived the decision in *Grieve v. Douglas-Home* (see above) on party political broadcasts.
97 The law is now governed by Part III of the Representation of the People Act 1983.
98 After the 1997 General Election, however, the result in the Winchester constituency (which had given the seat to the Liberal Democrats by two votes) was declared void: 55 ballot papers had not been stamped properly by the poll clerk at one polling station. The Speaker ordered a by-election, which was won by the Liberal Democrats with a majority of over 21,000.

– for example, peerage.[99] In such a case the court may, if satisfied that the incapacity existed, either declare the election void (so that a by-election has to be held) or, if satisfied that the voters for the successful candidate had had his incapacity sufficiently brought to their notice so that they must be deemed deliberately to have thrown their votes away, award the seat to the runner-up.[100] Normally the petition has to be lodged within three weeks of the date of the election.[101]

In form the judgment of an election court is a report to the Speaker, which the House is directed by statute to accept. By the act of resolving that the report be recorded in the Journals of the House, the empty shell of the ancient privilege of the House is preserved.

The other methods by which the qualification of an elected member to sit in the House may be challenged and determined have already been noted.[102]

99 See *Re Parliamentary Election for Bristol South-East* [1964] 2 QB 257 (the Stansgate Peerage case). See also the Northern Ireland cases of *Mitchell* and *Clarke* [1958] NI 143, 151 (successful candidates serving long sentences for felony, then a disqualification for election).

100 Thus, the Bristol South-East seat was awarded to Viscount Stansgate's (Mr Tony Benn's) defeated opponent after the by-election caused by the resolution of the House declaring the seat to be vacant.

101 Between 1970 and 1995 six election petitions were lodged: 267 HC Deb. *224* (written answers 22 November 1995).

102 See p. 251.

CHAPTER 14

The House of Commons: Functions and Procedure[1]

INTRODUCTION

Officers

The House of Commons has 659 members, including the Speaker. The first business of the House at the opening of a new Parliament is to elect a Speaker from among its members; the Queen formally signifies her approval of the Commons' choice. The Speaker is expected to be an absolutely impartial chairman of debate; in no sense is he a spokesman for the Government. In early days he was the spokesman for the Commons in relation to the Crown and the Lords. His function of presenting the views of the Commons to the monarch made his position fraught with hazard, and the show of reluctance that he puts up today as he is propelled gently to the Speaker's chair after his election is a reminder of things past.

His election is normally unopposed in the House, and he is not always a member on the Government side. In 1992 Miss Betty Boothroyd (who had been elected originally as a Labour MP and who had been Deputy Speaker in the previous Parliament) was elected the first woman Speaker. The election was contested, and she beat Mr Peter Brooke (a former Conservative Cabinet Minister) in a division. The previous contested election had been in 1951. The Speaker can be removed by a simple resolution of the House, but this state of affairs will arise only if he has comported himself with serious impropriety. The usual practice is to re-elect

---

1 See generally Rodney Brazier, *Constitutional Practice* (2nd edn, 1994), ch. 9, and *Constitutional Texts* (1990), ch. 9; J. A. G. Griffith and M. Ryle, *Parliament: Functions, Practice and Procedure* (1989), especially Parts I and III. A Select Committee on the Modernization of the House of Commons is considering how the practices and procedures of the House should be brought up to date.

the Speaker of the preceding Parliament if he has been returned at the General Election and is willing to stand for office again. As Speaker he detaches himself from his former party affiliations, although his seat will often be contested by other parties at a General Election.[2]

The Speaker does not participate in debate, even when the House is sitting in committee. Nor does he vote on a motion, unless a casting vote from the chair is required; the manner in which he is to cast such a vote is circumscribed by precedent. His main functions in the House are to maintain decorum in debate, to call upon members to speak, to give rulings on points of order and on a question whether a *prima facie* case of breach of privilege has been established, and to act as the servant of the House (for example, in directing the issue of writs for filling vacancies) or as its spokesman (for example, in delivering a reprimand or admonition to one found guilty of contempt of the House; or in communications with legislatures overseas or on ceremonial occasions). As the incarnation of the ancient dignity of the House, he is habitually treated with great respect, indeed deference. Important discretionary functions fall to be discharged by him from time to time – for example, certifying whether a bill is a money bill within the meaning of the Parliament Act 1911; suspending a member for a day for disorderly conduct, or naming a member (who may then incur a period of suspension) for persistent disregard of the authority of the chair;[3] appointing members of the panel of chairmen of committees at the beginning of each session;[4] deciding whether to accept a motion for the closure of debate, and whether to put to the House for debate a question raised as an urgent matter of public importance. He has the same rate of salary as a Cabinet Minister, charged on the Consolidated Fund so that it does not require annual renewal, and a house within the Palace of Westminster. When he retires he will be offered a peerage; the former custom of making a retiring Speaker a viscount was revived in 1983 for Mr George Thomas, but Mr Bernard Weatherill received a life peerage on his retirement in 1992.

The office of Deputy Speaker is filled by three members elected by the

---

2 Suggestions that the Speaker's constituents are in effect unrepresented in the House because of his non-political role overlook the fact that he will take up their problems with Ministers and in that capacity may carry greater weight than an ordinary backbencher. On the Speakership, see Lord Selwyn-Lloyd, *Mr Speaker, Sir* (1976); Philip Laundy, *The Office of Speaker* (1984).

3 See p. 328 note 55.

4 For the functions of the Business Committee of the House (consisting of the chairmen, and other members nominated by the Speaker), see pp. 269–70.

House – the Chairman and two Deputy Chairmen of Ways and Means. At least two belong to the party in office, but when in the chair they are expected to observe the same impartiality as the Speaker. Most of the Speaker's powers are exercisable by them.

The Speaker is assisted by the Clerk of the House of Commons, the other clerks at the table (whose functions are by no means merely clerical), a personal legal adviser, Speaker's Counsel, and an administrative officer, Speaker's Secretary. The Serjeant-at-Arms attends upon the Speaker; he executes orders of the House (for example, to clear the public galleries; to take a person into custody), and is generally responsible for the domestic staff arrangements of the House.

Records

The formal record of the transactions of the House is the Journal of the House, published annually. The Journals do not purport to summarize all that has occurred in debate. They are admissible in evidence in court. Each day the votes and proceedings of the House are recorded and circulated to members; they will record the decisions of the House and its committees, and in due course their substance will be entered in the Journals. The official report (*Hansard*) is a daily verbatim transcript of all that was said and done in the House in the course of parliamentary business; it includes, in what is in effect an appendix, written answers to questions. This is published by Her Majesty's Stationery Office with the authority of the House. It does not include reports of the proceedings of standing committees or select committees, which are published separately. Reports ordered to be laid before the House of Commons and published otherwise than in pursuance of royal or ministerial authority are called House of Commons papers, as distinct from Command papers. The Lords have their own Journals, minutes of proceedings, official reports, and series of papers.

The law and custom of Parliament

The main essentials of parliamentary procedure are contained in the standing orders[5] of the House, which are published by the Stationery Office from time to time and may be varied by a simple majority of the House, and in

5 The standing orders referred to are the 1997 version: see HC 1 (1996–7).

sessional orders which, for example, authorize the appointment of select committees which the House has not yet decided to establish on a permanent basis. Changes in these orders frequently emanate from recommendations of the Select Committee on Procedure. Separate standing orders for private bills are issued.

In addition, the conduct of parliamentary proceedings is regulated to a small extent by statute (for example, the procedure on consolidation bills) and common law; and to a large extent by resolutions of the House, Speakers' rulings and unwritten customs or conventions. Some of the most important practices governing the allocation of parliamentary time are not enshrined in any formal authoritative document.

Parliamentary privilege[6] stands in a slightly different category, though it is clearly part of the law and custom of Parliament. It is to be found partly in legislation and case law, mainly in resolutions of each House, and hardly at all in standing or sessional orders or in unwritten conventions.

The debating chamber

In many legislatures the chamber is in the shape of a horseshoe, and members are able to signify their ideological position by placing themselves on the far left, the far right, or at a suitable intermediate point; speeches are normally delivered from a rostrum. The chamber of the House of Commons is rectangular; the Government benches are on the right of the elevated Speaker's chair, the Opposition are to his left. Today this division symbolizes the character of parliamentary government. Ministers sit on the Government front bench and their supporters behind them; the Opposition front bench faces them. On each side of the House the undemarcated line between frontbenchers and backbenchers will be significant. Members speak from their places and do not declaim from a rostrum; this conduces to an informal style of debate, discouraging the rhetorical flourish. However, informality has its limits. Members must address themselves to the chair; when referring to other members they are to mention them not by name but by description ('the honourable member for Stretchford East'); pejorative epithets are out of order; smoking and reading newspapers are not permitted.

The House of Lords paved the way for the broadcasting of parliamentary

6 See ch. 16.

proceedings. Proceedings in both Houses, and in committees, are continuously recorded, and excerpts are broadcast in television and radio news and current affairs programmes. Prime Minister's Questions (held, under Mr Blair, in one weekly session on Wednesday afternoons) and important statements and debates are broadcast live.[7]

Facilities for members

The number of seats in the House is insufficient to accommodate all members at any one time. This dearth of space (which seldom gives rise to problems except immediately before an important division on a motion) is deliberately designed to foster the atmosphere of an intimate club; it also harks back to the days when for most members politics was far from being a full-time occupation. (Salaries were not paid to members till shortly before the First World War.) Up to 1988 MPs were embarrassed by having periodically to vote themselves pay rises. Now their pay is linked to a percentage of the salary earned by a senior civil servant, so that as civil service salaries rise, so automatically will those of MPs.[8] Currently MPs are paid £43,000 a year. They may also claim an office costs allowance for out-of-pocket office, secretarial and research expenses, up to a current maximum of £46,364 a year[9] MPs whose homes are outside London receive a London allowance of some £11,976 a year.[10] All travel within the United Kingdom on parliamentary business is either free or qualifies for a car mileage allowance, and telephone calls and postage from the House are free. The facilities provided for members outside the chamber are on the whole unimpressive: for example, just over half of all MPs have private offices, the rest having to share. It is planned that each MP will have a private office when the present building works are completed. There is, however, an excellent library and reference service.[11] The House frequently sits late into the night. Since members normally have a multiplicity of responsibilities besides attendance in the House, it is perhaps surprising that the quality of backbenchers is good and has almost certainly improved since the 1950s;

7 See Ryle (1991) 44 *Parliamentary Affairs* 185.
8 281 HC Deb. 533 (10 July 1996).
9 This, too, is indexed and so rises automatically.
10 Those living in inner London receive only £1,324. See generally 281 HC Deb. 527–43 (10 July 1996).
11 See M. Rush and M. Shaw (eds.), *The House of Commons: Services and Facilities* (1974); M. Rush (ed.), *Services and Facilities of the House of Commons* (1983).

this is partly attributable to financial rewards,[12] but not to a sense of security[13] or leisured ease, or a feeling that a backbencher is likely to set the course of the ship of state, but rather to such factors as the hope of ministerial office one fine day, a sense of excitement at being 'in the know' and close to the hub of political activity, or a desire to attract public attention to one's causes, opinions or oneself. MPs are on the whole a good deal more articulate than the average member of the community, and it is unkind to criticize them for having sought a place in that forum which offers the most dignified platform for eloquence.

PARTIES IN THE HOUSE[14]

In 1937 the Ministers of the Crown Act formally recognized the status of the Leader of the Opposition, providing for a salary, charged on the Consolidated Fund, to be paid to him. This was right and proper, for he is the alternative Prime Minister, and a fundamental feature of the British parliamentary system is that the leadership of the largest opposition party really is an alternative Government and should therefore be encouraged to behave like one; in short, being Leader of the Opposition[15] is a full-time job. Under the Ministerial and other Salaries Act 1975, his salary is currently £98,000, and that of the Opposition Chief Whip in the Commons is £74,000. Salaries are also paid to two Assistant Opposition Whips, and to

12 On sponsorship and retainers by pressure groups, see pp. 253, 271, 321. Adverse public reaction to the level of MPs' outside earnings, fuelled by accusations of 'sleaze', led in 1995 to the appointment by the Prime Minister of the Committee on Standards in Public Life, and to the adoption of a new code of conduct for MPs. See the Committee's First Report, Cm 2850 (1995).

13 MPs do, however, qualify for a pension: see Parliamentary and other Pensions Act 1972; Parliamentary and other Pensions and Salaries Act 1976; Parliamentary Pensions etc. Act 1984; Parliamentary and Other Pensions Act 1987. If an MP loses his seat at an election he may also receive a resettlement grant: over £1 million was paid after the 1987 General Election.

14 See especially Peter G. Richards, *The Backbenchers* (1972), chs. 3, 11. This book is a valuable and concise work of reference. See also Dick Leonard and Valentine Herman (eds.), *The Backbencher and Parliament* (1972).

15 Defined (Ministerial and other Salaries Act 1975, s. 2(1)) as that member 'who is for the time being the Leader of the party in that House in opposition to Her Majesty's Government having the greatest numerical strength in the House . . .' Any dispute as to who is the occupant of this post is to be determined conclusively by the Speaker.

the Leader of the Opposition and the Chief Opposition Whip in the Lords.[16]

At a special Labour Party Conference in January 1981 it was decided that in future the Leader and Deputy Leader of the Labour Party would be elected by an 'electoral college', in which 40 per cent of the votes would be cast by trade unions, 30 per cent by the constituency parties and 30 per cent by the Parliamentary Labour Party. The Leader would, moreover, be subject to re-election every year, regardless of whether the Party was in or out of office.[17] Mr Kinnock was elected under this system in 1983 on the resignation of Mr Foot; Mr John Smith was elected in 1992 on Mr Kinnock's resignation, and Mr Tony Blair on Mr Smith's death in 1994. The percentages of votes in the electoral college were changed to equal thirds in 1993. The Chairman of the Parliamentary Party (a backbencher), eighteen MPs and three peers are elected annually by the Parliamentary Party; four seats at least must be filled by women. Collectively they form the Parliamentary Committee or Shadow Cabinet (when in opposition). Decisions of the Shadow Cabinet – the allocation of subject responsibilities to its members is a matter for the Party Leader – are reported weekly to the Parliamentary Party. Lurking in the background lie the National Executive Committee of the Party (elected by the party's annual national conference and including prominent trade unionists and other non-parliamentary figures) and the resolutions passed by the annual conference itself.

In the Conservative Party, the Party Leader is elected by the Parliamentary Party, and is then presented to a meeting of Conservatives drawn widely from the Party and which acts as a nominal electoral college: in effect its function is to acclaim the Leader. In 1975 Mr Heath accepted changes in

16 The House of Commons resolved in 1975 that money from public funds should be paid to Opposition parties to help their parliamentary work, calculated on the number of seats and votes won at the previous General Election: 888 HC Deb. 1869–1934 (20 March 1975). It is known as 'Short money' after the Leader of the House who introduced the concept. The present formula for fixing the allowance was approved in 1993: see 231 HC Deb. 593–615 (4 November 1993). A party can receive an annual maximum of £1.5m. The Report of the Committee on Financial Aid to Political Parties, Cmnd 6601 (1976), recommended a different system of state funding, but it has not been implemented. The Home Affairs Committee of the House of Commons recommended against any new state funding of political parties: HC 301 (1993–4). The Government is considering afresh the whole system of political funding, beginning with a review of the question by the Committee on Standards in Public Life. See further Michael Pinto-Duschinsky, *British Political Finance 1830–1980* (1982); K. Ewing, *The Funding of Political Parties in Britain* (1987).

17 One consequence of this change was the creation in 1981 of the Social Democratic Party.

the election rules, and offered himself for re-election: he lost to Mrs Thatcher. The rules require annual re-election, which (as Margaret Thatcher discovered) gives the Leader only a leasehold, which can be terminated by the Parliamentary Party.[18] The Leader appoints the Deputy Leader, the Chief Whip, the Party Chairman and the Shadow Cabinet; he also has ultimate control of the party bureaucracy, a function vested, within the Labour Party, in the National Executive Committee. The Party's annual conference has tended to be more deferential than the corresponding Labour Party conference, and indeed is contrived to appear as a telegenic party rally. Within the Parliamentary Party there are elected specialized and regional committees. All backbench members belong to the 1922 Committee, a body to which the leadership must pay careful attention despite the fact that in form this Committee is only a discussion group.[19]

Party organization within the House is therefore far from being a haphazard affair. Whether a party is in office or in opposition, the role of the whips is of crucial importance in conveying the views of the rank and file to the leadership and vice versa; in keeping members informed by circular of forthcoming parliamentary business; in giving the expected times of divisions in order to secure a high attendance – by underlining the matter once, twice, or thrice; failure to comply with a three-line whip without a very good excuse is often to be construed as an act of rebellion against the leadership – in arranging, in consultation with whips on the other side, for an indisposed member, or one with an urgent outside commitment, to absent himself by 'pairing' him with another member who also wishes to be absent from the division, so that neither party will obtain an advantage; in making informal recommendations to the leadership about the suitability of backbenchers for preferment; in supplying names of members to serve on committees of the House and in helping to impose party discipline by suasion, admonition and, if necessary, threats that the party whip may be withdrawn or that the ultimate sanction of expulsion from the Parliamentary Party may be imposed.[20] However, disciplinary penalties on Labour members may be imposed only by the Parliamentary Party itself and the Conservative whip is hardly ever withdrawn.[21] All

18 See above, p. 170. The Conservative Party is currently reviewing its leadership election rules, and will probably give a vote to every member of the party.
19 John P. Mackintosh, *The British Cabinet* (3rd edn, 1977), pp. 594–5, mentions some of the decisions influenced by the Committee.
20 See Donald Wade, *Behind the Speaker's Chair* (1978).
21 It was, however, withdrawn from eight Conservative MPs in 1994 over their refusal to support the Government on a three-line whip; and Mr Peter Temple-Morris left the party in 1997 when the whip was withdrawn after he had negotiated to join Labour.

Government whips are now salaried and the Chief Whip usually attends Cabinet meetings. The senior whips also have an important part to play in organizing the distribution of parliamentary time 'through the usual channels'.

BUSINESS OF THE HOUSE

The House normally sits from 2.30 p.m. till at least 10.30 p.m. from Monday to Thursday and from 9.30 a.m. to 3 p.m. on Friday.[22] Standing orders recognize that priority shall be given to Government business,[23] but allocate ten Fridays during a session to private members' bills and motions.[24] In practice private members are allowed to determine the course of business on other occasions – for example, in debates on the daily adjournment, and at question time. An approximately equal amount of time to that allocated to private members is placed at the disposal of the official Opposition, which chooses the topics for debates on Opposition Days. Twenty such days are so allotted, seventeen being at the disposal of the Leader of the Opposition, three being reserved for the second largest opposition party.[25] If, moreover, the Opposition wishes to put down a motion of censure on the Government it is incumbent on the Government to give up a day for such a debate unless the request is part of a campaign of obstruction.

Government business includes not only bills but also motions to debate reports of committees and royal commissions (on which the Government will express its views and submit to comment and criticism), motions to approve certain subordinate legislative instruments, formal Government statements, procedural motions (for example, to curtail debate on a bill), and more general motions which serve as a peg on which a debate may hang.

This picture hardly corresponds with the image of a legislative body dominated by the Executive, particularly when one recalls that the Executive has to pay regard to the views of powerful pressure groups, to stirrings among its backbenchers and party loyalists outside Parliament, and in

22 SO No. 11. The House adopted changes in 1995 (see 265 HC Deb. 405–9 (2 November 1995)) designed to reduce the number of all-night sittings, to provide for the House not to sit on ten Fridays each session, and to establish Wednesday morning sittings for private members' debates.
23 SO Nos. 13(1), 24.
24 SO No. 13(4), (7).
25 SO No. 13(2).

some contexts to the voice of public opinion – not to speak of international pressures, and political popularity polls and by-election results in so far as they may influence political morale. Furthermore, a good deal of the time spent on Government bills is absorbed by critical speeches and debates on amendments. On the other hand, not all parliamentary business is transacted on the floor of the House. And a Government with an overall majority in the House is almost certain to succeed, by marshalling support in the division lobbies and if necessary using its majority to alter the parliamentary timetable, in securing the enactment of the great bulk of its legislative programme.

Form and substance are therefore intertwined but in convoluted shapes. The main responsibility for the business of the House is vested in the Leader of the House of Commons (usually the Lord President of the Council but occasionally the Lord Privy Seal), assisted by the Government Chief Whip. They are expected to consult their opposite numbers 'behind the Speaker's chair'; parliamentary time is allocated 'through the usual channels' on a basis of bargain and compromise, on the understanding that, subject to standing orders and convention, the Government has the biggest claim and may be able to impose its own priorities by resolutions suspending standing orders or otherwise adjusting the normal timetable. Each Thursday in the chamber the Shadow Leader of the House asks the Leader of the House to announce the business of the House for the forthcoming week. This is a question to which he may know the answer already; if he or any other member is dissatisfied (as is invariably the case), there is then an opportunity for public protest, and the Government, anxious not to leave itself open to justifiable criticism, will have already taken this possibility into account.

The following devices are available to enlarge the amount of time available to the Government – and, indeed, the House generally – for debate on the floor of the House.

1 Bills may be debated in standing committee (and second reading committee), so that other proceedings can take place on the floor of the House. The use of these small committees, sitting 'upstairs', has become a very important feature of contemporary parliamentary procedure. Bills based on Law Commission recommendations are usually referred to a second reading committee.
2 Standing orders relating to times may be suspended to postpone the time of the daily adjournment or provide for special sittings on Friday evenings or weekends (a device unpopular in nearly all quarters). Again, the provisional date of adjournment for a recess may be postponed if urgent

business is incomplete; a motion for this purpose may be resisted by the Opposition.

3 Standing orders may be suspended so as to enable the Government to annex private members' time. Any proposal to this effect would be deeply resented today.

4 Procedural devices are available for shortening debate, and are sometimes used to prevent protraction of the proceedings by the official Opposition or backbenchers. The first is the *closure*.[26] In its simplest form, this involves a member (usually a Government whip, rising at a prearranged time) purporting to move, in the course of debate, that 'the question be now put'. Unless the Speaker (or Deputy Speaker) regards such a motion as an abuse of the rules of the House or an infringement of the rights of the minority, he must put this question forthwith without further discussion; if the motion is passed, with at least 100 members voting in favour, then the question then under debate (for example, that the bill be read a second time, or that the House do now adjourn) is put to the House and voted on immediately. The closure was first introduced into the House on the Speaker's responsibility in 1881 after a continuous filibuster of forty-one hours by Irish home rulers who had decided that if Britain would not let Ireland govern herself, the Irish would do their best to prevent Britain governing herself; standing orders were adopted in 1882 to regularize the situation. The *guillotine* is a form of closure by compartments. If debate on a bill, particularly in committee, is likely to be, or is being, unduly protracted, the Leader of the House tries to get agreement through the usual channels for a voluntary timetable; only if that fails will he introduce a resolution under which a prescribed maximum number of days will be allocated to each stage of the bill.[27] Debate on such a motion is likely to be acrimonious, and a tedious three-hour debate will follow usually ending in a Government victory in the division. When the resolution has been passed, detailed compart-mentalization of the bill will be effected by the Business Committee of the House, and in standing committee by a subcommittee.[28] The Business Committee is established *ad hoc* in relation to particular bills to deal with such allocation of time. When the appointed hour is reached the guillotine falls; the chairman must interrupt debate and the committee (or the

---

26 See SO Nos. 35, 36. See also SO No. 10, which enables a Minister to move suspension of a late sitting till the following day.
27 The provision to seek agreement was introduced in 1995.
28 SO Nos. 80, 81, 103.

House) must pass on to the next phase even though many amendments have not yet been reached. One should also mention in this context a separate matter – the power (formerly called the *kangaroo*) vested in the Speaker at report stage and the chairman in committee to select for discussion some amendments to a bill and not to call (thus jumping over) others covering substantially the same ground. This power is conferred by standing orders,[29] is frequently exercised, and rarely evokes serious controversy.

LEGISLATION[30]

Most of us want to see some parts of English law changed, so as to rectify an injustice or an anomaly, or to prohibit conduct of which we strongly disapprove, or to enable something to be done in the interests of the general public or a section of it or merely ourselves. But if we are to transform our prescriptions into remedial medicine, we need power, influence or persistence, or a combination of all three. If the general law of the land is to be altered, Parliament must pass an Act, or Ministers must be persuaded to make new regulations under powers already vested in them by statute. Most of the public bills introduced into Parliament emanate from government Departments; nearly all of them will be passed.[31] A fair number of bills are introduced by private members; not many of them will reach the statute book. The vast bulk of rules and regulations made under statutory authority are departmental, apart from local by-laws. If, then, one cannot be a Minister or a senior civil servant, one ought to start a campaign, or better still, form or join an organization likely to influence the lawmakers. One can hope to exercise some influence within a major political party, particularly if one is elected to the House of Commons; though party discipline will impose its constraints. Or one can join a pressure group. And perhaps one will be moved to form or join such a group in order to prevent the law being changed for the worse.

Pressure groups fall into two main classes, the sectional or interest groups and the promotional or 'cause' groups. To the former class belong such

29 SO Nos. 31, 89(3).
30 See I. Burton and G. Drewry, *Legislation and Public Policy* (1981); D. R. Miers and A. C. Page, *Legislation* (2nd edn, 1990).
31 A spectacular exception was the loss of the Shops Bill (which would have reformed the law on Sunday trading) at second reading by 296 votes to 282, despite a Government three-line whip: see 95 HC Deb. 584–702 (14 April 1986).

powerful groups as the Trades Union Congress, the Confederation of British Industry, the National Farmers' Union, the British Medical Association, and associations representing different categories of local authorities. The degree of influence wielded by some of these bodies may vary according as the Government is Labour or Conservative. In 1971 and 1972 individual unions demonstrated their power in resisting implementation of the Conservative Government's industrial relations and wages policies, and their part in the incomes policies of the Labour Governments from 1974 to 1979 was crucial. The withdrawal of union support for Government economic policies and the 1978-9 'winter of discontent' cost the Labour Government the 1979 Election. The influence of the Confederation of British Industry, less obtrusive but more pervasive, resting on technical expertise, ample funds, representation on numerous official, advisory and consultative bodies, familiarity with the corridors of power and contacts with Ministers, civil servants, MPs and peers, must obviously be greater under a Conservative Government. The major sectional pressure groups are always significant, because a Government needs their cooperation and sometimes cannot withstand their opposition; because they represent large organized elements of the community; because they are wealthy, and can use their funds to employ research staff and to mount extensive publicity campaigns if necessary; because they have, or may be able to obtain, active members and sympathizers in Parliament; because they are represented on advisory bodies connected with Departments; because their office-holders will have direct access to Ministers and senior civil servants. In order to avoid any conflict of interest, the House maintains a Register of MPs' Interests.[32] For a Department to introduce a bill directly affecting the interests of such an organization without prior consultation with its representatives is exceptional; it is still more exceptional for regulations to be made without such consultation. Consultation does not presuppose concurrence, but the content of the bill or the regulations will frequently be influenced by these

---

32 See Report of the Select Committee on Members' Interests (Declaration), HC 102 (1974-5). The Register is published periodically as a House of Commons Paper. MPs must register specified classes of pecuniary interest or benefit, now also including lobbying activities (namely, paid activity in public relations and political and parliamentary advice and consultancy). See generally Erskine May, *Parliamentary Practice* (21st edn, 1989), pp. 384-90. In 1990 Mr John Browne was suspended for twenty sitting days by the House for not properly registering all his registrable interests: see 168 HC Deb. 889-976 (7 March 1990). For issues of parliamentary privilege, see below, pp. 321-2. In 1995 Mr Graham Riddick and Mr David Tredinnick were suspended for ten and twenty days respectively for accepting money to ask parliamentary questions: see 258 HC Deb. 382 (20 April 1995).

discussions. In the case of bills, moreover, detailed amendments put down in Parliament often originate from a pressure group. And a few bills passed, and a larger number of regulations made, during the course of a year will be traceable to the initiative of pressure groups, operating on Departments and private members.

The pressure group which exists to promote a cause (for example, the RSPCA, the Howard League for Penal Reform, Justice) rather than a sectional interest is far less likely to be consulted at the formative stage of legislation, but it may help to procure the enactment of legislation (usually introduced as a private member's bill) or the amendment of bills. Relatively small but energetic and well-organized pressure groups, using special reports or adept propaganda directed towards influential persons rather than the general public, have been largely instrumental in converting parliamentary majorities to such causes as the abolition of capital punishment for murder, reform of the criminal law relating to abortion and homosexual acts, the abolition of theatre censorship, and the creation of the Parliamentary Commissioner for Administration. The European Movement played a part in converting sceptics into supporters of British accession to the European Community.

The end-product of legislation is an interplay of departmental initiative, party political policies, pressure group activities and initiative of individual MPs or groups of MPs. A glance through the Public General Acts for almost any year bears out this proposition.

This evidence suggests that the picture of parliamentary legislation as a function of government is slightly over-coloured but by no means a caricature; and that it is easy to overemphasize the parts played by party political programmes (except during the first year of a new Parliament) and pressure group activities in determining the content of the statute book.

LEGISLATIVE PROCEDURE[33]

There is a Future Legislation Committee of the Cabinet, which considers departmental and interdepartmental proposals for new Government bills in principle and arranges provisional priorities; the Cabinet Legislation

[33] The principal source of information is *The Process of Legislation*, Second Report of the Select Committee on Procedure, July 1971 (HC 538 (1970–71)). See also J. A. G. Griffith, *Parliamentary Scrutiny of Government Bills* (1974). A Select Committee on the Modernization of the House of Commons was set up in 1997. It has a broad remit to consider possible reform of legislative and other procedures.

Committee considers later approved bills in detail, allocates firm priorities and keeps the parliamentary timetable under close review. A senior member of the Cabinet is designated by the Prime Minister to be chairman of the Committees.

Consultation with interest groups is likely to be most active when a bill has been approved in principle, though it may take place before any firm decision has been made (for example, after publication of the report of an independent committee or royal commission) to which the group will almost certainly have submitted evidence. Governments issue a large number of Green Papers and consultation documents, setting out tentative legislative proposals for public discussion. White Papers, setting out firm decisions prior to publication of bills, may follow.

A memorandum of instructions will be prepared by the sponsoring Department, or possibly an interdepartmental committee, for submission to Parliamentary Counsel, who will prepare a first draft of the bill. The bill may undergo several drafts before it is introduced into Parliament. The final draft will be scrutinized by a Law Officer of the Crown as well as the Legislation Committee. Responsibility for the European Communities Bill was taken by the then Solicitor-General, Sir Geoffrey Howe.

Introduction and first reading

Bills may be introduced in the Commons or the Lords. In the interests of good tactical management, a number of Government bills which are not likely to arouse party political opposition begin their career in the Lords. The existence of the upper House makes it possible to have more adequate parliamentary debates on legislation than would be the case if we had a unicameral Legislature. Money bills, however, must normally be introduced in the Commons[34] and a tax bill must be preceded by resolution of the Commons approving its introduction.

The normal method of introducing a public bill into the Commons is by its ministerial sponsors presenting a dummy print of the bill at the table; one of the clerks then reads out the title of the bill, which is thus deemed to have been read a first time; the bill is ordered to be printed and published, and a date fixed for the second reading.

Public bills introduced by private members can obtain a first reading in one of three ways. The first is by obtaining a high place in the ballot for

34 But cf. p. 227.

the right to introduce private members' bills.[35] In practice a member needs a high place to have any real prospect of seeing his bill pass through all its stages into law. The ten MPs placed highest in the ballot may each claim up to £200 as drafting expenses. Promotional pressure groups and sometimes the Government whips will seek to induce a well-placed private member to introduce a bill of their own devising. Several Law Commission bills have been enacted in this way. If the Government is particularly well disposed to a bill, a Minister will move any necessary money resolution and the assistance of Parliamentary Counsel may be made available to its sponsor. Sometimes a Government may give up part of its own time to enable the bill to pass its final stages in the House.[36] Secondly, a private member's bill may be introduced without leave of the House under SO No. 58. If such a bill is unopposed and skilfully managed, it has a chance of becoming law. Thirdly, any member may get up in his place at the beginning of public business on Tuesdays or Wednesdays and ask leave of the House to introduce a bill.[37] The Speaker may allow him a few minutes to explain the nature and objects of the bill and also another member a similar opportunity to speak in opposition; the House then divides on the question whether to give leave. Even if this preliminary hurdle is cleared, bills introduced under the 'ten-minute rule' seldom pass into law because they cannot even be debated unless the Government is prepared to surrender some of its own time.[38]

Before a private bill – a bill of a local or personal character – can be introduced and read a first time, elaborate statutory provisions and special standing orders have to be complied with. Private bills of a personal character are now almost obsolete.[39] The bills were used extensively in the nineteenth century to provide for the naturalization of aliens and for divorces entitling the parties to remarry, until these changes in status could be effected by administrative action or judicial decrees under general enabling legislation. The nineteenth-century flurry of railway private bills is now part of economic history. In the 1990–91 session sixty-nine Public General Acts were

35 See SO No. 13(6), and see D. Marsh and M. Read, *Private Members' Bills* (1988).
36 Occasionally the Government may be forced into legislative action by the popularity of such a bill, as happened with a bill to end solicitors' conveyancing monopoly in 1985.
37 See SO No. 19.
38 On average eighty private member's bills were introduced, of which ten were enacted, each session from 1960 to 1986: see 109 HC Deb. *117–23* (written answers 26 January 1987).
39 Especially following the enactment of the Marriage (Prohibited Degrees of Relationship) Act 1986, s. 1, which removes some of the previous need for a private bill to sanction marriage between related people.

passed, but there were also eighteen 'Local and Personal' Acts. Private bills are promoted mainly by local authorities seeking to acquire special powers; some are promoted by other public corporations, and a few by large public companies.

The private bill procedure is time-consuming and expensive. Accordingly, a Joint Select Committee on Private Bill Procedure recommended[40] radical changes which would apply to the works which Parliament most frequently authorizes by private legislation – those affecting railways, rapid transit systems, inland waterways, harbours, and ports. The committee's recommendations were enacted in the Transport and Works Act 1992. Under that Act an application may be made to the Secretary of State requesting him to make an order by statutory instrument in relation to the construction or operation of any of those transport systems. He must then ensure that specified consultations take place, and that if objections are lodged, a public local inquiry is held. After that, he may make an order authorizing the construction or works to take place. This new system has reduced the amount of private legislation by about half.

A local authority cannot promote a private bill to alter a local government area or to alter its status or electoral arrangements.[41] If a county or district authority wishes to promote a bill, it must give public notice, pass the necessary resolutions by an absolute majority, and confirm the resolution after the bill has been deposited in Parliament. Within the House, the bill must pass the close scrutiny of the examiners of private bills, who have to be satisfied that all the preliminary formalities, including the giving of notice to persons directly affected,[42] have been complied with. If these obstacles are successfully overcome, the bill is given a first reading.

Second reading

The occasion provided for parliamentary debate on the principles of a bill is the second reading stage.[43] No amendment to individual clauses is permissible. Rejection of a bill at second reading may be moved either by a reasoned amendment explaining why the bill should not be read a second time or by an amendment to postpone second reading. A private member's

---

40 HC 625, HL 97 (1987–8); debated at 151 HC Deb. 474–548 (20 April 1989), 507 HL Deb. 1180–212 (17 May 1989).
41 Local Government Act 1972, s. 70.
42 cf. *British Railways Board* v. *Pickin* [1974] AC 765.
43 The Speaker may announce that, because of the large number of MPs wishing to speak, he will limit backbench contributions to ten minutes.

bill may be simply 'talked out' because the allotted time has expired. Private bills are normally unopposed at second reading.

Historically the second reading stage has always taken place in the House itself. The second reading debate on a bill may be conducted in committee in two sets of circumstances.

1 On the motion of a Minister, a bill certified by the Speaker as relating exclusively to Scotland or Wales may be referred to the Scottish Grand Committee or the Welsh Grand Committee for this purpose (SO Nos. 94, 98). (Once the Scottish Parliament is established, such Scottish legislation would be considered only by that Parliament, and not at Westminster at all. Primary Welsh legislation, however, would still be enacted there, and not by the Welsh Assembly.)

2 Any other public bill may now similarly be referred to a second reading committee, consisting of between sixteen and fifty members, provided that ten days' notice of the motion is given and fewer than twenty members object (SO No. 90). Few bills were at first so referred, but the use of the committees has increased markedly of late.[44]

The Committee reports to the House, which formally resolves that the bill be read a second time.

Money resolution

Till 1967 financial clauses in a bill had to be considered in Committee of the Whole House, with the Speaker out of the chair,[45] the Speaker then reoccupied the chair and the financial resolution was formally reported to the House. To save time, the financial resolution has now been telescoped into a single stage, the Speaker remaining in the chair. The necessary motion must still be moved by a Minister, a requirement which means that a backbench MP cannot introduce a bill designed to impose or increase a tax or to authorize expenditure.

---

44 SO No. 90(2) allows private members' bills to be referred to a second reading committee with the leave of the House. This could increase the workload of such committees, especially for uncontroversial private members' bills, but few have been so referred.

45 The need for the Speaker to leave the chair on such occasions was explicable on the grounds that the power of the Commons to withhold taxes and supplies from the Crown was historically of paramount importance, and the Speaker had at times been under the monarch's influence.

Committee stage

The committee stage of a bill follows second reading. It is the stage most likely to be guillotined if the two sides of the House are unable to agree on a timetable. All public bills other than the annual bills providing for public expenditure and bills for the confirmation of provisional orders[46] go to standing committees unless the House otherwise resolves; since 1968 the annual Finance Bill (providing for taxation) has been taken partly in standing committee. The alternative is for a bill to be taken in Committee of the Whole House, which means that the House cannot proceed with any other business while the committee is sitting. Bills that are thought by the Government to be straightforward and not seriously controversial, and bills of major constitutional importance (such as the European Communities Bill or a bill to reform the Lords or to provide for devolution of power to Scotland or Wales) will be debated in Committee of the Whole House. The prospect of massive expenditure of time on the Parliament (No. 2) Bill in Committee of the Whole House induced the Government to withdraw it in April 1969; if the bill had been sent upstairs to a standing committee in the first place, the Government might perhaps have maintained patience.[47]

Standing committees consist of between sixteen and fifty members, chosen by the Committee of Selection in accordance with party strengths,[48] and having regard to their special qualifications. They usually sit in the morning. Scottish bills may be committed to a Scottish standing committee unless the second reading has been opposed by more than six members,[49]

---

46 Certain public general Acts empower Ministers to make provisional orders conferring special powers on public authorities. These orders are provisional in that they do not have effect till confirmed by a Provisional Order Confirmation Act. A provisional order usually entails a local inquiry at which objectors may be heard; the provisional order confirmation bill is technically a public bill, but its committee stage is similar to the committee stage of a private bill (see below).

47 See pp. 312–13. But if a guillotine motion had become necessary at any stage, the Government would have been apprehensive about the outcome, given the opposition of many of their backbenchers to the bill.

48 If the Government does not have a majority in the House, the best it can hope for is parity with combined opposition parties on standing committees. This was the solution arrived at in 1976 when the Government, following the loss of a by-election and the defection of an MP to the Opposition benches, was put into a minority in the House of Commons.

49 SO No. 94. This will change once the Scottish Parliament is functioning.

and bills dealing purely with Wales and Monmouthshire to the Welsh Grand Committee including all MPs from that area.[50]

In committee amendments to individual clauses of the bill are debated;[51] if no amendment to a clause is put down, that clause cannot be discussed except on the motion that the clause stand part of the bill. Proceedings are rather less formal than in the House; members may speak more than once to the same question. The Law Officers of the Crown[52] have the right to attend standing committees and take part in their deliberations, but they are not entitled to vote unless they are members of the committee; their presence is often important, for obscurities in drafting need to be clarified and the implications of proposed amendments made clear. The Minister in charge of a bill (who can speak on a Finance Bill even if he is not a member of the committee) will frequently put down amendments to his own bill in committee in the light of afterthoughts by members of the Government or officials or parliamentary draftsmen, or other representations made from inside or outside the House following second reading. Amendments put down by backbenchers or the Opposition front bench will sometimes be accepted, or withdrawn on the understanding that the Minister will reconsider the matter in an attempt to meet the point in an alternative formulation.

To anyone at all familiar with American legislative bodies, it will be apparent that proceedings in committee on a bill are fundamentally different in the two countries[53] In 1980, however, the House took a small step in the direction of the United States. A special standing committee was appointed to which a small number of bills (about three each session) could be committed. For up to twenty-eight days it can send for persons, papers and records, and hold up to four morning sittings. The first such sitting is in private, but the others are *in public*, to receive oral evidence from interested groups.[54] Although provision for special standing committees is now in standing orders,[55] only a few bills have been considered in them. The only

---

50 SO No. 98. Up to five other MPs may be added. Not much use is made of this Committee for legislative purposes: see above, p. 48. There is also a Northern Ireland Grand Committee, consisting of all Northern Irish MPs and not more than twenty others, which considers such matters affecting the province as may be referred to it (SO No. 99).

51 Subject to the chairman's power to select amendments: see p. 270.

52 See pp. 385–7.

53 See Caspar (1978) 26 *American Journal of Comparative Law* 359.

54 See 991 HC Deb. 835–6 (30 October 1980).

55 See SO No. 91. The Select Committee on Procedure has urged that more use be made of such committees: see HC 49 (1984–5), paras 11–13.

other British analogy with the congressional legislative committee is the select committee. But only in exceptional circumstances will a bill be committed to a select committee; in Britain such a committee is used predominantly as a device for parliamentary scrutiny of administration. However, statute law repeal bills (to clear away dead wood from the statute book)[56] and consolidation bills (to bring together all the existing statute law on a matter in one Act, subject to minor modifications)[57] go to a joint select committee of the two Houses. Such bills now emanate mainly from the Law Commissions.

Proceedings in committee on an unopposed private bill and also on a hybrid bill,[58] and to a large extent on a provisional order confirmation bill,[59] are quite different from those on public bills. A private bill will be considered by a small committee, of four in the Commons or five in the Lords. The bill will have been drafted by parliamentary agents. The promoters must prove the preamble, stating the facts accounting for the bill and its objects, to the satisfaction of the committee; petitioners against the bill, having established their *locus standi*, may argue against the preamble and put down amendments to clauses; the parties may be represented by counsel, call evidence and make submissions. The proceedings of the committee have the outward trappings of a quasi-judicial contest between parties, though the committees may give paramountcy to extraneous factors directed to the furtherance of the public interests.[60]

Report stage

The bill, as amended, is reported to the House. The Speaker takes the chair. If it is a private bill, the report stage may be a formality. If a public bill considered in Committee of the Whole House emerges unamended, there is no report stage. If a bill has been considered in standing committee, other members may wish to put down their amendments on report, subject again to the Speaker's power of selection. Again, if the Government has

---

56 Statute Law (Repeals) Acts are now regularly drafted by the Law Commissions.
57 Some interesting variations from ordinary legislative procedure are prescribed by the Consolidation of Enactments (Procedure) Act 1949. *Quaere* whether observance of the special procedure laid down is mandatory. See Erskine May, op. cit., pp. 668–70.
58 A recent example was the Channel Tunnel Act 1987. As to hybridity, see SO No. 59. The furious parliamentary debates in 1976–7 over whether the Aircraft and Shipbuilding Industries Bill ought to have been passed by the special hybrid procedure cast light as well as heat on the subject of hybridity.
59 See below, p. 344. Such bills are almost obsolete.
60 See above, p. 274.

afterthoughts it may decide to put down amendments or new clauses or schedules on report. It is possible for a bill to be sent back to committee at report stage. Bills considered at second reading in standing committee or by the Scottish Grand Committee may have their report stage taken before such a committee if a Minister so moves and fewer than twenty members object.[61]

Third reading

More often than not, a bill is read a third time immediately the report stage is concluded. The third reading will not be debated at all unless six or more members give notice that they wish for a debate or a postponement.[62] If there is a debate, it will be brief and general in its terms. Only minor verbal amendments may be made; the bill may, theoretically at least, nevertheless be rejected at the end of the debate.

Lords' bills and amendments

The procedure on bills in the Lords is similar to that in the Commons, but there is no money resolution stage and the committee stage is taken in the whole House, with the Lord Chairman of Committees in the chair, and there is no provision in standing orders for the closure or guillotining of debate. A public bill passed by the Lords cannot become law unless the Commons also pass it. A public bill passed by the Commons can become law under the Parliament Acts procedure although the Lords fail to pass it without amendment or reject it. Disagreements between the two Houses on clauses of a bill may be resolved in this manner, but it is more usual for one House (normally the Lords) to give way or for a compromise to be reached; a small committee is appointed by one House to give reasons why it disagrees with the other's amendments.

Quorum in the Commons

The general rule (subject to exceptions for certain hours and days and certain types of business) is that the quorum of the House and in Committee of the Whole House is forty.[63] This means not that forty members have in

61 SO No. 92. A standing committee (other than the Scottish Grand Committee) so constituted must have between twenty and eighty members.
62 SO No. 75.
63 SO No. 40.

fact to be present in the chamber at all relevant times, but that if the House divides on a motion, the business under discussion stands over till the next sitting unless forty or more members have taken part in the division. It is the responsibility of the Government whips to ensure that a sufficient number of their backbenchers are in the vicinity of the chamber to scurry in when a vote is called for. In standing committee the quorum is one-third of its members or seventeen, whichever is the less.[64]

Royal assent

Under the procedure introduced by the Royal Assent Act 1967, the House is simply notified by the Speaker that the royal assent to a bill has been granted, and it does not have to interrupt its proceedings and adjourn to the Lords' chamber to hear the royal assent signified orally.

European legislation

Community legislation of the European Union which is directly applicable without further enactment in this country[65] does not pass through any of these stages. Such legislation consists of regulations made by the Council of Ministers or the Commission. In Community law, regulations are secondary legislation. In United Kingdom law they must rank as primary and not delegated legislation. Existing and new machinery has been used to scrutinize European Union matters. Thus it has become customary for part of question time to be given over to European Union matters; Ministers make statements to the House on their part in the Council of Ministers; and there are periodic debates. The machinery centres in the House of Commons (similar provision is made in the Lords) on the Select Committee on European Legislation, which considers draft Community legislation and other documents published by the Commission for submission to the Council. The Government prepares explanatory memoranda, and the Committee can seek information from Government Departments. The Committee is charged with drawing the attention of the House to documents which raise questions of legal or political importance, to report what matters of principle, policy or law may be affected thereby, and to make recommendations to the House. The Government finds time to debate those materials which the Committee recommends for debate.

---

64 SO No. 89(1). Private members' bills are no longer 'counted out'.
65 European Communities Act 1972, s. 2(1).

The Select Committee on European Legislation has been supplemented by two European standing committees.[66] The Select Committee refers to them such European Union documents as it thinks appropriate. Each standing committee consists of thirteen MPs (although any MP can take part in its proceedings, but with no vote). Each committee reports to the House on those documents referred to it. Ministers have accepted that they should not agree in the Council of Ministers to any proposal for legislation which was still under scrutiny in the committees, save for trivial, routine or confidential proposals.

FINANCIAL PROCEDURE

The main departmental responsibility for the management of the national economy rests with the Treasury, under the Chancellor of the Exchequer. A department bearing the main brunt of decisions affecting national income and expenditure, interest rates, the country's international balance of payments and the cost of living is necessarily of crucial importance.

The initiative in tax policy is vested in the Treasury alone.[67] The details of the Chancellor of the Exchequer's budget speech are revealed to all his Cabinet colleagues only on the day on which it is delivered in the House. Mr Gordon Brown, however, as Chancellor decided to make an annual Pre-Budget Report to the House of Commons to indicate the possible broad lines of his subsequent budget some months before its delivery. This was intended to invite public comment and debate. In matters of public expenditure, Treasury approval is required for all large-scale items, not only at the central departmental level but also by public corporations and, directly or indirectly, by local authorities. The hand of the Treasury extends to approval of the standard terms of Government contracts and pricing policies. The influence of the Treasury at any given time is, of course, partly dependent on the personal stature of the Chancellor, and his ability to carry the Prime Minister and the Cabinet along with him. That influence has traditionally been exercised in the interests of economy and caution. In 1958 Mr Peter Thorneycroft, unable to convince the Cabinet of the need for scaling down the annual estimates, resigned with his two junior Ministers; the Macmillan Government survived his departure.

---

66 See SO Nos. 102, 127.
67 Subject to European Union rules: see below.

Taxation

Taxes are collected by or under the Board of Inland Revenue, and the Board of Customs and Excise. Some taxes – for example, stamp duties – imposed by statute have effect till the statute is amended. Others – notably income tax – have effect only till the end of the tax year and require renewal by Parliament in the annual Finance Act. No charge may lawfully be levied on the subject by the Crown except under authority conferred by express statutory language; the fact that an Act may be unworkable unless charges are imposed in the course of its administration is irrelevant.[68]

Membership of the European Union has had major constitutional effects. First, the United Kingdom has adopted the common external tariff and the common agricultural policy (involving the imposition of import levies).[69] Secondly, the rates of customs duties and agricultural levies can be varied by directly applicable regulations.[70] Thirdly, the European Union is to be progressively financed out of its 'own resources', which comprise the proceeds of customs duties (less 10 per cent for the cost of administration), agricultural levies, and eventually up to 1 per cent of a harmonized value added tax, all collected by Member States for European Union purposes.[71] United Kingdom authorities levy and collect money under Community law as agents for the European Union. Moreover, payments required to meet Britain's European Union obligations are charged on the Consolidated Fund.[72]

Before 1968 the budget was introduced in the Committee of Ways and

68 The leading cases are *Att.-Gen.* v. *Wilts United Dairies Ltd* (1921) 37 TLR 884, and *Cape Brandy Syndicate* v. *IRC* [1921] 1 KB 64. Money paid as taxes pursuant to an *ultra vires* demand is recoverable immediately, together with interest thereon: *Woolwich Equitable Building Society* v. *Inland Revenue Commissioners* [1992] 3 All ER 737 (HL). See also *Liverpool Corporation* v. *Maiden (Arthur) Ltd* [1938] 4 All ER 200 (local authorities). The Bill of Rights provides that no charge on the subject should be levied by pretence of prerogative without the consent of Parliament, but the principle stated in the text above ranges beyond prerogative exactions and, indeed, beyond central government. However, charges may be imposed by the Crown on the subject without express statutory authority for providing services (*China Navigation Co.* v. *Att.-Gen.* [1932] 2 KB 197) which it is under no prior obligation to furnish.
69 An Intervention Board for Agricultural Produce implements the agricultural policy (European Communities Act 1972, s. 6).
70 European Communities Act 1972, ss. 2(1), 5, 6.
71 See European Communities Act, s. 1, sched. 1, para. 6; European Communities (Finance) Act 1995.
72 European Communities Act 1972, s. 2(3). See for Consolidated Fund Services, p. 286. The purpose of charging these moneys on the Consolidated Fund is to reduce parliamentary scrutiny over them. See further 831 HC Deb. 1137–242 (22 February 1972).

Means, a Committee of the Whole House, with the Speaker out of the chair. This committee has since been abolished and the budget speech is made by the Chancellor in the House itself. At the same time, a White Paper is published containing a Financial Statement and Budget Report ('the Red Book'); this includes economic data for the recent past and predictions for the immediate future, some of which have been transferred from the Budget speech, and other parts of which have been added as a result of parliamentary pressure.

The budget was normally introduced in late March or early April but in his 1992 budget the Chancellor of the Exchequer announced a major reform. From 1993 the budget would be presented in the autumn of each year, and now includes both the Government's revenue-raising measures and its spending plans. This change puts income and expenditure proposals into the same process, in line with most other states, thus abandoning the Gladstonian tradition of spring budgets followed by autumn expenditure plans.[73] For tax purposes the financial year runs from 6 April to 5 April in the following year. The Finance Bill, incorporating tax legislation, takes several months of parliamentary time. In order to bridge this gap, statutory authority exists[74] to enable essential taxes to be levied immediately after the budget. As soon as the Chancellor sits down, resolutions approving these tax proposals are passed and have statutory effect forthwith by virtue of the Provisional Collection of Taxes Act 1968. Under section 5 of this Act (as amended), resolutions can be (and are) passed, giving provisional statutory effect, for ten days,[75] to the proposed new rates of income tax, value added tax, corporation tax and customs and excise duties for the financial year; they must be confirmed by the House within ten days; the Finance Bill must be read a second time within thirty days and passed within three months, otherwise the collection of taxes on the basis of the resolutions becomes retroactively invalid. Mr Gordon Brown decided in his turn to revert to the old timing of spring budgets.

Debate on the budget will continue for several days on a general resolution which does not have to be passed forthwith. The Finance Bill is then

73 See Cm 1867 (1992).
74 It was needed because such taxes could not lawfully be imposed merely on the strength of budget resolutions: *Bowles* v. *Bank of England* [1913] 1 Ch. 57. The position was regulated for the future by the Provisional Collection of Taxes Act 1913.
75 See also s. 1 of the 1968 Act, under which the resolutions can be given firm statutory effect (subject to the provisos mentioned in the text above) without a confirming resolution. Even if the budget resolutions are not moved until after 5 April, s. 2 of the 1968 Act gives provisional effect to them.

published and read a second time. At the committee stage – if taken in standing committee, many additional days become available for the business of the House – a very large number of amendments will be put down and some will be accepted or compromise amendments put down by the Government. The Government cannot be too amenable, because the sum to be raised by taxation is geared both to its general economic policy and its commitments as to the quantum of expenditure, but minor concessions are possible. Since there will not have been a full range of prior consultations with interest groups or expert committees before the budget is introduced, the practical implications of the proposed changes in tax law will not always have been appreciated by the Treasury, and it may welcome suggestions – for example, that a particular tax will cause undue hardship or be too difficult or costly to enforce. The bill will usually also modify aspects of tax law which do not need annual enactment.

Amendments will again be put down when the bill is reported to the House. After third reading, proceedings in the Lords will be a formality.

Supplementary budgets and other legislation to levy money (for example, to introduce higher National Health Service charges) may be introduced during a parliamentary session.

National expenditure

Public expenditure also requires statutory authority. About two-thirds of central government expenditure is customarily authorized on an annual basis.

As expenditure in the public sector of the national economy has grown, new machinery for coordinating departmental programmes has had to be constructed. Under this system all forms of public expenditure, including those of nationalized industries and local government, are surveyed. At the heart of these arrangements is the Public Expenditure Survey Committee (PESC), a committee of civil servants chaired by a Treasury official, and including the department financial officers. The Treasury and Departments seek to agree on the projected cost over the next four years of existing departmental policies. The Minister responsible is the Chief Secretary to the Treasury (who is usually in the Cabinet), not the Chancellor of the Exchequer. PESC writes a report on the basis of these discussions projecting the cost of present policies and outlining remaining areas of disagreement. This report (which is highly confidential and is not published) goes to the Chancellor. The Cabinet decides on expenditure for the whole of the public sector. An annual report is published for each department at budget time and sets out the department's performance, objectives and spending. The general economic background to public spending will be explained in the Chancellor's budget statement, which is debated in Parliament.

Bulky volumes of the estimates are published in February and March. They are divided into classes, 'votes' (for individual Departments, sub-Departments, and certain other bodies financed out of central funds), sub-heads and further details; the corresponding figures for the current year are also set out. For the purpose of national expenditure, the financial year extends from 1 April to 31 March. Parliament has to debate the estimates – redress of grievances precedes supply – and the result of its deliberations (or rather, the deliberations of the House of Commons) will be embodied in the Appropriation Act, which is usually passed in July. The Act authorizes the withdrawal from the Bank of England, and the expenditure, of the sum total of the estimates, and appropriates in its schedules money for prescribed votes. But the Government needs drawing and borrowing powers before this. To bridge the gap, a sum (called the vote on account) authorizing the prospective expenditure of 35 to 40 per cent of the total sought will be granted by one or more Consolidated Fund Acts passed before the beginning of the financial year. These Acts will also authorize expenditure on supplementary estimates for the year just ending, and may ratify an excess vote to a Department which overspent its allotted sum in the previous year.[76]

Those items of expenditure for which annual authority is needed are called Supply Services; the others (comprising interest on the national debt, the Civil List, and the salaries of judges, the Speaker, the Leader of the Opposition and other persons whose conduct in office ought not to be the subject of annual debate, and sums required for the discharge of European Union obligations) are Consolidated Fund Services. The Consolidated Fund is a notional account kept at the Bank of England. In 1968 many of its functions and revenues were allotted to a new account, the National Transactions Capital Account.[77]

The estimates are prepared in Government Departments and are then vetted by the Treasury, which usually demands cuts in them. Recently a Cabinet committee known colloquially as the Star Chamber has achieved final agreement each year between individual Ministers and the Treasury over the estimates, if prior agreement has proved impossible. That commit-

---

76 Unappropriated sums can be made available in an emergency out of the Civil Contingencies Funds. Such grants are scrutinized by the Comptroller and Auditor-General and the Public Accounts Committee (see below) and are often the subject of a critical report.

77 See National Loans Act 1968.

tee has been replaced by a standing Ministerial Committee on Public Expenditure. Three Estimates Days are then devoted in the House before 5 August each year to debate selected estimates.

Another scrutiny mechanism is the Treasury Select Committee, one of the fourteen new select committees set up in 1979.[78] It consists of eleven members under the chairmanship of a senior MP, usually a former Treasury Minister.[79] Its terms of reference authorize it to examine the expenditure, administration and policy of (inter alia) the Treasury, Board of Inland Revenue and Board of Customs and Excise. It is authorized to appoint one subcommittee. The committee makes full use of its powers to require the presence of senior Ministers, including the Chancellor of the Exchequer, and officials, and actively seeks the production of departmental papers. Among the subjects of inquiry on which it has embarked are the general management of the economy, covering control of public expenditure, responsibilities of the Comptroller and Auditor-General, taxation and monetary policies. Its declared aims are to monitor the Treasury and economic policy, and to keep Parliament and public better informed so as to broaden discussion of economic policies.

The Public Accounts Committee[80] was established in 1861 and is composed of fifteen members. Although, as in all select and standing committees, they are selected according to party strengths, the committee is scrupulously non-partisan – so much so that there is a well-settled convention that its chairman shall be a member of the Opposition; he is usually a former junior Minister at the Treasury. Its task is to ensure that parliamentary grants have been applied to the objects which Parliament prescribed. It bases its examination of government spending and of departmental administration on the reports of the Comptroller and Auditor-General. Accordingly its reports are not confined to financial irregularities but also cover wasteful and extravagant expenditure and imprudent contractual transactions.[81] The fact that the Comptroller and Auditor-General sits with the Committee strengthens its position greatly when it interrogates departmental accounting and finance officers. Its reports are treated with the greatest respect in Whitehall and are debated annually by the Commons.

78 See below, pp. 292–6.
79 SO No. 130.
80 See Basil Chubb, *The Control of Public Expenditure* (1952); E. L. Normanton, *The Accountability and Audit of Governments* (1966).
81 For example, the Ministry of Defence was criticized in 1986 over the £880m wasted on the Nimrod early-warning system, which was then cancelled – 'a major example of how not to approach' the making of contracts: see HC 104 (1986–7).

The Comptroller and Auditor-General is a key figure in the system of parliamentary control of finance. He is an officer of the House of Commons, not a civil servant. He is appointed by the Crown on an address presented to the Crown by the Commons and moved by the Prime Minister acting with the agreement of the Chairman of the Public Accounts Committee.[82] He is removable only for misbehaviour in pursuance of an address from both Houses of Parliament, and his salary is charged on the Consolidated Fund. His department, the National Audit Office,[83] has a staff of several hundreds appointed by him.

The Comptroller and Auditor-General is empowered to carry out examinations into the economy, efficiency and effectiveness with which various authorities or bodies have used their resources in discharging their functions, but not to question the merits of their policy objectives.[84] His powers did not extend to the nationalized industries.[85] The Government has, however, used its powers under the Competition Act 1980, section 11, to refer the accounts of several nationalized industries for audit by the Monopolies and Mergers Commission. The estimates for the National Audit Office are laid before Parliament after being approved by the Public Accounts Committee which includes the Chairman of the Committee of Public Accounts[86] and the Leader of the House of Commons.[87] It works closely with the departmental accounting officers, who are normally the permanent secretaries, and the departmental financial officers who head departmental financial branches.

The Comptroller and Auditor-General is responsible as designated auditor for the annual examination and certification of some 450 accounts involving net annual expenditure in excess of £50,000m. In addition to the Appropriation Accounts, store accounts and trading funds and accounts of all Government Departments, these include the accounts of a wide range of statutory boards and authorities as well as of certain international bodies and UN agencies. The C & AG examines and reports to Parliament on Inland Revenue, Customs and Excise and other revenue accounts. Without being designated auditor he has been granted access to inspect the books of more than 500 bodies of widely varying types which depend to a greater or lesser extent on finance from public funds. This enables him to report

82 National Audit Act 1983, s. 1.
83 ibid., s. 3 and sched. 2.
84 ibid., ss. 6 and 7.
85 ibid., s. 7(4) and sched. 4.
86 ibid., s. 2 and sched. 1.
87 ibid., s. 4(2).

to Parliament in such cases where it might not be appropriate or necessary for him to be appointed auditor. The C & AG's responsibilities do not, however, extend, within the public sector, to local authorities or, within the private sector, to numerous companies and other businesses and organizations in receipt of voted moneys. His reports draw attention not only to financial irregularities but also to wasteful and extravagant expenditure and imprudent contractual transactions. Their weakness is that the malpractices or blunders to which they refer will have occurred not less than a year beforehand and sometimes a good deal farther back, and the money may have been squandered beyond recall. But the report of an inquest may be productive as a spur to remedial action; for instance, the adverse report of the Public Accounts Committee on excess profits made by an armaments firm under a contract for the supply of a guided missile led to a repayment by the firm and tighter contracting procedures.

One of the Committee's 1979–80 reports shows what an indispensable watchdog it is. It uncovered overpayments of offshore suppliers' interest relief grants of £16m with further contemplated overpayments of £44m in breach of Treasury guidelines and complained with 'great concern and amazement' that it was given 'grossly inaccurate and misleading evidence' by the Permanent Under-Secretary of the Department of Energy. On the other hand, the Committee was only able to act as coroner in 1984 over the ill-fated De Lorean car factory project in Northern Ireland, because the £77m of public money had been spent and lost. The Committee thought that this was 'one of the gravest cases of the misuse of public resources for many years'. And in 1987 the Committee reported that, despite the fresh provision in the National Audit Act 1983, 'Parliament's consideration of the annual estimates – the key constitutional control – remains largely a formality.'[88]

SCRUTINY OF POLICY AND ADMINISTRATION

The general role of the official Opposition has already been considered. Its main procedural opportunities for criticizing the Government or individual members arise in the debate on the address in reply to the Queen's speech at the beginning of a session, debates on the budget and on Opposition

---

[88] See HC 98 (1986–7); see the Government's response, Cm 177 (1987). And see J. McEldowney in J. Jowell and D. Oliver (eds.), *The Changing Constitution* (3rd edn, 1994), ch. 7.

Days, debates on motions of censure or other substantive motions (for example, on a formal motion for the adjournment) for which the Government gives up part of its own time, second reading debates, and at question time. But the time saved by procedural changes enabling more legislation to be considered in standing committees has been filled by Government legislation rather than general debate.[89] Backbenchers have their opportunities on the occasions set aside for private members' motions, on the motion for the adjournment each day, at question time and, if any succeed in catching the Speaker's eye, in the course of general debate. They can also put their names to 'early day motions', which are in the nature of demonstrations of protest, concern or occasionally loyalty; these motions are tabled but are hardly ever debated in the House.

Ordinary business may be interrupted to debate a matter of urgency under Standing Order No. 20. A motion to adjourn to discuss 'a specific and important matter that should have urgent consideration' can be moved by any member, at short notice, immediately after question time. It lies within the Speaker's discretion whether to allow the motion to be put; leave is not readily granted. If this obstacle is overcome, and if the motion is approved by the House or supported by forty members rising in their places, the motion will be debated either that evening or the following day.

Members and question time[90]

Members of Parliament receive hundreds of thousands of letters from members of the public each year, making complaints which usually call for some kind of remedial action or request for information. In addition, most members hold local 'surgeries' to deal with the personal problems of their constituents. If a matter calling for further action falls within the area of ministerial responsibility, the member will usually write to the Minister about it and perhaps talk to him personally; if no satisfactory answer is received, the member may well decide to raise the issue at question time, or pass a complaint alleging injustice caused by maladministration to the Parliamentary Commissioner for Administration to investigate. If a grave public scandal is suspected, and pressure is exerted on the Government, a

89 HC 538 (1970), para. 4.
90 See D. N. Chester and Nona Bowring, *Questions in Parliament* (1962); Helen Irwin in M. Ryle and Peter G. Edwards (eds.), *The Commons under Scrutiny* (1988); J. A. G. Griffith and M. Ryle, op. cit., pp. 366–74; M. Franklin and P. Norton (eds.), *Parliamentary Questions* (1993).

special independent inquiry or a formal tribunal of inquiry may be set up.[91]

Tabling questions in the House is one form of obtaining publicity for individual grievances; redress may be forthcoming because a parliamentary question is threatened, or because it has been put down, or because the answer given to the question is manifestly unsatisfactory and the Minister feels that he is appearing in a bad light, or because the member presses home his point by giving notice that he will raise the issue again on a half-hourly debate on the daily adjournment; but if no redress has been granted by question time, the likelihood is that no redress will be offered at all. A question to a Minister is rather a method of ventilating grievance than of securing a remedy.

Questions to Ministers may serve other purposes. They may even be put for the purpose of eliciting factual information, in which case an oral answer will seldom be requested; the answer will then be given in writing, and circulated together with answers to oral questions which there was no time to reach. (Question time lasts for some forty-five minutes, on Mondays to Thursdays.) They may be inspired questions; a member is asked to put down a question so that the responsible Minister can make a public statement.[92] They may be, and often are, carefully designed to cause a Minister the maximum amount of embarrassment. Although a question for which an oral answer is requested must normally be tabled two days in advance, the question may be an opening gambit, to be followed by a supplementary question of which no prior notice is given. (It does not, however, overtax a Minister's Private Office to work out in good time what the supplementary questions are likely to be.)[93] Parliamentary reputations have been made and marred in the rapid cut and thrust of question time. For a few minutes the House comes to life audibly and visibly: wit,[94]

91 See chs. 28 and 30 for the investigation of alleged abuses under the Parliamentary Commissioner Act 1967 and the Tribunals of Inquiry (Evidence) Act 1921.
92 But a Minister should not carry this practice to a point where opposition questions cannot be put; nor should departmental civil servants be induced to take part in such a game. See Report of the Select Committee on Parliamentary Questions (HC 393 (1971–2)); 1st Report from the Select Committee on Procedure (HC 379 (1989–90)).
93 Ministers do not, therefore, go like lambs to the slaughter: they are (or should be) ready with supplementary *answers*. 'One evening I found Churchill at the Cabinet table . . . "What are you doing, Prime Minister?" I asked. "Oh, Parliamentary questions. Preparing improvisations! Very hard work!" ': Harold Macmillan, *Tides of Fortune* (1969), p. 496.
94 Winston Churchill, still Prime Minister at seventy-nine, was asked to constitute a Ministry of Fisheries separate from the Ministry of Agriculture. Explaining his refusal, he observed that 'there are many ancient links between fish and chips' (528 HC Deb. 2274), 17 June 1954.

feigned or genuine outrage, cheers and jeers intrude upon the solemnity of the proceedings; Government and Opposition are briefly locked in fascinating verbal combat; the Prime Minister and the Leader of the Opposition may gain or lose a point or two in the public opinion polls; a backbencher shows his ministerial potential, and the House wonders how much longer the Minister of Cosmology can last.

Whatever may be the intrinsic value of parliamentary questions, their popularity with MPs is beyond doubt. Some two hundred questions for oral answer are submitted each day in the average session.[95] The average cost of answering a question orally is £244, and in writing £105. If the cost of answering a given question is likely to exceed £450 a Minister may refuse to answer it.[96]

As has already been pointed out,[97] questions may and normally will be refused if they relate to matters lying outside the field of ministerial responsibility. Among inadmissible questions[98] are those on matters *sub judice*, but the scope of this exclusionary rule has been narrowed so as to enable the Speaker to admit questions in his discretion though they relate to matters pending adjudication in a civil court, if the issue raised concerns a matter of national importance or the exercise of a Minister's discretion challengeable only on narrow grounds before the court.[99]

Departmental select committees of the House[100]

A serious weakness of the House of Commons is the ineffectual role of so many backbenchers – no less ineffectual because it cannot be quantified.

95 The House has restricted to a maximum of two the number of questions which each member may table to any particular Minister for oral answer. The number of questions to be printed on the order paper has also been limited, and those which are not printed lapse: 178 HC Deb. 376–400 (24 October 1990).

96 See 129 HC Deb. *429* (written answers 14 March 1988).

97 See p. 194.

98 See Erskine May, op. cit., pp. 289–91. See also the Scott Report on the export of defence equipment to Iraq, HC 115 (1995–6), ch. K8.

99 839 HC Deb. 1589–627 (28 June 1972), a relaxation directly related to controversial proceedings before the (since abolished) National Industrial Relations Court; see HC 298 (1971–2). But the relaxation in 1972 was intended to be a deliberate one by the House of the *sub judice* rule in the area of public policy, which was not confined to that Court or to the Act which established it, and the Speaker exercises his discretion in favour of freer debate in every case where he properly can: 916 HC Deb. 882–4 (29 July 1976).

100 See J. A. G. Griffith and M. Ryle, op. cit., ch. 11; D. Englefield, *Commons Select Committees: Catalysts for Change?* (1984); D. Hill, *Parliamentary Select Committees in Action* (1984); G. Drewry, *The New Select Committees* (2nd edn, 1989).

Able men and women discover that their opportunities to contribute significantly to debate are few, that their influence on Government policy from the backbenches or in opposition seems negligible, that even in the privacy of parliamentary party meetings the leadership is rarely moved by their arguments and that the conduct of public administration cannot be effectively scrutinized by the House. If Parliament is the grand inquest of the nation, the roles of coroner and corpse are apt to be confused. But, as the experience of the Public Accounts Committee has shown, it is possible, within the existing British parliamentary system, for members to *influence* the conduct of administration and to modify aspects of policy by their scrutiny of administrative activity as members of select committees.

Very modest moves in favour of backbenchers were made in 1967 when Select Committees on Agriculture and on Science and Technology were established. The experiment was not an unqualified success. The Select Committee on Agriculture was discontinued in 1969 by a decision of the Government which the House ratified. A few other specialized select committees were formed subsequently, including one on race relations and immigration and another on the Parliamentary Commissioner for Administration (which rapidly justified its existence).[101] These committees offered some detailed and imaginative suggestions for administrative reorganization, and made themselves, the House in general and interested members of the public better informed about central administration and the views of the administered.

It was not until 1979 that a bold experiment to extend the opportunity for MPs to scrutinize the Executive through specialized select committees was started. In its breadth and concept it was far more radical than anything which had gone before. Following a report of the Select Committee on Procedure[102] the incoming Conservative Government, committed to offering the House the chance to reform its methods, afforded the House the opportunity to set up twelve new committees to examine the expenditure, administration and policy of designated Government Departments, with the power to send for papers and witnesses and to appoint sub-committees. The House took that opportunity.[103] The new departmental select committees, each with a fixed membership of between nine and eleven (most have eleven) MPs, are now on Agriculture; Culture, Media and Sport; Defence; Education and Employment; Environment, Transport

---

101 See further ch. 30.
102 See HC 588–1 (1977–8).
103 969 HC Deb. 33–252 (25 June 1979).

and the Regions; Foreign Affairs; Health; Home Affairs; Northern Ireland; Public Service; Science and Technology; Scottish Affairs; Social Security; Trade and Industry; Treasury; and Welsh Affairs.[104] There was no committee to oversee the Lord Chancellor's Department, as a result of dubious Government claims that such a committee might prejudice judicial independence. In 1991, however, the House amended its standing orders at the Government's instigation to put the Lord Chancellor's Department and the Law Officers' Department under the aegis of the Home Affairs Committee, with the Lord Advocate's Department coming under the Scottish Affairs Committee.[105] Members of the committees are chosen by the Committee of Selection. This device has been criticized because that Committee is itself nominated by the whips: the uncharitable take the view not only that it would keep the most outspoken of the Government's critics away from such delicate work but also that frontbench patronage would be enhanced. In recommending MPs for membership the Committee of Selection reflects the party balance in the House as a whole. The other main scrutinizing select committees are the Select Committees on the Parliamentary Commissioner for Administration, Public Accounts, European Legislation, and Broadcasting (of Commons proceedings), together with the Joint Select Committee on Statutory Instruments, the Select Committee on Standards and Privileges and the Select Committee on Procedure.

A select committee, known as the Liaison Committee and consisting of the chairmen of the departmental select committees, was set up in 1980 to consider general matters relating to the work of the new scheme.[106]

The Committees decide for themselves which topics to investigate, in consultation with the Liaison Committee so as to avoid duplication of effort. The Foreign Affairs, Home Affairs and Treasury Committees may nominate subcommittees so that simultaneous investigations may be conducted by each of those Committees. The formal powers of the committees to send for persons, papers and records have only had to be

---

104 SO No. 130. The departmental committees on Northern Ireland, Scottish, and Welsh Affairs are not to be confused with the three Grand Committees. No Scottish Affairs Committee was set up in the 1987 Parliament because not all of the small band of Conservative MPs from Scottish constituencies would agree to serve. The committee was, however, re-established in 1992.

105 'Consideration of individual cases and appointments' remains outside the committees' terms of reference: see 195 HC Deb. 608 (18 July 1991).

106 977 HC Deb. 1687–718 (31 January 1980). For its general reports on the progress of the departmental committees, see HC 92 (1982–3), HC 363 (1984–5).

exercised once:[107] an informal invitation to give or supply evidence usually does the trick. Those formal powers embrace Ministers (even Prime Ministers) and civil servants (even the Head of the Home Civil Service and Secretary to the Cabinet).[108] But in the aftermath of the Westland affair[109] the Defence Select Committee wanted to examine named civil servants who had been involved in the improper leaking to the press of the Solicitor-General's letter: the Government opposed this, and the Committee (which at one stage threatened to invoke its formal powers) agreed to a compromise in which the Cabinet Secretary and the Permanent Under-Secretary at the Department of Trade and Industry attended instead.[110] At no stage during this episode, however, did any select committee concede that its ultimate legal powers (which had been conferred on the committees by the House and which were underpinned by the ability of the House to punish for contempt) were restricted in any way claimed by the Government.

The extraction of evidence from witnesses has, on the whole, been an easy process. But the Government continues to insist that civil servants remain subject to ministerial direction, and in any case may not give evidence at all on certain matters.[111] And, just occasionally, a Minister himself may refuse to answer questions – a refusal which amounted to stonewalling by Mr Leon Brittan during his evidence on Westland to the Defence Committee.[112] In 1992 Kevin and Ian Maxwell repeatedly refused to answer questions before the Social Security Committee which was investigating the massive pensions frauds committed by their late father, Robert Maxwell. They did so on the grounds that, as they faced imminent criminal charges, their answers might prejudice a fair trial. The Committee recommended

107 In 1982, when the Energy Select Committee made a formal order against Mr Arthur Scargill, with which he fully complied. Any refusal to comply would be referred to the House to deal with as a contempt of the House: see Erskine May, op. cit., ch. 10. If an MP were reluctant to testify, only the House itself could order his attendance (although this has not yet had to be done).

108 The Government promised in 1979 that Ministers would attend if asked: see 969 HC Deb. 45 (25 June 1979). Occasionally the Prime Minister has directed that a Minister other than the one sought should attend.

109 See above, p. 197.

110 See HC 519 (1985–6), paras. 225–33.

111 In particular, they must follow the guidance issued by the Cabinet Secretary (see above, p. 203 and note 58). This restriction has been heavily criticized by the Treasury and Civil Service Committee (see HC 62 (1986–7)) and by the Liaison Committee (see HC 100 (1986–7)). For the Government's defence of its attitude, see Cm 78 (1987), paras. 9–12.

112 See HC 519 (1985–6), paras. 203–4.

that they be brought before the bar of the House to answer questions, but the dissolution of Parliament intervened and this was not done.

The departmental select committees provide a forum in which Ministers, civil servants and others can be cross-examined at length and more thoroughly than in any other way at present open to the House of Commons. Their members have acquired knowledge and have developed expertise about departments; the committees usually publish unanimous reports which can cross party lines so as to present powerful all-party criticism of the Government;[113] and, according to the Liaison Committee, they have markedly improved the flow of information to the House as a whole. The Select Committee on Procedure has conducted a full review of the system, and has reported very favourably on the work of the committees. It recommended no significant changes.[114] A continuing weakness of the system is, however, that only a small number of the reports issued are debated substantively in the House.[115]

113 See, e.g., HC 533 (1979–80) – the Foreign Affairs Committee's critical reaction to a Government plan to increase university fees for overseas students; HC 36 (1989–90) – the Trade and Industry Committee's criticism of the Department's lack of diligence towards insider dealing (reporting 'astounding' delays and 'dilatoriness' in enforcing the law); there are several other examples. An unusual example of a report in which Government and Opposition members divided on party lines was the Foreign Affairs Committee's report on the sinking of the *General Belgrano* during the Falklands conflict: see HC 11 (1984–5); another was the Home Affairs Committee's report on judicial appointments procedures: see HC 52 (1995–6).

114 2nd Report from the Select Committee on Procedure, HC 19 (1989–90). The Government welcomed the report: see Cm 1532 (1991).

115 Several reports are debated on other occasions, such as during adjournment debates. But the Government does routinely publish a response to each committee report, usually as a White Paper.

CHAPTER 15

The House of Lords[1]

COMPOSITION

The following are entitled to membership of the House of Lords.

1 The Lords Spiritual. These are the Archbishops of Canterbury and York, the Bishops of London, Durham and Winchester, and the next twenty-one senior diocesan bishops of the Church of England, seniority being determined by the date of appointment to a see;[2] they cease to be eligible to sit as Lords Spiritual after retirement at seventy. The Lords Spiritual are not peers, but Lords of Parliament.[3] Other ecclesiastics may sit only if granted peerages. In early Tudor times the Lords Spiritual had constituted half the membership of the House.

2 Hereditary peers of England (before 1707), Great Britain (1707–1800) and the United Kingdom (1801–): they are dukes, marquesses, earls, viscounts or barons.[4] There are about eight hundred such peers; more than half of the hereditary peerages of the United Kingdom have been created (on the advice of the Prime Minister) since 1900, though none was conferred from 1905 to 1983.[5] Some of the surviving ancient hereditary peerages were created by the issue of a royal writ of summons followed by the actual taking of a seat; such peerages descended to heirs general,

---

1 See Rodney Brazier, *Constitutional Practice* (2nd edn, 1994), ch. 11, and *Constitutional Texts* (1990), ch. 10; J. A. G. Griffith and M. Ryle, *Parliament: Functions, Practice and Procedure* (1989), ch. 12.
2 The Bishop of Sodor and Man is excluded because the Isle of Man is not part of the United Kingdom: see Erskine May, *Parliamentary Practice* (21st edn, 1989), p. 9.
3 See Standing Orders of the House of Lords relating to public business, SO No. 6.
4 The holder of a peerage other than a dukedom may simply be known as 'Lord' X. A baron is almost invariably so styled. Some confusion can be caused by 'courtesy titles'; thus, the eldest son of the Duke of Marlborough has the courtesy title of the Marquess of (or Lord) Blandford, but he is not a peer.
5 When viscountcies were recommended for Mr George Thomas and Mr William Whitelaw. Mr Harold Macmillan was created Earl of Stockton in 1984.

including women. All modern hereditary peerages have been created by letters patent;[6] they do not descend to women unless there is an express provision in the letters patent for inheritance by heirs female. But although a woman might be a peeress in her own right, she had no right at common law to take a seat in the Lords; and this disability was not removed by the general words of the Sex Disqualification (Removal) Act 1919: see *Viscountess Rhondda's* case (1922).[7] Under the Life Peerages Act 1958 a life peerage conferring the right to sit can be bestowed upon a woman; and the Peerage Act 1963 enabled all peeresses in their own right to sit in the Lords.[8]

3 Peers of Scotland, who have inherited peerages created before the Act of Union.[9] Till the Peerage Act 1963 they elected sixteen of their own number to represent them for the duration of a Parliament; now they have an unrestricted right to take their seats. Peers of Ireland no longer have any right to sit in the Lords,[10] but may be elected to the Commons.

4 Life peers, created under the 1958 Act; they number over three hundred and eighty. Non-hereditary peerages had been created under the prerogative, but it was held in the nineteenth century that conferment of such a peerage bestowed no right to sit in the Lords; such a right could only be given by statute.[11] It was thought that a number of persons with radical sympathies who were prominent in public life would be willing to accept life peerages but not hereditary peerages; the Life Peerages Act was passed mainly in the hope of strengthening and broadening the composition of the House of Lords. Once a year a list of new 'working' life peers is

---

6 A writ of acceleration was issued to Lord Cranbourne, heir to the Marquess of Salisbury, in 1992 on the Prime Minister's advice so that he could become a member of the House of Lords and take up a junior ministerial appointment. That procedure had previously been used in 1951.

7 [1922] 2 AC 339 – an unconvincing report by a majority of the Committee of Privileges of the House of Lords, praying in aid the presumption of statutory intent against the indirect introduction of major constitutional change.

8 The wife of a peer is not, as such, a peeress in her own right. She may be elected to a seat in the Commons.

9 Any Scotsman on whom a peerage has been bestowed since the Act of Union has been a peer of the United Kingdom. Disputes over Scottish peerages are decided by the Court of the Lord Lyon in Edinburgh, as happened in 1996 over the Earldom of Selkirk.

10 *Re Earl of Antrim's Petition* [1967] 1 AC 691; Report of the Committee for Privileges on the Barony of Farnham (HL 85 (1994–5)). Before 1922, when the Irish Free State was constituted, peers of Ireland elected twenty-eight representative peers for life. The machinery for filling vacancies caused by death then lapsed.

11 *Wensleydale Peerage case* (1856) 5 HLC 958; see p. 310, below.

drawn up by the Prime Minister after consultation with the Leader of the Opposition (and occasionally with other party Leaders).

5 Lords of Appeal in Ordinary, appointed for life under the Appellate Jurisdiction Acts. They are appointed as judges, usually from the Court of Appeal, but are not precluded from taking part in general debate,[12] and they are indeed still entitled to sit in the House after they have retired from judicial office. The maximum number entitled to be paid as Lords of Appeal at any one time is twelve.

It will be seen that some members of the House of Lords (the Lords Spiritual) are not peers, and that not all peers (for example, peers of Ireland) are entitled to sit. Alienage, infancy, bankruptcy and imprisonment for treason are also disqualifications for sitting.[13] There is no provision for expulsion of a peer by resolution of the House in its legislative capacity.

The potential membership of the House is over one thousand. Some peers who have succeeded to hereditary peerages have never applied for writs of summons;[14] other peers have been granted, or have been deemed to obtain, leave of absence[15] under a standing order designed to discourage habitual absentees ('backwoodsmen') from descending on Westminster in strength to vote down a controversial measure emanating from the Commons. The average daily attendance is about three hundred,[16] but the number can still rise sharply on an important occasion. In 1971 the House voted 451 to 58 in favour of the principle of entry into the European Community. Five hundred peers turned out in 1988 to vote on a hostile amendment to the bill to introduce the poll tax. The amendment was defeated by 317 to 183. In 1993 621 peers voted on a motion requiring a referendum on the Maastricht Treaty; the motion was defeated.

12 See generally Louis Blom-Cooper and Gavin Drewry, *Final Appeal* (1972), ch. 10.
13 Mental disorder does not disqualify: see HL 254 (1983–4), pp. 5–6, and Leopold [1985] *Public Law* 9. If a peer is imprisoned, the Lord Chancellor informs the House; he did so after Lord Brocket had been jailed for five years for fraud in 1996.
14 The number in 1995 was eighty-five.
15 Erskine May, op. cit., p. 168. In 1994–5, sixty-eight members of the Lords had leave of absence. At the beginning of each Parliament the Clerk of the Parliaments writes to those peers who were on leave of absence during the previous session asking if they wish to renew their leave. Leave is granted only to those who apply. One who has obtained leave of absence for that Parliament or that session, or who has not replied to the letter, is expected not to attend the House during the relevant period unless he gives a month's notice of his desire to attend, though he cannot apparently be prevented from speaking or voting if he nevertheless presents himself.
16 In 1955 (before the Life Peerages Act 1958) it was only ninety-two. The attendance record of peers of first creation was, not surprisingly, better than that of peers by inheritance.

A peerage may fall into abeyance or become extinct, but cannot be alienated; nor could it be renounced at common law.[17] Mr Tony Benn's persistent campaign to disclaim the Stansgate peerage to which he had succeeded came to fruition in the Peerage Act 1963.[18] Under this Act a peer may disclaim for his own lifetime a hereditary peerage to which he has succeeded, provided that he makes the disclaimer within twelve months of succession or coming of age. If he is an MP, or a parliamentary candidate who is then elected to the Commons, he has only a month in which to make up his mind. After disclaimer, he becomes a commoner; he may subsequently be granted a life peerage but not a hereditary peerage. One upon whom a peerage has been personally conferred cannot disclaim it. Seventeen peers by inheritance have disclaimed their peerages; not surprisingly, Mr Benn was the first of the few. The Earl of Home soon disclaimed his peerages in 1963 and became an MP after having been appointed Prime Minister.[19] Viscount Hailsham (Mr Quintin Hogg) also rejoined Mr Benn in the Commons but returned to the Lords as a life peer on being appointed Lord Chancellor in 1970. The effect of the Act has not seriously affected the balance between the two Houses, but it has belatedly removed a source of injustice to reluctant peers.

Peers are not paid a salary for attendance, but they may claim reimbursement for all travel on parliamentary business, and for daily subsistence up to £33 a day, for overnight subsistence up to £75 a day and a general office, secretarial and research allowance of up to £32 a day.

The House of Lords allows its proceedings to be televised.

FUNCTIONS AND WORK OF THE HOUSE[20]

The Lord Chancellor, sitting on the woolsack, presides in the House,[21] but he lacks, and does not need, the coercive disciplinary powers of the Speaker of the Commons. Proceedings in the Lords sometimes resemble a game of cricket without an umpire; probably no other legislative body maintains

17 In 1989 the barony of Grey of Condor was revived after a 500-year abeyance.
18 See Tony Benn, *Out of the Wilderness: Diaries 1963–7* (1987), ch. 2.
19 He received a life peerage as Lord Home of the Hirsel on his retirement from the Commons in 1974.
20 See D. Shell, *The House of Lords* (2nd edn, 1992).
21 That part of his salary which he receives as Speaker of the House of Lords is not charged on the Consolidated Fund, though the salary of the Speaker of the House of Commons is so charged. See Ministerial and other Salaries Act 1975, s. 1.

so high a degree of gentle decorum. Another engaging eccentricity is that the Lord Chancellor often leaves the impartial (and extremely comfortable) cushion of the Woolsack to speak for the Government.[22] When the House is in committee the chair is taken by the Lord Chairman of Committees. The House has a Gentleman Usher of the Black Rod to attend on the Lord Chancellor and execute the orders of the House. The clerk of the House is styled Clerk of the Parliaments; he prepares and presents bills for the royal assent; he is removable only on an address by the Lords. The House sits for about 150 days in an average session.

The White Paper on reform of the House of 1968 referred[23] to seven functions of the House: (i) its appellate role; (ii) the provision of a forum for debate on matters of public interest; (iii) the revision of Commons bills; (iv) the initiation of less controversial public bills; (v) the consideration of subordinate legislation; (vi) scrutiny of the activities of the Executive; and (vii) scrutiny of private legislation.[24]

The judicial functions of the House (i) will be considered separately,[25] so will function (v).[26] Function (vi) is not performed adequately; a stronger, reformed second chamber could do better. Reference has already been made to function (vii). The second, third and fourth functions are of some consequence.

Several factors impair the efficiency of the Lords. The House is aristocratic and non-elective; its members do not represent any body of constituents and are thought of as speaking for a small section of the community. Moreover, as is well known, a peerage is often granted as a reward to party loyalists or as a consolation for Ministers who, no longer measuring up to their jobs, are 'kicked upstairs'. The Conservatives always form the largest group. Governments do not depend on the favour of the Lords for their continuance in office. The House has no power over money matters; it cannot impose its will on the Commons in legislation but can be overridden by the Commons; it is vulnerable to a hostile Labour Government because of lack of a firm basis of public support, and, conscious of this fact, is very reluctant to exercise the suspensory powers over legislation which it

22 Another Minister is Leader of the House of Lords.
23 House of Lords Reform, Cmnd 3799, pp. 2–3.
24 In the 1985–6 session the House divided its time as follows, in percentages: consideration of Commons bills: 58; general debates: 16; questions: 11; ministerial statements, subordinate legislation: each 4; debates on European Community Committee reports: 2.5; private bills: 0.5; other: 4.
25 See pp. 308–11.
26 See p. 349.

retains,[27] the Government can brush aside opposition in the Lords more readily than in the Commons, mainly because a high-handed attitude on its part is less likely to have adverse electoral repercussions; the Government front bench in the Lords is seldom strong[28] and much of the excitement aroused by questions and debates in the Commons is therefore lacking in the Lords.

On the other hand, the quality of members and speeches is often high. Those upon whom peerages are conferred are usually persons of considerable experience of politics,[29] the public service or industry or who have otherwise made their mark in public or intellectual life. They bring to the House a wide range of expertise. They tend to be elderly, but there is a leavening of young peers by succession. In recent years the House has become markedly more liberal in its outlook towards matters of social and penal reform; the effect of the Life Peerages Act has been conspicuously beneficial. For example, the original initiative in relaxing the law relating to homosexual conduct (the Sexual Offences Act 1967) came from the Lords, not the Commons; a big majority in the Lords against the abolition of capital punishment for murder in the early postwar period was converted to an abolitionist majority in the mid-1960s.[30] The leisurely timetable of the Lords gives the backbencher more opportunities to speak than in the Commons; and debates on matters which cut across party lines, raising controversial moral issues out of which the Government is more likely to incur odium than attract credit by adopting a positive position, can easily be arranged in the Lords. Again, the political balance has become more evenly weighted save on highly contentious party occasions. In 1997 there were 476 Conservative peers, 290 cross-benchers, 109 Labour and 52 Liberal Democrats. It is, however, the case that the Conservative Party forms the largest single group in an average day's attendance.

---

27 But see below, pp. 307–8.

28 Partly to attract peers to the Government front bench, an allowance was made payable for the first time to Ministers in the Lords under the Ministerial and other Pensions and Salaries Act 1991, s. 5. The Leader of the Opposition in the Lords also receives an allowance under the Act.

29 For example, very few of the former Cabinet Ministers who have left the Commons since 1964 remain outside the House of Lords.

30 This can be partly explained by reference to a change of attitude among the bishops and to some extent among the Law Lords. See the debates on the bill which became the Murder (Abolition of Death Penalty) Act 1965. See also Janet Morgan, *The House of Lords and the Labour Government 1964–1970* (1975). The House also voted to insert a clause in the 1991 Criminal Justice Bill to end the mandatory life sentence for murder, but the Government secured a reversal of that vote.

The House of Lords as at present constituted is a useful legislative chamber. As has been mentioned, many of the less controversial Government bills are introduced there; the debates will often be well informed; helpful amendments to law reform bills may be moved by Law Lords at committee stage. The Government's legislative output is thereby enlarged and its efficiency improved. (It should, however, be noted that a majority of Commons' bills are passed wholly unamended every session.) The utility of the Lords as a forum for the consideration of private bills is well recognized. Not so generally appreciated is its value as a chamber for the introduction of private members' bills which may be crowded out in the Commons; in every session two or three such bills, not usually of a controversial character, become law. A controversial backbench bill originating in the Lords is unlikely to pass into law that session, but by attracting publicity it can lead to the implementation of a reform soon afterwards; the Sexual Offences Act 1967 is an illustration. The function of the Lords in revising Commons' bills is potentially more important, but is not very satisfactory in practice, mainly because the Lords are apprehensive about the consequences of using their delaying powers by insisting on amendments to a Labour Government's bills.

Occasionally the revising powers of the Lords are used with significant effect. The House, for example, successfully insisted that the bill which became the Foreign Compensation Act 1969 should (contrary to the Government's original wishes) make provision for a limited right of appeal to the Court of Appeal from the Commission's determinations about its jurisdiction. That episode showed the potential value of a well-informed second chamber. It also illustrates, incidentally, how a second chamber may be used by the Government to interpolate into a bill its afterthoughts instead of having to introduce an amending bill later.

This last point was illustrated still more aptly in 1972, when 610 Lords' amendments were made to the controversial and complex Local Government Bill after it had been passed by the Commons. The vast majority of those amendments were introduced by the Government.

The House of Lords regularly appoints select committees to investigate matters of concern to it. Some of the reports of those committees are critical of the policies of the Government of the day, regardless of its political colour: so, for example, the Report of the Select Committee on Unemployment urged major changes in the Conservative Government's employment policies,[31] and the Select Committee on Science and Technology roundly

31 See HL 142 (1981–2).

condemned the Government's failure to support industry and to take a greater part in innovation and manufacture.[32] The reports are always a useful source of information, and the House routinely debates all select committee reports – an attribute which the other House does not enjoy in relation to the reports of its departmental select committees.[33]

DISAGREEMENTS BETWEEN THE TWO HOUSES

Till 1911 the Lords and the Commons had coordinate legislative authority except in money matters.[34] By convention, and according to the privileges claimed by the Commons, bills dealing wholly or mainly with taxation or public expenditure had to be introduced in the Commons, and their money clauses could not be amended by the Lords, though the Lords retained at least a formal right to reject them. Nor could the Lords amend the financial clauses of non-money bills, save where the Commons decided not to insist on but instead to waive their privilege of having exclusive cognizance of such matters. This is broadly the constitutional position in relation to financial matters today[35] but superimposed is the drastic rule introduced by the Parliament Act 1911.

In 1909 the House of Lords rejected the Finance Bill; they passed it in 1910 after the Liberal Government had been returned to office at a General Election. Following the second General Election of 1910, at which the Liberals retained power, the Lords were induced to pass the Parliament Bill under the threat of being swamped by a massive influx of new Liberal peers.[36] The Parliament Act 1911 was amended by the Parliament Act 1949, but not so as to affect its provisions relating to money bills.

Money bills. For the purpose of section 1 of the Parliament Act 1911, a money bill is one which in the opinion of the Speaker contains provisions *exclusively* relating to central government taxation, expenditure or loans. If before a bill leaves the Commons the Speaker certifies it as a money bill, then it may be presented for the royal assent notwithstanding that the Lords have failed to pass it without amendment after it has been before them for

---

32 HL 37 (1990–91).
33 See above, p. 296.
34 See Erskine May, op. cit., ch. 30; see Brazier (1988) 17 *Anglo-American Law Review* 131.
35 Though see p. 227.
36 For a readable account of the crisis, see Roy Jenkins, *Mr Balfour's Poodle* (1954).

one month. The Speaker's certificate is to be endorsed on the bill; once given, it is conclusive for all purposes;[37] before giving it, he must, if practicable, consult two members of the chairmen's panel. It will be noted that the statutory definition of a money bill is narrow; not every Finance Bill has been so certified. But the combination of strict law and convention has deprived the Lords of all effective authority over raising and spending money.

Other bills. Other public bills (including private members' bills) passed by the Commons may also be passed into law against the opposition of the Lords. (The Commons may kill a Lords' bill simply by not passing it.) Under section 2 of the Parliament Act 1911, a bill could be presented for the royal assent if (1) it had been passed by the Commons in three consecutive sessions (whether of the same Parliament or not) in the same form or subject only to such amendments as were certified by the Speaker as being necessary through the effluxion of time or to Lords' amendments agreed to in the preceding session by the Commons; (2) the Lords had failed to pass it in each of the three sessions; (3) two years had elapsed between the second reading of the bill in the Commons in the first session and its third reading in the Commons in the third session; (4) the bill had been sent up to the Lords at least one month before the end of each session; and (5) the Speaker had certified that the requirements of the Parliament Act had been complied with. By the Parliament Act 1949 the number of sessions was reduced from three to two and the interval of time from two years to one. Hence the suspensory veto of the Lords has been reduced to one year and one month.[38]

These provisions do not, however, apply to bills to prolong the maximum duration of a Parliament beyond five years, or to provisional order confirmation bills,[39] nor do they apply to private bills or to subordinate legislation. Only by resorting to the unlikely, and probably self-defeating, expedient of requesting the monarch to create a sufficient number of new peers for the purpose,[40] could a Government secure the passage of such a bill against the adamant opposition of the Lords.

37 Though cf. pp. 32, 92.
38 If the Lords neither reject the bill nor amend it in a manner unacceptable to the Commons but merely adjourn proceedings on the bill, the Speaker is likely to certify that the requirements of the Parliament Acts have been complied with immediately before the end of the session so that the bill can be presented for the royal assent. In practice the suspensory veto is unlikely to exceed a year.
39 cf. p. 277.
40 See pp. 126–7.

Only four Acts have been passed over the heads of the Lords under the Parliament Act procedure: the Welsh Church Act 1914 (disestablishing the Church of Wales); the Government of Ireland Act 1914 (providing for home rule for Ireland; the outbreak of the First World War followed at once, and this Act was never brought into operation; self-government was introduced after the war, along with partition); the Parliament Act 1949; and the War Crimes Act 1991 (conferring jurisdiction on United Kingdom courts to try certain war crimes committed during the Second World War in German-occupied territories). The 1949 Act was ostensibly designed to forestall prospective Conservative opposition to a measure for the nationalization of the iron and steel industry. A Parliament Bill was introduced late in 1947 and was passed by the Commons; the second reading in the Lords was adjourned while a conference of party leaders discussed schemes for the future composition and powers of the Lords; the conference broke down on the question of the period of delaying power over legislation; the Lords then rejected the bill on second reading by a large majority, and after the bill had again been passed and rejected in the next two sessions it was submitted for the royal assent.[41] The Government nevertheless found it expedient to accept a Lords' amendment to the Iron and Steel Bill, postponing its operation; the Government lost office soon afterwards and that measure did not come fully into effect.

The House of Lords used its suspensory veto to the full over the Labour Government's Trade Union and Labour Relations (Amendment) Bill. Only when it became clear that the Government would cause the Bill to be passed under the Parliament Acts did the House of Lords withdraw its strong objections and allow the measure to go for royal assent in 1976, having forced a delay of slightly under one year.[42] The opposition peers could claim that they had ensured the maximum time for the Commons to reconsider the measure in a proper exercise of the constitutional function enshrined in the Parliament Acts.

Under the Government's 1968 proposals for Lords' reform, the period of delay would have been reduced to sixty parliamentary days from the

---

41 Professor Hood Phillips has argued (*Reform of the Constitution* (1970), pp. 18–19, 91–2) that the Parliament Act of 1949 may be a nullity, because it was enacted by a 'delegate' with limited powers (i.e. the King and Commons under the Parliament Act 1911 procedure) and a delegate cannot enlarge its own powers. But even if one accepts the view (rejected above at p. 93) that legislation passed under the 1911 Act procedure is 'delegated' and subordinate, it is questionable whether the 1949 Act was *ultra vires* according to the canons of statutory interpretation.

42 The Bill became the Trade Union and Labour Relations (Amendment) Act 1976.

date of disagreement between the two Houses. Provision would also have been made for enabling the Commons to override by a simple resolution the Lords' disapproval of such delegated legislation as was subject to parliamentary proceedings.[43]

In practice full-scale collisions between the two Houses have been infrequent. The Lords have not rejected any of the nationalization bills passed by the Commons under Labour Governments; they have inserted many amendments, but most have been withdrawn after the Commons have insisted on their unacceptability, or a compromise has been reached after discussions between party leaders in the two Houses; some Lords' amendments to Government bills have been accepted on their merits or for reasons of prudence.[44] There have, however, been two recent exceptions to this accommodation which provide the boldest instances of the House of Lords holding up and amending major pieces of Government legislation (apart from the War Crimes Bill). First, the Aircraft and Shipbuilding Industries Bill was introduced in the 1975–6 session and passed the House of Commons. The Lords, however, attached amendments which would have withdrawn the ship-repairing industry from the Bill, and insisted on those amendments. That session of Parliament ended and the Bill was lost. It was reintroduced in the 1975–7 session and passed when the Government gave way over the ship-repairing clauses.[45] Secondly, the House of Lords passed by a majority of 48 a wrecking amendment to the Local Government (Interim Provisions) Bill in 1984, so that the Conservative Government was forced to reconsider its plan to abolish the 1984 elections to the Greater London Council and to the metropolitan county councils and to put in nominated boards pending the abolition of those authorities. In view of the general unpopularity of the proposed abolition of elections and the number of Conservative defections and abstentions which contributed to the majority of 48, the Government had to cause the Bill to be amended so as to extend the life of the authorities to 1986 without elections in 1984

43 Cmnd 3799 (1968), pp. 21–3. See ch. 17.

44 In 1947–8 the Commons, on a free vote, inserted in the Criminal Justice Bill a clause moved by a backbencher which would have abolished the death penalty; the backwoodsmen emerged, and the Lords passed an amendment by a large majority to delete the clause; the Government dropped the clause from the bill. It is unlikely that the Parliament Act procedure would be invoked to secure the passage of any private member's bill.

45 The House of Lords had also effectively killed the House of Commons (Redistribution of Seats) Bill in 1969. The Government, unwilling either to accept the Lords' amendments or to resort to the Parliament Acts, decided to withdraw the Bill: see further pp. 241–3 and 349.

and to dispense with the expedient of nominated boards; the episode caused some regular critics of the existence of the House of Lords (such as Mr Ken Livingstone, Leader of the GLC) for a while to become its most ardent champions.

The House of Lords is, indeed, tending to behave in a more even-handed manner towards the legislation of Governments of both parties. The 1979 Conservative Government sustained its one hundredth legislative defeat in the Lords in October 1986 – roughly at the same rate of setback as that inflicted on the 1964 Labour Government. The two hundredth defeat was inflicted in 1992. This attitude has enhanced the House in the eyes of the general public.

In the last analysis the most important reason why a non-Conservative Government has seldom run into serious trouble with the Lords as at present constituted is a fear of the consequences of self-assertion which the Conservative leadership in the Lords rightly entertains. The Prime Minister might, for example, obtain a dissolution of Parliament in an endeavour to distract public attention from more embarrassing and relevant problems, and the Government might then contrive to win a sufficient measure of support to be returned to power, pledged to end the Lords (under the Parliament Acts procedure, if necessary).[46]

JUDICIAL DUTIES OF THE LORDS[47]

The Lords have functions of a judicial nature incidental to their capacity as a legislative body, though inasmuch as the House is a superior court of record, their determinations may be reported in the law reports. Claims to peerages[48] and to a right to sit in the House by virtue of the grant of a peerage are referred to the Committee of Privileges of the House; the House traditionally adopts the Committee's report.[49] This procedure is also adopted when allegations of breach of the privileges of the House are made.

---

46 On whether the House of Lords could lawfully be abolished, see Mirfield (1979) 95 *LQR* 37 and Winterton, ibid., 386.
47 See Robert Stevens, *Law and Politics: The House of Lords as a Judicial Body 1800–1976* (1979); Alan Paterson, *The Law Lords* (1982).
48 Disputes as to the validity of the creation of a new peerage are decided by the House of its own motion. Disputes as to who (if anyone) is entitled to an old peerage are determinable by the Attorney-General on behalf of the Crown but are normally referred, in practice, to the House.
49 See, e.g., *Ampthill Peerage case* [1977] AC 547; *Annandale and Hartfell Peerage Claim* [1986] AC 319 (earldom revived after almost 200 years in abeyance).

Magna Carta had laid it down that a free man was entitled to trial by his peers. This principle survived in the House of Lords till 1948; a peer (or his wife) charged with treason or felony was tried by the whole House of Lords; this expensive anachronism was abolished by the Criminal Justice Act 1948 and peers are now tried in the ordinary courts.

The process of impeachment is obsolete but has never been abolished. If a person were to be impeached today he would be tried by the whole House of Lords, with the House of Commons as his accusers.

Another function of a judicial nature, harking back to the days when the High Court of Parliament was a judicial as well as a legislative body, was the enactment of a bill of attainder, not by the Lords alone but by the Queen in Parliament. An act of attainder is a legislative judgment declaring a person to have been guilty of treason or other high crimes. Over 270 years have passed since this ugly manifestation of 'parliamentary judicature' was last expressed. The offences of which a man was attainted were not necessarily crimes at the time when the acts complained of were committed. Modern constitutional bills of rights will usually debar the Legislature from enacting *ex post facto* penal laws,[50] and the constitution may also, either expressly[51] or by implication,[52] invalidate bills of attainder.[53]

The House of Lords is also a court of appeal, at the apex of the ordinary hierarchy of courts in the United Kingdom.[54] In this capacity it exercises the ancient jurisdiction of the High Court of Parliament. It ceased to exercise original jurisdiction in the seventeenth century. The exercise of its appellate jurisdiction gave rise to some awkward problems; the quorum of the House in its judicial as in its legislative capacity is three, and there were not always three hereditary peers with judicial experience available to sit; the judges of the common law courts could, however, be called in to offer advice.[55]

50 For example, Constitution of India, art. 20(1).
51 For example, Constitution of the United States, art. 1, s. 9.
52 For example, where the constitution vests the judicial power exclusively in the Judiciary. And before Ceylon became the Republic of Sri Lanka under a new constitution in 1972, the power of the Ceylon Parliament to make laws for the peace, order, and good government of Ceylon did not import a power to pass an Act for the condemnation of a particular individual: *Liyanage* v. *R.* [1967] 1 AC 259; though *cf. Kariapper* v. *Wijesinha* [1968] AC 717.
53 Express references to 'bills of attainder' in modern constitutions are uncommon because of the ambiguity of the phrase – an ambiguity emphasized by trends of interpretation in the United States Supreme Court.
54 For a full study, see Louis Blom-Cooper and Gavin Drewry, *Final Appeal* (1972).
55 The last case in which such advice was sought was *Allen* v. *Flood* [1898] AC 1. The advice given by the judges in that case was not accepted.

An attempt was made to strengthen the judicial element in the Lords in the mid-nineteenth century by conferring a life peerage on a judge of the Court of Exchequer, Sir James Parke; the Committee of Privileges reported that a life peer was unable to take his seat,[56] and Parke had to be given a hereditary peerage. The idea of diluting the hereditary peerage with lawyers and their progeny was unattractive to the Lords; and the need for a second and not very distinguished appellate court was not readily apparent to laymen or indeed the bar. Under the Judicature Act of 1873 the appellate jurisdiction of the Lords was to be abolished; but after the Conservatives had ousted the Liberals at the General Election of 1874 a determined and successful campaign to restore that jurisdiction was mounted.[57] The Appellate Jurisdiction Act 1876 provided for the appointment of two (there may now be twelve) Lords of Appeal in Ordinary, life peers who have a right of audience in all proceedings in the Supreme Court;[58] they were given a *statutory* right to sit in the Lords. They retire at seventy-five[59] but may still be asked by the Lord Chancellor to sit. By convention, at least two must be Scots lawyers. The Lord Chancellor, ex-Lords Chancellor and other peers who hold or have held high judicial office may also make up the necessary judicial quorum; in practice five Law Lords normally sit to hear an appeal. Lay peers are not precluded by statute from sitting uninvited with the Law Lords to hear an appeal, but by convention they abstain from doing so; the last time when such a peer sat was in 1883 and his participation in the proceedings (including his vote on the appeal) was simply ignored.

In its capacity as a court of appeal the House sits as an appellate committee; it adjourns to the chamber of the House for the formal delivery of opinions, which have been handed out in writing shortly beforehand and are not now read out by their Lordships. It may sit during a prorogation or dissolution of Parliament.

The House entertains civil and criminal appeals, with leave of itself or the court below, from the Court of Appeal. It also hears appeals from the Courts-Martial Appeal Court and in certain cases direct from the Divisional Court of the Queen's Bench Division, and individual High Court judges, under restrictive conditions. It exercises civil but not criminal appellate

---

56 *Wensleydale Peerage case* (1856); above, note 11. Sir James Parke was a Baron of the Exchequer, but not the holder of a title of baronage.
57 See Stevens (1964) 80 *LQR* 343.
58 Courts and Legal Services Act 1990, s. 71 and sched. 10; see below, p. 362, note 20.
59 Lords of Appeal appointed after 1993 are subject to a retirement age of seventy: Judicial Pensions and Retirement Act 1993, s. 26 and sched. 5.

jurisdiction in respect of the Scottish courts, and hears both civil and criminal appeals from Northern Ireland.

APPROACHES TO REFORM

The preamble to the Parliament Act 1911 recited the intention 'to substitute for the House of Lords as it at present exists a second chamber constituted on a popular instead of a hereditary basis . . .' In 1917 the Bryce conference proposed[60] that three-quarters of the members of the second chamber should be indirectly elected on a regional basis by the House of Commons; this scheme, unpropitious in its timing and, like all other schemes for reform of the Lords, inconveniently controversial, was placed in a pigeon-hole, and there it remains. The inter-party conference convened after the second Parliament Bill had been passed by the Commons reached a substantial measure of agreement on an outline plan for a reconstituted upper House; the principle of indirect election, and inheritance as an automatic qualification for membership, were alike rejected; it was accepted that the House ought to be complementary to rather than a rival of the Commons, and that as far as possible matters should be so contrived that no party had a permanent majority in it.[61] Nothing was done to implement these proposals. Subsequent reforms have not undermined the hereditary principle, but the Life Peerages Act 1958 has led to an improvement in the quality of debate, an increase in the number of regular attenders and a modification in the political complexion of the more conscientious body of participants,[62] and standing orders providing for leave of absence have also helped. But a vote strictly along party lines on a matter attracting a large attendance will almost invariably give the Conservatives a majority.[63]

Discussions about the reform of the Lords have cut across party divisions without bringing about the impetus or sense of urgency needed to carry a scheme through the Commons. Agreement in principle amongst the sophisticated tends to be less than whole-hearted and to beget new disagreements when principle is translated into detail.

Real enthusiasm for Lords' reform is too often to be found among the eccentric and the naïve, who may have little idea of the mediocre

---

60 Cd 9038 (1917).
61 Cmd 7380 (1948).
62 This was also influenced, of course, by life peerages granted on the advice of Mr Wilson and Mr Callaghan during 1964–70 and 1974–9.
63 See above, p. 302, for party allegiances in the House of Lords.

performance of second chambers in so many other countries or of the limited expectations that can reasonably be reposed in a reconstituted British second chamber. Party political considerations also inhibit a determined approach to reform. Conservatives would, on the whole, like to see a less unrepresentative upper House brought into existence, but preferably by agreement and under a Labour Government; for a stronger upper House would be readier to exercise its authority, and if this were used to the detriment of a Labour Government (for example, by delaying bills) the Conservatives would not have to incur the unpopularity that would be attached to the reformed House's progenitor. Radicals have tended either to favour abolition of the Lords or to let sleeping dogs lie; an unrepresentative second chamber is now unlikely to do more than growl, and occasionally bark, at a Government of the Left, whereas a renovated and more self-assured body might bite hard.

In this context the Government's abortive scheme of 1968[64] was an imaginative effort to grapple with an elusive set of problems. Briefly, it envisaged a House stronger in its composition (though with reduced delaying powers), so constituted that no party would have a permanent overall majority; but the Government of the day would have a 10 per cent majority over the combined opposition parties, with crossbench peers (including the Law Lords) and bishops holding the balance. The House would, in effect, have two tiers – those members with voting rights and those who would be entitled to sit and speak but not vote. The voting House would have 200 to 250 members apart from bishops and serving Law Lords; the members would be those hereditary peers of first creation and life peers who were prepared to attend regularly; about eighty new Labour life peers would have had to be created if the bill had become law in 1969, in order to bring the Government side up to strength. There would be a retiring age for voting members and they would be paid a salary. Non-voting members would be those peers of first creation who were unable or unwilling to meet the attendance requirements, and all existing peers by inheritance; subsequently, however, inheritance of a peerage would no longer of itself qualify for membership of the House at all.

By June 1968 a large measure of agreement had been reached. Then the Government, irritated by the refusal of the Lords to approve (at the first time of asking) an Order in Council imposing mandatory UN sanctions against Rhodesia, broke off the talks and produced its own scheme, closely

<hr/>

64 House of Lords Reform, Cmnd 3799 (1968).

based on what had already been agreed. A White Paper embodying the Government's proposals was debated in November 1968. It was approved in principle by the Commons by 270 votes to 159. The breakdown of the voting figures is remarkable; although the Government had put on a three-line whip, and although the Opposition front benches were in general sympathy with the proposals, 45 Labour backbenchers, 104 Conservatives, 8 Liberals and 2 other members voted in the Noes lobby. The Lords agreed to the proposals by 251 votes to 56.

Nevertheless (or perhaps consequently) trouble lay ahead for the Government. A bill to implement the proposals, the Parliament (No. 2) Bill,[65] was read a second time in the Commons. But when it went to Committee of the Whole House, a multitude of amendments were put down by backbenchers. Many members objected to the excessive patronage that the scheme would have placed in the Prime Minister's hands; some Conservatives objected to the erosion of the hereditary principle or the weakening of the party's strength in the upper House; some Labour members saw the proposals as a means of shoring up a crumbling citadel of aristocratic privilege and wealth which ought to be demolished altogether or left alone to crumble away. In the end the Government gave up. In April it withdrew the bill, to make room for a still more controversial Industrial Relations Bill which was never introduced at all during that Parliament.

There have been no Government-sponsored measures to seek reform of the House of Lords since 1968.[66] The Labour Party conference in 1977 adopted a policy of abolition of the House in favour of a unicameral Parliament consisting of the Commons alone. That policy was subsequently reversed, and by the time of the 1992 General Election the Party had become reconverted to bicameralism. It advocated an elected second chamber, but with power to delay Commons bills for only a month – save for any bill designed to amend specified civil rights statutes, in which case the chamber would have the power to delay it until after the following General Election.[67] Labour is now committed to removing the hereditary peers from membership of the House of Lords (using the Parliament Acts if necessary) as a first stage towards the creation of an elected chamber. When the hereditaries had been ousted Labour Ministers would consult (through a Joint Select Committee of both Houses) on the composition of such an elected House,

---

65 The text is in Rodney Brazier, *Constitutional Texts* (1990), pp. 529–40.
66 For a Lords' debate on the desirable powers of a second chamber, see 518 HL Deb. 606–37 (25 April 1990).
67 See Brazier (1990) 41 *NILQ* 74. The Lords' veto over bills to extend the life of Parliament would be enjoyed by the new chamber.

which might be elected by proportional representation. The Liberal Democrats favour the replacement of the Lords by an elected Senate of about a hundred members, elected by proportional representation, and with the power to delay bills for up to two years.[68] The Conservatives have no plans for change.[69]

68 See *Here We Stand* (Liberal Democrat Federal White Paper No. 6, 1993).
69 A Conservative Party committee under Lord Home in 1978 recommended reform based on 268 members directly elected by proportional representation and 134 members nominated for life by the Queen on the Prime Minister's advice. See The House of Lords: Report of the Conservative Review Committee (1978).

CHAPTER 16

Parliamentary Privilege

GENERAL

Parliamentary privilege[1] is part of the law and custom of Parliament. It consists of special rules evolved by the two Houses in order to protect themselves collectively, and their members acting in their public capacities, against outside interference, so as to enable them to carry out their constitutional functions effectively. Most of these special rules are non-statutory; they have been laid down by resolutions of the two Houses or by Speakers' rulings. Some are statutory. They are part of the common law in so far as their existence and validity are recognized by the courts, but they are, in general, enforced not by the courts but by each House. The two Houses justify the special rights, powers and immunities conferred by parliamentary privilege as being necessary for the welfare of the nation. Citizens denied legal redress against MPs, or adjudged by the House of Commons to have committed a high contempt and a breach of its privileges, tend to be less impressed by these claims. The connotation of the word 'privilege', is, moreover, unattractive. A select committee of the House of Commons, appointed to review the law of parliamentary privilege, recommended in 1967 that the expression 'parliamentary privilege' should be sent to the lumber room, and that the House should instead speak of its 'rights and immunities',[2] but the committee's recommendations for the relinquishment of particular rights and immunities were extremely cautious. As will be

---

1 For an authoritative study, see Erskine May's *Parliamentary Practice* (21st edn, 1989), chs. 5–11. For valuable critiques, see *Report from the Select Committee on Parliamentary Privilege*, HC 34 (1967–8), and *Third Report from the Committee of Privileges: Recommendations of the Select Committee on Parliamentary Privilege* (HC 417 (1976–7)). See also J. A. G. Griffith and M. Ryle, *Parliament: Functions, Procedures and Practices* (1989), ch. 3. A Joint Select Committee was established in 1997 to consider whether parliamentary privilege is in need of reform.
2 HC 34 (1967–8), vi, viii, xlix.

seen at appropriate points in this chapter, the House took some action in 1978 on the committee's report.

The privileges of the Lords closely resemble those of the Commons, and will not be considered separately.

PRIVILEGES OF THE COMMONS

At the commencement of a Parliament the newly elected Speaker claims from the Crown 'all the ancient and undoubted privileges' of the House, and in particular freedom of speech in debate, freedom from arrest and freedom of access to the monarch through the Speaker; and he requests that a favourable construction be placed on the Commons' proceedings.[3] The most important privileges not specifically claimed are the right of the House to regulate its own composition, its right to have exclusive cognizance of matters arising within its precincts, the right to punish for contempt and breach of privilege, its privileges in relation to the Lords in financial matters,[4] and its claim to be the sole judge of the extent of its own privileges.[5] The difference between the privileges expressly claimed and those not expressly claimed is one of form, not of substance.

Freedom of speech

This is the most crucial and controversial parliamentary privilege. Article 9 of the Bill of Rights provided

that the freedom of speech, and debates or proceedings in Parliament ought not to be impeached or questioned in any court or place out of Parliament.

This is the basis of the modern law. Its interpretation and implications are of primary importance.

1 No action or prosecution can be brought against a member for any words used in the course of parliamentary proceedings. This rule is absolute. Thus, a member cannot be prosecuted or threatened with

---

3 These last two privileges (or claims) relate back to the days when the attitude of the monarch towards petitions by the Commons and its spokesman was apt to be tempestuous.
4 See ch. 15.
5 Among the less important privileges are immunity from attendance in court as jurors or (with certain exceptions) as witnesses; and the right of impeachment. The Select Committee (note 1 above) recommended that the right of impeachment be abolished by statute.

prosecution for sedition[6] or a breach of the Official Secrets Acts[7] for such words; a prosecution or threat to prosecute would probably be treated by the House as a breach of its own privileges.[8] If a member were to be sued for libel or slander in respect of words used in Parliament (other than in casual conversation not connected with parliamentary business) the writ should be struck out as disclosing no cause of action; if the case were to come to trial the court would hold that the member was protected by absolute privilege in the law of defamation[9] – i.e. that no action would lie against him even if his remarks were shown to be defamatory, untrue and unfair. The defence of absolute privilege (which has no necessary connection with parliamentary privilege) also extends to judges acting in their official capacities; the risk that the immunity from suit may be abused is considered less than the risk that the absence of absolute privilege might deter MPs and judges from speaking bluntly, even harshly, when it is their duty to do so.

2 Parliamentary privilege (and absolute privilege in the law of defamation) also attaches to statements in official reports of the proceedings of the two Houses and their committees, and to other papers published by order of the House. This rule was laid down by the Parliamentary Papers Act 1840, passed in consequence of a judicial decision (*Stockdale* v. *Hansard*)[10] that parliamentary papers were protected not by parliamentary privilege but only by qualified privilege in the law of defamation – i.e. that untrue and libellous statements made in such documents were actionable if shown to have been actuated by malice.

3 What is the meaning of 'proceedings in Parliament'? A partial answer has been accepted by the House on the recommendation of the Committee of Privileges,[11] namely, that any communication between an MP and a Minister or an officer of the House concerning the business of the House should be absolutely privileged – but the House realizes that the crucial

---

6 *Eliot's* case (1629) 3 St. Tr. 294.

7 *Case of Duncan Sandys* (1938). See HC 101 (1938–9). Sandys had complained that he had been threatened with prosecution for refusing to divulge his sources of information in connection with a parliamentary question he had put down about a shortage of anti-aircraft equipment.

8 This is to be inferred from the report of the Select Committee on the *Sandys* case and its adoption by the House. Members can be prosecuted for these offences in respect of disclosures or utterances which are not part of proceedings in Parliament.

9 *Dillon* v. *Balfour* (1887) 20 Ir. LR 600; *Goffin* v. *Donnelly* (1881) 6 QBD 307.

10 (1839) 9 A. & E. 1; see p. 331.

11 HC 417 (1976–7), iii; 943 HC Deb. 1155–98 (6 February 1978). That committee has been succeeded by the Select Committee on Standards and Privileges: see below p. 327.

phrase 'business of the House' needs to be defined by legislation. That legislation has not been forthcoming. Contributions to debate and committee discussions, oral questions, answers to parliamentary questions and voting are clearly within the definition; so are the execution of the orders of the House and the tabling of parliamentary questions. An MP's appointment to, promotion within, or removal from parliamentary committees is also within the definition: thus a letter written by another MP complaining about such an appointment is covered by parliamentary privilege.[12] Acts done and words spoken within the precincts of Parliament which have nothing whatsoever to do with parliamentary proceedings[13] are clearly not protected. In between lie many transactions and situations that do not lend themselves easily to classification.[14] If a member tables a question and a Minister invites him to discuss it with him, the correspondence or conversations appear to be covered by parliamentary privilege. It is arguable that unsolicited communications with a Minister are also covered if they are immediately related to a question or motion already tabled or a matter currently being debated in the House. If the issue has ceased to be before the House, such communications are probably no longer to be regarded as part of a proceeding *in* Parliament.

Communications with Ministers in respect of matters which may never arise in the House will not normally be covered by parliamentary privilege. Not every act done by a member in his capacity as a member is so protected.[15] So, for example, it is not a proceeding in Parliament when a member arranges for a film to be shown in a private room at the House, that film being the subject of an injunction which prevented it from being shown publicly.[16] A member's letter to or interview with a Minister, raising an issue of concern to an individual member of the public or a group of his constituents or any other section of the community, *may* lead to the putting down of a parliamentary question if no satisfactory

12 See *Rost* v. *Edwards* [1990] 2 All ER 641; the Privy Council decision in *Prebble* v. *Television New Zealand Ltd* [1994] 3 All ER 407 and Leopold (1995) 15 *Legal Studies* 204.
13 See, e.g. *Rivlin* v. *Bilainkin* [1953] 1 QB 485 (member of the public posting a defamatory letter within the House, not protected). But see Lock (1983) *Industrial Law Journal* 28.
14 See, for example, *Ex p. Wason* (1869) LR 4 QB 573 (no private prosecution for alleged conspiracy to deceive the House of Lords by false statements in the House; the matter lay within scope of parliamentary privilege). See also *Att.-Gen. of Ceylon* v. *Livera* [1963] AC 103 at 120–22 for judicial comment on marginal situations.
15 See generally de Smith (1958) 21 *Mod. L. Rev.* at 477–82.
16 The Committee of Privileges so decided after the Speaker had directed that the film (about a secret spy satellite, 'Project Zircon') be not shown at the House of Commons pending a decision on the matter by the House as a whole: see HC 365 (1986–7); Bradley [1987] *Public Law* 1 and 488.

informal answer is forthcoming; the issue thus raised may be a substitute for a *formal* parliamentary question (which would be privileged); but where is the line to be drawn between proceedings *in* Parliament and matters merely antecedent to possible proceedings in Parliament?

The leading modern case is that of *G. R. Strauss* (1957–8). Mr Strauss, Labour MP and formerly Minister of Supply, wrote to a Minister complaining about certain activities of an area board of a nationalized industry. The Minister disclaimed responsibility on the ground that the matter was one of day-to-day administration, and passed the letter on to the board. The board threatened to sue Mr Strauss for libel. Mr Strauss then raised this threat in the House as a question of privilege. The question was referred to the Committee of Privileges, which reported[17] that in writing his letter Mr Strauss was engaged in a proceeding in Parliament, and that the members of the board and their solicitors, by threatening legal proceedings against him in respect of his allegations, were in breach of parliamentary privilege. They recommended (some-what inconsistently) that the question whether Article 9 of the Bill of Rights, restating the privilege of freedom of speech, had been impliedly repealed by an obscure eighteenth-century statute should be referred to the Judicial Committee of the Privy Council for an advisory opinion. The question was so referred; the Judicial Committee advised that the Bill of Rights (whatever it might mean) stood intact.[18] The House accepted this advice and then debated the Report of the Committee of Privileges. On a free vote it rejected by 218 to 213 the Committee's finding that in writing his letter Mr Strauss had been engaged in a proceeding in Parliament.[19]

The decision is not binding on the House when future cases arise. And the Select Committee on Parliamentary Privilege in 1967 was 'strongly of the opinion' that the decision of the House in the *Strauss* case should be reversed by legislation.[20] At present the probability is that a court would hold a letter written by an MP to a Minister on a matter lying within the Minister's general area of responsibility[21] to be protected

---

17 HC 305 (1956–7).

18 *Re Parliamentary Privilege Act 1770* [1958] AC 331.

19 591 HC Deb. 207–346 (8 July 1958). See also Lock [1985] *Public Law* 64.

20 HC 34 (1967–8), xxvii. Some of its main recommendations have been implemented by the House by resolution – but then only after a delay of ten years, and necessary legislation is still awaited: see 943 HC Deb. 1155–98 (6 February 1978), and D. G. T. Williams [1978] *Camb. LJ* 1.

21 e.g. a letter by an MP to the Lord Chancellor complaining of solicitors' conduct, even though the Lord Chancellor has no direct disciplinary authority over them: *Beach* v. *Freeson* [1972] 1 QB 14.

only by qualified privilege in the law of defamation, unless the letter was ancillary, or an immediate preliminary, to proceedings within Parliament itself. Public policy considerations can be canvassed on either side. Letters from members of the public to MPs (and presumably from MPs to members of the public) on matters of public concern[22] enjoy only qualified privilege.[23] So do fair and accurate newspaper reports of parliamentary proceedings.[24] A statutory extension of the scope of parliamentary privilege to ease the minds of MPs potentially threatened with libel actions (and heavy bills of costs) would be widely interpreted as a self-endowed licence to make maliciously defamatory comments with impunity.[25] On the other hand, in 1967 communications between MPs and the Parliamentary Commissioner for Administration were accorded absolute privilege by statute.[26]

4 Matters arising in the course of parliamentary proceedings cannot be challenged or relied on for the purpose of supporting legal proceedings based on events that occurred outside Parliament; for example, if an MP is sued for libel in connection with his remarks in a television interview, and he pleads qualified privilege or fair comment, the plaintiff is not allowed to use the defendant's comments in the House to show that the latter was actuated by malice.[27] But now if an MP's conduct in Parliament is in issue in defamation proceedings he may waive, for the purpose of those proceedings, the legal protection which prevents proceedings in Parliament being impeached or questioned in any court or place out of Parliament.[28]

5 A member of the Commons who abuses his privilege of freedom of

22 Unless the MP is communicating to a complainant a report from the Parliamentary Commissioner for Administration (Parliamentary Commissioner Act 1967 s. 10(5)), in which case he will enjoy absolute privilege.
23 *R.* v. *Rule* [1937] 2 KB 375 (complaint by constituent to MP about public officers); see also *Beach* v. *Freeson* (note 21 above; complaint by MP to Lord Chancellor and Law Society).
24 *Wason* v. *Walter* (1868) LR 4 QB 73.
25 It would seem that in an action for defamation, an MP who passes on a letter from a member of the public will not lose his qualified privilege by becoming automatically infected with the malice of his informant: *Meekins* v. *Henson* [1964] 1 QB 472; *Egger* v. *Chelmsford* [1965] 1 QB 248.
26 Parliamentary Commissioner Act 1967, s. 10(5).
27 *Church of Scientology of California* v. *Johnson-Smith* [1972] 1 QB 522; *R.* v. *Secretary of State for Trade, ex p. Anderson Strathclyde plc* [1983] 2 All ER 233. See also *Dingle* v. *Associated Newspapers Ltd* [1960] 2 QB 405 (action for libel against newspaper; plaintiff not entitled to contend that proceedings of select committee of House, on which offending comments were based, were void for procedural irregularity).
28 Defamation Act 1996, s. 13.

speech may be subjected to disciplinary sanctions by the House; it is only outside Parliament that his parliamentary freedom of speech cannot be impeached.

6 The House still reserves to itself the right to treat the institution of legal proceedings against a member in respect of a matter covered, in its opinion, by parliamentary privilege, as a breach of its own privileges; but the Select Committee on Parliamentary Privilege recommended in 1967 that save in exceptional circumstances (for example, where a member is being improperly obstructed in the performance of his parliamentary functions) such matters should be left to the ordinary processes of the courts.[29] No action has been taken on that recommendation.

7 Substantial interference with the exercise of a member's freedom of speech and action in his parliamentary capacity, by threats, molestation, bribes or other improper inducements may be treated by the House as a contempt or breach of privilege. What if a member agrees to act as the parliamentary spokesman for an outside pressure group? The inconclusive case of *W. J. Brown* (1947)[30] neatly stated the problems. Brown, who had been general secretary of the Civil Service Clerical Association, was elected as an Independent MP. He entered into an agreement with the Association whereby he became their salaried 'parliamentary general secretary' but would retain full freedom to engage in his own political activities. The executive committee of the Association later became dissatisfied with his political attitudes and proposed to recommend the termination of the agreement. Brown claimed that this proposal was a breach of parliamentary privilege in that it was calculated to influence him in his conduct as an MP by threatening him with a financial penalty. The Committee of Privileges, dividing (unusually) along party lines, reported[31] that on the facts no breach of privilege had been committed, but it recognized that the exertion of outside financial pressure on a member for the purpose of influencing his conduct as a member could well be a breach of privilege. The House, adopting the report, resolved that it was inconsistent with the maintenance of the privilege of freedom of speech for a member to *enter into* a contractual agreement with an outside body fettering his freedom of action or stipulating that he was to act as that body's parliamentary representative. The duty of a member is to his constituents and to the country as a whole, rather than to any

---

29 HC 34 (1967–8), xvi-xvii. See generally de Smith (1958) 21 *Mod. L. Rev.* 465.
30 HC 118 (1946–7).
31 ibid.

particular section thereof. In any event a court would almost certainly refuse to enforce such a contract on grounds of public policy.[32]

A clearer case arose in 1975. The Yorkshire Area Council of the National Union of Mineworkers resolved to restrict the parliamentary conduct of MPs sponsored by the Area branch, in particular by requiring that such MPs *should not vote* on any issue contrary to union policy on the industry. The threat of withdrawal of sponsorship for recalcitrant MPs was suggested. The Committee of Privileges found that there had been a serious breach of privilege – but the National Executive of the NUM passed a motion to nullify the Yorkshire Area Council's resolution, so no further action was needed.[33] It is impossible to believe that financial aid tendered to members by sectional interest groups has always been granted on the understanding that a member is under no kind of obligation whatsoever to promote the interests of that group. The Select Committee on Parliamentary Privilege accepted as a fact the existence of such relationships and pointed out that a member speaking on a topic in which he had a financial interest might be guilty of a contempt of the House if he failed to disclose his interest. The Select Committee on Members' Interests, reporting in 1969,[34] expressed itself still more guardedly, emphasizing the distinction between improper inducements held out to or accepted by members for the promotion of *specific* matters in their parliamentary capacities, and *regular* financial assistance offered to members by outside organizations; the latter type of relationship was regarded (subject to the formal qualification interposed by the resolution of the House in *Brown*'s case) as being quite proper. Nevertheless, concern about MPs' outside earnings and other extra-parliamentary behaviour has led to changes in their rules of conduct. There is now a code of conduct for MPs, a Parliamentary Commissioner for Standards, and a Select Committee on Standards and Privileges. The Commissioner is in charge of the Register of MPs' interests, and the Committee, as well as succeeding to the duties of the former Committee of Privileges, considers any matter relating to the conduct of MPs and oversees the working of the code of conduct.[35]

Threats of disciplinary action against members by party whips have

32 See *Amalgamated Society of Railway Servants* v. *Osborne* [1910] AC 87 at 110–15 for the rationale of such a judicial attitude.
33 HC 634 (1974–5).
34 HC 57 (1969–70), viii–x. See also above, p. 271 on the Register of Members' Interests.
35 See SO No. 121A, 121B.

been ruled not to constitute infringements of the privilege of freedom of speech because they are part of the conventionally established machinery of political organization within the House. Nevertheless, pressure exerted on a member by whips may influence his conduct far more significantly than any connection he may have with an outside interest group.

8 In order to protect its freedom of speech, the House asserts ancillary privileges. It may resolve to clear the visitors' gallery by excluding strangers; in wartime it has often gone into secret session. Leave of the House had to be obtained for evidence to be given in court of anything that occurred in the course of parliamentary proceedings, until the rule was discontinued in 1980. (The courts have relaxed their own rule against considering material in *Hansard* in order to construe ambiguous statutes.)[36] The House used to treat publication of its debates as a breach of privilege; assertion of this privilege has been discontinued. The publication of leaks from the private deliberations of select committees, or of their draft reports, remains a breach of privilege, based on a resolution of the House passed in 1832. So in the case of *Richard Evans* (1985–6) a draft report of the Environment Select Committee about nuclear waste disposal was prematurely leaked to Mr Evans, a newspaper journalist. His newspaper published an article based on the leak. This was an admitted breach of privilege, but publication was defended on the ground that it was in the public interest. The leaker's identity was never established. The Committee of Privileges recommended that Mr Evans be suspended from Westminster for six months, but the House, while acknowledging that it would be proper to punish an MP who leaked in such circumstances, sensibly refused to punish Mr Evans who was 'merely doing his job'.[37]

Freedom from arrest

This immunity has lost most of its early importance, and in 1967 the Committee on Parliamentary Privilege recommended its abolition.[38] It does not protect members from arrest on criminal charges,[39] or from preventive

36 *Pepper (Inspector of Taxes)* v. *Hart* [1993] I All ER 42 (HL).
37 See HC 376 (1985–6); 98 HC Deb. 293–332 (20 May 1986).
38 HC 34 (1967–8), xxix.
39 The court which sentences an MP to imprisonment informs the Speaker, who informs the House. See, e.g., 125 HC Deb. 3 (11 January 1988). A warrant for the arrest of Mr Ron Brown MP was issued in 1988 after he had failed to appear to face private prosecution alleging criminal damage to the Commons' mace. The DPP, however, took over the proceedings and discontinued them.

detention as security suspects in wartime;[40] though their arrest or detention must not be based on anything they have said in the course of parliamentary proceedings. The privilege protects members from arrest in civil matters for wilful disobedience to a court order – for example, refusal to comply with the terms of a maintenance order.[41] It extends for the period of a session and forty days before and after. Imprisonment of defendants in civil proceedings, and in particular of debtors who were unavoidably prevented from discharging their obligations, was a commonplace matter till the latter part of the nineteenth century; nowadays arrest in civil cases is confined to a narrow range of situations where the defendant is as a rule seriously at fault.

Right of the House of Commons to provide for its own composition

This privilege is now partly regulated by statute. For example, the trial of disputed election returns has been committed to an election court; the question whether a member is subject to a legal disqualification may be determinable by an election court or the Judicial Committee of the Privy Council. Within its narrowed field, the privilege is nevertheless important. The House has the exclusive right, while it is sitting, to determine by resolution when a writ for the holding of a by-election shall be issued. It can declare a member's seat vacant on the ground that he has incurred a legal disqualification or for any other reason it thinks fit and the courts cannot interfere; this is why it would be lawful for the Government to use its majority in the House to expel all Opposition members.[42] Self-restraint, influenced by fair-mindedness and expediency, alone prevents abuse of its privilege. The inexpediency of abuse was illustrated by the case of *John Wilkes*, the rake, wit and radical demagogue, who was elected to the House of Commons; the corrupt House decided that he was unfit to share their company, and expelled him. But the House has no privilege to prevent any person from standing as a candidate at a by-election. Wilkes was duly

---

40 *Ramsay's* case (1940).
41 *Stourton* v. *Stourton* [1963] P. 302 (where privilege from arrest was successfully claimed by a peer). Members are privileged from arrest for civil but not criminal contempt of court: Erskine May, *Parliamentary Practice*, op. cit., ch. 7, *Wellesley* v. *Earl of Beaufort* (1831) 2 Russ. & M. 639; Leopold [1989] *Public Law* 398. There are difficult marginal cases (see Enid Campbell, *Parliamentary Privilege in Australia* (1966), 59–63; Sawer (1971) 7 *U. of Queensland LJ* 226), but broadly it seems that members are immune from detention imposed by a court if the purpose of the detention is coercive as distinct from punitive.
42 Under a written constitution, the grounds for expulsion could be judicially reviewable, cf. *Powell* v. *McCormack* 395 US 486 (1970).

re-elected, and his seat was again declared vacant by the House; after this absurd process had been repeated, the House resolved in 1770 that his election was void and that the seat be awarded to the runner-up. Wilkes was again elected in 1774; the House took no step to unseat him, and in 1782 the House resolved to expunge the resolution of 1770 from its Journals.

The only modern examples of expulsion for reasons other than legal disqualification are of members who had been convicted of criminal offences involving moral turpitude or who have committed gross contempts of the House.[43]

Right to have exclusive cognizance of matters arising within the House

This right is closely linked with the rule that proceedings in Parliament cannot be called in question in any court. The leading case is *Bradlaugh* v. *Gossett* (1884).[44] Bradlaugh, a militant atheist, was elected to the House. After some vacillation, the House decided to allow him to make an affirmation of allegiance in lieu of taking an oath. A common informer then sued Bradlaugh for penalties on the ground that he was not qualified to sit and vote because he did not come within the classes of persons permitted by statute to affirm instead of taking an oath; and the courts held that Bradlaugh was not entitled to affirm.[45] Bradlaugh's seat became vacant; he was re-elected, and then sought to take the oath rather than be excluded from sitting. The House refused to allow him to do so, although on a proper construction of the Parliamentary Oaths Act 1866 he appeared entitled to take the oath if he chose, despite his position as a non-believer. Subsequently it resolved to exclude him from the House until he undertook not to disturb its proceedings. Bradlaugh brought an action, claiming a declaration that the resolution was void, and an injunction to restrain the Serjeant-at-Arms (Gossett) from excluding him. The court held that it had

43 In 1947 Garry Allighan MP was expelled for contempt. He had made unsubstantiated allegations that MPs had given particulars of parliamentary party meetings, held within the precincts of the Palace of Westminster, to journalists for money or while under the influence of drink. He was himself receiving payments from a newspaper for disclosing such information and had given false answers to questions put to him in the Committee of Privileges.

44 12 QBD 271.

45 *Clarke* v. *Bradlaugh* (1881) 7 QBD 38. It was later held, however, that only the Crown could recover the penalties prescribed by statute: *Bradlaugh* v. *Clarke* (1883) 8 App. Cas. 354.

no jurisdiction to interfere. Assuming that the House had misinterpreted the Act, the matter would still fall within the exclusive privilege of the House to regulate its own proceedings. Similarly, if the House had resolved to allow Bradlaugh to take the oath, the courts would have had no power to pronounce upon that decision. But if proceedings were brought to recover a penalty from him as a disqualified person, it would be incumbent on the court to interpret the Act. In such a case the jurisdiction of the courts could not be excluded even by a resolution of the House purporting to protect Bradlaugh against an action for penalties, for the privileges of Parliament did not extend to such a matter arising outside the House.[46]

The House has not asserted a general jurisdiction over matters arising within the walls of the House if they have no direct connection with its proceedings. Theft, rape or murder are issues to be left to the criminal courts; in any event, the penal powers of the House are inadequate to deal with ordinary crimes.[47] If two members came to blows in the House, the courts and the House would have a *concurrent* jurisdiction; a magistrate could properly issue a summons for assault and try the case,[48] and the House might also decide that the fracas amounted to a contempt of the House. But when in doubt a court may elect to tread warily for fear of encroaching on what the House may deem to be its own exclusive preserve. When A. P. Herbert, who was campaigning to liberalize the liquor licensing laws and who was soon to become an Independent MP, decided to embarrass the members of the Kitchen Committee of the House by applying for summonses against them for selling drinks in the members' bar without a justices' licence, the chief metropolitan magistrate refused to issue summonses; and the Divisional Court of the King's Bench Division, taking a remarkably generous view of the scope of the internal affairs of the House of Commons, held that he had been right to decline jurisdiction because of parliamentary privilege.[49]

---

46 (1884) 12 QBD at 281–2, *per* Stephen J. See also *Papworth* v. *Coventry* [1967] 1 WLR 663 at 669–70.

47 See p. 328. In 1970, CS gas was projected into the chamber by a member of the public as a gesture of protest. The House left the matter to be dealt with by the police and the courts.

48 In *Eliot*'s case (note 6 above) where the conviction for *sedition* was ultimately quashed on a writ of error, the defendants' conviction for assaulting the Speaker in the House still stood. See also *Bradlaugh* v. *Gossett* (above) at 283–4.

49 *R* v. *Graham-Campbell, ex p. Herbert* [1935] 1 KB 594.

Right to punish for breach of privilege and contempt

The House can vindicate its own privileges by taking disciplinary action against members and others whom it adjudges to have broken them. All breaches of privilege are contempts of the House. But there is also a wide range of contempts that do not fall within the scope of any nominate privilege. The following are examples of contempts:[50] offering bribes to members; molesting or otherwise obstructing members or officers of the House in the performance of their duties; casting imputations reflecting on the dignity of the House by, for example, insulting the House or its members; attempting to disrupt the proceedings of the House; tampering with witnesses before select committees of the House; refusing to give evidence, or giving false evidence, before a committee of the House. These contempts are often called breaches of privilege; this usage is misleading, for the House has accepted that it cannot by resolution enlarge the scope of its own privileges, but has not closed the categories of contempt; and – to take but one example – if demonstrators shouted down witnesses giving evidence before an itinerant select committee, they would be guilty of a contempt of the House. No matter whether the offence is styled a breach of privilege or a contempt or both, the penal powers of the House are the same.

A complaint of 'breach of privilege' must be raised by a member as soon as is reasonably practicable.[51] If the Speaker rules that a *prima facie* case has been made out, the matter is referred to the Committee on Standards and Privileges, a select committee which is appointed for the duration of a Parliament and which is nominated in proportion to party strengths. In investigating the complaint, the Committee can require the attendance of witnesses and the production of documents; refusal to comply with its commands or to answer questions is a contempt. It does not, in practice, afford the persons against whom the complaints have been made any opportunity of being legally represented, and has sometimes reported that a complaint has been established although the 'defendant' has not been given any hearing at all. In the *Strauss* case[52] the Committee condemned

---

50 See Erskine May, *Parliamentary Practice*, op. cit., ch. 9.
51 The earlier rule – that the complaint had to be raised 'at the earliest opportunity' – was thought to be too restrictive, and was altered to the formulation given in the text: see 943 HC Deb. 1155–98 (6 February 1978). The Speaker may decide not to pursue it if an immediate, unqualified apology is made to him: see, for example, 902 HC Deb. 1392–3 (17 December 1975).
52 See p. 319.

the members of the area board without hearing them. Since, moreover, the members of the Committee are in a sense judges in their own cause, this disregard of the elements of natural justice is open to severe criticism. In 1967 the Select Committee on Parliamentary Privilege recommended a number of procedural reforms, which would give all persons directly concerned a right to attend its hearings, make submissions, and call, examine and cross-examine witnesses; and rights to seek the Committee's leave to be legally represented and to ask for legal aid.[53] These necessary reforms have not been introduced. There is also a case (which the Select Committee did not accept) for codifying contempts so as to introduce certainty at the expense of flexibility.[54] In some Commonwealth countries, not only are breaches of privilege and contempts codified by statute but allegations of breach of privilege and contempt are triable by the courts.

The Committee on Standards and Privileges may find that a complaint has been established but recommend that no further action be taken. It may recommend that the House resolve that the person guilty of contempt be admonished or reprimanded by the Speaker at the bar of the House; or that a member found guilty of contempt be suspended[55] or expelled from the House; or that a member, or a member of the public, be committed to prison for contempt. The recommendations of the Committee are nearly always, but not invariably, adopted by the House. The power of the House to impose fines for contempt was last exercised three hundred years ago and is now obsolete; the Select Committee in 1967 recommended that this power be revived by statute.[56] No person has been committed to prison for contempt since 1800 (and then only for one night). Imprisonment terminates on prorogation though it can be renewed in the next session. The House of Lords, as a court of record, may impose fines and may commit for a

---

53 HC 34 (1967–8), xiv–xlvii.
54 The House has, however, accepted guidelines on when its power to punish should be used. These are (a) that the power should be resorted to as sparingly as possible, and (b) then only when the House is satisfied that to exercise the power is essential to provide reasonable protection for the House, its members or its officers, from such improper obstruction or attempt at or threat of obstruction as causes, or is likely to cause, substantial interference with the performance of their respective functions: see 943 HC Deb. 1155–98 (6 February 1978). This change was designed to ward off petty complaints.
55 The Speaker may also order a member to withdraw from a day's sitting for grossly disorderly conduct (SO No. 42); and if he names a member for persistent disregard of the authority of the chair or other serious misconduct in the House, that member may be suspended forthwith upon a resolution of the House, the period of suspension for a first offender being five days (SO No. 43). These provisions do not affect the general inherent power of the House to suspend a member for contempt.
56 The House accepted this recommendation in 1978, but no bill has been introduced.

fixed term extending beyond prorogation. Offenders may be taken into the custody of the Serjeant-at-Arms (or Black Rod) and thence committed to prison if the House has so directed. Provided that the order of the House or Speaker's warrant is duly made out, the Serjeant at Arms may forcibly enter private property to carry out an arrest,[57] and is entitled to call upon the police or even the armed forces for any necessary assistance in executing the orders of the House.[58]

The Select Committee of 1967 confirmed what was already apparent – that some members had been too ready to invoke the jurisdiction of the House to deal with personal affronts as questions of privilege. It recommended that recourse to this jurisdiction should be confined to those cases where the exercise of the functions of the House was liable to be seriously impeded and, as has been seen above, the House has accepted this recommendation,[59] that where members considered themselves to have been defamed by newspaper comments or statements by individuals, they should normally be content to pursue their remedies in the ordinary courts – but the House has expressly retained the right of a member to bring an alleged breach of privilege to the Commons even if he has a civil remedy;[60] and that where proceedings were brought in the House for contempt, justification or reasonable belief in the allegations complained of should be admissible as defences.

Since 1967 the number of trivial complaints of breach of privilege has diminished. But it is incongruous, to say the least, that members of the House of Commons should be more sensitive than judges to hostile criticism.[61] It is also noteworthy that, whereas an appeal lies from a conviction for contempt of court, no such appeal lies from a finding of contempt of the House; this rule would be left unchanged by the Select Committee's proposals. Fortunately the House has on the whole dealt sensibly with contemnors; where the Committee on Standards and Privileges has found a complaint proved, it has usually recommended that no disciplinary action be taken and the House has regularly accepted such a recommendation.

---

57 *Burdett* v. *Abbot* (1811) 14 East 1.
58 ibid. See further HC (1967–8), pp. 115–65, 206–9 for details of the procedure adopted.
59 See above, note 54.
60 943 HC Deb. 1155–98 (6 February 1978).
61 For a modern (and tolerant) judicial attitude towards the concept of contempt of court, see *R.* v. *Metropolitan Police Commissioner, ex p. Blackburn (No. 2)* [1968] 2 QB 150.

PARLIAMENTARY PRIVILEGE AND THE COURTS

There are points of similarity between the royal prerogative and parliamentary privilege. Both are recognized as part of the law of the land; both embody special rules evolved for public purposes. The Crown cannot enlarge its own prerogatives within the realm; the two Houses have recognized that they cannot extend their privileges, though their attitude towards 'contempts' not falling within the scope of a nominate privilege is ambiguous. But there are material differences between prerogative and privilege. The prerogative is essentially a residuum of ancient common-law attributes, attenuated by judicial decisions and legislation. The growth of parliamentary privilege can be traced in resolutions and rulings recorded in the Journals of the two Houses; and privilege has been and can still be expanded, as well as abrogated by statute. Acts done within the recognized area of prerogative may be reviewed by the courts: acts done by either House within its acknowledged field of privilege are unreviewable.[62] The Crown cannot commit persons to prison for infringing its prerogatives; the two Houses can commit for breach of privilege, or enforce obedience to privilege by milder forms of direct action. The most interesting difference between the two bodies of law is that, whereas the Crown has long since ceased to claim to be the sole judge of the limits of its prerogative, the two Houses (and the House of Commons in particular) still assert that they are the sole judges of the *extent* of their own privileges – a claim to which the courts do not accede. For example, a decision by the House of Commons that Mr Strauss's letter to the Minister *was* a 'proceeding in Parliament' would not have been treated as binding by the courts if the board had sued Mr Strauss;[63] the House, on the other hand, might have not only rejected the courts' interpretation but also treated it as an encroachment on its own privileges, and therefore a contempt, on the part of the plaintiffs, their legal advisers and the judges.

The claim of the House to be the sole interpreter of its own privileges has given rise to two major constitutional conflicts. In the first of them, the House of Lords (as an appellate court) held (*Ashby* v. *White*)[64] that a voter at Aylesbury, whose vote the returning officer had maliciously refused

---

62 See *Bradlaugh* v. *Gossett* (1884) 12 QBD 271.

63 The situation in *Bradlaugh* v. *Gossett* was different in as much as the resolution of the House in that case, ill-founded or well-founded, undoubtedly fell within the scope of the privilege of the House to regulate its own internal affairs.

64 See 2 Ld. Raym. 938, 3 Ld. Raym. 320; 14 St. Tr. 695.

to accept, was entitled to damages. The House of Commons protested that this decision violated their exclusive privileges relating to parliamentary elections. Other Aylesbury voters brought similar actions against the returning officer; the House ordered them to be committed to prison. An application was made for writs of habeas corpus to secure their release from unlawful detention. In *Paty*'s case (1704) the court refused the writ;[65] counsel for the applicants, who intended to bring the case before the House of Lords, was promptly committed by the Commons to join his clients. The deadlock was broken only by a prorogation of Parliament.

The central issue revived, in a more spectacular form, at the beginning of Victoria's reign. One Stockdale published an illustrated treatise on the reproductive system. The book was found circulating among prison inmates. Stockdale considered himself to have been defamed by comments on his work made in a report by prison inspectors, published by order of the House of Commons, and sued Hansard, the parliamentary printers (then a commercial firm) for libel. The defendants were ordered by the Commons to plead that the publication was covered by parliamentary privilege. The Court of Queen's Bench rejected this plea, holding that as a matter of law such a publication was not comprised within the area of parliamentary privilege and awarded damages to Stockdale (*Stockdale* v. *Hansard*);[66] no resolution of the House could deprive the courts of their authority to interpret and apply the law of the land in a matter affecting the rights of subjects. Stockdale brought another action against Hansard; the defendants, on the instructions of the House, entered no plea, and the plaintiff was again awarded damages. There were two sequels.[67]

(i) Execution had been levied by the Sheriff of Middlesex on Hansard's property to recover the damages. The House resolved to commit the Sheriff for breach of privilege and contempt. He applied for habeas corpus on the ground that he was being unlawfully detained (*Sheriff of Middlesex*'s case (1840)).[68] The Speaker's warrant was 'general', in that it had not recited the facts allegedly constituting the contempt. The court dismissed the application, on the ground that it would be unseemly to inquire further. Even if the House of Commons were not a superior court of record, it

---

65 Ld. Raym. 1105, Holt CJ (rightly) dissenting on the ground that the cause of commitment stated in the return of the writ was insufficient in law; the facts alleged to constitute the contempt of the House had been explicitly averred.

66 (1839) 9 A. & E. I.

67 Four, if one includes the commitments of Stockdale and his solicitor for contempt of the House (cf. *Howard* v. *Gossett* (1845) 10 QB 359, 411).

68 11 A. & E. 273. In fact the two Sheriffs of Middlesex were committed by the House.

was entitled to as much respect as if it were; and on a habeas corpus application one superior court would not investigate the truth of the facts stated by another as a cause of commitment for contempt.[69] If, however, the facts constituting the alleged contempt had been set out by the respondent to the application, and they could not reasonably be construed as amounting to a contempt of the House, the court would be at liberty to intervene.[70] (ii) Parliament passed the Parliamentary Papers Act 1840, conferring absolute privilege on statements in parliamentary papers, and thus achieving what could not be attained by a mere resolution.

The refusal on the part of the courts to award habeas corpus to release the Sheriff from arbitrary detention is obviously open to criticism.[71] It was supported by precedent and was defended on grounds of principle; but the court had chosen to blind itself to notorious reality, and to countenance injustice. Although 'the old dualism remains unresolved',[72] in the sense that the courts still do not accept the conclusiveness of the House's pronouncements as to the scope of its own privileges and the House denies that the courts have jurisdiction to determine such a matter at all, it is not unfair to say that the courts have 'yielded the key of the fortress'[73] by accepting that the House can enforce its own view by first committing an innocent offender to prison and then refusing to give particulars of his alleged breach of privilege. Fortunately the House of Commons has not acted in such an overbearing manner since Stockdale's time; it has, moreover, acquiesced in the assumption of jurisdiction by the courts in several marginal cases, and the courts have shown circumspection when called upon to exercise jurisdiction.

69 The precedents were the *Earl of Shaftesbury*'s case (1677) 1 Mod. 144; *Murray*'s case (1751) 1 Wils. 299; and a considered dictum in *Burdett* v. *Abbot* (1811) 14 East at 150. In *Paty*'s case (above) a majority of the court had held their jurisdiction to be excluded even though the facts constituting the alleged contempt were specified in the return to the writ. The *Sheriff of Middlesex*'s case was followed by the High Court of Australia in *R.* v. *Richards, ex p. Fitzpatrick and Browne* (1955) 92 CLR 157 (held, also, that a House of Parliament in the Commonwealth of Australia could commit for a fixed term). See Enid Campbell, *Parliamentary Privilege in Australia* (1966), ch. 7.
70 Adopting Holt CJ's view in *Paty*'s case (above) and Lord Ellenborough's dictum in *Burdett* v. *Abbot* (1811) 14 East at 150.
71 Contrast the decisions of the Supreme Court of India in *Special Reference No. 1 of 1964* AIR 1965 SC 746, where a general warrant of commitment for breach of privilege was held not to exclude the court's jurisdiction to inquire into the legality of the commitment. See *Annual Survey of Commonwealth Law for 1965*, pp. 41–4.
72 *Re Parliamentary Privilege Act 1770* [1958] AC 331 at 354 (quoting Erskine May).
73 Keir and Lawson, *Cases in Constitutional Law* (6th edn, 1979), p. 225.

Nevertheless, the House has, more than once, reiterated its own position in recent years, and only by a narrow margin was the prospect of a similar conflict averted in 1958.[74] Judges are not always better equipped than other persons to decide questions of law set in political contexts. But the unhappy combination of uncodified contempts, an unsatisfactory procedure for investigating allegations of contempt, and the insistence of the House that it must have the first and last word in matters touching the interests of its members as members, irrespective of the impact of its decisions on the interests of members of the public, suggests that the House ought to relinquish its jurisdiction over breaches of privilege and contempts to the courts, as it has in effect relinquished its privilege to determine disputed election returns.

74 If the House had endorsed the report of the Committee of Privileges in the *Strauss* case, it is not at all certain that this would have deterred the board from proceeding with an action against Mr Strauss. In the 'Project Zircon' affair (see above, p. 318) in 1987 the Attorney-General's application for an injunction to prevent a named MP from showing the film complained of at the House of Commons was rejected by the court on the ground that it is for the House to regulate its own proceedings. It was astonishing that the Attorney-General made that particular application at all.

CHAPTER 17

Subordinate Legislation

GENERAL

Parliament is not the sole source of new law. The superior courts make new law by laying down rules in decided cases which form binding precedents – binding till they are overruled (by statute or in a later case), or distinguished, or otherwise explained away. Judicial law-making is almost surreptitious; a new departure is usually rationalized as a rediscovery of a long-lost principle, or as an application of an established rule to a novel set of material facts, or as the ascertainment of an unexpressed parliamentary intent. Although the idea that the courts merely declare and apply pre-existing norms may be a polite fiction, the supposed need for this verbal camouflage rests on a widely held assumption that it is for Parliament, not for the Judiciary, to bring the law up to date. The room for judicial manoeuvre is restricted by the framework of constitutional thought within which the courts operate.

As has been noted already,[1] such Community legislation as has direct effect in Britain is really *primary*, not *subordinate*, legislation, because the European Union organs are not subordinate to Parliament in the eyes of Community law and their legislative output does not derive its legal force from any delegation of authority by Parliament. Community legislation is indeed normally 'secondary' in the sense that it consists of regulations made by the Council or the Commission in pursuance of powers conferred by the European Union treaties, and it is therefore subordinate *within the Community legal order*, but not within our legal order.

There are other legislative institutions, forming part of the executive branch of government. The Crown, Ministers, some Departments of State, public corporations and local authorities have law-making powers. When we speak of subordinate legislation, we mean primarily the rules and

1 See pp. 25–7, 83–7, 112–4.

regulations made by these executive bodies. We also include rules of court made by independent statutory committees composed mainly of judges. Such legislation is *subordinate* in that it is made by bodies endowed with limited powers (usually conferred by Parliament), and is always subject to abrogation or alteration by Act of Parliament. Unlike legislation by the Queen in Parliament, it may, moreover, be held by a court to be *ultra vires*.

The only significant source of subordinate legislation made otherwise than in pursuance of powers delegated by Parliament is the royal prerogative. But the Crown has no general inherent power to alter the law of the land.[2] It has limited prerogative powers to make new constitutions and to legislate for the few remaining dependent territories acquired by conquest or cession, and to regulate the affairs of the civil service and the armed services.

The great bulk of subordinate legislation is made by virtue of parliamentary authority. Parliament delegates powers to legislate; the end-product is *delegated legislation*. The average annual output of delegated legislation easily exceeds the amount of parliamentary legislation. The Public General Acts cover, on average, over 2,000 pages each year, and published *Statutory Instruments* almost 6,000 pages. (*Statutory Instruments*[3] do not include by-laws made by local authorities or public corporations.) Roughly 2,000 sets of rules and regulations are made by Ministers or the Crown in Council or other central rule-making authorities in the course of a year; the total number of public and private Acts of Parliament will be about 100.

Some have depicted this state of affairs as an abdication by Parliament from its principal constitutional role in favour of the Executive.[4] Acts of Parliament, sponsored by Government Departments and passed into law with the acquiescence of a docile parliamentary majority, give the Executive sweeping legislative powers; and safeguards against the abuse of those powers are inadequate. The most celebrated denunciation of delegation to the Executive came in 1929 from Lord Hewart, the then Lord Chief Justice of England. In his book, *The New Despotism*, he attributed overgenerous delegations of legislative power to a deep-laid bureaucratic conspiracy. The Committee on Ministers' Powers, hastily appointed in anticipation of

2 *Case of Proclamations* (1611) 12 Co. Rep. 74.
3 For the meaning of this term, see p. 343. There are also half a dozen pages of prerogative instruments each year.
4 See especially Lord Hewart of Bury, *The New Despotism* (1929); C. K. Allen, *Bureaucracy Triumphant* (1931); *Law and Orders* (though the 3rd edn (1965) of this work was more restrained than the first); G. W. Keeton, *The Passing of Parliament* (1952). For more detached appraisals, see C. T. Carr, *Delegated Legislation* (1921); *Concerning English Administrative Law* (1941); John Willis, *The Parliamentary Powers of English Government Departments* (1933).

the furore that Hewart's book would arouse, reported in 1932 that the conspiratorial allegations were unsupported by the 'smallest shred of evidence'.[5] Nevertheless, the idea still persists in some quarters that delegation of legislative power to the Executive is at best a necessary evil, a constitutional impropriety to be half-heartedly condoned on grounds of expediency, but a potentially serious threat to the liberties of the subject. A few elementary and corrective points can be made.

1 Executive initiative is the dominant feature of parliamentary legislation. It is a still more dominant feature of delegated legislation. The difference is one of degree. Differences of degree can indeed be extremely important. Delegated legislation, unlike parliamentary legislation, has no committee stage at which amendments can be put down;[6] seldom is it debated in Parliament at all. None the less, prior consultation with advisory bodies and organized interest groups is a more conspicuous characteristic of delegated legislation than of parliamentary legislation.[7]

2 Most of the doom-laden prophecies were based on the experience of war and its immediate aftermath. In both the world wars of this century, vast law-making powers were delegated to the Executive. The Defence of the Realm Acts 1914–15 conferred a general power to make Orders in Council for securing the public safety and the defence of the realm. The Emergency Powers (Defence) Acts 1939–40 were more explicit but equally permissive, and the 1940 Act specified that Defence Regulations could make provisions 'requiring persons to place themselves, their services, and their property at the disposal of His Majesty'. These enormous powers were not always exercised reasonably. Some Defence Regulations remained in force too long after the war was over; and new regulations and orders, sometimes unpopular or ill-conceived, were made under postwar emergency legislation.[8] However, most of them were revoked or lapsed long ago (although the Import, Export and Customs Powers (Defence) Act 1939 was made permanent by the Import and

5 Cmd 4060 (1932), p. 59.
6 With the exception of special procedure orders; see p. 344.
7 See generally S. A. Walkland, *The Legislative Process in Great Britain* (1968), ch. 5.
8 Food rationing regulations were naturally among the least popular. According to a well-authenticated story. Churchill, on his return to office as Prime Minister in 1951, gave instructions that the food ration be constructed in the form of a model so that he could assess the quantity better. When the model was laid before him, he remarked 'Not a bad meal!' On being told that the model represented a week's rations he exploded: '. . . the people are starving . . .' (Harold Macmillan, *Tides of Fortune* (1969), pp. 490–91).

Export Control Act 1990). This fact does not, of course, imply that contemporary criticism was groundless or had no effect.

3 Open a recent volume of *Statutory Instruments* and read the first hundred pages. The tedium of wading through a mass of abstruse technicalities, barely comprehensible to anyone lacking expert knowledge of the subject-matter, is at least an instructive experience; and if one has the moral stamina, one can plough on through another five thousand pages. With such subject-matter, delegated legislation is in fact a dull subject for many of us.

4 Parliamentary scrutiny of delegated legislation admittedly tends to be perfunctory. But a select committee of the House of Commons examines statutory instruments which may be open to objection on constitutional grounds.[9] This committee, however, reports adversely on only a tiny number of instruments scrutinized. Before launching into a general denunciation of the content of delegated legislation, it is best to equip oneself with a sense of proportion.

5 Root and branch attacks on delegated legislation have often been prompted by a hearty dislike of public encroachments on freedom of property and contract. The assailants would have found the regulatory provisions no less objectionable if they had been embodied in Acts of Parliament rather than in rules and regulations.

There is one further preliminary point. Delegated legislation is sometimes confused with the establishment and work of administrative tribunals. Their only common feature is that both are substitutes: delegated legislation may be resorted to instead of Acts of Parliament, and administrative tribunals instead of courts. If substitutes are always a poor second best, if Parliament and the ordinary courts are the only acceptable media for legislation and adjudication, and if administrative law means delegated legislation plus administrative adjudication and is a negation of the rule of law, then it is right to place the two phenomena side by side in the same rogues' gallery. If one disagrees with these propositions, there is little point in discussing delegated legislation in conjunction with special tribunals. Such a discussion also generates confusion. The line between legislation and adjudication may often be thin, but legislation is basically the making of new rules of general application[10] for the future, and adjudication is the determination of individual claims and controversies. If new general rules emerge from

9 See pp. 349–51.
10 The difference between 'general' legislation and 'particular' executive action or judicial decisions is one of degree and sometimes imperceptible.

adjudication, this is incidental to the main purpose of the process. Obviously, statutory regulations laying down a new procedure for determining claims to social security benefits are different in kind from a decision by a social security appeal tribunal that X is or is not entitled to a benefit he has claimed in reliance on the existing rules.[11] Moreover, new tribunals are almost invariably constituted by Acts of Parliament; the normal role of delegated legislation in relation to tribunals will be to lay down detailed rules of procedure and to express in more precise terms the general functions confided in the tribunals by the enabling Act.

DELEGATED LEGISLATION: FUNCTIONS AND FEARS

Historical note[12]

Before 1832 Parliament delegated rule-making powers to the Executive spasmodically and, on the whole, sparingly. The plenitude of legislative authority devolved on Henry VIII by the Statute of Proclamations 1539 was not to be rivalled till 1914; the functions of central government were not wide enough to justify delegation on the grand scale. The Poor Law Amendment Act 1834, empowering the Poor Law Commissioners generally to make regulations for the management of the poor, marked the beginning of a new epoch. As the trend towards collectivism gathered momentum after 1870, so did delegations of legislative authority to the central government rapidly increase. But if this development threatened to undermine the fabric of the constitution, the dangers were hardly perceived. Dicey, among constitutional lawyers the most articulate exponent of Whiggish individualism, thought that Parliament was far too conservative in its attempts to unburden itself of detail; and, uncharacteristically, he commended the example of France, where executive decrees amplifying the general principles of legislation ranged over large areas of the law.[13] The phase of vehement denunciation began in the 1920s. Temperatures were lowered by the Report of the Committee on Ministers' Powers in 1932[14]

11 Some special tribunals have the duty of deciding in their discretion whether to *vary* existing rights (for example, by fixing fair rents) or to grant new rights and privileges (for example, licences).

12 See also Cmd 4060 (1932), pp. 10–15.

13 *Introduction to the Study of the Law of the Constitution* (10th edn, 1959), pp. 52–3.

14 Cmd 4060 (1932). The Committee is often called the Donoughmore Committee, after the name of its first chairman.

and have never reached the same height again. The Report provided an entirely convincing account of the reasons why the delegation of legislative powers to Ministers was indispensable, as well as indicating some real or potential dangers in the practice and suggesting safeguards against abuses. Amid the torrent of regulations descending from Whitehall between 1939 and 1950, few voices were raised to question the constitutional propriety of delegation. The main constitutional issues were: Where should the lines be drawn between parliamentary and delegated legislation? And how could safeguards against the misuse of delegated powers be improved?

Purposes of delegation

The reasons for delegating legislative powers to the Executive can be summed up in one phrase: the promotion of efficiency.

1 It is inefficient and unnecessary to incorporate a mass of complex detail in a parliamentary bill, or indeed in the schedules to such a bill, unless such provisions are designed to make really important changes in the law (for example, imposing substantial criminal liabilities or altering taxes), in which case they ought to be exposed to full parliamentary scrutiny. Few members of any Parliament will have the expert knowledge required to table and debate amendments to highly technical legislation; but a dogged group of the initiated can consume parliamentary time in this way, often for the ulterior purpose of impeding a Government's general legislative programme. Delegation saves parliamentary time.

2 The enactment of tortuous and cumbersome legislation, bulging with minutiae, disfigures the statute book and tends to detract from the prestige of Parliament. One can admire the diligence of the draftsmen of the Land Commission Act 1967[15] without being entranced by their product; some of the provisions of this convoluted statute should have been left to subordinate legislation.

3 It may be impossible to bring a major Act (for example, on town planning, social security, or reform of local government structure) into operation the day it receives the royal assent. Postponement may be necessary in order to undertake administrative reorganization or to conduct detailed consultations with various bodies with a view to modifying the general principles of the Act in their application to particular areas or sections of the community. Sometimes this can be effected by fixing the operative

15 Now repealed: Land Commission (Dissolution) Act 1971.

date when the bill is passed.[16] Sometimes this is impracticable, and the Act will therefore provide that it will come into force on such day as Her Majesty by Order in Council (or a Minister by statutory instrument) shall appoint. In any event, powers to make supplementary regulations on aspects of the new design will almost certainly be needed in the interest of flexibility, fairness and efficiency.

4 When an Act is passed, it is often reasonable to suppose that new contingencies (such as cases of special hardship, or technological developments) will arise although their exact form cannot be predicted at the date of enactment. It will be more sensible to give the responsible Minister powers to make regulations to amplify the Act should such contingencies arise than to compel him to rely on the chance of finding a place for amending legislation in an already long legislative queue.

5 Swift emergency action may have to be taken during a parliamentary recess or at a time when serious damage may be done if the normal processes of parliamentary legislation have to be followed. Sudden outbreaks of epidemics, natural disasters, or the discovery and introduction of new dangerous drugs or poisons may call for the immediate exercise of rule-making powers. Sometimes, of course, it is feasible to rush a bill through all its stages in both Houses within a few hours; the Emergency Powers (Defence) Act 1939 and the Southern Rhodesia Act 1965 (consequential on UDI) fell into this exceptional category. Sometimes a possible need for urgent action can be provided for by the enabling Act in the form of a grant of *executive* powers if *general* emergency regulations are unlikely to be required. However, when in 1972 the United Kingdom Government decided that it was imperative to impose direct rule on Northern Ireland and suspend the institutions of Stormont, the Northern Ireland (Temporary Provisions) Act 1972 not only vested *executive* authority in respect of Northern Ireland in the Secretary of State, but also provided that Orders in Council could be made on any matter within the competence of the Northern Ireland Parliament. A series of important legislative changes have been made under this wide-ranging delegated power.[17]

6 Changes in the constitutions of dependent territories, and constitutions adopted immediately before independence, are better embodied in Orders in Council than in Acts of Parliament. This is not because they are unimportant but because they are almost invariably the outcome of

16 Different dates may be fixed for bringing into operation different parts of an Act.
17 See further above, ch. 3.

an intergovernmental negotiation, and if it were open to Parliament to delete or modify individual provisions of the constitution a delicate balance might be upset and the political consequences could then be very serious.

Where delegation is open to criticism

1 It is a primary function of Parliament to determine the guidelines of legislative policy.[18] Parliament should not, therefore, delegate to Ministers power to make regulations on matters of general principle unless it lays down in the enabling Act standards delimiting the boundaries of the delegate's discretion. Skeleton legislation is justifiable only in order to deal with a state of dire emergency (such as the Northern Ireland situation since 1972) or a quite exceptional situation. In countries with written constitutions, a blanket delegation of legislative power to the Executive may be held to be unconstitutional.[19]

2 Grants of delegated power ought not to be so expressed that it becomes impossible in practice for the courts to review the limits of the powers exercised. Statutory formulae purporting to oust the jurisdiction of the courts by express language[20] are now uncommon. Less uncommon are statutory provisions endowing Ministers with powers which in their opinion are requisite or expedient for a broadly framed statutory purpose. When the validity of regulations made in pursuance of such powers is challenged, very strong grounds will have to be adduced before a court will be persuaded to intervene.[21] Moreover, Ministers, and their advisers, endowed with so large a discretion may be unable to resist temptations to stretch their powers beyond reasonable limits. Such delegations may thus offend against proposition (1).

3 Criticism has been levelled against the so-called 'Henry VIII clause', under which Parliament delegates authority to make regulations amending Acts

18 See generally Griffith (1951) 14 *Mod. L. Rev.* 279, 425.
19 See, for example, *Kent* v. *Dulles* 357 US 116 (1958) (United States); *Re Delhi Laws Act* (1951) SCR 747 (India), though see H. M. Seervai, *Constitutional Law of India* (2nd edn, 1975), pp. 874–86.
20 See pp. 355–6.
21 The point is well made by Lord Diplock *obiter* in *McEldowney* v. *Forde* [1971] AC 632 at 659–61, though see *Utah Construction and Engineering Co.* v. *Pataky* [1966] AC 629; *Customs and Excise Commissioners* v. *Cure and Deeley Ltd* [1962] 1 QB 340. See also pp. 353–4.

of Parliament.[22] This formulation is normally innocuous if the grant of power is confined to a limited period for the purpose of enabling draftsmen to make consequential adaptations to miscellaneous enactments that may have been overlooked when the principal Act was passed.[23] The Secretary of State's powers under the Deregulation and Contracting Out Act 1994 are exceptional. Subject to safeguards, he may repeal by statutory instrument any enactment on the ground that it imposes an unnecessary burden on business.[24]

4 Seldom if ever will a grant of power to make regulations imposing liabilities with retroactive effect be justified.[25]

5 The power to impose or vary taxation is, in general, too important to be delegated by Parliament. But a flexible power to make regulations modifying, for example, rates of indirect taxation or customs duties may be a valuable ancillary instrument for the management of the economy.[26]

6 In the interests of certainty, Parliament ought to identify the recipient of its delegated powers, and when delegating legislative authority it should not authorize sub-delegation of those powers to unnamed persons. In and immediately after the Second World War, when sub-delegation was expressly authorized by the Emergency Powers (Defence) Acts and their successors, instances of five-tier delegation arose.

The European Communities Act 1972

Quite apart from European regulations which are directly applicable of their own force (section 2(1)), further regulations are made in this country under powers delegated by the Act (section 2(2)) to give effect to European Union directives and decisions and also to implement in fuller detail some European Union regulations. Orders in Council and departmental

---

22 cf. Cmd 4060 (1932), pp. 36–8, 59–61, 65. For example, see Courts and Legal Services Act 1990, s. 3.

23 See, for example, Kenya Independence Act 1963, s. 5(4). An unusual power to amend the parent Act itself was conferred by section 16(2) of the Race Relations Act 1968 (see now the Race Relations Act 1976, s. 71). And see the extraordinary device in the Remuneration, Charges and Grants Act 1975, s. 1 (which lapsed in 1978).

24 Deregulation and Contracting Out Act 1994, ss. 1–6.

25 Such legislation is likely to be held to be *ultra vires* unless retroactive operation has been expressly authorized by the enabling Act. cf. authorities cited in *The Abadesa* [1968] P. 656 at 659. See also *Master Ladies Tailors Organisation* v. *Minister of Labour and National Service* [1950] 2 All ER 525 at 528. See, however, *Sabally & N'Jie* v. *Att.-Gen.* [1965] 1 QB 273.

26 cf. Excise Duties (Surcharges or Rebates) Act 1979, s. 1.

regulations made under these delegated powers *have the effect of Acts of Parliament* and can include any provision that might be made in an Act of Parliament (section 2(4))[27] except that they are not to impose or increase taxation[28] or have retroactive effect or sub-delegate legislative powers (other than power to make procedural rules for courts and tribunals) or create a new criminal offence punishable with more than two years' imprisonment or a fine of more than £5,000. This is probably the most sweeping grant of delegated legislative powers to the Executive in modern times except under emergency conditions.

STATUTORY INSTRUMENTS

Subordinate legislation may be designated as rules, regulations, orders, by-laws, schemes, measures, or by a variety of other appellations. The most important generic description is 'statutory instrument'. The definition of this term is complex and raises difficult points of interpretation.[29] Broadly, the term covers delegated legislation made under (1) powers conferred by statutes after 1947 on Her Majesty in Council, or on Ministers or Departments, to make, confirm or approve subordinate legislation where the enabling Act says that the power shall be exercisable by statutory instrument, and (2) powers conferred by statutes before 1948 on these authorities or other rule-making authorities (such as the Rule Committee of the Supreme Court) to make subordinate legislation, and on Ministers to confirm or approve instruments of a legislative (but not of an executive) character which also have to be laid before Parliament. A statutory instrument comes into effect when made unless (as is nearly always the case) the instrument specifies a later date on which it is to come into operation.

By-laws of local authorities and public corporations are not statutory instruments. Nor are measures of the General Synod of the Church of England.[30] Nor are provisional orders, which do not have legal effect till

---

27 For s. 2(4), see pp. 84–7. Clearly such regulations can repeal or amend Acts of Parliament in force at the time when they are made. But it is arguable that the regulations will be *ultra vires* unless related to European Union affairs.

28 But taxation can be imposed by directly applicable instruments (s. 2(1)).

29 For a full analysis, see Griffith and Street, op. cit., pp. 42–56, considering the meaning of the Statutory Instruments Act 1946 and regulations and an Order in Council made thereunder in 1947.

30 Made in pursuance of the Synodical Government Measure 1969; these measures are submitted for the royal assent if approved by both Houses of Parliament.

confirmed by Act of Parliament and are therefore not a form of delegated legislation at all. For most legal purposes, 'special procedure orders', which have replaced provisional orders under a number of Acts of Parliament, are statutory instruments; they will normally have legal effect without a confirmation Act.[31] Compulsory purchase orders, being of an executive rather than a legislative character, are not usually classified as statutory instruments. Nor, in general, are instruments made in pursuance of sub-delegated powers, but it is possible for them to fall within the definition of statutory instruments.[32] Nor, of course, are resolutions of the House of Commons statutory instruments; normally their legal effect is confined to matters arising within the House; but under some modern Acts of constitutional importance such resolutions have been accorded legislative effect.[33]

Statutory instruments must be printed, numbered, published and sold. They are also published in annual volumes in chronological sequence. However, local or temporary instruments, instruments made available in a separate series to persons directly concerned, and very bulky schedules, may be exempted from the requirement of publication. The annual volumes were called *Statutory Rules and Orders* before 1948;[34] since 1948 they have been entitled *Statutory Instruments*. Prerogative legislative instruments are unnumbered but are published and appear in an appendix to each volume.

Government statements of policy and intent, departmental circulars giving instructions to local authorities, and procedural rules issued by certain other public bodies, may be legislative in effect and will usually be published; but they will not be published as statutory instruments even if made in

---

31 See Statutory Orders (Special Procedure) Acts 1945 and 1965; the procedure on such orders (which is attracted where an Act prescribes that an order authorized to be made shall be 'subject to a special parliamentary procedure') involves opportunities to object to the order at a local inquiry and also by petition to Parliament; the order may be amended in pursuance of a report by a joint committee of the two Houses.

32 Regulations made by designated Ministers under the European Communities Act 1972 are statutory instruments (s. 2(2); sched. 2, para: 2(1)).

33 See Provisional Collection of Taxes Acts 1913 and 1968 (temporary authority to collect income tax and other annual taxes); Exchequer and Audit Department Act 1957, s. 1(3) (increase in salary of Comptroller and Auditor-General); Parliamentary Commissioner Act 1967, s. 2(2) (increase in salary of Parliamentary Commissioner for Administration). See also House of Commons Disqualification Act 1975, s. 6(2), (3) (relieving MPs from effect of disqualification); Murder (Abolition of Death Penalty) Act 1965, s. 1.

34 There is also a consolidation entitled *Statutory Rules and Orders and Statutory Instruments Revised*, comprising subordinate legislation in force at the end of 1948.

pursuance of statutory powers.[35] The extra-statutory concessions offered by the Inland Revenue in favour of taxpayers are clearly legislative in substance[36] but, just as clearly, are not within the definition of statutory instruments. The Immigration Rules are not classified as statutory instruments, perhaps because it is not clear that the power to make them is directly conferred by statute. Nor are the Codes of Practice made under the Police and Criminal Evidence Act 1984, and the Highway Code, which do not have quite the same legal force.

SAFEGUARDS

Contraceptive and antenatal

The most effective safeguard against the abuse of delegated powers is not to delegate them in such terms as to invite abuse. When a bill is first drafted by parliamentary counsel on instructions given by the sponsoring Department, it will go to that Department, to the Legislation Committee of the Cabinet (of which the Lord Chancellor and the Law Officers of the Crown are members) and may go to a specialized Ministerial Committee or an interdepartmental committee.

A number of policy and technical decisions have to be taken: where the lines should be drawn between matters explicitly to be set out in the bill and matters to be left for amplification by the exercise of delegated powers; how precisely the limits of delegated power are to be worded; whether the Act should require subordinate legislation to be laid before Parliament at all, and if so, whether it should also be subject to annulment by resolution of either House, or should require approval by affirmative resolution of one or both Houses; and so on. To what extent general criteria have been formulated as guides to making these decisions is far from clear though it can be assumed that the parliamentary draftsmen have regard to precedents and do not accede automatically to every eccentric departmental request. If the draftsmen consider an aspect of a draft bill to be objectionable on grounds of constitutional principle, they may succeed in carrying the sponsoring Department's legal advisers with them. If this is not enough

---

35 cf. *Blackpool Corporation* v. *Locker* [1948] 1 KB 349.
36 cf. *R.* v. *Customs and Excise Commissioners, ex p. Cook* [1970] 1 WLR 450 at 454–5 (where attention was drawn to the lack of any legal basis for concessions made by the Customs and Excise).

and they wish to press their point, they will have a further opportunity when the final draft of the bill is examined by the Law Officers.

The Legislation Committee of the Cabinet also reviews departmental drafts of statutory instruments which are of exceptional importance or special interest to other Departments or may give rise to criticism on the grounds that they are unusual in their content or of doubtful constitutional propriety. The departmental legal advisers may obtain the aid of parliamentary counsel in preparing the draft of a particularly important instrument.[37]

Before regulations are made by a Department, prior consultation with advisory bodies and organized interest groups is the general practice. Statutes often require that named bodies, or organizations identified by description (for example, representative of local authorities) be consulted in advance. Procedural regulations for tribunals and inquiries have to be submitted in draft to the Council on Tribunals.[38] Drafts of social security regulations have to be submitted to the Social Security Advisory Committee, a statutory body; the Committee must notify persons and bodies likely to be affected and give an opportunity for objections to be lodged; the Committee submits its report to the Secretary of State who, when he makes the regulations, must also lay the report before Parliament and state how far he has given effect to the Committee's recommendations and why he has not accepted them. In practice he has almost invariably accepted them.[39]

Under a few statutes, the initiative in preparing draft rules and regulations (for example, for agricultural marketing schemes) is given to bodies representing persons engaged in the occupation, and occasionally to individuals so engaged; such schemes cannot normally be given legislative effect without the responsible Minister's approval.

By-laws made by local authorities are subject to confirmation by the appropriate Minister, who is in most cases the Secretary of State for the Environment. Sets of model by-laws are available, and local by-laws deviating widely from these without special reasons are unlikely to be confirmed.

Publicity

'Does any human being read through this mass of departmental legislation?' asked Lord Hewart.[40] Perhaps not; but since ignorance of the law is, in general, no excuse for breaking it, regulations ought to be readily available

---

37 S. A. Walkland, *The Legislative Process in Great Britain* (1968), pp. 63–5.
38 Tribunals and Inquiries Act 1992, ss. 8, 9.
39 Social Security Act 1980, ss. 9(1), 10, sched. 3
40 *The New Despotism* (1929), pp. 96–7.

to members of the public and their legal advisers as soon as they come into force. The principles governing publication have already been noted.[41] An instrument may nevertheless have legal effect before it is published and available for sale at a government bookshop.[42] This is unusual; indeed, Departments now try to follow a general rule that an instrument shall not come into operation for twenty-one days after being laid before Parliament.[43] But to mitigate the hardship that may still arise, section 3(2) of the Statutory Instruments Act 1946 provides that it shall be a defence to criminal proceedings for contravening an instrument to prove that the instrument has not been issued at the date of the contravention unless the prosecution proves that reasonable steps have previously been taken to bring its purport to the notice of the public or persons likely to be affected or the person charged.[44]

In the best of all possible worlds, statutory instruments would be not only available but also intelligible. This desideratum may be unattainable, but the opaque has become translucent by the practice of appending brief explanatory notes at the end of statutory instruments, indicating their general purport and effect.

Parliamentary proceedings[45]

The parent Act may or may not require the instrument to be laid before Parliament. If there is no requirement as to laying,[46] a member of Parliament who gets to know of the instrument may still put down a question about it to the responsible Minister or seek to raise the matter in debate. If the instrument has merely to be laid, or laid in draft, before Parliament, it will be delivered to the Votes and Proceedings Office of the House of Commons.[47] No opportunity is provided by parliamentary procedure for

---

41 p. 344.

42 See R. v. Sheer Metalcraft Ltd [1954] I QB 586. Contrast Johnson v. Sargant & Sons [1918] I KB 101 (statutory order held not to have effect till it became known; the authority of this decision is now doubtful). See further Lanham (1974) 37 Mod. L. Rev. 510.

43 HC 475 (1971–2), para. 62. But not all instruments have to be laid before Parliament: see below p. 348.

44 The substance of that is unaffected by the Statutory Instruments (Production and Sale) Act 1996, a purely technical measure.

45 See Brazier, Ministers of the Crown (1997), ch. 11.3; Report of the Joint Select Committee on Delegated Legislation (HC 169 (1977–8)); Hayhurst and Wallington [1988] Public Law 547.

46 The large majority of statutory instruments in this category are instruments of a local nature.

47 SO No. 138; Laying of Documents before Parliament (Interpretation) Act 1948, s. 1.

the instrument to be discussed, but its existence will at least be brought to the notice of members and the Minister is more likely to be questioned about it than if it is not laid before Parliament at all. Moreover, any instrument required to be laid before Parliament does not become operative until so laid, unless it is essential for it to become operative at once, in which case the reason must be notified to the Lord Chancellor and the Speaker forthwith.[48]

It is more common for the enabling Act to provide that an instrument shall be laid, or laid in draft, subject to the negative resolution procedure. This means that it is open to any member to move a prayer to annul the instrument (or, if it has been laid in draft, to move that it not be made) within forty days of being laid.[49] Such motions are put at the end of the day's business; debate on such a motion must be terminated or adjourned not later than 11.30 p.m. in the Commons.[50] Statutory instruments against which a negative resolution has been moved, or which are subject to the affirmative resolution procedure (see below), are considered on their merits by a Standing Committee on Delegated Legislation – but this procedure can only be invoked *at the instance of a Minister*.[51]

A minority of instruments are required to be laid, or laid in draft, subject to an affirmative resolution of one or both Houses; unless a resolution approving the instrument is passed within the period (if any) prescribed by the enabling Act, the instrument ceases to have effect or cannot be made.[52] Instruments made subject to that procedure are normally those regarded as being of special constitutional importance (for example, varying constituency boundaries) or imposing taxation (in which case an affirmative resolution of the Commons alone will be needed). A statutory instrument made under the European Communities Act *may* be laid in draft subject to the affirmative resolution procedure; if not so laid in draft, it shall be subject to the negative resolution procedure.[53]

The value of the negative resolution procedure is not easily assessed. Motions to annul statutory instruments are infrequent; rarely are they

---

48 Statutory Instruments Act 1946, s. 4(1). See also above, and SO No. 139.
49 ibid., s. 5(1).
50 SO No. 15.
51 SO No. 101. The procedure can be blocked by twenty or more MPs; this enables the Opposition to ensure that the most controversial statutory instruments are debated on the floor of the House.
52 Passing a negative resolution or failing to pass an affirmative resolution does not have the effect of invalidating anything already done in pursuance of the instrument.
53 1972 Act, sched. 2, para. 2(2).

successful,[54] and it is open to the Minister to present the instrument afresh; but from time to time a Minister withdraws an instrument in the face of hostile criticism and may perhaps submit it in a revised form. One substantial criticism of this procedure is that because of pressure on parliamentary time it is not always possible to debate a prayer to annul an instrument.[55] Hardly ever does an Act make provision for the amendment of a statutory instrument. But the possibility that damaging parliamentary publicity may result from a debate on an ill-drafted or otherwise objectionable instrument is of some utility as a safeguard against the misuse of delegated power.

The affirmative resolution procedure is more important, in that the Government must find time to explain why the instrument should be approved and thus lays itself open to critical comment. In November 1969 the Home Secretary laid himself open to acrimonious criticism by moving (successfully) that four draft Orders in Council purporting to give effect to Boundary Commission recommendations be not approved by the Commons.[56] But if all statutory instruments were made subject to this procedure, a primary object of delegating legislative powers to the Executive – to make for economical use of parliamentary time – would be frustrated.

Parliamentary scrutinizing committees

The Joint Select Committee on Statutory Instruments replaced both the House of Commons Select Committee on Statutory Instruments and the House of Lords Special Orders Committee.[57] The terms of reference of the Joint Select Committee today are to consider every statutory instrument of a general character and various other instruments which, under the parent Act, were laid or laid in draft before the House subject to the negative or affirmative resolution procedure, with a view to deciding

54 A spectacular exception to the general rule was the rejection of the revised Immigration Rules (not technically a statutory instrument, but the distinction is immaterial) made under section 3(2) of the Immigration Act 1971: see 34 HC Deb. 355–440 (15 December 1982). Revised Immigration Rules had to be introduced. The House of Lords has *never* carried a negative resolution (HC 475 (1971–2), para. 13), although (or because) their opposition cannot be overridden under the Parliament Acts procedure.

55 HC 538 (1970–1), paras. 41–6; HC 475 (1971–2), paras. 95–128, for proposals for enlargement of the opportunities.

56 See pp. 241–3. Instruments subject to the affirmative procedure can be referred to a Standing Committee on Delegated Legislation: SO No. 101.

57 Although the function of the latter of examining instruments against which persons whose interests are directly affected may petition is now vested in the Lords' Hybrid Instruments Committee, set up in 1975. See SO No. 124.

whether the special attention of the House should be drawn to the instrument on any of these grounds: that (i) it imposes charges on the subject or the public revenue; (ii) it is ostensibly immunized by the parent Act against challenge in the courts; (iii) it purports to have retrospective effect in the absence of express authority given by the parent Act; (iv) there appears to have been unjustifiable delay in publication or laying before Parliament; (v) where it is essential for an instrument to come into effect before being laid, there has been unjustifiable delay in notifying the Speaker of this fact and the reasons; (vi) where the instrument gives rise to doubts whether it is *intra vires*, or where it appears to make an unusual or unexpected use of the powers conferred by the parent statute; (vii) where it requires elucidation; or (viii) where the draftsmanship appears to be defective; or any ground 'which does not impinge on its merits or on the policy behind it; and to report their decision with the reason thereof in any particular case'.[58]

Before deciding to draw the attention of the House to an instrument on any of these grounds, the Committee must give the Department concerned an opportunity of putting its case.

The Committee consists of seven members of each House, of whom two are a quorum. It is assisted by Counsel to the Speaker and by Counsel to the Lord Chairman of Committees. That its function is strictly technical and non-partisan is emphasized by the convention that the chairman shall be a member of the Opposition. Its concern is with efficiency and constitutional propriety, extending beyond (but including) consideration of the strict legality of the powers exercised by the prescribed authority. It can comment, and has commented, on inconsistencies in legislative practice (for example, in providing for parliamentary proceedings on some instruments but not on others of a similar character) and on unsatisfactory features of sub-delegation of powers. In its early years many of its adverse reports were based on undue delay in publication or laying before Parliament; departmental procrastination suddenly became very rare. The fact that regulations are on the whole less obscurely drafted than they used to be can be partly attributed to its influence. Perhaps the patient drudgery of the Committee has had a highly salutary effect on overweening bureaucrats; perhaps the dangers of abuse of delegated legislative powers were greatly exaggerated by some critics. That a few instruments made an unusual use of the powers granted, and that others were obscurely worded – these had

58 The words in quotation marks had been added in 1971. MPs consider without peers those instruments which the parent Act directs to be laid before and to be subject to proceedings in the House of Commons only.

become the main grounds for adverse reports by the 1960s – was hardly surprising. What was surprising was the small size of this problem viewed by an experienced scrutinizing committee.[59]

No special opportunity has been provided by parliamentary procedure for debating the Committee's reports; this must have detracted from its efficiency. But an adverse report delivered swiftly enough may lead to a prayer for annulment, or opposition to an affirmative resolution; or such a report may persuade a Department to amend or revoke an instrument.

Judicial review

The courts may hold a subordinate legislative instrument to be invalid if it is *ultra vires*, i.e. in excess of powers. This jurisdiction extends to prerogative instruments as well as statutory rules, regulations and by-laws. The validity of such instruments may be impugned directly or indirectly. Direct frontal challenges are unusual and are seldom successful; a plaintiff may find it impossible to establish that his personal interests are sufficiently affected by a general legislative instrument to give him title to sue.[60] Collateral, or indirect, attack is more common; a person is prosecuted for breach of a regulation or by-law, or is sued for breach of a contract the binding force of which is dependent on the validity of a regulation or by-law, and his defence is that the regulation or by-law is invalid. Under Community law this appears to be the only method by which European Union instruments can be impeached before national courts as being *ultra vires* the treaties.[61]

An instrument may be invalid because of a formal or procedural defect, or because it goes beyond the limited scope of delegated authority on a matter of substance. Challenges based on defects of form or procedure present difficulties in that not every such defect is a source of invalidity. Formal or procedural requirements are classifiable as either mandatory or directory. Non-compliance with a mandatory requirement is a potentially vitiating defect; if, however, the requirement is construed as being merely

---

59 That said, however, the Committee (in HL 51 and HC 169 (1977–8)) criticized the Government for giving Ministers wide discretionary powers in certain statutory instruments to amend statutory instruments, for omitting essential detail from statutory instruments, and for allowing inadequate time to elapse between the laying, publication and coming into force of some instruments.

60 But see *R. v. HM Treasury, ex. p. Smedley* [1985] QB 657 (taxpayer had standing to challenge draft Order in Council which would authorize spending from Consolidated Fund); *Hotel and Catering Industry Training Board v. Automobile Proprietary Co.* [1969] 1 WLR 697 (declaration that a statutory instrument was *ultra vires* granted).

61 Hartley [1981] *Crim. L. Rev.* 85.

directory, the courts may take the view that substantial compliance is enough or even that total non-compliance is a mere error that does not affect the validity of what has been done. Prediction of how a court will regard non-compliance is difficult; precedents afford little guidance, and although the practical importance of non-compliance with the duty is the main criterion, a court will sometimes take a stringent view of failure to observe a minor formality.[62] Non-observance of duties to consult with a specified body[63] or consider objections or give an opportunity to be heard[64] are likely to be held to render regulations invalid. Rather surprisingly, it appears that mere failure to publish an instrument does not render it invalid if other prescribed preliminaries have been observed;[65] the effect of breach of a duty to lay a statutory instrument before Parliament is doubtful, but this may well be held to render the instrument inoperative.[66]

If power is delegated only to do X, the delegate cannot do Y, unless Y is necessarily implicit in or incidental to the power to do X. Power granted for purpose A cannot be used instead for purpose B. These ostensibly straightforward questions of statutory interpretation may give rise to considerable problems in practice – for example, where the statutory purpose is not clearly defined,[67] or where the existence of a link between the subject-matter of the delegated power and the statutory purpose is expressed by the parent Act to be determinable by the delegate himself.[68] Again, a strictly literal interpretation of the enabling section may frustrate the general object of the Act or wreak injustice; a court will not necessarily shut its eyes to this possibility. Nor will a court disregard the context in which regulations have been made; regulations made in a state of grave emergency may be construed more benevolently in favour of the Executive than regulations made under the same powers when the seriousness of the emergency has diminished.

Forecasts of how a court may construe the validity of regulations are further complicated by other factors. Thus, ordinary literal interpretation

---

62 See, for example, *Patchett* v. *Leathem* (1949) 65 TLR 69.

63 *Agricultural etc. Training Board* v. *Aylesbury Mushrooms Ltd* [1972] 1 WLR 190.

64 *R.* v. *Housing Appeal Tribunal* [1920] 3 KB 334 at 342, 343, 346.

65 See pp. 346–7; but note the mitigating effect of s. 3(2) of the Statutory Instruments Act 1946.

66 *R.* v. *Sheer Metalcraft Ltd* [1954] 1 QB 586 at 590. It is still open to the courts to resolve these difficult issues.

67 cf. the 3:2 division of opinion in the House of Lords in *McEldowney* v. *Forde* [1971] AC 632, a case arising under the Northern Ireland Civil Authorities (Special Powers) Act 1922 (now repealed).

68 See pp. 341–2, 381–2.

may be modified in the light of common-law presumptions of legislative intent. For instance, there is a presumption that express statutory authority is needed to validate the exercise of delegated powers interfering with the liberty of the person, or excluding the citizen from access to the ordinary courts for the determination of his legal rights and liabilities,[69] or imposing taxation,[70] or taking away property rights without compensation.[71] The circumstances in which these presumptions will carry decisive weight are not easy to predict.[72] In the First World War, power to make regulations for securing the public safety and the defence of the realm was held to justify the making of a regulation for the preventive detention of British subjects on security grounds without trial,[73] notwithstanding the strong common-law presumption in favour of individual liberty. Three years later a court held that the same statutory power was not wide enough to validate a wartime regulation prohibiting landlords from taking legal proceedings for possession orders, against tenants who were munition workers, without the prior consent of a Minister.[74] In the Second World War, an undoubtedly valid defence regulation, providing that a Secretary of State could make orders for the detention of persons whom he had 'reasonable cause' to believe to be of hostile origin or associations and in need of subjection to preventive control, was not construed by the courts as importing an objectively determinable test of reasonableness. To establish the invalidity of a detention order, a detainee would have to discharge the impossible burden of proving that the Secretary of State did not genuinely believe he had 'reasonable cause'.[75] In a number of cases in which the validity of subordinate legislation and executive acts affecting property rights was challenged during and immediately after the Second World War, the courts

---

69 *Chester* v. *Bateson* [1920] 1 KB 829; *Customs and Excise Commissioners* v. *Cure & Deeley Ltd* [1902] 1 QB 340.

70 *Cure & Deeley's* case (above); see also *Att.-Gen.* v. *Wilts United Dairies Ltd* (1921) 37 TLR 884 (CA), but see p. 283, above.

71 For example, *Newcastle Breweries Ltd* v. *R.* [1920] 1 KB 854.

72 Contrast, for example, in the field of town planning decisions (executive acts), the case of *Hall & Co.* v. *Shoreham-by-Sea UDC* [1964] 1 WLR 240 (presumption against deprivation of property rights without compensation applied) with *Westminster Bank Ltd.* v. *Beverley BC* [1971] AC 508 (presumption not applied).

73 *R.* v. *Halliday, ex p. Zadig* [1917] AC 260.

74 *Chester* v. *Bateson* [1920] 1 KB 829.

75 *Liversidge* v. *Anderson* [1942] AC 206. Contrast, on the meaning of 'reasonable cause' or 'reasonable grounds', *Nakkuda Ali* v. *Jayaratne* [1951] AC 66 at 76–7. The only other ground on which a detention order could be challenged was that it had been improperly made out: *R.* v. *Secretary of State for Home Affairs, ex p. Budd* [1942] 2 KB 14 at 22. See ch. 24.

adopted a strictly literal interpretation of the enabling legislation in favour of the Executive. The enabling Act was typically expressed in the form: 'If it appears to' or 'if in the opinion of' the Minister, or 'if the Minister is satisfied that' a given state of affairs existed, he could make such orders as appeared to him necessary or expedient for a generally worded purpose.[76] By the early 1950s this self-denying ordinance had been slightly modified. The Judicial Committee of the Privy Council could state that a power so exercised had to be 'capable of being related to one of the prescribed purposes.'[77]

In 1961 the pendulum had swung far enough for a High Court judge (invoking common-law presumptions of legislative intent) to hold that a statutory power authorizing the Commissioners of Customs and Excise to make regulations 'for any matter for which provision appears to them necessary for the purpose of giving effect to the Act' was too narrow to validate a regulation by which they gave themselves power to determine conclusively what amount of purchase tax was payable in individual cases.[78] This is perhaps an extreme case of judicial activism. Nowadays the courts are unlikely to review the matter *de novo* but to ask whether the competent authority had misdirected itself and whether the regulations were reasonably capable of being related to the grant of power.[79]

Judicial tests for the validity of by-laws have generally been understood to be stricter than the tests for the validity of regulations made by Ministers or Her Majesty in Council. Although by-laws made by elected local authorities for the general welfare are to be benevolently construed,[80] they may be still held *ultra vires* and invalid if they are excessively uncertain in

76 For example, *R.* v. *Comptroller General of Patents, ex p. Bayer Products Ltd* [1941] 2 KB 306; *Point of Ayr Collieries Ltd.* v. *Lloyd-George* [1943] 2 All ER 547. In *Carltona Ltd* v. *Commissioners of Works* [1943] 2 All ER 560 at 564, Lord Greene MR said, 'All that the court can do is to see that the power . . . falls within the four corners of the power given by the legislature and [is] exercised in good faith. Apart from that, the courts have no power at all to inquire into the reasonableness, the policy, the sense, or any other aspect of the transaction.'

77 *Att.-Gen. for Canada* v. *Hallet & Carey Ltd* [1952] AC 427 at 450.

78 *Customs and Excise Commissioners* v. *Cure & Deeley Ltd* [1962] 1 QB 340 (*per* Sachs J). See to like effect, *Reade* v. *Smith* [1959] NZLR 996 (applied in *Labour Department* v. *Merrit Beazley Homes Ltd* [1976] 1 NZLR 505). cf., however, *Marsh (Wholesale) Ltd* v. *Customs and Excise Commissioners* (1970) 2 QB 206.

79 See note 21 above; *Hallet and Cary's* case (note 77); *Secretary of State for Employment* v. *ASLEF (No. 2)* [1972] 2 QB 455.

80 *Kruse* v. *Johnson* [1898] 2 QB 91 at 99–100; applied in *Burnley Borough Council* v. *England* (1978) 77 LGR 227 (by-law made by local council banning dogs from parks and children's playgrounds not unreasonable).

their terms or repugnant to the general law of the land or manifestly unreasonable. The English courts have yet to hold a statutory instrument to be *ultra vires* explicitly on these grounds alone. But a court might hold an instrument to be too vague to be capable of being related to a permitted purpose;[81] so offensive to the general principles of the law as to be beyond the contemplation of the enabling Act;[82] or so unreasonable that it could not be ascribed to the enabling provisions.[83] Perhaps, then, the differences in the scope of judicial review of by-laws, on the one hand, and statutory instruments, on the other, are only matters of degree or even verbal distinctions.

Although no English authority directly covers the point it is highly probable that the courts, applying the maxim *delegatus non potest delegare*, will hold that the recipient of delegated legislative power cannot validly sub-delegate any part of its rule-making power to another in the absence of express statutory authorization.[84] But a power vested in a Minister or a Department to make regulations can validly be exercised by an official authorized by his superiors to act in that behalf; this is not an example of sub-delegation, for the official is the Minister's other self, his *alter ego*.[85]

In the past a great deal of heat was generated by statutory provisions purporting to oust judicial review of the validity of regulations, orders and administrative decisions and determinations. The formula providing that a regulation or order, when made, was to have effect 'as if enacted in the Act', has fallen into desuetude. Whether the courts regarded it as excluding them from determining the *vires* of a subordinate instrument was never entirely clear.[86] A provision that the making or confirmation of an order was to be 'conclusive evidence' that the requirements of the Act had been complied with was probably effective to exclude judicial review,[87] despite the traditional disfavour shown by the courts to language ostensibly

---

81 *McEldowney* v. *Forde* [1971] AC 632 at 643, 645, 653, 665.
82 For example, by authorizing the condemnation of a person without allowing him an opportunity of being heard on his own behalf (*R.* v. *Housing Appeal Tribunal* [1920] 3 KB 334) or by taking away his common-law right of access to the courts: *Chester* v. *Bateson*; *Cure & Deeley's* case (note 77 above).
83 See note 81, above.
84 See *Jackson, Stansfield & Sons* v. *Butterworth* [1948] 2 All ER 558 at 564–6, and below, pp. 543–4.
85 *R.* v. *Skinner* [1968] 2 QB 700.
86 *Institute of Patent Agents* v. *Lockwood* [1894] AC 347 supported the view that such a provision barred judicial review; *Minister of Health* v. *R., ex p. Yaffe* [1931] AC 494 indicated that it did not. Various intermediate positions are possible.
87 *Ex p. Ringer* (1909) 73 JP 436.

depriving them of their inherent supervisory jurisdiction. Exclusionary formulae create a bad impression and are seldom used today unless finality is all-important.

The Extradition Act 1989 and the Parliamentary Constituencies Act 1986 have provisions to the effect that Orders in Council made thereunder shall not be questioned in any legal proceedings; the subject-matter of such Orders (application of an extradition treaty to a foreign State, and the determination of constituency boundaries) may justify the exclusion of judicial review.[88] Similar formulae purporting to protect judicial-type administrative determinations against judicial review are made nugatory (with certain exceptions) by the Tribunals and Inquiries Act 1992, if contained in Acts passed before August 1958.[89] In the present climate of opinion, one would not expect to see delegated legislation afforded special statutory protection save in highly exceptional circumstances. As we have seen, Orders in Council and regulations made in this country under the European Communities Act 1972 for the fulfilment of European Union obligations enjoy extraordinary protection inasmuch as they are assimilated for most purposes to Acts of Parliament.[90]

---

88 Extradition Act 1989, s. 4(3); Parliamentary Constituencies Act 1986, s. 4(7). See also Parliament Act 1911, s. 3; Parliament Act 1949, s. 2(2) (Speaker's certificates); West Indies Act 1967, s. 18. Judicial review of subordinate legislation is not excluded merely because provision has been made by the parent Act for the affirmative or negative resolution procedure (*R. v. Electricity Commissioners* [1924] 1 KB 171), but judicial intervention while an instrument was still before either House might be regarded as an encroachment on parliamentary privilege.

89 See Tribunals and Inquiries Act 1992, s. 12.

90 See p. 342. But, as was indicated, jurisdiction to determine the *vires* of such instruments is not entirely excluded.

PART FOUR

JUSTICE AND CIVIL RIGHTS

This Part incorporates analysis of the system of justice followed by chapters on fundamental human rights.

First, in chapter 18 some features of the administration of justice in England are considered. For detailed accounts of the structure and working of the English legal system, readers should consult textbooks devoted to the subject; here only an outline sketch is presented. The working of the Crown Prosecution Service is explained, and the roles of the amateur in the legal system – as magistrates and jurors – are touched on. More detail is devoted to the rules of law and convention, professional traditions and political practices, that help to sustain the independence of the Judiciary. The Lord Chancellor's policies and practices in relation to the appointment and promotion of the Judiciary have become clearer and are explained. The impact of the Courts and Legal Services Act 1990 is noted, and the chapter is a convenient place for considering the law of contempt of court, both in the Contempt of Court Act 1981 and in the case law upon it. The roles of Ministers (including the Attorney-General) and the Director of Public Prosecutions in the administration of justice are also considered. Every one of these topics is of constitutional interest and distinguishes the English system from a great many other legal systems.

Chapter 19 considers fully the European Convention on Human Rights (which is being incorporated into English law by the Human Rights Bill), evaluates the arguments in favour of and against a new bill of rights for the United Kingdom, and takes in the law relating to racial and sexual discrimination.

Chapter 20 begins with a discussion of the concept of British citizenship and the implications of that status. The complex rules governing the immigration and deportation of Commonwealth citizens and aliens, and the distinction drawn between those with and without the right of abode, are also outlined. Among the statutes considered are the British Nationality Act 1981 and the Immigration Act 1971, and the rules made under the latter Act (which give special rights to nationals of Community members). Further restrictions enacted against immigration in recent years are noted. Some aspects of the concepts of allegiance and protection (already touched on in the latter part of chapter 7) and the rules about British passports are then discussed. The law on the extradition of fugitive offenders is also brought into chapter 20, because it tends to raise the same *kinds* of issues covered in the early part of the chapter.

Chapter 21 is concerned with liberty of the person. It examines the main features of English law on liberty of the person, and the major – and controversial – Police and Criminal Evidence Act 1984 is considered. Special reference is made to police powers of arrest, interrogation, search and seizure; the offence of wilfully obstructing a police officer in the execution of his duty; and remedies against unlawful physical restraint, including the writ of habeas corpus. The chapter includes a brief note on the law of privacy, and of confidentiality, the latter having been propelled to prominence in recent years.

Chapter 22 is concerned with another basic freedom – freedom of expression. In order to ascertain the scope of this freedom, the circumstances in which a person may be prevented from expressing himself at all (such as the operation of the Official Secrets Act) or through particular media – for example, the cinema, the press, the broadcasting services – have to be considered first. Then there is the miscellany of criminal or civil wrongs that may be committed by speech or written words or pictorial representations – for instance, treason, sedition, breaches of the Official Secrets Act, blasphemy, defamation, contempt of court or of a House of Parliament, the offences under the Public Order Act 1986, sections 4 and 5, incitement to racial hatred, and, of course, offences in connection with 'obscene' publications.

In chapter 23 freedom of assembly and association are examined, substantially omitting the big subject of trade union law. Here again, what one is allowed to do depends on whether any other person is entitled to prevent one, and what specific wrongs one is liable to commit in attempts at self-expression. The law is closely related to that stated in chapter 22 but has a number of special features. There is no general right to conduct a public meeting in a street or an open space. Police powers over processions and public assemblies provided for in Part II of the Public Order Act 1986 are noted, together with the new statutory offences of riot, violent disorder and affray contained in Part I of that Act.

Part Four concludes with a chapter on states of emergency (which are clearly regulated by statute), the powers of the Crown in wartime, and the nature of a state of martial law.

CHAPTER 18

The Administration of Justice

COURTS[1]

Criminal jurisdiction

The most striking feature of the English legal system is the part played by the layman, as justice of the peace, as juror or as the initiator of criminal proceedings. It is open to an aggrieved member of the public to lay an information before a magistrate asking him to issue a summons, or in some cases an arrest warrant, against another person for a criminal offence (for example, assault). In practice most of these members of the public are police officers and prosecutions are largely conducted by the Crown Prosecution Service, but purely private prosecutions are not uncommon. For some serious offences (for example, against the Official Secrets Acts) the Attorney-General's leave must be obtained before a prosecution can be instituted. There are other offences for which only the Director of Public Prosecutions, or only a local authority, may prosecute.

Before 1986 criminal prosecutions were mainly conducted by or on behalf of the police. This unsatisfactory state of affairs, involving the police in both the detection and the prosecution of crime, was widely recognized and was ultimately condemned by the Royal Commission on Criminal Procedure.[2] The Government accepted the case for transferring the main prosecution role to an independent body,[3] and it secured the passage of the Prosecution of Offences Act 1985. The right to bring a private prosecution is

---

1 Only a brief outline of the system in England and Wales is offered in this chapter. Some important questions, like the cost of litigation and the award of costs, are omitted. The leading text is P. F. Smith and S. H. Bailey. *The Modern English Legal System* (2nd edn, 1991). See also R. L. Abel, *The Legal Profession in England and Wales* (1988); *The Judiciary: A Report by JUSTICE* (1992).
2 Cmnd 8092 (1981).
3 See Cmnd 9074 (1983).

expressly retained under the Act[4] so that, as well as the individual citizen keeping that right, the power of local authorities, Government Departments and others to prosecute under existing legislation is retained. It is still for the police to decide whether to initiate a public prosecution and, if they decide to do so, to lay an information. But the Crown Prosecution Service (CPS) actually conducts criminal prosecutions on behalf of the Crown, and may also decide which prosecutions should be discontinued.[5]

The Director of Public Prosecutions (the DPP)[6] is at the head of the CPS.[7] It is his duty to take over and to conduct all criminal proceedings which have been instituted by the police, to take over all criminal proceedings which appear to him to be important or difficult, and also to appear for the prosecution when directed to do so by a court in certain criminal appeals. He may also advise police forces on all matters relating to offences. The actual daily conduct of proceedings is in the hands of Crown Prosecutors[8] under a Chief Crown Prosecutor in each prosecution area. They operate under a Code for Crown Prosecutors issued by the DPP[9] and which is annexed to his annual report to Parliament.[10] The Crown Prosecutors have all the DPP's powers in relation to the institution and conduct of criminal proceedings, including the important power to discontinue cases in the magistrates' court.[11]

Apart from the issue of summonses and warrants, the chief functions of magistrates are the trial of summary offences, and the conduct of preliminary inquiries into indictable offences which are triable by a higher court.[12] Magistrates may be either lay justices of the peace – the office originated over six hundred years ago – or professional stipendiary magistrates. There are over 30,000 active justices of the peace in England and Wales, sitting in over a thousand magistrates' courts, but just seventy-six stipendiaries, of whom all but twenty-six are metropolitan magistrates sitting in the London

---

4 1985 Act, s. 6.
5 This power to discontinue, when exercised, may affect police decisions whether to initiate proceedings in similar cases in the future.
6 See further below, p. 386.
7 1985 Act, ss. 1–3.
8 ibid., ss. 4, 5.
9 ibid., s. 10.
10 This is published as a House of Commons Paper.
11 1985 Act, s. 23.
12 This is an oversimplification, especially since the enactment of the Criminal Law Act 1977 and later legislation which provides for specified offences to be tried either only summarily (before magistrates), or only on indictment (in the Crown Court), or 'either way'. See Criminal Justice and Public Order Act 1994, s. 44 and sched. 4.

area. There are no juries in magistrates' courts; in trying offences, magistrates are judges of law and fact and impose sentence. Metropolitan stipendiary magistrates always sit alone to hear summary cases; other stipendiaries usually sit unaccompanied by lay justices; the size of a lay bench will be between two and seven (and will usually be two or three), under a chairman elected by the magistrates. Magistrates must normally sit in open court, but when they sit as examining justices conducting a preliminary inquiry to determine whether there is sufficient evidence to commit a defendant for trial before a higher court, the evidence given at these proceedings cannot be reported contemporaneously except at the defendant's request, unless the magistrates discharge him.[13]

On conviction, magistrates cannot, in general, impose a sentence of more than six months' imprisonment or a fine of more than £5,000; they may, however, commit an offender for sentence at the Crown Court if the offence is one punishable by a heavier sentence and their own powers are inadequate to meet the case. They may also remand defendants in custody; in certain circumstances they may make recommendations for deportation upon conviction; they may bind over a defendant by requiring him to enter into recognizances, with or without sureties, to be of good behaviour or to keep the peace, and send him to prison if he refuses.[14] These are formidable powers to vest in amateurs[15] whose knowledge of legal technicalities and techniques may be rudimentary. The picture is not in fact quite as alarming as it may appear. Magistrates are advised on points of law and procedure by a clerk of the court, who is normally a full-time officer and who is legally qualified. All newly appointed justices are obliged to undergo a course of preliminary training; they are also obliged to attend refresher courses and conferences; they are kept informed by advisory Home Office circulars about sentencing policies and problems and other

13 Magistrates' Courts Act 1980, ss. 4(2), 8. If there are two or more accused and one objects to contemporaneous reporting, the court will only order that reporting restrictions be lifted if it is satisfied that it is in the interests of justice to do so: Magistrates' Courts Act 1980, s. 8(2A). In certain circumstances committal proceedings may be (and frequently are) based on written depositions: 1980 Act, s. 102.
14 This is really a form of preventive justice. Other alternatives after a case has been proved include absolute discharge, conditional discharge, community service orders and putting on probation: Powers of Criminal Courts Act 1973, as amended. For young offenders, a different set of sanctions or welfare orders is prescribed; see Children and Young Persons Act 1969, Criminal Justice Act 1982, ss. 1–28, Criminal Justice Act 1988, Criminal Justice and Public Order Act 1994, Part I.
15 The 'great unpaid' receive travelling and subsistence allowances for loss of earnings. The governing provision is now the Justices of the Peace Act 1997, s. 10 (itself a major consolidating measure).

developments on the treatment of offenders. The infirm and incompetent can be placed on a supplemental list where they will be ineligible to perform judicial functions. In any event, magistrates are now retired or placed on the supplemental list at seventy. Except in the City of London, the *ex officio* magistrate has almost disappeared.[16] The asperity of criticism formerly levelled against lay magistrates has been softened in the last forty years and there is a dearth of enthusiasm for the professional magistrate sitting alone.

Young offenders, and young persons in need of care and protection, are normally brought before youth courts, differently constituted from ordinary magistrates' courts and following a less formal procedure. They are composed predominantly of lay magistrates.[17]

Fundamental changes in the system of criminal courts were introduced by the Courts Act 1971. The reforms were based on the Report of the Beeching Commission on Assizes and Quarter Sessions.[18]

The Crown Court, which replaced other criminal courts, the most important of which were Assizes and Quarter Sessions, is part of the Supreme Court of Judicature.[19] It consists of High Court judges, Circuit judges, part-time Recorders and Assistant Recorders and, in certain circumstances, justices of the peace. There are over 500 Circuit judges who are now appointed exclusively from the ranks of Recorders (of whom some 800 are in office), and who sit in the Crown Court and the county court. Recorders are required to sit for twenty days a year in the Crown Court. They must have possessed a Crown Court or county court qualification (that is, a right of audience in all proceedings in those courts) for at least ten years.[20] Recorders are appointed by the Lord Chancellor from the pool of Assistant Recorders (of whom there are about 500), who must possess the qualification to be appointed a Recorder and who sit part-time mainly in the Crown Court. After about three to five years of such work an Assistant Recorder is considered for promotion to Recorder; if he is not

16 See Justices of the Peace Act 1997, s. 21.
17 The emphasis has shifted from criminal responsibility and sanctions towards civil responsibility and remedial orders.
18 Cmnd 4153 (1969).
19 See generally the Supreme Court Act 1981.
20 Courts and Legal Services Act 1990, s. 71 and sched. 10. That Act changed the criteria for judicial and certain other appointments. Previously, qualification as a barrister, solicitor or (in Scotland) advocate for a specific period was the main criterion. Now an advocacy qualification is required based on rights of audience granted by authorized bodies. The change has opened up more senior judicial appointments to be filled by solicitors.

promoted, his judicial assistance is dispensed with.[21] The qualification for appointment as a Circuit judge is to have had a Crown Court or county court qualification for at least ten years, or to be a Recorder.[22]

The Crown Court sits in twenty-four main provincial centres, staffed by High Court and Circuit judges, and by Recorders and Assistant Recorders. Here the High Court judge will wear two hats. Sitting in the *High Court*, he will hear civil cases; sitting in the *Crown Court*, he will hear the most serious criminal cases. But there is flexibility: the very serious criminal cases can be assigned to a Circuit judge, and a Circuit judge can also hear certain *High Court* civil cases. There is a second tier of centres, served by High Court and Circuit judges where only criminal cases are heard. Then there is a third tier, staffed by Circuit judges only. There are over 100 major centres for the administration of criminal justice outside London.

Offences are divided into four classes. Indictable offences in the first class must be tried by a High Court judge (although murder trials may be released to a Circuit judge); in the second class they must be tried by a High Court judge unless the judge presiding over a circuit releases a case to another judge; in the third class they may be tried by a High Court judge or Circuit judge or Recorder. The fourth class of offence (cases triable 'either way' under the Criminal Law Act 1977, together with a few other specified offences) will normally be tried by a Circuit judge or Recorder.[23] There are detailed rules directing or guiding magistrates as to the class of centre to which a particular case should be committed. All trials on indictment are by jury.

Juries are now selected more or less at random[24] from among registered electors between the ages of eighteen and sixty-five who have resided for

---

21 Information about the Lord Chancellor's appointments policy has been published in *Judicial Appointments* (Lord Chancellor's Department).

22 See above, note 20.

23 Criminal Law Act 1977, ss. 14–17; Practice Note: Crown Court Business [1995] 2 All ER 900.

24 But the controversial issue of 'jury vetting' has made the choice less random and has produced conflicting judicial attitudes towards its constitutionality: see, for example, *R. v. Sheffield CC, ex. p. Brownlow* [1980] QB 530, CA; cf. *R. v. Mason* [1980] 3 WLR 617, CA; 979 HC Deb. 948 (25 February 1980), and the Attorney-General's statement and new guidelines 989 HC Deb. 1929–40 (1 August 1980) and (1988) 138 *NLJ* 358–60. The Attorney-General authorized jury vetting in relation to eighteen defendants between 1980–85: see 72 HC Deb. 383–5 (4 February 1985). Since 1988 he has only approved Crown objections to potential jurors in cases involving terrorism or national security. A judge cannot discharge competent jurors in an attempt to secure a racial balance: *R. v. Ford* [1989] 3 All ER 445.

five years or more in the British Islands since childhood.[25] The right of a defendant to object to a potential juror without cause ('the peremptory challenge') was finally abolished in 1988. The jury is perhaps the most venerated English institution, lauded as a bulwark against oppression and the common-sense voice of twelve ordinary citizens. But uneasiness about the merits of jury trial has grown of late.[26] In civil cases trial by jury is now rare – hardly 30 cases a year. In criminal cases the accuracy of findings by juries and the processes by which they are reached are not infrequently questioned. Bribery and intimidation of jurors are thought to be extremely uncommon; nevertheless, because this problem arose in trials involving members of London gangs, the rule that a jury's verdict in criminal proceedings had to be unanimous was varied in 1967; a majority verdict may be accepted by the court if ten jurors agree that the accused is guilty.[27] In civil cases majority verdicts are acceptable with the consent of the parties, and without their consent subject to safeguards similar to those laid down in criminal proceedings.[28]

The system of appeals in criminal cases is complicated.[29]

1 A person convicted by a magistrates' court can appeal to the Crown Court on a question of law, fact or sentence; the appeal is by way of rehearing without a jury.

2 Alternatively, either the prosecutor or the defendant may appeal on a point of law by case stated[30] from a conviction by a magistrates' court, or a determination by the Crown Court *on appeal or a committal for sentence,*

---

25 See generally Juries Act 1974. Electors aged between sixty-five and seventy may now serve as jurors, but they have the right to decline: Criminal Justice Act 1988, s. 119. Jurors are paid travelling and subsistence allowances and compensation for loss of earnings. Subject to certain exceptions, service is compulsory. Juries are still used in coroners' courts: see Coroners' Act 1988, ss. 9–12.

26 A number of dreadful miscarriages of justice became apparent in the late 1980s and early 1990s, and the Government accordingly established a Royal Commission on Criminal Justice, which in 1993 recommended major changes: see Cm 2263 (1993).

27 See now Juries Act 1974, s. 17. If there are only ten jurors – the normal size of a jury is eleven or twelve – nine must concur in the finding of guilt. The court must not accept a majority verdict unless the jury has deliberated for at least two hours. Moreover, people who have been sentenced to or served prison and other penalties are disqualified from service for specified periods: Juries Act 1974, sched. 1, Part III, as substituted by the Juries (Disqualification) Act 1984.

28 Juries Act 1974, s. 17.

29 Part of this branch of the law was consolidated in the Criminal Appeal Act 1968. It was modified by the Courts Act 1971.

30 The clerk of the court draws up a statement of the facts found and the basis of the decision, and this is signed by the magistrates.

to a Divisional Court of the Queen's Bench Division, consisting of two or more (usually three and occasionally five) judges of that Division of the High Court. This course is followed where an authoritative legal ruling is sought.

3 From the Divisional Court, a further appeal on a point of law will lie direct to the House of Lords, but only with leave, which is not to be granted unless the Divisional Court certifies that a point of law of general public importance is involved, and that court or the House of Lords is of the opinion that it should be considered by the House.

4 From convictions in the Crown Court appeals lie against conviction or sentence to the Criminal Division of the Court of Appeal, but only with the leave of the Court of Appeal or the trial judge.[31] The Criminal Division sits in at least two courts, composed partly of Lords Justices of Appeal and partly of Queen's Bench judges. It must allow the appeal if the conviction was unsafe. If new relevant evidence is received by the court, it has discretion to order the appellant to be retried.[32]

5 A further appeal on a point of law will lie from the Court of Appeal to the House of Lords, subject to similar conditions to those in paragraph 3 above.

Ancillary points, not directly linked with appeals, need to be mentioned.[33] First, the Home Secretary may advise the Queen to exercise the prerogative of pardon: he may ask the advice of the Criminal Cases Review Commission on individual cases. Secondly, a prisoner may be released on licence on the recommendation of the Parole Board after serving a part of his sentence.[34] Thirdly, the Attorney-General may refer to the Court of Appeal a point of law arising out of an acquittal in a trial on indictment.[35] Fourthly, sentences passed for certain serious offences may be referred to the Court of Appeal by the Attorney-General if he thinks that the trial judge had been unduly lenient; the Court of Appeal may then substitute any sentence which it

---

31 Criminal Appeal Act 1995, s. 1. The Court of Appeal cannot increase the total period of sentence already imposed, except on an Attorney-General's reference against an 'unduly lenient' sentence: see below.

32 Criminal Appeal Act 1968, ss. 7, 8, 23; Criminal Justice Act 1988, s. 43; Criminal Appeal Act 1995, s. 2.

33 The Home Secretary's former power to refer a conviction to the Court of Appeal has been abolished, and references can now be made to the Criminal Cases Review Commission: Criminal Appeal Act 1995, ss. 3, 8–16.

34 Criminal Justice Act 1991, ss. 32–51 and sched. 5.

35 Criminal Justice Act 1972, s. 36. Whatever be the opinion of the court, the acquittal will still stand.

thinks appropriate.[36] Fifthly, determinations by magistrates' courts and the Crown Court are subject to review by the Divisional Court of the Queen's Bench Division exercising its supervisory jurisdiction – for example, an order of certiorari to quash a conviction (other than a conviction by the Crown Court in a trial on indictment) can be obtained if the court has exceeded its jurisdiction or broken the rules of natural justice.[37] Sixthly, a person deprived of his liberty without lawful authority may procure his release by the award of a writ of habeas corpus.[38]

Civil jurisdiction

Many justiciable claims and controversies in non-criminal matters are determined by bodies other than the ordinary courts – by special statutory tribunals or local authorities, or Ministers (through departmental officials), or named classes of officials, or domestic tribunals (committees of clubs, trades unions and so on). Businessmen often provide in their commercial contracts that disputes shall be submitted to arbitration. Informal small claims courts have also been set up. There are also specialized courts such as the Restrictive Practices Court and the Patents Court, outside the mainstream of the ordinary judicial system. But in almost all cases the general superior courts preserve an appellate or a supervisory jurisdiction.

Magistrates' courts have a limited civil jurisdiction. They have power to make maintenance and separation orders and decisions as to custody of children in matrimonial cases; appeal on points of law lies to a Divisional Court of the Family Division of the High Court. They also have various functions in the general field of administrative law, particularly in respect of licensing and the hearing of appeals against local authority licensing decisions; appeal usually lies to the Crown Court, with a further (or alternative) appeal by case stated on points of law to the Divisional Court of the Queen's Bench Division.

The county courts are the main courts of civil jurisdiction.[39] There never has been any necessary connection between a county court area and an administrative or geographical county. In the county courts undefended

---

36 Criminal Justice Act 1988, ss. 35, 36. The offences are those which are triable only on indictment or as are specified by statutory instrument. To 1996 nearly 300 cases had been referred; of the cases heard 85 per cent resulted in an increased sentence: 276 HC Deb. 765 (29 April 1996).

37 See ch. 27.

38 See pp. 439–43.

39 See County Courts Act 1984.

divorce petitions are heard, but their main function is to determine small monetary claims. To an increasing extent judicial functions in minor county court cases have been devolved upon District Judges (formerly called registrars). In practice most of the two million cases that come before county courts each year are undefended; these are mainly plaints issued in respect of debts.

Their monetary jurisdiction in contract and tort has been progressively raised; in 1990 the financial limits were finally abolished.[40] A plaintiff claiming less than £50,000 in a personal injury action must start proceedings in a county court; in other types of action the presumption is that actions for less than £25,000 will also start there, and that those over £50,000 will start in the High Court: criteria exist to provide for the transfer of cases between the two systems. County courts also exercise a miscellany of functions in the fields of equity, bankruptcy, and landlord and tenant (notably applications for possession orders), and a wide range of jurisdiction, mainly original but sometimes appellate, arising under collectivist legislation. Appeals lie, normally on points of law only, to the Court of Appeal (Civil Division).

The Supreme Court of Judicature consists of the Court of Appeal, the High Court and the Crown Court. The Court of Appeal has two divisions, civil and criminal: it is presided over by the Master of the Rolls, and has up to thirty-five Lords Justices of Appeal. It normally sits with a bench of two or three; the Lord Chief Justice presides in one court of the Criminal Division; other High Court judges are often called upon to sit to hear criminal appeals, but less frequently to hear civil appeals. Appeals on the civil side lie mainly from county courts and the High Court; the court may be leapfrogged and an appeal raising a point of law of exceptional difficulty or importance calling for a reconsideration of a binding precedent may, with leave of the House of Lords, lie direct from the High Court to the Lords.[41]

The High Court sits in three divisions: the Queen's Bench, the Chancery, and the Family Divisions. The Family Division replaced the Probate, Divorce and Admiralty Division in 1971. On appointment, a judge is assigned to one of the three divisions. The Lord Chief Justice presides in the Queen's Bench Division; the Lord Chancellor, who never sits, is

---

40 Courts and Legal Services Act 1990, s. 1, and High Court and County Courts Jurisdiction Order, SI 1991, No. 724.
41 Administration of Justice Act 1969, ss. 12–16. A certificate must first be given by the trial judge, and the parties must consent to the leapfrogging appeal.

nominally president of the Chancery Division and there is a Vice-Chancellor who is a Chancery judge; there is a President of the Family Division. The maximum number of other High Court judges (called puisne judges) is ninety-eight.[42] The original civil jurisdiction of the High Court is unlimited as to amount and persons but subject to territorial limitations. Distribution of work between the three divisions is governed partly by statute, partly by rules of court, partly by custom, and there is a substantial area of concurrent jurisdiction; for example, actions claiming injunctions or declarations are usually brought in the Chancery Division but can be instituted in the Queen's Bench Division or even the Family Division. The High Court also has appellate and supervisory jurisdiction in relation to inferior tribunals, a jurisdiction normally exercised by a Divisional Court of the Queen's Bench Division, and power to issue writs of habeas corpus.[43] The High Court, like the Court of Appeal, sits in the Royal Courts of Justice (the Law Courts) in London, and also (as has been seen) juxtaposed with the Crown Court at the top-tier provincial centres. There Queen's Bench judges sit as Crown Court judges for criminal cases too.[44]

The House of Lords as a 'final' appellate court has already been mentioned.[45] In 1966 it reasserted power to overrule its own decisions.[46]

INDEPENDENCE OF THE JUDICIARY[47]

It is clearly of great importance that justice be dispensed even-handedly in the courts and that the general public feel confident in the integrity and the impartiality of the Judiciary. Where the Government of the day has an interest in the outcome of judicial proceedings, the court should not act merely as a mouthpiece of the Executive. The Judiciary must therefore be secure from undue influence and autonomous within its own field.

These propositions may seem platitudinous. But in some countries some of them would be rejected. Whereas all governments would agree that

---

42 Supreme Court Act 1981, s. 4; Maximum Number of Judges (No. 2) Order 1993, SI 1993, No. 1255.
43 See pp. 555–6.
44 See p. 363.
45 pp. 308–11 and above. But see pp. 110–12 on the European Court of Justice.
46 Practice Statement [1966] 1 WLR 1234.
47 See Rodney Brazier, *Constitutional Practice* (2nd edn, 1994), ch. 12, and *Constitutional Texts* (1990), ch. 11.

there should be public confidence in the administration of justice, and that judges ought not to accept bribes or decide cases on the basis of personal friendship or animosity, some would not agree that the Judiciary ought to be independent of the Executive. On the contrary, they would say that the judges have not to be impartial between the people and the enemies of the people; that since the Government (or the Party) is the voice of the people, critics of the regime or bourgeois elements or other classes of persons stigmatized as antisocial must be dealt with severely by the courts, which are instruments of State policy. And judges who talk out of turn or acquit persons charged with sedition or refuse to join the Party or (as the case may be) fail to uphold and apply the edicts of the military regime may be dismissed.

In many other countries, the principles of judicial independence are acknowledged but are substantially qualified in practice. This is hardly surprising when one considers the implications that can be and have been read into the concept. Does judicial independence imply that the Executive must have no voice, or a muted voice, in the appointment or promotion of judges? Does it imply that neither the Executive nor the Legislature shall be competent to remove judges? If the principle carries these implications – and it is arguable that it should import them – it is imperfectly realized in Britain. Does it imply that judges should be entirely aloof from public sentiment and always disregard the strength of local feeling on an issue before them? If not, to what extent should judges take into account considerations of public policy, and how far can the Government or its unruly supporters or opponents be permitted to determine what is the public interest? In Britain these questions seldom arise in an acutely controversial form,[48] but judges not infrequently have to determine what is in the public interest, or whether a transaction is contrary to public policy, or whether it is necessary to impose a deterrent sentence because of the prevalence of a social evil; and in coming to such decisions they are expected

---

48 Though cf. the controversies which arose in 1972 out of the application of the Industrial Relations Act 1971 (since repealed). See, for example, John Griffith, 'Reflections on the Rule of the Law', *New Statesman*, 24 November 1972, for sharp criticism, and his *The Politics of the Judiciary* (5th edn, 1997); *Churchman* v. *Joint Shop Stewards' Committee* [1972] 1 WLR 1094; and see p. 384, on the Official Solicitor. When in 1975 a High Court judge ordered the fees of counsel and solicitors in a case before him to be reduced because of their conduct of the case, his decision was reversed by the Court of Appeal: *R.* v. *McFadden*, *The Times*, 11 December 1975. But, undeterred, the judge called an unprecedented press conference and wrote to *The Times*. A motion was tabled in the Commons to remove him, but no debate ensued and the matter lapsed.

to have some regard to the general sense of the community and not to rely merely on idiosyncratic opinions.[49] Moreover, in some political contexts the courts allow the Executive[50] or the House of Commons[51] the first and last word. Here we are enmeshed in the thicket of questions of degree, where generalizations are not very helpful.

Can we not at least agree that the protection of judicial independence in a liberal democracy demands that it should be unconstitutional for the Legislature to invade the domain of the Judiciary by pronouncing judgment (as in a bill of attainder)[52] or reversing a judicial decision with retroactive effect,[53] or enabling the Executive to designate which judges shall sit to hear a particular case,[54] or abolishing a judicial office while it has a substantive holder,[55] or reducing judicial salaries?[56] In Britain such measures would generally be regarded, in the absence of extraordinary circumstances, as unconstitutional in the sense of being contrary to constitutional convention. But in a number of Commonwealth countries they would be not only 'unconstitutional' but also invalid. And in some Commonwealth countries it would also be unconstitutional to impair the independence of the Judiciary by endowing them with functions extraneous to the judicial,[57] or to purport to oust the jurisdiction of the courts to decide the constitutionality of legislative or executive action.[58]

49 There have been a number of instances since the late 1970s in which individual judges have been publicly criticized because of remarks made or attitudes displayed in court to which exception was taken either by MPs or by their superiors. See further Brazier, op. cit., pp. 288–95.

50 See, for example, *Chandler* v. *DPP* [1964] AC 763; and other cases cited above, pp. 149–53.

51 See, for example, the *Sheriff of Middlesex*'s case (1840) 11 A. & E. 273; *Bradlaugh* v. *Gossett* (1884) 12 QBD 271.

52 See *Liyanage* v. *R.* [1967] 1 AC 259 (Ceylon); though cf. *Kariapper* v. *Wijesinha* [1968] AC 717; *Australian Communist Party* v. *Commonwealth of Australia* (1951) 83 CLR 1.

53 cf. *Burmah Oil Co.* v. *Lord Advocate* [1965] AC 75; War Damage Act 1965.

54 *R.* v. *Liyanage* (1963) 64 New LR 313 (Ceylon); see Thomas M. Franck, *Comparative Constitutional Process* (1968), pp. 384–98. The court held that this power was one properly reposed only in members of the Judicature.

55 See, for example, Constitution of Jamaica (SI 1952, no. 1550, sched. 2), s. 97(3).

56 For example, Constitution of India, art. 124(2), proviso.

57 *Att.-Gen. for Australia* v. *R. and the Boilermakers' Society of Australasia* [1957] AC 288. See also *Hinds* v. *R.* [1977] AC 195.

58 For example, *Balewa* v. *Doherty* [1963] 1 WLR 949 (PC, Nigeria).

Appointment[59]

Appointments of High Court and Circuit judges, Recorders, Assistant Recorders and stipendiary and lay magistrates are made either by or on the advice of the Lord Chancellor. He also decides whether to renew part-time judicial appointments. Since the Lord Chancellor is himself a political appointee and a member of the Cabinet, there appears to be ample scope for political patronage. Appointments to the Court of Appeal and to the House of Lords, and to the offices of Lord Chief Justice, Master of the Rolls and President of the Family Division, are made on the advice of the Prime Minister after consultation with the Lord Chancellor.[60] In a number of Commonwealth countries judicial appointments other than Chief Justice are made on the advice of a Judicial Service Commission, presided over by the Chief Justice and composed mainly of judicial members. In practice appointments in England and Wales are no longer made on political grounds, except to the lay magistracy. Justices of the Peace are appointed by the Lord Chancellor on the recommendation of local advisory committees whose membership is published. In a circular to advisory committees in 1966, the then Lord Chancellor made it clear that political affiliations ought not to be disregarded because it was important that 'justices should be drawn from all sections of the community and should represent all shades of opinion'.[61]

Before 1914 it was quite common for MPs belonging to the party in office to be appointed to the High Court.[62] Since 1945 hardly any judicial appointment in England appears to have been influenced by political considerations.[63] Professional standing at the bar and personal suitability are ostensibly the sole criteria. The Lord Chancellor is likely to consult the Lord Chief Justice, the Master of the Rolls, the Vice-Chancellor and the President of the Family Division before submitting a recommendation.

---

59 See *Judicial Appointments*, which describes the Lord Chancellor's principles and practices in some detail in relation to the lower judiciary, but much less fully in relation to the senior judiciary.

60 See Lord Hailsham, *The Door Wherein I Went* (1975), p. 254; the Prime Minister at 263 HC Deb. *391* (written answers 10 July 1995). For senior appointments in Scotland see 574 HL Deb. *60* (written answers 16 July 1996).

61 In the counties the chairman of the advisory committee is the Lord Lieutenant; in districts the chairman is appointed by the Lord Chancellor. The main political parties will be represented on the Committee.

62 See generally, H. J. Laski, *Studies in Law and Politics* (1932), pp. 168–80.

63 This comment does not apply to Scottish judicial appointments. See Willock (1969) 14 *Juridical Review* (NS) 193.

Not so long ago the Attorney-General was understood to have the first refusal of a vacancy in the office of Lord Chief Justice. In 1922 Lord Hewart, then Attorney-General, was appointed; in 1940 he was succeeded by Lord Caldecote, formerly Attorney-General and at the time Lord Chancellor. But in 1946 Caldecote was succeeded by Lord Goddard, a Law Lord who was far from being a Labour sympathizer[64] and in 1958 Lord Parker, a Lord Justice of Appeal, assumed the office. All subsequent holders of that office have come either from the Court of Appeal or from the judicial House of Lords. There is no reason, however, why the Law Officers of the Crown, and other lawyers in politics, should not be eligible for appointment to high judicial office, provided that they possess the appropriate qualities of character, temperament and intellect. Political affiliations may nevertheless operate as a disqualification inasmuch as an active proponent of revolution may be regarded as unsuitable to occupy what is in one aspect a high office of State.

Vacancies for Circuit and District Judges are advertised, and the Lord Chancellor is to extend that practice to vacancies on the High Court bench. A lawyer seeking appointment as a Recorder or professional magistrate should make the fact known to the Lord Chancellor's Department; candidates for such appointments are not easily identified.[65] Under the Courts and Legal Services Act 1990,[66] the barristers' monopoly on appointments to senior judicial positions has been broken: solicitors are now eligible for them, provided that they hold the relevant advocacy qualification. Solicitors have also exercised judicial functions as Masters of the Supreme Court, District Judges and chairmen of special tribunals. It has traditionally been claimed that the Bar's historical monopoly had a number of advantages. Members of the Bar alone have had the right of audience in the superior courts; they rub shoulders out of court with the judges, who remain members of their Inns; the Bar is an autonomous, individualistic but tightly knit profession, maintaining extraordinarily high standards of professional

64 Viscount Jowitt, Lord Chancellor under the Attlee Governments (1945–51), went to great pains not to afford any ground for suspicion that appointments to high judicial office were politically influenced.
65 The Home Affairs Select Committee has rejected the case for reform of the system of judicial appointments: see HC 52 (1995–6).
66 Section 71 and sched. 10; see above, p. 362, note 20. To be appointed a High Court judge, an individual must have had a right of audience in all proceedings in the High Court for ten years (or to have been a Circuit judge for two years); to be appointed a Lord Justice of Appeal requires the same High Court qualification (or to have been a High Court judge); to be appointed a Lord of Appeal in Ordinary requires a Supreme Court qualification, that is, to have a right of audience in all proceedings in the Court of Appeal and the High Court.

conduct, partly, perhaps, because the number of barristers in private practice in England and Wales is still only some seven thousand. Women and the ethnic minorities remain absurdly under-represented on the bench.[67] One class of lawyer, the full-time academic lawyer, is still in practice excluded from serious consideration for appointment to a superior judgeship. On this matter there are real difficulties to overcome. It would be a risk to appoint a person with little experience of advocacy to be a judge of first instance. To appoint him to the Court of Appeal or the House of Lords might evoke serious resentment among the puisne judges.

Promotion

In Britain the Judiciary is not a career service. In many countries a young person will join the judicial service, starting at the bottom and working upwards through the hierarchy. Such a system may tend to inhibit forthright independent-mindedness, particularly if promotion is determined by a Minister of Justice.[68] But in Britain appointments to the High Court are made from the ranks of successful practitioners;[69] professional magistrates are not promoted to the High Court, and promotions of Circuit judges are still unusual;[70] advancement from the High Court to the Court of Appeal may be gratifying, but it carries little increase in salary;[71] appointment to the House of Lords means a relatively small increment in salary, though by some a peerage is highly valued. There is no great material inducement to encourage a member of the Judiciary to curry favour with the politicians or his judicial superiors; any attempt to procure advancement by such means would bring a judge into disfavour. Moreover, a Prime Minister or Lord Chancellor has little incentive to take political considerations into account when recommending promotion or, indeed, the initial appointment of a judge. Matters might be different if we had a written constitution with entrenched guarantees and prohibitions subject to judicial interpret-

67 In 1997 there were no women Lords of Appeal in Ordinary, only one woman Lord Justice of Appeal, and seven women High Court judges.
68 In Commonwealth countries where there is a Judicial Service Commission, promotion is a matter for the Commission. This system may induce a different kind of deference.
69 They may well have served as deputy High Court judges, and will certainly have performed in some part-time judicial office.
70 Promotions of Circuit judges to be High Court judges may well, however, become more common in future. At the present time there are indications of hierarchical tendencies at the lower end of the scale – for example, a magistrates' clerk may become a professional magistrate and then a deputy Circuit judge or Circuit judge.
71 Every new Lord Justice is, however, made a Privy Counsellor.

ation, especially if it were difficult to procure constitutional amendments overturning the effect of inconvenient decisions.

Since the early 1980s the Lord Chancellor's policy has been to appoint and to promote to full-time judicial offices only those who have satisfactorily served in relevant part-time appointments. So a career progression has developed, from Assistant Recorder to Recorder to Circuit judge, and it is being extended to take in High Court appointments as well.[72] A similar progression is discernible in the senior judiciary, appointments being made to the Court of Appeal exclusively from the High Court, and to the House of Lords from the Court of Appeal.

Salaries

Judicial salaries and pensions are substantial by international standards. A puisne judge of the High Court is paid £110,000 a year, and is a charge on Consolidated Fund Standing Services.[73] Salaries may be increased, but not reduced, by the Lord Chancellor with the consent of the Minister for the Civil Service.[74] After twenty years' service a judge can retire on a pension equal to half his salary.[75] Practitioners are often earning much more in fees than a judicial salary when appointed to the bench, but a judgeship affords not only great dignity but financial security.[76]

The Act of Settlement 1701 had provided that judges' salaries were to be 'ascertained and established'. Till well into the eighteenth century judicial salaries were nevertheless low. Judicial incomes were supplemented by fees from suitors and other sources, sundry perquisites of office and the exercise of patronage.[77] These standing temptations to corruption – which had been all the greater so long as judicial salaries had to be met out of the King's privy purse[78] – under the Stuarts they were often in arrears – were finally

---

72 See *Judicial Appointments*.

73 See above, p. 286.

74 Administration of Justice Act, 1973 s. 9(1); Supreme Court Act 1981, s. 12. Lords of Appeal in Ordinary and the Master of the Rolls each receive £128,000 a year; Lords Justices of Appeal, the President of the Family Division and the Vice-Chancellor, £122,000. Circuit judges each receive £82,100 and stipendiary magistrates £70,000. The Lord Chief Justice receives £136,000.

75 Judicial Pensions and Retirement Act 1993, ss. 2, 3.

76 In 1970 a High Court judge resigned and became a member of a firm of merchant bankers; his decision aroused some professional criticism.

77 See generally W. S. Holdsworth, *History of English Law*, vol. 1, pp. 252–5.

78 For this reason William III had refused his assent in 1692 to a bill to increase judicial salaries to £1,000: Sir Kenneth Roberts-Wray, *Commonwealth and Colonial Law* (1966), pp. 485–6.

removed by an Act of 1826 which raised the salaries of superior judges to £5,000 and abolished their income from fees.

Rules tending to protect judicial independence

Insulation from politics. First, full-time judges are disqualified from membership of the House of Commons.[79] Secondly, by convention judges must refrain from politically partisan activities; and although they can criticize the wording and content of legislation and the conduct of members of the Executive, they should be careful not to take sides in matters of political controversy—a precept more easily formulated than followed,[80] for ostensibly non-political matters of public concern are apt to become party issues unexpectedly. Thirdly, by convention members of the Executive are expected to preserve a reciprocal restraint when commenting on the words and deeds of judges, though if criticized by a judge they are not obliged to remain mute, and if a judge makes politically controversial remarks a robust answer can be offered. Fourthly, in parliamentary practice members of the House of Commons are not permitted to cast aspersions on the conduct of a judge at question time, or in the course of debate except on a motion specifically criticizing the judge or supporting an address for his removal,[81] and in general a matter cannot be raised in Parliament if it is *sub judice*.[82] Fifthly, the courts disclaim jurisdiction to inquire into proceedings in Parliament.[83] Sixthly, the charging of judicial salaries on the Consolidated Fund means that since Parliament does not authorize them annually, there is no adequate opportunity to censure judges in the debates on the estimates.

Some hold the view that the independence of the Judiciary may be prejudiced if judges are entrusted with functions alien to the judicial; or if

---

79 House of Commons Disqualification Act 1975, ss. 1(1)(*a*), 1(2); First schedule. The disqualification of part-time Recorders for election in those constituencies where they exercised jurisdiction was repealed by the Courts Act 1971, sched. 11, and, it would seem (despite the general words of sched. 8 to that Act), not replaced. For Law Lords in the upper House, see ch. 15. The last judge (other than the Lord Chancellor) to hold Cabinet office was Lord Ellenborough, Chief Justice of the King's Bench, in 1806.

80 It tends to be followed more rigorously in England than in Scotland.

81 For a slight relaxation of this rule, see the Speaker's Ruling 935 HC Deb. 1381–4 (19 July 1977). If a judge writes a letter to an MP, its contents may be criticized by MPs: see 128 HC Deb. 166 (23 February 1988). (An MP had written to the Master of the Rolls about one of his judgments; Lord Donaldson MR replied; the Speaker ruled that MPs could comment on that reply.)

82 For an exception introduced in 1972, see p. 292.

83 See pp. 316–23, 330–33.

provision is made for courts to give advisory opinions to the Executive on questions of law. The former view does not seem to be generally accepted by the present generation of English judges; they sit in the Restrictive Practices Court and sat in the National Industrial Relations Court during its brief life from 1971 to 1974, and they accept appointments as chairmen of inquiries into alleged public scandals, major industrial disputes, police pay and conditions in the prisons and other politically contentious matters; they conceive these functions to be aspects of their duty towards the State.[84] There are various objections to the advisory judicial opinion, but they have only a tenuous connection with judicial involvement in executive policy. The fact that the Stuarts used judges as advisers and brought undue pressure to bear on them in private consultation does not imply that a publicly delivered advisory opinion on a specific question of law would prejudice judicial impartiality today.[85]

Judicial immunities in legal proceedings.[86] The majority in a Court of Appeal case[87] decided that every judge of the superior and inferior courts – including magistrates – was entitled to protection from liability in damages for anything done while acting judicially. As long as he acted under the honest belief that his conduct was within his jurisdiction, he was protected even though a mistake of law or fact led him outside his jurisdiction. The House of Lords reluctantly held that that decision must be overruled at least to the extent that magistrates would be held liable if they exceeded their jurisdiction.[88] Legislation was subsequently passed[89] which protects magis-

---

84 For a helpful catalogue and critique, see Zellick [1972] *Public Law* 1 and, for an exhaustive list of extra-judicial inquiries carried out by judges, see David Butler and Gareth Butler, *British Political Facts 1900–1994* (7th edn, 1994), pp. 291–301. It has been estimated that the equivalent of the time of three High Court judges is devoted to extra-judicial duties at any given time: see Report of the Committee on the Deployment of the High Court Bench (Lord Chancellor's Department, 1988), para. 3.2.

85 Advisory opinions may be obtained from the Judicial Committee of the Privy Council under section 4 of the Judicial Committee Act 1833; see also Criminal Justice Act 1972, s. 36 (p. 365). In Canada advisory opinions on the constitutionality of legislation have frequently been delivered by the courts. The International Court of Justice has also given several advisory opinions.

86 See Margaret Brazier [1976] *Public Law* 397; A. Olowofoyeku, *Suing Judges* (1993).

87 *Sirros* v. *Moore and others* [1975] QB 118.

88 *McC.* v. *Mullan* [1985] AC 528. See also *R.* v. *Waltham Forest JJ, ex p. Solanke* [1986] QB 479 (held, justices acted in execution of their office by committing man to prison for non-payment of money due to his wife under a High Court order, even though the order had not been registered).

89 Justices of the Peace Act 1997, Part V.

trates (and their clerks) against any proceedings brought against them while acting within their jurisdiction; while acting beyond their jurisdiction there is liability only if bad faith can be proved. While acting *within their jurisdiction*, members of other tribunals closely resembling courts[90] enjoy a similar immunity in respect of defamatory words, but a right of action may possibly lie against such officers for malicious *acts*,[91] and will lie for tortious acts done outside their jurisdiction where jurisdiction has been exceeded because of an error of law or an unreasonable mistake of fact.[92]

Judicial immunities from suit are conferred not for the benefit of judges but for the benefit of the administration of justice. The risk that a judge may abuse his privilege by making gratuitously defamatory remarks for reasons of personal rancour is considered to be less than the risk of his abstaining for reasons of prudence from condemning iniquity in appropriate language. In the public interest, absolute privilege also attaches to words used by the parties, counsel and witnesses in the course of judicial proceedings.[93] Nor can jurors be punished for their verdict.[94]

There may be circumstances in which a judge wrongfully declining to hear a case within his jurisdiction will incur civil liability to a person aggrieved.[95] Under the Habeas Corpus Act 1679 a judge wrongfully (and

90 See, for example, *Addis* v. *Crocker* [1961] 1 QB 11 (Disciplinary Committee of the Law Society). The courts have, in general, refused to hold members of administrative tribunals to be protected by absolute privilege; they enjoy qualified privilege which is destroyed by proof of malice.

91 See, on this difficult topic, *Everett* v. *Griffiths* [1921] 1 AC 631; *O'Connor* v. *Isaacs* [1956] 2 QB 288; Justices of the Peace Act 1997, ss. 51–2: see note 89). Amnon Rubinstein, *Jurisdiction and Illegality* (1965), pp. 128–33; Sheridan (1951) 14 *Mod. L. Rev.* 267; Thompson (1958) 21 *Mod. L. Rev.* 517; Margaret Brazier [1976] *Public Law* 397.

92 *Houlden* v. *Smith* (1850) 15 QB 841; *Palmer* v. *Crone* [1927] 1 KB 804. Even before *Sirros* v. *Moore and others* (above, note 87), a magistrate who had had to pay damages or costs in respect of proceedings instituted against him in the purported exercise of his duties has since 1964 been entitled to be indemnified out of public funds provided that he had acted reasonably and in good faith: see now Justices of the Peace Act 1997, s. 54.

93 Neither a barrister nor a solicitor can be sued for negligence in respect of his conduct of a client's case as an advocate: *Rondel* v. *Worsley* [1969] 1 AC 191; *Somasundaram* v. *M. Julius Melchior & Co.* [1989] 1 All ER 129. See also Courts and Legal Services Act 1990, s. 62. Solicitors are liable for professional negligence in other contexts, and in *Saif Ali and another* v. *Sydney Mitchell & Co.* [1980] AC 198 the House of Lords held that the immunity of barristers in respect of pre-trial acts or omissions was not to be given any wider application than was absolutely necessary in the interests of the administration of justice, although on the facts the barrister could not be said to have been negligent.

94 *Bushell's* case (1670) Vaugh. 135.

95 See *Ferguson* v. *Earl Kinnoull* (1842) 2 Cl. & F. 251.

presumably wilfully) refusing to issue a writ of habeas corpus is liable to a penalty of £500 recoverable by the prisoner.

The general rules of judicial immunity do not extend to giving a judge or magistrate an open licence to be corrupt or oppressive. Corruption would be a ground for prosecution. Oppressive conduct would result in the removal of a magistrate, and the same fate might befall an oppressive judge.

Contempt of court.[96] Disobedience to a court order is a civil contempt, punishable in the discretion of the court by imprisonment. This rule has nothing to do with judicial independence. Criminal contempts fall into three main categories. First, there are contempts in the face of the court – for example, the interruption of a High Court libel action by a group of Welsh nationalist student demonstrators,[97] or a wilful refusal by a witness to answer questions put to him.[98] Secondly, there is conduct which creates a substantial risk that the course of justice in a case will be seriously impeded or prejudiced[99] – for example, publishing newspaper comment or broadcasting a television programme tending to show (in criminal

96 See G. J. Borrie and N. V. Lowe, *The Law of Contempt* (2nd edn, 1983); A. Arlidge and D. Eady, *The Law of Contempt* (1982); C. J. Miller, *Contempt of Court* (2nd edn, 1990). See further the *Phillimore Report on Contempt of Court*, Cmnd 5794 (2nd edn, 1989), and *Contempt of Court: a Discussion Paper*, Cmnd 7145 (1978).

97 *Morris* v. *Crown Office* [1970] 2 QB 114 (power of judges to sentence summarily), *Balogh* v. *St Albans Crown Court* [1975] QB 73 (a gross interference with the course of justice in a case tried or about to be tried can be punished either by the judge who had seen the contempt or by a judge in another court to whom it had been reported: the jurisdiction is not limited only to contempt committed 'in the face of the court').

98 It is not contempt for a person to refuse to disclose a source of information contained in a publication for which he is responsible, unless the court decides that disclosure is necessary in the interests of justice or national security or for the prevention of disorder or crime: Contempt of Court Act 1981, s. 10 and *Secretary of State for Defence* v. *Guardian Newspapers Ltd* [1985] AC 339: held 'necessary' was to be construed strictly, not as a synonym for 'convenient'; followed in *Maxwell* v. *Pressdram Ltd* [1987] 1 All ER 656; *X Ltd* v. *Morgan-Grampian (Publishers) Ltd* [1990] 2 All ER 1. 'Prevention of crime' means crime generally, rather than any particular crime: *Re an Inquiry under the Company Securities (Insider Dealing) Act 1985* [1988] 1 All ER 203.

99 1981 Act, ss. 1, 2(2). In *Att.-Gen.* v. *News Group Newspapers Ltd* [1987] QB 1 an injunction to restrain further publication of allegedly defamatory material was refused because the trial would not begin for at least ten months and a *substantial* risk of serious prejudice would not be caused by such publication. If the proceedings are to be heard by a judge without a jury, or by an appellate court, there is less likelihood of a substantial risk that the course of justice in those proceedings would be seriously impaired: *Re Lonrho plc and others* [1989] 2 All ER 100. See also *Att.-Gen.* v. *Times Newspaper Ltd* [1991] 2 All ER 398.

proceedings) that a person not yet convicted, but who is either wanted under an arrest warrant, or who has been arrested or charged, is guilty, or (in civil proceedings) ascribing liability after arrangements for a hearing have been made, or after a hearing has begun – at the earliest of which events the proceedings become 'active';[100] or disclosing a party's past convictions; or putting pressure on witnesses to alter their evidence or not to give evidence; or publishing a report of legal proceedings in which the court has, in order to avoid a substantial risk to the administration of justice in them, ordered the publication of any report to be postponed for as long as it thinks fit;[101] or obtaining, disclosing or soliciting opinions expressed, arguments advanced or votes cast by members of a jury in the course of its deliberations.[102] Thirdly, there is conduct scandalizing the court by scurrilous criticism or imputations of partiality.[103] The limits of permissible criticism have been extended by the courts themselves in recent years. In a case report in 1936, the Judicial Committee, allowing an appeal against a conviction and fine imposed on the author of a newpaper article criticizing sentences imposed by local judges, held that members of the public were immune provided that they refrained from imputing improper motives to the judges and were not actuated by malice. 'Justice must not be a cloistered virtue; she must be allowed to suffer the scrutiny and respectful, even the outspoken, comments of ordinary men.'[104] Today, even disrespectful comments will not necessarily be construed as contempts of court. In a case decided in 1968,[105] the Court of Appeal declined to hold that an article by a QC (soon to be Lord Chancellor) in *Punch*, embodying robust, jocular and inaccurate denunciations of judgments by the court, was a contempt. Lord Denning MR said that the court would 'never use this jurisdiction as a means to uphold our dignity. We do not fear criticism, nor do we resent it.' Salmon LJ said that 'no criticism of a judge, however vigorous, can amount to contempt of court, providing it keeps within the limits of courtesy and good faith'. Judges may adopt differing standards, but the tendency is to

---

100 ibid., s. 2 and sched. 1. Even if proceedings are not 'active', where the conduct complained of is specifically *intended* to impede or prejudice the administration of justice the courts have a common-law power to commit for contempt which is saved by the 1981 Act, s. 6(*c*): see *Att.-Gen.* v. *Associated Newspapers plc* [1987] 3 All ER 276.

101 ibid., s. 4(2). See Practice Direction [1982] 1 WLR 1475; *R.* v. *Horsham Justices, ex p. Farquharson* [1982] QB 762.

102 ibid., s. 8, see, e.g., *Att.-Gen.* v. *Associated Newspapers Ltd* [1994] 1 All ER 556.

103 *McLeod* v. *St Aubyn* [1899] AC 549; *R.* v. *Gray* [1900] 2 QB 36; *R.* v. *Editor of the New Statesman* (1928) 44 TLR 301. See Walker (1985) 101 LQR 359.

104 *Ambard* v. *Att.-Gen. for Trinidad and Tobago* [1936] AC 322 at 335.

105 *R.* v. *Metropolitan Police Commissioner, ex p. Blackburn (No. 2)* [1968] 2 QB 150.

show more indulgence towards outspoken criticism alleging ignorance of the law or excessive harshness or leniency in sentencing. The Law Commission has recommended that this aspect of contempt be narrowed by the creation of a new offence of making false statements alleging corruption in the performance of judicial duties.[106]

Magistrates' courts can punish for contempt in connection with their proceedings. Any person who wilfully insults the justices or any witness before them or an officer of the court or any solicitor or barrister having business in the court during their sitting, or attendance, or in going to or returning from the court, or who wilfully interrupts the proceedings or misbehaves in court, is liable to a maximum penalty of one month in prison or a £5,000 fine or both.[107]

The maximum penalty for contempt of other courts[108] is two years' imprisonment.[109] An appeal against conviction lies to a higher court. It is a defence that a publisher or a disseminator of a contempt, having taken all reasonable care, did not know and had no reason to suspect that relevant proceedings were 'active', or that the publication contained a contempt.[110] A publication made of a discussion in good faith of public affairs or other matters of general public interest is not a contempt if the risk of impediment or prejudice to particular legal proceedings is merely incidental to the discussion.[111]

Security of judicial tenure

Before 1688 judges generally held office during the King's pleasure. When they incurred his displeasure they were apt to be summarily dismissed.

After the 'Glorious Revolution' of 1688 all superior judges were appointed during good behaviour. The Act of Settlement 1701 placed the terms of appointment on a statutory basis: judges' commissions were to be made *quamdiu se bene gesserint* (as long as they behave themselves), 'but upon the address of both Houses of Parliament it shall be lawful to remove

---

106 Law Com. No. 96 (1979).
107 Contempt of Court Act 1981, s. 12.
108 Defined as any tribunal or body exercising the judicial power of the State; ibid., s. 19 (e.g. a coroner's court: see R. v. *West Yorkshire Coroner, ex p. Smith (No. 2)* [1985] 1 All ER 100; or a mental health review tribunal: *Pickering* v. *Liverpool Daily Post* [1991] 1 All ER 622.
109 ibid., s. 14(1). Consecutive sentences are appropriate for each of a number of acts of contempt: *Lee* v. *Walker* [1985] 1 All ER 781.
110 ibid., s. 3(1), (2).
111 ibid., s. 5. See *Att.-Gen.* v. *English* [1983] 1 AC 116.

them'. This has often been understood to mean that a judge is irremovable except for misbehaviour, in pursuance of an address submitted to the Crown by both Houses praying for his removal on that ground. However, the better interpretation of the Act, and of modern Acts replacing it with slightly different wording,[112] is that a judge is in strict law removable by the Crown *either* for misbehaviour *or* on any other ground in pursuance of a parliamentary address.[113] Misbehaviour would include conviction for an offence involving moral turpitude, and persistent neglect of duties; it does not appear to cover mental infirmity. Removal from an office held during good behaviour has traditionally been effected by proceedings commenced by a writ of *scire facias*. Probably this procedure still survives;[114] it would seem that alternatively the Attorney-General could move for an injunction in the High Court to restrain the judge from continuing to act in an office to which he was no longer entitled, but the judge would have to be given prior notice and a fair opportunity to be heard before being removed.[115]

In practice no judge is likely to be removed except upon a parliamentary address based on the judge's misbehaviour. Only one judge has in fact been so removed since the Act of Settlement – Sir Jonah Barrington, an Irish judge, in 1830.[116] A few other addresses were moved unsuccessfully in the nineteenth century; the judges were permitted to defend themselves and be represented by counsel.[117] But the strictly legal safeguards of security of tenure are weak. The dearth of parliamentary addresses is attributable to the self-restraint of politicians and the circumspection maintained by the Judiciary.[118] It would be more satisfactory to introduce a new procedure whereby a judge would be removable either for mental or physical incapacity or misbehaviour in pursuance of the report of a judicial tribunal of inquiry, and on no other ground. Such a procedure has been incorporated in a

---

112 Supreme Court Act 1981, s. 11(3) (tenure 'during good behaviour, subject to' a power of removal by the Crown upon an address by both Houses); Appellate Jurisdiction Act 1876, s. 6 (Lords of Appeal in Ordinary).

113 See the discussion in Sir Kenneth Roberts-Wray, *Commonwealth and Colonial Law* (1966), pp. 486–90.

114 Despite the wording of the First Schedule to the Crown Proceedings Act 1947 the repeal of the writ may refer only to its use for the recovery of Crown debts.

115 In accordance with the rules of natural justice: see authorities quoted in *Ridge* v. *Baldwin* [1964] AC 40.

116 Half-hearted attempts to remove the President of the National Industrial Relations Court never reached the stage of putting down a motion, cf. notes 48 and 49.

117 See Alpheus Todd, *Parliamentary Government in England*, vol. 2, pp. 726–44, for particulars of the nineteenth-century cases.

118 From time to time senior judges have doubtless persuaded their aberrant or infirm brethren to resign.

number of Commonwealth constitutions since 1957.[119] The Lord Chancellor may, with the concurrence of senior judges, declare vacant the office of a superior judge who is subject to permanent medical incapacity and who is, through illness, unable to tender his resignation.[120]

Till 1959 tenure during good behaviour was tantamount to life tenure. In that year statutory provision was made for compulsory retirement. Superior judges appointed since 1993 must retire at seventy.[121] Circuit judges and Recorders are removable by the Lord Chancellor for incapacity or misbehaviour;[122] they have an implied right to be heard on their own behalf.[123] The normal age for compulsory retirement of a Circuit judge is seventy.

Magistrates have no legal security of tenure, but they may be placed on the supplemental list for infirmity or non-judicial behaviour or removed altogether from the commission of the peace. About a dozen lay magistrates are dismissed each year.[124] Both lay and stipendiary magistrates are placed on the supplemental list or retired at seventy.[125]

THE EXECUTIVE AND THE ADMINISTRATION OF JUSTICE

There is no Minister of Justice in England. Executive responsibilities in relation to the administration of justice are distributed among several Ministers – the Lord Chancellor, the Home Secretary, and the Law Officers of the Crown (the Attorney-General and the Solicitor-General for England and Wales).[126] The Scottish Law Officers are the Lord Advocate and the Solicitor-General for Scotland; the Secretary of State for Scotland also has responsibility for aspects of the Scottish legal system, which differs in many ways from the English.

---

119 Roberts-Wray, op. cit., pp. 490–501.
120 Supreme Court Act 1981, s. 11(8), (9).
121 ibid., s. 11(2) and Judicial Pensions and Retirement Act 1993, s. 26 and sched. 5.
122 Courts Act 1971, ss. 17(4), 21(6). A Circuit judge was removed in 1983 following his conviction for smuggling and a £2,000 fine. The Lord Chancellor is directed to satisfy himself before recommending a person for appointment as a Circuit judge that that person's health is satisfactory (s. 16(4)).

A Recorder may also be removed for failure to comply with the conditions of his appointment as to requirements to officiate (s. 21(3), (6)). He will be appointed for a fixed term, which may be renewed but not beyond the age of seventy.
123 Ex p. Ramshay (1852) 18 QB 173.
124 For the removal of sheriffs in Scotland see Stewart v. Secretary of State for Scotland 1995 SLT 895.
125 Justices of the Peace Act 1997, ss. 7, 12.
126 See Brazier [1989] Public Law 64.

The Lord Chancellor's duties[127] are multifarious, demanding the utmost delicacy and an extensive familiarity with lawyers and the law. As we have seen, he is head of the Judiciary, a Cabinet Minister and Speaker of the House of Lords. He seldom sits as a judge, but is responsible for arranging who shall sit to hear cases in the House of Lords and the Judicial Committee of the Privy Council. Many of his functions in relation to judicial appointments have been mentioned, but there are others; thus he appoints Chancery Masters, the senior Master of the Queen's Bench Division, judges' clerks, District Judges and the legally qualified chairmen of certain statutory tribunals. He is chairman of the committees that make rules of procedure for the Supreme Court[128] and the Crown Court and appoints the members of the corresponding body for county courts. To an increasing extent he has assumed responsibilities for matters connected with the administration of criminal justice. It was he, not the Home Secretary, who was the progenitor of the Courts Act 1971, and it is he who appoints the officials of the Crown Court. Responsibility for magistrates' courts has been transferred to the Lord Chancellor from the Home Secretary. He is also the Minister responsible for law reform on the civil side. In this context by far the most important advisory body is the Law Commission,[129] composed of a High Court judge as chairman and full-time Commissioners appointed by the Lord Chancellor. The Commission has a small but highly qualified research staff, and parliamentary counsel are attached to it as draftsmen. Before the Commission issues a formal report with firm proposals, it will hold extensive consultations, produce a preliminary consultation paper, and invite comments from representative bodies of lawyers and individuals. The Commission has produced detailed schemes ranging from divorce law reform to codification of the criminal law (through a draft Criminal Code) and statute law revision, and its reports have strengthened the position of

---

127 They are summarized in R. F. V. Heuston, *Lives of the Lord Chancellors 1885–1940* (1964), Introduction. For Lord Mackay's account of the office, see [1991] *Current Legal Problems* 241. Partly to reflect his heavy workload, he is paid more than his colleague the Prime Minister, at a rate fixed at £2,500 a year more than the Lord Chief Justice: Ministerial and other Pension and Salaries Act 1991, s. 3. His salary is currently £139,000. Doubts as to whether a Roman Catholic may hold the office have been removed in favour of adherents of that faith: Lord Chancellor (Tenure of Office and Discharge of Ecclesiastical Functions) Act 1974.

128 cf. *Bates* v. *Lord Hailsham of St Marylebone* [1972] 1 WLR 1373. Under the Civil Procedure Act 1997 a single Civil Court Rule Committee will replace the separate committees for the Supreme Court and the county courts. An advisory Civil Justice Council is also to be set up under that Act.

129 See Law Commissions Act 1965. There is a separate Law Commission for Scotland. The Commissions have also made numerous reports on criminal law reforms.

the Lord Chancellor, jostling with his ministerial colleagues for places in the legislative queue. Several bills emanating from the Law Commission have been passed as private members' bills. The Law Reform Committee is one of the part-time bodies which advises the Lord Chancellor. Again, he appoints the members of the Council on Tribunals[130] which has various supervisory, consultative and advisory functions with regard to statutory tribunals and inquiries; the Council makes reports to him. He exercises a general superintendence over the legal aid and advice scheme in civil matters for persons of modest means; the scheme is administered by the Legal Aid Board, which is appointed by him.[131] Administrative responsibility for the legal aid scheme in criminal matters has been transferred to the Lord Chancellor from the Home Secretary; decisions to grant legal aid orders are made by the criminal courts themselves.[132] If the Lord Chancellor has not enough to occupy his time, he can make speeches for the Government in the House of Lords or address his mind to his extensive ecclesiastical patronage or his responsibilities for the Land Registry and the Public Record Office.

Another function of the Lord Chancellor is to appoint the Official Solicitor to the Supreme Court and to give him general directions as to the performance of his duties. Among the multifarious duties performed by the Official Solicitor as a 'general sweeper-up of messes'[133] is representation of minors, mental patients and persons committed for contempt of court, particularly if they are unrepresented in forthcoming judicial proceedings.

The Home Secretary is in effect the Minister of the Interior, though he also has responsibilities for Westminster's relations with the Channel Islands[134] and the Isle of Man. Some of his responsibilities with regard to law and order have only a tenuous connection with the administration of justice – for example, implementing the reports of constituency boundary commissions; superintending the machinery for the conduct of elections; immigration, deportation, extradition, naturalization and the general regulation of aliens and immigrants; control of firearms, poisons and dangerous drugs. The Director-General of the Security Service (MI5) is personally answerable

130 See ch. 28.
131 See Legal Aid Act 1988, Part II; and Parts IV (advice and assistance), IV (civil legal aid) and V (criminal legal aid).
132 Legal Aid Act 1974, Port II. See further R. v. Derby JJ, ex p. Kooner [1971] 1 QB 147 (implied duty of magistrates to provide counsel in committal proceedings for murder).
133 The Then Official Solicitor's own description (1966) 63 Law Society's Gazette at 338.
134 In 1992 the Home Secretary advised the Queen to dismiss the deputy Bailiff of Jersey on account of his delay in delivering judgments.

to him. Other functions impinge on the administration of justice; he is the police authority for the Metropolitan Police and supervises local police forces; he is generally responsible for the penal system and the treatment of offenders, and looks after prisons, other custodial establishments and the probation service. It is he who advises the Queen on the exercise of the prerogative of mercy in England and Wales.[135] He is broadly responsible for not only the administration but also the reform of the criminal law, and is advised by a Criminal Law Revision Committee.

The Attorney-General[136] is the principal legal adviser to Government Departments. He appears in court on their behalf in important cases, and gives them formal and informal opinions on difficult questions of law out of court. Reference has already been made to his important role in scrutinizing drafts of bills; he is also a valuable member of committees on bills. These functions, and all of his other responsibilities,[137] are dischargeable by the Solicitor-General (who is not a solicitor). The Law Officers, though members of the Government, do not have seats in the Cabinet.

The Attorney-General has a number of non-political functions. As guardian of the public interest, he may institute civil proceedings in the High Court for the vindication of public rights – for example, to restrain a local authority from exceeding its powers, or a private individual from perpetrating repeated breaches of by-laws or other minor criminal offences. He may take such proceedings on his own initiative or at the request of other persons or bodies lacking a sufficient personal interest to sue on their behalf; he has an absolute discretion whether to proceed.[138] Again, he appears as an independent officer of State before judicial tribunals of inquiry. His role in criminal proceedings is of special constitutional importance. He can select the place of trial on indictment.[139] He can enter a *nolle prosequi* to stop any trial of an indictable offence: this incidentally allows him to grant immunity from prosecution, frequently in return for information. His leave is required before certain classes of criminal proceedings (for example, for breaches of the Official Secrets Acts) can be instituted. He can institute criminal proceedings, or instruct the Director of Public Prosecutions to take over a private prosecution and offer no evidence if a *nolle prosequi*

---

135 From 1979 to 1994, 1,256 pardons were granted on ministerial advice: 254 HC Deb. *217* (written answers 7 February 1995).
136 For the fullest accounts, see J. Ll. J. Edwards, *The Law Officers of the Crown* (1964) and *The Attorney-General: Politics and the Public Interest* (1984).
137 See Law Officers Act 1944; Law Officers Act 1997.
138 See *Gouriet* v. *Union of Post Office Workers* [1978] AC 435.
139 He can also determine the venue in civil cases involving the Crown.

cannot be entered or if it is preferable not to go through the formality of entering a *nolle prosequi*. These discretionary powers are probably unchallengeable in any court,[140] and they could be abused to serve party political purposes. But in performing these functions he is obliged by convention to exercise an independent discretion, not dictated by his colleagues in the Government, though he is at liberty to (and sometimes should) consult them and obtain their views in a case with political implications. In 1985 the Attorney-General's decision (taken after he had consulted the Solicitor-General and the Director of Public Prosecutions) to prosecute Clive Ponting under section 2 of the Official Secrets Act 1911 for leaking confidential information to Tam Dalyell MP about the sinking of the *General Belgrano* in the Falklands conflict aroused much controversy. Mr Ponting was acquitted.[141] Similarly, his role in the decision in 1987 to investigate possible breaches of that section arising out of an article in the *New Statesman* on the parliamentary funding of a spy satellite, 'Project Zircon', caused considerable parliamentary debate.[142] In 1924 the circumstances in which the Attorney-General was suspected of having yielded to Cabinet pressure in withdrawing a prosecution for sedition led to a successful vote of censure on the Government and its downfall.[143] He appoints, is politically answerable for, and 'superintends' the Director of Public Prosecutions.[144] The Director of Public Prosecutions himself instructs counsel and solicitors to conduct prosecutions in cases referred to him by Departments and in other serious or important cases (in some of which he alone is entitled to prosecute, or proceedings cannot be undertaken except with his leave),[145] and can take over prosecutions from private persons. He undertakes about three thousand such prosecutions a year. He also advises the police at their request whether there is sufficient evidence to justify a prosecution. His advice, though not binding, carries great weight.

In a number of Commonwealth countries with politically appointed

---

140 See *R.* v. *Allen* (1862) 1 B. & S. 850 on the prerogative power to enter a *nolle prosequi*. cf. Dickens (1972) 35 *Mod. L. Rev.* 347, suggesting that in some contexts his discretion may not be unlimited.

141 See 73 HC Deb. 737–830 (18 February 1985); Clive Ponting, *The Right to Know* (1985). *R.* v. *Ponting* [1985] *Crim. L. Rev.* 318.

142 See 109 HC Deb. *330* (written answers 29 January 1987); 109 HC Deb. 815–62 (3 February 1987). No prosecutions followed.

143 Edwards, *Law Officer of the Crown* (1964), chs. 10 and 11; Geoffrey Wilson, *Cases and Materials* (2nd edn, 1976), pp. 514–19.

144 Prosecution of Offences Act 1985, s. 2. See above, p. 360.

145 There are about a hundred statutory references to the DPP's consent being required for specified prosecutions: see 533 HL Deb 55–72 (written answers 18 December 1991).

Attorney-Generals, the Director of Public Prosecutions is given judicial security of tenure by the constitution and is vested with an exclusive independent responsibility for decisions to take over, continue or discontinue prosecutions. Where he decides to institute criminal proceedings himself, the constitution will provide that he shall not act under the direction of any other person. This constitutional device – and there are others designed to produce a similar effect[146] – emphasizes both the importance attached to the maintenance of public confidence in the process of prosecution and the precarious delicacy of the balance achieved by habits of political self-restraint in Britain. It is not too much to say that in Britain the independence of the Judiciary and the impartiality of the administration of criminal justice are maintained *in spite of* the strictly legal powers vested in Parliament and the Executive.

146 cf. Roberts-Wray, op. cit., pp. 354–5.

CHAPTER 19

The Protection of Human Rights

FUNDAMENTAL RIGHTS

'Now, most foreign constitution-makers have begun with declarations of rights. For this they have often been in no wise to blame.'[1] Here Dicey seems almost as patronizing as Mr Podsnap of *Our Mutual Friend*: other countries 'do – I am sorry to be obliged to say it – *as* they do'. But he was at least more restrained than his mentor, Jeremy Bentham, to whom the French revolutionary Declaration of the Rights of Man was 'rhetorical nonsense – nonsense upon stilts'. There is indeed something peculiarly exasperating about a broad affirmation of fundamental human rights unaccompanied by any machinery for giving them effective legal protection. This is what Dicey had in mind: 'The Habeas Corpus Acts declare no principle and define no rights, but they are for practical purposes worth a hundred constitutional articles guaranteeing individual liberty.'[2] Had he been alive in 1948, he might have added 'or a thousand Universal Declarations of Human Rights'.

The traditional legal approach to civil liberties in Britain can be summed up in three propositions. First, freedoms are not to be guaranteed by statements of general principle. Secondly, they are residual. Freedom of public assembly, for example, means the liberty to gather wherever one chooses except in so far as others are legally entitled to prevent the assembly from being held or in so far as the holding or conduct of the assembly is a civil wrong or a criminal offence. To define the content of liberty one has merely to subtract from its totality the sum of the legal restraints to which it is subject. Thirdly, for every wrongful encroachment upon one's liberty

---

1 A. V. Dicey, *Introduction to the Study of the Law of the Constitution* (10th edn), p. 198.
2 ibid., p. 199. See also Sir Ivor Jennings, *The Approach to Self-Government*, p. 20. See generally S. de Smith, *The New Commonwealth and its Constitutions* (1964), pp. 161–77.

there is a legal remedy awarded by an independent court of justice. *Ubi jus, ibi remedium.*

These are still the formal legal foundations of most of our civil liberties – but the Labour Government is currently sponsoring the Human Rights Bill which (as will be seen later) will incorporate the European Convention on Human Rights into domestic law. The traditional foundations for civil liberties have not made for the best of all possible worlds in the United Kingdom. If the constitution of Northern Ireland had been equipped from the outset with more detailed guarantees against religious discrimination, coupled with efficacious machinery for their enforcement, it is just conceivable that the worst of the current troubles might have been averted.[3] If the American constitutional Bill of Rights had been transported to Britain along with Marshall Aid in the late 1940s, our laws relating to police powers of interrogation, search and seizure, legal aid for persons suspected or accused of crime, obscene publications, passports and the delimitation of electoral constituencies might have been more satisfactory though more uncertain. For the American Bill of Rights has reasonably effective machinery for judicial interpretation and enforcement of its provisions. Its terms would also have made it more difficult for Parliament and the Government to nationalize industries and implement town and country planning policies; it might have led to more criminals escaping justice; it would surely have struck down some of our immigration legislation; it might have prevented – or at least made more difficult – some of the 1979 Conservative Government's legislation which reduced the powers of local government.

Objections to effective constitutional guarantees of human rights may be still more vehement than objections to pious platitudes. Effective guarantees obstruct governments from doing what they want to do and are expected to do. They are therefore said to be undemocratic because they obstruct fulfilment of the will of the people as expressed by their elected representatives. They lead to 'government by judges', if the constitution is hard to amend. There will be political appointments to the bench, and public confidence in the impartial administration of justice may dwindle. Justiciable guarantees and prohibitions induce delay and uncertainty, because politicians will not be sure what they are entitled to do until the judges have told them; they engender a litigious spirit; they are irreconcilable with our ancient traditions; they are, moreover, unnecessary.

These objections cannot be disregarded. However, a number of comments must be made to put those points into a United Kingdom context and

---

3 For constitutional guarantees in Northern Ireland, see ch. 3.

to show that the protection of human rights through a special constitutional document is neither unknown to the United Kingdom nor entirely alien to British experience.

1 It is possible to have a bill of rights enacted as an ordinary statute without constitutional entrenchment. Canada adopted this course from 1960 to 1982. Federal legislation was to be so construed and applied as to conform to the Canadian Bill of Rights except in an emergency or unless an Act expressly stated that it was to have effect notwithstanding the Bill of Rights. Its overt impact was not at first impressive. The courts held that it did not prevail over subsequent inconsistent Acts of the Federal Parliament. But it served as a guide to interpretation; and legislative draftsmen were at pains to conform to the standards it laid down. Its indirect effect on the content of legislation may have been considerable. Thus discussion about possible new constitutional guarantees for the United Kingdom need not run into the sands of unnecessary argument about whether, in English law, they could be entrenched.

2 The constitutions of a large majority of newly independent and partly self-governing Commonwealth countries have been equipped with full-scale entrenched bills of rights, based on the general pattern of the European Convention on Human Rights.[4] During its declining years, the Colonial Office moved from apathy or hostility towards this idea and began actively to press it on colonial politicians. The unmentionable became indispensable. What was obnoxious to the Westminster model has been the glory of Westminster's export models. Perhaps, after all, time-honoured Anglo-Saxon attitudes towards constitutional guarantees of fundamental rights have been slightly exaggerated. True, in some Commonwealth countries the guarantees existed – if they survived at all – only on paper. Yet nobody reading the judgments of the Judicial Committee of the Privy Council in two appeals (holding invalid a Maltese ministerial circular restricting freedom of the press,[5] and the discriminatory citizenship legislation in Sierra Leone)[6] can doubt that (to put it at its lowest) there is something to be said in favour of restricting legislative and administrative competence by constitutional guarantees.

3 As was seen in chapter 5, United Kingdom membership of the European

---

4 The beginnings of the trend are explained and analysed in de Smith, op. cit., ch. 5.
5 See *Olivier* v. *Buttigieg* [1967] 1 AC 115.
6 *Akar* v. *Att. Gen. of Sierra Leone* [1970] AC 853. With these two decisions there should be studied the remarkable judgment in *Liyanage* v. *R.* [1967] 1 AC 259 (Ceylon; implied prohibition read into a constitution not containing a wide range of guarantees).

Union has allowed individual British citizens to take advantage of certain rights under Community law. Such law is, therefore, an additional source of human rights.

4 The United Kingdom has, since 1953 in fact, been subject to a modern bill of rights with its own machinery for interpretation, and during that time United Kingdom law and practice has on occasion been altered so as to conform to it. That bill is the European Convention on Human Rights. It will now be looked at in some detail, especially because under the Human Rights Bill now before Parliament that Convention will become enforceable in the courts of this country.

THE EUROPEAN CONVENTION ON HUMAN RIGHTS[7]

The European Convention on Human Rights came into force in 1953 in the States (including the United Kingdom) that had ratified it. Those States form the Council of Europe, which had itself been established in 1949 and which today has thirty-two members.[8] The United Kingdom is bound by the Convention as a treaty in international law:[9] it is only now being enacted as part of United Kingdom law, but because of the international law obligation to observe its terms the Convention provides both a restraint on the legislative authority of the United Kingdom Parliament[10] and a fruitful source of rights for the individual.

The Convention specifies certain basic rights which the West European liberal democracies were able to agree on in the early 1950s.[11] Following the collapse of Communism many former Soviet bloc states acceded to the Convention. Those rights and freedoms, in summary, include the right to life (art. 2); freedom from torture or inhuman or degrading treatment or punishment (art. 3); freedom from slavery or forced labour (art. 4); the right to liberty and security of the person (art. 5); the right to a fair trial by

---

7 See Cmnd 8969 (1953); Cmnd 9221 (1954); Ian Brownlie, *Basic Documents on Human Rights* (3rd edn, 1992); R. Beddard, *Human Rights and Europe* (2nd edn, 1980); A. H. Robertson, *Human Rights in Europe* (3rd edn, 1993); J. E. S. Fawcett, *The Application of the European Convention on Human Rights* (2nd edn, 1987); F. G. Jacobs, *The European Convention on Human Rights* (2nd edn, 1996); T. H. Jones [1995] *Public Law* 430.
8 Members include all Western European states, many Eastern European states, Iceland, Estonia, Finland, and Lithuania; Russia is in the process of joining.
9 See above, p. 147.
10 See above, ch. 4.
11 Thus some rights which might appear in a comprehensive modern document, such as rights of property, are omitted.

an impartial tribunal (art. 6); the prohibition of retrospective criminal laws (art. 7); the right to respect for a person's private and family life, his home and correspondence (art. 8); freedom of thought, conscience and religion (art. 9); freedom of expression (art. 10); freedom of peaceful assembly and association, including the right to join a trade union (art. 11), and the right to marry and found a family (art. 12). Those rights are to be enjoyed without discrimination on any ground such as sex, race, colour, language, religion, political or other opinion, national or social origin, association with a national minority, property, birth or other status. Further rights were added by the First Protocol to the Convention. Thus every person is entitled, under that Protocol, to the peaceful enjoyment of his possessions (art. 1), to education (and States must respect parents' rights to the education of their children in conformity with their religious and philosophical convictions) (art. 2),[12] and to take part in free elections by secret ballot (art. 3).

The Convention also explains (lest this all seems too good to be true) the circumstances in which a protected right can be abridged or removed. Thus there is, for example, no blanket guarantee of freedom of speech, which can never mean what it appears to say; nor is there any guarantee of 'due process of law' which can mean anything a judge thinks fit. Freedom of expression is qualified by a number of provisos: the State may license broadcasting and cinemas; such restrictions on freedom of expression may be imposed 'as are necessary in a democratic society, in the interests of national security, territorial integrity or public safety, for the prevention of disorder or crime, for the protection of health or morals, for the protection of the reputation or rights of others, for preventing the disclosure of information received in confidence, or for maintaining the authority and impartiality of the judiciary' (art. 10). Derogation from some rights and freedoms is permissible in time of grave emergency, but only 'to the extent strictly required by the exigencies of the situation' (art. 15) – a derogation which has taken place in relation to Northern Ireland. Any derogation must be reported to the Secretary-General of the Council of Europe. No derogation from certain rights (for example, freedom from torture or inhuman or degrading punishment or treatment) is permissible at all. Because up till now the terms of the European Convention have not been incorporated as part of United Kingdom law, the courts in the United Kingdom have been unable to apply them directly.[13] If there is no British

---

12 The United Kingdom limited its acceptance of that article.
13 See, e.g., *Malone* v. *United Kingdom* [1981] Ch. 344; *Kaur* v. *Lord Advocate* [1981] SLT 322; *R.* v. *Secretary of State for the Home Department, ex p. Weeks*, the *Guardian*, 17 February 1988.

legislation on the subject-matter of a dispute, it seems that the courts *need not* take the Convention into account,[14] and, plainly, the terms of the Convention could not prevail over inconsistent statutory provisions. On the other hand the courts, in construing legislation passed since 1953, have been able to take note of the Convention and presume that Parliament did not intend to legislate inconsistently with it.[15] Until the Human Rights Bill becomes law an aggrieved British citizen must, therefore, continue to go to the European machinery which is provided for the vindication of his rights under the Convention.

The *European Commission of Human Rights* is elected by the Committee of Ministers of the Council of Europe (although, once elected, Commissioners serve as independent officers, not as representatives from the State parties to the Convention). The Commission receives and investigates alleged breaches of the Convention, either at the request of one State party against another (art. 24), or at the petition of an individual against his own State (art. 25) – provided in the latter case that his State has recognized the right of individual petition (as the United Kingdom has done since 1966).[16] Individual petitions are numerically much the more important: very few cases have been considered so far by the Commission, as against thousands of individual petitions. If the Commission decides that a petition is admissible[17] the Commission inquires into it, attempting in the first instance to achieve a friendly settlement (art. 28). If that does not succeed the Commission reports to the State concerned and to the Committee of Ministers (art. 31); the Committee, by a two-thirds majority vote, may then decide whether there has been a breach and, if so, may refer the case to the European Court of Human Rights.

The *European Court of Human Rights* is composed of twenty-one judges sitting in Strasbourg. It can consider, in a bench of seven judges, a case

---

14 *Malone* v. *United Kingdom* (above).

15 See, *Brind* v. *Secretary of State for the Home Department* [1991] 1 All ER 720. There is, however, no corresponding presumption that, as a matter of English law, the courts would review the exercise of an administrative discretion on the basis that the discretion had to be exercised in conformity with the Convention: ibid. See also *Garland* v. *British Rail Engineering Ltd* [1983] 2 AC 751; *R.* v. *Secretary of State for the Home Department, ex p. Bhajan Singh* [1976] QB 198; *R.* v. *Secretary of State for the Home Department, ex p. Phansopkar* [1976] QB 606; *Derbyshire County Council* v. *Times Newspapers Ltd* [1993] 2 WLR 449.

16 It has been renewed for five-year periods.

17 The petitioner must first have exhausted local remedies, and his petition must be brought within six months of the final local decision (art. 26); manifestly ill-founded petitions and any which abuse the right of petition will be rejected (art. 27).

only if (*a*) the State involved has accepted the compulsory jurisdiction of the Court (art. 46)[18] or has consented to the court hearing the particular case (art. 47), and (*b*) the Commission or a State has referred it. An individual cannot, therefore, take his petition straight to the Court. The Court's decision is final, and it can award compensation to a successful petitioner (art. 50); although the Court has no coercive powers, the State parties undertake to abide by its rulings, the implementation of which is overseen by the Committee of Ministers. As a result of the increasing workload the Committee of Ministers decided in 1993 to merge the Commission and the Court into a single body.

The Commission has dealt with a number of individual petitions alleging that United Kingdom immigration law was in breach of the Convention. So, for instance, a number of East Africans who were refused permission to enter the United Kingdom petitioned on the ground that the law was degrading, interfered with family life and was discriminatory (thus violating arts 3, 8 and 14). The Commission agreed.[19] Many petitions against the United Kingdom have been withdrawn when the British Government has agreed to take action in particular cases, or to change the general law. The European Court of Human Rights had ruled against the United Kingdom in some fifty cases by 1997.[20] The first of those cases to be considered by the Court on an individual petition was *Golder* v. *United Kingdom*,[21] in which it was held that the refusal of legal advice to a prisoner who was contemplating a defamation action against a prison officer infringed the right of respect for private life and correspondence (art. 8), and the guarantee of a fair hearing (art. 6).[22] In *Campbell and Fell* v. *United Kingdom*,[23] the procedure of a prison board of visitors was also held to violate that latter right. In *Tyrer* v. *United Kingdom*[24] and in *Campbell and Cozans* v. *United Kingdom*[25] the Court held respectively that birching in the Isle of Man was a degrading punishment (contrary to art. 3), and that corporal punishment

18 The United Kingdom accepted it in 1966.
19 The Commission so reported to the Commission of Ministers. The UK allowed the petitioners to enter, thus ending the particular complaint.
20 See 564 HL Deb. *86–90* (written answers 5 June 1995). The first inter-State case was *Republic of Ireland* v. *United Kingdom* (1978) 2 EHRR 25, in which the UK admitted that certain interrogation techniques which had been used in Northern Ireland violated art. 3 – but they had been abandoned.
21 (1975) 1 EHRR 524.
22 A similar breach was found in *Silver* v. *United Kingdom* (1983) 5 EHRR 347.
23 (1985) 7 EHRR 165.
24 (1978) 2 EHRR 1.
25 (1982) 4 EHRR 293.

in Scottish schools infringed the right of parents to have their children educated according to their philosophical convictions (under art. 2 of the First Protocol). Legislation in Northern Ireland which penalized consenting adult homosexual conduct was held in *Dudgeon* v. *United Kingdom*[26] to infringe the individual's right to respect for his private life (art. 8). The law of contempt of court[27] was declared to be in breach of the guarantee of freedom of expression (contrary to art. 10) in *Sunday Times Ltd* v. *United Kingdom*.[28] The procedure for the recall of mentally ill patients who had been conditionally released was declared to contravene the right to liberty of the person (art. 5) in *X.* v. *United Kingdom*[29] and in *Young, James and Webster* v. *United Kingdom*[30] provisions of the Trade Union and Labour Relations Act 1974 were held to violate the worker's right not to join a trade union (contrary to art. 11). And in *Abdulaziz and Others* v. *United Kingdom*[31] a provision of United Kingdom immigration law was declared discriminatory as between the rights of wives and of husbands to join spouses lawfully settled in the United Kingdom.

As a consequence of all these cases the British Government was either able to inform the Court that the law complained of had already been changed, or that appropriate legislative or administrative action would be taken to comply with the Court's judgments. The effect of the European Convention must obviously be considered when legislation is being drafted, and that effect will have to be considered even more closely when the Convention becomes part of domestic law under the Human Rights Bill.

---

26 (1981) 4 EHRR 149.
27 As it had been declared in *Att.-Gen.* v *Times Newspapers Ltd* [1974] AC 273.
28 (1979) 2 EHRR 245. But the Obscene Publications Act 1959 was held to conform to the right of freedom of expression in *Handyside* v. *United Kingdom* (1976) 1 EHRR 737. Several British newspapers had been denied their right to freedom of expression when the Government obtained injunctions in the British courts to prevent them publishing extracts from the book *Spycatcher* after it had been published abroad: *Sunday Times* v. *United Kingdom*, 26 November 1991, ECHR.
29 (1981) 4 EHRR 188. The absence in the United Kingdom of judicial procedure to enable prisoners serving life sentences to challenge, at reasonable intervals, the continued lawfulness of their detention was held to be in violation of art. 5 in *Thynne, Wilson and Gunnell* v. *United Kingdom* (1991) 13 EHRR 666.
30 (1981) 4 EHRR 188.
31 (1981) 4 EHRR 38.

A NEW BILL OF RIGHTS?

The lack of a comprehensive and easily accessible statement of fundamental rights and freedoms enforceable in the United Kingdom, the delay and inconvenience of going to Strasbourg, reliance on the accidents of litigation to disclose enforceable Community rights, among other factors, has led to discussion since the 1970s of whether the United Kingdom should adopt a new bill of rights of her own.[32] In 1977 the Standing Advisory Commission on Human Rights in Northern Ireland recommended that a bill of rights for the whole United Kingdom would be the best way to protect rights in the province.[33] The Home Office had published a Green Paper in 1976.[34] A select committee of the House of Lords in 1978 considered the desirability and possible form of a bill of rights,[35] and recommended that (if one were to be adopted) the way forward would be to incorporate the European Convention into domestic law.[36] There have been a number of attempts by backbench peers and MPs to do just that,[37] one being the Human Rights Bill which narrowly failed to obtain a second reading in the House of Commons in 1987.[38] The Conservative Party does not believe that a new bill of rights is necessary or desirable; the Labour Party has now embraced the idea, which is also advocated by the Liberal Democrats.

There are various models to hand for a new bill of rights, ranging from (for example) an Act incorporating the European Convention into United Kingdom law, to a statute which declared certain rights and provided that they would prevail over *prior* inconsistent legislation, to one which would go further and entrench those against *subsequent* inconsistent attempts at legislation.[39] What is lacking is not a serviceable scheme, but any political consensus for its adoption. Some lawyers and others object to the greater

---

32 See Lord Scarman, *English Law – the New Dimension* (1974); M. Zander, *A Bill of Rights?* (3rd edn, 1985); P. T. Wallington and J. McBride, *Civil Liberties and a Bill of Rights* (1976); H. W. R. Wade, *Constitutional Fundamentals* (1980).

33 Cmnd 7009 (1977).

34 Legislation on Human Rights (1976).

35 HL 176 (1977–8).

36 On this, see J. Jaconelli, *Enacting a Bill of Rights: The Legal Problems* (1980), ch. 9.

37 The House of Lords approved bills sponsored by Lord Wade in 1981 and by Lord Scarman in 1985.

38 109 HC Deb. 1123–89 (6 February 1987). The House of Lords gave a second reading to a backbench peer's Human Rights Bill early in 1997: it lapsed on the dissolution of Parliament.

39 The latter is the least likely to be taken up because of doubts about its efficacy in the face of the orthodox doctrine of parliamentary sovereignty: see above, ch. 4.

power which a new bill could give to unaccountable judges to the detriment of Parliament.[40] Others believe that only a fully entrenched and comprehensive new bill would be worth the effort.[41] Some politicians are nervous that a bill of rights might hamper the implementation of their manifesto promises. And there would be general dissent, if a new bill were drafted from scratch, over some issues which are likely to remain of party political controversy – the electoral system, private medicine, trade union rights and so on. On purely pragmatic grounds there is a sound argument that, as the United Kingdom is a party to the European Convention, it would be better for the parties to disputes under it to have them resolved in the United Kingdom, saving delay, inconvenience, expense and the occasional condemnation of the Government of the day by a 'foreign' court. There would be drawbacks in such a course, for the Convention is over forty years old, is not comprehensive,[42] and because account might still have to be taken of the European Court's interpretation of it.[43]

The new Labour Government published the Human Rights Bill late in 1997. Under the Bill it would be unlawful for any public authority (a concept which is widely defined) to act in a way incompatible with Convention rights. A person aggrieved by such alleged unlawfulness would be able to challenge the public authority in the courts in this country, and at any appropriate level of court. In trying such litigation the courts would be bound to take account of relevant decisions of the European Court of Human Rights (but those decisions would not be binding on English courts). As far as interpretation is concerned, Acts and secondary legislation would have to be interpreted by the courts so far as possible so as to be compatible with the Convention, a requirement that would apply to future as well as to existing legislation. If a court found that a rule of statute law conflicted with Convention rights it would not have the power to strike it down, but it could issue a declaration of incompatibility. The Government and Parliament would thereby be placed under political pressure to alter the statute law. Legislation to be so amended could be changed by Order in Council, so that the usual delay in passing an ordinary Bill would be avoided. In future Ministers would be under a duty, in introducing any Bill into Parliament, to declare that its provisions were compatible with the Convention.

40 See, e.g., J. A. G. Griffith (1979) 42 *Mod. L. Rev.* 1.
41 See, e.g., Lord Scarman, op. cit.
42 See note 11, above.
43 See, however, Arnhill [1985] *Public Law* 378.

RACIAL DISCRIMINATION[44]

Britain has no laws which discriminate against persons on account of their race or colour. Jewish, Chinese and black people, for example, all enjoy the same voting rights: they must merely comply with the same rules about nationality and residence as everybody else. They are equally entitled to the facilities for education and to the benefit of social services. The law does not order segregation in public transport or anywhere else. In these respects Britain is free from the legal restraints which agitated the United States so much. In this limited sense, there is equality before the law.

An equally important practical question is the effectiveness with which the law takes positive steps to ensure that persons are not discriminated against on account of race or colour. To say that the law does not discriminate is one thing, but does the law compel persons not to discriminate, or otherwise protect those who are liable to be discriminated against?

It was to deal with this question that Parliament for the first time introduced legislative controls in the Race Relations Act 1965. That Act had limited application and was based on inadequate research, but experience of its operation was helpful in preparing the much more comprehensive Race Relations Act 1968 which replaced it.

The main emphasis of the 1965 Act was placed not on punishment but on rendering certain discriminatory practices unlawful and devising machinery to reduce friction and promote conciliation. The Act made it unlawful for the proprietors, managers or other employees of certain places of public resort – hotels, restaurants, cafés, public houses, theatres, cinemas, dance halls, sports grounds, swimming pools and other places of public entertainment or recreation – and public transport undertakings to practise discrimination on the ground of colour, race or ethnic or national origins against persons seeking to use these facilities. Complaints of discrimination were to be made to local conciliation committees of the Race Relations Board, a body of three members appointed by the Home Secretary; the Board was to make annual reports to be laid before Parliament. A committee would investigate the complaint and try to reach a settlement and obtain an assurance that discrimination would cease. If it was unsuccessful it would report to the Board; the Board was to report to the Attorney-General if it considered that a course of discriminatory conduct in contravention of the

44 See I. A. MacDonald, *Race Relations: the New Law* (1977); L. Lustgarten, *The Legal Control of Racial Discrimination* (1980).

Act was likely to continue, and the Attorney-General could then apply to the High Court or a county court for an injunction to restrain its continuance. Neither the committees nor the Board had any power to obtain information or subpoena witnesses, and no new civil remedy was given to a person aggrieved by discriminatory acts. Section 5 of the Act invalidated discriminatory restrictions on the disposal of tenancies other than in premises occupied by the owner or head tenant.

In 1967 there was published a penetrating critique of the Act with suggestions for legislative reform drawing on the experience of civil rights legislation in the United States and Canada.[45] The Race Relations Act 1968 (the enactment of which was doubtless accelerated by the bad impression created by the Commonwealth Immigrants Act 1968) gave effect to a number of these suggestions. The Act defined discrimination so as to include segregation and a single act of discrimination could be unlawful. The ambit of unlawful discrimination was extended to cover the provision to the public, or to a section of the public, of goods and facilities (including trading, banking, insurance, credit, education and professional services); employment, and trade unions and business associations; the provision of housing accommodation and business premises; and advertisements and other notices. A number of exceptions to the general rule were introduced for particular employment and housing situations.[46] The provisions of the Act were made generally applicable to the Crown and the police.[47]

The Act posed some difficult problems of interpretation. Discrimination on the grounds of a person's present nationality (as distinct from his 'national origins') was not contrary to the Act.[48] The House of Lords held that private social or political clubs with a genuinely selective membership did not discriminate unlawfully within the meaning of the Act by operating a colour or racial bar inasmuch as they were not providing facilities to 'the public or a section of the public'.[49]

The Act altered the procedure for investigation of complaints, strengthening the powers and enlarging the size of the Race Relations Board. Complaints might be made direct to the Board; the Board could also decide

45 Harry Street, Geoffrey Howe and Geoffrey Bindman, *Report on Discrimination Legislation* (1967).
46 ss. 1–9.
47 s. 27; subject to various exceptions – for example, the Crown was not placed under a duty to employ aliens on the same basis as British citizens (s. 27(9)(a)).
48 *Ealing LBC* v. *Race Relations Board* [1972] AC 342.
49 *Race Relations Board* v. *Charter* [1973] AC 868 (Indian excluded on racial grounds from local Conservative club).

to undertake an inquiry into suspected discrimination of its own motion, and it could appoint assessors to assist it. Conciliation and investigation procedures were spelt out, but were essentially informal, and the Board and area committees had no power to compel attendance or the production of information. Complaints about employment, unions and employers' associations were referred in the first instance to the Secretary of State for Employment; in certain circumstances the Board would carry out the investigation. The Act also provided for the establishment of a Community Relations Commission, an advisory, research, coordinating and promotional body.

Under the 1968 Act, the power to bring civil proceedings for an injunction to restrain a course of discriminatory conduct was transferred from the Attorney-General to the Race Relations Board. The Board might also be awarded a declaration that a discriminatory act was unlawful and special damages and damages for loss of opportunity (but not damages for humiliation and distress) on behalf of a person damnified by such an act (sections 19–22). Courts, moreover, were expressly empowered (section 23) to revise the terms of contracts in such proceedings so as to bring them into conformity with the Act. The county courts in which these proceedings were brought were specially designated by the Lord Chancellor, and the judge had to be assisted by two expert assessors.

The 1968 Act was replaced in its turn by the Race Relations Act 1976. This Act has two aims, to harmonize with the machinery for sex discrimination put into operation in 1976 (and examined below) and to make good some of the defects revealed in the 1968 Act. The Act abolished both the Race Relations Board and the Community Relations Commission, and one body alone, the Commission for Racial Equality, administers the Act. The Commission consists of a chairman and not more than fourteen members appointed by the Home Secretary; the various ethnic minorities are substantially represented in its composition.

A person discriminates if on racial grounds he treats another less favourably than he treats or would treat other persons. The 'racial grounds' are extended so as to include nationality and citizenship.[50] A new provision makes it unlawful to apply a requirement or condition which (irrespective of motive) is such that the proportion of persons of a particular colour, race, nationality

---

50 Reversing *Ealing LBC* v. *Race Relations Board*, above. In *Mandla* v. *Dowell Lee* [1983] 2 AC 584, the House of Lords held that Sikhs were a 'racial group' within s. 3(1) of the 1976 Act, and in *Commission for Racial Equality* v. *Dutton* [1989] 1 All ER 306 gipsies were also held to be a racial group.

or ethnic or natural origins able to comply with it is considerably smaller than the proportion of other persons able to do so, and which is not justifiable on racial grounds. The ambit of the Act is substantially the same as before, but certain anomalies are removed. Where principals engage somebody personally to execute labour or work, or where a firm of six or more partners offers new partnerships, the Act applies. Bodies which confer authorization to engage in a particular trade or profession are covered. Clubs with twenty-five or more members are affected.[51] Advertisements for jobs outside the UK are brought within its scope.

It is the aggrieved individual, not the Commission, who instigates a complaint of discrimination. The Commission will, on application, be able to give assistance to a claimant or potential claimant where the case raises an issue of principle or it is unreasonable, for instance, by reason of the case's complexity, or the respective positions of the parties to the dispute, to expect the claimant to proceed on his own behalf. 'Assistance' includes advice, conciliation, arranging for legal advice and assistance, and representation.

If the alleged discrimination is in the field of employment, the aggrieved person complains to an industrial tribunal. The complainant has the burden of proving discrimination before the tribunal. If he wins, the tribunal may declare his right, or award compensation, or recommend that the employer take action to obviate or reduce the adverse effect on the complainant of the act of discrimination.

Complaints regarding bodies over which the Secretary of State for Education and Employment exercises powers are first made to him, and he has two months in which to act. Subject to that, all complaints regarding education, housing and the provision of goods, facilities and services are made to county courts. The complainant has the burden of proving discrimination. If he succeeds the court has power to award damages (including damages for injured feelings) and to grant an injunction restraining the defendant from discriminating unlawfully against the plaintiff.

Complaints about discriminatory advertisements are handled by the Commission, which can if necessary institute proceedings in the county court, seeking an injunction. One of its main functions is to conduct investigations into discriminatory practices. It has powers to require the furnishing of information and the production of documents; it can seek an order in the county court ordering anyone who refuses to produce the

---

51 Reversing *Race Relations Board* v. *Dockers' Labour Club and Institute Ltd* [1976] AC 285.

information. If its investigation (after hearing the person investigated) reveals discrimination it may issue a non-discrimination notice requiring him to cease, but an appeal lies to the county court or industrial tribunal, as the case may be. It is empowered to ensure that in the subsequent five years the notice is complied with, and if necessary, to apply to the county court (in the field of employment) for an injunction. It collects information about all individual complaints and monitors the legislation generally.

Much in the 1976 Act is an improvement on the earlier Acts. Particularly welcome is the power of the Commission to enforce production of documents. For the first time the Commission is able to uncover any widespread discriminatory practices and secure their cessation. The power of the courts to grant injunctions restraining discriminatory activities is also important. What causes most disquiet in this Act is the imposition on the aggrieved of the task of pursuing his complaint, without legal aid, before an industrial tribunal. There has always been difficulty about overcoming the fear of an aggrieved person to report discrimination. In the past he has known that the case would be handled for him at every stage by the central body; all he had to do was to report his complaint. Some unlawful discrimination must now go unchecked because timid, harassed, ignorant or poor victims will not take cases themselves.

Nobody should believe that law alone can create racial harmony; yet without legal sanctions, the prospects are much worse. This Act creates the legislative framework for better race relations in all those areas of potential conflict.

The 1976 Act also extended the scope of the criminal law. Succumbing to pressure consequent on incidents at Fascist meetings, the Government in the Race Relations Act 1965 made it a crime for a person to publish or distribute threatening, abusive or insulting words, if the matter or words were likely to stir up hatred against any section of the public in Great Britain on grounds of colour, race or ethnic or national origins, or citizenship. There was disquiet when this new crime was introduced in 1965 especially because the content made the publication criminal even though no public disorder resulted. The offence under section 70 of the 1976 Act was wider in that it was no longer necessary to prove an intention to stir up hatred. The Public Order Act 1986, Part III, now provides for these offences (see p. 472).

SEX DISCRIMINATION

Not until 1976 had Britain any laws in force designed to counter sex discrimination. Now there are two interrelated Acts, the Equal Pay Act 1970 and the Sex Discrimination Act 1975, which became operative simultaneously.

The Equal Pay Act provides that women are to have equal pay in three circumstances. The first is when they are doing 'like' work. If the jobs are not identical, but the differences in job content are not significant or, though significant, do not recur frequently (for example, a man would lift heavy weights once a month), then it is 'like work'. The second is where an official job evaluation study has been made and this rates the work as equivalent to men's work. The third case is where a collective bargaining agreement has been made between employer and trade union which provides different rates for men and women.

A woman who believes that she is not getting equal pay has to make a claim to an industrial tribunal. She will have to satisfy the tribunal that her work is the same as or similar to a man's. Once she proves that, the onus is then on the employer to prove that there are material differences between the man's situation and the woman's other than sex, which constitute a genuine reason for the difference in the treatment awarded them: an obvious example of a material difference would be where the woman worked day shifts, but the man worked regular night shifts. If the woman wins she is awarded compensation which may include up to two years' arrears of pay. In 1982 the European Court of Justice held that the United Kingdom had failed to apply the principle of equal pay for work of equal value for which no system of job classification existed.[52] Changes were then made in English law.[53]

The Act applies not only to basic pay but to other matters in a woman's contract of employment. It therefore may extend also to overtime pay, bonus payments, sick pay schemes, health insurance, holiday pay, and length of holidays, luncheon vouchers, other fringe benefits and rest periods provided for in her contract. A successful claimant will be also awarded the appropriate cash damages to compensate her for having been deprived of any such benefit. The House of Lords has held that a woman cook at

[52] *European Commission* v. *UK* (1982) 3 CMLR 284.
[53] Equal Pay (Amendment) Regulations 1983. And see Townshend-Smith (1984) 47 *Mod. L. Rev.* 201. See generally D. Pannick, *Sex Discrimination Law* (1985).

Cammell Laird Shipbuilders was entitled to the same pay as a carpenter, or a joiner, or a thermal insulation engineer, employed by the company, because she did work of equal value to them.[54]

The Sex Discrimination Act 1975 covers much more ground than the Equal Pay Act. Like the Equal Pay Act it applies to employment, but if the complaint is about money under a contract of employment, the Equal Pay Act governs the matter. Its concern on employment is with every aspect of an employer's relations with his workers. It may be his recruiting policy (say advertising only for boy school-leavers), his advertisements for vacancies, arrangements for interviewing, training methods, selection for promotion or transfer, lay-offs, redundancy or dismissal. Complaints about matters other than money, such as company cars or cheap loans, fall within either Act. Trade unions and employment agencies are also within the net of the 1975 Act. A printing union operating where there is a closed shop cannot keep a male preserve by barring women from the union. The Sex Discrimination Act 1975, section 6(3), exempted from its provisions private households and businesses employing not more than five workers. That exemption was held to be contrary to European Community law,[55] and the Sex Discrimination Act 1986 was passed to repeal it and to exempt employment where work is done in a private house involving a degree of contact which might reasonably involve an objection by a worker of a particular sex.[56]

As the title of the Act indicates, its concern is discrimination. This it defines under four heads: treating a woman less favourably than a man on account of sex; conversely treating a man less favourably than a woman (maternity excepted); treating a married person less favourably, on grounds of marriage, than a single person; and fourthly, victimization because someone has invoked either of the Acts. Indirect discrimination is also outlawed when tests are applied which appear neutral but place one sex (or married people) at a disadvantage; for example, stipulating that all clerks must be at least 5 ft 8 in. tall. Complaints about discrimination in employment and training are made to an industrial tribunal which may award compensation.

The 1975 Act also affects education. It is unlawful for those responsible for an educational establishment – other than single-sex institutions – (including school governors and university governing bodies) to discrimi-

---

54 *Hayward* v. *Cammell Laird Shipbuilders Ltd* [1988] 2 All ER 257.
55 *Commission* v. *United Kingdom* [1984] 1 All ER 353.
56 See 1986 Act, s. 1.

nate on grounds of sex in admissions policy – no medical school can lawfully operate a quota system for girls – or require higher A-levels from them, or in the benefits and facilities offered. A local education authority may not provide worse science laboratories in its girls' schools than in its boys' schools. Other matters where sex discrimination is outlawed include: the provision to the public of goods, facilities or services, including facilities offered by building societies, insurance companies, banks, credit institutions and loan companies; restaurants, public houses and places of entertainment;[57] local authorities and transport authorities. The disposal of residential or business premises is affected. These changes in the law affect many common business practices, such as making the husband sign a consumer credit contract when the wife, who has a good job of her own, is buying the article, or the building society that looks askance at women borrowers. Pubs are not allowed all-male bars; hotel cocktail bars cannot deny admission to unaccompanied women. Local authorities cannot throw out of her council flat the separated wife who can pay the rent. Complaints may be made to the county court.

Another innovation of this Act is the establishment of the Equal Opportunities Commission. This has power to conduct formal investigations into any person it believes to be discriminating unlawfully. It may compel him to give evidence or to produce documents. It may apply to court for an injunction, disobedience to which would be a contempt of court in various circumstances. It may have served a non-discrimination notice against someone it is satisfied is discriminating, and who has not successfully appealed against it; within five years it may seek an injunction to prevent his continuing to discriminate. It may also do so against someone whom an individual has successfully sued for discrimination.

It may itself sue an individual and seek an injunction if his unlawful discrimination is proved. If someone publishes an advertisement which indicates an intention to discriminate unlawfully, it may seek to prevent him by obtaining an injunction. In effect the Commission is expected to see that the law is complied with, even though individual victims do not themselves choose to seek its protection. Had the Act merely left it to aggrieved individuals to sue, its impact might have been negligible. The Commission has the chance to unearth sex discrimination in all the areas

---

57 A local council which provided free swimming facilities for people of pensionable age was guilty of unlawful discrimination in charging a man (aged 61) an entrance fee when his wife (also aged 61) was admitted free: *James* v. *Eastleigh Borough Council* [1990] 2 All ER 607.

covered by the Act, not only employment, to investigate where it has
suspicions and to confront offenders with the prospect of imprisonment
for defying a court order to desist from discriminatory practices.

The Employment Act 1989 was passed to meet the requirements of the
Equal Treatment Directive.[58] Sections 1 to 6 of the Act are designed to
amend or repeal most legislation that discriminates between men and
women in employment and vocational training. Discriminatory requirements in pre-1975 legislation which had been left in place by the 1975 Act
are now subject to that Act.[59] But there are a number of circumstances
where statutory requirements which discriminate between the sexes are
still lawful: thus, for example, pre-1975 discriminatory requirements in
fields other than employment and vocational training are preserved, as also
are provisions which protect women in respect of pregnancy, maternity or
other circumstances giving rise to risks specifically affecting women.[60]

58 Directive 76/207/EEC.
59 1989 Act, s. 1.
60 1989 Act, ss. 3, 4. Specified educational establishments are also allowed to discriminate
when making certain appointments: s. 5 declares such practices to be lawful in the case,
e.g. of Oxford and Cambridge women's colleges, and religious schools.

CHAPTER 20

Citizens, Aliens and Others

BACKGROUND

The concept of a British subject at common law was rooted in the idea of allegiance, the bond which linked a man with his feudal lord. In return for allegiance a man was entitled to his lord's protection. Persons born within His Majesty's dominions owed the King natural allegiance and were his subjects.[1] Aliens within those dominions owed a temporary local allegiance. No one could divest himself of his natural allegiance; and violation of the duty of allegiance might constitute treason.

The common law has been greatly altered by a series of statutes. Until 1983 the principal statute was the British Nationality Act 1948. That Act was part of a complex arrangement between the independent Commonwealth countries whereby each was to have its own nationality laws but would recognize as British subjects nationals of other Member States. The British Government chose the United Kingdom and Colonies as the composite unit of citizenship whose members became British subjects.

A rapid rise in the influx of British subjects from the West Indies, Pakistan and India led to the passing of the Commonwealth Immigrants Act 1962 which imposed for the first time restrictions on the freedom of Commonwealth citizens to migrate to the United Kingdom. Other statutory restrictions followed, until in 1971 the Immigration Act superseded these Acts by a detailed control of immigration and deportation of aliens as well as of Commonwealth citizens. The consequence was that citizenship under the 1948 Act no longer clearly indicated who was free to settle in the United Kingdom. The British Nationality Act 1981 (which came into force in 1983) was intended to create a closer relationship between citizenship and

---

1 *Calvin*'s case (1607) 7 Co. Rep. 1a (Scotsman born after the union of the Crowns was not an alien in England).

the right to enter the United Kingdom.[2] It created three main forms of status: British citizenship, British Dependent Territories citizenship and British Overseas citizenship.

Anyone who at the end of 1982 was a citizen of the United Kingdom and Colonies and had the right of abode in the United Kingdom under the Immigration Act 1971 became a British citizen. A person had the right of abode if (a) he were born, adopted, naturalized or registered in the United Kingdom or the Islands (the Channel Islands and the Isle of Man); or (b) his parent had that citizenship at the time of birth or adoption, provided that the parent had either acquired citizenship in the United Kingdom or the Islands or been born to or adopted by a citizen parent (that is, our citizen's grandparent) who at that time had citizenship acquired in the United Kingdom or the Islands; or (c) settled at any time in the United Kingdom and Islands and had been ordinarily resident there as a citizen for the last five years or more; or if (d) though not a citizen of the United Kingdom and Colonies, was a Commonwealth citizen born to or adopted by a parent who had that citizenship of the United Kingdom and Colonies by birth in the United Kingdom or Islands; or if (e) being married to someone having the above right of abode, had obtained registration as a citizen.

From 1983 birth in the United Kingdom ceased to be a sufficient qualification. If either parent at the time of the birth is either a British citizen or ordinarily resident in the United Kingdom, British citizenship is acquired. Others born in the United Kingdom are entitled to be registered if they have spent the first ten years of their life here, or if a parent subsequently becomes a citizen or ordinarily resident here while the child is still a minor. A child adopted through a United Kingdom court order becomes a British citizen if an adopter is a British citizen.

A child born abroad to parents either of whom is a British citizen other than by descent will be a British citizen by descent. If a parent is a British citizen (even by descent) serving overseas in Crown or European Community service, the child born abroad is also a British citizen.

There are complex rules about obtaining British citizenship by registration. Certain classes of minor may seek registration.[3] At his discretion the Home Secretary may naturalize certain categories of applicant intending

2 What follows is a general summary of the law regarding nationality and immigration. The rules are hedged about with exceptions and qualifications. It is impossible to include these in this brief account. For a more detailed review see Blake (1982) 45 *Mod. L. Rev.* 179; White and Hampson [1982] *Public Law* 6.
3 See British Nationality Act 1981, ss. 3, 4, 5 and 7.

to make their principal home here and whom he is satisfied to be of good character and to have a good knowledge of the English language. They include those with five years' residence in the United Kingdom or those married to British citizens.[4] There is no appeal against his refusal. The Home Secretary can deprive a naturalized or registered citizen of his citizenship if he is satisfied that the registration or certificate of naturalization was obtained by means of fraud, false representation or the concealment of any material facts.[5] He also has power to deprive on grounds of disaffection, assisting the enemy in wartime, and of certain terms of imprisonment.[6] He must be satisfied that it is not conducive to the public good that he remain a British citizen.[7]

The second category of citizenship is that of British Dependent Territories citizenship. It is, in essence, a colonial citizenship and carries no right of entry into the United Kingdom. If a citizen of the United Kingdom and Colonies acquired that citizenship through his own connection with the dependent territory (by birth, naturalization or registration) he qualifies. This applies to people in Hong Kong in particular, of whom some 3.25 million are British Dependent Territories citizens. Following the agreement to retrocede Hong Kong to China in 1997,[8] provision was made[9] to allow such citizens in Hong Kong to acquire a new status of British National (Overseas), and for their current status to end in 1997. Many Falkland Islanders were also British Dependent Territories citizens, but in the wake of the Argentinian invasion the British Nationality (Falkland Islands) Act 1983 was passed: it conferred British citizenship on Falkland Islanders born before 1 January 1983. People born in the Islands after that date acquire their citizenship status through the provisions of the British Nationality Act 1981. And Gibraltarians who have British Dependent Territories citizenship and who are nationals of the United Kingdom for the purpose of European Union treaties may register as British citizens.[10]

---

4 ibid., ss. 4, 44, and sched. 1.
5 ibid., s. 40(1).
6 ibid., s. 40(3).
7 ibid., s. 40(5). For the right to have the matter referred to a committee of inquiry, see s. 40(7). See R. v. *Secretary of State for the Home Department, ex P. Akhtar* [1981] QB 46.
8 See the Joint Declaration made between China and the United Kingdom.
9 SI 1986, No. 948, made under the Hong Kong Act 1985: see Cmnd 9637 (1985); 89 HC Deb. 1270–306 (16 January 1986); 97 HC Deb. 655–78 (13 May 1986). Up to 50,000 Hong Kong people could have been registered as British citizens before 1997 by the Secretary of State on the recommendation of the Governor of Hong Kong. See note 11.
10 British Nationality Act 1981, s. 5.

British Overseas citizenship is a residual and transitional status acquired from 1983 by all citizens of the United Kingdom and Colonies who have not become British or British Dependent Territories citizens. The largest groups are living in Malaysia, India and East Africa and may number about 1.5 million. Every person who under the 1981 Act is a British citizen, a British Dependent Territories citizen or a British Overseas citizen has the status of a Commonwealth citizen.[11]

THE IMMIGRATION ACT 1971[12]

The Immigration Act 1971 (as amended by the British Nationality Act 1981),[13] together with statutory instruments made in pursuance of it, and supplemented by detailed Immigration Rules,[14] now regulates immigration and deportation.

The critical issue now is whether a person has a right of abode for the purpose of the 1971 Act. All British citizens have that right.[15] In addition Commonwealth citizens who before the 1981 Act had a right of abode retain a right of abode for their lifetime.[16] The latter group, when seeking to enter, have to prove their right of abode by a certificate of entitlement.[17] Little special significance is attributed to the holding of a United Kingdom passport.[18] British citizens are free from immigration control. Citizens of

---

11 Section 37(1). To avoid a British Dependent Territories citizen, or a British Overseas citizen, becoming stateless on the retrocession of Hong Kong to China, the British Nationality (Hong Kong) Acts 1990 and 1997 permit a Hong Kong resident who qualifies under the 1997 Act to be registered as a British citizen.

12 See I. A. MacDonald, *Immigration Law and Practice in the United Kingdom* (3rd edn, 1991); A. Dummett and A. Nicol, *Subjects, Citizens, Aliens and Others* (1990); D. Jackson, *Immigration: Law and Practice* (1996).

13 Section 39 and sched. 4.

14 Statement of Changes in Immigration Rules, HC 169 (1982–3); HC 503 (1984–5).

15 Immigration Act 1971, s. 2(1) as amended by s. 39(2) of the 1981 Act.

16 ibid.

17 Section 2(3) and s. 3(9) of the 1971 Act as amended by s. 39(2) of the 1981 Act.

18 Except that citizens holding UK passports not endorsed to the effect that the holder is subject to immigration control are admitted without proof of patriality, and should be admitted (even though their passports are so endorsed) if they hold a special voucher or entry certificate. See also SI 1972, No. 1613, r. 5.

However, the United Kingdom Government's responsibility under the European Convention on Human Rights for indignities caused to United Kingdom passport holders who are refused entry is not excluded merely by designating them as 'non-patrial'. Under the European Convention the European Commission on Human Rights in 1974 reported to the Committee of Ministers that, in relation to twenty-five East African Asian citizens the Republic of Ireland and other European Union nationals also have rights to enter and settle in the United Kingdom which Commonwealth citizens without a right of abode lack.[19]

Three special comments ought to be made at this point about those other than European Union nationals who have no right of abode. First, those who were already settled in this country on 1 January 1973 (that is, being ordinarily resident here without any time limit imposed by immigration legislation: see Immigration Act 1971, sections 2(3)(*d*), 8(5), 33) are regarded as having been given indefinite leave to enter and remain here (section 1(2)); and although this does not in itself exempt them from liability to deportation, they may become exempt after five years' residence here, provided that they are Commonwealth or Irish citizens (section 7). Secondly, the immigration rules must not render a Commonwealth citizen or his wife or children any less free to come and go than before the Act (section 1(5)). Thirdly, Commonwealth citizens with a *grandparent* born here (but not qualifying for the right of abode) are allowed under the immigration rules to enter without a work permit to seek work here, provided that they have an entry clearance,[20] though they remain liable to deportation. This concession, which benefits several million Commonwealth citizens, placated Conservative critics who objected to the preference given by the former draft rules to European Union nationals over citizens of the old Commonwealth countries.

A prospective immigrant who is not a British citizen, whether he be a Commonwealth citizen or an alien, is refused entry to take up employment unless he can produce a work permit[21] and permits are issued by the Department of Education and Employment for a specific post for a limited period (normally not more than twelve months[22] in the first instance) with a particular employer. The period for which a work permit will be extended

---

of the UK and Colonies whom the UK had refused to admit for settlement in the UK, the UK Government had violated art. 3 of the Convention relating to degrading treatment. A lengthy extract from the report is set out in HC 434 (1979–80), First Report from the Home Affairs Committee, Appendix 2. The Committee of Ministers took no action on the report; Appendix 3.

19 It is a criminal offence for the owner of a ship or aircraft, or a carrier, to allow any person who requires leave to enter the UK to arrive in the UK without any necessary passport and visa: Immigration (Carriers' Liability) Act 1987.

20 HC 169 (1982–3), § 29. Entry clearances are obtainable through the appropriate UK representative in the country concerned (§ 11).

21 HC 169, § 115.

22 HC 169, § 116.

is normally three years.[23] Work permits are not needed for certain specialized forms of employment. There are rules[24] for sea and air crews, visitors, returning residents, students, au pairs, businessmen and self-employed persons, writers and artists, young Commonwealth citizens coming for working holidays, fiancés, fiancées and family dependants.[25] A very wide range of entry conditions may be imposed. Visitors from Ghana, Nigeria, Bangladesh, India and Pakistan must have a visa issued by the British High Commission in those countries before they will be allowed to enter the United Kingdom.[26] Since 1988 people of independent means, writers and artists, businessmen and the self-employed may obtain leave to enter and remain for one year, and au pairs for up to two years; the maximum period for a visit has been reduced to six months.[27] Persons with diplomatic or similar status are exempt from control.[28]

Political asylum should be granted, under the immigration rules, to a person seeking entry if the only country to which he could be removed is one to which he is unwilling to go owing to a well-founded fear of persecution for reasons of race, religion, nationality, membership of a particular social group or political opinion.[29] The decision is made by the Home Office but leave to enter will not be refused if removal would be contrary to the provisions of the Convention and Protocol relating to the Status of Refugees.[30]

In respect of persons seeking to come here for *settlement*, the rules contain very complicated and detailed provisions.[31] Two sets of exceptions to these immigration controls are of major importance.

23 ibid.
24 See generally HC 169 (1982–3). Under HC 208 (1987–8), visitors may stay for a maximum of six months, and businessmen and the self-employed for up to one year (and they may then apply for an extension of a further three years).
25 The wives (and children) of male Commonwealth citizens who were settled in the UK before 1973 no longer have an unqualified right to join their husbands (and fathers): Immigration Act 1988, s. 1.
26 Statement of Changes to Immigration Rules, Cmnd 9914 (1986).
27 Statement of Changes to Immigration Rules, HC 208 (1987–8).
28 1971 Act, s. 8 (2), (3); SI 1972, No. 1613, and SI 1977, No. 693.
29 HC 169, §§ 65 and 73. See *R.* v. *Secretary of State for the Home Department, ex p. Bugdaycay* [1987] 2 AC 514.
30 Asylum and Immigration Appeals Act 1993. See also the Asylum and Immigration Act 1996.
31 HC 169. A British Overseas citizen coming here for this purpose needs a special voucher or corresponding entry certificate issued to him by a British Government representative overseas (HC 169, § 45); there is no express corresponding provision for aliens. The issue of vouchers is rigorously controlled.

(a) *Citizens of the Republic of Ireland.* Citizens of the Republic of Ireland are not aliens in United Kingdom law.[32] Immigration controls have not been applied to them except under emergency conditions in Northern Ireland. The British Islands and the Republic of Ireland now form a Common Travel Area, and *bona fide* local journeys within that area by persons already resident there are not restricted by immigration requirements.[33] However, it is open to the Home Secretary to refuse entry to an Irish citizen if he deems it conducive to the public good in the interests of national security, or if that citizen has already been refused leave to enter, and it is possible under the 1971 Act for him to exclude the Republic from the Common Travel Area.[34] Under the Prevention of Terrorism (Temporary Provisions) Act 1989 the Home Secretary may exclude from the UK anyone (including Irish citizens but excepting one who has been ordinarily resident throughout the last three years) if it appears to him that he is or has been concerned in the commission, preparation or instigation of acts of terrorism,[35] and many Irish citizens have been so excluded.

(b) *European Union Nationals.* The immigration rules, purporting to implement European Union obligations,[36] provide that when a European Union national (other than an Irish citizen) is given leave to enter, no condition may be imposed restricting his employment or occupation in the United Kingdom.[37] Prospective workers, businessmen and self-employed persons are admitted without a work permit or other prior consent,[38] and the rights of their dependants to accompany or join them are appreciably wider than those with respect to others who are not British citizens.[39] In Community law, restrictions of freedom of migration of European Union nationals can be imposed by Member States only for reasons of public security, public health and certain facets of the public interest.[40]

---

32 British Nationality Act 1981, s. 50(1).
33 Immigration Act 1971, ss. 1(3), 9; sched. 4; SI 1972, No. 1610.
34 1971 Act, s. 9(4), (6).
35 1989 Act, s. 7.
36 For which see EEC Treaty, arts. 3(c), 48–58 and regulations and directives issued thereunder.
37 HC 169, § 67.
38 Admission of European Union nationals for employment will normally be for six months. If they establish themselves they will normally be given a residence permit for five years. See generally HC 169 § 70, 140–46.
39 HC 169 (1982–3), § 68.
40 And see HC 169, § 69.

STATUS WITHIN THE UNITED KINGDOM OF THOSE
HAVING NO RIGHT OF ABODE

(a) *Commonwealth citizens*. They are liable to deportation for breach of entry conditions (for example, overstaying their period of entry or taking up a different job without leave) and on other grounds, though there is no formal restriction of movement within the country and they are not required to register with the police. Nevertheless, given the type of condition that is imposed on them, they suffer a substantial curtailment of their civil liberties.

(b) *Citizens of the Republic of Ireland*. Although not British citizens, they are entitled to exercise the franchise and be elected to public office; and rules of law applicable to British subjects before the British Nationality Act 1948 still apply to them unless subsequently excluded.[41] They are, however, liable to deportation, and it is an offence to re-enter the United Kingdom while subject to a deportation order; though given the absence of effective immigration controls this is not exactly a rigorous sanction.

(c) *Aliens (other than European Union nationals)*. In order to enter the country at all, an alien must normally have an acceptable national passport or travel document, and in some cases he needs a visa or other entry clearance.[42] If he is given limited leave to enter, he may be subject to a condition requiring him to register with the police, and if he is granted an extension enabling him to remain longer than six months such a condition will then normally be imposed.[43]

Aliens cannot exercise the franchise, sit in either House of Parliament or hold any office under the Crown within the United Kingdom unless the responsible Minister certifies either that suitably qualified British citizens are not available for such a post or that the alien has exceptional qualifications.[44] Nor, in general, may they hold other public office.[45] Aliens are subject to a limited range of other occupational, professional and proprietary

---

41 On the last point, see British Nationality Act 1948, s. 3(2); Ireland Act 1949, s. 3(1). See also note 32, above.
42 HC 169 (1982–3).
43 HC 169, § 74.
44 Aliens Employment Act 1955, s. 1.
45 Act of Settlement 1701, s. 3.

disabilities. Certain classes of aliens (members of visiting forces[46] and persons enjoying diplomatic and other privileges)[47] enjoy immunities from the operation of various rules of United Kingdom law and in some instances are exempt from amenability to the jurisdiction of the courts.

An 'enemy alien', in the sense of a citizen of a country with which Her Majesty is in a state of war, is liable to internment or expulsion under the prerogative;[48] but if he is registered and allowed to remain within this country[49] he has an implied licence from the Crown to take legal proceedings for the protection of his interests. The term 'enemy alien' may alternatively refer to a person or company carrying on business in an enemy country. Such a person or corporation need not be an enemy alien in the first sense of the term, or indeed an alien at all. But an alien in this second sense cannot sue in British courts, though if sued he can defend an action and lodge an appeal.[50] His property within the realm can be confiscated and handed over to a Custodian of Enemy Property.

(d) *European Union nationals.* Their rights to enter and remain in this country, surpassing those citizens without right of abode, have already been noted. Within this country the general rule is that they cannot be discriminated against by reason of their non-citizen status except in relation to employment in the public service: a European Union national may become a civil servant, except in a specified 'central core'.[51]

DEPORTATION

Not until the passing of the Commonwealth Immigrants Act 1962 were Commonwealth citizens subject to deportation, although the Home Secretary already had that power in respect of aliens by virtue of the Aliens Order 1953. The Immigration Act 1971, as amended by the British Nationality Act 1981, now regulates the deportation of all who are not British citizens.

Apart from those Commonwealth citizens (and Irish citizens) who were

---

46 Visiting Forces Act 1952; p. 224.
47 See p. 150.
48 See p. 151. A state of war for this purpose does not appear to cover a mere state of armed conflict in the absence of a prerogative declaration.
49 At large or as an internee, but not as a combatant.
50 *Porter* v. *Freudenberg* [1915] 1 KB 857.
51 European Communities (Employment in the Civil Service) Order 1991, SI 1991, No. 1221 (made under EEC Treaty, art. 48).

ordinarily resident in the United Kingdom on 1 January 1973,[52] and special groups like diplomats and their households and consuls, anyone who is not a British citizen is now subject to deportation if (i) the Home Secretary deems it to be 'conducive to the public good' or (ii) the person is over seventeen and recommended for deportation by a court on conviction for an offence punishable with imprisonment, and the recommendation is accepted by the Home Secretary,[53] or (iii) he breaks entry conditions or overstays his permitted period of entry or (iv) he or she is the infant child or wife of a person against whom a deportation order is made.[54] Grounds (i) and (iv) were new for Commonwealth and Irish citizens. Deportation of the family with their head is not automatic; they may be allowed to stay on compassionate grounds.[55] A person liable to deportation as a 'family deportee', or as a result of a recommendation of a court, may be given financial assistance to leave instead of being deported.[56]

The deportation provisions of the 1971 Act do not exclude European Union nationals from their application. On reference from the UK the European Court has held that deportation on the ground of a criminal conviction is justified only if there is a genuine and serious threat to a fundamental interest of society going beyond the disturbance of the social order which every crime inevitably involves.[57] A European Union directive

---

52 Who, if at all times ordinarily resident here since then, cannot be deported on grounds of 'public good', and if ordinarily resident here for the last five years, cannot be deported at all (Immigration Act 1971, s. 7), unless they are in UK unlawfully: see R. v. Pentonville Prison Governor, ex p. Azam [1974] AC 18.

53 For the factors which the Home Secretary considers, see Immigration Rules HC 169 (1982–3) § 150. In R. v. Nazari [1980] 1 WLR 1366 the Court of Appeal laid down the guidelines for courts when making recommendations for deportation. The court should give reasons for its recommendation: R. v. Home Secretary, ex p. Santillo [1981] QB 778. In R. v. Home Secretary, ex p. Dannenberg [1984] QB 766, the Court of Appeal quashed a deportation order for an EC citizen on the ground that the court gave no reason for its recommendation.

54 1971 Act, ss. 3(5), (6), 5, 6: sched. 3. See R. v. Secretary of State for the Home Department, ex p. Khawaja [1984] AC 74; R. v. Secretary of State for the Home Department, ex p. Cheblak [1991] 2 All ER 319 (courts will only review Home Secretary's statement that deportation is necessary on national security grounds if there is evidence of bad faith or excess of statutory powers); R. v. Immigration Appeal Tribunal, ex p. Patel, the Independent, 5 May 1988 (deportation is conducive to the public good both where a person has obtained entry by deception, and where, having entered lawfully, a person obtains leave to stay by deception).

55 H.C. 169 §§ 160–64.

56 1971 Act, s. 5(6). Financial contributions may also be made to assist non-British citizens wishing to leave this country to live permanently elsewhere (s. 29).

57 R. v. Bouchereau [1978] QB 732, where the magistrate decided that possessing a small quantity of drugs did not justify deportation.

provides that deportation must be exclusively on the ground of the individual's personal conduct whereas the Act allows for deportation because another member of his family has been ordered to be deported.[58]

APPEALS

The appellate system laid down by the Immigration Act 1971 is too complex to describe in detail but some features are of constitutional interest.

The normal channel of appeal from the decision of an immigration officer is to an adjudicator, and thence with leave to the independent Immigration Appeal Tribunal.[59] An appeal against a decision given in conformity with the immigration rules must be dismissed, except in so far as there is a disputed question of fact; but except where otherwise stated, the adjudicating body may review the exercise of a discretion by an immigration officer or the Secretary of State himself.[60]

In brief, appeals lie[61] to an adjudicator against (a) exclusion from the United Kingdom (by refusal of entry or an entry clearance), but not while the appellant is in the UK unless (in certain circumstances) he is refused leave at the port of entry; (b) variation of or refusal to vary the conditions of entry (for example, duration of stay or location or type of employment); (c) deportation orders (other than orders made in pursuance of a recommendation by a court after a conviction), and refusals to revoke a deportation order already in force (provided that the appellant is out of the country), but the appeal lies to the Appeal Tribunal and not to an adjudicator if the deportation order was made on grounds of 'public good' or if the appellants are 'family deportees'; (d) directions for removal, including objections to being removed to a particular country or territory. Small disbursements have been made out of public funds (section 23) to enable the Immigrants Advisory Service, a voluntary body, to assist immigrant appellants. If on an appeal it is alleged that an entry document is a forgery, and that disclosure of the method of its detection would be contrary to the public interest, the investigation of that allegation takes places in the absence of the appellant and his representative (section 22(4)). A person who appeals against refusal

---

58 Directive 64/221 and *R* v. *Bouchereau*, above. Section 3(5) of the Immigration Act 1971.
59 For the procedural rules, see SI 1972, No. 1684. Members of the tribunal are appointed by the Lord Chancellor and adjudicators by the Secretary of State.
60 Immigration Act 1971, ss. 19, 20.
61 ibid., ss. 13–17.

of leave to enter and does not hold entry clearance or a work permit may exercise his right of appeal only whilst he is outside the United Kingdom.[62]

There is no right of appeal at all against:

1 Refusal of entry if the Secretary of State certifies that he personally directed that the applicant be excluded because exclusion would be conducive to the public good, or if entry was refused in obedience to such a direction (section 13(5)).

2 Reduction of or refusal to increase the permitted period of entry, if (a) the Secretary of State certifies that the appellant's deportation would be conducive to the public good in the interests of national security or good international relations or for other political reasons, or (b) the Secretary of State took the decision in person (section 14(3)).

3 A decision to make a deportation order against him on 'conducive' grounds as in 2(a) above (section 15(3)), except that appeal lies as to the destination.

4 Refusal to revoke an existing deportation order if revocation has been refused by the Secretary of State in person or if he certifies that exclusion was conducive to the public good (section 15(4)).

It is most unusual – it may indeed be an innovation – for legislation to attribute special effects to the fact that a Minister has taken a decision in person. No less interesting is the method of dealing with the delicate situations mentioned in (2) and (3) above where the 'public good' is allegedly bound up with security or political factors. But although there is no provision for *appeal* in such cases, there is an extra-statutory reference, at the request of the person aggrieved, to the Three Advisers who deal with civil servants' appeals against security dismissals and transfers.[63] The immigrant may state his case before them. Their advice to the Home Secretary is neither disclosed nor binding on him.[64]

A person would normally be expected to exhaust his rights of appeal under the Immigration Act before seeking judicial review.[65] Where appropriate an

---

62 ibid., s. 13(3).

63 819 HC Deb 375–7 (15 June 1971).

64 In *R. v. Home Secretary, ex p. Hosenball* [1971] 1 WLR 766 two journalists were deported for publishing information harmful to the security services. They challenged the validity of the deportation order; the Court of Appeal held the normal rules of natural justice did not apply so that the order was valid even though they were not given the evidence against them or the panel's report to the Home Secretary. The European Commission of Human Rights subsequently held that their application regarding that decision was inadmissible.

65 *R. v. Chief Immigration Officer, Heathrow, ex p. Salamat Bibi* [1976] 1 WLR 979.

aggrieved person might make an application for judicial review under the Supreme Court Act 1981 section 31, and Order 53[66] or seek a writ of habeas corpus.[67] He might, for example, establish an excess of power by the Home Office[68] or by an immigration officer. Where an immigration officer has exercised his power to detain and remove an illegal immigrant, the court has to be satisfied, on the civil standard of proof to a high degree of probability, that in fact the applicant was an illegal immigrant when removed.[69] If he could discharge the heavy onus of proving that the Home Secretary abused his discretionary powers he could challenge a decision.[70] He could challenge as a question of law the official interpretation of the Act[71] or presumably of the Immigration Rules. Proof that an immigration officer conducted his investigation unfairly would make the decision reviewable as a breach of the rules of natural justice.[72] On the other hand, when interpreting the now repealed Aliens Order, the courts held that the Home Secretary need not give a hearing before deporting an alien.[73] The Court of Appeal has, however, decided that judicial review is not to be used so as to avoid the appeal procedures in the Immigration Act 1971.[74] If, on the other hand, the Home Secretary acts unreasonably according to *Wednesbury* principles[75] in deciding a question of status (such as that of refugee), then judicial review may be successfully sought.[76] A person may appeal on a point of law to the Court of Appeal from the Immigration Appeal Tribunal: Asylum and Immigration Appeals Act 1993, section 11.

The power of the Home Secretary to make exclusion orders under the Prevention of Terrorism (Temporary Provisions) Act 1989 preventing

66 See p. 556.

67 See p. 439. The House of Lords discussed this remedy in relation to immigration law in *R. v. Secretary of State for the Home Department, ex p. Khawaja* [1984] AC 74.

68 *R. v. Governor of Richmond Remand Centre, ex p. Asghar* [1971] 1 WLR 129. And see *R. v. Home Secretary, ex p. Phansopkar* [1976] QB 606.

69 *R. v. Secretary of State for the Home Department, ex p. Khawaja* [1984] AC 74.

70 *R. v. Brixton Prison Governor, ex p. Soblen* [1963] 2 QB 243 shows how difficult it is to satisfy the courts of that. The applicant unsuccessfully maintained that the Home Secretary's dominant purpose in deporting him was to effect extradition to the United States for a non-extraditable offence. And see *R. v. Home Secretary, ex p. Hosenball* [1977] 1 WLR 766, above.

71 *In re Abdul Manan* [1971] 2 All ER 1016.; *R. v. Immigration Appeal Tribunal, ex p. Singh* [1986] 1 WLR 910.

72 *Re HK* [1967] 2 QB 617.

73 *Soblen's* case, above and *Schmidt v. Home Secretary* [1969] 2 Ch. 149.

74 *R. v. Secretary of State for the Home Department, ex p. Swati* [1986] 1 WLR 477.

75 See below, p. 549.

76 See *R. v. Secretary of State for the Home Department, ex p. Bugdaycay* [1987] 2 AC 514, HL.

those concerned with acts of terrorism from entering or remaining in Great Britain, Northern Ireland or the UK has been previously mentioned.[77] A person served with an exclusion order may object to the Home Secretary within seven days and, if he requests, may be interviewed by an adviser nominated by the Home Secretary. The Home Secretary then reconsiders the case after receiving a report from his adviser.[78] This procedure is executive only and so is not subject to any effective judicial review.

ALLEGIANCE AND PROTECTION[79]

At common law, one who owes allegiance to the Crown is entitled to the Crown's protection; allegiance and protection are said to be correlative duties. The basic legal consequences of these principles at common law are as follows.

1 Violation of allegiance by levying war against the Queen within the realm or adhering to the Queen's enemies[80] is high treason, an offence still attracting the death penalty.

2 One who enjoys the protection of the Crown (a) is entitled to be physically protected by the Crown against armed attack within Her Majesty's dominions;[81] (b) is entitled to be afforded diplomatic protection by the Crown,[82] (c) may be made a ward of court, if a minor,[83] and (d) can sue the Crown or its officers if the Crown commits or orders, authorizes or ratifies unlawful acts in relation to him, inasmuch as act of State is not generally available as a justification for *prima facie* wrongful interference with the legal rights of a person owing allegiance.[84]

Allegiance is owed by:

---

77 See above, p. 413.

78 1989 Act, s. 4(4) and sched. 2.

79 See H. Lauterpacht (1947) 19 *Camb. LJ* 330; Glanville Williams (1948) 10 *Camb. LJ* 54.

80 Acquisition of enemy nationality by a British citizen in wartime is treasonable: *R. v. Lynch* [1903] 1 KB 444.

81 See generally *China Navigation Co. v. Att.-Gen.* [1932] 2 KB 197, and *Mutasa v. Att.-Gen.* [1980] QB 114. Hence the Crown cannot demand payment as a condition of granting such protection; *aliter* if such protection is granted outside Her Majesty's dominions to a person voluntarily exposing himself to a special hazard.

82 *Joyce v. DPP* [1946] AC 347 (treason); but see below.

83 *Re P. (GE) (an Infant)* [1965] Ch. 568.

84 *Johnstone v. Pedlar* [1921] 2 AC 262; see also *Nissan v. Att.-Gen.* [1970] AC 179 and pp. 156–8 above, indicating possible exceptions to the general rule.

1 British citizens wherever they may be;
2 friendly aliens within Her Majesty's dominions;
3 friendly aliens outside Her Majesty's dominions if they are (a) ordinarily resident within them but are temporarily absent and evince an intention to return by leaving family or property there; or (b) are in possession of a current British passport or a travel document entitling them to return,[85] and
4 enemy aliens within Her Majesty's dominions with the express or implied licence of the Crown; this appears to cover all enemy aliens except combatants[86] other than prisoners of war.

The local allegiance of an alien does not cease to be owed merely because the part of Her Majesty's dominions in which he is resident is occupied by hostile forces.[87] It is not clear what is the legal foundation for the suggestion[88] that the Crown may expressly withdraw its protection from a friendly alien within Her Majesty's dominions.

This pattern of rules, founded on conceptual reasoning, is nevertheless irregular. For example, it is impossible to believe that the Crown has any kind of legal *duty* to afford diplomatic protection to an alien outside Her Majesty's dominions, even if he has obtained a United Kingdom passport by misrepresenting his citizenship.[89] Nor, it is thought, would the Crown be incapacitated from pleading act of State in defence to an action in tort brought by him for ostensibly wrongful acts outside Her Majesty's dominions. Resident enemy aliens can commit treason, but they do not enjoy that modest degree of protection against the Crown which would render them immune from being interned or expelled under the prerogative. Allegiance and protection are not fully correlative duties for every purpose and the implications of protection may vary according to the content.

A Commonwealth citizen who is not a British citizen is not guilty of any offence in United Kingdom law in respect of any act or omission committed either in his own country or in a foreign country unless it

---

85 *Joyce's* case; *Re P. (GE)* (see above).
86 *Joyce's* case [1946] AC at 368.
87 *De Jager* v. *Att.-Gen. of Natal* [1907] AC 326 (treason).
88 Made *obiter* in *Johnstone* v. *Pedlar* (above).
89 Williams (1948) 10 *Camb. LJ* 54, pointing out the flaw in the *ratio decidendi* of *Joyce's* case. Joyce, an American citizen, had obtained a British passport in 1939; he went to Germany and, as 'Lord Haw-Haw', broadcast Nazi propaganda; held, he owed allegiance by virtue of the passport and was guilty of treason. Clearly, however, the Crown owed no *duty* to protect him by the *fact* of his having the passport. Why, then, did Joyce owe allegiance while in Germany?

would be an offence if committed by an alien in a foreign country (section 3(1) of the 1948 Act). This means that a citizen of Canada or India, for instance, cannot be convicted of treason in the United Kingdom for anything done in Canada or India unless his conduct would have been equally treasonable if perpetrated by a Frenchman in France (for example, because he was ordinarily resident in the United Kingdom or perhaps held a current United Kingdom passport).

Passports: a note

United Kingdom passports are issued under the royal prerogative by the Passport Agency (an executive agency within the Home Office). They may be refused, revoked and impounded in the absolute discretion of the Crown, and there is no formal machinery for appeal, but a person aggrieved can obtain judicial review of a decision adverse to his interests.[90] In form a passport is a request in the Queen's name to afford the holder free passage and any necessary assistance; it is also a certificate of identity and citizenship. A holder (provided, at least, that he is in fact a citizen) is entitled to the diplomatic protection of the United Kingdom Government in a foreign country, though any such duty cast upon the Crown does not appear to be directly enforceable in judicial proceedings. The Government has stated that in practice passports are withheld in four classes of case: (i) a minor whose journey is known to be contrary to a court order, to the wishes of a parent or other person or authority to whom a court has awarded custody, care and control, or to the provisions of section 25(1) of the Children and Young Persons Act 1933, as amended, or section 52 of the Adoption Act 1958, as amended; (ii) a person for whose arrest a warrant has been issued in the United Kingdom, or who is wanted by the United Kingdom police on suspicion of a serious crime; (iii) in very rare cases, a person whose past or proposed activities are so demonstrably undesirable that the grant or continued enjoyment of passport facilities would be contrary to the public interest; (iv) a person repatriated at public expense, until the debt has been

---

90 R. v. *Secretary of State for Foreign and Commonwealth Affairs, ex p. Everett* [1989] 1 All ER 655. This moves English law nearer the position in the USA and India, where the highest courts have held that the Executive has not an arbitrary discretion to refuse or revoke a passport and thus derogate from a citizen's freedom of movement. See, for example, *Kent* v. *Dulles* 357 US 116 (1958). JUSTICE, *Going Abroad: A Report on Passports* (1975), is a good summary of practice, which recommends the enactment of a statute conferring upon all citizens the legal right to a passport. And see Jaconelli (1975) 38 *Mod. L. Rev.* 314.

repaid. Under successive Administrations it has been extremely rare to refuse a person under category (iii). Decisions in these cases are always taken personally by the Secretary of State.[91]

In practice it is extremely difficult to travel outside the country without a valid passport or national identity card, because carriers will demand production of passports by passengers, and immigration authorities elsewhere will not normally accept the entry of non-holders. (Passports of European Union nationals are not, however, examined at all closely by immigration officials when such nationals travel from one European Union country to another. Indeed, all passport controls are being abolished by many European Union states for travel within the European Union – although the United Kingdom is retaining passport controls for European Union citizens entering the country.) Since any decision not to grant or to revoke or withhold, a passport may seriously restrict freedom of movement, there should be a statutory procedure for appeal or review, with special arrangements for politically sensitive cases.

FUGITIVE OFFENDERS

Special statutory rules govern the surrender from the United Kingdom of fugitives from criminal justice in other countries. The ease of modern travel, especially by air, and the continuing scourge of international terrorism mean that effective arrangements for the extradition of alleged criminals must be maintained, and from time to time updated and improved. To those ends the Government made proposals for reform in 1985,[92] which were contained in the Criminal Justice Act 1988, and are now in the consolidating Extradition Act 1989. These rules apply, in general, to all persons, irrespective of their citizenship. The 1989 Act applies to all foreign countries, Commonwealth states, and colonies; it does not apply to Ireland: rendition to the Republic of Ireland is effected by a single procedure under the Backing of Warrants (Republic of Ireland) Act 1965. As has been noted,[93] a deportation order may, in certain circumstances, have the same practical effect as an extradition order.

Extradition to foreign countries is regulated by statute and treaty. There

91 416 HL Deb. 558 (22 January 1981).
92 Green Paper on Extradition, Cmnd 9421 (1985); Criminal Justice: Plans for Legislation, Cmnd 9658 (1986).
93 *Soblen*'s case above, p. 419.

can be no extradition (as distinct from deportation) to a foreign State in the absence of a bilateral treaty to which effect is given in United Kingdom law by an Order in Council made in pursuance of the Extradition Acts.[94] The terms of such an Order in Council must be compatible with the Acts – for example, it cannot provide for surrender of a person charged with an offence that is not an extradition crime scheduled to the Act – but there is scope for variation; thus, some extradition treaties exclude the rendition of nationals of one or both of the contracting states.

Extradition proceedings are started by an overseas government issuing a request for extradition to the Home Secretary.[95] He may, if satisfied that the request is lawfully made, issue a warrant to proceed to a metropolitan stipendiary magistrate (or, in Scotland, to the sheriff of Lothian and Borders), who in turn may issue an arrest warrant.[96] On arrest the wanted person is brought before the metropolitan magistrate and, if he is satisfied that the authority to proceed relates to an extradition crime and that the person is the one named, he must issue a certificate to commit him to the Home Secretary's custody.[97] (Before the passage of the Criminal Justice Act 1988 the magistrate had to consider the evidence against the accused and satisfy himself that there would, in English law, be a *prima facie* case to answer. That judicial process was removed by the 1988 Act, except in relation to extradition requests from Commonwealth countries.) An extradition crime is one which, if committed in the United Kingdom, would be an offence punishable by twelve months' imprisonment or more and which is so punishable in the requesting State (or which is an extraterritorial offence against the law of that State) – all subject to certain conditions.[98] In no case may a person be returned to a foreign State under the 1989 Act if it appears that the offence alleged is of a political character or is an offence only under military and not under civil law, or that the request is in fact made in order to punish the accused on account of his race, religion, nationality or political

---

94 Orders in Council made under the Extradition Act 1870 and later statutes passed before the consolidating Extradition Act 1989 are continued in force, unless and until fresh arrangements are made under the 1989 Act: s. 37(3).

95 1989 Act, s. 7.

96 ibid., s. 9; Criminal Justice and Public Order Act 1994, ss. 158, 159.

97 ibid., s. 8.

98 ibid., s. 2. The conditions are that (i) the offence must carry 12 months' imprisonment or more; and *either* (ii) in corresponding circumstances equivalent conduct outside the UK would be an extraterritorial offence against the UK, *or* (iii) the foreign State bases jurisdiction on the nationality of the offender, and the offence occurred outside the UK and would be an offence in UK law.

opinions.[99] If the magistrate refuses to commit the accused to the Home Secretary's custody the requisitioning State may 'question' the proceedings in the High Court;[100] if the accused is committed, he may apply for habeas corpus.[101] The Home Secretary must give the accused a written notice explaining that he may make representations to him why he should not be returned; the accused may seek judicial review of the Home Secretary's decision (but not on the ground that he did not have evidence before him to justify return).[102] If at least fifteen days elapse after committal, and any judicial proceedings are completed, the accused may be returned under the Home Secretary's warrant.[103]

Some of the cases on the former law will continue to be relevant. So, the metropolitan magistrate (and the High Court on a habeas corpus application) may consider whether the offence was one within the Act, the Order of Council and the treaty; whether the surrender of the accused is being sought for the purpose of detaining or trying him for a different offence; and whether it is being sought for an offence of a political character or in order to try or punish him for an offence[104] of a political character.[105] The House of Lords has, however, held that the courts have no jurisdiction to refuse extradition on the ground that surrender would be oppressive,[106] or even on the ground that the accused had been convicted by the foreign court without an opportunity to defend himself and hence in breach of natural justice;[107] it lies within the discretion of the Home Secretary[108] to decide whether, in all the circumstances, the extradition order should be enforced. The courts are also extremely reluctant to attribute ulterior motives to an overseas government with which the United Kingdom

99 ibid., s. 6(1).

100 ibid., s. 10.

101 ibid., s. 11. The High Court may order his discharge if it would be unjust or oppressive to return him by reason of the triviality of the offence, or the passage of time since the alleged offence, or if the accusation against him is not made in good faith: ibid., s. 11(3). He may waive the right to apply: ibid., s. 14.

102 ibid., s. 13.

103 ibid., s. 13.

104 *R.* v. *Bow Street Magistrates, ex p. Mackeson* (1982) 75 Cr. App. R. 24.

105 1989 Act, ss. 1, 6 and sched. 1, para. 1. It would seem that for extradition to be refused on this last ground the 'political' offence must have already been committed. See *R.* v. *Brixton Prison Governor, ex p. Keane* [1972] AC 204 (a case decided on the similar but not identical wording of section 2(2) of the Backing of Warrants (Republic of Ireland) Act 1965).

106 *Atkinson* v. *United States Government* [1971] AC 197.

107 *R.* v. *Brixton Prison Governor, ex p. Kotronis* [1971] AC 250.

108 Extradition Act 1989, ss. 1, 6 and sched. 1, para. 8.

maintains diplomatic relations; consequently they will accept assurances that the accused will not be tried or detained for any other offence or on political grounds upon his surrender.[109] The Home Secretary may exercise a political discretion after the court proceedings have terminated.

The magistrate, or the court on a habeas corpus application, will direct the release of the accused if of the opinion that the offence with which he has been charged is of a political character. Indeed, the Home Secretary should refuse to proceed with a request for surrender in the first place if the offence is political. To this extent the law does recognize a right, and not merely a privilege of political asylum.[110]

For a long time it was thought that an offence could not be political unless it was committed in pursuance of a struggle for power between contending factions within a State. The murder of a Swiss official in furtherance of an uprising was an offence of a political character;[111] a murder committed by a bomb-throwing anarchist whose destructive impulses were directed against organized society at large was not.[112] Up to a point this test is serviceable; thus, a family dispute about the religious education of children in Israel, leading to perjury, kidnapping and a national political controversy did not fall within the concept of a political offence.[113] But no all-inclusive test is acceptable. For example, a mutiny and assault on the high seas designed to enable the criminals to escape to the West from a communist regime – an offence which in Poland would have been regarded as treasonable – was held to be of a political character, although there was no element of a struggle for power.[114] The murder of Jews in a Nazi concentration camp was an act of State policy, but it was not a political offence because the offenders would not have been entitled to political asylum in Britain,[115] Genocide is now an extradition crime and is deemed not to be of a political character (Genocide Act 1969, s. 2). Hijacking aircraft and unlawful acts against the safety of aircraft are also extradition crimes, but the ordinary exception for political offences remains (Aviation Security Act 1982, s. 9; see also the Aviation and Maritime Security Act 1990, s. 49).

109 R. v. Brixton Prison Governor, ex p. Kotronis (see above). cf. the differences in approach to this question in the judgments in R. v. Brixton Governor, ex p. Kolczynski [1955] 1 QB 540.
110 cf. p. 412. But to be 'political', the offence must be directed against the requisitioning State, not a third State: Cheng v. Governor of Pentonville Prison [1973] AC 931.
111 Re Castioni [1891] 1 QB 149.
112 Re Meunier [1894] 2 QB 415.
113 R. v. Brixton Prison Governor, ex p. Schtraks (see above).
114 R. v. Brixton Prison Governor, ex p. Kolczynski [1955] 1 QB 540, per Cassels J.
115 Re Extradition Act 1870, ex p. Treasury Solicitor [1969] 1 WLR 12.

In the eyes of the courts, the categories of offences of a political character have not been closed. In deciding whether an offence does fall within this general description, or within the list of extradition crimes, the courts are entitled to receive additional material and can review the determination of the magistrate *de novo*. If, of course, the offence (for example, espionage) is not one of the scheduled crimes, the question whether it is of a political character does not arise. The House of Lords has decided that, in considering the offence, a crucial factor is whether there was a sufficient and direct link between the crime and the alleged political purpose, which should be tested by examining the means used to achieve that purpose, whether the crime was aimed at a governmental or military target, and whether the crime would involve indiscriminate killing or maiming of civilians.[116]

The combined effect of the Suppression of Terrorism Act 1978 and the European Convention on the Suppression of Terrorism is to eliminate or restrict the possibility of terrorists evading extradition by pleading that their crimes are political offences. The listed offences include murder, kidnapping and use of imitation firearms. If the United Kingdom refuses to extradite in circumstances covered by the convention because the fugitive might suffer on account of his race, religion, nationality or political opinions, it can take jurisdiction itself to try the offence.[117]

Rendition must be refused if the offence is of a political character, or if the request has in fact been made for the purpose of prosecuting or punishing him on account of his race, religion or political opinions, or if the offender might[118] be prejudiced at his trial or detained on any of these grounds. References to offences of a political character do not include offences against the life or person of the Queen.[119] The Home Secretary may decide not to order the return to any state or dependent territory of any person who would face the death penalty there for an offence not carrying that penalty in the United Kingdom.[120]

Special arrangements between Northern Ireland and the Republic of Ireland exist under the Criminal Jurisdiction Act 1975 and equivalent Irish

---

116 *T.* v. *Secretary of State for the Home Department* [1996] 2 All ER 865.
117 For a reasoned criticism of this Act, see Schiff [1979] *Public Law* 353. And see Taking of Hostages Act 1982.
118 If the apprehended prejudice is grave, it is enough for the applicant for habeas corpus to show that a serious possibility of its occurrence exists; he does not have to show that the degree of possibility exceeds 50 per cent: *R.* v. *Pentonville Prison Governor, ex p. Fernandez* [1971] 1 WLR 987.
119 1989 Act, s. 6(8).
120 ibid., s. 12(2).

legislation. The 1975 Act allows Northern Ireland courts to try offenders in the province accused of serious crimes of violence committed in the Republic apparently with political motives. These extraterritorial offences are described in schedule 1 to the Act. A person accused in Northern Ireland of such an offence may choose to be tried in the Republic, and vice versa. From 1976 to 1991, thirty-two applications were made by United Kingdom prosecutors for proceedings to begin in Ireland; no applications were made by Irish prosecutors in that period requesting proceedings to begin in the United Kingdom.[121]

121 198 HC Deb. 352 (written answers 11 November 1991).

CHAPTER 21

Personal Freedom

LEGAL RESTRAINTS ON THE LIBERTY OF THE PERSON

A typical bill of rights in a Commonwealth country's constitution will provide that no person shall be deprived of his personal liberty save as authorized by law and on specified grounds: unfitness to plead on a criminal charge; sentence by a court for a criminal offence; committal for contempt of court; detention in pursuance of any other court order, or to bring him before a court, or on reasonable suspicion of having committed or being about to commit a crime; custody for care and protection, in the case of an infant; detention to prevent spread of certain diseases; detention for mental illness, drug addiction, alcoholism or vagrancy; detention for illegal immigration, or to secure deportation or extradition; or detention under a reasonably justifiable order restricting his movements or place of residence. With the exception of the last, these are roughly the grounds on which deprivation of personal liberty may be based in English law.

The constitution will go on to lay down minimum safeguards for persons detained, arrested or tried on criminal charges. They must be brought before a court without undue delay. If they are not going to be tried within a reasonable time, they must be released on bail. They and their property are not to be arbitrarily searched. Persons unlawfully detained are entitled to compensation. One charged with a criminal offence must be given a fair hearing before an impartial court. He is to be presumed innocent till proved guilty. He is to be informed as soon as is reasonably practicable of the offence with which he is charged; he must be given proper defence facilities, including the free assistance of an interpreter if needed. He cannot be subjected to retroactive, inhuman or degrading punishment. He cannot be compelled to give evidence at his trial; nor in general can he be tried twice for the same offence.

This is, in effect, an outline sketch of some basic principles of English criminal law and procedure, transposed into a constitutional text. In England the most important legal inhibitions on personal liberty consist in the powers and duties vested in those entrusted with the task of investigating and detecting crime. Special attention will be given to them, though other matters will also be introduced.

Powers of arrest

Unfortunately few branches of English law are more obscure or complex than that relating to powers of arrest.[1] The general common-law principles have been partly codified by the Police and Criminal Evidence Act 1984 but hardly clarified.[2]

To lay hands on another against his will and without lawful justification is an assault.[3] Unlawful detention (including arrest) is false imprisonment. Both are crimes and civil wrongs. In what circumstances, then, are the detention and arrest of suspected criminals justified by law?

The police have no general power to detain suspects for questioning unless they are arrested,[4] or even to require suspects or witnesses to accompany them to a police station or to give their names and addresses[5] or indeed to answer any questions, or to compel anyone to attend for an identity parade.[6] Apart from certain common-law powers, the police now have a general power, on reasonable suspicion, to search any person or vehicle for stolen or prohibited articles, to detain a person or vehicle for that purpose, and to stop and search persons and vehicles if a senior police officer believes it to be necessary to prevent anticipated serious violence.[7]

1 For detailed analyses of powers of arrest, see Glanville Williams [1954] *Crim. L. Rev.* 6, 408, 508; [1959] *Crim. L. Rev.* 73, 155; Thomas [1962] *Crim. L. Rev.* 520, 597; [1966] *Crim. L. Rev.* 639; Lidstone [1978] *Crim. L. Rev.* 332.
2 See ss. 24, 25. On the Act generally see V. Bevan and K. Lidstone, *The Investigation of Crime – A Guide to Police Powers* (1991); M. Zander, *The Police and Criminal Evidence Act 1984* (3rd edn, 1995); L. H. Leigh, *Police Powers in England and Wales* (2nd edn, 1985); St J. Robilliard and J. McEwan, *Police Powers and the Individual* (1986). The Human Rights Bill now before Parliament will add the direct protection in English law of the provisions of the European Convention on Human Rights on freedom of the person and the rights of arrested people.
3 Though cf. *Donnelly* v. *Jackman* [1970] 1 WLR 562 (see note 55, below).
4 *R.* v. *Lemsatef* [1977] 1 WLR 812; *R.* v. *Houghton and Franciosy* (1978) 68 Cr. App. R. 197.
5 *Rice* v. *Connolly* [1966] 2 QB 414; but see p. 432 how the general power of arrest may oblige a suspect to give his name and address.
6 Sargant [1966] *Crim. L. Rev.* 485.
7 Police and Criminal Evidence Act 1984, ss. 1–3; Criminal Justice and Public Order Act 1994, s. 60. Prohibited articles are defined (ibid.) as offensive weapons, articles to be used in specified offences under the Theft Act 1968, and include articles with a blade or sharp point, as defined by the Criminal Justice Act 1988, s. 139.

If a police officer decides to arrest a person on a criminal charge, he must normally obtain an arrest warrant from a magistrate by information supported by a sworn statement. The warrant must specify the name of the person to be arrested and general particulars of the offence. A general warrant, not naming the person to be arrested or failing to give adequate particulars of the offence, is illegal at common law.[8] Arrest warrants are hardly ever issued to persons other than police officers; and they are issued only in respect of arrestable offences[9] punishable (subject to various statutory exceptions) with a maximum of at least five years' imprisonment. If the issue of the warrant is outside the magistrate's jurisdiction but is *prima facie* valid, a constable executing it is protected from civil liability.[10]

An arrest involves an element of compulsion, though not necessarily physical seizure; a mere request by a constable that a person accompany him to a police station is not an arrest;[11] the arrest is not lawful unless the person arrested is informed that he is under arrest (even if the fact of arrest is obvious).[12] In effecting an arrest, no more physical force must be used than is reasonably required; otherwise the arrest becomes an actionable assault.

Special difficulties arise in ascertaining the legal grounds on which an arrest may be effected without a warrant.

Any member of the public may arrest without warrant:[13]

1 Anyone who is in the act of committing an arrestable offence.
2 Anyone whom he has reasonable grounds for suspecting to be committing such an offence.
3 Anyone who is, or whom he reasonably suspects to be, guilty of an arrestable offence, where such an arrestable offence has been committed.[14]

---

8 *Leach* v. *Money* (1765) 3 Burr. 1692, 1742. See also *Wilkes* v. *Wood* (1769) 19 St. Tr. 1406 (search warrant); *Entick* v. *Carrington* (1765) 19 St. Tr. 1030.
9 Police and Criminal Evidence Act 1984, s. 24(1), (2) (hereafter 'the 1984 Act'); both statutory and common-law offences are included under the Act.
10 Constables' Protection Act 1750.
11 *Alderson* v. *Booth* [1969] 2 QB 216. See, however, *Wheatley* v. *Lodge* [1971] 1 WLR 29 (defendant lawfully arrested although he failed to realize, because of deafness unknown to the police officer, that he was being required to go to police station under arrest). cf. *R.* v. *Inwood* [1973] 1 WLR 647.
12 1984 Act, s. 28(1), (2).
13 1984 Act, s. 24(4), (5).
14 If no arrestable offence exists, a private person (including a store detective) is liable in false imprisonment if he carries out an arrest, even if he reasonably believes that an arrestable offence has taken place: *Walters* v. *Smith* (*W.H.*) *and Son Ltd* [1914] 1 KB 595. And if a defendant is acquitted of an offence for which he has been arrested by a private citizen, that defendant cannot be convicted of, e.g., an assault committed while resisting arrest: *R.* v. *Self* [1992] 3 All ER 476.

A *constable, in addition*, may arrest without warrant:

1 Anyone whom he has reasonable grounds for suspecting has committed an arrestable offence – even though no such crime has been committed.[15]
2 Anyone who is about to commit an arrestable offence, or whom he has reasonable grounds for suspecting is about to commit such a crime.[16]
3 Any person, when the constable has reasonable grounds for suspecting that any offence which is not an arrestable offence is being or has been committed or attempted provided that service of a summons is impracticable or inappropriate because any of the specified 'general arrest conditions' is satisfied.[17]

The conditions are (i) that the suspected person's name is unknown to, and cannot be readily ascertained by, the constable; or (ii) that the constable has reasonable grounds for doubting whether a name furnished is correct; or (iii) that the address furnished is unsatisfactory for service; or (iv) that the constable has reasonable grounds for believing that, unless he arrests the person, he may cause physical harm to himself or another, or he may suffer physical injury or cause loss of or damage to property, or commit an offence against public decency, or an unlawful obstruction of the highway; or (v) that the constable has reasonable grounds for believing that an arrest is necessary to protect a child or other vulnerable person from the suspected person.[18] A member of the public is entitled to use reasonable force 'in the prevention of crime', or in effecting or assisting in the 'lawful arrest' of offenders or suspected offenders.[19] Given the uncertainty about the degree of force justifiable to prevent crime and the meaning of a lawful arrest – this includes arrest for specified arrestable offences (but few members of the public will carry the list in their heads) and arrest for breaches of the peace committed in one's presence[20] (but even the term 'breach of the

---

15 1984 Act, s. 24(6). See the consideration of common-law authority in *Barnard* v. *Gorman* [1941] AC 378 and *Wiltshire* v. *Barrett* [1966] 1 QB 312. The question whether a constable has 'reasonable cause' to suspect that a person is guilty of an offence is to be determined objectively on the basis of the information available to him at the time of the arrest; the constable need not also have an honest belief in the suspect's guilt: *Castorina* v. *Chief Constable of Surrey*, the *Independent*, 16 June 1988.
16 ibid., s. 24(7).
17 This is a new general power conferred by the 1984 Act, s. 25.
18 1984 Act, s. 25(3).
19 Criminal Law Act 1967, s. 3; or of persons 'unlawfully at large': this category includes not only escaped prisoners but detained mental patients.
20 For the powers of the police and citizens to arrest for suspected breaches of the peace, see *R.* v. *Howell* [1982] QB 416.

peace' has an uncertain meaning apart from acts of violence to the person) – it is obviously risky for the citizen to take a suspected offender into custody. To respond to the request of a police officer to help him apprehend a criminal may evince public spirit but does not confer immunity from liability if the arrest is unlawful. On the other hand, to refuse compliance with such a request without lawful excuse when two or more persons are actually committing a breach of the peace is an offence.[21]

If these prerequisites of a valid arrest are present, the arrest will still not be lawful unless, at the time of making the arrest, the person arrested is informed of the ground for the arrest, at that time or as soon as practicable afterwards – and if a constable makes the arrest, even if that ground is obvious, such as being caught red-handed.[22] He does not have to be told the technical name of the offence in question; nor is it necessary to say anything to him if it is reasonable to think that announcing one's presence before seizing him would cause him to run away from the scene; nor does one have to communicate the reasons to a person who, unknown to oneself, is deaf. The purpose of requiring communication, where practicable, is to enable the person arrested to clear himself by explanation at the first opportunity.[23]

A person who is unlawfully arrested may use reasonable force to free himself.[24] But although passive submission may not be required by law, active resistance is apt to be perilous, because a court may hold that excessive force has been used, and not every mistaken arrest by the police is unlawful.

Since 1974, Prevention of Terrorism Acts have been in operation with the aims of banning the Irish Republican Army and allied organizations, and of excluding from Great Britain any terrorists who might use violence for political ends.[25] Police are empowered to arrest without warrant on

---

21 *R.* v. *Brown* (1841) Car. & M. 314.

22 1984 Act, s. 28(3), (4). But if an arrested person is subsequently informed of the reason, the arrest is only unlawful from its inception until that moment: *Lewis* v. *Chief Constable of the South Wales Constabulary* [1991] 1 All ER 206.

23 See *Christie* v. *Leachinsky* [1947] AC 573; *John Lewis & Co.* v. *Tims* [1952] AC 672; *DPP* v. *Hawkins* [1988] 3 All ER 673; *Abbassy* v. *Metropolitan Police Commissioner* [1991] 1 All ER 193. For a marginal case, where a person was held to have been lawfully arrested although he was given the wrong legal ground for his arrest, see *Gelberg* v. *Miller* [1961] 1 WLR 138; the facts constituting the reason for his arrest were, however, apparent to the defendant, and he could have been arrested for an offence arising out of those facts. See also *R.* v. *Kulynycz* [1971] 1 QB 367 (original arrest wrongful, no proper reason having been given, but error rectified while defendant still in custody). Contrast *R.* v. *Holah* [1973] 1 WLR 127.

24 As in *Kenlin* v. *Gardiner* [1967] 2 QB 510.

25 The current Act is the Prevention of Terrorism (Temporary Provisions) Act 1989.

reasonable suspicion of terrorism. They are given powers to detain suspects pending investigation for two days at their discretion. The Home Secretary may authorize a further five days' detention.

Police detention

The powers of the police to detain a person after arrest and before charging him are subject to the Police and Criminal Evidence Act 1984.[26] As soon as the police decide there is sufficient evidence to support a charge the person must be charged. Otherwise he must be released, unless the police have reasonable grounds for believing his detention without charge is necessary to secure, preserve or obtain evidence.[27] After being charged the arrested person may be released, but may instead be further detained if specified conditions are satisfied, such as police suspicion about any name and address furnished.[28] In any event the Act imposes time limits on the period of detention without charge.[29] From the time at which the arrested person arrives at the police station, the police have twenty-four hours in which to charge him, failing which he must be released;[30] but the police may themselves authorize his detention for a total of up to thirty-six hours, and a magistrates' court for up to a total of ninety-six hours, if this is necessary to obtain evidence of a 'serious arrestable offence'.[31] The arrested person must be released within these limits unless he is charged.[32] Detention for questioning for such long periods must, in practice, endanger the right to silence.

Bail

A person arrested and charged must be brought before a magistrates' court as soon as practicable and in any event not later than the first sitting after he is charged (which will usually be the following day).[33] He may be remanded in custody or on bail pending further proceedings by way of summary trial, preliminary hearing, committal for trial on indictment or

26 1984 Act, Part IV.
27 ibid., s. 37.
28 ibid., s. 38(1).
29 ibid., ss. 41–4.
30 ibid., s. 41(1).
31 ibid., ss. 42, 43, 44; 'serious arrestable offence' is defined in s. 116 partly by reference to certain named crimes and partly by reference to other arrestable offences made serious by their consequences in the particular case.
32 See below, under *Bail*.
33 1984 Act, s. 46.

appeal. Release on bail may be granted by a police sergeant following arrest without warrant,[34] or by magistrates or by a High Court or Circuit judge. The powers of magistrates and judges to refuse release on bail were curtailed by the Bail Act 1976. There is a statutory presumption in favour of bail for an accused in custody who has not yet been convicted. He must be remanded on bail (whether or not he has applied for it) unless the court is satisfied that there is an unacceptable risk that if he were released on bail he would fail to surrender to custody or commit an offence while on bail, or interfere with witnesses or otherwise obstruct the course of justice.[35] Before being admitted to bail, the person arrested may be required to produce sureties for his appearance and other relevant conditions may be imposed. An accused can no longer be asked to provide a recognizance, to be forfeited should he not surrender for trial.[36] Instead the Act introduces a new offence of absconding while on bail.[37] A court must hear arguments in favour of granting bail on the first two occasions at which it is sought; thereafter a court need not hear arguments as to fact or law which it has heard previously.[38] If he is refused bail or objects to the conditions under which it is offered, he must be told the reasons, and of his right to apply to the Crown Court or a High Court judge, who have power to admit to bail or vary the conditions under which it has been offered.[39]

Binding over to be of good behaviour or to keep the peace[40]

A person convicted of crime may, instead of being sent to prison, be bound over. This power is ancillary to the exercise of criminal jurisdiction (Justices of the Peace Act 1968, section 1(7)) and does not presuppose the conviction of the person bound over. Alternatively, a bind-over order may be made

---

34 ibid., s. 47, and the Criminal Justice and Public Order Act 1994, ss. 27–8. For granting of bail by police to persons under 17, see Children and Young Persons Act 1969, s. 29; Bail Act 1976, s. 3(7).

35 Section 3.

36 Section 3(2).

37 Section 6, and the Criminal Justice and Public Order Act 1994, s. 29.

38 Criminal Justice Act 1988, s. 154. Codified the decision in *R.* v. *Nottingham Justices, ex p. Davies* [1981] QB 38: so preventing series of applications based on same arguments.

39 Criminal Justice Act 1967, s. 22; Supreme Court Act 1981, s. 81; Criminal Justice Act 1982, s. 60. The detainee cannot apply to successive judges in turn in the hope of obtaining bail; *R.* v. *Reading Crown Court, ex p. Malik* [1981] QB 451.

40 See generally Glanville Williams (1953) 16 *Mod. L. Rev.* 417; D. G. T. Williams, *Keeping the Peace*, ch. 4; [1970] *Camb. LJ* at 103–6; [1963] *Public Law* 441; D. A. Thomas, *Principles of Sentencing* (2nd edn, 1979), pp. 228–9. See also Law Commission Working Paper No. 103 (1987) which has an excellent review of the law.

by way of preventive justice. Under section 115 of the Magistrates' Courts Act 1980 the court may, on the complaint of X, bind Y over to enter into a recognizance, with or without sureties, to keep the peace or to be of good behaviour towards X. No such order may be made unless the complaint is properly proved. Magistrates also have a general power under the Justices of the Peace Act 1361 to bind persons over to be of good behaviour or to keep the peace; this power may be exercised without a formal complaint, and in the course of other proceedings, though if the order is to keep the peace, some threat to the peace must be disclosed by the evidence adduced.[41] If the person against whom an order is made refuses to give the required undertaking, or refuses or is unable to offer sureties for his conduct, he can be sent to prison for a period of up to six months even though he has committed no crime. Because such an order is not a conviction, no appeal against the merits of the decision lay till one was provided by statute in 1956.[42] Binding-over orders have been used not only to restrain political agitators from repeating or encouraging violence or from inciting other persons to break the law[43] but also to prevent persons from behaving in a way likely (though not intended) to provoke others to commit breaches of the peace[44] and to inhibit the activities of prostitutes, kerb-crawling motorists looking for prostitutes, protestors and peeping Toms.

Obstructing the police in the execution of their duty

Under section 89(2) of the Police Act 1996 (substantially reproducing the wording of an Act of 1885) it is an offence, punishable with up to a month's imprisonment, wilfully to obstruct a constable in the execution of his duty.[45] It will be considered further in the context of the law of public meeting,

---

41 See generally *R.* v. *Aubrey-Fletcher, ex p. Thompson* [1969] 1 WLR 872. The party against whom an order is made must first be given an opportunity to argue against it: *Sheldon* v. *Bromfield JJ.* [1964] 2 QB 573.
42 Magistrates' Courts (Appeals from Binding-Over Orders) Act 1956 as amended by the Courts Act 1971 (appeal on the merits to the Crown Court). But a bind-over made without jurisdiction may be quashed at common law by the High Court on an application for certiorari (*R.* v. *Aubrey-Fletcher*, above) and appeal lies by case stated on a question of law to a Divisional Court of the Queen's Bench Division: see, for example, *Beattie* v. *Gillbanks* (1882) 9 QBD 308.
43 For example, *Lansbury* v. *Riley* [1914] 3 KB 229.
44 *Wilson* v. *Skeock* (1949) 65 TLR 4128, approved in *Aubrey-Fletcher*'s case, above.
45 See *Lewis* v. *Cox* [1984] 3 All ER 672 for a discussion of the offence, especially in relation to the defendant's motive.

but the case law tells us something, albeit in discordant language, about the duties of the police. The general duty of the police is to preserve public order and secure due observance of the criminal law; and they cannot divest themselves of these obligations.[46] They have other specified statutory duties and numerous powers. The courts have attempted to strike a balance between facilitating the proper discharge of the functions of the police on the one hand and the maintenance of individual liberty on the other. Police powers and duties for securing public order have been widely interpreted; the police have a duty to break up public gatherings where serious disorders occur and to prevent reasonably apprehended breaches of the peace, and a refusal on the part of a member of the public to desist when called upon to do so is an obstruction of a constable in the execution of his duty.[47] Again, unreasonable use of the highway amounting to a public nuisance or wilful obstruction should be stopped by the police, and it will be an offence to refuse to comply with a police instruction to disperse.[48] In these circumstances the police have an implied power to arrest without warrant; but it would seem that there is no *general* power of arrest merely for wilful obstruction of the police,[49] though a summons may be issued. Obstruction of police investigations into suspected crimes is not necessarily an offence although the police may be acting in the general execution of their functions. Deliberately attempting to prevent the apprehension of one guilty of an arrestable offence, or wasting the time of the police by making allegations one knows to be false, are separate statutory offences.[50] To give other offenders prior warning of the approach of the police so as to enable them to escape detection is a wilful obstruction of a constable in the execution of his duty,[51] and the same is probably true of the deliberate destruction or removal of relevant evidence,[52] or having an extra drink in order to frustrate a breathalyser test that is about to be administered by a police officer to

---

46 See generally R. v. *Metropolitan Police Commissioner, ex p. Blackburn* [1968] 2 QB 118; ch. 20.

47 *Duncan* v. *Jones* [1936] 1 KB 218. See also *Piddington* v. *Bates* [1961] 1 WLR 162.

48 *Tynan* v. *Balmer* [1967] 1 QB 91. See also *Gelberg* v. *Miller* [1961] 1 WLR 153 (power to arrest for highway obstruction in the Metropolitan area), and see generally Highways Act 1980, s. 137.

49 *Gelberg* v. *Miller* (see above); but see pp. 432–3.

50 Criminal Law Act 1967, ss 4, 5(2).

51 *Hinchliffe* v. *Sheldon* [1955] 1 WLR 1207; *Betts* v. *Stevens* [1910] 1 KB 1; contrast *Bastable* v. *Little* [1907] 1 KB 59 (warning of speed trap).

52 Though cf. R. v. *Waterfield and Lynn* [1964] 1 QB 164 (attempt by police officers to prevent motor car suspected of involvement in serious offence from being driven off, held not part of their duties). See criticisms of that decision in *Ghani* v. *Jones* [1970] 1 QB 693 at 707–8.

oneself,[53] or giving misleading statements while under police interrogation. But it has been held not to be an offence simply to refuse to answer police questions[54] or to resist with reasonable force detention for the purpose of being so questioned.[55] Nor do police officers have a general licence to enter upon private premises without the occupier's permission in order to investigate suspected crime.[56] Even if they enter with permission, they become trespassers once consent is withdrawn,[57] unless they have entered in pursuance of a valid warrant or to effect a lawful arrest[58] or for the prevention of a reasonably apprehended breach of the peace[59] or under other, ill-defined, conditions furnishing justification for entry. The general duty to investigate suspected crime imports powers[60] limited in scope; and a member of the public is not inevitably guilty of an offence by deliberately making it more difficult for the police to exercise those powers or effectively to discharge this general duty.

Police interrogation

As has been noted, detention for questioning is generally unlawful except where it amounts to a lawful arrest; and a person interrogated by the police is not obliged to say anything. Moreover, confessions of guilt are inadmissible in evidence at a criminal trial if procured by oppression or in consequence of anything said or done which was likely to render them unreliable,[61] and other admissions detrimental to an accused are sparingly admitted. The accused is not required to give evidence at his trial.

The American constitutional Bill of Rights provides that no one shall be compelled to be a witness against himself, that an accused shall have the

---

53 *Dibble* v. *Ingleton* [1972] 1 QB 480.

54 *Rice* v. *Connolly* [1966] 2 QB 414.

55 *Kenlin* v. *Gardiner* [1967] 2 QB 510 (a case of alleged assault on the police). Contrast *Donnelly* v. *Jackman* [1970] 1 WLR 562 (where the police officer had merely touched his assailant on the shoulder with a view to questioning him).

56 For example, *Davis* v. *Lisle* [1936] 2 KB 434; p. 448 below. *Morris* v. *Beardsmore* [1980] 3 WLR 283 (constable entering driver's home an hour and a half after accident to conduct a breathalyser test a trespasser).

57 See the general discussion of legal principle in *Robson* v. *Hallett* [1967] 2 QB 393.

58 See Police and Criminal Evidence Act 1984, s. 17.

59 *Thomas* v. *Sawkins* [1935] 2 KB 249; see pp. 485–6, below.

60 *R.* v. *Prebble* (1858) 1 F. & F. 325 (constable turned persons out of public house at landlord's invitation; resistance to him held to be an assault, but not an assault committed while he was executing his *duty*, because there was no nuisance or danger of a breach of the peace).

61 Police and Criminal Evidence Act 1984, s. 76.

assistance of counsel, and generally that due process of law shall be observed. English law does not go so far as the law in the United States in restricting methods of police interrogation.[62] The procedure to be followed is prescribed partly by the exclusionary rules of evidence indicated above, and partly by the Police and Criminal Evidence Act 1984[63] and codes of practice made under it.

The codes are not rules of strict law in the ordinary sense. Non-compliance does not render statements by an accused person inadmissible in evidence, but the provisions of the codes must be 'taken into account' by a court when deciding any question to which they are relevant.[64] The details of the codes need not be examined here, but they are designed to ensure first that interrogation shall not be oppressive, secondly that statements to the police shall be voluntary, and thirdly that a person shall be notified, by formal cautions, that he is not obliged to say anything in answer to questions. A person must be allowed access to a solicitor, as soon as is practicable if he so requests, and in any case within thirty-six hours of arrival at a police station.[65] At least in form, the 'right to be silent' enjoys better protection under the American case law than under the 1984 Act and codes. A defence lawyer on the spot will tend to advise his client to say nothing to the police in the first instance. An arrested person has the right to have one person told, if he so requests, that he has been arrested. This must be done within thirty-six hours of arriving at the station.[66]

HABEAS CORPUS[67] AND OTHER REMEDIES

A person subjected to invalid or excessive physical restraint may exercise self-help, sue or prosecute for assault or false imprisonment. If he is prosecuted without reasonable or probable cause and for improper motives, he may sue for damages for malicious prosecution.

The most celebrated safeguard of the liberty of the subject is the preroga-

62 There is a valuable comparative study of American and Commonwealth (including English) law on these matters by H. J. Glasbeek and D. D. Prentice in (1968) 23 *Cornell L. Rev.* 473. And see Gooderson (1970) 48 *Can. Bar. Rev.* 270.
63 1984 Act, Parts V and VI.
64 ibid. s. 67(10), (11).
65 ibid., s. 58. The right to consult a solicitor is 'fundamental', and may only be delayed under the exceptions in s. 58 in very limited circumstances: see *R.* v. *Samuel* [1988] 2 All ER 135.
66 ibid., s. 56.
67 The leading monograph is R. J. Sharpe, *The Law of Habeas Corpus* (2nd edn, 1989).

tive writ of habeas corpus. Traceable beyond Magna Carta, in the fourteenth century the modern function of the writ emerged: to require a person having custody of a prisoner to bring him before the court together with grounds for detention. The court could then test the legality of the detention and direct release if the imprisonment was found to be unlawful. The Habeas Corpus Act 1679 made the writ an efficient remedy in criminal cases by providing stringent safeguards against lengthy imprisonment without trial. Time limits were laid down for entering a return to the writ, and for producing the prisoner before a superior court if there were *prima facie* grounds for supposing the imprisonment to be unlawful; the court was empowered or required to admit to bail or provide for speedy trial if detention were founded on a criminal charge; heavy financial penalties were imposed on judges wrongfully refusing to issue the writ,[68] on gaolers evading service or compliance with the writ (for example, by moving the prisoner from one gaol to another or overseas), and on persons recommitting a prisoner already discharged on an application for habeas corpus. An Act of 1816 extended some of these provisions to civil cases, and empowered the court to inquire into the truth of the return made to the writ.[69]

The modern law of habeas corpus[70] is governed partly by statute, partly by case law and partly by Rules of the Supreme Court.[71] An application is made to a Divisional Court of the Queen's Bench Division or, if no such court is then sitting, to a single judge of any division, even at his private house. Habeas corpus applications have priority over all other business. The application is to be made by or with the concurrence of the detainee unless he is incapable of consenting, in which case a relative, guardian or friend may apply on his behalf. It must be accompanied by an affidavit showing why his restraint is unlawful. If *prima facie* grounds are demonstrated, the person who ordered the detention or who has actual custody (for example, a prison governor, the Serjeant-at-Arms, the superintendent of a mental hospital, or a Minister) must then show cause, on a date fixed by the court, why the writ should not issue to release the detainee. Production of the record of an apparently valid conviction by a court places on the applicant the burden of proving that the court had exceeded its jurisdiction.

---

68 s. 10. This section of the Act is still in force. Some of the other sections have been repealed, amended or indirectly superseded by new statutory provisions for the granting of bail and the expedition of trials, cf. *R.* v. *Campbell* [1959] 1 WLR 646.

69 The history of habeas corpus is traced by Holdsworth, *History of English Law*, vol. 10, pp. 108–25. See also Jenks (1902) 18 *LQR* 64.

70 The only significant form of the writ now used is called *habeas corpus ad subjiciendum*.

71 Especially RSC Ord. 54.

On the other hand, in a case of private detention, or where a British citizen is being detained by the Executive, allegedly on grounds specified by statute, the onus of proving that there existed facts justifying the detention rests on the custodian.[72]

In general, habeas corpus cannot be used as a device for impeaching the correctness of a determination made by a court of competent jurisdiction, the only appropriate means of redress being appeal;[73] though not all decisions on habeas corpus are reconcilable with this principle.[74] On habeas corpus applications made by persons committed by magistrates for extradition or rendition as fugitive offenders, the court did not substitute its own opinion for the magistrate's on the question whether there was a *prima facie* case, but it might award the writ if satisfied that his conclusion on the facts as found was such as no reasonable magistrate properly directing his mind to the issues could have reached[75] or if it disagreed with his finding that the offence was not of a political character.[76] The scope of review will in practice vary according to the context. The courts have given short shrift to wartime security suspects;[77] they have flinched from questioning the validity of a Speaker's warrant alleging contempt of the House of Commons in general terms, even though the inadequacy in law of the true grounds for commitment has been notorious.[78] The House of Lords has held that where an immigration officer has exercised his power to detain and remove an illegal immigrant, the court will have to be satisfied, on the civil standard of proof to a high degree of probability, that in fact the applicant was an illegal immigrant when the power was exercised.[79]

Applicants for habeas corpus in recent years have mostly been persons in detention for the purpose of extradition, deportation or implementation of a refusal to admit as an immigrant.[80] The introduction of an immigration

---

72 *R. v. Brixton Prison Governor, ex p. Ahsan* [1969] 2 QB 222. Contrast *Green* v. *Home Secretary* [1942] AC 284, a wartime preventive detention case.

73 *Ex p. Hinds* [1961] 1 WLR 325. The court may admit to bail on an application on a criminal matter.

74 Amnon Rubinstein, *Jurisdiction and Illegality* (1965), pp. 105–16, 178–86.

75 See *R. v. Brixton Governor, ex p. Armah* [1968] AC 192, especially at 229–35, *per* Lord Reid, conceding that the scope of review is not confined to strictly jurisdictional grounds.

76 But see now pp. 423–8.

77 For example, *Green*'s case, note 72.

78 *Sheriff of Middlesex*'s case (1840); p. 331.

79 *R. v. Secretary of State for the Home Department; ex p. Khawaja* [1984] AC 74, overruling its own decision in *Zamir* v. *Home Secretary* [1980] AC 930.

80 The writ was unsuccessfully sought in 1984 by a prisoner held on remand who had not been produced from prison to court at the time fixed because of an industrial dispute at the prison: *R. v. Brixton Prison Governor, ex p. Walsh* [1985] AC 154.

appeals system has stemmed[81] the flow by providing an alternative remedy. The abolition of conscription for military service and the creation of a Courts-Martial Appeal Court have almost ended applications made by persons complaining that they are not subject to military law or that courts-martial have exceeded jurisdiction.[82] A new procedure for determining child custody cases has rendered habeas corpus applications almost superfluous. Alternative remedies do not necessarily exclude the right to apply for habeas corpus, but they make recourse to the writ less frequent. Unusual cases of paramount importance may yet arise; others have followed the 1974 example of Mr Milhench by seeking the writ to challenge the validity of the police detaining for questioning.[83] It was on a habeas corpus application that slavery was declared illegal in England.[84]

Successive applications and appeals

It used to be thought that an unsuccessful applicant could renew his application before each superior court and judge in turn till his funds ran out or he obtained a favourable ruling.[85] No appeal lay from a decision to *grant* habeas corpus except in cases of private civil detention (for example, child custody), or against a *refusal* of habeas corpus in a criminal cause or matter.

The Administration of Justice Act 1960 restated the law. No application for habeas corpus can be made on the same grounds to the same court or judge or any other court or judge unless fresh evidence is adduced.[86] The Act reformed the law relating to habeas corpus appeals. In civil matters the right of an unsuccessful applicant to appeal to the Court of Appeal and thence, with leave, to the House of Lords was retained, but the same rights

---

81 See ch. 20.

82 cf. pp. 223–4.

83 The police eventually charged Milhench two hours before the time fixed by the judge for the police to show cause why he should not be released. Unfortunately the judge usually adjourns the application for at least twenty-four hours to enable the police to be represented; meanwhile police questioning during unlawful detention may continue. And see Gifford and O'Connor (1979), *Legal Action Group Bulletin* 182.

84 *Somersett* v. *Stewart* (1772) 20 St. Tr. 1 (Negro slave brought to England; released though slavery still lawful in the territory from which he came).

85 See especially *Eshugbayi Eleko* v. *Government of Nigeria* [1928] AC 459. This view was aptly criticized by R. F. V. Heuston (1950) 66 *LQR* 79.

86 Administration of Justice Act 1960, s. 14(2). The fresh evidence must be relevant and admissible: *Ex p. Schtraks* [1964] 1 QB 191. Repeated applications can be struck out if they are being used vexatiously or in a manner amounting to an abuse of process: *R. v. Governor of Brixton Prison, ex p. Osman (No. 4)* [1992] 1 All ER 579.

were extended to the respondent where the application had been granted. In criminal matters (for example, extradition), a single judge may issue habeas corpus, but if minded to refuse he must refer the case for hearing by the Divisional Court. From a decision by the Divisional Court *to grant or refuse* an application in a criminal matter[87] an appeal lies, with leave either of that court or of the House of Lords, direct to the Lords at the instance of the applicant or respondent.[88] A curious feature of this type of appeal is that if the detainee is discharged on his original application, and the respondent's appeal is successful, the former detainee is nevertheless immune from recommittal unless the court below, having been notified of the respondent's intention to appeal, makes an order for his remand in custody or temporary release on bail.

Territorial scope

Habeas corpus will not issue from the High Court to Scotland or Northern Ireland[89] or, in general in respect of detention on foreign soil. It will not issue to a dependent territory where there is a court competent to award and supervise the execution of the writ.[90] Scots law has developed its own procedures to secure release from wrongful imprisonment.[91]

Emergency powers

In wartime there is provision for preventive detention of enemy aliens and security suspects. These powers will be briefly considered in a later chapter.[92] Powers of detention in Northern Ireland have been mentioned separately.[93]

---

87 An application by a compulsorily detained mental patient is deemed to be in respect of a criminal matter.
88 Possibly this change in the law is attributable to the problems created by the decision in *R.* v. *Board of Control, ex p. Rutty* [1956] 2 QB 109.
89 *Re Keenan* [1972] 1 QB 533. In this case the Court of Appeal assumed, it is thought erroneously, that habeas corpus was a discretionary remedy. cf. Yale [1972A] *Camb. LJ* 4. But Northern Ireland courts have jurisdiction to award habeas corpus.
90 Habeas Corpus Act 1862; Sir Kenneth Roberts-Wray, *Commonwealth and Colonial Law* (1966), pp. 612–15.
91 See J. D. B. Mitchell, *Constitutional Law* (2nd edn, 1968), pp. 339–41.
92 ch. 24.
93 ch. 3.

Habeas corpus and damages

Unlawful detention is false imprisonment. Consequently a person released on habeas corpus will normally be entitled to recover damages in tort against the persons responsible for his detention. To the general rule there is a limited range of exceptions. For example, the custodian may have a special statutory defence to an action for damages if he acted in good faith. Moreover, a person whose initial arrest was wrongful may be entitled to nominal damages for false imprisonment although he is subsequently convicted and cannot obtain release on habeas corpus.

PRIVACY AND SEARCH

Offensive invasion of personal privacy[94] is not yet recognized in English law as an independent tort.[95] (The courts may develop such a tort when the European Convention on Human Rights becomes part of English law.) An intrusion into one's private affairs may indeed constitute the torts of defamation, trespass, nuisance, conspiracy, injurious falsehood, breach of copyright or passing off, depending on the circumstances; or if it tends to prejudice the outcome of pending judicial proceedings it may be a contempt of court. Some intrusions on privacy are criminal offences – for example, using an electronic eavesdropping device in breach of the Wireless Telegraphy Act 1949; sending out unsolicited advertisements for sex manuals.[96] An injunction and possibly damages can be claimed for certain forms of breach of confidence[97] – a civil wrong which has a capacity for development. But

---

94 The primary sources are the Report of the Committee on Privacy (Cmnd 5012 (1972)) – the Younger Report; Reports of the Committee on Privacy and Related Matters (Cm 1102 (1990) and Cm 2135 (1993)) – the Calcutt Reports. See also T. Gibbons, *Regulating the Media* (1990), pp. 132–5. On press freedom, see below, p. 455. The text above is concerned only with English law.

95 Because English law recognizes no general right of privacy there is no right to have a telephone conversation in one's home without interruption: *Malone* v. *Metropolitan Police Commissioner* [1979] Ch. 344.

96 Unsolicited Goods and Services Act 1971, s. 4.

97 For example, *Argyll* v. *Argyll* [1967] Ch. 602; *Schering Chemicals Ltd* v. *Falkman Ltd* [1982] QB 1; *Att.-Gen.* v. *Jonathan Cape Ltd* [1976] QB 752, Cmnd 5012 (1972). In *Att.-Gen.* v. *The Observer Ltd, Guardian Newspapers Ltd, Times Newspapers Ltd* [1988] 3 All ER 545, the House of Lords rejected the Government's claim for a permanent injunction to restrain the newspaper publication of parts of Mr Peter Wright's memoirs, *Spycatcher*. The Government had asserted that members of the Security Services owe a lifelong duty of confidentiality to the Crown. The House of Lords, however, noted that, there is no legal redress available to one whose past life is mercilessly publicized, or who is accurately photographed in embarrassing circumstances, or whose conversations are deliberately recorded by mechanical or electronic devices in the absence of conspiracy, trespass or breach of the 1949 Act. Moreover, evidence obtained by an eavesdropping device is admissible in criminal proceedings;[98] so, indeed, is evidence procured as a result of an unlawful search which is a trespass.[99]

Parliament has intervened, however, to safeguard further the citizen's right not to have his telephone calls or mail interfered with, except according to the provisions of the Interception of Communications Act 1985.[100] It is an offence under that Act[101] to intercept unlawfully a communication sent by post or by means of a public telecommunications system, but it is a defence to show that such interception had been authorized by a warrant issued under the Act.[102] Such a warrant may only be issued by the Secretary

---

as the book had been published in many other countries, secrecy had been destroyed, and the public interest in freedom of speech meant that permanent injunctions should not be granted. The House of Lords had upheld the granting of interim injunctions at [1987] 1 WLR 1248. On the *Spycatcher* affair, see [1987] *Public Law* 626; D. G. T. Williams (1988) *Camb. LJ* 1. See also *Att.-Gen.* v. *Blake* [1996] 3 All ER 903. The Official Secrets Act 1989, s. 1, now makes it an offence for a person who is or has been a member of the security or intelligence services to disclose, without lawful authority, any information relating to his work.

98 *R.* v. *Maqsood Ali* [1966] 1 QB 688. Contrast *Katz* v. *US* 389 US 347 (1967).

99 *Kurama* v. *R.* [1955] AC 197; *King* v. *R.* [1969] 1 AC 304 (notwithstanding a constitutional guarantee of freedom from unreasonable search). Contrast the position in the United States: *Mapp* v. *Ohio* 367 US 643 (1961). But in *Lindley* v. *Rutter* [1981] 1 QB 128 it was held unlawful to remove a woman's brassière by force.

100 The interception of telephone calls and of the mails had been authorized before 1985 by the Secretary of State as an exercise of the prerogative: see Report of a Committee of Privy Counsellors, Cmnd 283 (1957) (the Birkett Report). In practice the Home Secretary issued (and continues to issue) most warrants, and the Foreign and Commonwealth Secretary and the Secretaries of State for Scotland and Northern Ireland issue some as well. In *Malone* v. *United Kingdom* (1985) 7 EHRR 14, the European Court had held that telephone tapping as authorized by the Home Secretary violated article 8 of the European Convention on Human Rights, because English law and practice contained inadequate safeguards for the individual. The Government then caused the 1985 Act to be passed, on which see Lloyd (1986) 49 *Mod. L. Rev.* 86; Prosser [1986] *Public Law* 8; Robilliard and McEwan, op. cit., pp. 31–6.

101 1985 Act, s. 1.

102 ibid., ss. 1(2), 2. See also Post Office Act 1953, s. 58(1) (as amended by the 1985 Act, s. 11(2)). The 1985 Act now covers the interception of overseas telegrams and cables, previously governed by the Official Secrets Act 1920, s. 4 (which is repealed: 1985 Act, s. 11(5)).

of State[103] if he considers it to be necessary in the interests of national security, or for the purpose of preventing serious crime[104] or for the purpose of safeguarding the economic well-being of the United Kingdom.[105] Unusually, the Act requires the Secretary of State himself to sign the warrant, except in urgent cases. Anyone who thinks that his communications have been unlawfully intercepted may apply to the Tribunal established by the Act.[106] It will investigate whether a relevant warrant had been issued, and if so whether there had been any breach of the Act. If it discovers a breach, the Tribunal must inform the complainant and the Prime Minister, and it may order that the warrant be quashed, that any copies of intercepted material be destroyed, and it may also award compensation. If the Tribunal finds that no warrant had been issued, the Tribunal must inform the complainant that there has been no breach of the Act[107] – a provision which amply shows that the Tribunal has no power over any interception conducted wholly unlawfully and without any attempt to stay within the law. A Commissioner holds office under the Act[108] to keep under review the Secretary of State's functions under the Act, and to assist the Tribunal.[109]

Powers of search and seizure ancillary to a valid arrest are exercisable by the police. Upon a person's arrest a constable can search him if he reasonably believes that he may present a danger to himself or others, or has on him anything which could help him escape, or has evidence relating to the suspected offence. He may also search any premises in which the arrest was carried out for evidence relating to the crime.[110] Reasonable force may be used for the purpose,[111] and the constable may detain anything for which the search was carried out.[112] An arrested person may be searched again at a

---

103 Warrants are issued to the police, Customs and Excise, and the Security Service (MI5).
104 Defined (Interception of Communications Act 1985, s. 10(3)) as the use of violence, or resulting in substantial gain, or conduct by a large number of people; or an offence which in the circumstances could carry a sentence of three years' imprisonment.
105 ibid., s. 4(1).
106 ibid., s. 7 and sched. 1.
107 The Tribunal's decisions cannot be questioned in any court, nor be subject to an appeal there: ibid., s. 7(8).
108 ibid., s. 8. He must be a senior judge.
109 In his Report for 1991, Cm 1942 (1992), the Commissioner reported that three telephones had been tapped other than those specified in warrants, the result of faulty British Telecom equipment or mistakes by BT engineers.
110 Police and Criminal Evidence Act 1984, s. 32.
111 ibid., s. 117.
112 ibid., s. 32(8), (9).

police station to ascertain what property he has, and it may be retained if it could be used to cause injury, damage, interference with evidence or to help him escape.[113] He may also be subjected to an 'intimate search'.[114] After arrest the police may enter and search, without a warrant, any premises of the arrested person on reasonable suspicion that there is evidence there about the crime for which he has been arrested.[115]

A constable in uniform may enter and search any premises without a warrant, using reasonable force if necessary, to execute an arrest warrant, to arrest a person for an arrestable offence (and for other specified and limited offences), to recapture one who is unlawfully at large and whom he is chasing, or to save life and limb or to prevent serious damage. All the common-law rules about entry without a warrant (save in relation to breach of the peace) have been abrogated.[116] Police officers and immigration officers have certain exceptional powers to stop and detain persons without effecting any arrest, for the purpose of search or examination.[117]

In the celebrated case of *Entick* v. *Carrington* (1765)[118] it was held that a general warrant issued by a Secretary of State to arrest a named person for sedition, and to search for and seize his papers, was illegal and could not be justified on the ground of State necessity[119] or reasonable suspicion. An Englishman's home was his castle. Indeed, the 'great end for which men entered into society was to secure their property. That right is preserved sacred . . . in all instances where it has not been abridged by some public law for the good of the whole.'[120] As Salmon LJ, a judge noted for robust assertions of individual rights, once observed, these words today have 'an odd ring – both archaic and incongruous'.

Here one moves from the theme of personal liberty to freedom of property – a topic with vast ramifications which will not be explored here. Powers of entry for the purpose of inspection, testing, survey, levying

---

113 ibid., s. 54.
114 ibid., s. 55, and the Criminal Justice and Public Order Act 1994, ss. 54, 55.
115 1984 Act, s. 18.
116 ibid., s. 17(5), (6).
117 See, for example, Misuse of Drugs Act 1971, s. 23 (police power to stop and search); Immigration Act 1971, s. 4; sched. 1 §§ 2, 16 (detention for examination or prior to removal). See also Customs and Excise Management Act 1979, s. 164.
118 (1765) 19 St. Tr. 1030.
119 A ground accepted as one justification for retention of papers seized in circumstances of doubtful legality in *Elias* v. *Pasmore* (above) at 173 (police entered premises to arrest H under warrant for a seditious offence; they had no search warrant, but impounded papers found there and used them in a successful prosecution of E for a similar offence).
120 *Per* Lord Camden at 1066. See also *Wilkes* v. *Wood* (1763) 19 St. Tr. 1153.

execution and distress, taking possession, destruction and demolition are vested by some 200 or so different statutory provisions in numerous officials.[121] Police powers of entry, like administrative powers, are not unfettered: there is, as we have seen, no general licence to enter or remain on private property in the investigation of a crime.[122] The police can enter premises without permission for the purpose of preventing or stopping a reasonably apprehended or actual breach of the peace[123] or for effecting an arrest for certain offences,[124] or for the execution of a search warrant. Search warrants may be issued by magistrates or judges under a number of statutes, some of them of constitutional importance (for example, the Official Secrets Acts, the Public Order Act); they do not invariably have to be ancillary to an arrest. The Police and Criminal Evidence Act 1984 is now the main statute. A magistrate may issue a search warrant if, on an application by a constable, he is satisfied that there are reasonable grounds for believing that a serious arrestable offence[125] has been committed; that evidence likely to be of serious value to the investigation of that offence is on the premises; that it is not 'excluded' or 'special procedure' material[126] and that entry without such a warrant (that is, by consent) would not be practical or possible.[127] A constable may use reasonable force, if necessary, in the execution of a search warrant.[128] Anything may be seized under the warrant, provided that it is not subject to legal privilege[129] and provided that the constable has reasonable grounds for believing that it is evidence about a crime he is investigating or any other crime, and that it is necessary to seize it to prevent its concealment, loss or destruction.[130] If premises are lawfully searched in

---

121 See generally R. Stone, *Entry, Search and Seizure* (3rd edn, 1996).

122 *Great Central Rly Co* v. *Bates* [1921] 3 KB 578; *Davis* v. *Lisle* [1936] 2 KB 434; *McArdle* v. *Wallace (No. 2)* (1964) 108 SJ 483.

123 As in *Thomas* v. *Sawkins* [1935] 2 KB 249, a power expressly preserved in the 1984 Act, s. 17(6).

124 ibid., s. 17(1).

125 Defined in the 1984 Act, s. 116.

126 Defined ibid., ss. 9–14, sched. 1: such material requires a warrant from a Circuit judge to authorize search and seizure. For the procedure to be followed, see *R.* v. *Central Criminal Court, ex p. Adegbesan* [1986] 3 All ER 113.

127 ibid., s. 8.

128 ibid., s. 117.

129 Defined ibid., ss. 10, 19(6) and including communications between a legal adviser and his client. But items held with the intention of furthering a criminal purpose are not protected: see s. 10(2) and *R.* v. *Crown Court at Snaresbrook, ex p. DPP* [1988] 1 All ER 315; *Francis & Francis* v. *Central Criminal Court* [1988] 3 All ER 775.

130 ibid., s. 19(3).

pursuance of a warrant specifying stolen property to be seized, the taking of property not included in the warrant is normally unlawful; but it appears that reasonable mistake, and reasonable suspicion that goods not specified have been stolen and are evidence on a charge of stealing or receiving against the person in possession or his associates, may justify seizure. The common-law rule that the police, having lawfully obtained entry, are not entitled to conduct a search of private property, without a warrant, in order to fish hopefully for evidence of a crime, is preserved.[131]

The risk remains after the enactment of the Police and Criminal Evidence Act 1984 that the courts, having formerly leaned over backwards in their solicitude for private property, may give too much weight to the public interest in crime detection and too little to the claims of personal privacy. That the apprehensions of the police must be shown to be reasonable is not much of a safeguard against abuse of powers given the notorious reluctance of magistrates[132] to reject assertions by the police as to the reasonableness of their own suspicions.

THE SECURITY AND INTELLIGENCE SERVICES

Of the covert government agencies concerned with maintaining national security, the two best known are the Security Service (MI5) and the Secret Intelligence Service (MI6). Their existence has, however, only been officially confirmed within the last few years, along with that of Government Communications Headquarters (GCHQ). Both the Security Service and the Secret Intelligence Service have been placed on a statutory footing.[133] Under the Security Service Act 1989, there continues to be a Security Service 'under the authority of the Secretary of State' – in practice, the

---

131 ibid., s. 19; *Ghani* v. *Jones* [1970] 1 QB 693 at 706 (detention of Pakistani passports obtained in police search without warrant held unlawful in absence of reasonable grounds for believing plaintiffs to be implicated in a suspected murder or for believing the documents to be material evidence to prove the offence); *Reynolds* v. *Metropolitan Police Commissioner* [1985] QB 881.

132 And often superior judges: see *Piddington* v. *Bates* [1961] 1 WLR 164 at 170. See also K. Lidstone [1984] *Crim. L. Rev.* 499.

133 For the historical perspective, see D. G. T. Williams, *Not in the Public Interest* (1972), chs. 7, 8; Cmnd 2152 (1963) (the Denning Report); T. Bunyan, *The History and Practice of the Political Police in Britain* (revised edn, 1977); C. Andrew, *Secret Service* (1985); and L. Lustgarten and I. Leigh, *In From the Cold: National Security and Parliament* (1996).

Home Secretary.[134] Its main function is expressed to be[135] the protection of national security; in particular MI5 protects national security against threats of espionage, terrorism and sabotage emanating from agents of foreign powers, and actions intended to overthrow or undermine parliamentary democracy by political, industrial or violent means. In 1992 MI5 was given the task (formerly entrusted to the Special Branch of the Metropolitan Police) of spearheading anti-IRA intelligence-gathering. Another purpose[136] is to safeguard the economic well-being of the United Kingdom against threats posed by the actions or intentions of persons outside the British Islands.[137] The final responsibility of the Security Service is to act in support of the police in the prevention and detection of serious crime.[138] The Director-General of the Security Service must ensure that information is only obtained for the proper discharge of its functions, and that the Service does not act to further the interests of any political party. The Director must report annually to the Prime Minister and the Secretary of State.[139] The Act states that no entry or interference with property by the Service shall be unlawful if it is authorized by the Secretary of State; a warrant can only be issued if the Secretary of State thinks it necessary to obtain information which is likely to be of substantial value to the Service and which cannot be obtained by any other means.[140] A Security Service Commissioner and Tribunal exist to review the use of warrants and to investigate complaints:[141] they are similar in concept to the Commissioner and Tribunal under the Interception of Communications Act 1985.[142] Much information about MI5 was officially published in 1993 for the first time in a book entitled *The Security Service*. The Secret Intelligence Service is continued in being, but by virtue of statute, under the Intelligence Services

---

134 s. 1(1), 2. The Director-General of the Service had been made responsible to the Home Secretary under a directive issued by Sir David Maxwell-Fyfe in 1952. There is no definition of the Service in the Act.

135 s. 1(2).

136 s. 1(3).

137 As it had been the task of MI6 to collect foreign intelligence, casting economic protection on to MI5 is odd.

138 Security Service Act 1996, s. 1.

139 s. 2(1), (2), (3). The first woman Director-General, Stella Rimington, was appointed under the Act in 1992.

140 s. 3. The Secretary of State must issue the warrant himself, save in an urgent case when a senior official may do so: s. 3(3). The Service has no power of arrest beyond that enjoyed by ordinary citizens.

141 ss. 4, 5 and sched. 1.

142 See above, p. 445.

Act 1994.[143] Its functions are expressed to be the obtaining of information relating to people outside the British Islands, and to perform other tasks relating to the actions or intentions of such people.[144] Those functions can be exercised only in the interests of national security, or in the interests of the economic well-being of the United Kingdom, or in the prevention or detection of serious crime.[145] MI6 operates under a Chief of the Service, appointed by the Secretary of State.[146] Under the Intelligence Services Act 1994 the Government Communications Headquarters (GCHQ) is also continued in being, and is subject to the authority of the Secretary of State.[147] Its task is to monitor, or to interfere with, electromagnetic and other 'emissions',[148] and to provide information to the Crown about cryptography, but it may do so only for the same purposes as MI6.[149] There is a Director of GCHQ.[150] Warrants may be issued by the Secretary of State to any of the three intelligence services to do in relation to property what would otherwise be unlawful.[151] A Commissioner reports annually under the Intelligence Services Act, and a Tribunal exists to investigate complaints.[152] And there is a statutory Intelligence and Security Committee, drawn from the membership of both Houses of Parliament, and appointed by the Prime Minister in consultation with the Leader of the Opposition.[153] It examines the expenditure, administration and policy of the three intelligence services.[154]

143 s. 1(1).
144 s. 1(1)(a).
145 s. 1(2).
146 s. 2(1). The Chief has statutory duties enumerated in s. 2(2).
147 s. 3.
148 s. 3(1).
149 s. 3(2).
150 s. 4.
151 s. 5.
152 ss. 8, 9.
153 s. 10.
154 This is another rare example of statutory references to the Leader of the Opposition. The Committee's duty mirrors that of the select committees which oversee government departments.

CHAPTER 22

Freedom of Expression

IN GENERAL

Bills of rights in modern Commonwealth constitutions include qualified guarantees of freedom of conscience and religion, freedom of speech and expression, and freedom of peaceable assembly and association. In practice these liberties are intimately related. If serious encroachments are made on any one of them, some or all will be diminished. Of all the basic freedoms in the world today the most precarious are the rights to express opinions and associate with like-minded persons for the purpose of opposing and eventually deposing the government in office. Fortunately in Britain these political rights, though not formally guaranteed, enjoy adequate protection in practice, and will be underpinned when the Human Rights Bill becomes law. In this chapter the outline of the law relating to freedom of expression will be considered.[1] In the next, aspects of the law of assembly and association will be dealt with. These areas of the law intersect but can be treated separately.

Freedom of conscience and religion does not call for an extensive discussion.[2] Freedom of conscience falls partly within the scope of freedom of expression, partly under freedom of assembly and association. The law does not concern itself with individual beliefs or disbeliefs unless a person propagates his views in scurrilous terms or in circumstances likely to give rise to a breach of the peace or in a place to which he is denied lawful access. There is no compulsory State religion, no obligation to submit to any form of religious instruction, no religious test for the tenure of public office save in the case of the monarch.[3] Religious disqualifications for the

---

1 See E. Barendt, *Freedom of Speech* (1985); H. Street, *Freedom, the Individual and the Law* (6th edn, 1989, by G. Robertson), chs 4–7; Boyle [1982] *Public Law* 574.
2 See generally St J. Robilliard, *Religion and the Law* (1984).
3 See pp. 129–30. Section 1 of the Lord Chancellor (Tenure of Office and Discharge of Ecclesiastical Functions) Act 1974 declares that for the avoidance of doubt, the office of Lord Chancellor is and shall be tenable by an adherent of the Roman Catholic faith.

franchise and sitting in Parliament had been abolished by the end of the nineteenth century. Not since the sixteenth century have men and women been burnt at the stake as heretics and the worst horrors of the Inquisition passed England by. Compassing or imagining the monarch's death is still a statutory offence, but treasonable conduct must be manifested by overt acts for a conviction to be obtained;[4] 'the devil himself knoweth not the thought of man',[5] and though a person's state of mind may be an essential ingredient of a specific criminal or civil wrong, the law refrains from imposing sanctions in the absence of a wrongful act or omission.[6] Potentially subversive political opinions may, however, be a ground for preventive detention in wartime,[7] and for dismissal from the civil service or removal to a non-sensitive post.[8]

PRIOR RESTRAINTS

'Freedom of discussion', in Dicey's words, was 'in England little else than the right to write or say anything which a jury, consisting of twelve shopkeepers, think it expedient should be said or written.'[9] It was subject to no prior restraint. Press censorship had lapsed in 1695. Press libels, moreover, were triable according to the ordinary law of the land by the ordinary courts; the rule of law prevailed.

This simple picture, portraying the laws of defamation, sedition and blasphemy as the main restrictions of freedom of expression, needs to be modified today. The restrictions, though not oppressive, are multifarious. Trial of offenders is not always by jury. Moreover, restraints may operate before any legal wrong has been committed. These prior restraints are not neatly segregated from offences arising from dissemination. For example, one needs a licence to transmit a radio broadcast; if one broadcasts without such a licence, one incurs a criminal penalty. Obscene literature can be seized, condemned and destroyed; if such literature escapes suppression it is still an offence to publish it. A public meeting held on private premises

---

4 Statute of Treasons 1351; *R.* v. *Thistlewood* (1820) 33 St. Tr. 681; Treason Act 1795, s. 1; Treason Felony Act 1848, s. 3.
5 *Per* Brian CJ in 1477.
6 Misprision (concealment) of treason is still a common-law offence, but misprision of another's felony has been superseded by section 5(1) of the Criminal Law Act 1967 which makes it an offence to accept a valuable consideration for concealment of an arrestable offence.
7 See p. 496.
8 See pp. 211–14.
9 *Introduction to the Study of the Law of the Constitution* (10th edn), p. 246.

is a civil trespass if conducted without the occupier's permission and an injunction may be obtained to prevent it from being held.

Prior restraints are not all of the same kind. Some are strictly legal prohibitions coupled with a sanction; others are extra-legal and have to be analysed in different terms. If there is a sanction annexed to disregard of a prohibition, it may range from imprisonment to loss of a licence or of promotion prospects. Such restraints are more easily tabulated than classified.

Accessibility of media for publicity

I may be at liberty to express an opinion but unable to obtain an audience because nobody will let a hall to me for the conduct of a public meeting, or because the competent authority refuses me a permit to hold a meeting in a public place under its control, or because the police (if no prior authority is required by law) threaten to prosecute me for obstruction of the highway or a similar offence if I proceed; or the police may simply assert their power to stop me because they reasonably apprehend a breach of the peace,[10] though by participating in a mass demonstration I may at once achieve more publicity and gain a measure of safety in numbers. I cannot compel newspaper editors to publish my letters, or editors and publishers to accept my articles and books. If I have the money and persistence I can have my work printed privately and distributed by post. Provided that it does not contain offensive or obscene material and it is not prejudicial to public safety or security[11] it will be immune from interception and seizure in the mails. But booksellers and public libraries may refuse to purchase it, and indeed blacklist it. I may offer to pay for or subscribe to the cost of an advertisement for the propagation of my opinions; newspapers may decline to print it and other bodies owning advertising space are not obliged to display it. I cannot set up a private broadcasting station to air my opinions to the public at large within the United Kingdom unless I am awarded a licence by the Independent Television Commission or by the Radio Authority.[12]

10 See ch. 23.
11 Post Office Act 1953, ss. 11, 58, 66.
12 See Wireless Telegraphy Act 1949; Marine etc. Broadcasting (Offences) Act 1967; Broadcasting Acts 1990 and 1996, p. 456.

Censorship and suppression[13]

The Press. Executive censorship of the press ended in 1695, to be revived only in wartime. The legal requirements as to the registration of newspapers and the printing of the names of their publishers and printers in each issue are not substantial restraints.

Offences committed by the publication of material by reason of its content will be considered separately, but it may be noted at this point that it is unlawful for the press to publish the evidence (otherwise than such as is disclosed by the judge's summing up or judgment) in divorce and nullity proceedings, or any indecent matter disclosed in judicial proceedings,[14] or (subject to limited exceptions) information divulging the identity of juveniles involved in court proceedings, or in general except at the defendant's request, a contemporaneous report of the evidence given at committal proceedings before magistrates.[15]

Reference can also be made here to the 'D' Notice system. There exists a non-statutory Defence, Press and Broadcasting Committee, with a senior civil servant as chairman; it includes other senior officials, but representatives of the press, press agencies and broadcasting services are in the majority among its members; it has a full-time secretary, a retired senior officer from the armed services. Its main function is to approve the issue of 'D' Notices, which are confidential letters initiated by Government Departments and addressed to newspaper, periodical and news-bulletin editors, requesting that material not be published because it would have an adverse effect on national defence or security.[16] Non-compliance with such a request is not an offence in itself, but it may result in a prosecution for a breach of the

13 See generally Paul O'Higgins, *Censorship in Britain* (1972) for radical criticism of the law and practice.
14 Judicial Proceedings (Regulation of Reports) Act 1926, s. 1. See also Domestic and Appellate Proceedings (Restriction of Publicity) Act 1968..
15 Criminal Justice Act 1967, s. 3, as amended by the Magistrates' Courts Act 1980, s. 8(2A) (see above, p. 361). The restrictions do not apply if the defendant is *not* committed for trial.
16 See generally Cmnd 1681 (1962), ch. 9; Cmnd 3309, 3312 (1967); D. G. T. Williams, *Not in the Public Interest* (1972), pp. 80 ff.; Marshall [1967] *Public Law* 261; Report of the (Franks) Committee on section 2 of the Official Secrets Act 1911 (Cmnd 5104 (1972)), §65: Minutes of Evidence, vol. 2, pp. 241−5, vol. 3, pp. 51−68; Report from the Defence Committee, HC 773 (1979−80), and Jaconelli [1982] *Public Law* 37. 'D' Notices are also sent to book publishers from time to time, requesting non-publication of certain matters or the submission of manuscripts for security clearance.

Official Secrets Acts,[17] compliance with the request being in practice a safeguard against a prosecution, though an assurance that an item of information is not covered by a 'D' Notice is not in itself such a safeguard.[18] Even if disclosure of the information is not a breach of the Acts, the news medium concerned may be publicly censured and may find that confidential information formerly supplied to it from official sources is thereafter withheld.

Broadcasting services.[19] The British Broadcasting Corporation, constituted by royal charter in 1926, provides all non-commercial radio and television services. Its functions are prescribed by its charter, the current licence and agreement[20] under which it operates, and any directions issued to it by the Home Secretary in pursuance of powers conferred on him by the governing instruments. Under the agreement he is empowered to require the Corporation to refrain from broadcasting any matter or class of matter at any time. If the Corporation fails to comply with a valid direction he may revoke its licence.[21]

He enjoys statutory powers of direction in relation to the Independent Television Commission,[22] which regulates commercial services provided by programme contractors. A number of positive duties (for example, to broadcast Government announcements but to maintain political impartiality) are cast on the BBC and the ITC.

In what circumstances (if any) can a breach of such duties by the broadcasting authorities give rise to judicial proceedings? This question has come before the courts once, in the important case of *Attorney-General ex rel. McWhirter* v. *IBA*[23] concerning the duty of the former IBA to satisfy themselves that so far as possible '. . . nothing is included in the programmes which offends against good taste or decency or is likely to . . . be offensive

---

17 See pp. 463−7.
18 This was the position in the *Sunday Telegraph* (or Biafra) case, 1970−71; see Jonathan Aitken, *Officially Secret* (1971).
19 See T. Gibbons, *Regulating the Media* (1991).
20 See Cm. 3152 (1996).
21 Licence, clauses 13(4), 23. In 1985 the BBC board of governors at the Home Secretary's 'request' cancelled the broadcast of a programme which included an interview with the IRA chief of staff. The Home Secretary had issued a directive banning the broadcasting of interviews with supporters of terrorist organizations: see 139 HC Deb. *1075* (2 November 1988); the ban was held to be lawful in *Brind* v. *Secretary of State of the Home Department* [1991] 1 All ER 722. It was lifted in 1994.
22 Broadcasting Act 1990, s. 10; see also note 21.
23 [1973] QB 639.

to public feeling'.[24] The court held that it could grant an injunction only if the decision of the Authority were wrong in law or one to which it could not reasonably have come. The Attorney-General seeks the injunction as guardian of the public interest, but a private citizen can do so only with the leave of the Attorney-General.[25] Whether breach of a particular duty is actionable depends on the nature and wording of the duty. The duties of the BBC to send out broadcasts 'efficiently' and of the ITC to maintain a 'high quality' in programmes are so vague that a court would be reluctant to enforce them. (It is, of course, possible for the Minister to cancel the BBC's licence, or to initiate the dismissal of the Governors of the BBC by the Crown or himself to dismiss the members of the ITC. Such drastic action, however, would hardly be conceivable unless there was direct disobedience of a specific ministerial direction; in the Republic of Ireland in November 1972 the members of RTE, the equivalent body of the BBC, were dismissed *en bloc* for refusal to comply with a direction.) Duties to broadcast Government announcements and to maintain political impartiality[26] are potentially enforceable in judicial proceedings by an order of mandamus awarded by the High Court on the application of the Minister.

Technological development in cable and (particularly) in satellite broadcasting[27] led to the passage of the Cable and Broadcasting Act 1984. The Cable Authority operated under the Act to license the provision of programmes by cable, and the Satellite Broadcasting Board oversaw programmes broadcast directly from satellites. The ITC was subsequently given responsibility for satellite[28] and cable[29] services, in place of that Authority and Board. Cable and direct satellite broadcasts are subject to similar standards imposed on the BBC and the ITC by the Broadcasting Act 1990. Satellite broadcasting is more widely available than cable transmissions; and also impossible to censor if broadcast by a foreign operator.

The broadcasting authorities are responsible for their own standards,

---

24 s. 4(1)(a).
25 *Gouriet* v. *Union of Post Office Workers* [1978] AC 435. The House of Lords expressly disapproved dicta in the *McWhirter* case to the effect that a private individual could seek the injunction himself in circumstances of urgency or where the Attorney-General wrongly withheld his permission.
26 In 1986 Ministers were critical of the BBC's coverage of the United States' bombing of Libya, on the ground that it was not 'impartial'.
27 See Cmnd 8679 (1982); Cmnd 8751 (1982); Cmnd 8866 (1983); Broadcasting Act 1996.
28 Broadcasting Act 1990, ss. 43−5.
29 ibid., ss. 2, 46−7.

subject to formal obligations and ministerial directives, in the presentation of films and plays and other programmes. The provisions of the Obscene Publications Act 1959 now apply to the provision of programme services.[30] A Broadcasting Standards Commission publishes a code concerning violence, sexual conduct, taste and decency in broadcasts,[31] and it receives complaints about such matters.[32] As we have seen, they are also included within the ambit of the 'D' Notice system.

Theatres and plays. Till 1968, stage performances and theatres had to receive a licence from the Lord Chamberlain before they could lawfully be performed and used; it was a criminal offence to stage a play in an unapproved form. A private member's bill was introduced to abolish the Lord Chamberlain's powers; it became the Theatres Act 1968. Premises still require a local authority licence if they are to be used for the public performance of a play, but no condition may be imposed restricting the content of the 'plays' to be performed other than an exhibition of hypnotism.[33] The law relating to criminal offences and civil wrongs committed in the course of a stage performance has been redefined. The immediate practical effects of the Act were an increase in plays dealing with controversial topics such as homosexuality, the production of nude musicals, and the use of earthier language than the Lord Chamberlain would formerly have permitted.

Films.[34] Film censorship is a blend of statutory and non-statutory regulation. Cinemas are licensed[35] by local authorities. Conditions may be attached to the grant of licences, restricting the admission of children, prohibiting the exhibition of films likely to be injurious to morality, and so on. A condition commonly imposed is that no film not approved by the British Board of Film Classification shall be exhibited without the express consent of the licensing authority. The Board is a non-statutory body constituted by the film industry; the president is appointed by a committee representing the industry after consultation with the Home Office and the local authority

30 ibid., s. 162.
31 ibid., Part VII.
32 Broadcasting Act 1996, Part V.
33 s. 1(2). Conditions may be imposed in the interests of physical safety and health. An appeal lies to a magistrates' court at the instance of a person aggrieved by a licensing decision (s. 14).
34 Street, op. cit., pp. 217–21.
35 Cinemas Act 1985.

associations, but he is independent of the industry. The full-time secretary of the Board has, in practice, been its most dominant figure. Films are classified as 'U' (suitable for universal exhibition), 'PG' (parental guidance; some scenes may be unsuitable for young children), '12' (no child under twelve being permitted to be present), '15' (no child under fifteen being permitted to be present), '18' (no person under eighteen being permitted to be present) or '18R' (restricted distribution through segregated premises, 18 and over). The Board may refuse a film a certificate altogether, or grant one only if prescribed cuts are made. A licensing authority cannot validly fetter its discretion by automatically following the Board's decisions[36] though it may elect to follow them unless exceptional circumstances are present. There is nothing, apart from the sanctions of the criminal law which may be applied to an exhibitor, to prevent a local authority from allowing a film to be exhibited to which the Board has denied a certificate or from permitting the restoration of cuts made at the insistence of the Board. Nor is an authority obliged to permit the exhibition of a film passed by the Board. It is not uncommon for different authorities to adopt various attitudes towards a particularly controversial film.

Having regard to the higher attendance of children at cinemas than theatres, there is a stronger case for film censorship than for theatrical censorship. Accordingly the Departmental Committee on Obscenity and Film Censorship recommended in 1979 a statutory body for censoring films.[37] That recommendation has not been acted on.

The Video Recordings Act 1984[38] provides for the censorship of video films before sale or hire to the public. It is an offence to supply an unclassified video cassette outside of the terms of the Act. The classification scheme is similar to that which applies to films, but there are complex definitions of 'exempted works'. The British Board of Film Classification is charged with the censorship of the thousands of different videos which were in circulation before the Act came into force, as well as new productions. The hire and purchase of video films is extremely popular, and it is right that potential viewers (and their parents) be adequately warned of the contents of any given video cassette.[39]

36 *Ellis* v. *Dubowski* [1972] 3 KB 621.
37 Cmnd 7772 (1979). Under s. 2 of the Local Government (Miscellaneous Provisions) Act 1982 any district council or London borough council may resolve to introduce a licensing system for sex cinemas as set out in sched. 3 of that Act.
38 See Street, op. cit., pp. 222–8.
39 For a critical view of such censorship, see Hunnings [1985] *Public Law* 214.

Official documents and civil servants' publications. As has been indicated, State papers (including Cabinet documents) are made available to public scrutiny only after the lapse of thirty years. Records may still be withheld after that period by the Lord Chancellor, with the approval or at the request of the relevant Ministers, or if they embody information received under a pledge of confidence.[40]

The former practice whereby whole classes of departmental documents relevant to judicial proceedings could be withheld from disclosure by virtue of a ministerial objection on the ground that that production would be injurious to the national interest has been substantially diminished in the last few years.[41] Moreover, departmental documents must be made available to the Parliamentary Commissioner for Administration for the purpose of his investigations.

Any student of central government administration in Britain will be aware of the difficulty experienced in persuading civil servants to divulge particulars of internal procedures or the undisclosed reasons for individual decisions if there is any likelihood of his publishing an account of his research. The ethos generated by the Official Secrets Act is still pervasive. Serving and retired civil servants must obtain official approval of the manuscript of any book they themselves write before it is published. A civil servant who writes a controversial letter to the press or gives a broadcast interview will be well advised to seek approval in advance; otherwise he risks contravening service regulations and earning the severe disapproval of his superiors.

Contempt of court. A news medium proposing to publish material which would tend to prejudice a fair trial may be restrained by an injunction in proceedings instituted by the Attorney-General.[42]

Miscellaneous. In 1971 leading American newspapers published extracts from the 'Pentagon papers', a record of top-secret policy discussions about Vietnam. An attempt by the United States Government to obtain an injunction to restrain further publication of the information was rejected

---

40 Public Records Acts 1958 and 1967. For a review of the law and practice relating to State secrets see Brazier (1996) 55 *Camb. LJ* 65.
41 See especially *Conway* v. *Rimmer* [1968] AC 910.
42 See Contempt of Court Act 1981, ss. 1–7, sched. 1, and above, pp. 378–80, and *Att.-Gen.* v. *Times Newspapers Ltd* [1974] AC 273.

by the United States Supreme Court.[43] This may be contrasted with the decision of Widgery L C J in the *Crossman Diaries* Case that the publication of Cabinet memoirs is a breach of confidence, which may be stopped by injunction, when the public interest demands it.[44]

Prior censorship, and the seizure and destruction of documents under legal powers, are the most obvious means of suppressing freedom of expression. The prospect of incurring penal sanctions *ex post facto* will also tend to inhibit free expression. So will the foreknowledge that one's communications may be intercepted and read or overheard.

Freedom of expression is not an end in itself. Doctrinaire absolutism is an inept instrument for evaluating the competing claims of the individual and society. John Stuart Mill, himself a powerful defender of human liberty, declared: 'The sole end for which mankind are warranted, individually or collectively, in interfering with the liberty of action of any of their number, is self-protection.' This grudging concession is a starting point, not the conclusion, of any attempt to define the proper limits of freedom of expression. But the onus to be discharged by one seeking to justify the stifling of opinion should be heavier than that cast upon one asserting the propriety of penalizing its expression after the event. History bears witness to the insidious effects of the suppression of dissent and the denial of free interchange of ideas. These effects are all the more insidious when the fact of suppression is itself suppressed or so concealed as not to be identifiable.

CRIMES, TORTS AND OTHER WRONGS

The following are the principal wrongs in English law that may be committed by words or pictorial demonstrations.

Treason and treason felony

These offences overlap. Treason is still punishable with death, treason felony with life imprisonment. It is treason to conspire or incite to kill or overthrow the monarch, to levy war against her by raising an insurrection,

---

43 *New York Times Co.* v. *United States* 403 US 713 (1971); *The Pentagon Papers* (Bantam Books, 1971). In *Secretary of State for Defence* v. *Guardian Newspapers Ltd.* [1985] AC 339 the Court of Appeal ordered the *Guardian* to return to the Minister a photocopy of a document leaked to it by a civil servant, on the ground that the Government had the copyright in the photocopy; see further above, p. 378.

44 *Att.-Gen.* v. *Jonathan Cape Ltd* [1976] Q B 752; Hugo Young, *The Crossman Affair* (1976).

or to adhere to her enemies[45] in time of war (for example, by broadcasting propaganda for the enemy).[46] Incitement to rebellion against the Government in the United Kingdom, or a conspiracy to deprive the Queen of her sovereignty in any part of her dominions, or an invitation to a foreigner to invade any part of them, is also treason felony.[47]

Seditious offences[48]

To publish spoken or written words with a seditious intention is a common-law misdemeanour. A seditious intention has been defined in very broad terms, including 'an intention to bring into hatred and contempt, or excite disaffection against . . . the government and constitution . . . either House of Parliament, or the administration of justice . . . or to raise discontent or disaffection among Her Majesty's subjects, or to promote feelings of ill-will and hostility between different classes of such subjects'.[49] This could encompass any forceful criticism of the existing structure of authority within the State.

In this century prosecutions for sedition have been so few that the ingredients of the offence cannot be stated with assurance, but it would seem that there must now be an intent to incite to violence against the institutions and laws of the State[50] or a section of the community[51] for a conviction to be obtained. Proof of an intention to cause ill will and hostility between different classes of Her Majesty's subjects does not of itself establish a seditious intention: there must be, in addition, proof of incitement to violence intended to disturb lawful authority.[52]

45 Within or without Her Majesty's dominions (*R.* v. *Casement* [1917] KB 98).
46 To be guilty of treason the accused must be a person owing allegiance; on which see *Joyce* v. *DPP* [1946] AC 347. There must be overt acts of disloyalty.
47 Treason Felony Act 1848. Again, only persons owing allegiance may commit the offence.
48 For good synopses, see Smith and Hogan, *Criminal Law* (7th edn, 1996), pp. 758–60. Ian Brownlie's *Law of Public Order and National Security* (2nd edn, 1981), pp. 234–44, and for proposals for reform, Law Commission Working Paper No. 72 (1977).
49 Sir James Stephen, *Digest of the Criminal Law* (3rd edn), art. 93.
50 *R.* v. *Burns* (1886) 16 Cox C. C. 355. See also *R.* v. *Aldred* (1909) 22 Cox C. C. 1, where the publication had been calculated to incite to violence but it was not made clear by the judge that an intent to provoke violence had to be established.
51 *R.* v. *Caunt* (1947) (*An Editor on Trial*, an offensive attack on British Jewry; jury directed that an intent to excite violence had to be demonstrated). Such an attack might still be indictable as a public mischief.
52 *R.* v. *Wallace-Johnson* [1940] AC 231 (Gold Coast); *R.* v. *Chief Metropolitan Magistrate, ex p. Choudhury* [1991] 1 All ER 306 (an attempt to prosecute Salman Rushdie (*inter alia*) for sedition over his book *The Satanic Verses*).

Some of the successor governments to colonial regimes have used a wide concept of sedition as an instrument for browbeating their opponents.[53]

There are several statutory offences akin to sedition in its broadest meaning. It is an offence to do any act 'calculated to cause disaffection' among the police.[54] Under the Incitement to Disaffection Act 1934,[55] it is an offence maliciously and advisedly to endeavour to seduce a member of the forces from his duty or allegiance to the Crown, or to have in one's possession, with intent to commit or counsel the offence, literature the dissemination of which would be such an offence. Prosecutions have been very rare, and leave of the Director of Public Prosecutions is required. A search warrant may be issued by a High Court judge in respect of an offence under the Act. The Act could be used against persons distributing pacifist literature to members of the forces. In this area of the law, restraint in instituting prosecutions, the prospect of a restrictive direction by a judge and an acquittal by a jury are the effective safeguards for the expression of political dissent.[56]

Breaches of the Official Secrets Acts[57]

Till 1889 there was no legislation making it an offence to disclose official secrets to foreign powers or to other unauthorized persons. The present law is contained in the Official Secrets Acts 1911, 1920, 1939 and 1989. The ambit of the Acts is by no means confined to espionage. The marginal note to section 1 of the 1911 Act reads 'Penalties against spying', and makes it an offence punishable by fourteen years' imprisonment for any person, 'for any purpose prejudicial to the safety or interests of the State', not only to engage in specified conduct calculated to be useful to an enemy but also

---

53 To that extent the Privy Council decision in *R.* v. *Wallace-Johnson* [1940] AC 231 that sedition under the laws of a colony could be committed without incitement to violence cannot apply in England.
54 Police Act 1996, s. 91, reproducing earlier legislation. See also Aliens Restriction (Amendment) Act 1919, penalizing forms of disaffection instigated by aliens.
55 See also Incitement to Mutiny Act 1797; D. G. T. Williams, *Not in the Public Interest*, pp. 102–3, 113–14.
56 The Law Commission has provisionally recommended the abolition of the crime of sedition: Working Paper No. 72 (1977), paras. 76–8.
57 The leading study is D. G. T. Williams, *Not in the Public Interest*. See now Report of the Committee on section 2 of the Official Secrets Act 1911 (Cmnd 5104 (1972)) and Minutes of Evidence in three volumes; these contain a mine of information, much of it previously undisclosed.

to approach, inspect or enter a 'prohibited place'[58] within the meaning of the Act. Nuclear disarmers who approached a military airfield with the intention of immobilizing it were convicted under this section,[59] although their purpose was not espionage but non-violent sabotage; the fact that in their opinion they were acting in the true interests of the State was held to be irrelevant, inasmuch as they were intentionally engaging in conduct prohibited by the Act and the policy behind the disposition and use of the armed forces of the Crown fell within the scope of the royal prerogative and could not be a subject of independent judicial scrutiny. It is also an offence to refuse to supply information to a senior police officer as to the commission of an offence under this section.[60] In a prosecution for the principal offence, the prejudicial purpose may be inferred from the circumstances in the absence of an overt act; and if information about a prohibited place is proved to have been obtained or communicated without lawful authority, the onus of proving that the purpose was not one prejudicial to the interests of the State is cast upon the accused.[61]

Under the catch-all section 2 of the 1911 Act (which has been repealed) it was an offence punishable with up to two years' imprisonment to retain without permission, or fail to take reasonable care of, information obtained as a result of one's present or former employment under the Crown or a government contract; or to *communicate* information so obtained, or entrusted to one in confidence by a person holding office under Her Majesty,[62] or obtained in contravention of the Act, to anybody other than a person to whom one was authorized to convey it or to whom it was one's duty to impart it in the interests of the State; or to *receive* such information, knowing or having reasonable cause to believe it had been given in contravention of the Act. These were wide-ranging prohibitions. The section was indeed convoluted and abstruse. The Franks Committee which reported in 1972 described it as 'catch-all' and a 'mess'.[63] Yet who could malign a section which created 2,324 separate offences?[64]

However, the section had undoubtedly many defects. For instance, it

---

58 s. 3 (for example, defence establishments and places used by or belonging to the Crown and declared by a Secretary of State to be prohibited places).
59 *Chandler* v. *DPP* [1964] AC 763; criticized by Thompson [1963] *Public Law* 201.
60 Official Secrets Act 1920, s. 6 (as amended by the Official Secrets Act 1939).
61 1911 Act, s. 1(2).
62 This term included a police officer: *Lewis* v. *Cattle* [1938] 2 KB 454; and a civilian computer operator employed by a local authority but taking instructions from a police inspector at the police station where he operated it: *Loat* v. *Andrews* [1985] ICR 679.
63 Cmnd 5104 (1972), §§ 17, 88.
64 Minutes of Evidence, vol. 2, p. 262 (Appendix to evidence of Bar Council).

was not clear whether guilty knowledge (*mens rea*) had to be proved for unauthorized communication to be an offence.[65] When was communication authorized?[66] What of 'leaks' by Ministers?[67] According to official doctrine, Ministers 'authorized themselves' to convey information about matters of government and administration; civil servants had implied authorization depending on the nature of their job and the circumstances of the case. All this was very vague. And in the absence of authorization, when was it my duty or a journalist's duty 'in the interests of the State' to publicize official information? No intelligible answer was ever produced. The Attorney-General had an absolute discretion in deciding whether to institute a prosecution; the criteria adopted in deciding whether to bring or authorize a prosecution were nebulous; there was a marked rise in the number of prosecutions from 1979 to the late 1980s, although most (but by no means all) involved elements of obvious impropriety.[68] But the deterrent effect of the Act on junior and middle-grade civil servants in particular may have been considerable.

The Franks Committee made detailed proposals for replacing section 2 by a new Official Information Act. The Committee's proposals would have restricted the ambit of the criminal law, but were not really radical. The Government introduced a Protection of Official Information Bill into the House of Lords in the 1979–80 session, but it was so heavily criticized (and faced almost certain defeat in Parliament) that it was withdrawn.[69] A backbench Conservative MP, Mr Richard Shepherd, introduced a liberalizing bill with the same title in the 1987–8 session, but thanks to the imposition of a Government three-line whip against it – an unprecedented Government interference in the fortunes of a private member's measure –

65 In the *Sunday Telegraph* case (1971, unreported; see Jonathan Aitken, *Officially Secret*) Caulfield J directed the jury that *mens rea* on the part of all involved in the chain of communication had to be proved. This interpretation was not universally accepted: it was, for example, rejected by McCowan, J. in the course of the trial of Clive Ponting (who was none the less acquitted by the jury); see Clive Ponting, *The Right to Know* (1985) and *R.* v. *Ponting* [1985] *Crim. L. Rev.* 318.
66 The burden was on the Crown to prove that the communicator had not been authorized: *R.* v. *Galvin* [1987] QB 862.
67 The Attorney-General did not prosecute the publishers of the Crossman Diaries under the Act, apparently because he concluded that the Act did not apply once Mr Crossman had died; Lord Lloyd of Hampstead (*semble*) took the opposite view: Young, op. cit., at pp. 21 and 33.
68 From 1978 to 1987 the Attorney-General authorized 23 prosecutions under s. 2: see 124 HC Deb. *606–9* (written answers 17 December 1987).
69 The fact that the truth about the traitor Anthony Blunt could not have been revealed by the press had the bill been law became the bill's death blow.

the bill was denied a second reading.[70] The Home Secretary announced that the Government had been working for some months on its own replacement for section 2 (a section which he conceded had become virtually inoperable). The Government published a White Paper in 1988;[71] a Bill was introduced in the 1988–9 session of Parliament; it became the Official Secrets Act 1989. Section 2 of the Official Secrets Act 1911 has been repealed by the Official Secrets Act 1989,[72] and has been replaced by six categories of official information, the unauthorized disclosure of which is an offence. Those categories cover security and intelligence, defence, international relations, information likely to result in an offence or other related consequences, information resulting from unauthorized disclosures, and information entrusted in confidence to other States or international organizations.[73] In relation to the first five categories the prosecution must prove that specified tests of harm have been satisfied, as well as the existence of an unauthorized disclosure;[74] and in prosecution against anyone who is not a Crown servant[75] or Government contractor it must also be proved that the accused knew or had good reason to know that the specified harm was likely to have been caused by the disclosure. The maximum penalty under the Act is two years' imprisonment. It is not an offence merely to receive information covered by the Act; disclosure of other official information is no longer a crime – although civil servants may face disciplinary proceedings for doing so. There is no defence that disclosure was in the public interest; the uncertainties inherent in the concept of 'authorization' remain;[76] the Act protects official information without any attempt to balance that through (for example) giving fuller publicity to innocuous official information.

Opposition parties often advocate open government and freedom of information. When they come to power they do not always give effect to

70 However, twenty Conservative MPs defied the whip to vote for the bill and others abstained: the Government's majority was cut to thirty-seven despite an actual Commons majority of 101: see 125 HC Deb. 563–637 (15 January 1988).
71 Cm 408 (1988); see also 137 HC Deb. 1412–81 (22 July 1988).
72 s. 16(4) and sched. 2.
73 ss. 1–6.
74 Except that *any* unauthorized disclosure by members of the security and intelligence services will always be treated as harmful: s. 1(1).
75 Defined (s. 12) as a Minister of the Crown, any person employed in the civil service of the Crown, any member of the armed forces and any constable.
76 A disclosure of information by a Crown servant is made with lawful authority if, and only if, it is made in accordance with his official duty: ibid., s. 7(1). What does this mean? Who defines the scope of that duty?

those policies. The 1979 Conservative Government made inroads into unnecessary secrecy: it published a Code of Practice on Open Government;[77] it published *Questions of Procedure for Ministers* and details about Ministerial Committees; and it instructed civil servants to classify documents as being Top Secret only when absolutely necessary.[78] The Labour Government has promised to publish a White Paper on a Freedom of Information Bill, and to enact such a Bill during the present Parliament.

Blasphemy

It is an offence at common law to outrage the feelings of a Christian by abusing Christ or by denying and attacking the Christian religion.[79] This crime is not obsolete[80] and in 1978 the House of Lords upheld a conviction and also ruled that it is unnecessary to prove an intention to blaspheme; the intention to publish is enough. The House of Lords also confirmed that there is no need to prove that the publication tended to lead to a breach of the peace.[81]

Defamations[82]

A defamatory statement is one which tends to expose another to hatred, ridicule or contempt or to cause him to be shunned by reasonable persons. Defamatory matter consisting of spoken words, or gestures, is slander; in permanent form it is libel. By statute,[83] words used in a broadcast or a public performance of a play are deemed to be libel. The distinction between slander and libel is of practical importance. In the first place although both

77 Cm 2290 (1993).

78 240 HC Deb. *259–60* (written answers 23 March 1994).

79 And only the Christian religion: *R.* v. *Chief Metropolitan Magistrate, ex p. Chaudhury* [1991] 1 All ER 306.

80 The Law Commission has recommended that the common-law offence of blasphemy be abolished, and that statutory offences be enacted of disrupting religious worship and of offensive behaviour in a place of worship: Law Com. No. 145 (1985).

81 *R.* v. *Lemon* [1979] AC 617. 'Indecent' behaviour in a place of religious worship (an offence under s. 2 of the Ecclesiastical Courts Jurisdiction Act 1860) includes interrupting a service by shouting political slogans: *Abrahams* v. *Cavey* [1968] 1 QB 479.

82 For details, see the latest editions of *Gatley on Libel and Slander*, and the leading textbooks on the law of tort (*Clerk and Lindsell*, *Salmond*, *Street*, and *Winfield and Jolowicz*). Only a very brief outline of this complex branch of the law is presented here. Reforms of the law were made by the Defamation Act 1996.

83 Defamation Act 1952, s. 1; Theatres Act 1968, ss. 4, 7.

slander and libel are torts, no action will lie for slander in the absence of proof of special pecuniary damage, save in a limited range of situations. Secondly, slander is not of itself a criminal offence. A conviction for libel may be obtained even though the statement was published only to the person defamed and was true (unless publication was for the public benefit). A libel may also be indictable, though not actionable as a tort, if it relates to a class of persons, or if it relates to a dead person. No prosecution against a newspaper proprietor, publisher or editor may be brought except with leave of a judge in chambers.[84]

For a civil action to lie, the defamatory statement must have been published to a third party. It is a defence that the statement was true, or was a fair comment on a matter of public interest, or was uttered on a privileged occasion. No action will lie in respect of an absolutely privileged statement even if it is false and malicious. Absolute privilege attaches to statements made in the course of judicial proceedings, proceedings in Parliament, parliamentary papers, and to communications between high officers of State and to fair and accurate newspaper or broadcast reports of judicial proceedings.[85] Qualified privilege is lost by proof of malice, which is not easily established. Among the numerous situations covered by qualified privilege are fair and accurate newspaper reports of parliamentary proceedings,[86] and of the proceedings of public meetings, local councils and administrative tribunals and inquiries;[87] and communications between members of the public and MPs and MPs and Ministers, on matters of public interest.[88] If a person is unintentionally defamed, the innocent publisher may defend himself successfully in an action by making an offer of amends

---

84 Law of Libel Amendment Act 1888, s. 8 (permission was given for Mr James Goldsmith to prosecute the publishers of *Private Eye*: *Goldsmith* v. *Pressdram Ltd* [1977] QB 83). Leave is not required to prosecute a television company or a journalist. The House of Lords has discouraged criminals from prosecuting by allowing the defence to adduce evidence of the general bad reputation of private prosecutors; *Gleaves* v. *Deakin* [1980] AC 477. In the same case the House of Lords went out of its way to advocate that leave of the Attorney-General should be required for all prosecutions for this crime. See also Newspaper Libel and Registration Act 1881, s. 4 (certain newspaper libels are triable summarily before magistrates). The Law Commission has recommended that criminal libel be abolished and replaced by a statutory offence of publishing defamatory material knowing it to be seriously defamatory: see Law Com. No. 149 (1985).

85 See above, p. 376. For the latter immunity see the Defamation Act 1996, s. 14.

86 Defamation Act 1996, s. 15 and schedule 1. *Wason* v. *Walter* (1868) LR 4 QB 73.

87 See generally Defamation Act 1996, s. 15 and schedule 1. In many of these situations qualified privilege will be a defence only if the newspaper has published, at the plaintiff's request, a reasonable statement by way of contradiction or explanation: ibid.

88 See p. 315.

(which means the publication of a correction and an apology) as soon as possible.[89]

The law of defamation still presents many hazards for the press; and juries are still apt to make heavy awards of compensatory damages to persons defamed by newspapers.[90] Many proprietors and editors of journals would doubtless welcome a judicial decision such as one delivered in 1964 by the United States Supreme Court, that false and defamatory press statements about the conduct of a holder of a public office were not actionable provided that the critic was acting in good faith.[91] At the present time some tabloid newspapers achieve a mass circulation by 'shocking revelations' about the private lives of persons in the news. As was mentioned earlier,[92] there is in general no legal remedy for the improper but non-defamatory invasion of privacy. But a complaint may be made to the Press Complaints Commission,[93] an investigatory body composed largely of representatives of the press, and this Commission can do no more than administer a public rebuke. When invoked, the sanctions of the law of defamation are quite severe, but they are not open to persons of modest means: actions for defamation cannot be brought in county courts, High Court costs may be extremely heavy and the legal aid scheme does not extend to such proceedings.

Contempt of court and of the Houses of Parliament[94]

In some respect these legal restrictions on free expression do bear harshly on journalists and broadcasters. Premature disclosure of the report of a parliamentary committee is a contempt of the House in question. The protection given to a journalist's sources by section 10 of the Contempt of Court Act 1981 is so set about with limitations that he may easily commit contempt by refusing to disclose his sources to a court.[95]

---

89 Defamation Act 1996, ss. 2–4.
90 For example, the £½m awarded to Mr Jeffrey Archer in 1987. Exemplary damages in tort can only be awarded in a limited range of situations: *Broome* v. *Cassell & Co.* [1972] AC 1027.
91 *New York Times Ltd* v. *Sullivan*, 376 US 255 (1964).
92 See p. 444.
93 This replaced the Press Council following a recommendation of the Calcutt Committee (Cm 1102 (1990)). The second Calcutt Report (Cm 2135 (1993)) recommended the setting up of a replacement press complaints tribunal with enhanced statutory powers, and the creation of new offences to protect privacy. See also Cm 2918 (1995).
94 See ch. 16.
95 See above, p. 378, note 98.

Miscellaneous wrongs involving speech or writing

A great number of criminal offences can be committed by the use of spoken words or writing. For example, it is an offence to incite another to commit a crime. A criminal conspiracy can hardly be effected without verbal communication. Intimidating words accompanied by threatening behaviour may be an assault although there is no physical contact with the person put in fear. Perjury, blackmail, fraud and attempting to pervert the course of justice by, for example, interfering with witnesses, all involve some form of verbal communication. It is an offence to waste the time of the police by knowingly making a false report;[96] or to pester people with false or offensive telephone calls;[97] or to publish a false description of articles and goods for sale.[98] Among torts, fraudulent misrepresentation, deceit, slander of title and passing off are essentially verbal misdeeds.[99]

Insulting words and behaviour[100]

Under a number of local Acts and by-laws it has long been an offence to use threatening, abusive or insulting words or behaviour in a public place with intent to provoke a breach of the peace or whereby a breach of the peace is likely to be occasioned.[101] Section 5 of the Public Order Act 1936 made this a general offence, and extended it to public meetings. In 1963 the maximum penalties for the offence were increased;[102] in 1965 the offence was extended to the distribution or display of written matter and signs;[103] and in 1968 to theatrical performances to which the public is admitted.[104] The Public Order Act 1986[105] altered the law further. Section 5 of the 1936

---

96 Criminal Law Act 1967, s. 5(2).

97 Telecommunications Act 1984, s. 43.

98 Trade Descriptions Act 1968.

99 It is an offence under s. 1 of the Malicious Communications Act 1988 (which was based on Law Com. No. 147 (1985)) to send a letter or article conveying an indecent or grossly offensive message, or a threat, or information which the sender knows or believes to be false, with the intention of causing distress or anxiety.

100 See D. G. T. Williams, *Keeping the Peace*, pp. 153–69; Brownlie, *The Law of Public Order and National Security* (2nd edn, 1981), pp. 3–15.

101 See, for example, *Wise* v. *Dunning* [1902] 1 KB 167.

102 Public Order Act 1963.

103 Race Relations Act 1965, s. 7. This provision (restating section 5 of the 1936 Act) had no direct connection with race relations: see below.

104 Theatres Act 1968, s. 6.

105 On which see generally below, pp. 482–90.

Act was repealed[106] and replaced by a new crime under section 4 of the 1986 Act. It is an offence (*a*) to use towards another person threatening, abusive or insulting words or behaviour; or (*b*) to distribute or display any writing, sign or visible representation which is threatening, abusive or insulting, in each case with intent to cause that other person to fear immediate unlawful violence, or to provoke such violence, or whereby that other person is likely to believe that such violence will be used or whereby it is likely to be provoked. The offence can be committed in a public[107] or private place, and it is potentially a much wider offence than the one which it replaced. The maximum penalty is six months' imprisonment and a fine of £5,000. Another crime was created by section 5 of the 1986 Act, that of using threatening, abusive or insulting words or behaviour, or displaying any writing, sign or other visible representation which is threatening, abusive or insulting, within the hearing or sight of a person likely to be caused harassment, alarm or distress thereby.[108] The maximum penalty is a £1,000 fine. The powers of the police at common law to deal with or prevent a breach of the peace are expressly preserved.[109]

The importance of the section 4 offence in the context of freedom of expression is that it restricts the freedom of speakers at political meetings. Judicial interpretation of some of the key words in that section is likely to be carried over from the 1936 Act provisions. So, the word 'insulting' is to be understood in its ordinary sense.[110] There need be no intention to insult: it is sufficient that an ordinary person might feel so insulted.[111] Putting one person in fear of unlawful violence is enough under section 4 of the 1986 Act, as is conduct likely to provoke such violence. In deciding what is 'likely', a 1963 decision will probably be followed. So if a speaker deliberately insults a hostile audience with the result that they are likely to commit a breach of the peace, it is immaterial that he may not have intended to provoke them to acts of violence or that they would not have resorted to violence had they been reasonably phlegmatic or decorous persons. When Colin Jordan, the British Nazi, insulted a hostile audience in Trafalgar

106 Public Order Act 1986, s. 9(2).
107 Defined (ibid., s. 16) as any highway, or any place to which at the material time the public has access, on payment or otherwise, as of right or by express or implied permission. See also *R.* v. *Horseferry Road Magistrates, ex p. Siadatan* [1991] 1 All ER 324.
108 Again, it can be committed in a public or private place: see note 106. See also *DPP* v. *Orum* [1988] *Crim. L. Rev.* 848.
109 ibid., s. 40(4).
110 *Brutus* v. *Cozens* [1973] AC 854 (anti-apartheid demonstration on tennis court during Wimbledon championships not an offence, though spectators angered).
111 *Parkin* v. *Norman* [1982] 3 WLR 523.

Square, calling them 'red rabble' and asserting that Britain had picked on the wrong enemy in 1939, that international Jewry was the real culprit and that 'Hitler was right', it was held that he had to take the audience as he found them; the gist of the offences was public insult, likely in the circumstances to give rise to a breach of the peace, and he was convicted.[112] The offence is not confined to political diatribes; it includes abusive language directed against a neighbour in public.[113] However, it is not enough to show that other people were annoyed or affronted.

Incitement to racial hatred

This was first made an offence in 1965; it was further refined by section 70 of the Race Relations Act 1976; it is now contained (with other offences) in the Public Order Act 1986, sections 17 to 23. 'Racial hatred' means hatred against a group of people in Great Britain defined by reference to colour, race, nationality or ethnic or national origins. It is an offence to use threatening, abusive or insulting words or behaviour, or to display any written material which is threatening, abusive or insulting, if done with intent to stir up racial hatred, or if in the circumstances racial hatred is likely to be stirred up.[114] Leave of the Attorney-General must be obtained before a prosecution can be instituted; the offences are triable summarily or on indictment, and if the defendant elects to be tried by jury on indictment, the possibility of acquittal or disagreement may be very real. The gist of these offences is the opprobrious nature of the words or conduct in question and the feelings of disgust they are likely to arouse. To this extent the offence is more akin to the old common law of obscenity than to other modern limitations imposed by the criminal law on freedom of expression.

Obscenity[115]

The law of obscenity is both complex and controversial. It encompasses a range of common-law offences, statutory offences, and provisions for search, forfeiture and destruction. And it bears on the limits of free expression and the relationship between the law and ideas about morality.

---

112 *Jordan* v. *Burgoyne* [1963] 2 QB 744.
113 *Ward* v. *Holman* [1964] 2 QB 580.
114 1986 Act, s. 18. Other offences include publishing or distributing written material with intent to stir up racial hatred or whereby racial hatred is likely to be stirred up (s. 19); to perform a public play, or distribute or play a recording, with similar intent or likelihood (ss. 20, 21), and to possess racially inflammatory material (s. 23).
115 The law is well reviewed by Smith and Hogan, op. cit., pp. 738–58.

In 1663 indecent exposure, coupled with the projection of urine from a balcony upon an audience at Covent Garden, was held to be common-law misdemeanour.[116] A common-law offence of obscene libel developed from this bizarre episode. The common-law crime appeared to have been largely superseded by statute, but in 1961 the House of Lords held that an obscene publication was also indictable as common-law conspiracy to corrupt public morals[117] and in 1972 it reaffirmed this proposition in a case where a majority of their Lordships were also of the opinion that a conspiracy to outrage public decency was an offence.[118] The defences now provided by the Obscene Publications Acts do not apply to such charges.

Statutory obscenity. Under the Obscene Publication Acts 1959 and 1964 it is an offence to publish an obscene article, or to have an obscene article for gain. Authors, photographers, artists, publishers, booksellers and other distributors may find themselves prosecuted under the Acts. Similarly, it is an offence under the Theatres Act 1968 to direct or present an obscene theatrical performance. The Criminal Law Act 1977 has extended the 1959 Act to films, and the Broadcasting Act 1990 to television and radio.[119]

The test of obscenity under these Acts is similar to that laid down in a mid-Victorian case, where it was held to be whether the matter in question had a tendency to deprave and corrupt those who were open to such influences and into whose hands it might fall.[120] Under the recent Acts, the prosecution must prove that the matter, *taken as a whole*, would tend to deprave and corrupt persons likely to read or see or hear it; hence a book is not now obscene merely because it contains a few obscene words or sentences. However, a magazine or other publication consisting of a number

---

116 *R.* v. *Sidley* (1663) I Siderfin 168; *sub nom. Sydlye's* case (1663) I Keb. 620, stating the facts more fully. See also Vagrancy Act 1824, s. 4; Criminal Justice Act 1925, s. 42.
117 *Shaw* v. *DPP* [1962] AC 220 (the *Ladies' Directory* case; publication of a guide to specified prostitutes for prospective clients). There could be a criminal conspiracy without publication. No prosecution can be brought in respect of a theatrical performance: Theatres Act 1968, s. 2(4), or a film (Criminal Law Act 1977, s. 53(3)); for this offence or for conspiracy to outrage public morals, see next note.
118 *Knuller Ltd* v. *DPP* [1973] AC 435 (agreement to publish advertisements in the *International Times* by person seeking homosexual relationships, although such conduct between consenting adult males was no longer unlawful). Held, also, that there was an insufficient element of *publicity* for the offence of conspiracy to outrage public decency to be committed; but that the latter common-law offence could also be committed publicly by an individual in the absence of conspiracy.
119 s. 53. The consent of the Director of Public Prosecutions is required for the prosecution of any feature film.
120 *R.* v. *Hicklin* (1868) LR 3 QB 360 (a seizure, not a prosecution).

of separate items may be obscene although only one item falls within that description.[121] A person may be convicted under the Acts even if he had no intention to deprave or corrupt;[122] though it is a defence[123] for him to prove that he had not examined the offending article and had no reasonable cause to believe that publication or possession would be an offence.

It is also a statutory defence to a prosecution under the Act of 1959 that the publication was for the public good in the interests of science, literature, art or learning[124] or other objects of public concern.[125] If a tendency to deprave and corrupt is proved, the defendant is entitled to acquittal if he can establish this defence on a balance of probabilities.[126] Expert opinion as to the scientific, literary or artistic merits of the book or article is admissible in evidence on both sides. However, such evidence is not admissible (save in highly exceptional circumstances[127]) on the primary issue of whether the article is obscene or not.[128]

What, then is meant by a tendency to deprave and corrupt? And deprave and corrupt whom? Judicial pronouncements on these matters have shown a conspicuous lack of uniformity. Depravity and corruption have generally been understood to imply the weakening of moral fibre. Nowadays a judge, magistrate or jury is unlikely to be persuaded that anything less than the explicit portrayal or description of sexual activity tending to evoke erotic desires and an inclination to imitate what has been described or depicted is obscene in this sense. Yet this approach raises many problems. It is almost impossible to establish a causal connection between an erotic book or film and subsequent conduct.[129] In the decisions of magistrates and juries, and the directions of judges, there have been elements of unpredictability amounting to caprice. In 1928 *The Well of Loneliness*, a discreetly written

---

121 *R.* v. *Anderson* [1972] 1 QB 304 (the *Oz* 'schoolkids' issue case).

122 *R.* v. *Calder & Boyars Ltd* [1969] 1 QB 151.

123 Obscene Publications Act 1959, s. 2(5); Obscene Publications Act 1964, s. 1(3)(a).

124 In *Attorney-General's Reference (No. 3 of 1977)* [1978] 3 All ER 1166 it was held that 'learning' meant 'the product of scholarship' so that evidence of the educational effect of sexually explicit material was not admissible.

125 1959 Act, s. 4. In *R.* v. *Jordan* [1977] AC 699 the House of Lords held that these words meant the value inherent in obscene material, so that evidence was not admissible that it was of therapeutic benefit to some readers. See also Theatres Act 1968, s. 3, and Criminal Law Act 1977, s. 53 (films).

126 See *R.* v. *Calder & Boyars Ltd* above.

127 As in *DPP* v. *A & BC Chewing Gum Ltd* [1968] 1 QB 159 (expert evidence as to effect on children).

128 *R.* v. *Anderson* [1972] 1 QB 304; see also *R.* v. *Stamford* [1972] 2 QB 391.

129 See, for example, the Report of the Committe on Obscenity and Film Censorship, Cmnd 7772 (1979).

literary work dealing with a sad theme of female homosexuality, was condemned as obscene. In the 1960s *Fanny Hill*, a well-written and amusing eighteenth-century erotic work, was condemned, and the publishers of *Last Exit to Brooklyn*, a book containing descriptions of male homosexual intercourse and brutal violence but in a manner calculated to arouse feelings of pity and disgust, were held by a jury to be guilty of obscene libel,[130] but the publishers of *Lady Chatterley's Lover* (a serious though unconsciously funny novel, liberally interspersed with four-letter words and descriptions of extra-marital intercourse) were acquitted,[131] and no proceedings were taken in connection with a book such as *Portnoy's Complaint*. In the mid-seventies administrative and police practice had become more indulgent as society had become more permissive. Since 1977 enforcement action by the police has been much more vigorous in some police areas, but the outcome of judicial proceedings remains a lottery.[132]

If the tendency of a book to deprave and corrupt is established, it is not refuted merely because the most likely purchasers would already be depraved; they may be capable of being further depraved by reading it.[133] If, on the other hand, the only person to whom it was shown, for example, a senior police officer, was unlikely to be depraved or corrupted, there should be no conviction unless there was an intention to publish to others.[134] It seems that only if a significant proportion of the persons into whose hands a book may fall (not merely well-brought-up fourteen-year-old girls)[135] are likely to be depraved or corrupted by it is the offence committed.[136] The circumstances of publication or offer for sale are therefore material. An expensive hardback book may not offend against the Acts, though a cheap and easily accessible paperback edition may. Erotic prints or sculpture in a shop window may offend against them though the same representations in an art gallery may not. But the matter may still be so

---

130 The conviction was reversed because of a misdirection by the recorder (note 126, above).

131 See C. H. Rolph, *The Trial of Lady Chatterley*.

132 The problems of the police in enforcing the law against 'hard-core pornography' are well depicted in *R. v. Metropolitan Police Commissioner, ex p. Blackburn (No. 3)* [1973] AC 849.

133 *DPP* v. *Whyte* [1972] AC 849.

134 *R. v. Clayton and Halsey* [1963] I QB 163; he had *mens rea* and might now be guilty of an offence under the Criminal Attempts Act 1981, s. 1(1); see also *R. v. Barker* [1962] I WLR 349; 1964 Act, s. 1(3)(b).

135 cf. *R. v. Martin Secker & Warburg Ltd* [1954] I WLR 1138 at 1139. Read as a whole, the direction given by Stable J to the jury in that case (a charge of obscene libel at common law) is remarkable for its eloquent common sense.

136 *R. v. Calder & Boyars Ltd* (note 126, above).

pornographic (for example, photographs of sexually deviant conduct) that the Act will be contravened despite the fact that display and distribution have been carefully restricted. Yet if the matter is so disgusting as to cause aversion or revulsion rather than corruption or depravity, the Acts are not contravened.[137]

The Acts are not confined to matters of sexual morality. A book extolling the pleasures of drug-taking may be an 'obscene' publication.[138] So, it seems, may a publication tending to induce violent behaviour,[139] but the publication of horror comics is a separate statutory offence.[140]

General. To outrage decency in public is a common-law misdemeanour. The offence may be committed not only by conduct, but also by words and pictures.[141] If the words or conduct are both insulting and likely to cause a breach of the peace, this is a separate statutory offence.[142] Under a number of local Acts and by-laws, the use of obscene language in public, the display of obscene signs and other reprehensible forms of public conduct are also offences.

Obscene articles reasonably suspected of being kept for publication for gain can be searched for and seized under a magistrate's warrant.[143] Forfeiture proceedings can then be brought before the magistrate; the occupier is entitled to appear and show cause why they should not be forfeited. The defence of public good is available, but there is no provision for trial by jury. The quantity of articles thus seized and condemned is very large; again, there is no uniformity of police or magisterial practice.

137 *R.* v. *Anderson* (note 121). Because the 'aversion' defence was not put properly to the jury, the conviction of the defendants under the Obscene Publications Acts (though not their conviction under the Post Office Act: see below) was quashed.
138 *Calder (John) Publications Ltd* v. *Powell* [1965] 1 QB 509.
139 *DPP* v. *A & BC Chewing Gum Ltd* [1968] 1 QB 159.
140 Children and Young Persons (Harmful Publications) Act 1955. No prosecution under this Act can be commenced without the consent of the Director of Public Prosecutions. The Protection of Children Act 1978 makes it an offence to take indecent photographs of children under sixteen or to distribute or exhibit such photographs.
141 A London cinema proprietor was convicted for exhibiting *More About the Language of Love* even though the GLC had given it an X certificate: *DPP* v. *Jacey Ltd*, the *Guardian*, 6 June 1975.
142 See pp. 470–72.
143 Obscene Publications Act 1959, s. 3. The warrant may be obtained only on information laid by the Director of Public Prosecutions or a constable (Criminal Justice Act 1967, s. 25), and criminal proceedings must be conducted by the DPP (Prosecution of Offences Act 1985, ss. 3(2)(d), 15(5)). A *prosecution* under the 1959 Act can be brought by a member of the general public, but leave of the Attorney-General is required in respect of plays and of the Director of Public Prosecutions in respect of films.

Indecent or obscene articles dispatched through the mails may be detained and destroyed. An article (for example a photograph) may be indecent for this purpose though not 'obscene'.[144] In this context 'obscene' is given its 'usual' meaning; an article may be obscene though repulsive, and there is no need to prove a tendency to deprave and corrupt, nor is the defence of public good available.[145] The importation of indecent or obscene works is prohibited under customs legislation and customs officers may seize them.[146] They are forfeited within a month unless the importer exercises his right of objection, in which case forfeiture can be ordered only by a magistrate; no defence of 'public good' is available in such a proceeding.

The Indecent Displays (Control) Act 1981 makes it an offence punishable by up to two years' imprisonment to display indecent material in public. Shops can display such material inside in a separate section prominently identified and to which under-eighteens are refused admission.

Much dissatisfaction with the law of obscenity has persisted. The scope of the law is uncertain and juries seem increasingly reluctant to convict on either obscenity or indecency charges.[147] Police enforcement has lacked consistency. Consequently, a Departmental Committee on Obscenity and Film Censorship was set up; it reported in 1979.[148] Its finding was that 'the law in short, is a mess'. It proposed the replacement of the 'deprave and corrupt' test by what it called the 'harm condition', i.e. that no conduct should be suppressed by law unless it can be taken to harm someone. It also proposed prohibition in those limited circumstances where harm can be assumed, and a statutory board for film censorship. No legislation has been forthcoming.

---

144 Post Office Act 1953, s. 11; *R.* v. *Stanley* [1965] 2 QB 327, where the court quoted with approval (at 333) the following dictum in a Scottish case: 'For a male bather to enter the water nude in the presence of ladies would be indecent but it would not necessarily be obscene. But if he directed the attention of a lady to a certain member of his body his conduct would certainly be obscene. The matter might perhaps be roughly expressed thus in the ascending scale: positive – immodest; comparative – indecent; superlative – obscene. These, however, are not rigid categories.' See also Unsolicited Goods and Services Act 1971, s. 4.
145 *R.* v. *Anderson* [1972] 1 QB 304; *R.* v. *Stamford* [1972] 2 QB 391.
146 Customs Consolidation Act 1876, s. 42; Customs and Excise Management Act 1979, ss. 139–44, sched. 3. See also Post Office Act 1953, ss. 16, 17, 26(6); Post Office Act 1969, s. 64; *Derrick* v. *Customs and Excise Commissioners* [1972] 2 QB 28.
147 e.g. the 1976 acquittals of an exhibition of *The Language of Love* and a publisher of *Inside Linda Lovelace*.
148 Cmnd 7772.

477

CHAPTER 23

Freedom of Assembly and Association

ASSOCIATION

Freedom of political association in Britain is subject to two main limitations, neither of which affects movements seeking to operate within the framework of the existing constitutional order. In the first place, there is section 2 of the Public Order Act 1936, subheaded 'Prohibition of quasi-military organizations'. The Act was passed mainly to cope with the situation created by the activities of the British Union of Fascists in the 1930s. Under section 2, it is an offence to take part in the control, management, organization or training of a body which is *either* organized or trained or equipped for the purpose of enabling it to usurp the functions of the police or the armed forces; *or* organized or trained, or organized or equipped, for the use or display of force in promoting any political object.[1] The offence is punishable, upon conviction on indictment, by a maximum two years' imprisonment and an unlimited fine. No prosecution can be instituted without the Attorney-General's consent, which has been very sparingly granted. In the 1960s, leaders of Spearhead, a neo-Nazi organization, and of the Free Wales Army, were convicted under section 2.

The Prevention of Terrorism (Temporary Provisions) Act 1989[2] bans the IRA and the INLA and other terrorist organizations and makes it an offence to belong to them or to invite others to contribute to their finances

---

1 For comment on this section, see Ian Brownlie, *The Law of Public Order and National Security* (2nd edn. 1981), pp. 184–6. This book and D. G. T. Williams's *Keeping the Peace* are the leading works on the topics covered by this chapter, although they pre-date the Public Order Act 1986, on which see Law Com. No. 123 (1983); Cmnd 9510 (1985); P. Thornton, *Public Order Law* (1987); R. Card, *Public Order: the New Law* (1987); A. T. H. Smith, *Offences Against Public Order* (1987).
2 See Clive Walker, *The Prevention of Terrorism in British Law*, (2nd edn, 1990). The police have other powers to combat terrorism under the Prevention of Terrorism (Additional Powers) Act 1996.

or to make or receive such a contribution.[3] To arrange or address a meeting of three or more persons knowing that the meeting is in support of such a proscribed organization is also an offence.[4] It is also a crime for anyone in a public place to dress or wear, carry or display any article, so as to arouse reasonable apprehension that he is a member of a proscribed organization.[5]

MEETINGS AND PROCESSIONS: PRIOR RESTRAINTS AND PREVENTIVE MEASURES

It is usually said that there is no 'right of public meeting', but that public processions are *prima facie* lawful.[6] These statements need to be explained and examined.[7]

Clearly there is no right to hold any kind of meeting on private premises without the consent of the owner or occupier; such conduct will be a trespass. A trespasser may be evicted by the use of such force as is reasonable in the circumstances. Police officers may render assistance, as private individuals, to the occupier, but they are not obliged to do so and will normally refuse, though they have a common-law duty to take such steps as are reasonably required to quell a breach of the peace and to prevent a reasonably apprehended breach of the peace. Trespass is a tort, for which nominal damages are recoverable; if the court considers that the case is serious enough and that repetition is likely, it may in its discretion award an injunction against the trespasser at the instance of the occupier. Disobedience to an injunction is a contempt of court. It is a crime to use or threaten violence for the purpose of securing entry into any premises.[8]

Does it make any difference if the premises are public buildings belonging to a local authority? Candidates at elections are entitled to have access to locally maintained schools and other public halls in order to hold campaign

---

3 s. 1, 2 and sched. 1.

4 s. 2(*c*).

5 s. 3.

6 See, for example, Goodhart (1937) 6 *Camb. LJ* 161; E. C. S. Wade (1939) 2 *Mod. L. Rev.* 177.

7 See especially Brownlie, op. cit., ch. 2, for criticism of the usual analysis of the law relating to meetings in public places. The freedoms of peaceful assembly and of association are expressly recognized in the European Convention on Human Rights and will become part of English law under the Human Rights Bill.

8 s. 6(1) Criminal Law Act 1977.

meetings.[9] For the rest, local authorities have an ostensibly free discretion whether to let premises to anybody wishing to hold a meeting there. Since, however, they are public bodies, the exercise of their discretionary powers is potentially subject to judicial review. A decision not to allow *any* political meeting, or a particular *class* of political meeting, to be held on any premises under their control might possibly be held to be an unlawful fetter on their own discretion. Again, the validity of a decision to refuse the promoters of a particular meeting permission to conduct it on such premises might conceivably be impugned as being based on legally irrelevant considerations or as being so arbitrary that no reasonable body of persons could have reached it.[10]

Is there a general right or liberty to hold demonstrations or meetings in public open spaces? To conduct such a meeting is not a criminal or civil wrong merely because a Minister, a local authority, a police officer or a magistrate purports to prohibit it[11] unless their prior permission is required by law. For example, the permission of the Secretary of State for the Environment has to be obtained before a meeting can be held in Trafalgar Square.[12] Provisions in local legislation requiring advance notice of processions are in effect in many local authority areas in England and Wales. The right to hold meetings at Speakers' Corner in Hyde Park is conferred only by statutory regulations.[13] The mere fact that an open space is dedicated to the public use does not apparently entitle persons to use it for holding a public meeting.[14] There is no procedure for banning open-air meetings as distinct from processions[15] even though serious disorder is feared – although as will be explained shortly the police may impose conditions on both assemblies and processions under the Public Order Act 1986, Part II so as to maintain public order.

The House of Commons regularly makes a sessional order instructing the police to keep the streets leading to the Houses of Parliament free from

---

9 Representation of the People Act 1983, ss. 95, 96, sched. 5. The courts will compel a local authority to make premises available: *Webster* v. *Southwark LBC* [1983] QB 698.

10 cf. *Associated Provincial Picture Houses Ltd* v. *Wednesbury Corporation* [1948] 1 KB 223. And see *Webster* v. *Newham London BC, The Times*, 22 November 1980.

11 *Beatty* v. *Gillbanks* (1882) 9 QBD 308; *M'Ara* v. *Edinburgh Magistrates* 1913 SC 1059.

12 Trafalgar Square Regulations 1952 (SI 1952, No. 776), r. 3. cf. *Ex p. Lewis* (1888) 21 QBD 191.

13 It is not a common-law liberty: *Bailey* v. *Williamson* (1873) LR 8 QB 118. See Royal Parks and Gardens Act 1872; Williams, op. cit., ch. 3.

14 See *De Morgan* v. *Metropolitan Board of Works* (1880) 5 QBD 155. See also *Llandudno UDC* v. *Woods* [1899] 2 Ch. 705 (religious services on the foreshore).

15 See p. 482.

obstruction to members. This order can have no legal effect outside the precincts of the House,[16] but the Commissioner of Police has statutory power[17] to give directions for the prevention of obstruction by assemblies in that vicinity and in various other places in the police district. Not every direction given with those purposes in view for the dispersal of a public assembly is necessarily valid, but the power is a wide one.[18]

Stationary gatherings on highways are generally regarded as trespasses at common law against the person or body in whom the highway is vested, unless the consent of the owner has been obtained. This is because the primary purpose to which a highway is dedicated is passage and repassage.[19] And since a public procession involves people marching down a highway, participation is *prima facie* lawful except perhaps while the procession is assembling. But a procession may well constitute an unlawful obstruction of the highway or a public nuisance.

The general rule that meetings on highways are trespasses is derived from private law. It gives no weight to the public interest in freedom of expression, and it seems ripe for reconsideration by the courts. In any event, the principle of dedication to passage and repassage is subject to exceptions indeterminate in scope – ancillary activities such as holding private conversations and shopping are not trespasses, nor are brief stoppages by motor cars,[20] but what of distributing leaflets or soliciting answers from passers by to questionnaires? It would be sensible to replace the prevailing concept by one which equates trespass with unreasonable use.[21] Seldom would a large meeting in a public thoroughfare be a reasonable use.

16 *Papworth* v. *Coventry* [1967] 1 WLR 663 at 669–70.
17 Metropolitan Police Act 1839, s. 52. It is an offence to contravene a valid direction (s. 54(9)).
18 See *Papworth* v. *Coventry* (note 16). The assembly in question in *Papworth*'s case comprised only seven stationary protestors against the Vietnam War. Although they were standing at the corner of Downing Street, it is doubtful whether they were reasonably capable of causing obstruction or annoyance.
19 See, for example, *ex p. Lewis* (1888) 21 QBD at 197; *Harrison* v. *Duke of Rutland* [1893] 1 QB 142; *Hickman* v. *Maisey* [1900] 1 QB 752. See also cases cited in note 14, and the Scottish cases *M'Ara* v. *Edinburgh Magistrates* 1913 SC 1059, and *Aldred* v. *Miller* 1924 SC (J.) 117. See, however, *Burden* v. *Rigler* [1911] 1 KB 337 where it was held that a meeting held on a highway was not necessarily unlawful.
20 See *Iveagh* v. *Martin* [1961] 1 QB 232 at 273; *Randall* v. *Tarrant* [1955] 1 WLR 255.
21 In *Hirst and Agu* v. *Chief Constable of West Yorkshire* (1987) 85 Cr. App. R. 143, the Divisional Court held that the reasonableness of user by protesters handing out leaflets in the street was a relevant consideration, such conduct not in itself being unlawful. See also the dissenting judgment of Lord Denning in *Hubbard* v. *Pitt* [1976] 1 QB 142 for a passionate defence of constitutional freedom, and Wallington (1976) 35 *Camb. LJ* 82.

If an employee attends at or near his place of work in contemplation of furtherance of a trade dispute for the purpose only of peacefully obtaining or communicating information or peacefully persuading any person to work or abstain from working, his conduct is lawful.[22] That rule applies also to recently dismissed employees and to trade union officials accompanying and representing their members. Subject to those statutory provisions pickets have no immunity from the impact of the various laws examined in this chapter. The law recognizes no right to demonstrate in a trade dispute; the picketing provisions do not protect anyone who does not work at the place being picketed. There is no authority to obstruct the passage of vehicles to and from the workplace.[23]

Of more practical importance than the law of trespass are the miscellany of local statutory restrictions already referred to, the law of obstruction and the regulatory powers of the police under the Public Order Act 1986, Part II. Wilfully to obstruct the free passage along a highway without lawful authority or excuse is a criminal offence.[24] If there has been an appreciable and unreasonable obstruction, it is no defence that a way round it could be found or that nobody was proved to have been obstructed,[25] nor is it a defence that a speaker holding a meeting did not wish to create an obstruction, or that other speakers holding meetings in the same place had not been prosecuted.[26] The prosecution must prove its case, but since the amount and duration of an obstruction that it needs to establish in order to obtain a conviction are slight, the police and the local authority have almost a *de facto* licensing power with regard to public meetings and even the distribution of leaflets in the streets. If they decide to take no action, their abstention from prosecution means that no proceedings are likely to be taken at all. If a police officer orders a speaker, distributor, vendor or audience to 'move along', non-compliance with this direction is likely to lead to a conviction for obstruction of the highway or obstruction of a constable in the execution of his duty.

Public processions were first made subject to general statutory powers

---

22 Trade Union and Labour Relations (Consolidation) Act 1992, s. 220.
23 *Thomas* v. *NUM* (*South Wales*) [1986] 1 Ch. 20; see generally Carty [1984] *Public Law* 600; Bennion [1985] *Crim. L. Rev.* 64.
24 Highways Act 1980, s. 137.
25 See generally *Horner* v. *Cadman* (1886) 55 LJMC 110; *Nagy* v. *Weston* [1965] 1 WLR 280.
26 *Arrowsmith* v. *Jenkins* [1963] 2 QB 561. Or that the local authority had acquiesced in the defendant's obstruction of the highway for a long period before deciding to prosecute: *Redbridge LBC* v. *Jacques* [1970] 1 WLR 1604.

of regulation by the Public Order Act 1936. Newer forms of public disorder over recent years, especially at some industrial disputes, riots in some cities and football hooliganism, gave an impetus for fresh and more effective preventative arrangements. These are contained in the Public Order Act 1986, Part II. First, advance written notice of a public procession[27] intended (a) to show support for (or opposition to) the views or actions of any person or body of persons, or (b) to publicize a cause or campaign, or (c) to mark or commemorate an event, must be given to the police.[28] That notice must be received by the police at least six clear days ahead, specifying the proposed date, route, time and the name and address of the organizer (or organizers). It is an offence for the organizers not to give such notice, punishable by a maximum fine of £1,000. Secondly, a senior police officer may give directions in relation to a planned or actual public procession if he reasonably believes that (a) the procession may result in serious public disorder, serious damage to property or serious disruption to the life of the community, or (b) the purpose of the organizers is to intimidate others.[29] The directions can be of any type which seems to him to be necessary to prevent his fears coming to fruition. Knowingly failing to comply with such directions is an offence,[30] and a constable in uniform may arrest anyone whom he reasonably believes is committing it. Organizers may well negotiate with the police (as was common before the 1986 Act) to get agreement about planned marches, rather than have conditions forced upon them. Thirdly, if a chief constable reasonably believes that his powers to impose conditions on a procession would not be enough to prevent serious public disorder, he may apply to the district council in whose area the procession would take place for an order prohibiting for a period up to three months the holding of all, or a specified class of, public processions in the area.[31] The council may make such an order with the Home Secretary's consent; it may be amended or revoked in the same way.[32] Knowingly contravening such an order is an offence,[33] and a constable in uniform may arrest for it.

27 i.e., a procession in a public place: 1986 Act, s. 16.
28 1986 Act, s. 11. If it is not reasonably practicable to do so (e.g. when a gathering is spontaneous), no such duty exists.
29 ibid., s. 12. The 'senior police officer' is the chief constable (for planned processions), or the senior officer present (at an actual procession).
30 The organizer, and an inciter, are liable to three months' imprisonment and a £5,000 fine; a participant to a £1,000 fine.
31 ibid., s. 13.
32 In the City of London or the Metropolitan Police District the two chief officers may each make an equivalent order with the Home Secretary's consent.
33 See note 30.

Fourthly, the police have a power to give directions in relation to public assemblies.[34] If the senior police officer[35] has the same fears about an assembly as were set out above in relation to public processions, he may impose similar directions upon it – although he cannot ban it. A public assembly is one of twenty or more persons in a public place which is wholly or partly open to the air:[36] meetings inside buildings are excluded. Offences may be committed as for breach of conditions for public processions,[37] and the same power of arrest exists. All these powers seek to balance, on the one hand, the rights to process and to assemble against, on the other, the rights of those not involved to live peaceful lives which are not unreasonably disrupted. Although the validity of conditions imposed on the organizers of a procession might be challenged in court on various grounds, it would seem that a prohibitory order could be impugned only if it were perverse or singled out an individual procession as distinct from a class of processions; the court cannot review the merits of an order.

Preventive justice may be (and quite frequently is) involved by the police in bringing potentially disorderly demonstrators or other 'agitators' before local magistrates, who may bind them over to be of good behaviour or to keep the peace.[38] If they refuse to enter into a recognizance or are unable to find sureties, they may be sent to prison for up to six months. If they break the conditions set out in the recognizance they become liable to forfeiture of the sum there specified.

If the police reasonably apprehend that the holding of a gathering in a public place will give rise to a breach of the peace, they are under a common-law duty to take reasonable steps to prevent that gathering from taking place or to break it up. This power was used, for example, to prevent disorder during the miners' strike of 1984–5. In *Moss and Others* v. *McLachlan*[39] four would-be pickets ignored police requests to turn back from their intended picket site while still some few miles away from it. They were convicted of obstructing the police, who had ample evidence to fear a breach of the peace at the intended destination. The common-law powers of the police to deal with a breach of the peace are unaffected by the Public Order Act 1986 or by the arrest provisions of the Police and Criminal Evidence Act 1984. The problems caused by the ambit of *Duncan*

34 1986 Act, s. 14.
35 See note 29.
36 1986 Act, s. 15.
37 See note 30.
38 Williams, op. cit., ch. 4; Law Com. No 103 (1987).
39 [1985] IRLR 77.

v. *Jones*,[40] however, have been greatly reduced by the Public Order Act 1986.[41]

If a public meeting is held on private premises, and the police reasonably apprehend that, should they not be present, a breach of the peace or an incitement to violence will occur, they are entitled to attend and insist on remaining in order to prevent such an occurrence. This is the narrowest possible *ratio decidendi* of *Thomas* v. *Sawkins*,[42] a decision that has been widely criticized, not least because the judgments included some unacceptably sweeping propositions about the extent of police powers.[43] Nevertheless, the principle set out above is reasonable, provided that it is confined to apprehended violence and the dissemination of incitements. The presence of a policeman on the spot can have a restraining influence at both indoor and outdoor meetings. An ordinary member of the public cannot claim a right to enter a meeting or to remain there after his invitation or licence to remain has been withdrawn, even though the meeting has been advertised as being open to the public.[44] But the police have special common-law responsibilities for the maintenance of public order, and it would be unreasonable to deny them a right of entry until a breach of the peace has actually occurred. It may be asked whether the same rule applies to

40 [1936] 1 KB 218.
41 See below, p. 488.
42 [1935] 2 KB 249. See also *McConnell* v. *Chief Constable of Greater Manchester Police* [1990] 1 All ER 423.
43 See, for example, Goodhart (1936) 6 *Camb. LJ* 22. A meeting was organized by the Communist Party to protest against the Incitement to Disaffection Bill, then before Parliament, and to demand the dismissal of the Chief Constable of Glamorgan. Uniformed police entered the meeting and refused to leave; the speaker laid hands on a police officer whom he wished to eject as a trespasser; the officer resisted; the speaker took out a summons against the police officer for assault; the magistrates dismissed the case, holding that the police officer was not a trespasser. The speaker appealed on a point of law by way of case stated to the Divisional Court. Some passages in Lord Hewart CJ's judgment were too loosely expressed. Avory J held that the police were entitled to remain if they reasonably apprehended that if they were not present seditious speeches and/or breaches of the peace would occur. He observed (at 256): 'In principle I think there is no distinction between the duty of a police constable to prevent a breach of the peace and the power of a magistrate to bind a person over to prevent a breach of the peace.'

In the text above, 'sedition' has been equateed with an incitement to violence (see p. 462). It should be noted that the magistrate found as a fact that the police had reasonable grounds for thinking that if they were not present there would be incitements to violence and breaches of the peace.

44 Subject to limited exceptions. Whether a person who has paid for admission to a public meeting can be ejected as a trespasser whenever the promoters think fit is questionable. A member of an organization may also have a legal right to attend a private meeting of that organization.

private gatherings on private premises. One has to balance the public interest in the prevention of disorder against (i) the public interest in the maintenance of personal privacy against unsolicited intrusion, (ii) the possibility that a power to insist on entry might be abused, and (iii) the probability that, where incitements to violence are apprehended, the presence of police officers might not serve any useful purpose because the group could quietly arrange another meeting at a different time and place. The point is not clearly covered by English authority, but it is thought that the powers of the police do extend to insistence on being present at such a meeting[45] where violence at or immediately after the gathering is reasonably apprehended.

OFFENCES

We have seen how the mere holding of a public meeting or procession may be wrongful. It may be a trespass. It will be a criminal offence if it is held without the permission required by a local Act or by-law, or in breach of the provisions of Part II of the Public Order Act 1986. Organizers of a procession commit an offence if a ban on public processions in that area is in force, or if they infringe conditions lawfully imposed by the police. A meeting held in a public place may well constitute an obstruction of the highway. So may a public procession if it causes significant obstruction.

A demonstration, mobile or stationary, may also be a public nuisance if it entails an unreasonable use of the highway, causing obstruction or excessive noise. Prosecutions for public nuisance in this context have been uncommon.[46] but in 1963 the leader of a political demonstration in Central London was sentenced to eighteen months' imprisonment for inciting other persons to commit a nuisance. The conviction was quashed on appeal because the jury had not been directed to consider whether the obstruction caused was an unreasonable use of the highway.[47] In that case there was evidence of obstruction by a large crowd. The decision of the appellate court may indicate a benign attitude towards processions (as distinct from meetings) or a difference in the degrees of obstruction

---

45 For example, a meeting of a student body on university premises. However, the possibility that the presence of police may provoke rather than dampen inflammatory statements is not to be disregarded.
46 The Attorney-General, on behalf of the general public, may also sue for an injunction to restrain the continuance or repetition of a public nuisance; see pp. 559–62.
47 *R.* v. *Clark (No. 2)* [1964] 2 QB 315.

needed to obtain convictions for a public nuisance and for wilful obstruction under the Highways Act 1980.[48] In any event, the most remarkable feature of the case was the sentence imposed by the court of first instance.

It is an offence to use or threaten violence for the purpose of securing entry into any premises.[49] Squatters or other persons who occupy premises and refuse to leave at the request of a displaced residential occupier of the premises also commit a crime.[50]

There is an obvious danger that a large number of people in a mobile or static demonstration may be so stimulated by the fervour of their cause that serious public order crimes result. So, for example, about 140 charges of riot and over 500 of unlawful assembly were brought during the miners' strike of 1984–5.[51] The common-law offences of riot, rout unlawful assembly and affray were, as the Law Commission concluded, unsatisfactory[52] and the law was modernized by the Public Order Act 1986, Part I. Those four common-law offences were abolished[53] and in their place statutory crimes of riot, violent disorder and affray were created; rout and unlawful assembly were not recreated (at least, not under those names).

Riot[54] is an offence in which twelve or more people who are present together use or threaten unlawful violence[55] for a common purpose,[56] and the conduct of them (taken together) is such as would cause a person of reasonable firmness present at the scene[57] to fear for his personal safety. That common purpose may be inferred from their conduct;[58] a riot may take

---

48 On the question of unreasonable obstruction, the case law does not point unambiguously to any such difference.

49 s. 6(1) Criminal Law Act 1977.

50 ibid., s. 7(1). There are several other possible offences relating to the misuse of another's land: see the Criminal Justice and Public Order Act 1994, Part V.

51 No evidence was offered, however, in a large number of cases, and there was a high rate of acquittals – partly as a result of the problems of establishing those offences, as Lord Scarman had warned in his report on the Brixton disorders would be the case: see Cmnd 8427 (1983).

52 See Law Com. No. 123 (1983).

53 1986 Act, s. 9. See the commentaries on the Act cited above, p. 478, note 1.

54 ibid., s. 1. See *R.* v. *Jefferson* [1994] 1 All ER 270.

55 'Violence' for purposes of riot and violent disorder means (s. 8) any violent conduct including violence towards property.

56 The mental element required is an intention to use violence, or that the accused is aware that his conduct may be violent: s. 6(1).

57 No such person need actually be, or be likely to be, present at the scene: ibid., s. 1(4).

58 ibid., s. 1(3).

place in a private or in a public place;[59] it carries a maximum penalty of ten years' imprisonment and a fine.[60] It is clearly the most serious public order offence, and the consent of the Director of Public Prosecutions is necessary for any prosecution of it.[61] Civil claims to compensation out of public funds under the Riot (Damages) Act 1886 will continue to be made for loss suffered by property-owners as a result of riots.

Violent disorder[62] is committed when three or more persons who are present together use or threaten unlawful violence[63] and the conduct of them (taken together) is such as would cause a person of reasonable firmness present at the scene to fear for his personal safety.[64] The maximum penalty on indictment is a five-year prison sentence and a fine, or on summary conviction six months' imprisonment or a fine of up to £5,000.[65] Violent disorder will be the usual charge following serious disorder. The crime replaces unlawful assembly, about which there was uncertainty as to its nature and scope: the Law Commission had identified no fewer than four ways of defining it.[66] Difficulties of interpretation existed about when an assembly became unlawful,[67] about what constituted a breach of the peace,[68] and about the liability of people in one group for unlawful acts which were likely to be provoked in or committed by others. That last problem was highlighted in the attempts to reconcile, in particular, *Beatty* v. *Gillbanks*,[69] *Wise* v. *Dunning*[70] and *Duncan* v. *Jones*.[71] No doubt the courts will find fresh problems in interpreting the Public Order Act 1986, although perhaps not of the same intellectual complexity.

---

59 ibid., s. 1(5): for the definition, see s. 16.
60 ibid., s. 1(6). It is therefore an arrestable offence under s. 24 of the Police and Criminal Evidence Act 1984. On the common-law offence, see *Field* v. *Metropolitan Police Receiver* [1921] 3 KB 334; *Munday* v. *Metropolitan Police District Receiver* [1949] 1 All ER 337.
61 ibid., s. 7(1).
62 ibid., s. 2. See *R.* v. *Jefferson* (note 54 above).
63 An accused must intend to use or threaten violence, or be aware that his conduct may be violent or threaten violence: s. 6(2).
64 Again, no such person need be, or be likely to be, present (s. 2(3)); it can be committed in public or private (s. 2(4)).
65 ibid., s. 2(5). It is an arrestable offence under s. 24 of the Police and Criminal Evidence Act 1984.
66 Law Commission Working Paper No. 82 (1982), paras. 2.43–2.50.
67 See *R.* v. *Caird* (1970) 50 Cr. App. R. 449.
68 Contrast *R.* v. *Howell* [1982] QB 416 and *R.* v. *Chief Constable of Devon and Cornwall, ex p. CEGB* [1982] QB 458.
69 (1889) 9 QBD 308.
70 [1992] 1 KB 167.
71 [1936] 1 KB 218. See the 5th edn, 1985, of this book, pp. 513–18.

Affray[72] is committed by one who uses unlawful violence towards another when his conduct is such as would cause a person present of reasonable firmness to fear for his personal safety. A threat cannot be made by words alone.[73] On indictment the maximum penalty is three years' imprisonment and a fine; summarily it is three months' imprisonment and a fine up to £5,000.[74] A constable may arrest without warrant anyone he reasonably suspects is committing an affray.[75]

It should be remembered that if none of these offences can be proved prosecutions could succeed under the Public Order Act 1986, sections 4 and 5,[76] and for obstructing a police officer in the execution of this duty.[77]

In the exercise of their powers the police must be aware of the importance of the right of assembly so that those who are lawfully conducting themselves but who encounter opposition should receive police protection. Under the old common-law position, the police were occasionally too ready to move against those who were exercising their constitutional rights, rather than to act against others who threatened them or the public peace.[78] The offences in Parts I and II of the Public Order Act 1986 are, on the whole, constructed so as to redress the balance in favour of freedom of assembly.

Finally, there are three points of some importance in the conduct of public meetings but not directly associated with the foregoing discussion.

1 Section 2(6) of the Public Order Act 1936 recognized the legality of employing a reasonable number of stewards to assist in the maintenance of order in public meetings on private premises. However, they are not to be so organized as to usurp the functions of the police or to display force in the promotion of a political object.

---

72 1986 Act s. 3. No such person need be present (s. 3(4)); it can be committed in public or private (s. 3(5)). If two or more people so act, it is their conduct taken together that must be considered: s. 3(2). See *R.* v. *Davison* [1992] *Crim. L. Rev.* 31.

73 ibid., s. 3(3).

74 ibid., s. 3(7).

75 ibid., s. 3(6). For the common-law offence, see *Button* v. *DPP* [1966] AC 591 and *Taylor* v. *DPP* [1973] AC 964 (HL); *Att.-Gen.'s Reference (No. 3 of 1983)* [1985] 1 QB 24.

76 See above, pp. 470–72.

77 Police Act 1996, s. 89(2): see above, pp. 435–6.

78 The Public Meeting Act 1908, s. 1 (which remains in force) makes it an offence to act in a disorderly manner for the purpose of preventing the transaction of business at a lawful meeting. A constable may take the name and address of a suspect; if he refuses to give it, or if the constable believes it is false, he may arrest him under the Police and Criminal Evidence Act 1984, s. 25.

2 It is an offence under section 1 of the Act punishable by three months'
   imprisonment and/or a fine up to £2,500 to wear a political uniform
   (except with the permission of the Home Secretary) in a public place or
   at a public meeting. Emblems, badges and armbands will not normally
   be understood to be uniforms, but a shirt with a colour signifying the
   wearer's political associations would be so regarded. Those who, in 1974,
   attended a London IRA funeral procession in black berets and dark
   glasses were convicted under the section.[79]

3 Under the Prevention of Crime Act 1953 it is an offence to have, without
   lawful authority or reasonable excuse, an offensive weapon in a public
   place. For this purpose, a public place includes a public meeting on
   private premises. The burden of proving lawful authority or reasonable
   excuse will lie on the defendant. An offensive weapon is an article made
   or adapted for causing injury to the person, or alternatively one that is
   intended by the person having it with him to be used for that purpose;
   in the latter case the prosecution must prove intent.[80]

The range of crimes and civil wrongs that may be committed by participants
in public gatherings is therefore impressive. And the miscellany of crimes
and torts described in the previous chapter may be committed on such
occasions. The ample scope of punitive, preventive and repressive powers
(which, as is to be expected, is far wider in Northern Ireland) implies that
considerable self-restraint must be shown by the police and magistrates if
the spokesmen of unpopular or eccentric or other causes are to be allowed
to ventilate their opinions.

---

79 *O'Moran* v. *DPP* [1975] QB 864. The Northern Ireland (Emergency Provisions)
Act 1996, s. 31 makes it a specific offence for members of the IRA or other proscribed
organizations to wear any item of dress or wear, carry or display any article in public
support of that organization.
80 See also the Offensive Weapons Act 1996.

CHAPTER 24

National Emergencies

CIVIL DISORDER[1]

Public order is now subject in particular to threats from political terrorists, and hijacking of aircraft.[2] The police are now trained in handling firearms to deal with political terrorists, and their internal rules regulate the circumstances in which they may use them. The sight of armed police patrolling airports is now commonplace. Senior police officers occasionally have to decide what degree of force to use against disorder, whether baton charges or even CS gas. When a chief officer of police believes that his force can no longer deal with a threat to public order he will consult the Home Office. The Home Secretary and the Secretary of State for Defence and, if the matter is serious enough, the Prime Minister and Cabinet will decide whether to sanction the use of force by troops. A combined operation of police and military will then be put into effect.[3] This is the kind of plan for protecting airports against terrorist attacks. Nevertheless, circumstances may arise where a military officer on the spot may have to make a snap decision whether to use force, and if so, how much, to quell a riot.[4] It may be sufficient to use batons, tear gas, rubber bullets or water cannon. If such methods are ineffective in the circumstances, he must decide whether to order his men to open fire with lethal bullets. Failure to give an order may lead to the triumph of the rioters and perhaps the capture of arms, followed

---

1 See D. Bonner, *Emergency Powers in Peacetime* (1985); G. Marshall, *Constitutional Conventions* (1984), ch. 9.
2 See above, p. 426.
3 See Report of the Metropolitan Police Commissioner for 1975 Cmnd 1976, app. 9; 91 HC Deb. *317* (written answers 10 February 1986). The General Officer Commanding British troops in Northern Ireland is subject to the political direction of the United Kingdom Government.
4 See the official *Manual of Military Law*. Relevant extracts are set out in Appendix 5 to Ian Brownlie's *Law of Public Order and National Security* (2nd edn, 1981).

perhaps by his being court-martialled and cashiered,[5] or even indicted for a common-law offence,[6] in respect of his breach of duty. If he orders deadly violence to be used when this is not justified under the conditions, he (and possibly his subordinates)[7] may be convicted of murder or manslaughter.

The officer's predicament is made more acute by the obscurity of the legal principles governing the scope of his duties. Judges and writers have insisted many times over that soliders are entitled, indeed obliged at common law, to use all necessary force, including deadly violence in the last resort, to disperse rioters, who are doing serious and extensive damage to property – for example, demolishing and setting fire to colliery buildings.[8] Is this still the law? Section 3 of the Criminal Law Act 1967 provides that a person may use such force as is *reasonable* in the circumstances in the prevention of crime; and it expressly replaces the common-law rules on this matter. Referring to this section,[9] the authors of a leading textbook on criminal law assert that it can rarely, if ever, be justifiable to use deadly force merely for the protection of property.[10] What if skinheads try to burn down the National Gallery, or if revolutionaries try to demolish No. 10 Downing Street? In the last analysis, answers to the question whether it can be justifiable to use lethal weapons to prevent the destruction of property, in the absence of an immediate threat to human life, may depend on value judgements which may reasonably differ. Soldiers can be expected to be equipped with common sense. They can hardly be expected to make fundamental judgements about social institutions when they are under stress in the face of mob violence; and their oath of loyalty implies an obligation to do what appears necessary for the preservation of the existing order and its physical manifestations.[11]

5 See Professor Heuston's account of the sequel to the Bristol Riots of 1831 in *Essays in Constitutional Law* (2nd edn, 1964), pp. 137–8. For a fuller account of the use of troops in aid of the civil power at that time and in the preceding years, see L. Radzinowicz, *A History of English Criminal Law and its Administration*, vol. 4, pp. 141–52.
6 cf. *R.* v. *Pinney* (1832) 3 B. & Ad. 947.
7 Subject to the doubtful defence of superior orders; see pp. 222–3.
8 See, for example, *Report of the Committee on the Featherstone Riots* (C. 7734 (1893)).
9 For an interpretation of the corresponding provision in Northern Ireland law see *Devlin* v. *Armstrong* [1971] NI 13 (organization of petrol-bomb throwing by Miss Devlin not reasonable to prevent invasion of Bogside by constabulary and suspected Protestant mob).
10 J. C. Smith and Brian Hogan, *Criminal Law* (8th edn, 1996), p. 262.
11 However, the potentially grave social consequences of resorting to deadly violence, even in a situation where troops are being subjected to physical assault by riotous demonstrators, were vividly illustrated by the events of 'Bloody Sunday' in Londonderry (30 January 1972). See the Report of the Widgery Tribunal of Inquiry (HC 220 (1971–2)), where it seems to have been assumed that instructions to the troops to fire without warning only against persons endangering or about to endanger life (see paras. 89 et seq.) were correct in law. A further inquiry is planned.

It is possible to analyse the duties of soldiers to quell local riots as being the duties of the ordinary citizen writ large.[12] But when riot passes into rebellion or guerrilla warfare, emphases shift and other principles intrude. Levying 'war' against the Queen in her realm is both treason and treason felony. The civil power primarily responsible for containing and suppressing an uprising must be the Government in office. The military authorities will be obliged to act in its support. The Crown, acting through its advisers, has, moreover, a prerogative power to direct the disposition and use of the armed forces. The exact limits of this prerogative are far from clear,[13] but it cannot mean that troops can lawfully be ordered to do whatever the Crown thinks fit whenever it thinks fit to maintain internal security, irrespective of what necessity requires. However, it may well imply that the strict tests of legality applied to the conduct of those entrusted with the preservation of order in local disturbances[14] should be slightly relaxed in time of extensive turmoil.

If the situation moves a stage further and the civil authorities become incapable of governing because of a large-scale insurrection, powers to do whatever may be needed to restore peace may be handed over to (or assumed by) the military authorities. This is a new situation, different both in degree and kind. A state of martial law will then exist, and the powers of the General Officer Commanding the Forces will, so it is usually thought, become non-justiciable and, for the time being, absolute, subject only to consultation (if this is feasible) with the civil power.

Martial law has been aptly described as 'a peculiar system of legal relations'[15] which arises in time of civil war or insurrection, or, it may be added, invasion. It is a state of affairs, not a settled body of rules, though rules and orders will be promulgated and enforced by the military authorities as they see fit. It must be sharply distinguished from military law, a settled body

---

12 In Reference under 48A of the Criminal Appeal (Northern Ireland) Act 1968 (No. 1 of 1975) [1977] AC 105 at 136 Lord Diplock said: '. . . when troops are called on to assist in controlling a riotous assembly . . . it may not be inaccurate to describe the legal rights and duties of a soldier as being no more than those of an ordinary citizen in uniform.'

13 The common-law rules on the prerogative in emergencies falling short of war are remarkably abstruse; see the inconclusive comments in *Halsbury's Laws of England* (4th edn), vol. 8, pp. 625–6.

14 See *Lynch* v. *Fitzgerald* [1938] IR 382; Keir and Lawson, *Cases* (6th edn, 1979) p. 206.

15 Keir and Lawson, op. cit., p. 217; also see generally pp. 217–50; Heuston, *Essays* (2nd edn, 1964), pp. 150–63; symposium in (1902) 18 *LQR* 117–58.

of rules applied in accordance with prescribed procedures to members of the armed forces and ancillary personnel. Military law is simply a specialized branch of United Kingdom law administered by military officers acting summarily or sitting in courts-martial, subject to the supervisory and appellate jurisdiction of the ordinary courts.[16] Courts-martial applying military law are regular courts. Courts-martial applying martial law are not: they are informal tribunals or committees of officers,[17] and appear to be no more subject to the supervisory jurisdiction of the superior courts than are 'drumhead courts' or soldiers meting out summary punishment to armed rebels, curfew-breakers or other supposed malefactors among the civil population.

Confusion of martial law and military law was far more common before a regular corpus of military law was introduced in the eighteenth century. In the Middle Ages the prerogative Court of the Constable and Marshal dispensed the 'law martial' against rebellious civilians as well as undisciplined soldiers; it lost most of its jurisdiction in 1640.[18] Under the Tudors and early Stuarts special commissions were issued from time to time under the prerogative for the trial by martial law of serious offenders against public order. The issue of such commissions was forbidden by the Petition of Right 1628. But the terminological confusion lingered on.

The term 'martial law' is also sometimes used to denote military rule over enemy territory occupied by British forces. Such a situation is regulated rather by the international law of war than by British municipal law.

Finally, 'martial law' can be used to describe an entirely different kind of situation – one where military officers overthrow the legitimate government establish a new regime and proclaim a state of martial law. The phenomenon is all too familiar in many countries. It has not arisen in Britain in modern times and our constitutional law books are silent on its legal consequences. Briefly, one can say that the judges and officials are not obliged to recognize

---

16 See pp. 223–4.

17 Hence the courts will not control them by issuing prerogative orders: *Re Clifford and O'Sullivan* [1921] 2 AC 570 (prohibition). This House of Lords decision skirted the main issue – whether the courts had any jurisdiction at all to interfere with the decisions of the military tribunals.

18 However, the ancient Court of Chivalry retains a minor aspect of the jurisdiction: see *Manchester Corporation* v. *Manchester Palace of Varieties Ltd* [1955] P. 133 (right to use a coat of arms).

the validity of such a proclamation any more than they are obliged to accept any other revolutionary *coup d'état*, but that if they defy the mailed fist, they cannot expect to retain office for long. If they do recognize the supersession of the old order as valid,[19] successful revolution has begotten its own legality.[20]

Propositions about martial-law situations, as reviewed by the courts, are deducible from cases arising out of the Irish troubles and the Boer War. They presuppose (i) the existence of civil authorities who (ii) are unable to cope with widespread disorders or armed conflict and who therefore (iii) authorize or acquiesce in the imposition of military government upon civilians for the purpose of restoring order.

1 A state of martial law may be introduced by or without a proclamation. A proclamation purporting to introduce a state of martial law is of no legal effect in itself; martial law is justified only by paramount necessity.

2 If the ordinary courts are still sitting, it seems that they have jurisdiction to determine whether 'a state of war' (not necessarily war in the international sense but a state of affairs requiring military 'pacification' by the imposition of martial law) exists in an area where they normally have jurisdiction. In determining this question, they will give heavy weight to the opinion of the local military commander, but his opinion is not binding on them.[21]

3 If they decide that a 'state of war' does exist, then (according to the present weight of legal opinion) they should decline to review the legality of anything done by the military authorities in the purported discharge of military responsibilities till, in their independent judgement, the 'state of war' has terminated.[22]

---

19 As they did in Pakistan in 1958 (*The State* v. *Dosso* PLD 1958 SC 533); though the prevailing conditions did not justify the initial proclamation of martial law in that year. Martial law was again declared in Pakistan in 1969 during a widespread breakdown of law and order, but after the collapse of the regime early in 1972 following the defeat of the Pakistan army by India, the Pakistan Supreme Court held (*Jilani* v. *Government of the Punjab* PLD 1972 SC 139; disapproving *Dosso*'s case) that the martial-law regime was unlawful.

20 See pp. 70–73.

21 See, for example, *R.* v. *Allen* [1921] 2 IR 241; *R.* (*Garde*) v. *Strickland* [1921] 2 IR 317; cf. the striking decision in *Egan v. Macready* (note 23, below).

22 *Ex p. Marais* [1902] AC 109; *Tilonko* v. *Att.-Gen. of Natal* [1907] AC 93; cases cited in note 21, above, and note 23, below.

4 The non-justiciability of acts done by the military authorities during the 'state of war' seems to embrace situations where they have exceeded emergency powers conferred on them by statute.[23]

5 When ordinary civil proceedings can be resumed, proceedings may be brought against the military authorities by persons aggrieved by acts done during the state of martial law. According to one view soldiers will be legally liable at common law in respect of any unnecessary use of force against persons or property.[24] A more realistic view is that liability should attach only to such conduct as was manifestly unreasonable in the circumstances.[25] In practice an Act of Indemnity is almost certain to be passed (assuming that the disturbances are quelled), exonerating from liability persons who were acting in good faith for the suppression of the uprising.[26]

WAR

The declaration and general conduct of war, as the term is understood in international law, are matters of prerogative. Among the specific prerogatives exercisable in time of war are powers to intern and deport enemy aliens,[27] to prohibit trading with the enemy except by licence, to requisition property (including land[28] and British ships[29]) for military purposes, to requisition neutral ships and chattels (the right of angary),[30] and to destroy property

---

23 R. v. Allen (above); but see Egan v. Macready [1921] IR 265, where the court held that the 'prerogative' powers exercised by the military authorities had been superseded by statute. See the valuable discussion of these cases in Keir and Lawson, op. cit., pp. 233–7. And note the courageous decision of a Pakistan court in Mir Hasan v. The State PLD 1969 (2) Lahore 786, interpreting a martial-law regulation and holding an order made by a martial-law authority to be invalid; see Dias [1970] Camb. LJ 49. It is arguable that public policy does not require a total abdication of judicial review during a state of martial law.

24 A. V. Dicey, Introduction to the Study of the Law of the Constitution (10th edn, 1959), pp. 289–91.

25 Keir and Lawson, op. cit., pp. 224–5.

26 For interpretation of such an Act, see Wright v. Fitzgerald (1798) 27 St. Tr. 759. But much will depend on the wording of the particular Act and a jury's view of the merits of the case: see O'Higgins (1962) 25 Mod. L. Rev. 413, discussing unreported Irish decisions on the activities of 'Flogger Fitzgerald'.

27 R. v. Bottrill, ex p. Kuechenmeister [1947] KB 41.

28 See discussion of the precedents in Att.-Gen. v. De Keyser's Royal Hotel Ltd [1920] AC 508.

29 The Broadmayne [1916] P. 64.

30 Commercial & Estates Co. of Egypt v. Board of Trade [1925] 1 KB 271.

in order to impede, or deny facilities to, an advancing enemy.[31] Compensation is payable at common law for requisitioning, damaging or destroying private property (except in battle);[32] but the War Damage Act 1965 abolished the duty to pay compensation for lawful *damage* to or *destruction* of property during, or in contemplation of the outbreak of, war.[33] The exact scope of the prerogative in time of war may never be exactly ascertained. Nor is it clear how far the war prerogatives extend to a state of immediately apprehended war. Again, some of the emergency powers exercisable by the Crown (for example, to enter upon private property and construct defence works to repel an invasion)[34] may be regarded as common-law powers exercisable by all citizens as a matter of necessity, and not peculiar to the Crown; hence they would not usually be classifiable as prerogatives. In practice most of the powers that the Crown is likely to exercise during war will be regulated by statute.

There seems to be no justification for the view that a state of martial law may be imposed within the realm whenever the Crown is at war; if the civil authorities are capable of governing, there is no legal warrant for the introduction of military rule by prerogative.

Reference has already been made to the vast powers conferred on the Crown in Council by the Defence of the Realm Acts 1914–15 and the Emergency Powers (Defence) Acts 1939–40.[35] The general words of the Defence of the Realm Acts, authorizing the making of regulations to secure the public safety and the defence of the realm, were construed as being wide enough to validate a regulation for the preventive detention of British subjects on security grounds.[36] The emergency legislation of the Second World War was more explicitly worded. It expressly saved the royal prerogative;[37] it authorized the sub-delegation of delegated powers and the imposition of charges on the subject,[38] and the making of regulations for

31 *Burmah Oil Co.* v. *Lord Advocate* [1965] AC 75 (destruction of British-owned oil installations in Burma in 1942, on orders of military commander, acting in pursuance of Government 'scorched earth' policy, so as to prevent Japanese army from taking them intact).
32 ibid.
33 The Act was severely criticized in that it had retroactive effect, overruling the actual decision of the House of Lords in the *Burmah Oil* case.
34 *Case of the King's Prerogative in Saltpetre* (1606) 12 Co. Rep. 12.
35 See above, p. 340.
36 *R.* v. *Halliday, ex p. Zadig* [1917] AC 260 (Regulation 14B).
37 Emergency Powers (Defence) Act 1939, s. 9.
38 ibid., ss. 1(3), 2; cf. *Att.-Gen.* v. *Wilts United Dairies Ltd* (1921) 37 TLR 884, where it was held that the Food Controller, purporting to act under emergency powers, could not validly require a milk purchaser to pay him 2d. a gallon as a condition of being granted a licence to purchase, since he had no express statutory authority to impose a charge.

the detention of persons on security grounds and for the amendment of any prior Act of Parliament.[39] The Emergency Powers (Defence) (No. 2) Act 1940 authorized the making of Defence Regulations for the trial of civilians by special courts if the military situation so required. No such regulation was in fact made. The Acts expired in 1946, but some of the Defence Regulations were continued in force and others were made under post-war emergency legislation. Those which had survived were placed on a permanent footing by statute in 1964. Regulation 18B, authorizing the internment of security suspects, had been revoked immediately after the termination of armed hostilities with Germany.

It should be noted that in neither world war was the right to apply for the writ of habeas corpus against the Executive expressly suspended. However, regulations authorizing a Secretary of State to detain persons of hostile origins or associations were so broadly interpreted by the courts as to leave a detainee hardly any room for successfully challenging an internment order by habeas corpus or any other means.[40]

DISRUPTION OF ESSENTIAL SERVICES

Permanent legislation gives the Executive power to deal with dislocation caused by strikes in essential services and by natural catastrophes.[41] Under the Emergency Powers Acts 1920 and 1964 Her Majesty may proclaim a state of emergency if at any time it appears to her that there have occurred, or are about to occur, events of such a nature as to be calculated to deprive the community, or any substantial part of it, of the essentials of life by interference with the supply and distribution of food, water, fuel or light, or with the means of locomotion. If Parliament is not sitting when such a proclamation is issued, it has to meet within five days. The proclamation will be in force for one month but may be revoked before the expiry of that time or renewed after it.

---

39 ibid., ss. 1(2)(a), 1(4).
40 *R.* v. *Halliday* (note 36, above); *Liversidge* v. *Anderson* [1942] A C 206; *Greene* v. *Home Secretary* [1942] A C 284; cf. *R.* v. *Secretary of State for Home Affairs, ex p. Budd* [1942] 2 K B 14 (release by habeas corpus where detention order defective in form, followed by valid detention under detention order properly made out). For a hostile critique of the implementation of a policy of preventive detention of security suspects, see C. K. Allen, *Law and Orders* (3rd edn, 1965), Appendix 1. Earlier editions were even more critical.
41 Local authorities may use Civil Defence resources in an emergency or disaster involving destruction of property or danger to life or property: Civil Protection in Peacetime Act 1986.

During the state of emergency, such regulations may be made by Order in Council as are deemed necessary for securing and regulating the supply and distribution of the necessities of life, for preserving the peace and for other essential purposes and incidental matters.

A court would probably hold the grounds for making the proclamation to be non-justiciable, and the power to make regulations is so widely drawn that it would be difficult to establish that any such regulation was *ultra vires*, though it might be less difficult to show acts done ostensibly in pursuance of a regulation were unlawful. Under a number of new Commonwealth constitutions which give power to the Executive to proclaim a state of emergency, derogation from certain guarantees of fundamental rights is permitted but only to the extent 'reasonably required' or 'reasonably justifiable' for the purposes of dealing with the emergency.[42]

In a state of emergency, troops may be employed on agricultural duties;[43] and there is a statutory power (not confined to formal states of emergency) vested in the Secretary of State to call out the reserve forces, if required, to assist the civil power at time of national danger, great emergency or attack on the United Kingdom.[44]

Several safeguards are provided against the serious abuse of statutory emergency powers. Regulations made under Acts of 1920 and 1964 must be laid before both Houses of Parliament as soon as may be, and expire seven days after being laid unless approved by affirmative resolutions of both Houses. They may create new criminal offences triable by magistrates' courts, but the maximum penalty is to be three months' imprisonment and a £5,000 fine and they cannot change existing criminal procedure or authorize punishment by imprisonment or the imposition of fines without trial.[45] Nor may any such regulation make it an offence to take part in a strike or peacefully to persuade others to take part in a strike or impose compulsory military service or industrial conscription.

States of emergency were proclaimed in 1921, 1924, and again in 1926 at a time of the General Strike followed by a miners' strike. From 1945 to

42 For reviews and critiques of 'emergency' powers in Northern Ireland, see Lord MacDermott (1972) 17 *Juridical Review* (NS) 1; Claire Palley, *The Evolution, Disintegration and Possible Reconstruction of the Northern Ireland Constitution* (reprinted from (1972) 1 *Anglo-American L. Rev.* 368–476); Fabian Soc., *Emergency Powers: A Fresh Start* (1972). See also the Northern Ireland (Emergency Provisions) Act 1996.
43 Emergency Powers Act 1964, s. 2.
44 Reserve Forces Act 1996, s. 52.
45 The late Sir Carleton Allen's suggestion (*Law and Orders*, op. cit., p. 378) that preventive detention orders might be made under the Emergency Powers Act 1920 is sustainable only if such detention is differentiated from punishment.

the end of 1984 they were proclaimed on eight occasions, five of them under the Heath Government (arising from a dock strike and 'work to rule' at electricity power stations in 1970, a miners' strike and a dock strike in 1972 and a ban on overtime by miners and electric power workers in 1973–4).[46] The content of the regulations has depended on the kind of emergency: wide powers to fix food prices, requisition property and prohibit public gatherings may be conferred, but in the periods of emergency since 1945 the action taken in pursuance of the regulations[47] has had only a mild impact on the ordinary citizen and the emergencies have not been accompanied by civil disturbances apart from some acts of mob violence and intimidation of non-strikers in 1972. Potentially, however, very extensive authority could be exercised by the police and the armed forces under the Acts,[48] quite apart from their common-law powers and duties to secure the maintenance of public order.

The miners' strike of 1984–5 was indicative of a change of tactics by the authorities faced by a major industrial dispute. There was widespread mob violence and intimidation especially at coalfields, involving in some instances thousands of miners and demonstrators, but the supply of coal was not disrupted to any significant extent and no state of emergency was declared: the police used their ordinary powers to the full to maintain public order and carry out arrests. And a 'national reporting centre' was set up at Scotland Yard to coordinate the necessary movements of large numbers of police from all over England and Wales, a development objected to by some as a blueprint for a national police force.[49]

---

46 See K. Jeffery and P. Hennessy, *States of Emergency: British Government and Strikebreaking Since 1919* (1983).

47 In 1948 the strikers went back to work before any regulations had been issued. The proclamation of emergency had an immediate psychological effect.

48 For critical comment, see Ronald Kidd, *British Liberty in Danger*, pp. 48–51.

49 Further moves in that direction may be seen in the establishment of the National Criminal Intelligence Service and the National Crime Squad (see the Police Act 1997).

PART FIVE

ADMINISTRATIVE LAW

In this Part there is an introduction to the most rapidly developing area of public law in this country – the law of public administration, or administrative law. The subject has vast ramifications; here the treatment is confined to those aspects which have general constitutional importance.

Chapter 25 explains what administrative law is about. It goes on to classify the different types and forms of decisions in the law of public administration and outlines their procedural characteristics. As will be seen, the picture is untidy.

Chapter 26 reflects the changing attitudes of the courts towards judicial review of administrative action and the flood of case law in a way which highlights the major principles and leaves sufficient detail to allow for wider reading. It deals with the general principles governing judicial review of administrative acts, orders, decisions and omissions. The principles are illustrated by a selection of judicial decisions. In the 1960s the courts became less reticent in reviewing administrative acts and decisions, laying down more exacting standards of legality and fair procedure to be observed by the Administration. In particular, the courts widened the scope of the duty to observe the rules of natural justice in the course of arriving at administrative decisions, and emphasized the importance of a more loosely formulated 'duty to act fairly'. The progress of the doctrine of legitimate expectation is noted.

Some of the principles applied by the courts have already been illustrated in earlier chapters, notably in that on subordinate legislation (chapter 17).

In chapter 27 the main features of the more important remedies in administrative law are outlined. The changes brought about by the application for judicial review are explained and evaluated, together with the effect of the cases on the public law/private law divide. The restrictions placed on leave to apply for judicial review if alternative remedies have been exhausted are noted.

Chapter 28 examines the part played by special tribunals and statutory inquiries in the general scheme of administrative law.

Chapter 29 is about civil proceedings for damages and other private law remedies by and against the Crown, with sidelong glances at proceedings against other public bodies. Here again the law has controversial features, and further developments in the operation of public interest immunity are traced.

The final chapter in this Part deals with redress of individual grievances outside the system of the courts, tribunals, formal inquiries, and proceedings in Parliament. In particular, it is concerned with the Parliamentary Commissioner for Administration (the Ombudsman). This chapter links up with earlier chapters on ministerial responsibility and the functions of the House of Commons.

CHAPTER 25

Administrative Law: Introduction

ADMINISTRATIVE LAW AS PART OF
CONSTITUTIONAL LAW

Administrative law[1] is the branch of public law dealing with the actual operation of government, the administrative process. When the constitutional process has resulted in a duly elected Government which has determined its policies and enacted any necessary primary legislation, the administrative process begins. It concerns the day-to-day administration of the country at central and local level and putting into practice constitutionally decided policies. Administrative law regulates that process. It relates to the organization, composition, functions and procedures of public authorities and special statutory tribunals, their impact on the citizen and the legal restraints and liabilities to which they are subject. It controls the making of subordinate legislation by public authorities.[2] In essence administrative law is that part of constitutional law which reveals what tangible and enforceable limits can be placed on administrative action. Today, when administrative action and decisions impinge on so many areas of the citizen's life, certain topics in administrative law have developed special statutory and judge-made rules peculiar to themselves and which have become independent legal topics. Local government, tax law, social security law and immigration are but a few examples. The aim here is to introduce the basic framework of administrative law in the context of a study of constitutional law.

1 The leading general works on administrative law are H. W. R. Wade and C. F. Forsyth, *Administrative Law* (7th edn, 1994); J. F. Garner, *Administrative Law* (7th edn, 1989 by B. L. Jones). A refreshingly new approach is taken by P. P. Craig, *Administrative Law* (3rd edn, 1994). See also D. Foulkes, *Administrative Law* (7th edn, 1990). The main specialist work is S. A. de Smith, *Judicial Review of Administrative Action* (5th edn, 1996 by Lord Woolf and Jeffrey Jowell).
2 See ch. 17.

It is sometimes said that there is no developed system of English administrative law and that in its function of regulating the powers of the Administration English administrative law compares unfavourably with France's *droit administratif*.[3] The French citizen personally aggrieved by an administrative decision simply submits his complaint to the nearest *Tribunal Administratif* which investigates the issue and then may quash the decision, and if necessary award compensation to the citizen. Appeal from the *Tribunal Administratif* lies to the source of French administrative law, the *Conseil d'État*. The French student simply applies himself diligently to the case law developed by the *Conseil d'État* and will be able to deduce a set of coherent and logical principles determining the rights and duties of the State and the limits of its powers in its relationship with individuals. The English student is less fortunate. In the latter part of the last century Dicey's polemic[4] against the tyrannical nature of *droit administratif* prejudiced whole generations against administrative law in any form. For the French courts applying *droit administratif* are completely separate from the ordinary courts of law and staffed by judges with an administrative, not a legal, background. This, declared Dicey, was contrary to the rule of law, sacred to all Englishmen, which demanded that the conduct of the Administration and its officials be judged in the same common-law courts and governed by the same principles applied to ordinary citizens in private disputes. The problem is that the second part of Dicey's thesis is impossible. Once government vests wider discretionary powers in public authorities and creates special tribunals outside the ordinary court system there are no private law principles which can be applied when the powers or proceedings of an authority or tribunal are called in question. Like it or not, the common-law courts were forced to develop a system of principles of administrative law.[5] Nor can identical rules apply to the Government even where on the face of it proceedings by the citizen against a public authority resemble an ordinary contract or tort action. If a local council is empowered to keep roads free of ice and an individual slips on the ice, the court, in determining whether the authority was negligent, cannot ignore the duty owed by the council to the whole community, the limited resources available to fulfil that duty and the consequent need for the council to determine priorities.[6]

3 See L. Neville Brown and J. Bell, *French Administrative Law* (4th edn, 1993).
4 *Introduction to the Study of the Law of the Constitution* (10th edn, 1959), chs. 4 and 12.
5 See Lord Denning MR in *Breen* v. *AEU* [1971] 2 QB 175 at p. 189: 'It may now truly be said that we have a developed system of administrative law.' See also *Mahon* v. *Air New Zealand* [1984] AC 808 at 816, *per* Lord Diplock.
6 See *Haydon* v. *Kent CC* [1978] QB 343.

Developments in relation to the remedies available in administrative law would probably cause Dicey to turn in his grave. Long overdue reform of the procedure for challenging administrative decisions[7] has caused the House of Lords to pronounce that public law rights are enforceable only through an application for judicial review. The distinction between public and private law rights has resulted in no little difficulty for the courts. In France, where the distinction has been entrenched for over a century, a special court, the *Tribunal de Conflits*, is required to make a final decision in case of dispute. The conceptual basis of any such distinction in English law has been vigorously attacked.[8] But its emergence, at the same time as administrative changes, has led to the creation of a separate court list for administrative cases, the Crown Office List, all of which must lead us to speculate whether an Administrative Court has been smuggled into our legal system by the back door.[9]

In attempting a survey of English administrative law the tendency is to concentrate on the role of the Judiciary in controlling statutory powers, introducing the concept of natural justice into administrative decision-making and on certain occasions genuinely fulfilling the role allocated to them by Dicey of involving the common law as a bulwark against tyranny. Nevertheless, the bulk of English administrative law is statutory in origin. This is not simply because Acts of Parliament create public authorities and confer their powers on them. Very often today a statute which grants powers of a nature likely to affect individual interests also builds in safeguards for the individual. It may be only the right to complain to a Minister. But most statutes with a substantial impact on individual interests provide either for a special tribunal to hear disputes arising between the authority and the citizen, or make provision for holding a public inquiry prior to the final decision. Tribunals and inquiries were once condemned as kangaroo justice far removed from the judicial atmosphere of the courts. Now their procedure is usually controlled by statutory instrument and provides for a fair hearing without the awesome formality of the common-law courts. More and more provision is made for an appeals system in the case of tribunals, and access to the High Court to determine disputed points of law is generally allowed from both tribunal decisions and decisions made after an inquiry

---

7 Supreme Court Act 1981, s. 31.
8 See Cane [1984] *Public Law* 16, and *Davy* v. *Spelthorne BC* [1983] 2 All ER 278 at 284 (Lord Wilberforce). See also Wade (1983) 99 *LQR* 166; for a defence of the distinction, see Woolf [1986] *Public Law* 220.
9 See Blom-Cooper [1982] *Public Law* 250.

has been held.[10] The statutory safeguards are far from perfect. Property rights are better protected than a man's legitimate right to or expectation of social security benefits. Immigrants get a raw deal, and once a murmur is raised about national security, safeguards against administrative abuse become minimal. It will be seen that the judges have similar priorities in their view of the protection of the citizen's interests.

The function of the judges is to invoke 'the justice of the common law to supply the omission of the legislature'.[11] The Judiciary first imposed elementary notions of justice on the proceedings of tribunals and inquiries using the remedies developed by their predecessors to curb over-mighty justices of the peace and inferior courts. They still intervene where no statutory rules exist or where those rules do not meet the judicial concept of natural justice. The courts, especially recently, have developed principles curbing the misuse of discretionary powers to a level equal to their French counterparts on the *Conseil d'État*. They do stand in a very real sense as the ultimate arbitrator of the balance between the demands of effective government and individual interests. In this capacity the judges wield political power, a feature of administrative law not to be overlooked by the constitutional law student. Whether they like it or not, a body of men with power to decide that the Secretary of State for Education may not intervene to prevent a local council reintroducing selective secondary education[12] and to ensure that, despite a new Government's opposition, Sir Freddie Laker's Skytrain takes off for New York,[13] and to declare valid although in breach of the rules of natural justice the Government's removal of trade union rights without prior consultation from civil servants at the Government Communications Headquarters at Cheltenham[14] are taking decisions of political significance. They cannot be surprised when some people question whether they have sufficient understanding of administrative problems to take such decisions,[15] and speculate whether in view of the predominantly upper-middle-class background of most judges it is possible for judges to be completely impartial in essentially political controversies.[16]

Finally, the extent of the discretionary powers of the judges in administrative law is as important constitutionally as the extent of discretionary

10 Note particularly the Tribunals and Inquiries Act 1992.
11 *Cooper* v. *Wandsworth Board of Works* (1863) 14 CB (NS) 180.
12 *Secretary of State for Education* v. *Tameside MBC* [1977] AC 1014.
13 *Laker Airways Ltd* v. *Department of Trade* [1977] QB 643.
14 *Council of Civil Service Unions* v. *Minister for the Civil Service* [1985] AC 374.
15 See, e.g., J. A. G. Griffith [1985] *Public Law* 564.
16 See generally J. A. G. Griffith, *The Politics of the Judiciary* (5th edn, 1997).

powers vested in public authorities. All remedies in administrative law are discretionary. The applicant may make out his case only to be told that he may have been prejudiced by lack of fairness but his own conduct was so deplorable he does not deserve any remedy.[17] The court may decide that this is an area of government into which they would rather not intervene save in the grossest case of abuse and so in its discretion refuse a remedy in the normal case.[18] The element of choice in judicial review is further developed in chapter 26 and is a vital feature of judicial review today.

DECISION-MAKING IN THE ADMINISTRATIVE PROCESS

The administrative process, and therefore administrative law, consists of the making of thousands of decisions each day. How far those decisions are open to challenge is a central issue in administrative law. Decisions are classified in various ways and the classification of a decision has an important effect on the degree to which it may be reviewed either as provided for in a statute or by the courts. The democratic nature of the constitution is tested by the extent to which an individual affected can challenge a decision and whether decision-making offers any real opportunity for the members of the public involved by the decision to participate in the process. Decisions in the administrative process can be classified in various ways. For example, is the decision legislative or non-legislative, judicial or non-judicial? Does the decision involve the exercise of a power or the performance of a duty? Which type of administrative authority makes the decision? Does it have to be made after a hearing, or is it subject to a subsequent hearing before it has final effect, or can it have effect without any hearing at all? Is it subject to appeal or review, and if so, what body is vested with the appellate or supervisory jurisdiction?

Classes of function[19]

Functions may be classified as legislative, administrative, judicial, quasi-judicial and ministerial. None of these terms is unambiguous or self-explanatory and there is often scope for appending two or more labels to

---

17 *Glynn* v. *University of Keele* [1971] WLR 487.
18 *R.* v. *Preston Supplementary Benefits Appeal Tribunal, ex p. Moore* [1975] 1 WLR 624.
19 For fuller analysis of the terminology used, see S. A. de Smith, *Judicial Review of Administrative Action* (5th edn, 1996), ch. 2.

a specific act or decision, to the confusion of all students. Briefly, the ingredients of a *typical* function belonging to the main classes can be stated.

1 A legislative function involves making rules of general application with prospective effect. Legislation is made by Acts of Parliament, statutory instruments, other regulations and by-laws.
2 An administrative (or executive) function may involve making policy or carrying out a policy or simply deciding what is the most appropriate thing to do in particular circumstances. Examples of administrative decisions are determining new standard terms of public contracts, placing public contracts, making decisions on public appointments, and allocating resources such as council housing.
3 A judicial function involves the determination of a question of law or fact by reference to pre-existing rules or standards.
4 A ministerial act is not normally something done by a Minister; it is the performance of a legal duty (for example, to refund overpaid income tax) into which no element of choice or discretion enters.

These terms have to be used because they are in common currency. The term 'legislative' does not give rise to a great deal of difficulty in practice, for most of us can recognize legislation when we see it; but we also know that legislative rules can have retrospective as well as prospective effect, that they may simply restate (by consolidation or codification) existing law, that the boundary line between a not very 'general' legislative rule and particular administrative decisions affecting many people can become so blurred as to be imperceptible, and that judges sometimes change the law under the guise of declaring or interpreting it.

Difficulties lurk in the term 'administrative', 'judicial' and 'quasi-judicial' when they are being contrasted with one another. 'Quasi-judicial' is, on the whole, a superfluous adjective which increases rather than diminishes confusion. Usually it means a discretionary (administrative-type) decision preceded by a judicial-type procedure (for example, confirming a compulsory purchase order after a local inquiry), but the term is also sometimes used to describe the final decision itself and sometimes to describe the preliminary procedure.

As we have seen, 'administrative' acts are what administrators *typically* do and 'judicial' acts are what judges typically do. This terminology does not preclude us from saying that officials (administrators) can perform analytically 'judicial' functions – for example, deciding (subject to appeal) that X is legally obliged to pay £100 in capital gains tax, or that publications imported by Y are obscene, or that Z is not legally entitled to jobseeker's allowance – or that judges, especially in administrative law, have to exercise wide discretionary powers. A law student's problem (sometimes so puzzling as to seem insoluble) lies in the fact that judges in the reported cases on administrative law use the terms inconsistently. A function that is judicial in one context is labelled 'administrative' in another context. Occasionally these discrepancies are nothing more than an inelegant use of language; occasionally they are attributable to the looseness of the concept of 'administrative' functions; more frequently they can be explained by looking for the legal *consequences* of calling a function 'judicial' or 'administrative' as the case may be.

Duty and discretion

The contrast between public duty and discretionary power is ostensibly clear-cut. A duty is an act that *must* be performed; thus, a tribunal has a duty to entertain an application or appeal in a matter within its jurisidiction; a local authority has a duty to grant a council tax rebate when prescribed conditions are satisfied. Performance of such a duty can normally be enforced in judicial proceedings.[20] Compliance with some of the statutory duties cast on local authorities is enforceable by Ministers exercising default powers.

A discretionary power implies freedom of choice; the competent authority *may* decide whether or not to act (for example, whether to order computers for local schools) and, if so, how to act (for example, with whom should the order be placed; how many computers should be bought?). In practice, duties and powers tend to be interwoven. Seldom does a public body have no discretion at all as to the circumstances in which it is to perform a duty. Police officers, who have a general duty to enforce the law, have a limited discretion to abstain from reporting particular offences. And discretionary powers are normally accompanied by express or implied duties. For instance, a licensing authority may have a discretion to attach such conditions as it thinks fit when granting a licence; but it will be under a legal duty to exercise a genuine discretion in each individual case, and not fetter its choice by adopting rigid rules; and the conditions imposed

---

20 See further pp. 518 and 559–62. But some public duties (for example, to provide 'a varied and comprehensive educational service') are so widely framed that no court will direct their enforcement at the suit of a member of the public; and others (for example, those which were imposed on certain public corporations administering the nationalized industries) are expressed to be unenforceable in any court. Duties unenforceable by a court obviously resemble statutory powers in this context.

must not be irrelevant to the purposes for which the power was conferred on it.

Decision-makers

Powers and duties to make decisions in public administration may be vested in the Crown, Ministers, Government Departments, civil servants, public corporations and their officers, local authorities, local government officers, tribunals and courts. The distribution of functions among them is not predetermined by any grand design; it is a product of historical accident, tenacious tradition, experiment, and largely uncoordinated decisions about the most appropriate ways of handling individual problems. Patterns are irregular, reflecting the untidy structure of administrative authority in England. A few points should be noted; some have already been mentioned in earlier chapters.

1 Government Departments with ministerial heads did not assume an important role in the provision and regulation of social services till the late nineteenth and early twentieth centuries. Even today, the main providers of public services (for example, education, environmental planning, housing, public health) are the elected local authorities. They have been joined by semi-autonomous public corporations (for example, for broadcasting) and statutory bodies such as hospital trusts. The primary initiative in the direction of national policy, particularly in legislative change and the allocation of financial resources, rests with the central government, but the immediate impact of administrative decisions on the individual citizen generally occurs at a lower level.

2 Decisions by Government Departments directly affecting individual rights are usually made by officials in the Minister's name. The courts recognize the reality of the situation by treating the Minister and his officials within the Department as one entity: thus the Minister may receive advice without having to disclose it to affected individuals in the same way as he would not have to disclose his own cerebral deliberations.[21] Powers are sometimes conferred by statute on specified classes of officials (for example, immigration officers, customs and excise officers, local authority auditors and inspectors conducting inquiries) to be exercised in their own official capacities.

3 Local authority decisions are usually taken by councils or committees of

21 *Bushell* v. *Secretary of State for the Environment* [1981] AC 75.

councils. Officials do not have a general power to act on the council's behalf, but very wide powers can be delegated to them. Some functions are vested by statute directly in specified officials (for example, directors of public health).

4 Decision-making by tribunals in the sphere of public administration has a long history. For centuries the local government authorities in the counties were the justices of the peace, who granted licences, regulated taverns, enforced the poor law and the upkeep of highways and bridges, and so on, under judicial forms. Most of their administrative functions passed to elected local authorities in the nineteenth century, but some survive – for example, liquor licensing – and other administrative jurisdiction has been vested in magistrates' courts, notably the hearing of appeals from certain decisions by local authorities.

5 The Justices of the Peace and borough corporations were subject, during the Tudor and early Stuart periods, to control by the King's Council and the Star Chamber. This was replaced after 1650 by the supervisory jurisdiction of the Court of King's Bench. The basic features of this supervisory jurisdiction survived and have been extended to other types of decision-making bodies.

6 Particularly since the Second World War, power to determine a wide range of claims and controversies in administrative law has been vested in specialized 'administrative' tribunals.[22] The jurisdiction of these tribunals may be original or appellate. The High Court has powers to review their determinations.

7 The functions of the superior courts in administrative law are varied:[23] they include appellate and supervisory review of determinations by inferior tribunals, and affording legal redress for wrongful acts committed by other administrative bodies.

Decisions with or without a hearing

Obviously most decisions in the fields of government and administration have to be taken without a formal inquiry or hearing. If a Minister has to make a major policy decision, he will normally consult the main interest groups likely to be affected – and in some situations he will be under a statutory duty to do so – but government could not be carried on if every

22 See ch. 28.
23 See chs. 26, 27, 29.

important decision had to await the outcome of a full-dress inquiry. Some policy decisions affecting a large number of private individuals in a locality – for example, a decision as to the route of a motorway, or whether to develop an area as a new town – will be preceded by a formal public inquiry. But a decision by a Minister to refuse an application for an export licence, an industrial grant or loan, can be made summarily, without any antecedent hearing, though informal representation before and after the decision may be entertained. And clearly decisions made on departmental initiative (for example, to vary rates of taxation) will not usually entail formal hearings either before or after the event.

Again, a great number of decisions made by other public bodies will be made without any formal hearing or inquiry – for example, decisions on the allocation of a council house or a place in an old people's home: or to place a contract with X rather than with Y or Z, or to promote P rather than Q or R. It does not follow that such decisions will be capricious; they may be regulated or influenced by administrative precedent or general guiding principles; they may be preceded by thorough investigations and personal interviews even though these are not required by law; in some instances they will be subject to appeal.[24]

Nevertheless, the formal pre-decision hearing or inquiry is an important feature of the administrative process in England.[25] Thus, one who applies for a licence to operate a commercial air service or a betting shop, or who claims compensation for injuries sustained as a result of violent crime, will be entitled or may be required to appear before a board or tribunal which will make the decision. If there are objectors to his application, they too will, in some instances, be entitled to a hearing. Of more general importance is the statutory procedure followed where public authorities wish to take away or restrict the exercise of private rights in land. A person whose property is the subject of a compulsory purchase order is entitled to be heard at a formal local inquiry before the order can be confirmed. Again, a local inquiry must be held if objections are lodged against proposals to impose certain types of street restrictions, and conservation and local interest groups often make a substantial contribution to inquiries.

24 For example, under the Sex Discrimination Act 1975. See above pp. 403–6.
25 See generally R. E. Wraith and G. B. Lamb, *Public Inquiries as an Instrument of Government* (1971).

Appeals

More common than a statutory right to a prior hearing is a right to be heard on appeal against an administrative decision. This must not be confused with the supervisory role of the courts exercised by a review of a challenged decision.[26] Three preliminary points need to be made.

1 A right of appeal is the creature of statute and it can only be conferred by express language. There is no such thing as an implied right of appeal to a court or any other body.
2 The absence of a right of appeal does not necessarily mean that a decision cannot be challenged at all in a court of law. The jurisdiction of the High Court in matters of administrative law is supervisory as well as appellate. This question will be examined in chapters 26 and 27.
3 There is no clear pattern of rights of appeal. This point emerges only too plainly from the following outline sketch.

Ministers and civil servants. In general, no appeal will be provided against discretionary decisions involving questions of national policy or the allocation of scarce resources. Reference was made earlier to discretionary decisions made without a prior hearing; no right of appeal is provided against any of the classes of decisions there illustrated. But there is no universal rule in this matter. The Immigration Appeals Act 1969 gave rights of appeal to adjudicators from discretionary decisions of immigration officers, and to an Immigration Appeal Tribunal from discretionary orders by the Secretary of State for the deportation of aliens. However, under the Immigration Act 1971 the more politically sensitive types of decision were removed from the scope of the appellate system.

Where a decision by a Minister or a civil servant entails the determination of a question of law, appeal often lies to an independent tribunal or the superior courts; rights of appeal to the courts are usually confined to the legal issues. From decisions on liability to income tax, an appeal lies to the Commissioners of Income Tax (a special tribunal), and thence to the Chancery Division of the High Court. If a local planning authority considers that planning restrictions have been contravened, it may issue an enforcement notice; the person aggrieved may appeal to the Secretary of State against the notice, and if dissatisfied with the Secretary of State's decision

---

26 The House of Lords emphasized and explained the distinction in *Chief Constable of the North Wales Police* v. *Evans* [1982] 1 WLR 1155.

he may appeal on a point of law to the Divisional Court of the Queen's Bench Division. A person dissatisfied with a decision of an officer of the Department of Social Security holding that he is not entitled to a social security benefit may appeal to a social security appeal tribunal and thence to a Social Security Commissioner.

Local authorities. Here again, allocative decisions – decisions on the discretionary allocation of limited resources – are not, as a rule, appealable, but there are a number of exceptions. The statutory designation of appellate bodies can only be described as bizarre. For example, a full appeal lies to magistrates' courts against the merits of various kinds of licensing decisions (for example, the licensing of theatres, street traders, massage establishments); to the Crown Court against decisions on cinema licensing; and to a county court against a decision to make an order for the demolition of an individual insanitary house. Appeals against decisions to refuse planning permission (i.e. permission to 'develop' land by making a material change of use), or to grant such permission subject to conditions to which the applicant objects, lie to the Secretary of State for the Environment or, in cases of minor development raising no big policy issue, to an inspector exercising delegated powers.

Special tribunals

Some administrative tribunals exercise original jurisdiction; some are appellate bodies. There is usually (but not always) an appeal on the merits of the decisions from a tribunal exercising original jurisdiction to a superior tribunal; in a few cases the appellate authority is a Minister. Appeals lie on points of law to the superior courts from the decisions of a majority of tribunals of last instance. In most cases the appellate tribunal is the Divisional Court of the Queen's Bench Division, but even in this context there is no uniform pattern; appeals lie in income tax cases to a Chancery judge; from service pensions appeal tribunals to a Queen's Bench judge; from the Transport Tribunal, the Lands Tribunal and the Foreign Compensation Commission to the Court of Appeal; and from some professional disciplinary bodies to the Judicial Committee of the Privy Council.

IN GENERAL

We appear to be losing ourselves in a labyrinth through which even the most expert guide could not be relied on to conduct us. Are there, then, no general principles of English administrative law? Is there but a wilderness of individual instances? An answer can be offered at two levels. In the first place, to achieve a full mastery of the subject one requires an encyclopaedic range of knowledge which is hardly worth while acquiring. So much depends on the wording of particular legislation, which is influenced by a motley array of policy considerations. Development of the law has been pragmatic, empirical, even adventitious; only occasionally do broad general principles intrude into the devising of a legislative scheme, and these intrusions tend to operate in the area of the *procedure* followed in decision-making rather than in the substantive structure and interrelationship of authority. Secondly, if one concentrates on the part played by the *courts* in affording legal redress for grievances, the law is still complex and rather confusing, but it is possible to elicit general principles according to which the courts will afford remedies and redress to a person aggrieved by administrative action. These principles sometimes have to be stated at a high level of generality, but they are at least intelligible.

CHAPTER 26

Judicial Review: Principles

This chapter is about the general principles applied by the superior courts in reviewing the validity or legality of the acts, decisions and omissions of administrative authorities, including statutory tribunals. In the chapter on delegated legislation we have already been introduced to this subject.[1] In chapter 27 some special features of judicial remedies in administrative law will be considered. Actions for damages for civil wrongs committed by public authorities, particularly the Crown, will be considered in chapter 29.

Four preliminary words of warning are needed. First, this is an extremely complex subject with intricate ramifications.[2] Every aspect cannot be considered here, even in outline. And some matters will have to be oversimplified if they are to be explained at all. They may still seem rather mysterious. Secondly, a grasp of general principles is obviously important. But to apply these principles to concrete situations demands flexibility and subtlety. In approaching the solution to a particular case, the crucial questions will often be: What are the context and purpose of the legislation in question? What significance is to be attributed to the language in which a grant of statutory power is worded? To a large extent judicial review of administrative action is a specialized branch of statutory interpretation. Thirdly, administrative law is not very coherent. For example, the laws of town and country planning, social security and immigration have some points of contact but far more points of dissimilarity. Precedents laid down in one area of the law may be treated by a court as irrelevant if cited as authorities in another area. One needs to be an expert forecaster to be able to predict how a court will react to such citations in any given case.

---

1 Ch. 17.
2 See S. de Smith, *Judicial Review of Administrative Action* (5th edn, 1996); H. W. R. Wade and C. F. Forsyth, *Administrative Law* (7th edn, 1994); P. P. Craig, *Administrative Law* (3rd edn, 1994); R. Gordon, *Judicial Review: Law and Procedure* (2nd edn, 1996).

Fourthly, from time to time the courts shift their position, and they are apt not to be entirely consistent in their attitudes.

Hence, if one is asked what legal principles a public authority is obliged to observe when exercising a specific discretionary power, one's answer may often have to be hedged about by words like 'probably' and 'perhaps'. The state of the law is elusive and fluid.

One further point must always be borne in mind – a point more obvious to the uninstructed layman than to a law student grappling with an intractable body of legal material. In deciding individual cases the courts will try to do justice by balancing the needs of administration and the public interest against the claims of the private citizen to fair treatment. Some judges are prepared to 'bend' the law by manipulating precedent and principle in order to achieve and vindicate what appears to them a just solution to the case in hand. Judges exercise more freedom of manoeuvre here than in most of the other branches of English law.

GOING TO COURT

Judicial review of administrative action may be invoked for a wide range of purposes by a person claiming to be aggrieved.

1 To obtain damages or another private law remedy (for example, an injunction) for a civil wrong, such as a breach of contract or a tort.
2 To have an order, act or decision of a public body quashed or declared invalid on the ground that it is *ultra vires* or outside jurisdiction. This purpose may be achieved by means of an appeal (if one is provided by statute), or a statutory application to quash (for example, a decision to confirm a compulsory purchase order), or an application to the High Court for judicial review and an order of certiorari to quash a decision, or a declaration that the act, order or decision is invalid. Already one sees that substantive administrative law is interwoven with the law of remedies.
3 To procure, on appeal, the reversal or variation of an order or determination for error of law. This overlaps with (2); the difference between *invalidity* and *error* will be explained shortly.
4 To restrain the performance or continuance of unlawful action. This may be achieved by an application for an order of prohibition or for an injunction or a declaration, or a statutory application to restrain (for example) the making of an invalid compulsory purchase order.

5 To obtain release from unlawful detention. The appropriate remedy will be either appeal or an application for habeas corpus.
6 To secure an authoritative statement of the law governing a specific legal dispute by means of a binding declaration awarded by the courts. Consequential relief (for example, damages) does not have to be claimable as well.
7 To secure the performance of a public duty (for example, to make reimbursement; to exercise a discretion according to law; to hear an application or appeal within a tribunal's jurisdiction). Normally the judicial remedy for a wrongful omission will be an order of mandamus; a declaration, or even a mandatory injunction, are possible remedies. Sometimes non-performance of a public duty will give rise to an action for damages.
8 To defend oneself in proceedings which rely on the validity of an administrative act or order. If, for example, one is prosecuted for breach of a by-law, one can set up the defence that the by-law is *ultra vires*.

Public authorities may appear in the courts for other reasons. For instance, many enforcement powers vested in public authorities (for example, to abate nuisances) are exercisable only with leave of a court or magistrate; and in most of these situations the prospective victim can be heard on his own behalf. Again, sometimes criminal proceedings can be brought *against* public authorities (for example, for breaches of public health legislation).

ULTRA VIRES AND EXCESS OF JURISDICTION

The starting point for judicial review of administrative action is that public authorities will be restrained from exceeding their powers (acting *ultra vires*) and inferior tribunals will be prevented from exceeding the limits of their jurisdiction. This important constitutional function of containing both the Executive and inferior tribunals within the limits of their authority has long been exercised by the courts. In the seventeenth century it was established that the Crown could not set itself above the law by a bare assertion of prerogative.[3] Today the *ultra vires* doctrine prevents public authorities from doing anything which the law forbids, or taking any action for which they have no statutory authority.

A dramatic example of the *ultra vires* rule in practice can be seen in *Laker*

3 See pp. 73–6, 134–7.

Airways Ltd v. *Department of Trade*.[4] Freddie Laker wanted to operate his Skytrain service across the Atlantic. Two obstacles stood in his way. He had to obtain a licence for the service from the Civil Aviation Authority, and he had to be accepted as a 'designated air-carrier' by the British and United States Governments in order to fly Skytrain into the USA. The Civil Aviation Act 1971 empowered the Civil Aviation Authority to license air services and laid down criteria for them to follow in fulfilling this function. These included the principle that British Airways should not have a monopoly on any air route. The Act also empowered the Secretary of State for Trade to give guidance to the Authority. Any guidance had to be approved by both Houses of Parliament. Skytrain was granted a licence in 1972 to operate from Stansted to New York and the then British Government started the process to have Laker Airways accepted as a designated air-carrier by the United Staff Government. In 1975 a new British Government adopted a complete reversal of policy towards Skytrain. The Secretary of State for Trade subsequently issued guidance to the Civil Aviation Authority directing them in effect that British Airways were to retain a monopoly on scheduled transatlantic routes. Both Houses of Parliament gave their approval. Skytrain's licence was withdrawn by the Authority and the process to have Laker Airways accepted as a designated air-carrier by the USA was stopped. The Court of Appeal held that the Secretary of State had acted *ultra vires*. He had authority merely to guide the Authority, not to direct it. The guidance was itself unlawful in that it was directly contrary to the objectives set out in the Civil Aviation Act. The withdrawal of the designation might be the exercise of a prerogative power arising under a treaty with the USA, but prerogative powers could not be used in order to deprive Laker Airways of rights which they were granted by statute. Prerogative powers were discretionary powers and subject to judicial control. The Secretary of State had exercised the power unlawfully in an attempt to do indirectly what he was unable to do directly, that is, prevent Laker Airways competing on the transatlantic route. So Laker Airways were successful in their action.

The general principle underlying the *ultra vires* doctrine is easy to illustrate. Acts reasonably incidental to powers expressly granted may be construed as falling within the grant of power. So when a local authority in the performance of its statutory duties regularly needed a certain amount of printing work done it did not exceed its powers by establishing its own

4 [1977] QB 643.

printing machinery and personnel for internal work.[5] But a local authority empowered to provide wash-houses where local people could bring their own washing and do it themselves acted *ultra vires* when it proceeded to open a laundry service trading for profit.[6] As far as local authorities are concerned their incidental powers have been enlarged by statute.[7]

The problem of whether an act is reasonably incidental to the power granted is relatively easily solved by examination of the enabling statute. A more intractable problem is what effect should be given to an order which is partly *ultra vires* and partly lawful. An authority may lawfully issue a licence, or order, but attach to that licence conditions which it is not entitled to impose. Can the court sever the invalid conditions, leaving operative the grant of the licence?[8] If it is apparent that the invalid condition is peripheral to the grant of the licence, or that even in the absence of the *ultra vires* condition the licence would still have been granted by the licensing body, then this is the course which may be taken.[9] When the condition is part and parcel of the reasons for granting the licence then the court faces a dilemma. If it severs the invalid condition from the licence the result will be that the applicant obtains an unconditional licence which the authority entrusted with the power to license would never have given. If it strikes down the entire decision on the grounds of the unlawful nature of the attached conditions then the applicant has to start all over again before the licensing body. Nevertheless this last course has more than once commended itself to the Court of Appeal[10] and has the attraction that it does not detract from the powers conferred on the licensing body; the price is no more than inconvenience and delay to the applicant.

Action taken by a public authority not only runs the risk of being *ultra vires* in substance but may in certain cases be *ultra vires* in form. Certain powers are exercisable only subject to procedural safeguards enshrined in the enabling statute. The relevant Act may require that some person or

---

5 *Att.-Gen.* v. *Smethwick Corporation* [1932] 1 Ch. 562.

6 *Att.-Gen.* v. *Fulham Corporation* [1921] 1 Ch. 440. See also *R.* v. *Richmond upon Thames Council, ex p. McCarthy and Stone Ltd* [1992] AC 48; *Hazell* v. *Hammersmith and Fulham Council* [1992] 2 AC 1.

7 See especially the Local Government Act 1972.

8 See *R.* v. *Secretary of State for Transport, ex p. GLC* [1986] QB 556.

9 See *Kingsway Investments (Kent) Ltd* v. *Kent CC* [1971] AC 72.

10 *Hall & Co.* v. *Shoreham-by-Sea UDC* [1964] 1 WLR 240; *R.* v. *Hillingdon LBC, ex p. Royco Homes Ltd* [1974] QB 720. See also *DPP* v. *Hutchinson* [1990] 2 All ER 836; by-laws were wider than the enabling Act authorized, severance was impossible and convictions under them were quashed.

organization be consulted before action is taken or an order made. Notice of intention to act may have to be given in a particular form or by a specified date. What happens if the procedure laid down is not complied with by the authority? First the courts will classify the procedural or formal requirement *as mandatory* or *directory*. If a requirement is merely directory then substantial compliance with the procedure laid down will suffice to validate the action; and in some cases even total non-compliance will not affect the validity of what has been done. If a mandatory requirement is not observed then the act or decision will be vitiated by the non-compliance with the statute. This does not mean that the act or decision has no legal effect and can be ignored or treated as void. The House of Lords has stressed that the use of such terms as 'void' and 'voidable' has little practical meaning in administrative law where the supervisory jurisdiction of the High Court operates to ensure the proper exercise of powers by public authorities. Non-compliance with a mandatory procedural requirement results in the act or decision being susceptible to being quashed by the High Court which will then make whatever order to the public authority it sees as appropriate to remedy the unlawful action taken.[11]

Determining whether a requirement is mandatory or directory is not simple. Where the impact of the action taken on private rights is material then an ostensibly small deviation from statutory requirements may render the action invalid. And where the procedural requirement can be seen to be intended to assist the citizen in enforcing his rights, then it is likely to be regarded as mandatory. Examples of procedural requirements which have been held to be mandatory include failure to give notice of a right to appeal within a specified period,[12] failure to give the address to which an appeal must be lodged,[13] failure to notify persons affected by a proposed administrative order *in due time*,[14] and where a person aggrieved is substantially prejudiced by non-compliance with a requirement to give adequate, proper, clear and intelligible reasons for a decision where reasoned decisions are required by statute.[15] The aim of the courts is to try to deduce (a) what Parliament intended in instituting a particular procedural requirement, and (b) what effect on the validity of the process Parliament would have desired

---

11 *London & Clydeside Estates Ltd*. v. *Aberdeen DC* [1980] I WLR 182.
12 ibid.
13 *Agricultural etc. Training Board* v. *Kent* [1970] 2 QB 18.
14 *Lee* v. *Department of Education and Science* (1967) 66 LGR 211.
15 *Givaudan & Co*. v. *Minister of Housing and Local Government* [1967] I WLR. 250; *French Kier Developments Ltd* v. *Secretary of State for the Environment* [1977] I All ER 296.

to result from non-compliance.[16] Consequently the practical results of holding compliance to be mandatory will be weighed in the balance. In an extreme example, when the Governor-General of New Zealand issued his warrant for the holding of a General Election at a later date than the law prescribed it was contended that the ensuing General Election was therefore invalid. Not surprisingly the courts held that the rules about time were only directory. For if they had held otherwise there would have been a legal vacuum which nobody within New Zealand could have filled, for no Parliament could lawfully have been summoned and the administration of the country might have ground to a halt.[17] And no sane Parliament would have intended or desired this result.

When no question of any statutory provision excluding judicial review arises the narrow and literal view of *ultra vires* adopted by some of their Lordships in *Smith* v. *East Elloe RDC*[18] would now appear obsolete. In that case a property-owner challenged a compulsory purchase order confirmed by a Minister on the grounds that it had been procured by fraud. The enabling statute permitted the confirmation of the order to be challenged in the High Court within six weeks of it being made on the grounds that the authorization of the order 'was not empowered to be granted under the Act'. The House of Lords held that any form of judicial review was precluded once the prescribed six weeks had elapsed. Certain Law Lords also expressed the view that even within the six weeks allowed the order could be challenged only if it was *ultra vires* in the sense that it was an order outside the competence of the Minister to confirm, and that irregularities in the decision-making process culminating in the confirmation of the order did not render it *ultra vires*. The views of Lord Radcliffe and Lord Reid that powers abused or misused are powers exercised *ultra vires* now prevail. But the narrow view of *ultra vires* cannot be relegated to history because it may be that in some later case a return to the narrow construction of *ultra vires* will be invoked as a device to determine a case in favour of the public authority when a court feels that the merits of the dispute lie on the Government side. And it is clear that the distinction between acts entirely outside the authority of the relevant body and acts founded on a misuse of power within that authority is still crucial in some instances when a statutory provision excluding judicial review is in question.

16 *London & Clydeside Estates Ltd* v. *Aberdeen DC* [1979] 3 All ER 876, *per* Lord Hailsham at p. 881.
17 *Simpson* v. *Att.-Gen.* [1955] NZLR 271.
18 [1956] AC 736.

This problem is dealt with in the penultimate section of this chapter.[19]

Discussion so far has been generally in terms of *vires* or powers. When considering judicial control of tribunals and similar bodies whose function is to decide the outcome of a dispute, rather than exercise a specific power, it is more appropriate to talk in terms of jurisdiction. All inferior tribunals (magistrates' courts, county courts, special tribunals, professional disciplinary bodies, committees of clubs and trade unions, Ministers determining legal disputes) have a limited jurisdiction. Since the end of the seventeenth century certiorari could be issued to quash a decision of an inferior tribunal outside its jurisdiction and the writ of prohibition lay to prevent an anticipated departure by the tribunal from its proper jurisdiction. Jurisdiction might be exceeded if the tribunal tried a case outside its competence, for example because it had no authority to deal with the subject-matter of the dispute, or no authority over the particular persons before it, or tried a case beyond its territorial jurisdiction. Failure to comply with essential procedural steps in instituting the hearing, or incorrect composition, or grave defects in the manner of the hearing, or a final order which the tribunal was not empowered to make – all such errors resulted in the decision of the tribunal being quashed as being in excess of its jurisdiction. But mistakes made within the jurisdiction whether of fact or law did not lay the tribunal open to certiorari for excess of jurisdiction. Jurisdiction to determine a dispute necessarily includes the authority to determine the merits of the dispute. If every error in assessing the arguments presented to the tribunal were to be subject to review by the High Court the intention of Parliament to create the tribunal as the decision-making body in a particular field would be frustrated. For example, the membership of rent assessment committees is balanced so as to combine lay and expert opinion. This is the kind of body to which Parliament has chosen to entrust rent disputes. Unlimited access to the High Court for the disappointed party would result in effective jurisdiction being transferred to that institution.

Yet equally judicial review which operated only a narrow view of the jurisdiction of the tribunal, considering only whether the tribunal was properly constituted, complied with the proper procedure and began its inquiry into the correct matter, would be inadequate. The supervisory jurisdiction of the High Court over tribunals has been extended in the following ways.

1 From most inferior tribunals an appeal on points of law lies to the High Court.[20]

19 At pp. 550–54.
20 See especially the Tribunals and Inquiries Act 1992, s. 11.

2 Certiorari will issue not only for excess of jurisdiction but also in respect
   of an 'error of law on the face of the record'.[21] The 'record' consists of
   the written statement of the tribunal's decision, read in conjunction with
   relevant statutory provisions. If the decision sets out reasons for the
   decision, or findings and inferences of fact, these form part of the 'record'
   and so do any documents referred to in the statement of the decision.[22]
   Since the Tribunals and Inquiries Act of 1958 the giving of reasons has
   been required from many tribunals if requested by the parties[23] and the
   reasons given, whether orally or in writing, form part of the record and
   an important means of ensuring that tribunals do not err on questions
   of law.[24]

3 Provided no statutory provision excluding judicial review is operative
   the extension of the *ultra vires* doctrine to include any misuse of the
   power has been applied to jurisdiction to determine disputes or appeals.
   In the case of Ministers deciding planning appeals and other disputed
   issues in relation to the control of land use, the statutory rights of challenge
   on the grounds that the Minister's order is outside the powers conferred
   by the enabling Act, or that some procedural requirement has not been
   observed, has been interpreted by the courts to mean that any decision
   erroneous in law is a decision taken in excess of his jurisdiction.[25] The
   Minister's jurisdiction is to determine the dispute on the correct legal
   basis only.

4 Allied to this last extension of the powers of the High Court to superintend
   the jurisdiction of inferior tribunals is the view of jurisdictional error taken
   by the House of Lords in *Anisminic* v. *Foreign Compensation Commission*.[26] It
   was held that even when a tribunal had engaged within the limits of its
   jurisdiction on a proper inquiry into the dispute before it, its decision
   could be quashed and regarded as a nullity if in the course of its deliberations the tribunal deviated from the rules of natural justice, or asked itself

21 R. v. *Northumberland Compensation Appeal Tribunal, ex p. Shaw* [1951] 1 KB 711;
affirmed [1952] 1 KB 338, C A. See Emery and Smythe (1984) 100 *LQR* 612.
22 *See R. v. Southampton JJ, ex p. Green* [1976] QB 11, CA, as to when the 'record'
may be supplemented by affidavits disclosing errors of law on the part of the tribunal.
23 See now the Tribunals and Inquiries Act 1992, s. 10.
24 And see R. v. *Knightsbridge Crown Court, ex p. International Sporting Club (London) Ltd*
[1982] QB 304.
25 *Ashbridge Investments Ltd.* v. *Minister of Housing and Local Government* [1965] 1 WLR
1320.
26 [1969] 2 AC 147. See also R. v. *Monopolies and Mergers Commission, ex p. South
Yorkshire Transport Ltd* [1993] 1 All ER 289: if a decision is so aberrant that it cannot be
classed as rational the decision-maker will have acted outside his jurisdiction.

the wrong questions, or took into account irrelevant matters. Parliament conferred jurisdiction on the tribunal to consider the dispute in a fair and proper manner and act on relevant and material considerations. Departure from these conditions would take the tribunal outside its jurisdiction for it would cease to be making the inquiry directed and intended by Parliament.

The distinction between jurisdictional and non-jurisdictional error has lost some of its importance in modern times. Its relevance lies mainly in relation to statutory exclusion of judicial review which is discussed later and as a possible means of retreat from extending judicial control of administrative action and adjudication when a particular area of the administrative process is one where judges fear to tread.

LAW AND FACT

Although the distinction between jurisdictional and non-jurisdictional matters is so hard to draw or define, perhaps we can hope to explain the important distinction between matters of law and matters of fact more easily. Unfortunately this is not so: the latter distinction is fiendishly difficult to define or even to illustrate at all clearly.

The superior courts will afford redress for errors of fact in two main situations: first, in those rare circumstances where rights of appeal are not restricted to questions of law; and secondly, where a factual error causes a tribunal to step outside its jurisdiction. The courts will be somewhat reluctant to make an independent determination of a question of pure fact if the issue turns upon conflicting evidence and they have not heard the oral testimony themselves.[27]

Whether X hit Y on the head is a question of fact. The state of X's mind at the time is also a question of fact (or of opinion). These questions will be left to the jury to answer. Whether X's conduct is *capable* of being construed as maliciously causing grievous bodily harm to Y is a question of law on which the judge directs the jury; the words 'maliciously' and 'grievous bodily harm' have acquired technical legal meanings. We can describe the whole issue as one of mixed law and fact.

Decisions by special tribunals and public authorities are made without juries; so one convenient line of demarcation is absent. Still, administrative

---

27 See generally Jones [1990] *Public Law* 507.

law controversies may sometimes be compartmentalized as questions partly of law and partly of fact for the purposes of judicial review. Other approaches to analysis may be adopted. An entire question may be characterized as one of law, or as one of fact (or fact and degree, which means 'fact'). The technical meaning of a term used in a public contract may be a pure question of law, because only a trained lawyer could be expected to understand it in the light of principle and decided authority. If a tribunal is obliged to observe the rules of evidence or specified statutory procedures, and there is no dispute as to what actually took place, a question whether the rules were duly observed is again purely one of law. But suppose that the question is whether a building is a dwelling-house, or 'of special architectural or historic interest', or is 'unfit for human habitation', or whether an industrial injury arose 'out of or in the course of employment', or whether consent to a particular act was 'unreasonably withheld', or whether there was a 'material change in the use' of land for which planning permission was required. The tribunal or other deciding body finds the basic or primary facts (for example, who did which and with what and to whom?); it may draw inferences from the facts; it has to go on to decide whether the facts as found *fall within the ambit of the statutory description*. A court, on review or appeal, can choose whether to characterize the conclusion as one of fact or as one of law; either form of characterization is possible, for here we are in a 'grey zone'. Generally speaking, the following are categorized as questions of fact: questions decided by specialized expert tribunals in which the courts repose confidence; questions on which reasonable persons might arrive at divergent conclusions; questions which the courts consider to have been correctly decided; questions on which the courts would find it very difficult to form an independent judgment without hearing all the evidence. But where the crux of the issue is a question of the interpretation of the language adopted in a statute or statutory instrument the courts reserve the final say in the matter to themselves. So the Court of Appeal held that it was entitled to overrule the Price Commission on the meaning of the term 'costs' in the Price Code.[28]

Findings of fact may still be held to embody reviewable errors of *law* if they are made without any supporting evidence at all, or if the conclusions drawn from them are perverse (in that the facts as found point unmistakably the other way) or are based on the application of a wrong legal test or if the reasons given for the findings or conclusions are unintelligible or inadequate in law; in these cases the tribunal will be held to have misdirected

28 *HTV* v. *Price Commission* [1976] ICR 170.

itself in law. Nevertheless, the courts will be slow to interfere with erroneous findings, inferences or conclusions of fact. For instance, in one case the question was whether land had been developed without planning permission; the central issue was whether the change of use to which it had been put was 'material'. The only change was the installation of an automatic egg-vending machine in the forecourt of a petrol-filling station. The court held[29] that whether a change of use was 'material' was a question of 'fact and degree',[30] not a question of law; the local planning authority's decision that there had been a material change of use was surprising, but it was not so perverse as to justify the court's interference. If the question had been categorized as one of law, the court could have substituted its own opinion. Now, if the court had adopted a slightly different approach – if it had applied the following test: there is an error of law if the inference or conclusion drawn from the facts found could not *reasonably* have been arrived at[31] – it might possibly have set the decision aside. Sometimes the courts do apply this broader test to conclusions of fact.

NATURAL JUSTICE

The rules of natural justice are minimum standards of fair decision-making, imposed by the common law on persons or bodies who are under a duty to 'act judicially'. They were applied originally to courts of justice and now extend to any person or body deciding issues affecting the right or interests of individuals where a reasonable citizen would have a legitimate expectation that the decision-making process would be subject to some rules of fair procedure. The content of natural justice is therefore flexible and variable. All that is fundamentally demanded of the decision-maker is that his decision in its own context be made with due regard for the affected parties' interests and accordingly be reached without bias and after giving the party or parties a chance to put his or their case. Nevertheless some judges now prefer to speak of a duty to act fairly rather than a duty to observe the rules of natural justice. Often the terms are interchangeable. But it is perhaps now the case

---

29 *Bendles Motors Ltd.* v. *Bristol Corporation* [1963] 1 WLR 247 (enforcement notice) an appeal on a question of law.
30 See the valuable articles by Wilson in (1963) 26 *Mod. L. Rev.* 609; (1969) 32 *Mod. L. Rev.* 361.
31 See *Ashbridge Investments Ltd.* v. *Minister of Housing and Local Government* [1965] 1 WLR 1320 at 1326 *per* Lord Denning, MR; adopted in *British Dredging (Services) Ltd.* v. *Secretary of State for Wales* [1975] 1 WLR 687.

that while a duty to act fairly is incumbent on every decision-maker within the administrative process whose decision will affect individual interests, the rules of natural justice apply only when some sort of definite code of procedure must be adopted, however flexible that code may be and however much the decision-maker is said to be master of his own procedure. The rules of natural justice are generally formulated as the rule against bias (*nemo judex in causa sua*) and the right to a fair hearing (*audi alteram partem*). They will be examined first and then a brief explanation of the duty to act fairly, inasmuch as it has a separate existence from natural justice, will be considered.

Rule against bias (nemo judex in causa sua)[32]

The rule has two main aspects. First, an adjudicator must not have any direct financial or proprietary interest in the outcome of the proceedings. Secondly, he must not be reasonably suspected, or show a real likelihood, of bias.

In its first aspect, the rule is very strict. No matter how small the adjudicator's pecuniary interest may be, no matter how unlikely it is to affect his judgment, he is disqualified from acting and the decision in which he has participated will be set aside,[33] unless (i) the parties are made fully aware of his interest in the proceedings and clearly waive their right to object to his participation, or (ii) he is empowered to sit (or the validity of the proceedings is preserved if he does sit) by a special statutory dispensation, or (iii) in very exceptional circumstances, all the available adjudicators are affected by a disqualifying interest, in which case they may have to sit as a matter of *necessity*. Perhaps we should classify under the same heading the rule that nobody should act as both judge and prosecutor, plantiff or advocate in a controversy. But here we begin to move towards the second aspect of the rule.

If an adjudicator is likely to be biased he is also disqualified from acting. Likelihood of bias may arise from a number of causes: membership of an organization or authority that is a party to the proceedings; partisanship expressed in extrajudicial pronouncements; the fact of appearing as a witness for a party to the proceedings; personal animosity or friendship towards a

---

32 de Smith, op. cit., ch. 5.
33 In *Dimes* v. *Grand Junction Canal Proprietors* (1852) 3 HLC 759 a decree made by the Lord Chancellor was set aside because he was a shareholder in the company which was a party to the proceedings. But a judge's shares in a bank are no bar to the judge trying an alleged robber of that bank: *R.* v. *Mulvihill* [1990] 1 WLR 438.

party; family relationship with a party; professional or commercial relationships with a party; and so on. The categories of situations potentially giving rise to a likelihood of bias are not closed.

The test of likelihood of bias must be applied realistically. If a controversy has aroused strong local passions, one cannot reasonably demand that every member of a local bench of magistrates deciding the issue must have maintained a total and lofty detachment from the controversy from the time when it first arose. When a Minister (like the Minister in the *Stevenage* case) is placed by a statute in a position where he must inevitably incline toward confirming his own provisional decision notwithstanding the force of objections subsequently expressed, he cannot be subjected to the rigorous standards of impartiality rightly imposed on a superior judge or indeed on a member of an independent statutory tribunal.[34]

How should the test of disqualification for likelihood of bias be formulated? The strict test of disqualification for personal interest is based on the principle that public confidence in the administration of justice must not be impaired by even the smallest suspicion of judicial impropriety; the rule looks to the *appearance* of the matter to an outsider. Occasionally the courts have adopted a similarly exacting approach to the 'likelihood of bias' test. A magistrates' clerk retired with the bench while they were considering their verdict in a case of dangerous driving; the defendant was convicted; he applied, successfully, for certiorari to quash the conviction, on the ground that the clerk belonged to a firm of solicitors acting in civil proceedings on behalf of the other party to the accident out of which the criminal proceedings arose. It was 'of fundamental importance that justice should not only be done, but should manifestly and undoubtedly be seen to be done'.[35] Yet in that case there was no evidence at all that the clerk had influenced or attempted to influence the decision. A more common formulation of the test is: Would a member of the public, looking at the situation as a whole, *reasonably suspect* that a member of the adjudicating body would be biased? Another common formulation is: Is there in fact a *real likelihood* of bias? That test has been approved by the House of Lords.[36] There is no need, on either formulation, to prove *actual* bias; indeed, the courts may refuse to entertain submissions designed to establish the actual bias of a member of an independent tribunal, on the ground that such an

---

34 *Franklin* v. *Minister of Town and Country Planning* [1948] AC 87.

35 *R.* v. *Sussex JJ*, *ex p. McCarthy* [1924] 1 KB 256 at 259, *per* Lord Hewart CJ

36 *R.* v. *Gough* [1993] AC 646. See also *R.* v. *Secretary of State for the Environment, ex p. Kirkstall Valley Campaign Ltd* [1996] 3 All ER 304, and *R.* v. *Camborne JJ, ex p. Pearce* [1955] 1 QB 41 and 51.

inquiry would be unseemly. In practice the tests of 'reasonable suspicion' and 'real likelihood' of bias will generally lead to the same result. Seldom indeed will one find a situation in which reasonable persons adequately apprised of the facts will reasonably suspect bias but a court reviewing the facts will hold that there was no real likelihood of bias. Neither formulation is concerned wholly with appearances or wholly with objective reality. In ninety-nine cases out of a hundred it is enough for the court to ask itself whether a reasonable person viewing the facts would think that there was a substantial possibility of bias. So the decision of a rent assessment committee was quashed because the chairman, a solicitor, was acting for his father and other tenants in a separate dispute with the landlords. Reasonable people would have seen his conduct as unwise and unjudicial.[37]

Clearly the nature of these criteria offers scope for the exercise of judicial discretion. In *Hannam* v. *Bradford Corporation*[38] it was held that it was contrary to natural justice for school governors to sit as members of a local education authority's subcommittee which had to decide whether to confirm a decision of the governors to dismiss a teacher. This was so even though the relevant governors had been absent from the meeting of governors which took the decision to dismiss. But in *Ward* v. *Bradford Corporation*[39] the court refused to interfere with the decision of the governors of a teachers' training college to expel a girl student who had had a man in her room for several weeks, despite the fact that the same body instituted the disciplinary proceedings against the girl. The court's disapproval of the applicant's conduct was unveiled. Nevertheless it seems better to regard *Hannam* as the rule and *Ward* as the exception. The Divisional Court in 1978 quashed a decision of the Leicestershire Fire Authority reducing an officer to the ranks after evidence that the Chief Fire Officer, who had brought the disciplinary charge, had spent five minutes or so with the committee after they had retired. Justice, said the court, must be seen to be done and it was inevitable that the applicant would infer that the Chief Fire Officer had influenced the committee. There was no reason to treat the case as one of those exceptional instances requiring some degree of flexibility in the rule against the likelihood or suspicion of bias.[40]

---

37 See *Metropolitan Properties Co. (FGC) Ltd* v. *Lannon* [1969] 1 QB 577.
38 [1970] 1 WLR 937.
39 (1971) 70 LGR 27.
40 *R.* v. *Leicestershire Fire Authority, ex p. Thompson* (1978) 77 LGR 375. Contrast *R.* v. *Board of Visitors of Frankland Prison, ex p. Lewis* [1986] 1 WLR 130 (Board member not disqualified from adjudicating despite knowledge of prisoner's previous criminal record: such knowledge is common in such members).

Subject to the qualifications already indicated, the principles apply to the conduct of all statutory tribunals, to bodies other than tribunals deciding matters analogous to the judicial (for example, local authorities deciding whether to grant a permit after objections have been lodged, or to revoke a licence)[41] and to Ministers deciding disputes between parties. If the deciding body is a large one (for example, a local council), the pecuniary interest of a single member will disqualify[42] although it may be that the likelihood of his being biased will not be material unless he took an active part in influencing the decision. This is still a doubtful point.

The right to a fair hearing (audi alteram partem)[43]

The right to a fair hearing requires at least that nobody be penalized by a decision affecting his rights or legitimate expectations unless he has been given (a) notice of the case he has to meet and (b) a fair opportunity to answer the case against him and put his own case. The enforcement of this right has a long and chequered history. In 1723 a Dr Bentley obtained an order of mandamus to secure his reinstatement to degrees of which he had been deprived by the University of Cambridge without notice or hearing.[44] When a local authority exercised a statutory power to demolish a house without giving the owner notice or an opportunity to make representations on his own behalf he was awarded damages for trespass, for the authority had failed to observe a rule 'of universal application and founded on the plainest principles of justice'. The court claimed that it 'invoked the justice of the common law to supply the omission of the legislature' which had failed to give the property-owner any right to be heard. So in *Cooper* v. *Wandsworth Board of Works* the foundations of the rules of natural justice were laid.[45]

Natural justice binds Ministers and officials in departmental adjudication. They must 'act in good faith and fairly listen to both sides, for that is a duty lying upon anyone who decides anything'.[46] Did the rules of natural justice then bind all decision-makers? The authoritative statement is to be found

---

41 *R.* v. *Barnsley MBC, ex p. Hook* [1976] 1 WLR 1052, CA.
42 *R.* v. *Hendon RDC, ex p. Chorley* [1933] 2 KB 696 (unanimous decision by council on application to change use of land quashed because one councillor was an estate agent acting for an interested party).
43 de Smith, op. cit., ch. 4.
44 *R.* v. *Chancellor of the University of Cambridge* (1723) 1 Str. 557.
45 (1863) 14 CB (NS) 180.
46 *Board of Education* v. *Rice* [1911] AC 179.

in the judgment of Atkin LJ in *R.* v. *Electricity Commissioners.*[47] Certiorari, the remedy used to correct a breach of the rules of natural justice, lay to 'any body of persons having legal authority to determine questions affecting the rights of subjects, and having the duty to act judicially'. From 1920 to 1960 this much-quoted passage was used to limit the application of natural justice to the extent that the rules of natural justice almost faded into obscurity. A series of decisions held that only if the decision-making body was similar in nature to a court of law or obliged to follow a judicial procedure was there any duty to 'act judicially'. To take one example, the Commissioner of Metropolitan Police had a discretionary power to cancel taxi-drivers' licences. The Divisional Court held that he was not obliged to observe the rules of natural justice because his powers were of an administrative and disciplinary nature.[48] In no sense did the deprivation of a licence by the Commissioner resemble proceedings in court – that is, judicial proceedings. Effectively, only if the decision-making body was required to determine a dispute between parties independent of itself did any question of granting a fair hearing arise.

The House of Lords in *Ridge* v. *Baldwin*[49] breathed new life into natural justice. They held that the Chief Constable of Brighton, who held an office from which by statutory regulations he could only be removed on grounds of neglect of duty or inability, could not validly be dismissed in the absence of notification of the charge and an opportunity to be heard in his defence. The duty to act judicially could be inferred from the nature of the decision to be taken and was not dependent on the nature of the decision-making body.

Since *Ridge* v. *Baldwin* the general trend has been to extend the application of the rules of natural justice to any decision-maker who determines questions affecting the rights or legitimate expectations of individuals. The content of the rules has been adapted and rendered sufficiently flexible to meet the needs of the wide spectrum of decision-making now subject to natural justice. Public policy is openly considered in determining whether the rules should apply to a body and what constitutes a fair hearing in a particular instance.[50] And as the remedies available to those who allege a breach of natural justice are discretionary, the courts may refuse a remedy despite a breach of natural justice, because in the circumstances it is felt

---

47 [1924] 1 KB 171 at p. 205.
48 *R.* v. *Metropolitan Police Commissioner, ex p. Parker* [1953] 1 WLR 1150.
49 [1964] AC 40.
50 *R.* v. *Hull Prison Board of Visitors, ex p. St Germain* [1978] QB 678, CA.

that there is no merit in the applicant's case or it is clear that even if natural justice had been scrupulously observed the applicant would still have met the same fate.[51]

A few examples will illustrate the general trend of extending the scope of natural justice. The right to a hearing was said by the Privy Council to apply to the dissolution of a local council for incompetence by the Minister of Local Government in Ceylon.[52] Three matters were important in determining whether a right to be heard must be granted: the nature of the benefit of which the applicant was deprived by the decision, the circumstances in which the decision-making body could intervene, and the severity and effect of the sanction which could be imposed. So a Scottish schoolteacher dismissible at pleasure had to be afforded an opportunity to be heard before dismissal.[53] A local constituency party was entitled to a hearing before final suspension or disaffiliation from the party organization.[54] Before it was held that exclusive jurisdiction over university students as members of the university vested in the Visitor,[55] students were said to be entitled to a hearing before being sent down on either academic or disciplinary grounds.[56] In R. v. *Hull Prison Board of Visitors*[57] the Court of Appeal found that prisoners appearing before the Board of Visitors to answer serious disciplinary charges which could result in severe punishment had the right to a proper hearing. Despite their deprivation of general liberty the prisoners retained rights which the Board of Visitors had power to affect materially either by punishment within the prison through solitary confinement or loss of privileges, or by effectively extending their period of incarceration through loss of remission.[58] The Board's power to intervene was in cases of gravity where judicial conduct would be expected of a decision-making body and the sanctions at their disposal were severe. Nor did their Lordships see that the extension of natural justice to the

---

51 *Glynn* v. *University of Keele* [1971] 1 WLR 487.
52 *Durayappah* v. *Fernando* [1967] 2 AC 337.
53 *Malloch* v. *Aberdeen Corporation* [1971] 1 WLR 1578, HL.
54 *John* v. *Rees* [1970] Ch. 345.
55 See *Thomas* v. *University of Bradford* [1987] 1 All ER 834. Disputes between academic staff and their university used to be decided by the Visitor, but the Education Reform Act 1988, s. 206, gave the courts jurisdiction in such disputes. See *Pearce* v. *University of Aston (No. 1)* [1991] 2 All ER 461; *Hines* v. *Birkbeck College (No. 2)* [1991] 4 All ER 450; *Page* v. *Hull University Visitor* [1993] 1 All ER 97. See also R. v. *Visitors to the Inns of Court* [1993] 2 All ER 876.
56 R. v. *Aston University Senate, ex p. Roffey* [1969] 2 QB 538.
57 [1978] QB 678.
58 See also *Raymond* v. *Honey* [1983] AC 1.

deliberations of Boards of Visitors would disrupt the efficiency of the prison service, although they admitted that demanding the same standards from the governor in his day-to-day disciplinary role might do so.[59] In *Hone* v. *Maze Prison Board of Visitors*[60] the House of Lords held, however, that this does not imply an absolute right to legal representation before the Board, and that such representation would never be required on a charge heard by the governor of a prison. The rigid application of predetermined policy without allowing representations for a change in the policy may be a breach of the rules of natural justice.[61]

Natural justice is not confined to decisions depriving citizens of existing rights. Dicta suggest that when a citizen has a legitimate expectation that his application for a discretionary benefit such as a licence or permit will not be refused without a chance for him to put his case then he is entitled to some sort of hearing.[62] Where he already enjoys the benefit, the expectation that he should not be deprived of it arbitrarily and unheard by the decision-maker makes his case morally and legally stronger.[63] But this is an area where judges tend to speak in terms of the duty to act fairly, a more fluid and less formalized duty than the duty to observe the rules of natural justice.

While finding against the trade union members of GCHQ who had been deprived by the Government of their right to belong to their unions on the grounds of national security, some at least of their Lordships held that, but for national security, the trade unionists would have had a legitimate expectation of consultation before the ban was imposed.[64] The GCHQ case illustrates two important trends in judicial attitudes towards the expectation of a fair hearing. First, it may open the door to a wider practice of requiring consultations with groups rather than with individuals. Secondly,

59 That qualification was subsequently accepted in *R.* v. *Deputy Governor of Camphill Prison, ex p. King* [1985] QB 735, but that case was later overruled by the House of Lords in *Leech* v. *Parkhurst Prison Deputy Governor* [1988] 1 All ER 485, the House refusing to give special immunity to a prison governor's 'management function'. See further Richardson [1988] *Public Law* 183.

60 [1988] 1 All ER 321.

61 *R.* v. *Secretary of State for the Environment, ex p. Brent LBC* [1983] 3 All ER 321.

62 *McInnes* v. *Onslow-Fane* [1978] 1 WLR 1520; *O'Reilly* v. *Mackman* [1983] AC 237.

63 *Schmidt* v. *Home Secretary* [1969] 2 Ch. 149 at p. 170; *R.* v. *Gaming Board, ex p. Benaim and Khaida* [1970] 2 QB 417, at p. 430; *Att.-Gen. of Hong Kong* v. *Ng Yuen Shiu* [1983] 2 AC 829.

64 *Council of Civil Service Unions* v. *Minister for the Civil Service* [1985] AC 374, applied on the legitimate expectation point in *R.* v. *Secretary of State for Transport, ex p. GLC* [1986] QB 556.

once again the courts have shown a great unwillingness to go behind the Government's view of what national security requires.[65]

Today it can be assumed that the rules of natural justice will apply in the following cases.

1 Where the decision-making body is a court or tribunal. Such a body may nevertheless be empowered or required to act *ex parte* (hearing one side only) in special circumstances – for example, to order that a person suffering from a prescribed infectious disease be detained in hospital.

2 Where the decision-making body has as its functions the holding and hearing of inquiries, or the determination of disputes between parties.

3 In any case where a decision-making body is required to determine questions of law or fact in individual cases and its decisions will have a direct impact on the interests of the individuals concerned.

4 When a decision-making body vested with discretionary powers in the exercise of those powers will take a decision seriously impinging on individual rights and expectations. But it may well be that today such bodies will be characterized as under a duty to act fairly rather than to observe the rules of natural justice.

So wide is the class of cases when it will be presumed that the rules of natural justice apply that it is the exceptions which repay more careful attention and analysis.

1 Where a body conducts an investigation but has no power to decide,[66] providing that the investigation is truly only a preliminary fact-finding exercise and there are no circumstances to suggest that it would be unfair to prevent the aggrieved individual putting his case at this stage. But a duty to act fairly will attach to such bodies.[67] The stringency and content of this duty will depend to what degree the preliminary investigation is of a kind where some degree of disclosure of the case against him and opportunity to put his case would reasonably be expected by the person under investigation. So if the investigation exposes a person to legal hazard and is a necessary prelude to other proceedings which may seriously affect the person's rights or interests then the investigator must

65 But in R. v. *Secretary of State for the Home Department, ex p. Ruddock* [1987] 2 All ER 518, Taylor J held that the courts would not decline to intervene merely because a Minister asserted that national security would be prejudiced if there were a hearing, and that the doctrine of legitimate expectation imposed a duty to act fairly.

66 *Herring* v. *Templeman* [1973] 3 All ER 569.

67 *Norwest Holst Ltd* v. *Department of Trade* [1978] Ch. 201, CA; *Lewis* v. *Heffer* [1978] 1 WLR 1601, CA.

at least inform the person of adverse imputations against him and give him an opportunity to reply.[68] The requirements of 'fairness' will depend on the circumstances of each case. Where the function of the investigating authority is akin to that of the police gathering evidence in order to determine whether further proceedings are necessary, even a suspicion of bias may not affect the validity of the action taken.[69] The duty to act fairly in such circumstances is a duty not to misuse the discretionary powers vested in the investigating body, not a duty to attempt to achieve a fair procedure.

2 Where an exhaustive statutory procedural code has been prescribed.[70] Since the establishment of the Council on Tribunals, such codes have proliferated. But the courts may hold that an ostensibly exhaustive code imports further duties to act fairly in accordance with natural justice.

3 Where a decision affects so many people that it is really a legislative act;[71] or where the range of public policy considerations that the deciding body can legitimately take into account is very wide.[72] This proposition has to be expressed guardedly, for the idea of procedural fairness is not necessarily thus restricted, and in such cases judges will often state that there is a duty to act fairly even though the rules of natural justice are not applicable.

4 Where an employer decides to dismiss an employee. Unless contractual or statutory procedural duties are cast on the employer, the courts may confine the employee to damages for breach of contract if the dismissal is wrongful.[73] But there are now large exceptions to the general rule,[74] particularly since the concept of 'unfair dismissal' was introduced by the

---

68 *Re Pergamon Press* [1971] Ch. 388; *Maxwell* v. *Department of Trade and Industry* [1974] QB 523.

69 *R.* v. *Secretary of State for Trade, ex p. Perestrello* [1980] 1 All ER 28.

70 *Wiseman* v. *Borneman* [1971] AC 297; *Pearlberg* v. *Varty* [1972] 1 WLR 534; *Furnell* v. *Whangarei High Schools Board* [1973] AC 660.

71 See, for example, *Essex CC* v. *Ministry of Housing and Local Government* (1967) 66 LGR 23 (designation of third London airport); *Bates* v. *Lord Hailsham* [1972] 1 WLR 1373 (making statutory rules for solicitors' charges).

72 *Schmidt* v. *Home Secretary* [1969] 2 Ch. 149 (non-renewal of entry permits for alien scientology students).

73 See, for example, *Vidoydaya University Council* v. *Silva* [1965] 1 WLR 77; *Pillai* v. *Singapore City Council* [1968] 1 WLR 1728. The decision in *Ridge* v. *Baldwin* [1964] AC 40 is not inconsistent with the principle; a chief constable is nobody's servant and enjoys a special legal *status*.

74 See *Malloch*'s case (note 53); *Hill* v. *Parsons (C. A.) & Co.* [1972] Ch. 305 (injunction to restrain wrongful dismissal).

Industrial Relations Act 1971 and preserved by subsequent employment legislation.

5 Where a decision entails the allocation of scarce resources – for example, university places, council houses, industrial grants, certain discretionary licences – for which there are numerous competitors. But withdrawal or non-renewal of any such advantage *may*, in justice, have to be preceded by notice and an opportunity to make representations.[75]

In addition, as we have seen, factors such as urgency or an overriding need for confidentiality or national security may negative the existence of a *prima facie* duty to observe the rule or aspects of the rule. Nor need the rule be observed in the exercise of those prerogative powers which are not justiciable.

6 Where the conduct of the person claiming to be affected by the denial of a hearing was such that he could have 'no legitimate expectation of a hearing'. Minicab drivers who had persistently flouted the law and regulations concerning touting for custom at London Airport were found to have only themselves to blame when they were denied any opportunity to make representations to the authority when it acted to exclude all persons from the airport who were not bona fide passengers.[76]

What is a fair hearing?

When a person has a right to a hearing he must know what evidence has been given and what statements made against him and he must be given a fair opportunity to correct or contradict them.[77] There is no fixed rule that the right to be heard means a right to be heard orally; in some situations a case can fairly be concluded in writing.[78] But there is a rebuttable presumption in favour of the duty to afford an oral hearing if one is requested. All relevant information, including information gathered by the decision-maker on his own initiative or as a result of his own expertise or consideration of the case,[79] must be disclosed to persons likely to be affected by its concealment,

75 See notes 62 and 63. See also *R.* v. *East Berkshire Health Authority, ex p. Walsh* [1985] QB 152; CA, and *R.* v. *BBC, ex p. Lavelle* [1983] 1 WLR 23.
76 *Cinnamond* v. *British Airports Authority* [1980] 1 WLR 582; and see *Lovelock* v. *Secretary of State for Transport* [1979].
77 *Kanda* v. *Government of Malaya* [1962] AC 322 at pp. 337–8.
78 *Local Government Board* v. *Arlidge* [1915] AC 120; *Brighton Corporation* v. *Parry* (1972) 70 LGR 576.
79 *Sabey* v. *Secretary of State for the Environment* [1978] 1 All ER 586 (refusal of permission to extract gravel based on conclusions reached by the inspector at the inquiry which he had never put to the applicants for their consideration).

except when full disclosure may injure the individual affected or the public interest.[80] The Gaming Board was not required to disclose its sources of information suggesting that applicants for gaming licences had underworld connections.[81] And in *R. v. Secretary of State for Home Affairs, ex p. Hosenball*,[82] when a young American journalist sought to have a deportation order quashed on the grounds that his presence in the United Kingdom was not prejudicial to national security, Cumming Bruce LJ said, '. . . the field of judicial scrutiny by reference to the enforcement of the rules of common fairness is an extremely restricted field in the sphere of operations necessary to protect the security of the state'. So Mr Hosenball was deported, despite the fact that when he was afforded an opportunity of appearing before a panel advising the Home Secretary on his decision to deport, he was given totally inadequate information on which to answer the general charge against him.

Generally when an oral hearing is granted, parties must be allowed to call witnesses and make submissions. They must have a fair chance to put their case and an adjournment of the hearing should be granted if necessary to prevent a party being taken by surprise,[83] but where there are a large number of parties (as in a public inquiry) the prejudice to one party must be weighed against the inconvenience to everyone else.[84] Cross-examination of witnesses should generally not be prevented[85] and hearsay evidence should not be allowed if it results in a person being effectively disabled from answering the points made against him in the hearsay testimony.[86] There are no hard and fast rules on either cross-examination or hearsay. The crucial factors are the nature of the decision and process challenged and whether at the end of the day the persons affected did have a proper opportunity to put their case. A refusal by the inspector at a public inquiry to allow cross-examination of departmental witnesses giving evidence on national road policies did not result in a breach of natural justice.[87] But prisoners appearing on disciplinary charges before a Board of Visitors should

80 R. v. *Kent Police Authority, ex p. Godden* [1971] 2 QB 662 (distressing medical report disclosed to the applicant's medical adviser only and withheld from him); *Re WLW* [1972] 1 Ch. 456 (psychiatric reports held back in a case where an infant would suffer if published).
81 R. v. *Gaming Board, ex p. Banaim and Khaida* [1970] 2 QB 417.
82 [1977] 1 WLR 766.
83 R. v. *Thames Magistrates, ex p. Polemis* [1974] 1 WLR 1371.
84 *Ostreicher* v. *Secretary of State for the Environment* [1978] 1 WLR 810.
85 *Ceylon University* v. *Fernando* [1960] 1 WLR 223.
86 R. v. *Hull Prison Board of Visitors, ex p. St Germain (No. 2)* [1979] 1 WLR 1401.
87 *Bushell* v. *Secretary of State for the Environment* [1980] 2 All ER 608.

be allowed to cross-examine any witness the reliability of whose evidence is material to the case against them.[88]

It has been said that a party who is entitled to be heard is *prima facie* entitled to be legally represented.[89] The number of circumstances in which this implied right can be excluded[90] makes it more accurate to say now that there is probably a right to be legally represented when a fair hearing is not possible without legal representation. The more that the person affected has at stake and the more severe the potential sanction then the more likely it is that legal representation may become a right enforced by the rules of natural justice.[91] And so where prisoners faced charges of mutiny before the prison Board of Visitors, the Board was held to have acted wrongly in refusing them legal representation. The requirements of a fair hearing demand that the tribunal exercise its discretion over the issue of representation. No reasonable Board could refuse legal representation to men facing charges of such gravity and complexity.[92]

In some situations there is an oral hearing conducted by a small committee or tribunal but the decision is made by a larger body. The general rule is that he who decides must also hear.[93] This requires that those who listen to the evidence and make recommendations must deliver to the deciding body an adequate report on which that body can discharge its obligation to hear as well as decide. The stringency with which this requirement is enforced will depend on the nature of the decision-making process under review. The more closely it resembles proceedings in the ordinary courts then the more strictly the rule will apply.[94] Departmental adjudication, where it is obvious that the Minister cannot hear and decide every case remitted to him, has always been outside the scope of the rule.[95] With the decision the fair hearing is complete. The common law has not as yet enforced any general rule that fairness demands that those affected be told the reasons for the decision, nor did it oblige Ministers to disclose the

88 *R.* v. *Hull Prison Board of Visitors (No. 2)* [1979] 1 WLR 1401.

89 *R.* v. *Assessment Committee of St Mary Abbots, Kensington* [1891] 1 QB 378.

90 See *Enderby Town FC Ltd* v. *Football Association Ltd* [1971] Ch. 591; *Fraser* v. *Mudge* [1975] 1 WLR 1132; *Hone* v. *Maze Prison Board of Visitors* (1988) 1 All ER 321 (prisoners on disciplinary charges).

91 *Pett* v. *Greyhound Racing Association Ltd* [1969] 1 QB 125; *(No. 2)* [1970] 1 QB 46.

92 *R.* v. *Secretary of State for the Home Department, ex p. Tarrant* [1985] QB 251; but see *Hone* v. *Maze Prison Board of Visitors* (above, p. 534 note 60).

93 *Jeffs* v. *New Zealand Dairy Production & Marketing Board* [1967] 1 AC 551.

94 *R.* v. *Race Relations Board, ex p. Selvarajan* [1975] 1 WLR 1986. And see *Chief Constable of the North Wales Police* v. *Evans* [1982] 1 WLR 1155, HL.

95 *Local Government Board* v. *Arlidge* [1915] AC 120.

reports of inspectors at public inquiries.[96] In the case of the decisions of most special statutory tribunals, and of Ministers reaching decisions after the holding of inquiries, statute has filled the gap.[97] The courts enforce the giving of reasons when required by statute but the full rigour of the statutory rule is not always brought to bear on public authorities. For example, in one case concerning an application that the plaintiff's houses be rehabilitated rather than demolished a statement of reasons read: 'for the reason that the premises should be demolished and the site used for the erection of new housing accommodation'. The Court of Appeal held this to be sufficient although the Court also said that their finding did not mean that such a formula would always fulfil the duty to give reasons.[98]

In making sense of the inconsistencies in the application of the rules of natural justice it should never be forgotten that natural justice is not and is not intended to be a precise and uniform code of procedure. What the courts seek to enforce is substantial justice. The whole of the decision-making process under review is examined. In *Calvin* v. *Carr*[99] the appellant had been accused of being a party with his jockey to stopping his horse running a fair race. It was assumed that he had been denied a fair hearing by the course stewards but his appeal to the Australian Jockey Club was conducted with scrupulous fairness. The Privy Council held that the unfairness of the first hearing did not necessarily vitiate the entire decision-making process.

Duty to act fairly

The duty to act fairly is not rationally distinguishable from the duty to observe the rules of natural justice. Judges on occasion use the terms interchangeably. Examples have been noted in which it has been suggested that although there is no right to a hearing, in the sense discussed in the previous section, the decision-maker is still bound to act fairly. This duty to act fairly prohibits the decision-maker from acting capriciously and here it merges with principles preventing misuse of discretionary powers. But it is in the area of decisions which either (1) affect large groups rather than

96 ibid.
97 Tribunals and Inquiries Act 1992, s. 10.
98 *Elliot* v. *Southwark LBC* [1976] 1 WLR 499. The Higher Education Funding Council was held to be under no duty to give reasons for reducing an institution's grant, because such decisions were a matter of academic judgement: *R.* v. *Universities' Funding Council, ex p. Institute of Dental Surgery* [1994] 1 All ER 651.
99 [1979] 2 WLR 755.

individuals, or (2) appear to be part and parcel of everyday administration, or (3) are made by bodies so very different in form and function from those usually subject to natural justice, that the courts appear happier to use the flexible notions of fairness rather than stretch the rules of natural justice even further.

In *R. v. Liverpool Corporation, ex p. Liverpool Taxi Fleet Operators' Association*[100] the town clerk of Liverpool assured bodies representing taxi-drivers that no increase in the number of taxi licences would be made without consulting them. A subcommittee of the council recommended graduated increases after hearing representations from lawyers representing the taxi-drivers. An undertaking was given in the council that there would be no increases made until forthcoming legislation was passed. The council was then advised that this restriction acted as an improper fetter on their discretion and the numbers of taxi-licences increased. The Court of Appeal held that although the council was indubitably exercising an administrative function in determining the number of taxi licences to be allocated in the city the court should not hesitate in a suitable case to intervene to ensure fairness. A similar attitude has been taken to the functions of an immigration officer determining whether an immigrant in front of him is truly under sixteen and entitled to enter the United Kingdom as a dependant;[101] and to a magistrate condemning potatoes as unfit for human consumption.[102] In *HTV v. Price Commission*[103] the Commission had regularly treated payments made by commercial television companies to the Exchequer as part of their total costs even though the scale of the payments was calculated as a percentage of advertising profits. In 1975 the Commission changed its mind and in determining an application for a price increase calculated HTV's profits as including those payments, refusing to treat them as costs. The Court of Appeal held that the Commission was obliged to act consistently and fairly and, having regularly interpreted costs in one manner, must allow representations from the affected company before reversing their policy.

These examples, and those cited earlier where 'the duty to act fairly' was preferred to the rules of natural justice as a tool of judicial control, illustrate the three points made at the beginning of the section. They are examples of decision-making processes so far removed from the original sphere of natural justice that even after *Ridge v. Baldwin* it would stretch the English

100 [1972] 2 QB 299.
101 *Re HK* [1967] 2 QB 617.
102 *R. v. Birmingham City Justice, ex p. Chris Foreign Foods (Wholesalers) Ltd* [1970] 1 WLR 1428.
103 [1976] ICR 170.

language to say that the decision-makers must 'act judicially'. Additionally they are decisions taken in a context where the effect of requiring fairness to one group or individual must be considered in the light of the administration's general policy and conduct. Speaking of a duty to act fairly frees the judge to consider whether his decision will result in a general improvement in standards of fairness in that area of government without causing inefficiency, or delay, or insuperable administrative difficulties. Only if he is satisfied that this is so will the individual be afforded a remedy.

DISCRETIONARY POWERS

General

Discretion implies power to choose between alternative courses of action. If X applies to a local council for a licence to open a massage establishment, the council may grant the licence unconditionally or subject to such conditions as it thinks fit to impose, or refuse the application. But its discretion is not unlimited; and it must exercise a genuine discretion in each individual case. Thus, it has an implied duty not to refuse the application on legally irrelevant grounds (for example, that X is a Jehovah's Witness) or to attach legally irrelevant conditions to the grant of a licence (for example, that X shall employ only persons resident in the district); nor must it adopt a rigid rule not to grant any new applications for licences irrespective of the merits of the individual case. If no appeal lay from its decisions, X would be entitled to go to the High Court for an order of mandamus to compel it to perform its public duty. Mandamus would lie not to compel the council to give him a licence but to exercise its discretion according to law.

In fact mandamus is unnecessary, for an appeal against the merits of the decision lies to a magistrates' court. If the magistrate wrongfully refuses to entertain the appeal at all, he has declined jurisdiction in breach of his public duty and mandamus will issue to him. If he listens to submissions and then erroneously dismisses the appeal, the question might arise on an application for mandamus whether he had wrongfully declined jurisdiction or made an error of law on a matter within his jurisdiction; in this context the answer is unimportant, for an appeal will lie to the Divisional Court by case stated. In arriving at his decision, he can substitute his own opinion for that of the local authority, giving due weight to the council's knowledge of local conditions. Indeed, he has a legally enforceable duty to exercise an independent discretion.[104]

It is fairly unusual to provide a full right of appeal to a court against the merits of a statutory discretionary decision. Judicial control of the exercise of discretion is normally limited to two questions: Has the discretion been exercised at all? If so, has it been exercised according to law?

Failure to exercise a discretion

1 The general rule is that, unless expressly authorized to do so, an authority cannot sub-delegate its powers to another person or body: *delegatus non potest delegare*. Application of this principle gives rise to a number of difficult problems – for example, what exactly is meant by 'delegation'? – which we need not pursue. But it is not hard to illustrate the application of the general rule. A local authority empowered to issue cinema licences subject to conditions cannot validly impose a condition that *no* film shall be exhibited unless approved by the British Board of Film Classification;[105] it must preserve a residual discretion to override the rulings of the Board in an individual case; otherwise it will be held to have abdicated from its statutory duty to exercise its own discretion.[106] Again, in deciding an appeal, Minister X must not dispose of the matter solely on the basis of Minister Y's policy; otherwise the decision becomes Minister Y's.[107]

2 One authority cannot lawfully act under the dictation of another unless the other is a superior in the administrative hierarchy or is empowered by law to give instructions to it.[108]

3 An authority must not so fetter its own discretion by self-created rules as to preclude itself from applying its mind to the merits of an individual case before it. The council, in our hypothetical illustration, could,

---

104 *Sagnata Investments Ltd* v. *Norwich Corporation* [1971] 2 QB 614. The same principles apply to the Crown Court hearing an appeal from a magistrates' court.
105 *Ellis* v. *Dubowski* [1921] 3 KB 621. But see *R.* v. *Greater London Council, ex p. Blackburn* [1976] 1 WLR 550 (authority may adopt policy of approving all films passed by the British Board of Film Censors unless a specific objection is made); *R.* v. *Police Complaints Board, ex p. Madden* [1983] 2 All ER 353 (Board could not decline to act on a complaint merely because the DPP had decided against a criminal prosecution).
106 *Mills* v. *LCC* [1925] 1 KB 213.
107 *Lavender (H.) and Son Ltd* v. *Minister of Housing and Local Government* [1970] 1 WLR 1231 (planning appeal dismissed because Minister of Agriculture always opposed such development).
108 See *Laker Airways Ltd* v. *Department of Trade* above, p. 519, and *R.* v. *Secretary of State for the Environment and Cheshire County Council, ex p. Halton DC, The Times,* 14 July 1983.

however, adopt a general policy of not granting any further massage establishment licences for the time being (because, for example, some of these establishments had been improperly conducted), provided that it was prepared to make an exception in a particular case.[109] It must keep its mind open. But an authority entitled to take general considerations of national policy into account may be entitled to refuse to consider any application belonging to a particular class. For example, the Home Secretary may validly instruct immigration officers not to admit any alien wishing to enter the country as a student member of a cult which he deems to be harmful to the public welfare.[110]

4 An authority cannot validly bargain away, or otherwise undertake not to exercise, powers vested in it for the purpose of fulfilling an important public purpose. A local authority cannot disable itself from making a particular by-law or revoking a grant of planning permission;[111] and in general public bodies cannot be estopped from exercising their powers by erroneous assurances given to members of the public.[112] In matters of national policy, the Crown cannot fetter its own freedom to act for the public good.[113] But these rules are easier to formulate than to apply in practice.

Misuse of discretion

The courts have demonstrated that they can if they wish review the legality of the exercise of virtually any discretionary power. That a power derives from the prerogative or is subject to the approval of Parliament will not deter judicial examination of the propriety of the decision to act and the action taken.[114] The Judiciary choose not to intervene on occasion. This is especially the case when the statutory power challenged concerns national security or the operation of the immigration rules. In times of emergency the ordinary rules of judicial review are naturally modified, and in some sensitive political areas such as industrial relations the courts will back away

---

109 See, for example, *Cumings* v. *Birkenhead Corporation* [1972] Ch. 12 (allocation of pupils to denominational schools); *British Oxygen Co.* v. *Board of Trade* [1971] AC 610 (policy on investment grants).
110 See *Schmidt* v. *Home Secretary* [1969] 2 Ch. 149.
111 See, e.g., *Cory (William) & Son Ltd* v. *City of London Corporation* [1951] 2 KB 475.
112 On assurances given by Crown servants, see *Howell* v. *Falmouth Boat Construction Co.* [1951] AC 837 at 845, 849 (contrast *Robertson* v. *Minister of Pensions* [1949] 1 KB 227).
113 *Rederiaktiebolaget Amphitrite* v. *R.* [1921] 3 KB 500; and see pp. 600–601.
114 *Laker Airways Ltd* v. *Department of Trade* [1977] QB 643.

from intervening in controversy. Unfortunately, rather than stating clearly that their view of public policy inhibits them from investigating certain areas of government, judges too often fall back on earlier notions of the limited power to review administrative acts or the presumption that an authority granted powers in subjective terms has satisfied itself of the necessary conditions for the lawful exercise of its discretion.

How far may the courts go in examining the exercise of discretionary power? All statutory powers must be exercised in good faith and to promote the objects of the enabling Act. Statutory discretions are potentially reviewable on these grounds at the instance of a person aggrieved by their exercise. Bad faith – the intentional abuse of power for extraneous motives – may be virtually impossible to prove. Misuse of powers in good faith – by using them for an unauthorized purpose or without regard to legally relevant considerations or on the basis of legally irrelevant considerations – need not be so difficult to establish. If a power expressly granted for one purpose is in fact used for a different purpose the administrative act is invalid.[115] If such a power is used to achieve its proper purpose and another unauthorized purpose the court must consider what was the 'dominant' purpose of the action taken.[116] Was the exercise of the power a colourable sham or has the purpose for which the power was granted been substantially fulfilled?[117] If the statutory purpose has not been spelt out, the courts may read implied limitations into an ostensibly unfettered grant of power.[118] As was pointed out in an earlier chapter, the courts are nowadays reluctant to hold that an administrative authority is the sole judge of the legality of the purpose for which it exercises a discretionary power. They may interpret a statute restrictively, relying if necessary on common-law presumptions of legislative intent; and they may draw adverse inferences from the conduct of the administrative authority.[119]

---

115 *Congreve* v. *Home Office* [1976] QB 629.
116 *Westminster Corporation* v. *L & NW Railway Co.* [1905] AC 426. See also *R.* v. *Inner London Education Authority, ex p. Westminster City Council* [1986] 2 WLR 28 (purpose of the exercise of a power held improper so irrelevant that a proper purpose had been achieved as well).
117 *Asher* v. *Secretary of State for the Environment* [1974] Ch. 208.
118 *R.* v. *Barnet & Camden Rent Tribunal, ex p. Frey Investments Ltd* [1972] 2 QB 372 (local council could not use its power to refer contracts of letting to a rent tribunal for the purpose of using the tribunal as a general rent-fixing agency irrespective of the circumstances of individual cases).
119 *Congreve* v. *Home Office* [1976] QB 629 (and note the effect of a finding of maladministration by the Parliamentary Commissioner for Administration in proving the invalidity of an administrative act).

Perhaps the most outstanding recent example of judicial activism in this field of the law was the decision of the House of Lords in *Padfield* v. *Minister of Agriculture* (1968).[120] Under a statutory marketing scheme, the Milk Marketing Board fixed prices to be paid to producers in each of eleven regions in England and Wales. Producers from the south-east region wanted an increase in the basic price paid to them by the Board. They could not get a majority on the Board for their view. But under the Act they could, and did, make a complaint to the Minister. The Act provided that, 'if the Minister . . . so directs', a committee was to be appointed to investigate and report on such a complaint. The Minister refused to appoint a committee. He claimed that he had a free discretion to do as he thought fit. But he was induced to give reasons for his refusal: the complaint raised issues affecting other regions; he would be expected to implement the report of such a committee, and this could lead to political difficulties. The House of Lords held that the Minister had had regard to irrelevant considerations and had failed to promote the implied purposes of the Act; and an order of mandamus was issued to direct him to consider the appellants' complaint according to law.[121]

Thus the House of Lords subjected a wide executive discretion to judicial standards. *Padfield* was hailed as the dawn of a new era of judicial review, showing that English administrative law did recognize a principle akin to the French *détournement de pouvoir*, or misuse of administrative power. Moreover, misuse of power might be inferred from inadequate reasons or, so the Law Lords observed *obiter*, from the absence of any reason given in rebuttal when an aggrieved person had established a *prima facie* case. Alas, once again the courts failed to demonstrate a consistent policy. In the years that followed *Padfield* there appeared to be a retreat from the implications of that decision. Either the terms in which the discretion was granted or the circumstances of its exercise were held to preclude the rigours of the *Padfield* approach[122] or the complainant was required to establish that the authority was motivated by an improper purpose.[123]

---

120 [1968] AC 997.
121 The Minister then set up the committee; the committee reported in favour of the south-eastern producers; the Minister rejected the report. A local authority which banned stag-hunting on its land on moral grounds was held to have failed to take into account whether such a ban would be for the general public benefit: *R.* v. *Somerset County Council, ex p. Fewings* [1995] 3 All ER 20.
122 See *Secretary of State for Employment* v. *ASLEF* [1972] 2 QB 455.
123 See *Asher* v. *Secretary of State for the Environment* [1974] Ch. 208; and see *Hoveringham Gravels Ltd* v. *Secretary of State for the Environment* [1975] QB 754.

In 1976 in *Congreve* v. *Home Office*[124] and in the *Tameside* case[125] the courts reasserted judicial willingness to examine the reasons advanced in support of an exercise of discretion and to infer misuse of discretion in the absence of good reasons to support a decision. Mr Congreve, anticipating a price rise in colour television licences, renewed the licence before the date on which renewal was due in order to avoid paying the increased charge. The Home Secretary, after Mr Congreve had refused to pay an additional sum equivalent to the increase, revoked his television licence. The Court of Appeal held that the Minister's reasons – loss of revenue, dissatisfaction on the part of licence holders less financially astute than Mr Congreve – were quite insufficient and the revocation consequently unlawful. More important, the court reiterated that had the Minister hidden behind a refusal to give reasons, then they would have been prepared to infer that his reasons were inadequate.

The *Tameside* decision reduced the efficacy of the device of excluding judicial review by granting a discretion in subjective terms, which apparently requires only that the Minister, or other authority, be satisfied, or form an opinion and so at first sight exclude judicial review. Framing a power in subjective terms will no longer prevent judicial examination of the exercise of that power. The 1944 Education Act authorized the Secretary of State for Education to intervene and give directions to a local education authority if he 'is satisfied' that the authority has acted or proposes to act 'unreasonably'. In 1976 the Secretary of State for Education applied for an order of mandamus to enforce directions which he had given to the newly elected Conservative council for Tameside requiring them to go ahead with comprehensive plans scheduled to come into effect that September, and not to continue with the eleventh-hour reintroduction of selection. Counsel for the Secretary of State argued that the opinion of the Secretary of State was conclusive as to whether Tameside's action was unreasonable. All Parliament demanded for the lawful exercise of this power granted in subjective terms was that the Secretary of State himself form a judgment. The House of Lords rejected this argument. They held that when the exercise of a power requires the formation of a judgment which depends on the existence of certain facts, then although the evaluation of those facts is a matter for the relevant authority, the courts are entitled to inquire whether the facts exist and whether the authority in reaching its judgment has done so in accordance with the usual principles governing the exercise

124 [1976] QB 629.
125 *Secretary of State for Education and Science* v. *Tameside MBC* [1977] AC 1014.

of discretionary powers. In the *Tameside* case the Secretary of State lost because he was unable to show that a reasonable Minister, applying the proper criteria to the circumstances, and disregarding any irrelevant considerations, would have been satisfied that Tameside were acting unreasonably.

The Courts have at their disposal a formidable armoury for investigating and controlling administrative action. When they choose not to unleash their weapons they may take three courses of action. The Court of Appeal in the *Hosenball*[126] deportation appeal frankly admitted that judicial scrutiny of matters touching on national security was extremely limited and no assistance would be given to the applicant in proving his case that the Home Secretary had misused his discretion. The Minister would not be required to disclose his reasons and no inferences would be drawn from his silence. Less admirably the court may state that although it is open to the courts to review the exercise of a subjectively framed decision there are no grounds for them to do so unless the applicant for review can advance positive evidence that the Minister did not have proper grounds to be satisfied, or form an opinion, that he was entitled to exercise his discretion.[127] The *Tameside* case was unusual because it was the Minister who applied to the court seeking aid to enforce his statutory powers. When a citizen alleges that powers have been misused the court may decide to presume that the Minister has acted properly until the contrary is proved. This attitude frustrates any coherent growth in judicial enforcement of reasoned decision-making and in the absence of reasons the task of determining whether a power has been exercised lawfully is very much a matter of guesswork. Where an immigration officer's power to detain depends on the existence of certain facts, even though he had reasonable grounds for believing that the facts existed, the court will, on challenge of the detention by habeas corpus or judicial review, uphold the detention only if it is satisfied that the facts did exist.[128]

If a statutory power is expressed to be exercisable only where there exist 'reasonable grounds', 'reasonable cause' or 'reasonable suspicion', the courts can properly inquire independently whether these conditions precedent were satisfied.[129] And when the Secretary of State for Education purported

126 R. v. Secretary of State for Home Affairs, ex p. Hosenball [1977] 1 WLR 766.
127 See note 122, above.
128 R. v. Secretary of State for the Home Department, ex p. Khawaja [1984] AC 74, HL overruling Zamir v. Secretary of State for the Home Department [1980] AC 934, HL.
129 Nakkuda Ali v. Jayaratne [1951] AC 66 at 76–7, distinguishing Liversidge v. Anderson [1942] AC 206.

to give directions to a local authority in the exercise of his power to intervene if the authority had acted 'unreasonably' the House of Lords held that the courts could inquire whether there was evidence to support the Minister's finding of unreasonableness.[130]

If there is no express statutory obligation cast on the competent authority to act reasonably, the courts may nevertheless impose minimum standards of reasonableness. The Poplar councillors who voted to pay unskilled employees a minimum wage of £4 a week in the early 1920s were held to have exercised their discretion unlawfully by taking irrelevant considerations into account and failing to have regard to relevant considerations.[131] To say that they had acted unreasonably would come to the same thing. But suppose that an authority vested with a wide discretion is not deflected into the paths of irrelevancy; instead, it gives too much weight to one relevant factor and too little to others, and ends by coming to an unreasonable decision. In the *Wednesbury Corporation* case[132] a local authority, empowered to attach such conditions as it thought fit to the grant of a permit for Sunday cinema opening, imposed a condition that no child under fifteen should be admitted to a Sunday performance at all. The condition was attacked as being void for unreasonableness. The Court of Appeal held that it was valid; the courts should be slow to substitute their own opinion for that of the competent authority, and only if the condition were such as no reasonable body of persons could have imposed should they be prepared to pronounce it invalid. This seems to suggest that only a preposterous decision ('something overwhelming') could be successfully impugned on its merits; and a preposterous decision would in any event probably be characterized as having been made in bad faith or for an improper purpose. The test thus formulated appeared to be every bit as narrow as that adopted to determine the validity of by-laws alleged to be void for manifest unreasonableness.[133] However, cases of conditions annexed to grants of planning permission and caravan site licences show that the *Wednesbury* test of unreasonableness need not be a formality, and it has been invoked to

130 *Secretary of State for Education and Science* v. *Tameside MBC* [1977] AC 1014, HL cf. *Luby* v. *Newcastle-under-Lyme Corporation* [1965] 1 QB 214.
131 *Roberts* v. *Hopwood* [1925] AC 578. See *Pickwell* v. *Camden LBC* [1983] 1 All ER 602; *R.* v. *London Transport Executive, ex p. GLC* [1983] 2 All ER 262.
132 *Associated Provincial Picture Houses Ltd* v. *Wednesbury Corporation* [1948] 1 KB 223.
133 *Kruse* v. *Johnson* [1898] 2 QB 91 at 99–100. From time to time local authority by-laws have been held invalid for manifest unreasonableness, though the test of validity may appear similar to the *Wednesbury* test. See, for example, *Parker* v. *Bournemouth Corporation* (1902) 66 JP 440; *Repton School Governors* v. *Repton RDC* [1918] 2 KB 133.

strike down clearly unreasonable conditions.[134] But the courts are, on the whole, still chary of holding the exercise of local authority discretionary powers to be void for unreasonableness *per se*, especially if they contain a significant policy element.[135]

In *Council of Civil Service Unions* v. *Minister for the Civil Service*[136] Lord Diplock suggested that judicial review could be said to be available on three grounds (while not denying that there might be others). These were 'illegality', 'irrationality' and 'procedural impropriety'. He saw irrationality as a more appropriate term for '*Wednesbury* unreasonableness' – 'a decision which is so outrageous in its defiance of logic or of accepted moral standards that no sensible person . . . could have arrived at it'.[137]

Statutory exclusion of judicial control

The gradual extension of judicial control over administrative action has been demonstrated in the preceding pages. How far can Parliament limit judicial intervention in government? We are concerned in this section with direct exclusionary formulae which are generally worded 'The decision of X shall not be called into question in any court of law'. The courts will normally construe very strictly any statutory provision ousting or restricting their ordinary jurisdiction. If such a provision is reasonably capable of having more than one meaning, the meaning preserving the courts' ordinary jurisdiction will be adopted.[138] But the presumption against judicial review does not apply where the tribunal vested with exclusive jurisdiction is itself a court of law, albeit an inferior court.[139]

---

134 *Mixnam's Properties Ltd* v. *Chertsey UDC* [1965] AC 735; *Hartnell* v. *Minister of Housing and Local Government* [1965] AC 1134.

135 See, for example, *R.* v. *Barnet & Camden Rent Tribunal, ex p. Frey Investments Ltd* [1972] 2 QB 372 (power to refer private tenancies to rent tribunal); *Cumings* v. *Birkenhead Corporation* [1972] Ch. 12 (allocation of pupils to secondary schools). The courts will not review the reasonableness of a Minister's decision if it requires and receives the approval of the Commons, unless both Minister and House misconstrue the Act under which it was made, or unless he deceived the House: *R.* v. *Secretary of State for the Environment, ex p. Nottinghamshire County Council* [1986] AC 560. But in *Tower Hamlets LBC* v. *Chetnik Developments Ltd* [1988] 1 All ER 961, the House of Lords held that a local authority's statutory discretion to refund overpaid rates was a power which had to be exercised according to the purpose for which it had been conferred.

136 [1985] AC 374 at 410.

137 His classification is being used in judgments: see, e.g., *R.* v. *Secretary of State for Social Services, ex p. Association of Metropolitan Authorities* [1986] 1 All ER 164 at 169.

138 *Anisminic Ltd* v. *Foreign Compensation Commission* [1969] 2 AC 147, at p. 170.

139 *Re Racal Communications Ltd* [1980] 2 All ER 634.

To some extent excluding judicial review has ceased to be a burning issue. The Tribunals and Inquiries Act 1992, s. 12, provides that with one exception any provision in an Act passed before 1 August 1958 seeking to oust the jurisdiction of the courts shall not prevent the removal of proceedings to the High Court by way of certiorari or mandamus. But by section 12(3) this provision has no effect on statutes providing for access to the High Court for a limited period (usually six weeks), and thereafter excluding judicial review. What we must consider is the potential effect of any new attempt to oust the courts' jurisdiction altogether, and whether there are any circumstances in which a decision can be challenged after a limited period of access to the High Court which had been permitted by statute had expired. A series of judicial decisions has to be analysed.

In 1956, in *Smith* v. *East Elloe RDC*,[140] the House of Lords refused to allow the validity of a compulsory purchase order to be challenged when the applicant alleged bad faith in the procuring of the order. Their Lordships gave literal effect to the statutory provision that once the six weeks allowed to challenge the confirmation of the order by the Minister had expired the decision could not be questioned in any legal proceedings whatsoever. Twelve years later the House of Lords considered the case of *Anisminic Ltd* v *Foreign Compensation Commission*.[141] The dispute arose from the agreement between the Governments of Egypt and the United Kingdom that a sum be paid by Egypt to provide compensation for those British companies and persons whose property had been lost or damaged in the 1956 Suez incident, and subsequent expropriations of British property by the Egyptian Government. The United Kingdom Government entrusted the distribution of compensation to the Foreign Compensation Commission and section 4(4) of the Foreign Compensation Act provided that 'The determination by the Commission of any application made to them under this Act shall not be called into question in any court of law.'

The statutory instrument defining the powers of the Commission in relation to applications arising out of the Suez incident contained complicated and obscure provisions as to the nationality of applicants for compensation. The object was to ensure that only those of British nationality received compensation, be they the original owners of the property lost or damaged, or their successors in title. Anisminic was a British company but its property had been first sequestrated and then sold to an Egyptian organization. The Commission interpreted the statutory instrument

---

140 [1956] AC 736.
141 [1969] 2 AC 147.

defining proper applicants for compensation as excluding Anisminic because their successor in title was of Egyptian nationality. The House of Lords held that the Commission had misconstrued the instrument because where the original owner of the property claimed he was British the nationality of his successor in title was irrelevant. The Commission had considered a matter totally irrelevant to the questions which they had been granted jurisdiction to determine. They had embarked on an inquiry beyond the limited inquiry directed by Parliament. Accordingly they had exceeded their jurisdiction and their purported determination was invalid and not protected by the provision preventing proper determination of the Commission being questioned in the courts.

Anisminic established the basic principle that if an authority or tribunal exceeds its jurisdiction then its decision is regarded by the courts as invalid and beyond the protection of any exclusionary formula yet devised by Parliamentary draftsmen. It reinforces the importance of the distinction between error depriving a tribunal of jurisdiction and error within the jurisdiction. Lord Denning's suggestion in *Pearlman* v. *Keepers and Governors of Harrow School*[142] that the distinction be disregarded has been firmly rejected by the Privy Council.[143] The Malaysian Industrial Relations Act 1967 provided that awards of the Industrial Court should be 'final and conclusive, and no award shall be challenged, appealed against, reviewed, quashed or called into question in any court of law'. The Industrial Court's original award depended on a finding that a strike by employees did not terminate their contracts of employment. This was clearly a question which the Industrial Court had jurisdiction to determine. The Privy Council held that they had no jurisdiction to review the Industrial Court's decision on the grounds of an error of law within the jurisdiction in the face of the clear and express exclusionary formula in the governing statute.

More common now than a complete ouster of the courts' jurisdiction is the provison of a short time in which a decision may be challenged on the expiry of which the courts are excluded from reviewing the decision. In *R.* v. *Secretary of State for the Environment, ex p. Ostler*[144] there was a proposal to build an inner relief road in Boston, Lincs. An inquiry took place to consider the new road in the course of which it was alleged that a secret promise had been made to an objector that access to his business would be

---

142 [1979] QB 56, at p. 70.
143 *South East Asia Fire Bricks* v. *Non-Metallic Mineral Products Manufacturing Union* [1981] AC 363.
144 [1977] QB 122.

ensured by widening a subsidiary road, Craythorn Lane. The general scheme for the trunk road was approved by the Secretary of State and a second inquiry into consequent changes to subsidiary roads was held. Mr Ostler objected because his business would be badly affected by the widening of Craythorn Lane. Later he found out about the alleged promise made at the first inquiry and sought to challenge the order concerning the trunk road made nearly two years earlier. But the Highways Act of 1959 provided that such schemes might be questioned in the High Court within six weeks of being made and thereafter should not be questioned in any legal proceedings whatsoever. The Court of Appeal dismissed Mr Ostler's application for certiorari. They held that *Smith* v. *East Elloe R D C* was still a good authority. *Anisminic* was distinguished on the following grounds. (1) The confirmation of a compulsory purchase order was an administrative decision, not a genuinely judicial decision as was the case in *Anisminic*. It followed that the public interest in swift and conclusive decision-making had to be considered. Six weeks were allowed to challenge the decision and, after that, action in the form of acquiring land, demolishing buildings and erecting others should not be left at the mercy of some later judicial intervention. (2) What was impugned by Mr Ostler was not the jurisdiction of the Minister to make the order but the alleged fraud or unfairness which procured the order. Lord Denning also considered it relevant that the jurisdiction of the courts was limited to six weeks and not ousted altogether.

From this survey of case law the following guidelines can be put forward. When a statutory provision excludes the ordinary jurisdiction of the courts it will prevent judicial review of errors of law within the jurisdiction of the authority or tribunal. If a tribunal has considered the questions entrusted to it by Parliament, and not embarked on consideration of matters outside its authority, then a mistake in its evaluation of those questions cannot be reviewed or corrected when an authority in the exercise of an administrative power, requiring swift and irrevocable action, has exercised that power within the limits set by Parliament, and its decision cannot be challenged on the grounds that the process leading up to the decision was affected by bad faith or want of natural justice. Two questions remain and allow the courts room to enlarge their jurisdiction in the face of exclusionary formulae. First, exactly what type of error deprives an authority or tribunal of jurisdiction to make a valid decision has not been conclusively decided. For example, certain judges in *Anisminic* thought a decision procured by fraud or want of natural justice was a decision outside jurisdiction. Jurisdiction was not limited simply by what matters an authority had power to decide but by an implied requirement to follow a proper procedure and to conduct oneself lawfully in exercising jurisdiction. Secondly, the well-tried device of characterizing a power as administrative or judicial enables the judges to juggle terms in order to arrive at a decision which they believe to be fair and in the public interest.

Compensation for unlawful administrative action

When an unlawful administrative decision results in the commission of an actionable wrong, a citizen suffering loss as a result of that decision may be able to claim damages[145] as well as obtaining an order to quash or declare the decision invalid. But if the decision or action taken does not fall into any category of actionable wrong recognized at common law, then no compensation is payable even though the decision may be found to be invalid and to have resulted in financial loss to individual citizens.[146] The absence of a logical theory of compensation for unlawful administrative action is one of the main defects of English administrative law.[147]

145 See below, p. 606.
146 See *Dunlop* v. *Woolahra Municipal Council* [1982] AC 158 (PC).
147 See Craig (1980) 96 *LQR* 413. For a comprehensive reform programme for judicial review, see Woolf [1992] *Public Law* 220.

CHAPTER 27

Judicial Review: Remedies

This chapter attempts no more than a preliminary survey of the judicial remedies available against administrative bodies.[1] Remedies may be statutory or non-statutory and the practical importance of the former should not be ignored, despite the fact that only a brief mention of statutory remedies will be made in the following pages.

Statutory remedies

1 Rights of appeal to the courts. From most statutory tribunals appeals lie to the High Court (normally the Divisional Court of the Queen's Bench Division) or the Court of Appeal on points of law.
2 Statutory applications to quash, or restrain the making of, compulsory purchase and similar orders, and decisions on planning appeals, on the ground that the order or decision is *ultra vires* or that the applicant has been substantially prejudiced by non-compliance with a procedural or formal requirement on the part of the competent authorities. Applications lie to a single judge of the High Court,[2] and must be brought within a brief period, normally six weeks. The statutory procedure excludes the non-statutory grounds for challenge.

Sometimes the classes of persons and bodies entitled to lodge an appeal or bring an application to quash are specified by the Act. Unfortunately, it is more common for the Act merely to afford these rights to a 'person aggrieved', leaving it to the courts to interpret what this expression means. The courts used to adopt a restrictive interpretation requiring that a 'person aggrieved' be some person or body whose existing legal rights had been interfered with or upon whom a new legal obligation

---

1 S. de Smith, *Judicial Review of Administrative Action* (5th edn, 1996), Part III.
2 In practice in the Queen's Bench Division. See further, Order 94 of the Rules of the Supreme Court.

was to be imposed.[3] Now the trend is towards a more liberal policy. Loss of amenity has been held to render a householder a 'person aggrieved'.[4] An amenity society which was *permitted* by the inspector in his discretion to make representations at a public inquiry has been found to have a sufficient interest to qualify as a 'person aggrieved'.[5] In some statutory contexts, a 'person aggrieved' must clearly be given a wider meaning than usual: if a right of appeal lies from decisions of a licensing body, an unsuccessful applicant must obviously be a person aggrieved and entitled to appeal although he has not been deprived of existing legal rights by the adverse decision.[6]

3 In some contexts statutory default powers, exercisable by Ministers to enforce compliance with public duties, particularly duties imposed on local authorities, may involve applications to the courts.[7]

Application for judicial review

The main non-statutory remedies in administrative law are the prerogative writ of habeas corpus, the prerogative orders of certiorari, prohibition and mandamus, the injunction, the declaration and damages. Actions for damages are touched on in the next chapter. The prerogative writ of habeas corpus remains subject to its own procedure. Until 1978 applications for the other remedies also had their own and diverse procedural rules. Combining proceedings for more than one form of relief and claiming damages in addition to the desired remedy was not always possible and was always fraught with technical hazard. Nor was the discovery of documents in the possession of a public authority available. Cross-examination of witnesses was not provided for, and if the aggrieved citizen sought compensation he was forced to institute a separate claim for damages by writ. Important reforms, introduced in 1978 and now embodied in section 31 of the Supreme Court Act 1981 and a revised Order 53 of the Supreme Court, provide at last for a common procedure for instituting claims for

---

3 *Ealing Corporation* v. *Jones* [1959] 1 QB 884; *Buxton* v. *Minister of Housing and Local Government* [1961] 1 QB 278.
4 *Maurice* v. *LCC* [1964] 2 QB 362 (and hence entitled to lodge an appeal). See also *Att.-Gen. of the Gambia* v. *N'jie* [1961] AC 617 at 634; *Arsenal Football Club* v. *Smith (Valuation Officer)* [1979] AC 1, at p. 17.
5 *Turner* v. *Secretary of State for the Environment* (1973) 72 LGR 380.
6 *Stepney BC* v. *Joffe* [1949] 1 KB 509.
7 For example, for an order of mandamus or a declaration against the defaulter. But such proceedings are rare. On the effect of default powers on the rights of *individuals* to go to court, see pp. 569–71.

relief against public authorities.[8] An application for mandamus, prohibition or certiorari, or for a declaration or injunction in relation to public law rights, is to be made by way of an application to the High Court for judicial review.[9] The rules provide for discovery to be ordered, for cross-examination to be permitted and most importantly for a claim for compensation to be annexed to the application for review. Where a claim for damages is joined with the application for judicial review the court may award damages if satisfied that a separate claim for damages would have succeeded had it been instituted.[10] The applicant still has to establish a common-law claim for damages. The Supreme Court Act introduces no new principle of compensation for unlawful administrative action. But the applicant is at least spared the expense of two distinct sets of proceedings. The procedure also provides for substantial safeguards for the administration. Leave of the High Court must be sought before the application can proceed. The applicant must show a sufficient interest in the matter to which the application relates.[11] And he must act with speed. The Act provides that where the court considers that there has been undue delay in making an application, it may refuse to grant leave for the making of the application, or any relief sought under the application, if it considers that the granting of the relief sought would be likely to cause substantial hardship to, or substantially prejudice the rights of, any person, or if to do so would be detrimental to good administration.[12] Order 53 provides that applications have to be made promptly and in any event within *three* months from the date when the grounds for the application first arose, unless the court considers that there is a good reason for extending that period.

Finally, the award of any of the remedies to be discussed below is discretionary and the applicant must show that he has a moral as well as a legal case to be granted relief.

The reformed procedure has led to a profound change of direction in administrative law in England. The House of Lords has interpreted the

---

8 See generally R. J. F. Gordon, *Judicial Review: Law and Procedure* (2nd edn, 1996); G. Aldous and J. Alder, *Applications for Judicial Review: Law and Practice* (1985). See also Law Commission, *Remedies in Administrative Law* (Law Com. No. 73 (1976)), *Administrative Law: Judicial Review and Statutory Appeals* (Law Com. Consultation Paper No. 126 (1993)). If the body complained of is not a public body then judicial review will not lie: see, e.g., R. v. *Disciplinary Committee of the Jockey Club, ex P. Aga Khan* [1993] 2 All ER 853.
9 Supreme Court Act 1981, s. 31(1), (2).
10 ibid., s. 31(4).
11 ibid., s. 31(3). See *Equal Opportunities Commission* v. *Secretary of State for Employment* [1994] 1 All ER 910.
12 Supreme Court Act 1981, s. 31(6).

provisions of Order 53 and of the Act as meaning that a claim which relates solely to public law rights may be pursued only by way of an application for judicial review: the general power to apply to the courts for a declaration or injunction by way of ordinary proceedings instituted by a writ is no longer available in public law claims. In *O'Reilly* v. *Mackman*[13] some prisoners alleged that they had lost remission after a disciplinary hearing which had failed to comply with the rules of natural justice. They started a claim for a declaration by way of service of writ. Proceeding by writ had two major advantages for them. First, they would not be subject to a three-month time limit, but rather the usual six-year limitation period; and secondly they would not need leave to start their action. The House of Lords struck out the action as an abuse of the process of the court. Lord Diplock said that, *as a general rule*, where a claim related to the infringement of rights protected exclusively by public law, then that claim must be brought by way of an application for judicial review. Lord Diplock said that the disadvantages to the claimant which encumbered the pre-1978 procedure for application for the prerogative orders had been swept away by the reforms of 1978 and 1981. The safeguards for good administration, particularly in relation to the need for leave, the short time limit and the discretionary nature of the availability of remedies embodied in the new procedures were not to be circumvented by claimants bringing their actions via a different route. The House of Lords has held that, in deciding whether an action is properly brought by way of private law, the overriding question is whether the proceedings constitute an abuse of the process of the court, and stressed the importance of retaining some flexibility between the two systems.[14]

But what are rights protected exclusively by public law? In *O'Reilly* v. *Mackman* the claimants' rights depended entirely on the principles related to fair hearings developed in the public law domain: it was most unlikely that those rights could be asserted through actions in contract or tort. In *Cocks* v. *Thanet D C*[15] the plaintiff brought an action for breach of statutory duty in relation to the defendant council's failure to house him as a homeless person. His action, too, was struck out. His private law remedy for breach of statutory rights would succeed only if he could successfully challenge the refusal of the council to house him as being *ultra vires*. His claim related essentially to his right to require a discretionary decision of a public authority

---

13 [1983] 2 AC 237; and see [1983] *Public Law* 190; Cane [1992] *Public Law* 193.
14 *Mercury Communications Ltd* v. *Director-General of Telecommunications* [1996] 1 All E R 575.
15 [1983] 2 AC 286.

to be taken lawfully according to the principles developed, once again, in the public law domain. The claim for damages was subsidiary. But once the claimant is asserting essentially private rights, arising from the general law of, say, tort or contract, the fact that a public authority is the defendant will not force the claimant to rely on an application for judicial review. So in *Davy* v. *Spelthorne DC*[16] the plaintiff sued the defendant council for negligence. He alleged that he had suffered loss because he had relied on misleading advice from the council's planning officers in not appealing against an enforcement order in respect of the use of his premises. He did not challenge the validity of the order. The House of Lords refused to strike out his claim. They held that he did not seek to impugn any decision of the council. None of the traditional public law remedies would help him. His claim purely and simply related to the alleged negligence of the officers for whom the council was vicariously liable, and was founded in the general law of negligence. Lord Wilberforce in a forceful judgment made two points. First, a claimant could not be required to proceed by application for judicial review where none of the prerogative orders was appropriate to enforce his rights. Secondly, he stressed that, even where a public law remedy was available to the claimant, Lord Diplock in *O'Reilly* v. *Mackman* had expressed a general rule to prevent plaintiffs improperly and flagrantly evading the safeguards for good administration embodied in the procedure for judicial review. Exceptions are available to the general rule. Where issues of private rights arise and when the procedure for judicial review would cause serious procedural obstacles to the claimant, exceptions will be made.[17] In *Roy* v. *Kensington and Chelsea Family Practitioner Committee*[18] Lord Lowry noted that Order 53 was not primarily designed for use by applicants who sought a monetary remedy, and he stressed that the courts have a discretion to refuse to entertain an application.

Mandamus

Mandamus, to compel the performance of a public duty, was evolved by the King's Bench early in the seventeenth century to restore persons to public offices of which they had been unlawfully deprived.[19] For the next

---

16 [1984] AC 262; see Cane [1984] *Public Law* 16, and *Wandsworth LBC* v. *Winder* [1985] AC 461; *An Bord Bainne Co-operative Ltd (Irish Dairy Board)* v. *Milk Marketing Board, The Times,* 22 May 1984, CA.

17 See *Wandsworth LBC* v. *Winder* [1985] AC 461.

18 [1992] 2 WLR 239.

19 The leading case is *Bagg's* case (1615) 11 Co. Rep. 93b.

two hundred years or more it enjoyed vast popularity as a means of prodding inert and inept officials, magistrates and borough corporations into fulfilment of their public obligations. A synopsis of the case law, published in 1848, ran to 252 pages. But its importance was already dwindling as local government was reformed; and it shrivelled as new statutory remedies by way of appeal, complaint or objection to Government Departments, tribunals or courts, were introduced. For mandamus was always an 'extraordinary' remedy, awarded only if no alternative remedy was equally convenient or effective.

However, it will still lie in quite a wide range of situations. It may be issued to compel a tribunal or Minister or a local authority to entertain an appeal or application in respect of which they have wrongfully declined jurisdiction. It will lie to compel a body to carry out a duty to give reasons for a decision or to give adequate reasons; and to require a local authority to produce minutes and accounts for inspection. If an authority required to exercise a discretion in a matter fails to consider it on its merits because it has improperly sub-delegated its powers or acted under dictation or fettered its own discretion by unauthorized promises or a rigid self-imposed rule, mandamus will lie. It will also lie to order an authority which has abused its statutory discretion (for example, by rejecting an application on the basis of legally irrelevant considerations) to hear and determine the matter according to law: see *Padfield*'s case.[20] Although on an application for mandamus, the courts are not supposed to direct the competent authority *how* to exercise its jurisdiction or discretion (for example, to issue a licence to X), they may in effect achieve this result by holding that only one avenue of approach to a particular case is legally permissible.[21]

Mandamus will not lie against the Crown, nor will it lie to a Crown servant to order the performance of a duty owed *only* to the Crown; but it will lie to a Minister to carry out a duty in the performance of which a member of the public has a substantial personal interest.

There are important limitations on its availability. It cannot be obtained (except in some instances on the application of a Minister) to compel a local authority to provide a public service. The courts might refuse to issue such an order on a number of different grounds – that enforcement could

20 *Padfield* v. *Minister of Agriculture* [1968] AC 997; see above p. 546.
21 See *R* v. *Derby JJ, ex p. Kooner* [1971] 1 QB 147 (where 'may' was treated as meaning 'must'). See also *R* v. *Home Secretary, ex p. Phansopkar* [1976] QB 606 (effect of court's order was to force the Home Office to reconsider procedure concerning the admission to the United Kingdom of wives of patrials).

not be adequately supervised; that the matter is non-justiciable because judicial review has been expressly excluded or because the duty is merely descriptive of a general administrative function; that there are adequate alternative remedies.

Who may apply for mandamus? In other words, who has *locus standi*? Section 31(3) of the Supreme Court Act 1981 enacts that the court shall not grant leave to make an application for judicial review unless it considers that the applicant has a sufficient interest in the matter to which the application relates. *Locus standi* to apply for mandamus has been equated with *locus standi* to apply for certiorari and prohibition in *R v. IRC, ex p. National Federation of Self-Employed and Small Businesses Ltd.*[22] The Revenue reached an agreement with casual workers on Fleet Street that they would be granted an amnesty in respect of past tax avoidance in return for agreement to arrangements to ensure that tax could be properly collected from them in the future. The National Federation of the Self-Employed objected to such preferential treatment and in an application for judicial review sought a declaration that the Revenue had acted unlawfully and mandamus to compel the Revenue to do their duty according to law and collect the tax owing. The Court of Appeal (Lawton LJ dissenting) held that as taxpayers the Federation had a genuine grievance in the unfairness to them caused by the Revenue allowing other taxpayers to be free of part of the normal burden of taxation. The House of Lords held that no taxpayer or group of taxpayers had *locus standi* to ask the court to investigate the affairs of other taxpayers or to complain that other taxpayers had been over- or under-assessed. The existence of sufficient interest to apply for mandamus depended on evidence of an alleged breach of duty or illegality which when related to the position of the claimant made it clear that he had an *individual* interest to pursue and protect. This test is wider than that laid down in some earlier cases that the applicant must have a specific legal right to the performance of the duty. It may be assumed that all earlier cases accepting *locus standi* remain authoritative, but some denying it may have to be reconsidered in the light of the House of Lords' decision. The House of Lords agreed that on all applications for judicial review standing and merits may have to be considered together. Under the Supreme Court Act, the court will ordinarily hear applications for leave *ex parte*. The applicant may make a *prima facie* case for leave. At the later hearing the court will consider the whole legal and factual context, including the nature

22 [1982] AC 617.

of the duty and the breach in order to decide whether the applicant has a sufficient interest in the matter.

The applicant for mandamus must have demanded performance and been met by a wrongful refusal, communicated directly or by conduct evincing an intention not to comply or a failure to understand what compliance means.

There are several discretionary bars to the award of the order. Alternative remedies, unreasonable delay in making an application, the absence of any useful purpose in issuing a judicial command, and the unacceptable motives of the applicant are among the most common. For example, the Commissioners of Customs and Excise had allowed bookmakers to pay a new and heavy licensing duty on betting premises by monthly instalments. But the Finance Act 1969 had provided that the tax was to be paid in one sum or by two half-yearly instalments. There was no statutory authority for the concession made by the Commissioners acting under the responsible Minister's instructions. Two bookmakers who had paid their duties in accordance with the Act applied for mandamus to compel the Commissioners to administer the Act according to law. The court dismissed the application.[23] Even assuming that the applicants had *prima facie* a sufficient legal interest to maintain the proceedings, their ulterior purpose was to put less affluent competitors out of business, and this was not a purpose for which mandamus should be granted for non-compliance with this statutory obligation.

Certiorari and prohibition

Certiorari will issue to quash, and prohibition to prevent, an order or decision on any of the following grounds.

1 Excess or want of jurisdiction. If part of an impugned order is quite distinct and severable from the rest of the order, the invalid part may be quashed, leaving the remainder intact.
2 Breach of the rules of natural justice or of the duty to act fairly.
3 Error of law on the face of the record.
4 Fraud, perjury or duress in procuring a decision.

Certiorari has become less important in administrative law because of the extension of alternative remedies. But within its own field it has been fortified by the revival of the concept of review for error of law on the

---

23 R. v. *Customs and Excise Commissioners, ex p. Cook* [1970] 1 WLR 450.

face of the record, by the statutory enlargement of the 'record', by the extension of duties to give reasons for decisions and by the nullification of statutory formulae purporting to exclude judicial review.

In the *Electricity Commissioners* case Atkin LJ said[24] that certiorari and prohibition may issue to 'any body of persons having legal authority to determine questions affecting the rights of subjects, and having the duty to act judicially . . .'

A 'body of persons' included one person – for example, a Minister. 'Legal authority' was generally understood to mean authority derived from statute or royal charter. In 1967, however, it was held[25] that certiorari would lie to a judicial-type body (the Criminal Injuries Compensation Board) fulfilling public functions but created by purely administrative action. (The Board is financed out of moneys provided by Parliament, and was placed on a statutory footing in 1988.) Decisions by a *private* non-statutory tribunal (for example, the committee of a club or trade union) are challengeable not by certiorari but by injunctions and declarations.[26]

The courts in the past sometimes refused to award certiorari and prohibition against bodies with no power to make a final decision; such bodies are not 'determining questions'.[27] And a narrow view of questions 'affecting rights' was taken. A licence was not a right even though its revocation resulted in a man losing his livelihood.[28] The qualification that the body must be under a duty to 'act judicially' was used to exclude decisions characterized as administrative in nature.[29] The modern approach is to examine the decision-making process and determine whether the body deciding any question, even a preliminary matter,[30] which affects the rights, legitimate interests or expectations of citizens is required to act fairly in their dealings with affected persons.[31] If they are so required and fail to meet the requisite standard of fairness which their kind of decision-making of its nature demands, then certiorari will issue to quash their decision.

---

24 *R.* v. *Electricity Commissioners* [1924] 1 KB 171 at 204–5.
25 *R.* v. *Criminal Injuries Compensation Board, ex p. Lain* [1967] 2 QB 864.
26 See, e.g. *R.* v. *City Takeover Panel, ex p. Datafin plc* [1987] 2 WLR 699.
27 *Jayawardne* v. *Silva* [1970] 1 WLR 1365.
28 *Nakkuda Ali* v. *Jayaratne* [1951] AC 66 at p. 78.
29 *R.* v. *Metropolitan Police Commissioner, ex p. Parker* [1953] 1 WLR 1150.
30 See *R.* v. *Kent Police Authority, ex p. Godden* [1971] 2 QB 662.
31 *R.* v. *Hull Prison Board of Visitors, ex p. St Germain* [1979] QB 425; *O'Reilly* v. *Mackman* [1983] 2 AC 237, HL; *Att.-Gen. of Hong Kong* v. *Ng Yuen Shiu* [1983] 2 AC 629 (PC); *R.* v. *Greater Manchester Coroner, ex p. Tal* [1985] QB 67.

The duty to act fairly as much as the rules of natural justice is now enforced by the orders of certiorari and prohibition.[32]

The requirement to 'act judicially' is no longer a prerequisite to control of an authority by certiorari. In *Ridge* v. *Baldwin*[33] Lord Reid found that the inclusion of a duty to 'act judicially' in the conditions precedent for the award of the order of certiorari was itself devoid of authority. Excess of jurisdiction, error of law on the face of the record or improper procuration of a decision may form grounds for an order of certiorari against any public authority determining questions affecting the rights of subjects. Certiorari lay to quash a decision of a local authority attaching *ultra vires* conditions to a grant of planning permission.[34] In that case Lord Widgery CJ went so far as to say that he saw 'no general legal inhibition on the use of such orders, although no doubt they must be exercised only in the clearest cases and with a good deal of care on the part of the court'.[35] Whether public policy will be served by making an order of certiorari to control the proceedings of a particular authority is expressly considered by judges dealing with applications for certiorari.[36] It is to be hoped that if a case arises when certiorari should *not* issue on the grounds that it is inappropriate to extend judicial intervention into the relevant part of the administrative process, this will be openly admitted and the subterfuge of retreating to a narrow interpretation of the governing dictum of Atkin LJ in the *Electricity Commissioners* case be avoided.

The courts, before application for judicial review was introduced, took a liberal view of *locus standi* in relation to certiorari. Any person with a substantial personal interest to vindicate, and members of a local community who have a special grievance by virtue of their membership of that community, had a sufficient interest to challenge a decision affecting them by way of certiorari. In *R.* v. *GLC, ex p. Blackburn*[37] the Court of Appeal held that Mr and Mrs Blackburn had a sufficient interest as citizens of London and ratepayers to apply for prohibition to prevent the exhibition of allegedly pornographic films. Lord Denning MR seemed to abandon any precise definition of *locus standi* in favour of the principle that any person offended or injured by a decision on the part of a public authority should have

32 *R.* v. *Birmingham City Justice* [1970] 1 WLR 1428; *R.* v. *Liverpool Corporation, ex p. Liverpool Taxi Fleet Operators' Association* [1972] 2 QB 299.
33 [1964] AC 40, at pp. 71–9.
34 *R.* v. *Hillingdon LBC, ex p. Royco Homes Ltd* [1974] QB 720, at p. 728.
35 ibid., at p. 728.
36 *R.* v. *Hull Prison Board of Visitors* (note 31, above).
37 [1976] 1 WLR 550.

access to the courts who 'in their discretion can grant whatever remedy is appropriate'. With the enactment of the Supreme Court Act 1981, standing for certiorari is affected only to the extent mentioned when considering *locus standi* for mandamus.[38]

The principles governing the discretion of the court to award certiorari have partly crystallized. The courts exercise discretion in practice when deciding whether the applicant had *locus standi*. An application may be refused for waiver of or acquiescence in an excess of jurisdiction or a breach of natural justice; or (exceptionally) because there is a more appropriate alternative remedy; or because the applicant had delayed unreasonably before instituting the proceedings, the normal time limit being three months. The Aston University students who had been denied natural justice lost their case on the ground of delay.[39] Certiorari may also be refused because to award it would serve no useful purpose, or because of the applicant's unreasonable behaviour.[40]

Prohibition does not call for special discussion. In administrative law it will lie to the same bodies as certiorari, and on similar grounds,[41] though a case for prohibition for error of law on the face of the record could hardly ever arise because by the time the error had become apparent the order would nearly always be final. Occasionally certiorari and prohibition may be awarded in conjunction – certiorari to quash a decision already taken by a tribunal and prohibition to prevent the tribunal from proceeding or continuing to entertain other like cases outside its jurisdiction.[42]

Injunction

Injunctions may be prohibitory (to restrain the commission or continuance of unlawful conduct) or mandatory (to compel the performance of a duty). Mandatory injunctions are granted sparingly; and in administrative law they are of little practical importance.[43] An interim or interlocutory

---

38 See p. 561, above.

39 *R.* v. *Aston University Senate, ex p. Roffey* [1969] 2 QB 538. And see *R.* v. *Herrod, ex p. Leeds City Council* [1976] QB 540.

40 *Glynn* v. *University of Keele* [1971] 1 WLR 223.

41 See especially the *Godden* case, note 30; *R.* v. *Board of Visitors of Dartmoor Prison, ex p. Smith* [1987] QB 106 (appeal dismissed).

42 *R.* v. *Paddington & St Marylebone Rent Tribunal* [1949] 1 KB 666.

43 See, for example, *Att.-Gen.* v. *Colchester Corporation* [1955] 2 QB 207 (no mandatory injunction to compel continued operation of ferry service); and see generally *Glossop* v. *Heston and Isleworth Local Board* (1879) 12 Ch. D. 102. See, however, *Ghani* v. *Jones* [1970] 1 QB 693 (mandatory order to police to return wrongfully detained Pakistani passports).

injunction may be awarded as a matter of urgency *ex parte* (on the strength of the plaintiff's representation alone) to restrain the commission or repetition of an allegedly wrongful act which is liable to do very serious harm, pending a full hearing of the case.

The injunction is essentially a discretionary private law remedy, awarded where damages would not be a sufficient form of redress. It is also obtainable against public authorities and of officials, including now the Crown and Crown servants acting in that behalf,[44] not only for actionable wrongs (such as trespasses or nuisances) but also to restrain acts which are *ultra vires* but give no right of action for damages. Who may sue? Local authorities are entitled to take proceedings on behalf of the local community.[45] A private individual can sue to restrain 'a public wrong' if his own legal rights have been encroached upon, or are threatened by the defendant, and perhaps in exceptional circumstances when the individual is threatened with special damage over and above that which the 'wrong' inflicts on the rest of the public.[46] In all other cases only the Attorney-General acting in his sole discretion can institute proceedings to vindicate public rights. The citizen aggrieved by a public wrong must seek the Attorney-General's consent, obtain his *fiat*, to the proceedings which are then conducted in the Attorney-General's name. These actions are known as 'relator' actions and effectively the citizen, the 'relator', is in control of the proceedings, for having given his consent the Attorney-General takes little active part in the proceedings. Nevertheless if he refuses to consent to a 'relator' action the citizen cannot proceed. In *Gouriet* v. *Union of Post Office Workers*[47] Mr Gouriet had sought the Attorney-General's consent to proceedings for an injunction to restrain the Union of Post Office Workers from breaking the law by blacking mail from this country to South Africa. The Attorney-General refused. Mr Gouriet went to court asserting that the Attorney-General had acted unlawfully in refusing his consent and/or he was entitled to proceed for an injunction in his own right. There was never any suggestion that Mr Gouriet had any special interest in the free passage of mail or would suffer any special damage by the blacking. The House of Lords rejected his application. Their decision established that (1) the courts would not question the discretionary decision of the Attorney-General whether or not to consent to a 'relator' action, and (2) in no circumstances could a citizen

---

44 See the *Factortame* case (above, p. 85, n. 77).
45 Local Government Act 1972, s. 222, and see *Solihull MBC* v. *Maxfern Ltd* [1977] 1 WLR 127; *Stoke-on-Trent City Council* v. *B & Q Ltd* [1984] AC 754.
46 *Boyce* v. *Paddington Corporation* [1903] 1 Ch. 109.
47 [1978] AC 435.

whose sole standing in the matter was his concern as a m
public that a breach of the criminal law was threatened pro
action for an injunction except by way of a 'relator' action.

The Attorney-General himself may sue for an injunction
repeated breaches of regulatory legislation where the sanction
criminal law have proved inadequate.[48] He has also been awarded inju...ions
against individuals breaking or proposing to break the criminal law where
the matter is very urgent, notwithstanding that the criminal courts have
not yet dealt with the issue.[49] The House of Lords in *Gouriet* said that this
was a power which should be exercised only in exceptional cases and for
this reason was entrusted to the Attorney-General, who was obliged to
consider the public interest as a whole, and would not be afforded to
individuals who might have genuine grievance at the prospect of criminal
behaviour by others but be unable to judge what action would best serve
the national interest. *Gouriet* was decided before application for judicial
review was introduced. The effect of the Supreme Court Act 1981 will be
examined in the next section on the declaration.

Declaration[50]

The declaratory judgment is basically a twentieth-century judicial remedy
and has come to be used for a great variety of purposes in public and
private law.[51] Declarations can be awarded in almost every situation where
an injunction will lie – the most important exception is that interim relief
cannot be granted by way of a declaration – and they extend to a number of
situations where an injunction would be inappropriate (for example, because
there is nothing to prohibit) or could not be obtained for other reasons.

Where civil proceedings in private law for a declaration (or an injunction)
are appropriately brought without the need to apply for judicial review
under the Supreme Court Act 1981,[52] the pre-Act rules about *locus standi*
continue to apply. Infringement of a private right or special damage flowing
from the infringement of a public right has to be proved.[53] Those rules are

48 *Att.-Gen.* v. *Harris* [1961] 1 QB 74 (Manchester flower-seller repeatedly breaking local Act but preferring to pay fines rather than desisting).
49 *Att.-Gen.* v. *Chaudry* [1971] 1 WLR 1614 (breach of fire safety law).
50 See de Smith, op. cit., ch. 10.
51 See I. Zamir, *The Declaratory Judgment* (1962).
52 See p. 557, above.
53 *Gouriet* v. *Union of Post Office Workers* [1978] AC 435; *Barrs* v. *Bethell* [1982] 1 All ER 186.

of greatly reduced importance in administrative law now that application for judicial review is normally required in public law, even where an injunction or declaration is sought.[54] In the *IRC* case the House of Lords interpreted the *Gouriet* case as one solely in private law, so that it was not binding in the *IRC* case, where an application for judicial review was required. In effect the *IRC* case must be taken as deciding that on an application for judicial review, if the applicant proves sufficient interest to seek a prerogative order then an injunction or declaration may be granted even though the common-law requirements about standing for an injunction or declaration would not have been met.

The declaration is also a discretionary remedy; thus, the courts may refuse a declaration if its award would serve no useful purpose or if there are more appropriate alternative remedies.[55] Subject to those cautionary reservations, there are few limits to the potential scope of declaratory relief in public law. For example, declarations can be obtained that administrative orders or notices directly affecting the plaintiff are invalid;[56] that conditions annexed to a grant of planning permission are invalid;[57] that one's products are exempt from tax;[58] that one enjoying a special statutory or public[59] status has been invalidly dismissed[60] or suspended[61] (though the courts will be very reluctant to make a declaration entitling an ordinary employee to reinstatement);[62] and that the decision of a tribunal is invalid for excess of jurisdiction[63] or breach of natural justice[64] or (possibly) that it is wrong in law, provided at least that the error is patent and the tribunal has power to

---

54 See p. 558, above.

55 See *Maxwell* v. *Department of Trade and Industry* [1974] QB 523.

56 *Dyson* v. *Att.-Gen.* [1911] 1 KB 410 (court had jurisdiction to declare that a tax form requiring submission of certain particulars under threat of a penalty was *ultra vires*). This was the effective starting-point for the rise of the declaratory judgment in administrative law. *Gillick* v. *West Norfolk and Wisbech AHA* [1986] AC 112 (departmental circular based on incorrect interpretation of the law).

57 *Hall & Co.* v. *Shoreham-by-Sea UDC* [1964] 1 WLR 240.

58 *Sebel Products Ltd* v. *Customs and Excise Commissioners* [1949] Ch. 409.

59 *Ridge* v. *Baldwin* [1964] AC 40 (chief constable); *Malloch* v. *Aberdeen Corporation* [1971] 1 WLR 1578.

60 *Vine* v. *National Dock Labour Board* [1957] AC 488 (dock labourer); *Hanson* v. *Radcliffe UDC* [1922] 2 Ch. 490 (schoolteacher).

61 *Barnard* v. *National Dock Labour Board* [1953] 2 QB 18.

62 See, for example, *Pillai* v. *Singapore City Council* [1968] 1 WLR 1278. For an exceptional case, see *Hill* v. *Parsons* (*C. A.*) *& Co.* [1972] Ch. 305.

63 For example, *Anisminic Ltd* v. *Foreign Compensation Commission* [1969] 2 AC 147.

64 For example, *Cooper* v. *Wilson* [1937] 2 KB 309. Many decisions of non-statutory domestic tribunals have been declared invalid on this ground.

rescind its determination.[65] A bare declaration that natural justice had not been observed where no other relief is asked for, and no decision exists to be quashed, will be granted only in the most exceptional circumstances.[66] The declaration does not, however, have to be accompanied by a claim for consequential relief (for example damages), nor is it necessary that such relief be claimable at all. Indeed, it does not have to be a declaration of invalidity. A person may obtain a declaration as to his nationality or marital status. Declarations may be sought by one public authority to resolve a legal dispute with another (for example, as to financial obligations), or by a public authority wishing to obtain a judicial pronouncement as to the scope of its own powers or duties before it acts in relation to a specific matter.[67] And a declaration may be awarded as to the true construction of a statute or other legal document which is the subject of a controversy between parties.

Declarations granted by the courts may be formulated in a number of different ways to meet the particular circumstances of a case. This is yet another characteristic of the flexibility of declaratory judgments. Where a declaration is sought that a tribunal has as a result of an error of law made a perverse determination of the question entrusted to its jurisdiction, the court has a discretionary power to do more than quash the determination as a nullity: it may issue a positive declaration of the applicant's rights. This power is only to be exercised in the clearest of cases as the courts are wary of cutting down the jurisdiction of inferior tribunals.[68]

Effect of alternative remedies

Reference has been made to the exclusion of judicial remedies in the High Court by special statutory formulae or the provision of alternative remedies. The latter type of exclusion is still important. Despite the presumption against excluding the right of access to the courts for the determination of civil rights and obligations, there is a well-known principle that the *original*

---

65 This is a difficult question, still unresolved. See especially *Healey* v. *Minister of Health* [1955] 1 QB 221. The main difficulty lies in the principle that an erroneous determination *within* jurisdiction is *not* invalid but binding till properly set aside. See also *Punton* v. *Ministry of Pensions and National Insurance (No. 2)* [1964] 1 WLR 226.

66 See *Maxwell's* case (note 55, above).

67 See, for example, *Central Electricity Generating Board* v. *Jennaway* [1959] 1 WLR 937, where the Board obtained a ruling on the question whether it had power (disputed by the landowner) to erect lines over private property. See also *CEGB* v. *Dunning* [1970] Ch. 643.

68 *Barty-King* v. *Ministry of Defence* [1979] 2 All ER 80.

jurisdiction of the superior courts is ousted where a statute creates a *new* legal right or obligation and *that same Act* prescribes a specific method for it enforcement.[69] The method of enforcement may be by taking proceedings in an inferior court or tribunal[70] or by complaint or appeal to an administrative authority or by the potential exercise of administrative default powers.[71] Particularly in declaratory proceedings or on applications for mandamus, persons attempting to obtain judicial declarations of their rights or the enforcement of public duties have often found the courts refusing to entertain their claims for these reasons. But if it is possible to hold that the alternative remedy is only optional – for example, because *pre-existing* legal rights are in issue[72] or because the prescribed remedy is inadequate or less convenient[73] or if there is inordinate delay in the domestic disciplinary process[74] or if the interests of justice call for intervention by the High Court[75] – the result may be different. Moreover, even if the courts hold that their *original* jurisdiction to determine the issue in the first instance has been excluded, they can still exercise a *supervisory* jurisdiction after the appointed body or tribunal has acted, so as to see that the law has been duly observed. In exercising that supervisory jurisdiction the court will sometimes go on to declare what the correct decision is or should have been.[76] The courts will intervene in appropriate cases to quash decisions taken *ultra vires* by the original authority even though an alternative remedy exists to correct mistaken decisions taken within the limits of that authority's powers. Certiorari, for example, lay to quash a decision of a planning authority to grant planning permission subject to invalid conditions despite the statutory

---

69 *Barraclough* v. *Brown* [1897] AC 615.

70 For example, an income tax tribunal (*Inland Revenue Commissioners* v. *Pearlberg* [1953] 1 WLR 331), or an industrial tribunal (*Road Transport Industry Board* v. *Wyatt (Haulage) Ltd* [1972] 3 All ER 913). See also *Department of Health and Social Security* v. *Walker Dean Walker Ltd* [1970] 2 QB 74.

71 For example, complaints about alleged breaches of duty by education authorities: *Cumings* v. *Birkenhead Corporation* [1972] Ch. 12.

72 *Pyx Granite Co.* v. *Ministry of Housing and Local Government* [1960] AC 260 (property rights affected by planning legislation).

73 *Ealing LBC* v. *Race Relations Board* [1972] AC 342 (council could test legality of its housing policies in High Court instead of waiting to be sued by Race Relations Board in county court).

74 *R.* v. *Chief Constable of Merseyside Police, ex p. Calveley* [1986] QB 424.

75 *Enderby Town FC Ltd* v. *Football Association Ltd* [1971] Ch. 591 (dicta) (High Court could give ruling on difficult and important point of law).

76 *Cooper* v. *Wilson* [1937] 2 KB 309 and the *Anisminic* case [1969] 2 AC 147 (declarations as to plaintiff's rights consequential on declaration that decision of tribunal was void); *Barty-King* v. *Ministry of Defence* (above). And see *R.* v. *Sheffield CC* (1978) 77 LGR 26; *Meade* v. *Haringey LBC* [1979] 1 WLR 637.

system of appeals in the Town end Country Planning Act 1971.[77] On the other hand the existence of a comprehensive appeals system provided by statute has led the courts to declare that judicial review should not be available to immigrants[78] or to applicants for social security[79] who had exhausted their statutory rights of appeal. The existence of such rights will, therefore usually preclude judicial review.[80] And the House of Lords has said that leave to apply for judicial review should be granted only sparingly when Parliament has intended that a public body be the judge of matters of fact, for to do otherwise could lead to the courts' usurpation of that function. So, in *R. v. Secretary of State for the Environment, ex p. Puhlhofer*[81] the applicants were denied leave as the local authority had properly decided that the applicants were not homeless. (The sympathy expressed by the courts for would-be immigrants, seekers after social security and of homes does not detract from the fact that it is precisely such groups who need the greatest measure of protection which the courts can allow.)

77 *R. v. Hillingdon LBC* [1974] QB 720.
78 *R. v. Secretary of State for the Home Department, ex p. Swati* [1986] 1 WLR 477.
79 *R. v. Secretary of State for Social Services, ex p. Connolly* [1986] 1 WLR 421.
80 *R. v. Inland Revenue Commissioners, ex p. Preston* [1985] AC 835.
81 [1986] AC 484.

CHAPTER 28

Tribunals and Inquiries

IN GENERAL[1]

In 1957 the Report of the Franks Committee on Administrative Tribunals and Enquiries went a long way to remove certain misconceptions contained in the Report of the Committee on Ministers' Powers which had been published twenty-five years earlier.[2] By 1957 statutory tribunals appointed by Ministers had proliferated. The Committee like its predecessor did indeed prefer to see judicial functions vested in the courts rather than special tribunals, and in special tribunals rather than in Ministers. However, it did not label special tribunals as 'Ministerial tribunals'. It insisted that tribunals were not 'appendages of Government Departments'. It considered that tribunals 'should properly be regarded as machinery provided by Parliament for adjudication rather than as part of the machinery of administration',[3] and it made detailed proposals designed to integrate them more closely with the general judicial system of the country. It drew a sharp distinction between 'administrative' adjudication, on the one hand, and discretionary decisions reached by Ministers following a local inquiry, on the other. Its proposals for reforming procedures involving inquiries in matters affecting the regulation of land use were radical but far better informed and more realistic than those of the 1932 Committee. Its detailed recommendations

---

1 The best general review is R. M. Jackson's *Machinery of Justice in England* (8th edn, 1989 by J. R. Spencer), ch. 6. The Report of the Committee on Administrative Tribunals and Enquiries (the Franks Committee (Cmnd 218 (1957)), is prescribed reading. The published Minutes of Evidence of the Committee also contain a wealth of information. See also the Tribunals and Inquiries Act 1992 and any of the Annual Reports of the Council on Tribunals (HMSO). See further R. E. Wraith and P. G. Hutchesson, *Administrative Tribunals* (1973); G. Ganz, *Administrative Procedures* (1974), ch. 4; J. A. Farmer, *Tribunals and Government* (1974); J. Bowers (ed.), *Tribunals: Practice and Procedure* (1985).
2 Cmd 4060 (1932).
3 Cmnd 218 (1957), § 40.

were too persuasive to be ignored, and most of them have been implemented. Today no reasonably well-read student has any excuse for confusing tribunals with inquiries. Whitehall's terrible twins are neither terrible nor twins.

The Franks Committee itself was an outstanding example of a particular type of public inquiry. Its members were appointed by the Lord Chancellor, not under statutory authority but in virtue of the prerogative. They were judges, former high-ranking civil servants, practising lawyers, leading academics, trade unionists, elder statesmen, active politicians. It was directed to inquire into and make recommendations on matters raising broad issues of public policy. It sat in public to receive oral evidence from officials and others; it obtained a number of written memoranda; it accumulated and published a mass of factual information, much of which had not previously been divulged to the public; it was a new clearing-house for informed opinion and original ideas. Its reports stimulated public debate and refertilized official thinking. In substance it fulfilled the role of a Royal Commission (the members of which are appointed by Her Majesty on the Prime Minister's advice) and unlike so many Royal Commissions, its recommendations were not disregarded.[4]

Public inquiries are basically instruments of government[5] (using the term 'government' in the broadest sense) or Parliament. As instruments of Parliament, or a House of Parliament, their role may be to investigate an alleged public scandal, or a national disaster such as the Aberfan catastrophe. Upon a resolution of both Houses, a 'tribunal' headed by a superior judge may be appointed under the Tribunals of Inquiry (Evidence) Act 1921.[6] The practice of setting up a select committee of the House of Commons to inquire into such a matter fell into disuse after the partisan report and debate on the Marconi scandal in 1913. There are other alternatives.

4 The appointment of a Royal Commission is sometimes prompted by a Government's desire to avoid making a decision on an awkward question. The matter can be shelved till the Commission has reported; the Government may then spend several months formulating its own reactions to the recommendations, and may find itself supplied with new reasons why nothing of importance should or could be done. See T. J. Cartwright, *Royal Commissions and Departmental Committees in Britain* (1975).

5 See R. E. Wraith and G. B. Lamb, *Public Inquiries as an Instrument of Government* (1971) – the fullest study of the subject.

6 cf. G. W. Keeton, *Trial by Tribunal* (1960); and the report of the Royal Commission on Tribunals of Inquiry, Cmnd 3121 (1966) suggesting procedural reforms, which the Government accepted: Cmnd 5313 (1973). So far no such reforms have been enacted. For the controversial Vehicle and General Inquiry (Report, HC 133 (1971–2)) see p. 195. These tribunals (unlike most of the other types of inquisitorial bodies) have powers to subpoena witnesses and to require the production of documents.

Covert official telephone tapping, security leaks, 'D' notices, interrogation techniques in Northern Ireland, the use made by former Ministers of 'confidential' information for their memoirs and the lessons to be drawn from the Falklands conflict have all led to the appointment by the Prime Minister of *ad hoc* committees of Privy Counsellors to inquire and report; the outcome has sometimes been embarrassing to the Government. Lord Denning investigated aspects of the Profumo affair.[7] Major security leaks are now referred to a Security Commission under a superior judge. Another non-statutory technique, commonly employed, is for Ministers to appoint a departmental or interdepartmental committee of inquiry into a particular issue – for example, section 2 of the Official Secrets Act 1911,[8] and the fertilization of human embryos.[9] Again, a Minister may appoint a committee or an independent person to inquire into serious complaints about the conduct of officials. The Crichel Down inquiry, conducted by a QC, was such a case.[10] The publication of the Report led to the censure and transfer of some officials, to the resignation of the Minister of Agriculture on his own initiative, and indirectly to the appointment of the Franks Committee (from whose terms of reference the Crichel Down type of situation was, nevertheless, excluded).

Other types of formal inquiry may be held under statutory authority to investigate allegations of suspicions of malpractice or culpable negligence or organizational deficiencies – for example, an inquiry by Department of Trade and Industry inspectors into the affairs of a company; or an inquiry into the causes of an aircraft, shipping, railway or mine disaster or a factory accident; or a military 'court of inquiry' into an untoward incident that requires special investigation; or an inquiry into complaints against police officers.

7 For his report, see Cmnd 2152 (1963).
8 For the second Franks Report (Cmnd 5104 (1972)), see ch. 22. The first Franks Committee was also, in a sense, a departmental committee, though the Lord Chancellor, who appointed it, occupies a kind of 'crossbench' position.
9 The Warnock Committee: see Cmnd 9314 (1984).
10 See Cmd 9176, 9220 (1954); Griffith (1955) 18 *Mod. L. Rev.* 557, (1987) 1 *Contemporary Record* 35; Chester (1954) 32 *Public Administration* 389. Crichel Down had been compulsorily acquired by the Air Ministry as a bombing range. After the war it was handed back to the civil authorities. Lieut.-Commander Marten, the son-in-law of the former owner, wished to buy it or alternatively to become the tenant farmer of the area. The civil servants concerned decided to re-equip the estate, to let it to another tenant, and not to accede to Marten's requests, but failed to keep him properly informed and created false impressions in his mind. Marten pursued his grievance through political channels. The procedure for dealing with the disposition of such land was not regulated by statutory rules.

The common features of these inquiries are (i) that the persons conducting them are expected to hold hearings and ascertain facts about specified matters of public concern and (ii) that they do not make *decisions*, though their findings and recommendations may be a foundation for decisions by others, including decisions to institute legal proceedings. Indeed, in some situations a finding of culpability, or of a *prima facie* case of culpability, may be a necessary condition for the institution or continuance of such proceedings. But the fact that the investigating body may be called a 'court' or 'tribunal' does not endow it with the characteristic power of a judicial body to make decisions. On the other hand, an inquisitorial body may exceptionally be endowed with such powers. The verdict of a coroner's inquest in a case of homicide may assert that X was legally culpable but does not amount to a conviction though it may be the foundation of criminal proceedings against X; a verdict that Y committed suicide does, however, have binding legal effect.[11] Inspectors conducting inquiries in town planning law are generally restricted to finding and reporting on facts, and recommending a decision to be taken by or on behalf of the Minister; since 1968, however, power to make decisions in consequence of certain types of inquiries has been delegated by the Minister to the inspectors themselves.[12] In these few intermediate zones the distinction between tribunals and inquiries disappears; the investigator *is* the tribunal.

The typical inquiry – one which does not culminate in a binding decision by the person who presides at the hearing – may be directed to a very wide range of public purposes. The point is well illustrated by an Order made in 1967,[13] bringing within the purview of the Council on Tribunals no fewer than sixty-five types of discretionary inquiries held in pursuance of statutory powers. They ranged from inquiries held in pursuance of section 5 of the renowned Fisheries (Oyster, Crab and Lobster) Act 1877 to the committee of inquiry appointed by the Home Secretary to advise him before he decides whether to deprive a naturalized or registered citizen of his citizenship.[14] And they included inquiries that may be held by a person appointed by a Secretary of State for a large number of administrative purposes in local government law – for example, before the Secretary of State confirms various statutory schemes. Add to these all the sundry types of inquiries which a Minister *must* cause to be held when a prescribed state

---

11 A coroner's jurisdiction over the finding of treasure trove was ended by the Treasure Act 1996.
12 See now Local Government Act 1972, s. 101.
13 SI 1967, No. 451.
14 British Nationality Act 1981 s. 40(7).

of affairs exists (for example, when he entertains an appeal against certain administrative decisions taken at a lower level), and the indeterminate miscellany of situations in which a discretionary inquiry may be set up *without* statutory authority,[15] and one has a very mixed bag. One finds, for example, Acts providing that before certain kinds of subordinate legislation can be made or confirmed a statutory inquiry may or must be held.[16] If one can offer any useful generalizations in this variegated field of public law, they ought to be focused rather on the public local inquiry. Local inquiries are used for three main purposes.[17]

1 As a means of consulting and informing local opinion, and gleaning local information as to the likely impact of a proposed administrative decision (for example, to alter constituency or local boundaries, or to amalgamate police forces) affecting the interests of persons and bodies in that locality. This slows down the pace of decision-making but provides the decision-maker with a better fund of knowledge.

2 As a means of giving those whose interests will be most directly affected by a proposed or provisional decision (for example, to make an order for the compulsory purchase of their land or to designate an area as the site of a new town) the legal right to put their objections orally, and through legal representatives, to a person appointed by the Minister or another competent authority before a final decision is made. Other points of view may be expressed at the inquiry, and the outcome should (as in (1)) be conducive to better decision-making. Purposes (1) and (2) are complementary. In some cases the scope of inquiry will be confined to the objections and not directed to the general merits of the proposed order.

3 As a stage in the process of determining appeals against an administrative decision that has already been taken. The best-known examples arise in planning law.

For instance, X applies to his local planning authority for permission to make a material change in the use of his land; planning permission is refused, or is granted subject to conditions that X dislikes; X is entitled to appeal to the Secretary of State for the Environment; the Secretary of State

---

15 In general, persons conducting inquiries in pursuance of statutory powers have authority to compel the attendance of witnesses and the production of documents, and those conducting non-statutory inquiries have not.

16 J. A. G. Griffith and H. Street, *Principles of Administrative Law* (5th edn, 1973), pp. 127ff.

17 Neat classification is impossible. See Wraith and Lamb, op. cit., chs. 3, 4, 8.

causes a local inquiry to be held through an inspector; the inspector makes a report and the Secretary of State (or a civil servant on his behalf) decides.[18]

In situations (1) and (2) one can speak of judicialized administration; in the third type of situation, judicialized administration merges into administrative adjudication.

SPECIAL TRIBUNALS[19]

One tends to use the terms 'special tribunals', 'administrative tribunals' and 'statutory tribunals' interchangeably. Terminological inexactitude does not matter much in this field, because no single term could be all-embracing; but a few preliminary points should be borne in mind.

1 Some tribunals that are commonly called 'administrative' deal with disputes between private landlords and tenants. These tribunals are the rent assessment committees and agricultural land tribunals.[20]

2 A small number of tribunals which can well be described as 'administrative' (in the sense that they deal with claims and controversies involving public authorities) are non-statutory. But the most important of them – the Criminal Injuries Compensation Board (which makes discretionary awards out of funds provided by Parliament to claimants who are victims of criminal violence) – has been placed on a statutory basis.[21]

3 Not all 'special' tribunals are in any conceivable sense 'administrative'. Commercial and industrial arbitrators, the disciplinary committees of trade unions and clubs, professional statutory disciplinary bodies,[22] the stewards of the Jockey Club and the Greyhound Racing Association are obviously not 'administrative'; the disciplinary committees of private organizations are called *domestic* tribunals.

4 Tribunals exercising functions in administrative law may be designated as tribunals, courts, boards, committees, commissioners, referees,

18 Unless the power of decision has been delegated to the inspector; see note 12, above.
19 The body of literature on this subject is now extensive. W. A. Robson, *Justice and Administrative Law* (3rd edn, 1951) is the classic pioneering work.
20 The Lands Tribunal (see below) also has a private law jurisdiction to vary restrictive covenants.
21 Criminal Justice Act 1988, Part VII. It had operated for twenty years without such a footing.
22 See, e.g., *R. v. General Medical Council, ex p. Gee* [1986] 1 WLR 1247.

umpires; the name is unimportant. The Lands Tribunal is more court-like than the local valuation courts from which it entertains appeals.

5 Tribunals dispensing 'administrative justice' may in substance be doing exactly the same kind of work, in a specialized field, as an ordinary court of law, and doing it with the same degree of freedom from political pressure and influence.

Neither the creation of specialized courts nor the hostility of the legal profession to them need cause any surprise. And any new specialized tribunal, set up to serve a general public purpose, could be assured of an ample measure of initial hostility following the struggle against the Star Chamber, especially if it neither looked nor functioned like a court of common law. Military courts-martial, professional disciplinary bodies and commercial arbitrators could be tolerated. Tribunals adjudicating informally in disputes arising out of social welfare legislation were another matter. The rules they applied interfered with freedom of property and contract; their members were appointed and removable by Ministers; often they exercised discretionary powers which could only be reposed with safety in the hands of Chancery or Circuit judges; if lawyers appeared before them at all, everyone tended to be ill at ease. To some, their very existence was a slur upon the legal profession and a constructive contempt of court. Dicey and Hewart were right: the rule of law was in jeopardy. So ran the train of thought – one that the Committee on Ministers' Powers did little to disturb. Nevertheless, the Committee grudgingly conceded[23] that 'Ministerial tribunals' might, in exceptional circumstances, be preferred to the ordinary courts on five grounds: cheapness, accessibility to the parties, freedom from technicality, speed, and expert knowledge of their particular subject-matter.

The climate of opinion has now changed. No longer must exceptional circumstances be present to justify the establishment of a special tribunal to determine controversies arising under regulatory or welfare legislation. We have about fifty different *types* of these tribunals and some 2,000 tribunals altogether. If, for instance, the question of how disputes about the entitlement of dismissed workers to redundancy payments from their employers ought to be decided under a new Act, there is an *expectation* that the deciding body will be a special tribunal. The alternatives would be (1) a Minister, (2) one of the ordinary courts, (3) a specially constituted court,

---

23 Cmd 4060 (1932), p. 97. See also the Franks Report, Cmnd 218 (1957), § 38, making the same point in less grudging terms.

and (4) an independent arbitrator. Giving the power of decision to a Minister means in practice that the parties may not know who takes the decision in the Minister's name and will not be entitled to be heard before that person:[24] and they will not usually feel confident that departmental adjudication is justice according to law. There is, therefore, a presumption in favour of vesting the power of decision in a person or body conducting oral hearings; this presumption may be rebutted only if considerations of national or regional policy, for which the Minister is responsible, are likely to condition the manner in which an individual issue ought to be determined, or if uniformity of decision is of primary importance. A possible compromise – and not a very satisfactory one – is to set up an independent tribunal with an appeal to the Minister.[25] Setting up a specialized court, rather than a tribunal, may be to make heavy weather of small issues. The outstanding modern example of a specialized court in the strict sense is the Restrictive Practices Court; this is a court because it is expressed to be a superior court of record and is presided over by a superior judge (though it includes expert laymen); its jurisdiction (to nullify restrictive trading agreements which are contrary to the public interest) *could* have been vested in a body styled as a tribunal, and when it was first constituted there are many who would have preferred to see that course adopted.[26] Committing issues to independent arbitrators – the last alternative – is most appropriate where the number of issues arising is relatively small and a high level of expertise, likely to be found only among specialists willing to act as part-time adjudicators, is required.

The grounds, already indicated, for giving jurisdiction to tribunals rather than courts are sometimes overstated. Certainly it would be absurd to make applicants for benefits go before a High Court judge; the cost, delay and formality would thwart the objectives of social security schemes and would clog up the general administration of justice. These considerations do not apply with anything like the same force to the county courts, which are more accessible and expeditious than some special tribunals and hardly more expensive. County courts do, moreover, have jurisdiction in some matters of administrative law. Where the county courts have been bypassed

24 They will have no such entitlement at common law: *Local Government Board* v. *Arlidge* [1915] AC 120 (housing appeal). But they may be entitled to be heard before a person appointed by the Minister to report to him.
25 For example, the Civil Aviation Authority, from which an appeal lies to the Secretary of State for Trade and Industry.
26 See R. B. Stevens and B. S. Yamey, *The Restrictive Practices Court* (1965).

and new statutory tribunals established instead, the reasons have generally been as follows.

1 Circuit and District judges are generalists, not specialists. There is no reason to expect them to be experts in transport licensing or the rating of property or to be familiar with the problems of the sick and needy or to have the time and opportunity to acquire the necessary expertise or familiarity. A special statutory tribunal may include persons with the desired initial qualifications and others who will acquire them through specialization and experience.

2 Courts are formal. The kind of person who is aggrieved by refusal of a social security benefit or who wants to make a complaint arising out of the administration of the National Health Service may be overawed by the atmosphere of a judicial proceeding and reduced to incoherence or silence if he is precluded by the rules of evidence from telling his story in his own way. In some situations justice can be dispensed only in an informal environment. Special tribunals can be very informal. And none of them is obliged to follow all the strict rules of evidence and procedure of a court of law.

3 Tribunals usually take an active part in finding the facts for themselves; they may adopt 'inquisitorial' procedures, probing away with questions, not acting as detached umpires who rely almost entirely on the material as presented to them by the parties or their advocates. Some of them (for example, valuation courts) regularly conduct site inspections. And though they must observe those minimum requirements of procedural fair play called the rules of natural justice they can draw on their own expert and acquired knowledge in drawing inferences from the facts found.

4 Courts are bound by precedent. Tribunals, though bound by judicial precedents laid down in their own field of the law, and capable of evolving a body of 'case law' themselves, can be more flexible in formulating standards (for example, what is reasonable under local conditions; whether premises are educationally suitable) and departing from them when the circumstances of a case warrant relaxation.[27] Indeed, one of the more formal special tribunals was warned by the Court of Appeal that it ought *not* to adopt a rigid body of case law.[28]

---

27 A point well made by H. Street, *Justice in the Welfare State* (2nd edn, 1975), pp. 6–9.
28 *Merchandise Transport Co.* v. *British Transport Commission* [1962] 2 QB 173 at 186, 192–3.

One of the most significant legal developments in the immediate post-war period was the replacement of the Workmen's Compensation Act by the national insurance (industrial injuries) scheme.[29] Not only was private insurance replaced by public social insurance; the tribunals constituted to administer the new scheme were special tribunals before which legal representation was at first excluded; such representation is now allowed. The jurisdiction of county court judges was ousted and the massive body of case law evolved in the many legal battles fought as far as the House of Lords was deprived of binding authority. This was a drastic repudiation of technical legalism in which social justice had too often been overlooked.

Types of tribunals[30]

No attempt will here be made to present a full synopsis. Only a broad outline under general headings will be offered.

Fiscal liability and claims, property and land. Appeals against administrative assessments to income tax, corporation tax and capital gains tax are heard either by special commissioners of income tax (who are civil servants) or by general commissioners (who are not).[31] Appeals against value added tax assessments by the Customs and Excise lie to special value added tax tribunals. Persons aggrieved by assessments may object before a local valuation court, which is composed largely of unpaid local councillors and magistrates. Appeal lies to the Lands Tribunal, a body which could easily be styled an administrative court; its members are professional lawyers and surveyors appointed by the Lord Chancellor; its procedure is fairly informal but its judgments are often reported. The jurisdiction of the Tribunal also includes the assessment of compensation for compulsory acquisition of land where this is not agreed between the acquiring authority and the property-owner.

Industrial tribunals are possibly the most important group of tribunals today. They have jurisdiction over a wide range of questions, including claims to compensation for unfair dismissal, disputes concerning redundancy payments, appeals against assessments to the industrial training levy and appeals for compensation for loss of public office under statutory

---

29 W. A. Robson, *Justice and Administrative Law* (3rd edn, 1951), pp. 209–22.
30 Figures of cases heard by most of the various tribunals are supplied in an Appendix to the Annual Report of the Council on Tribunals.
31 Appeals concerning capital transfer tax are heard only by the special commissioners or by the High Court.

reorganization schemes. They sit in London and over sixty other centres in England and Wales.[32]

The Foreign Compensation Commission entertains claims to the award of compensation out of funds received by the British Government from foreign Governments for the expropriation or destruction of British-owned property overseas, and allocates the money to successful claimants on a discretionary basis. The Criminal Injuries Compensation Board makes discretionary awards to claimants who are victims of criminal violence.

The informal rent assessment committees fix fair rents between private landlords and tenants; they are appellate bodies, an initial determination having already been made by a rent officer. Reasonable rents for council tenants under the Housing Rents and Subsidies Act 1975 are determined not by tribunals but by the local authorities themselves. Agricultural land tribunals deal with disputes between landlords and tenant farmers about notices to quit.

Social welfare. Post-war legislation has substantially enlarged the number and jurisdiction of such tribunals. Most are appellate bodies hearing appeals lodged by persons aggrieved by initial administrative decisions; and in most of the cases before them the monetary sums at issue are small, though often of major importance to the poor and disabled. There are the social security appeal tribunals (dealing with claims to jobseeker's allowance, sickness benefit, industrial injuries benefit, retirement pensions, child benefit and so on), and medical appeal tribunals on industrial injuries claims.[33] Appeals in respect of disability pensions claimed by ex-servicemen lie to separate pensions appeal tribunals. From the social security appeal and medical appeal tribunals, appeals lie to senior full-time lawyers, the social security commissioners. A complex network of tribunals (including the Secretary of State for Health and the Health Service Commissioners) exists to hear complaints and allegations against practitioners in the National Health Service and to entertain appeals. Persons compulsorily committed to a mental hospital can seek their release from custody by application to a mental health review tribunal.

Among other tribunals concerned with social welfare in a broad sense are the industrial tribunals, rent assessment committees, agricultural land tribunals, the Criminal Injuries Compensation Board, independent schools

---

32 The Annual Report of the Council on Tribunals gives the latest figures of cases disposed of.

33 For a good critique of the social security tribunals see Street, op. cit., pp. 10–32.

tribunals (which determine whether a private school or its proprietor or any of its teachers ought to be struck off the official register or disqualified as the case may be) and tribunals exercising roughly similar functions with regard to voluntary children's homes.

Regulatory. Regulation by licensing, normally coupled with powers of inspection, is a familiar feature of public supervision of private activity. Powers to grant licences will be accompanied by powers to impose conditions, to refuse renewal of a licence, and to revoke a licence when prescribed violations of the terms of the licence are established: powers to revoke in the absolute discretion of the licensing authority are rarely conferred today. Licensing powers may be vested in Government Departments, public corporations or local authorities.[34] Aspects of the regulation of transport communications have been committed, for reasons of practical convenience, to independent tribunals. For example, applications for licences to operate commercial air routes are heard by the Civil Aviation Authority; objectors have a right to be heard in opposition; an appeal lies to the Secretary of State for Trade and Industry. Regulation of carriage of goods and passengers by road follows a curious pattern. There are area licensing authorities. Appeal lies from decisions on passenger road services to the Secretary of State for Transport, on goods carriers' licences to the Transport Tribunal. The latter is an anomalous body; till 1969 it also heard applications for variations of railway passenger charges in the London transport area. It is a court with judicial trappings and procedure; its rate-functions (still exercisable for limited purposes) are successors to the jurisdiction exercised from 1921 by the Railway Rates Tribunal, the antecedents of which can be traced to the Railway and Canal Commission, a superior court and an arbitral body, set up in 1873.

Among other regulatory bodies are the Comptroller-General of Patents, Designs and Trade Marks (from which an appeal lies to the Patents Court), the Plant Variety Rights Tribunal exercising similar functions, the Performing Rights Tribunal, the tribunal appointed to consider alleged violations of the Prevention of Fraud (Investments) Act 1958 by dealers in securities, and the Wireless Telegraphy Appeal Tribunal set up to consider complaints of undue interference with radio broadcasts on the part of private operators.

Tribunals to consider complaints about the conduct of voluntary schools and children's homes are also regulatory bodies. Perhaps one should include

34 ibid., ch. 4.

the immigration appellate bodies in this category too. The Gaming Board for Great Britain, which decides on the basis of police reports and other information whether to grant a certificate of consent to gaming-club proprietors, thus enabling them to apply for a local licence, is a regulatory body which may be regarded as a kind of informal tribunal.

This is not a complete list,[35] and some classes of tribunals defy classification. Informal adjudication within Government Departments is also of practical importance. Civil servants in Britain are more accessible to informal interviews than in many foreign countries.

Franks and after

The Franks Committee found nothing fundamentally wrong with the system and working of statutory tribunals, and it did not seek to put tribunals into a strait-jacket. But its bias in favour of judicialization led it to make a number of recommendations designed to assimilate tribunals more closely to specialized courts. For example, it deprecated undue informality, and stressed the need for settled rules of procedure, reasons for decisions, rights to legal representation, proper channels of appeal and the removal of any suspicion of political dictation of or influence over decisions. The procedures of tribunals ought to be characterized by 'openness, fairness and impartiality'.[36] Openness implied not only reasoned decisions but also public hearings (except where the interests of the public – for example, in security – or the parties demanded privacy, as in potentially embarrassing social security appeals and complaints against National Health Service practitioners), with evidence given orally. Fairness demanded that the parties knew their rights in advance, had proper notice of the case they had to meet, an adequate opportunity to put their own case in person or through their representatives, and rights to appeal against and obtain review of decisions. Impartiality required new safeguards for the appointment and tenure of members, and to preserve the appearance of impartiality, independent tribunals ought not to sit in departmental premises. To maintain some degree of coherence and surveillance over the tribunal system, there should be a standing Council on Tribunals.

The Tribunals and Inquiries Act 1958 provided for the establishment of the Council on Tribunals, to keep under review the constitution and working of specified tribunals; other tribunals have been added to the list.

35 The latest Annual Report of the Council on Tribunals gives a full list.
36 Cmnd 217 (1957), § 23.

The current Act is the Tribunals and Inquiries Act 1992. The Council[37] consists of up to fifteen members appointed by the Lord Chancellor and the Secretary of State for Scotland, and the Parliamentary Commissioner for Administration *ex officio*. The chairman is salaried; the other appointed members receive fees; but the Council is essentially a part-time supervisory body with a minute official staff. It meets once a month. More specifically, the functions of the Council in respect of tribunals – it has powers in connection with inquiries too[38] – are as follows.

1 To consider and report on the statutory tribunals under its supervision, and on such particular matters concerning these and other tribunals as may be referred to it by the Lord Chancellor and the Secretary of State.

   Within the limited scope of its resources, it has attempted to conduct general reviews of specific classes of tribunals and has reported on special matters such as the power to award costs and the law of defamation. It organizes conferences with tribunal chairmen.

2 To receive and investigate complaints about tribunals made by members of the public.

   In its first ten years the Council received only 242 complaints relating to tribunals. This small figure probably indicates a widespread ignorance of the Council's very existence or whereabouts rather than a general satisfaction of consumers with the work of tribunals. The Council has no power to alter a tribunal's decision and in most cases the tribunal would have no jurisdiction to rescind its own decision even if it wished to do so. However, individual complaints may lead to further investigations and recommendations for reform. The Council can get to know where the shoe pinches.

3 To make an annual report to the Lord Chancellor and the Secretary of State. The Report is laid before Parliament and is published as a House of Commons paper. It attracts little public comment but is a very useful source of information.

4 To be consulted by the responsible Minister before procedural rules for tribunals and inquiries are made.

   This is probably its most important function – one in which the minority of lawyers on the Council play a leading role. It has helped to promote a higher degree of uniformity in tribunal procedures, and in particular to instil the essentials of judicial fairness into procedural

37 See Bernard Schwartz and H. W. R. Wade, *Legal Control of Government* (1972), pp. 179–80; D. G. T. Williams [1984] *Public Law* 73.
38 See pp. 595–6.

regulations – for example, adequate notification of rights of appeal, proper notice of hearings and disclosure of the case to be answered; rights of cross-examination; rights to legal representation at oral hearings.

The Council is also consulted by the Department sponsoring legislation under which a new tribunal is to be constituted or an existing one abolished or reorganized. It has complained that in these matters it is sometimes consulted too late for its representations to have any effect, and has urged that more thought be given to coordinated rationalization of the tribunal system, involving the amalgamation of some types of tribunals and reallocations of jurisdiction.[39] The Council has asked for statutory provision to be made to give it the right to be consulted whenever legislation is being drafted affecting its jurisdiction and, if the Council's opinion were not accepted by the Minister, the new statutory provision should oblige him to disclose the Council's view when introducing the legislation.[40]

5 To make *general* recommendations to the appropriate Minister as to the appointment of members of tribunals.

In practice this has not been an important function of the Council. However, the Franks recommendations have had a significant effect on appointments and tenure. The chairmen of certain tribunals have to be legally qualified, and appointed either by the Lord Chancellor or by the Minister generally concerned with the area of administration in question from a panel maintained by the Lord Chancellor. Members of most tribunals cannot be removed except with the Lord Chancellor's concurrence;[41] they may, however, be refused reappointment after their term of office has expired.

Tribunals are not cast in a common mould, but some general points are important.

(i) Most tribunals are not composed of officials,[42] though there are some exceptions – for example, Ministry inspectors deciding planning appeals, special commissioners of income tax, the Comptroller-General of Patents, Designs and Trade Marks; these officers nevertheless act independently.

39 Annual Report for 1969–70 (HC 72 (1970–71), pp. 10–11, 29–32; and for 1973–4 (HC 289 (1974–5)), pp. 4–5, 6, 18–19.
40 Council on Tribunals Special Report on Functions, Cmnd 7805 (1980).
41 See Tribunals and Inquiries Act 1992, ss. 5, 7. For the Franks recommendations on these matters, see Cmnd 218 (1957), ch. 5.
42 See further R. E. Wraith and P. G. Hutchesson, op. cit.; H. W. R. Wade and C. F. Forsyth, *Administrative Law* (7th edn, 1994), ch. 23.

(ii) A fairly typical tribunal is composed of a legally qualified chairman, appointed by one of the procedures indicated above, and two lay members, one of whom will perhaps be an employer and another a trade union official; or both may be independent specialists or local worthies.

(iii) They are bound by regulations made by the Minister, but only in highly exceptional circumstances defined by legislation will the Minister be legally entitled to give them specific directions for the determination of a particular case.

(iv) For a variety of reasons the position of a legally qualified chairman may be of crucial importance. The legislation which a tribunal has to interpret and apply may be just as complicated as law in the courts. Although the parties will nearly always be *entitled* to legal representation;[43] they will seldom be so represented before tribunals like social security tribunals dealing with small matters. Unfortunately, the legal aid and advice scheme has not been applied to proceedings before tribunals except the Lands Tribunal, the Commons Commissioners and the Employment Appeal Tribunal.[44] If one party is legally represented, the chairman will have to do his best to help the unrepresented party put his case without shedding his own impartiality as a fact-finder and adjudicator. Obviously this is a difficult task.

Before some tribunals legal representation may, however, be a mixed blessing to a party. Clearly, such representation is important if a party is accused of culpability or if his vital interests are in serious jeopardy. But advocates appearing before tribunals can also sow confusion and protract the proceedings unnecessarily by reading documents at length, conducting long examinations and cross-examinations of witnesses, making elaborate submissions and generally frustrating the object of an informal hearing. Few practising lawyers appear regularly before the minor tribunals, and unfamiliarity with the atmosphere can be a serious disadvantage. There is a real dilemma: in certain cases it is very desirable for all interested parties to have the right kind of legal representation; that kind of representation may simply not be available, and the chairman has to do his best to supply the omission or remedy the deficiency.

6 The last function of the Council on Tribunals in this context is concerned with reasons for decisions. Under section 10 of the Tribunals and Inquiries

43 The Franks Report (§ 87) recommended that the right to legal representation be curtailed only in the most exceptional circumstances.
44 The Lord Chancellor's Legal Aid Advisory Committee recommended that legal aid be extended to all tribunals within the supervision of the Council on Tribunals in which representation is permitted. Twenty-fourth Annual Report, HC. 20 (1974–5).

Act 1992, tribunals under the superintendence of the Council are required, when requested, to supply oral or written reasons for their decisions when giving or notifying their decision, unless exempted by order made by the Lord Chancellor after consultation with the Council. Only one class of tribunal has been accorded exemption.

The general statutory duty to give reasons[45] is, however, subject to qualifications. The tribunals in question are not obliged to volunteer reasons or to inform the parties of their right to request them. Some tribunals interpret their statutory duty literally and, in the absence of a request, simply do not give reasons.[46] Moreover, the duty to give reasons does not import a duty to summarize the evidence or state findings of fact. Reasons may properly be withheld on grounds of national security, or if they are asked for by somebody not primarily concerned with the decision and it would be contrary to the interest of any of the parties to supply them.[47]

Appeal and review

There is no common appellate structure. From most tribunals of last resort an appeal lies to the superior courts on questions of law,[48] but there is no such appeal from determinations by, for example, the social security commissioners or the immigration appeal tribunal. On questions of fact and discretion the pattern is irregular. Appeal may lie to a superior tribunal or to a Minister, or there may be no appeal on the merits at all; there is no such appeal, for instance, from decisions of mental health review tribunals or the Foreign Compensation Commission.

Judicial review may be exercisable although no appeal is provided by statute or in addition to appellate review. A determination by a tribunal may be quashed if it is made without jurisdiction or in breach of the rules of natural justice, or if it exhibits an error of law on the face of the 'record'. A tribunal may be restrained from exceeding its jurisdiction or commanded to hear a case within its jurisdiction; it can also be ordered to perform a duty to give reasons for its decision. These matters were discussed in chapter 26.

---

45 Some tribunals were already under a duty to give reasons for decisions and they cannot be exempted from this duty. Their duty was not subject to all the qualifications mentioned in the text below.
46 See Street, op. cit., pp. 67–9.
47 Tribunals and Inquiries Act 1992, s. 10(2), (3).
48 See p. 513, and Tribunals and Inquiries Act 1992, s. 11.

INQUIRIES AND LAND USE

The Franks Committee emphasized the need for openness and fairness in inquiries held on behalf of a Minister, but it recognized that a procedure culminating in a discretionary decision by a Minister responsible for national policy could not be expected to exhibit the same degree of impartiality as proceedings before an independent tribunal.[49]

The difference is best illustrated by situations where the purpose of the inquiry is to investigate, for the information of the Minister, objections to the Minister's own proposals.[50] The New Towns Act 1946 provided for the establishment of new towns to attract population and industry from the metropolis. Before the bill had been introduced, the Minister had already provisionally decided, as a matter of policy, to designate Stevenage as the site of a new town. While the bill was before Parliament, he imprudently made a speech in Stevenage, proclaiming that he intended to carry out a daring exercise in town planning there, and affirming (amid hostile interruptions . . . 'Gestapo' . . .) that the project would go forward. Subsequently a draft order was made, designating Stevenage; objections were lodged; a public local inquiry into the objections was held by a Ministry inspector; the Minister, having received the report on the inquiry and considered the objections, finally made the order. In *Franklin* v. *Minister of Town and Country Planning*[51] objectors challenged the validity of the order in the courts, claiming that the Minister had failed to act judicially. He had manifested bias or a real likelihood of bias in favour of his proposal from the outset; and the fact that he had made the final order while important technical problems (water supply and sewage disposal) remained unsolved showed that his bias had continued to the end. The House of Lords held that the standard of impartiality imposed on an independent tribunal was inapplicable to this type of situation; the Minister's role made it inevitable that he would incline in favour of his own scheme. The only duties cast upon him were to cause a properly conducted inquiry to be held and to consider the objections and the report fairly, with a mind not closed to argument. The Minister's functions were 'purely administrative'.

49 Cmnd 218 (1957), § 25.
50 On the difficulty in applying judicial standards to procedures involving public inquiries held as part of a process in arriving at a discretionary decision, see *Wednesbury Corporation* v. *Ministry of Housing and Local Government (No. 2)* [1966] 2 QB 275; and *Essex CC* v. *Ministry of Housing and Local Government* (1967) 66 LGR 23.
51 [1948] AC 87.

The decision in this case was sensible, though the term 'purely administrative' may have been unfortunate. A duty to act fairly may imply a duty to behave like an adjudicator *for certain purposes* – for example, in ensuring that everyone directly concerned is adequately informed of his rights, knows the case he has to meet and has a proper chance to put his case, and that reasons are given for decisions.[52]

A more typical situation in administrative law is where a Minister, X, has to decide a dispute between Y, a local authority, and Z, a property-owner.[53] This 'triangular' situation may arise where Y makes an order for the compulsory purchase of Z's property and Z objects; or where Z applies to Y for permission to make a material change in the use of his land or premises (planning permission), Y refuses, or consents subject to conditions, and Z appeals to the Minister, X, against the refusal or the conditions. In certain respects the Minister resembles an adjudicator determining a *lis inter partes*, a dispute between parties. Long before the Franks Committee had ever been thought of, the courts had recognized that certain *implied* duties ought to be cast on the Minister when deciding whether or not to confirm a compulsory purchase order initiated by a local authority in so far as his role was analogous to the judicial. They divided his functions into three stages. First, before objections were lodged, he had no duty to 'act judicially'; thus, if relevant communications were made to him by the local authority, he had no obligation to divulge them to the objectors; he was acting in an 'administrative' capacity.[54] Secondly, after objections had been lodged and up to the time of the final decision, he had to 'act judicially' in accordance with the minimum standards of natural justice; hence, the inspector conducting the public local inquiry had to behave impartially, and the Minister could not communicate with one party behind the other's back (for example, by viewing the site, through his officials, in company with representatives of the local authority, without giving the objectors the opportunity to be present) on evidential matters raised at the inquiry.[55] In making his final decision the Minister cannot be regarded as separate and distinct from his Department. He is entitled to consult his officials, and

---

52 The inquiry procedure rules have been changed subsequently by statutory instrument.
53 Z may also be a public authority.
54 *Johnson (B.) & Co. (Builders) Ltd* v. *Minister of Health* [1947] 2 All ER 395. The leading judgment by Lord Greene MR contains the fullest review of the case law up to that time.
55 *Errington* v. *Minister of Health* [1935] 1 KB 249 (a slum clearance case; the same principles applied). For an acute analysis see Griffith and Street, *Principles of Administrative Law*, op. cit., pp. 171–5.

advice (including technical advice), tendered to him within the Department is not new evidence of the kind which he would be required to disclose to the objectors had he received it from sources outside his Department.[56]

The courts recognize that over-judicialization of the procedure at inquiries will lead to delay and unnecessary technical fetters on the inspector's conduct of the inquiry. Their aim is to ensure that objectors at an inquiry are able to take 'an active, intelligent and informed part in the decision-making process'.[57] In putting their case and answering the points made on behalf of the public authority, objectors must be given 'a fair crack of the whip'.[58] When an inspector based his recommendations on a substantial matter which, although it had been mentioned at the inquiry, had not been treated as part of the case for denying the applicants permission to extract gravel, so that they had not had a chance to deal with the question, the Minister's decision, based on the inspector's findings, was quashed.[59] But the Court of Appeal refused to treat the inclusion of the inspector's own opinion of the architectural value of a house as new evidence which should have been disclosed at the inquiry or which should have caused the inquiry to be reopened.[60] Any sensible person would have expected the inspector to form an opinion based on such a fact. Considering the effect of refusal by an inspector to adjourn an inquiry, that same court took into account the multiplicity of parties at an inquiry and found that the inspector must be allowed to weigh the possible unfairness to one objector against the delay to the inquiry and consequent inconvenience to all the other parties.[61] The inspector is master of the procedure at an inquiry. While actual prejudice need not always be proved for an objector to succeed in getting an order consequent upon an inquiry quashed for lack of natural justice,[62] absence of any real prejudice to the objector may be used as a ground for denying him relief.[63]

Judge-made safeguards left some gaps in the protection afforded to the citizen. The House of Lords had held that even while the Minister was acting 'judicially', he did not have to disclose the inspector's report.[64] The

56 *Bushell* v. *Secretary of State for the Environment* [1981] AC 75; *R.* v. *Secretary of State for Transport, ex p. Gwent County Council* [1987] 1 All ER 161.
57 *Nicholson* v. *Secretary of State for Energy* (1977) 76 LGR 693.
58 *Fairmount Investments Ltd* v. *Secretary of State for the Environment* [1976] 1 WLR 1255.
59 *Sabey* v. *Secretary of State for the Environment* [1978] 1 All ER 586.
60 *Winchester CC* v. *Secretary of State for the Environment* (1979) 77 LGR 715.
61 *Ostreicher* v. *Secretary of State for the Environment* [1978] 1 WLR 810.
62 *Hibernian Property Co. Ltd* v. *Secretary of State for the Environment* (1973) 72 LGR 350.
63 *George* v. *Secretary of State for the Environment* (1979) 77 LGR 689.
64 *Local Government Board* v. *Arlidge* [1915] AC 120.

Franks Committee recommended disclosure of the fact-finding sections of inspectors' reports before they were submitted to the Minister, so as to enable the parties to propose corrections of fact; and full disclosure of the report with the Minister's reasoned letter of decision.[65] The recommendation for disclosure *prior* to the decision has not been implemented by legislation because it would lead to too much delay in decision-making, but subsequent disclosure must now be made on request. Most of the other Franks recommendations have been implemented. For instance, an acquiring authority must give advance particulars of its case; if a Department has expressed a view in support of the local authority's proposal or decision and this fact is stated in the local authority's submissions, a representative of the Department must be available at the inquiry to give evidence, in the absence of special statutory rules, but natural justice does not require that objectors be permitted to cross-examine him on questions of national policy, or on the accuracy of the material on which the policy is based. The inspector has a discretion to determine whether cross-examination serves any useful purpose.[66] There are statutory codes for the conduct of inquiries, specifying who has a right to be heard and who may be heard, embodying rules of procedure analogous to those for a judicial-type proceeding, and dealing with the procedure before and after the hearing.[67]

All this seemed eminently reasonable; and it was. But in practice judicialization tended to slow down the process of making decisions. Inspectors' reports, for example, and reasoned letters of decision setting out the inspectors' main findings had to be carefully composed; otherwise the decisions might be struck down in the courts for failure to comply with the requirements of the legislation.[68] This could be quite serious in the case of compulsory purchase orders, because judicial review meant uncertainty, and the work of building roads, schools or houses could not safely be begun while judicial proceedings were pending (though they had to be instituted within a few weeks of the confirmation of the order).

For a different reason, delay was serious in the context of planning

65 Cmnd 218 (1957) §§ 343–5. Partial disclosure of reports prior to the decision is the practice followed in Scotland. The rules governing reasoned decisions by the tribunals named in the Tribunals and Inquiries Act were applied to decisions in pursuance of mandatory statutory inquiries (see now 1992 Act, ss. 10(1), 14(1)) and to a number of voluntary inquiries held on behalf of a Minister.

66 *Bushell* v. *Secretary of State for the Environment* [1981] AC 75.

67 These include rules on inquiry procedures generally, and on planning appeals.

68 See *Givaudan & Co.* v. *Minister of Housing and Local Government* [1967] 1 WLR 250 (decision quashed because the reasons given in the letter of decision, read together with extracts from the inspector's report, were unintelligible).

appeals; they were very numerous, and private development of property was held up while a backlog piled up in the Ministry. In 1967 it was taking an average of nine months to determine those planning appeals where the appellant had asked for an oral hearing.[69] One answer to the latter problem was decentralization of decision-making; hence power to decide minor appeals has been delegated to inspectors, who do not have to make a full-scale report but can simply issue a short letter of decision containing reasons.[70] Another device was to encourage appellants to agree to having the matter decided by written representations coupled with an unaccompanied site inspection. There have been other reforms in planning procedure.[71] Instead of having area planning policy settled by a development plan to which hundreds of objections could be entertained at a massive public inquiry, the larger planning authorities now prepare outline structure plans subject to ministerial approval. The Secretary of State can decide which aspects of the plan shall be considered at 'an examination in public' and whom to invite to be heard; and he has a free discretion whom to consult when he is considering the plan.[72]

In some respects implementation of the Franks recommendations did not go far enough. For example, the Government refused to carry out the proposals that there should be an express duty to acquaint the parties with relevant statements of policy and changes in policy prior to the decision. Again, at first nothing was done to implement recommendations about reopening the inquiry where the Minister proposed to disagree with the inspector's recommendations. The latter issue came to a head in the Saffron Walden chalkpit case.[73] A company sought permission to quarry chalk in a pit. Neighbouring farmers claimed that these operations would seriously damage their land and livestock. The local planning authority refused the application for planning permission; the company appealed, and an inspector, having conducted a local inquiry on behalf of the Minister and heard expert evidence, recommended that the appeal be dismissed. The

69 Cmnd 3333 (1967), p. 7.

70 See notes 12 and 67.

71 Richard Buxton, *Local Government* (2nd edn, 1973), ch. 7.

72 Town and Country Planning Act 1990, s. 35. *Local* plans do not necessarily have to be confirmed by the Secretary of State at all (1990 Act, ss. 36, 43), unless the Secretary of State so directs, in which case he is free to consult with any interested party without having to go back to the others (1990 Act, s. 35(6)); cf. *Errington*'s case, note 55. See also SI 1974. No. 1486. The 1990 Act provides for local publicity and participation in the preparation of structure and local plans (ss. 33, 39).

73 See J. A. G. Griffith and H. Street, *A Casebook of Administrative Law* (1964), pp. 142–92.

Minister overruled the inspector and allowed the appeal, having consulted other experts. Naturally this created a bad impression in so far as an open inquiry had been followed first by closed consultations behind the back of the parties and then by a decision overruling the weight of the body of expert opinion already tested by public interrogation. A neighbouring landowner, Major Buxton, challenged the Minister's decision in the High Court; he failed on the technical ground that he was not a person aggrieved by the decision,[74] though certainly he thought he had a legitimate grievance. The Council on Tribunals took up the issue with the Lord Chancellor and the Minister. Eventually new rules were laid down to be applied in the future. Major Buxton had lost his private battle, but he triumphed in defeat. Now, if the Minister is minded to disagree with an inspector's recommendation on a planning appeal, he must normally notify the applicant, the local planning authority, and any other person with a direct interest in the land who gave evidence at the inquiry, and must give them an opportunity of making fresh representations to him.[75] If, moreover, the reason for the proposed disagreement is that the Minister has received new evidence, including expert opinion on a matter of fact, or has considered any new issue of fact (not being a new issue of Government policy) which was not raised at the inquiry, he must be prepared to reopen the inquiry if requested to do so.[76] This change could, of course, slow down decision-making still further. In practice it has not been particularly important.[77] A White Paper stated that the Minister agreed with thirty-nine out of forty recommendations by inspectors.[78]

Not many people had suggested that under the old procedure decisions were in fact unfair. Now they *look* fairer. Furthermore, the liberalization

---

74 *Buxton* v. *Minister of Housing and Local Government* [1961] 1 QB 278 (B was only a 'third party' in the appeal to the Minister).

75 If the Minister simply disagrees with the inspector's views about what planning policy *is*, or how that policy should be *applied* to the facts found at an inquiry, or on a matter of aesthetic taste, this decision is final: *Luke of Pavenham* v. *Minister of Housing and Local Government* [1968] 1 QB 172; *Vale Estates (Acton) Ltd* v. *Secretary of State for the Environment* (1970) 69 LGR 543. If there is disagreement between the Minister and inspector on a material *finding of fact*, an opportunity to make further written representations must be afforded.

76 This is required by the planning appeal rules.

77 It has led to several unsuccessful applications to the courts to quash Ministers' decisions for refusing to reopen an inquiry; see *Luke's* and *Vale's* cases; *Continental Sprays Ltd* v. *Minister of Housing and Local Government* (1968) 67 LGR 147, 19 P & CR 774; *Boyer (William) & Sons Ltd* v. *Minister of Housing and Local Government* (1968) 67 LGR 374; 20 P & CR 176 (complaints of inadequate findings of fact in inspectors' reports).

78 Cmnd 3333 (1967), §§ 33, 34.

in the procedure of inquiries, in particular the discretion given to the inspector to hear anyone with a genuine grievance, has led to a corresponding liberalization in the attitude of the courts to the issue of who is entitled to challenge a decision before them. Any person appearing at the inquiry, whether by right or at the discretion of the inspector, may now seek a final ruling from the courts on the legality of the decision.[79]

Scrutiny of inquiries

The functions of the Council on Tribunals are of some importance. It considers and reports on such matters as the Lord Chancellor or the Secretary of State may refer to it; on its own initiative it may also raise particular questions affecting inquiries; it has to be consulted before procedural rules are made for inquiries; it receives complaints from members of the public. It is not entrusted with the task of keeping the general working of statutory inquiries under review, nor is it empowered to make recommendations as to the kind of person who should be appointed to conduct them; in these respects its functions are narrower than its functions relating to tribunals, but the impediment is not a serious one.

Its tendency to emphasize the need for procedural safeguards, particularly after the termination of an inquiry,[80] and its criticisms of the procedure adopted in two controversial cases,[81] brought it into intermittent conflict with Ministers of Housing and Local Government; the Lord Chancellor, more sympathetic to its objectives, was at times hard pressed to maintain the principle of collective ministerial responsibility. Procedures involving inquiries held on behalf of Ministers tend to evoke stronger feelings than matters affecting tribunals, not only among local inhabitants but also in the Departments concerned. The potential conflict between the needs for affording fair play to individuals and for speedy implementation of policy decisions in compulsory purchase cases is apt to develop into a heated battle in which an independent scrutineer can hardly fail to earn obloquy as a busybody, a nonentity or a supposed partisan. Relations between the

---

79 See *Turner* v. *Secretary of State for the Environment* (1973) 72 LGR 380 and SI 1974, No. 420, r. 7. (What would be the position of a person with a substantial grievance who had not appeared at the inquiry? Would the *Buxton* decision still bar him from the courts?)

80 It was instrumental in securing a more satisfactory final draft of the procedural rules for planning appeals and compulsory purchase order inquiries in 1962.

81 The *Saffron Walden Chalkpit* case (p. 593) and the *Packington Estate* case [1966] *Public Law* 1; Annual Report of the Council on Tribunals for 1965, §§ 77–82.

Council and the Departments are not generally hostile, and Departments voluntarily consult the Council when introducing bills providing for new inquiry procedures. But when conflicts arise the Council is handicapped by its lack of a political powerbase.

The Parliamentary Commissioner for Administration[82] can also entertain complaints about injustice caused by maladministration in connection with procedures involving inquiries held on behalf of a Minister; and because of the jurisdictional overlap he has been made an *ex officio* member of the Council. However, he cannot investigate a complaint unless it is addressed to him through a Member of Paraliament.[83] He has no power to investigate complaints of decisions by tribunals or by Ministers acting in a judicial capacity,[84] but may, in his discretion, investigate a complaint of departmental 'administrative' maladministration in presenting or otherwise handling the matter.

82 See ch. 30.

83 But for an amendment to this procedure, see below, p. 620. For the procedure adopted for passing on to him complaints addressed to the Council and vice versa, see Annual Report of the Council for 1968 (HC 272 (1968–9)), §2.

84 Parliamentary Commissioner Act 1967, s. 5(2). He is concerned only with the 'administrative' functions of Ministers and officials. Determination of a planning appeal or confirmation of a compulsory purchase order is to be regarded as 'administrative' for this purpose.

CHAPTER 29

Crown Proceedings

Aspects of civil proceedings to which the Crown is a party have been
referred to earlier in this book. The Crown Proceedings Act 1947 made
substantial changes in the law. Archaic forms of proceedings advantageous
to the Crown were abolished;[1] various privileges and immunities of the
Crown were abridged; the Crown was at last made liable in tort. But on
a number of issues we have to look at the common-law and equitable
principles evolved before the Act and left unaltered by it. Some of these
principles are still remarkably obscure. New puzzles have been added by
the wording of certain provisions of the Act; some of these are highly
technical, and we shall not trouble to examine them in any detail[2] except
where they are of general practical importance.

CONTRACTS[3]

Before the Crown Proceedings Act, claims against the Crown for breach of
contract had to be brought by way of petition of right[4] in the High Court.
The plaintiff was a 'suppliant'; the procedure was unsatisfactory – for example,
the Home Secretary's fiat had to be granted before proceedings could be
commenced – and too favourable to the Crown. The 1947 Act repealed the
Petitions of Right Act 1860 and provided that claims formerly brought by
petitions of right (with the exception of proceedings against Her Majesty in

---

1 In particular by section 13 of the Act and the First Schedule to the Act.
2 The leading works are Glanville Williams, *Crown Proceedings* (1948), P. W. Hogg,
Liability of the Crown (2nd edn, 1989), and Harry Street, *Governmental Liability* (1953).
H. W. R. Wade and C. F. Forsyth, *Administrative Law* (7th edn, 1994), ch. 21, offers a lucid
review of the main features of the law. See also J. Jacob, *The Republican Crown* (1996).
3 Colin Turpin, *Government Procurement and Contracts* (1989).
4 Petitions of right also lay for recovery of land and chattels, for compensation due under
a statute (for example, the *De Keyser* case [1920] A C 508) and in quasi-contract, but not
for pure torts.

her private capacity)[5] were to be enforceable through ordinary civil proceedings against the Crown. These proceedings could be instituted in county courts; this was perhaps the most salutary innovation introduced by the Act. The substantive law of Crown liability in contract was left unchanged.

How far does Crown liability in this sphere differ from that of local authorities or private persons?

1 The Crown, as a corporation sole at common law, has a potentially unrestricted competence to enter into contracts, save in so far as it is disabled from so doing by the terms of a statute or an overriding common-law principle. Statutory corporations can contract only for purposes within the defined scope of their authority.

2 If the Crown is to be able to discharge its obligations under a contract, funds for this purpose must have been appropriated by Parliament. It is sometimes said that the Crown is under no contractual liability at all in the absence of such an appropriation.[6] This view seems to be correct only where a statute or the terms of a contract have expressly provided that the supply of parliamentary funds shall be a condition precedent to the validity of a contract with the Crown.[7] Normally there is, of course, no such provision. The proper analysis of the normal situation appears to be that if money is not made available to meet the Crown's obligations, the contract is not void but unenforceable against the Crown.[8]

5 Which are maintainable only by petition of right and in respect of matters for which petitions of right could be brought. Section 39(1) and the Second Schedule having repealed the Petitions of Right Act 1860, it is arguable that such petitions must now be brought under the still more archaic pre-1860 procedure. However, section 40(1) of the 1947 Act provides that *nothing* in the Act shall apply to proceedings against the Sovereign in his or her private capacity. This may well be understood to mean that the repeal of the 1860 Act does not include such proceedings. A petition of right under the pre-1860 procedure may still be brought under the Colonial Stock Act 1877 to sue for interest due from the Crown: *Franklin* v. *Att.-Gen.* [1974] 2 QB 185, 205.

6 See especially *Churchward* v. *R.* (1865) LR 1 QB 173 at 209; cf. *Commercial Cable Co.* v. *Government of Newfoundland* [1916] 2 AC 610 at 617.

7 As was the position in *Churchward*'s case, where a long-term government contract for the carriage of mails was discontinued; the annual Appropriation Act indeed expressly stated that no more money was to be applied towards payments to Churchward. SO No. 55 of the House of Commons now expressly provides that in government contracts for the carriage of mails by sea, extending over a period of years, there shall be inserted the condition that the contract shall not be binding till approved by a resolution of the House.

8 See *New South Wales* v. *Bardolph* (1934) 52 CLR 455 (Australia); Wilson, *Cases and Materials*, p. 626. For an incisive analysis, see Street, op. cit., pp. 85–92. It is still not clear whether 'unenforceable' means unenforceable by the other party in an action or merely that judgment against the Crown could be awarded but not executed; if the latter is the correct interpretation, the position is the same as with any other contract with the Crown.

3 Crown contracts are made by agents acting on its behalf. The agent cannot be sued on the contract; only the Crown, as principal, is liable.[9] The agent's authority to bind the Crown may be express or implied. But what if the agent has no such authority? In private law the principal will still be liable if he has held the agent out as having the authority he lacks; this is called 'ostensible' authority. In certain situations a principal will also be liable if the agent was acting in the course of his 'usual' authority although that authority was neither implied nor ostensible. It is still unclear whether, and if so when, the Crown is bound in such cases. Possibly the Crown will be estopped from denying that its servant or agent has authority to bind it in these situations, provided that (i) the other party could not reasonably have been expected to know the limits of the agent's authority;[10] (ii) the limits of the agent's authority were not defined by legislation;[11] and (iii) the Crown itself was not precluded from entering into the contract.[12] But nobody can be sure of the legal position at the present time. It has been held that if a Crown agent exceeds his authority and the Crown is not bound, the other party to the 'contract' cannot recover damages against the agent for breach of warranty of authority,[13] though the agent would be so liable in private law.

4 As has been seen,[14] the Crown is in a different legal position from other employers. The common-law rule is that civil servants hold office at the pleasure of the Crown and cannot sue for damages for wrongful dismissal, though they are legally entitled to be paid for the work they have done and they can obtain a statutory order for reinstatement or re-engagement

---

9 *Macbeath* v. *Haldimand* (1786) 1 TR 172.

10 In *Robertson* v. *Minister of Pensions* [1949] 1 KB 227 (not a case of contract) the Crown was held to be estopped from denying through one Department the binding force of assurances (about entitlement to a service pension) which another Department had given without authority but on which the other party had relied to its detriment. (Followed in *Re L. (An Infant)* [1971] 3 All ER 743.) Even today the authority of this proposition is uncertain (cf. *Howell* v. *Falmouth Boat Construction Co.* [1951] AC 837).

11 *Att.-Gen. for Ceylon* v. *Silva* [1953] AC 461 (Crown not bound). In that case the agent had held *himself* out as having the authority he lacked; the principal would therefore not have been bound in private law according to the doctrine of ostensible authority. It has nevertheless been suggested that the Crown might have been bound if a superior officer had held the agent out as having authority; or alternatively that the Crown should have been bound according to the doctrine of 'usual' authority. There are wide differences of opinion among commentators.

12 For example, because of a statutory restriction or the *Amphitrite* principle; see below.

13 *Dunn* v. *Macdonald* [1897] 1 QB 401, 555, a much criticized decision, but applied in *The Prometheus* (1949) 82 Ll.L. Rep. 859.

14 pp. 209–10 and 217–18.

and an award of compensation for unfair dismissal.[15] Military servants of the Crown cannot even sue for their pay.

5 In the *Amphitrite* case the rule that Crown servants are dismissible at pleasure was ascribed to a general principle of law that the Crown 'cannot by contract hamper its freedom of action in matters which concern the welfare of the State'.[16] In that case, which arose during the First World War, the Crown had assured the owners of a neutral ship that if it put into a British port with cargo, it would be given a clearance and allowed to depart. The ship was nevertheless detained and the owners brought a petition of right for breach of contract. It was held that there was no contract, first because the assurance given by the Crown was to be construed as no more than a statement of intent,[17] and secondly, because the Crown was incapacitated from binding itself in the manner contended by the suppliants, though it could have bound itself to perform an ordinary commercial contract. The decision raises a number of problems, and some critics have denied that any principle of law precluding a Government from fettering its future executive action exists. Nevertheless, there is no doubt that such a principle does exist;[18] the question is how to formulate it and determine its scope. The Crown, like other public authorities, ought not to be able to bind itself to abstain from exercising discretionary powers or performing public duties in matters of primary importance.[19] If it were to purport to bind itself in such ways, then the undertaking should be either of no legal effect at all or capable of being repudiated by the Crown when the national interest so demanded. But the courts must retain power to determine when, for example, executive necessity justifies the Crown in repudiating an ostensibly binding contract. It is not reasonable to insist that engagements with established civil servants must be subject to the *Amphitrite* principle – a point originally (and albeit indirectly) conceded by the Industrial

15 Employment Rights Act 1996, ss. 111–32, 191. See above, p. 210.
16 *Rederiaktiebolaget Amphitrite* v. *R.* [1921] 3 KB 500 at 503–4.
17 See also *Australian Woollen Mills Ltd* v. *Commonwealth of Australia* [1956] 1 WLR 11. But in *Amphitrite* the ingredients of a contract were present.
18 It has seldom been relied on by the Crown in reported cases, and in *Robertson*'s case (see above) Denning J held that it was applicable only where there was an implied term introducing it, but the principle was both recognized and applied in *Board of Trade* v. *Temperley Steam Shipping Co.* (1927) 27 Ll.L. R. 230 (charter party of a ship to the Government) and *Crown Lands Commissioners* v. *Page* [1960] 2 QB 274 (requisitioning of land in wartime and for some years after the end of the war): see especially Devlin LJ's judgment at 291–4.
19 See p. 543; and J. D. B. Mitchell, *The Contracts of Public Authorities* (1954).

Relations Act 1971[20] – nor, on the other hand, does it follow that all commercial contracts are excluded from its scope (for example, in time of grave emergency). Where the principle does apply, the other party to the 'contract' has no right to damages or compensation. It would be a useful law reform to give the courts jurisdiction to award compensation (but not an injunction or a decree of specific performance) to a party damnified by the repudiation of a contract by the Crown on the grounds of executive necessity in cases where the Crown was initially bound by the agreement.

6 The Government is a large-scale purchaser and is often able to impose its own terms on a contractor. There is no special body of case law governing the standard term contract; the quasi-legislative character of such contracts should be recognized and their terms subject to a measure of judicial review.

TORT

Before the Crown Proceedings Act, the individual Crown servant was personally liable as a tortfeasor even though he was purporting to act in the execution of his official functions. But if sued he might not be able to pay the damages or indeed the costs. The Crown was immune from liability; the King could do no wrong and hence was immune from liability for the wrongful acts of his servants although in the same circumstances other employers (including autonomous public authorities) would have been liable. Ministers and superior officials were not legally liable either,[21] unless they had authorized or otherwise participated in the wrongdoing, in which case they were personally liable as joint tortfeasors in their private capacities.

The Crown would often pay damages awarded against its servants for torts committed in the general course of their employment. It would submit some claims to arbitration and abide by the result. If liability were disputed, it would sometimes put up a Crown servant as a nominated defendant though the real defendant should have been the Crown, and it would stand behind him. In two cases, where no legal duty towards the plaintiff had been owed by the nominated defendant, the courts disapproved of this convenient practice;[22] these strictures expedited the introduction of the Crown Proceedings Bill.

20 See now the Employment Rights Act 1996, s. 191.
21 *Bainbridge* v. *Postmaster-General* [1906] 1 KB 178.
22 *Royster* v. *Cavey* [1947] KB 204; *Adams* v. *Naylor* [1946] AC 543.

The Act preserved the personal immunity of the Sovereign. It did not state in general terms that the Crown was to be liable in tort; instead, it made the Crown liable in the same manner as a private person of full age and capacity for specified classes of torts which, subject to certain exceptions, cover the general field.[23] The Crown is now liable for torts committed by its servants or agents[24] acting in the general course of their functions, and for breach of the common-law duties owed by employers and those owed by owners or occupiers of property. In cases of vicarious liability (liability for acts of a servant or agent) there must also be a right of action against the servant himself. Were public corporations administering the remaining nationalized industries servants or agents of the Crown? Almost certainly none of them was; the point was latterly made clear by statute, but even if it was not, they had the requisite degree of autonomy in relation to Ministers for them to be excluded from the category of Crown servants.[25] Certain public corporations providing social services may be in a more ambiguous position. So may incorporated bodies promoting or regulating economic activity as instruments of the central government. The Act providing for their constitution and functions is not always clear on this matter; a corporation may be a Crown servant or agent for certain purposes but not others. The question may assume practical importance only if the corporation is sued and claims a special Crown immunity (for example, from injunctions) or if the Crown is sued instead of the corporation because the latter lacks adequate funds. In determining whether a corporation is a Crown servant the court will scrutinize not only the constituent instrument but also the degree of ministerial control over the corporation.[26]

Section 2(6) has a curious look about it. It renders the Crown liable for the Acts or omissions only of such of its officers as are (i) appointed, directly or indirectly, by the Crown and (ii) paid wholly out of central government funds. The main practical effect of this subsection was to exempt the Crown from liability for acts of the police.[27] Under the Police Act 1996, chief constables are vicariously liable for the torts of police officers.[28] But section

23 Crown Proceedings Act 1947, s. 2. Detailed analysis is not included in the text below.
24 'Agent' was defined (s. 38(2)) as including an independent contractor (i.e. one who was doing the work for the Crown otherwise than a servant). The term 'officer' of the Crown includes a Crown servant.
25 See especially *Tamlin* v. *Hannaford* [1950] 1 KB 18.
26 See generally pp. 142–3.
27 Assuming, of course, that they were officers of the Crown.
28 s. 88. They are indemnified out of local funds.

2(6) leaves the Crown immune from liability for the torts of borrowed 'servants'.

The Crown is liable in tort for breaches of statutory duty in situations where breach gives rise to a right of civil action.[29] However, its position is not quite the same as that of other public authorities on this matter. A statutory duty will not be held to bind the Crown unless it does so expressly or by a very necessary implication.[30] Moreover, the Crown will not be liable unless the statute is also binding on persons *other* than the Crown and its officers; there seems to be no good reason for this limitation. On the other hand, the Crown is liable for breaches of statutory duties imposed on its servants; this goes beyond the liability of other public bodies.

The Crown is not, of course, liable in respect of acts of State or acts done by virtue of the royal prerogative.[31] Section 11(2) of the Act provides that where, in proceedings under the Act, it is material to determine whether anything was properly done (or left undone) in the exercise of the prerogative, a certificate given by the responsible Minister that the act or omission was necessary for the defence of the realm or for training or maintaining the efficiency of the armed forces shall be conclusive. The exact effect of this provision, like so many other matters touching the prerogative, is obscure; the certificate will be conclusive of the facts stated but cannot conclusively determine, as a matter of law, whether the act or omission in question fell within the scope of the prerogative.

Under section 10 of the Act, no action in tort lay against a member of the armed forces, who, while on duty, caused death or injury to another member of the forces on duty or on land, premises or transport being used for the purposes of the forces, provided that the responsible Minister certified that the death or injury was attributable to service for entitlement to a pension. Nor was the Crown liable in these circumstances. Similarly, no action would lie against the Crown for death or personal injury suffered by a member of the forces as a result of the condition of such land, premises or transport, or equipment or supplies (for example, through the crash of a defective transport plane or the premature explosion of a shell or food poisoning in the cookhouse), provided that the appropriate certificate of pensionability was awarded. The right of civil action was barred even

29 For those situations a student should consult a textbook on the law of tort.
30 See pp. 139–40.
31 See ch. 7.

though in the end no pension was in fact awarded to the claimant.[32] In recent years it became generally accepted that section 10 could cause injustice: for example, pension payments and disability allowances for members of the armed forces no longer compared favourably with the levels of damages recoverable in civil actions. The courts showed some subtlety in interpreting the section so as to restrict its scope,[33] and the Government supported a private member's bill which became the Crown Proceedings (Armed Forces) Act 1987. Under it section 10 was repealed[34] except in relation to anything suffered by a person in consequence of an act or omission before the date on which the Act was passed: the 1987 Act is therefore not retrospective.[35] Section 10 may, however, be revived by the Secretary of State by statutory instrument, either generally or for such purposes as the instrument may describe; it must, in any case, be expedient to revive it by reason of imminent national danger or great emergency or warlike preparations outside the United Kingdom.[36]

Section 9 excluded liability of the Crown and its officers in tort for any default in connection with postal, telephone or telegraphic services, apart from a limited financial liability for wrongful loss or damage to registered inland postal packets.[37] This immunity was justifiable on grounds of public policy; to introduce the principle of liability would probably encourage a great number of unmeritorious claims. When the Post Office ceased to be a Government Department and became a public corporation, section 9 was replaced by sections 29 and 30 of the Post Office Act 1969 which reproduced similar immunities. Immunities in favour of British Telecom (BT) have since been repealed.[38]

The Crown is also exempt from liability for the acts or omissions of persons discharging or purporting to discharge responsibilities of a judicial nature or in connection with judicial process (section 2(5)). But for this subsection (which is presumably intended to emphasize the independence of the judicial function), interesting problems would arise in determining

32 *Adams* v. *War Office* [1955] 1 WLR 1116.
33 See *Bell* v. *Secretary of State for Defence* [1986] QB 322; *Pearce* v. *Secretary of State for Defence* [1988] 2 All ER 348.
34 1987 Act, s. 1.
35 The Government agreed, however, to make *ex gratia* payments relating to claims made during the few months before its enactment.
36 1987 Act, ss. 2(1), (5), 2(2). The instrument is subject to parliamentary approval.
37 On the interpretation of this section, see *Triefus* v. *Post Office* [1957] 2 QB 352; *Building & Civil Engineering Holidays Scheme Management Ltd* v. *Post Office* [1966] 1 QB 247.
38 Telecommunications Act 1984, s. 109 and sched. 7.

whether a person performing judicial functions was a Crown servant.[39] Individual liability is not affected.[40]

Subject to these exceptions, the tortious liability of the Crown is much the same as that of local authorities[41] and other public bodies. In other words, it is not set apart from the private law of tort. The doctrine of 'sovereign immunity', which in American law exempts governmental bodies from civil liability for discretionary acts, forms no part of English law. And, although in particular classes of situations liability without fault may be attributed,[42] there is as yet no *general* principle of English law that public authorities are liable without fault (as they are in France) for damage caused by an exceptional risk created by a public activity.

Reasonable care has to be exercised in the discharge of statutory powers and duties so as to prevent the occurrence of reasonably foreseeable damage to private rights or unnecessary aggravation of such damage as must inevitably be caused. But this general principle cannot be applied mechanically without reference to the context. For example, it would be futile for a farmer, whose fertile land had been compulsorily acquired under statutory powers, to claim damages for trespass against the acquiring authority on the ground that it was unreasonable to take his land. Even if the jurisdiction of the courts to entertain such a claim were not ousted by the provision of an exclusive alternative remedy (a statutory application to quash the order within a limited period), he would still have to show that the order was not merely unreasonable but tainted with a vitiating defect.

Liability in negligence for the careless exercise of, or failure to exercise, discretionary powers is still at an embryonic stage. The basic principle emerging from *Dorset Yacht Co. Ltd* v. *Home Office* and *Anns* v. *Merton LBC*[43] is that an individual claiming damages for loss sustained as a result of the negligent operation of a discretionary power, or failure to exercise such a power at all, must prove that the conduct of the public authority was not simply negligent but amounted to a misuse of the relevant discretionary

39 cf. *Ranaweera* v. *Ramachandran* [1970] AC 962 (PC). Clearly officers sitting as members of a court martial administering military law, and Crown servants such as the special commissioners of income tax, are officers of the Crown exercising judicial functions. Are judges officers of the Crown? And which (if any) licensing authorities exercise functions of a 'judicial' nature?

40 See p. 376.

41 See, e.g., *Fisher* v. *Oldham Corporation* [1930] 2 KB 364.

42 For example, under the rule in *Rylands* v. *Fletcher* (1866) LR 1 Ex. 265 and in certain cases of breach of statutory duty.

43 [1970] AC 1004, and [1978] AC 822.

powers. But in *Murphy* v. *Brentwood Council*[44] the House of Lords held that *Anns* had been decided wrongly, and that the defendant council owed no duty of care to the plaintiff when it approved plans for defective foundations for his house.

PROCEDURE AND EVIDENCE

Crown proceedings must be brought by or against an 'authorized Department' – the Department concerned with the general field of conduct in issue; or if none of the authorized Departments is appropriate or if it is not clear which is appropriate, proceedings must be brought against the Attorney-General. A list of authorized Departments is published by the Cabinet Office (section 17).

In general, the same periods of limitation apply to proceedings against the Crown as against other persons. Damages and costs may likewise be awarded against the Crown. However, execution of a judgment cannot be levied against Crown property; this is not a matter of any consequence, for the Crown does comply with judgments against it. Coercive orders – for the specific restitution of land and property, for the specific performance of contracts, and injunctions – cannot issue against the Crown; instead, the court may make an order declaratory of the plaintiff's rights (section 21(1)).[45] Moreover, the court cannot grant an injunction against an officer of the Crown if the effect of granting it would be to give relief against the Crown which could not have obtained in proceedings against the Crown itself (section 21(2)).[46] Interpretation of the latter subsection presents difficulties. It appears to preclude the award of an injunction against Government Departments, those public corporations which are Crown servants, Ministers and other officers of the Crown for acts done in the purported exercise of their statutory functions,[47] save perhaps where the unlawful act is not

---

44 [1991] 1 AC 398.

45 See, e.g., *R.* v. *Secretary of State for the Home Department, ex p. McAvoy* [1984] 1 WLR 408.

46 See, e.g., *R.* v. *Secretary of State for the Home Department, ex p. Kirkwood* [1984] 1 WLR 913; *R.* v. *Secretary of State for the Home Department, ex p. Yaqood* [1984] 1 WLR 920.

47 *Merricks* v. *Heathcoat-Amory* [1955] Ch. 567. See also *Harper* v. *Home Secretary* [1955] Ch. 238, where the question was not firmly decided. And see *M.* v. *Home Office* [1993] 3 All ER 537; cf. Hogg, op. cit., pp. 24–6, putting the case for a more restrictive interpretation of section 21(2).

merely *ultra vires* but also a tort, in which case an injunction might be awarded against an offending Crown officer in his *personal* capacity if the act was far removed from his field of lawful authority. But in *M.* v. *Home Office*[48] the House of Lords established that in judicial review proceedings, coercive orders such as injunctions can be awarded against Ministers acting in their official capacities. The state of the law before the Act was by no means crystal clear. What is clear, unfortunately, is that where the courts have no jurisdiction to issue a final injunction, they have no jurisdiction to issue an interim injunction either; and although a declaration may be an effective substitute for a final injunction (because the Crown will comply with it) the courts do not issue interim declarations.[49] It would seem that unless the Crown consents to a specially expedited hearing of a declaratory action,[50] a person aggrieved may be unable to invoke the jurisdiction of the courts as a matter of urgency to restrain the Crown or its officers from inflicting irreparable damage on private rights by unlawful conduct.

A blanket exclusion of injunctive relief against the Crown and its servants was hard to justify. Mandamus (also a coercive remedy, disobedience to which is likewise a contempt of court) will lie against a Minister in his official capacity on the application of a person with a sufficient interest in the performance of the duty. So will an order of prohibition, and a statutory order to restrain the making or confirmation of a compulsory purchase order; these remedies are closely analogous to injunctions. The arguments against giving the courts a general jurisdiction to award injunctions seem to be (i) that injunctions cover a wider field than these classes of orders and (ii) that the Crown through its servants might find it necessary to disobey the strict letter of the law in an unpredictable emergency and ought not to be impeded or embarrassed by an adverse court order. But injunctions are discretionary and judges are not in the habit of ignoring the existence of a grave national emergency. Fortunately, in *M.* v. *Home Office* the House of Lords made it clear that injunctive relief is now available against Ministers.

---

48 [1993] 3 All ER 537.

49 *Underhill* v. *Ministry of Food* [1950] 1 All ER 591; *International General Electric Co. of New York* v. *Customs and Excise Commissioners* [1962] Ch. 784.

50 In *Marsh (Wholesale) Ltd* v. *Customs and Excise Commissioners* [1970] 2 QB 206, where final declarations were claimed, the case was tried only three weeks after the issue arose. In *Lee* v. *Department of Education and Science* (1967) 66 LGR 211, judgment was delivered within three *days* of the institution of proceedings.

Public interest immunity

By section 28 of the 1947 Act the courts could make an order for discovery of documents against the Crown and require the Crown to answer interrogatories, but this new power was subject to important qualifications. It was not to affect any rule of law about the withholding of any document or refusal to answer any question on the ground that disclosures or answers would be injurious to the public interest; nor was it to affect any rules made to secure non-disclosure of the very existence of a document if in the opinion of a Minister it would be injurious to disclose its existence.[51]

The first proviso referred to the broad rule laid down in *Duncan* v. *Cammell, Laird & Co.*,[52] propounding the common-law doctrine of Crown privilege. The rule was not confined to proceedings to which the Crown was a party. In *Duncan*'s case dependants of men lost when the submarine *Thetis* sank on its trials sued the shipbuilders for negligence. The plaintiffs sought production of various documents in the possession of the defendants. Some of these would in fact have revealed unique features of the submarine which would, if openly divulged, have been of considerable advantage to the enemy; the proceedings were brought during the Second World War. The defendants, under Government instructions, objected to their production, and the First Lord of the Admiralty swore an affidavit to the effect that he had considered the documents and had formed the opinion that their disclosure to anybody would be injurious to the public interest. All the courts upheld this objection and declined even to inspect the documents. Viscount Simon LC, speaking for a unanimous House of Lords, stated the principle at a high level of generality. Documents otherwise relevant and liable to production in judicial proceedings were not to be produced if the public interest required that they be withheld. The objection to production should be taken personally by the Minister in charge of the Department, or, if he were unavailable, by the permanent head of the Department. An objection properly taken should be accepted by the courts as conclusive. The test of injury to the public interest might be satisfied by reference either to the contents of the particular document or to the fact that the document belonged to a class which, as a class, had to be withheld from production. Examples of classes of documents which could properly be withheld were those where disclosure would be injurious to national defence, good diplomatic relations or the proper functioning of the public

51 See now Rules of the Supreme Court, Order 77, r. 12(2).
52 [1942] AC 624.

service. The public interest might well require 'a particular class of communication with, or within, a public department to be protected from production on the ground that the candour and completeness of such communications might be prejudiced if they were ever liable to be disclosed in subsequent litigation . . .'[53] The same consideration applied to oral evidence of the contents of such documents,[54] but they did not necessarily apply to criminal proceedings.

It will be noted that 'Crown privilege', as thus formulated, was not confined to those proceedings to which the Crown was a party. Indeed, the principle was not so much a privilege of the Crown as an exclusionary rule of evidence based on the public interest, of which the Minister was deemed to be the sole judge if he expressed a view in the appropriate form; but if the Minister did not object, the judge himself ought to exclude evidence contrary to the national interest.

Probably no modern rule of English law has attracted so much criticism.[55] The courts had abdicated in favour of the Executive at the expense of the interests of litigants and the public interest in the due administration of justice. And privilege was claimed as a matter of principle for most classes of communications within and between central Government Departments and many types of communications between Departments and outside bodies. In *Ellis* v. *Home Office* (1953), where a prisoner on remand, who had been assaulted and severely injured by a mentally disturbed patient in the prison hospital, sued the Crown for negligence, privilege was successfully claimed for prison medical reports on the assailant;[56] the action had to fail, and doubts were expressed by judges themselves whether justice had in fact been done.

In 1956, and again in 1962 and 1964, administrative concessions were announced: privilege would no longer be claimed for various classes of documents, including those in issue in *Ellis*'s case. The law was not modified, but the basis of the broad rule in *Duncan*'s case was being questioned. Critics harked back to a Privy Council decision (disapproved in *Duncan*'s case) where it had been held that the courts had an inherent power, exercisable in exceptional circumstances, to inspect documents for which privilege had been claimed and to disallow the claim altogether if it were

53 At 635.
54 *Gain* v. *Gain* [1962] 1 WLR 1469.
55 One of the best critiques is by Clark (1967) 30 *Mod. L. Rev.* 489.
56 [1953] 2 QB 135. Privilege was also successfully claimed for documents affecting international relations on an application for habeas corpus: *Soblen*'s case [1963] 2 QB 243.

clearly unreasonable.[57] The Scottish courts reasserted a somewhat similar residuary power (denied in *Duncan*'s case) to overrule a claim to privilege if the interests of the administration of justice so demanded.[58] In the mid-1960s, courts in some Commonwealth countries rejected the general rule laid down in *Duncan*'s case. And the Court of Appeal, in three cases decided in 1964,[59] began to undermine the authority of the rule in English law, declining to accept 'the proper functioning of the public service' as a sufficient reason for withholding disclosure and affirming that the court did have a reserve power, if dissatisfied with the Minister's reasons, to inspect and order disclosure. But the court refrained from overruling the Minister's claim in any of these cases.

In *Conway* v. *Rimmer* (1968) a probationary police constable had been prosecuted for theft; the charge was dismissed, but he was dismissed from his post soon afterwards. He brought an action for malicious prosecution against his former superintendent, and in the course of preliminary proceedings for discovery the Home Secretary objected to the disclosure of certain reports relevant to the case. His objection was made in proper form, particularizing the classes of documents into which they fell (confidential reports on police officers and reports concerning investigation into crime) and specifying that in his opinion the production of documents of each class would be injurious to the public interest. The House of Lords held[60] unanimously that the Minister's assertion as to the effect of disclosure was not to be accepted as conclusive; that although *Duncan*'s case was rightly decided on its own facts, the broader propositions for which that case had been regarded as an authority were wrong;[61] that the courts had a residuary power to inspect the documents in question privately in order to determine whether the public interest in suppressing them outweighed the interests of parties to proceedings and the general public in the unfettered administration of justice; and this power should be exercised in the instant case.

57 *Robinson* v. *South Australia (No. 2)* [1931] AC 704, applied in *Burmah Oil Co. Ltd* v. *Bank of England* [1980] AC 1090.
58 *Glasgow Corporation* v. *Central Land Board* 1956 SC (HL) 1; *Whitehall* v. *Whitehall* 1957 SC 30.
59 *Re Grosvenor Hotel, London (No. 2)* [1965] Ch. 1210; *Merricks* v. *Nott-Bower* [1965] 1 QB 57; *Wednesbury Corporation* v. *Ministry of Housing and Local Government* [1965], 1 WLR 261.
60 [1968] AC 910.
61 If these propositions are to be regarded as part of the *ratio decidendi* in *Duncan*'s case, then the House of Lords was exercising its newly asserted power to overrule its own binding precedents. Some judges and commentators have regarded those propositions merely as *obiter dicta*. I prefer the first of these opinions.

Having inspected the documents, their Lordships overruled the Minister's claim of Crown privilege and ordered disclosure.

This important decision – the most striking example of judicial activism in administrative law since the war – left some questions unanswered. Five separate judgments seldom elicit a clear-cut *ratio decidendi*. Opinions differed on the criteria to be adopted by courts in evaluating claims to Crown privilege, but it can be inferred that judges ought not even to call for inspection of documents described as belonging to certain classes (for example Cabinet papers, and documents concerned with diplomatic relations).[62] Documents belonging to other classes (for example, concerning the formation of policy, or methods used in the investigation of crime) might be inspected but should not normally be disclosed.[63] Official documents of a more routine nature would be inspected and, if relevant, normally disclosed. It was still not clear what standards judges should apply in balancing the possible injury to the public interest caused by disclosure (or the prospect of disclosure) against the claims of the administration of justice in an individual case; or what criteria or procedure should be used if a claim for privilege were to be raised before an inferior court. But there was no obvious reason for differentiating claims on a 'class' basis from claims for privilege based on the *contents* of a particular document. It had already been held[64] that a claim to exclude a subpoenaed witness from giving any *oral* evidence at all should be disallowed; objection should be taken to individual questions and answers on behalf of a Minister at the hearing.

Conway v. *Rimmer* has substituted absolute judicial discretion for absolute executive discretion. There was no obvious reason why judicial wisdom and experience should be surer guides to the public interest on these matters than the judgments formed by the Executive. That Ministers and civil servants have tended to give far too much weight to the interests of secrecy and confidentiality and too little weight to the hardship caused to individual litigants can at once be conceded. On the other hand, the implementation of judicial policy is now unpredictable, whereas executive policy in relation to the withholding of relevant evidence was at least regulated by intelligible principles. Consistency is not an end in itself, but problems of such public importance ought not to be left to be dealt with merely on a case-to-case

62 The courts will not inspect documents when a Minister's certificate shows that an actual or potential risk to national security would be caused by disclosure: *Balfour* v. *Foreign and Commonwealth Office* [1994] 2 All ER 588.
63 Though disclosure of a report concerned with an investigation of a particular suspected crime was ordered in *Conway* v. *Rimmer*.
64 *Broome* v. *Broome* [1955] P. 190.

basis. A primary purpose of Crown privilege was to maintain the efficient conduct of affairs or 'the proper functioning of the public service'. Some important information cannot be obtained at all except under a pledge of secrecy. Many persons will not write completely candid appreciations if they have reason to think that their comments may be subsequently divulged.[65] To some people, including judges, who ought to know better, the latter statement is apparently incredible, at any rate when it is made with reference to civil servants. One can only reply by dogmatic assertions.

1 If, for example, a Department is to place a contract worth £10 millions, it must have the fullest possible information about the standing of potential contractors and any personal characteristics of their directors and managers which cast doubt on their suitability to be entrusted with a major project.
2 Similarly, if a Minister has to conduct personal negotiations with a group of people with whom he is unacquainted, he ought to be briefed by frank appreciations prepared by his advisers.
3 These comments will sometimes be disparaging and defamatory.[66]
4 They ought to be put in writing, not left to oral communication. Memory fades and Ministers change.
5 Senior civil servants do in fact express themselves on paper far more fully and bluntly on 'personnel' matters than, for example, local government officers or most university teachers.
6 The prospect of disclosure to the persons disparaged will tend to transfer comments from the departmental file to private conversations in the office or the club.
7 This tendency is not limited to a handful of moral cowards: many of us are afflicted with this foible.

And why do defamatory comments by judges in court, and MPs in parliamentary proceedings, need to be protected by absolute privilege?

Developments in the courts since *Conway* v. *Rimmer* have been surprising. In 1972 the Law Lords described the very term 'Crown privilege' as 'wrong',

---

65 This point emerges in the selection of candidates for university places. Head teachers' confidential assessments are occasionally wrong-headed, but they are usually quite frank. Disclosure of such assessments would probably be self-defeating while we maintain a system of selective admissions, because some head teachers would 'pull their punches'. Testimonials for graduate students coming from certain countries where 'open testimonials' are the rule (and actions for libel against the authors of testimonials have not been uncommon) are seldom worth the paper they are written on.

66 There is admittedly a risk that disparaging comments will be unfair, irrelevant or founded on inadequate information.

'misleading', 'not accurate' and 'a misnomer'.[67] The courts now prefer the term public interest immunity. But in the case in question they were unanimously upholding a claim by the Home Secretary and the Gaming Board to set aside a witness summons obtained by a gaming club proprietor for the purpose of procuring disclosure of a confidential police report on him to the Gaming Board so as to enable him to prosecute a police officer for libel.[68] What they were trying to emphasize was that the withholding of evidence on grounds of public interest was not really a 'privilege' of the Crown at all. Two revenue cases in the Lords have touched on some especially awkward problems about the scope of 'public interest'.[69] There has been a belated acknowledgement that what used to be called Crown privilege can be justified in some circumstances on the grounds indicated above – that if certain communications were thought to be likely to be revealed, they would either not be made candidly or not be made at all – and that this might be a very undesirable state of affairs. Recognition of these elementary facts has also been shown in other contexts.[70] But prediction of how the courts will react to claims of public interest immunity is not easy. So, for example, in *Peach* v. *Commissioner of Police for the Metropolis*[71]

---

67 *R.* v. *Lewes JJ, ex p. Home Secretary* [1973] AC 388 at 400, 406, 412.

68 There had been doubts whether 'Crown privilege' applied to criminal proceedings. Public interest immunity can extend to criminal proceedings: see *Re Barlow Clowes Gilt Managers* [1992] Ch. 208. See also *Rogers* v. *Home Secretary* [1973] AC 388. For the approach of the Australian courts on this point, see *Sankey* v. *Whitlam and others* (1978) 53 ALJR 11, and of the New Zealand Court of Appeal see *Environmental Defence Society* v. *South Pacific Aluminium Ltd* [1981] NZLR 146, 153.

69 *Crompton (Alfred) Amusement Machines Ltd* v. *Customs & Excise Commissioners (No. 2)* [1974] AC 405 (Court of Appeal overruled: disclosure of the documents asked for considered contrary to public interest). *Norwich Pharmacal Co.* v. *Customs and Excise Commissioners* [1974] AC 133 (discovery allowed: documents not highly confidential and would relate to persons who were probably tortfeasors). *Inspection* of documents was allowed in *Burmah Oil Co. Ltd* v. *Bank of England* [1980] AC 1090 because it was considered that the documents, although containing confidential information about the Bank's financial dealings, would not, if disclosed, be 'prejudicial to state policy'. On inspection, however, discovery was refused: the documents did not contain material necessary to dispose fairly of the case.

70 See *R.* v. *Gaming Board, ex p. Benaim and Khaida* [1970] 2 QB 417 (p. 538, above); *Collymore* v. *Att.-Gen.* [1970] AC 538 at 549–51 (confidential information about industrial disputes); *Re D (infants)* [1970] 1 WLR 599 (local authority case records of children under care).

In *Blackpool Corporation* v. *Locker* [1948] 1 KB 349 it was held that Crown privilege could not be claimed by local authorities. Now it seems that a local authority may object to the production of evidence on grounds of public interest and that the material excluded does not even have to emanate from the central government (*Re D*, above).

71 [1986] QB 1064.

the Court of Appeal decided that documents must be admitted in a civil action in which it was alleged that a policeman had unlawfully killed the deceased, for the public interest in establishing the cause of a violent death outweighed the claim to confidentiality. And in *Conerney* v. *Jacklin*[72] the immunity was held not to attach to a complaint made against a police officer when he wished to sue the complainant in libel. Information obtained by an adoption society about the child of an unmarried couple was held admissible in affiliation proceedings against them in *R.* v. *Bournemouth Justices, ex p. Grey.*[73] On the other hand, in *Evans* v. *Chief Constable of Surrey*[74] a report sent by the chief constable to the Director of Public Prosecutions in the course of a murder investigation was held to be covered by public interest immunity and so could not be disclosed in a later civil action for damages against the police for false imprisonment.

The current leading decision is that of the House of Lords in *R.* v. *Chief Constable of the West Midlands Police, ex p. Wiley.*[75] The House of Lords reviewed the law on public interest immunity and certificates claiming it. Their Lordships made clear that any claim for immunity was a matter for the court, not an individual litigant, and that the claim should be determined by the court weighing the competing public interests (i) in preserving the confidentiality of the evidence and (ii) in securing justice for the other party.

Following the publication of the Scott Report on the export of defence equipment to Iraq[76] the Government instituted a review of the law on public interest immunity. The Government subsequently committed itself[77] to the principle that there should be the maximum disclosure consistent with protecting essential public interests. Ministers would focus directly on the damage that disclosure would cause. The former division into class and contents claims would be abandoned. Ministers would only claim public interest immunity when it was believed that disclosure of a document would cause real damage or harm to the public interest. It would be impossible in advance to describe the types of damage exhaustively, but it might relate to the safety of an individual (such as an informant), or to a regulatory process, or it might relate to damage to international relations

---

72 [1985] *Crim. L. Rev.* 234.

73 *The Times*, 31 May 1986.

74 *Independent*, 21 January 1988.

75 [1994] 3 All ER 420.

76 HC 115 (1995–6). That Report is the fullest independent investigation into the law and practice of public interest immunity certificates.

77 See the Lord Chancellor's statement at 576 HL Deb. 1507–8 (18 December 1996).

caused by the disclosure of confidential diplomatic communications. The Government stated that the test of serious harm would mean that Ministers would not, for example, claim public interest immunity to protect either internal advice or national security material merely by pointing to the general nature of the document. The only basis for a claim would be the belief that disclosure would cause real harm.

CHAPTER 30

Redress of Grievances: The Ombudsman and Others

FORMS OF REDRESS AGAINST OFFICIAL CONDUCT

Judicial redress

The main features of judicial review have been outlined in the last four chapters and need not be recited again. The most obvious defects are: (a) the centralization of the main forms of proceedings (other than actions for damages) in the High Court; this conduces to delay and expense; (b) the still quite wide range of unreviewable administrative action; (c) the difficulty in penetrating to the merits of an administrative decision; challenges to validity often have to be based on a technical, procedural or formal flaw; it is very hard to impugn an act or decision for unreasonableness or even for an error of fact; the procedure of the courts is not well adapted to finding out the facts of a case, particularly where relevant material is in departmental files; (d) the limited scope of duties to give reasons for administrative decisions; (e) various gaps in the law governing the civil liability of public authorities; (f) perhaps above all, the fact that a successful challenge to an invalid order or decision may prove a Pyrrhic victory; the winner may find himself back at 'square one', with a heavy bill of costs and no statutory entitlement to any form of compensation.[1]

Some defects have been eliminated or diminished since 1958 by statutory reform, and as has been seen, the Judiciary in recent years has once again shown itself to be willing to adapt the limited methods available to exercise

---

1 For the doubtful blessings of victory in the courts, see, for example, *Hall & Co.* v. *Shoreham-by-Sea UDC* [1964] 1 WLR 240 (plaintiff obtained declaration that conditions annexed to grant of planning permission were void; but the court refused to sever the conditions and the grant fell with them).

where possible effective review of administrative action. There is still room for much improvement. There is also strong resistance to significant change, as was shown when the Law Commission's attempt[2] to instigate widespread reform was resisted by the Government. Proponents of larger changes fall into two main groups. First, there are those who think in terms of reform within the framework of the existing legal system; they may advocate amalgamation or simplification of judicial remedies, some extension of the scope of review and of administrative liability to pay damages and compensation, and the creation of a special Administrative Division of the High Court, which might include members or assessors with experience in public administration.[3] Secondly, there is a more radical school of thought, consisting mainly of admirers of the French *Conseil d'État*, who despair of piecemeal reform within the existing system and urge the creation of a separate administrative court staffed by members with specialized qualifications in law and administration and applying a separate body of administrative law. Only thus, so they claim,[4] can the law free itself from superficiality, burdensome precedent and inadequate fact-finding techniques and develop rules of administrative justice consonant with the needs of public authorities as well as of the citizen. Their point of view has, however, made little headway during the last few years.

Appeals to tribunals and Ministers

These have been considered in chapter 28.

Parliamentary safeguards

The various opportunities to ventilate individual grievances in Parliament, and in particular in the House of Commons, by invoking the doctrine of individual ministerial responsibility at question time and in debate, have also been considered. Departmental select committees concern themselves only incidentally with *individual* grievances. Occasionally a parliamentary storm over an alleged scandal leads to the appointment of a special tribunal

---

2 *Administrative Law* (Law Com. No. 20, 1969).
3 See note 1.
4 The most eloquent exponent of this point of view is Professor J. D. B. Mitchell. See his articles in [1965] *Public Law* 95; (1966) 15 *ICLQ* 95; (1967) 38 *Political Quarterly* 360; [1967] *Camb. LJ* 46. See also *Let Right Be Done* (Inns of Court Conservative and Unionist Society, 1966), pp. 16–23.

or committee of inquiry, but sledgehammers have too often been used to crack nuts.

Other safeguards

Letters to MPs[5] (which may result in informal written questions to Ministers and, if satisfaction is not obtained, a question in the House), complaints to local councillors, to consumers' councils, to the regulators of privatized industries (such as Oftel and Ofgas), and to the Council on Tribunals; rights of objection at formal statutory inquiries to proposed administrative orders; opportunities to make informal representations against departmental decisions and proposals where no statutory machinery has been provided – these are among the media for voicing protest and, from time to time, securing redress in respect of administrative acts and omissions. The activities of national and local opposition political parties, of pressure groups agitating on behalf of their members, of the press and broadcasting media and of a body such as Liberty (formerly the National Council for Civil Liberties), and, at a different level, the work of the Citizens' Advice Bureaux, impose constraints on the exercise of public power and afford prospects of redress by a person injured by its abuse.

Nevertheless, in the early 1960s a widespread body of opinion had been converted to the view that a new institutional safeguard was needed. This development sprang from at least six sources. First, the report of the Franks Committee, and the detailed implementation of its recommendations, showed that a good deal of valuable work could be done in improving the facilities already provided in the area covered by statutory tribunals and inquiries. Secondly, it was noted that no comparable review had been undertaken of situations typified by the Crichel Down affair, where there was no machinery at all for statutory appeal against or review of discretionary decisions. Thirdly, there was a feeling in some quarters that Crichel Down was but the tip of an iceberg; horrendous things were being done to the detriment of the little man by faceless bureaucrats. To put the matter more conservatively, there had been an increase in State control and regulation of national resources and economic activity since 1939; the State had become a massive provider of social services and financial benefits; these developments seemed to be irreversible, and many cases of injustice arising from maladministration would surely occur. Fourthly, disenchantment with judicial and parliamentary methods of redress had grown. A new phase of

5 See Page [1985] *Public Law* 1.

judicial activism was about to begin, but commentators were more conscious of the long period of judicial self-restraint, particularly in relation to acts done by Ministers. Parliamentary questions and the like were of limited efficacy; it was noted that Commander Marten of Crichel Down was wealthy, well connected and tenacious, but that even so he did not get his wrong redressed. Fifthly, the Danish Ombudsman, Professor Hurwitz, made a lecture tour in this country in 1958. Publicity was gradually built up; perhaps a cure-all would emerge from Scandinavia? Sixthly, the Labour Party was eventually persuaded to incorporate a version of the Ombudsman idea in its electoral programme.

THE PARLIAMENTARY COMMISSIONER FOR ADMINISTRATION[6]

In 1965 the Labour Government, rejecting the view of its Conservative predecessor, published a White Paper proposing the appointment of a Parliamentary Commissioner for Administration.[7] The Parliamentary Commissioner Act 1967 was the outcome.

The Commissioner (hereinafter called the PCA) is appointed by the Crown on the Prime Minister's advice; his salary is charged on the Consolidated Fund; he holds office during good behaviour, subject to a retiring age of sixty-five and a power of removal on addresses from both Houses of Parliament. The first PCA was the retiring Comptroller and Auditor-General, Sir Edmund Compton.[8] He has his own Office, and appoints his own staff subject to Treasury approval. He has a small staff, drawn from the civil service; none of them, astonishingly, is a professional lawyer.

His terms of reference are to investigate complaints by individuals and bodies corporate (other than local authorities and other public corporations) who claim to have 'sustained injustice in consequence of maladministration', while they were in the United Kingdom, at the hands of scheduled central Government Departments or persons or bodies acting on their behalf,

---

6 For the background to the establishment of this office, see R. Gregory and P. G. Hutchesson, *The Parliamentary Ombudsman* (1975).
7 Cmnd 2767 (1965).
8 His two immediate successors were also civil servants, but some subsequent PCAs have been lawyers.

performing or failing to perform administrative[9] functions, or at the hands of specified non-departmental public bodies ('quangos').[10]

He cannot act on his own initiative, nor can he be approached directly by a member of the public. But since 1978 the PCA has adopted the practice of forwarding any letter sent by a citizen straight to him to an MP, stating that he is willing to investigate. The citizen's consent to this is still necessary. His investigations must be conducted in private, and the official head of the Department concerned and any other official implicated in the complaint must be notified and given the opportunity of commenting on the allegations. No set form of inquiry is prescribed, but the PCA has adequate powers to investigate a complaint thoroughly. He can administer oaths and compel the attendance of witnesses and documents. Wilful obstruction of his investigations is punishable as if it were a contempt of court. His reports on investigations, and communications with MPs on the subject-matter of a complaint, are protected by absolute privilege in the law of defamation.[11] Irrespective of the Official Secrets Acts and the law relating to Crown privilege, he must be allowed access to any relevant document other than one relating to the proceedings of the Cabinet and its committees (section 8),[12] though public interest immunity may be asserted to prevent the PCA and his officers from *disclosing* information thus obtained (section 11(3)), and the Official Secrets Acts apply to disclosures other than for the purposes of investigations and reports (sections 11(1), (2)).

The PCA has no power to alter or rescind decisions. His statutory powers are confined to making reports on his investigations, or giving to the MP who referred the complaint his reasons for not investigating. Reports on investigations go to the MP who referred the complaint, and the official against whom the allegations were made and his departmental head. If it appears to the PCA that an injustice has been caused by maladministration and has not been rectified, he may make a special report to both Houses; he may make other special reports, and must make an Annual Report, to each House. His Special and Annual Reports are

9 As distinct from judicial or legislative.

10 1967 Act, s. 4 and sched. 2, as substituted by the Parliamentary and Health Service Commissioners Act 1987, s. 1 and sched. 1. See also the Parliamentary Commissioner Act 1994.

11 s. 10(5). The MP also enjoys absolute privilege in respect of such communications and in the communication of the PCA's report to the complainant.

12 It has, however, been recommended that he should have access to Cabinet and Cabinet committee papers, but Parliament has not yet given such authority: see *Fourth Report from the Select Committee on the PCA* (HC 444 and 615 (1977–8)).

considered by a small Select Committee of the House of Commons on the Parliamentary Commissioner for Administration. Occasionally his special reports have been debated on the floor of the House. A considerable quantity of published material about his work is now available.

Jurisdictional limitations

'Injustice' and 'maladministration' were deliberately left undefined.[13] 'Injustice' means something wider than legally redressable damage; it includes hardship and a sense of grievance which ought not to have arisen. 'Maladministration' covers a multitude of administrative sins, sins of commission and omission – corruption, bias, unfair discrimination, harshness, misleading a member of the public as to his rights, failing to notify him properly of his rights or to explain the reasons for a decision, general high-handedness, using powers for a wrong purpose, failing to consider relevant materials, taking irrelevant material into account, losing or failing to reply to correspondence, delaying unreasonably before making a tax refund or presenting a tax demand or dealing with an application for a grant or licence, and so on. The Commissioner is not allowed to question 'the merits of a decision taken without maladministration . . . in the exercise of a discretion . . .' (section 12(3)). He interpreted this limitation as meaning that he could not consider whether a decision was manifestly unreasonable or even, apparently, based on a clear mistake of fact, if the appropriate procedures had been followed and there was no evidence of impropriety. He was persuaded by the Select Committee that in an extreme case he ought to infer maladministration from the 'thoroughly bad' *quality* of a decision;[14] but he has shown extreme circumspection in this matter. The Committee also persuaded him to consider the 'bad rule' – an internal departmental rule which caused undue hardship to individuals – and to find maladministration if hardship had arisen in a subsequent case arising under the same rule where it had not been properly reviewed by the Department. There are indications that his activities in this area have induced some Departments to re-examine their rules and give them better publicity. The PCA has also accepted that he can investigate the administrative procedures attendant on the making and review of statutory orders other than statutory instruments.

---

13 See *R*. v. *Local Commissioner for Administration, ex p. Bradford City Council* [1979] QB 287, especially Lord Denning MR's judgment, for an attempt to give a judicial definition of maladministration.
14 HC 350 (1967–8), 11–14.

Until 1973 the PCA had no jurisdiction to investigate complaints about the National Health Service. The National Health Service Reorganization Act 1973, Part III[15] provided for the appointment of a Health Service Commissioner for England and one for Wales, and the PCA was given these additional posts on 1 October 1973. The relevant statute is now the consolidating Health Service Commissioners Act 1993. The procedures are broadly similar to those under the 1967 Act, although an improvement is that a complaint may be made direct to the Commissioner. Subject to exceptions, he may investigate an alleged failure in a service, or failure to supply a service provided by specified National Health Service bodies, or any other action taken by or on behalf of such bodies. The 1993 Act, like its predecessor, does not go as far as some might have wished; several matters are not subject to investigation. But the Commissioner may now investigate complaints which arise from an exercise of clinical judgement.[16]

Among the matters excluded from his jurisdiction under the Third Schedule to the Parliamentary Commissioner Act 1907 are matters arising in external relations and overseas territories (except for complaints against consular officials),[17] extradition, action taken for the investigation of crime or the protection of national security (including the withholding or impounding of passports), judicial proceedings, the prerogative of mercy, government contractual and commercial transactions (subject to limited exceptions), personnel matters in the armed forces and the civil service, the award of honours and the granting of royal charters. Nor can he investigate complaints against local authorities, public corporations (other than instruments of the Crown) or the police. These are very big exclusions. If the subject-matter of a complaint lies within the jurisdiction of a special tribunal or a court of law, the PCA has a discretion: normally he should abstain from investigating the matter, but he may waive the rule if it is unreasonable in the particular circumstances to expect the complainant to resort or to have resorted to the tribunal or court (section 5(2)). We cannot all be experts in administrative law. In practice, wittingly or otherwise, he has frequently investigated complaints of procedural maladministration which would have been judicially reviewable. This makes it all the more incongruous that he should be so averse from treating manifest unreasonableness as maladministration. There is no bar to investigating matters that

15 See also Cmnd 5055 (1972), pp. 44–5, 55–6; National Health Service (Scotland) Act 1972, Part VII, and the current National Health Service (Scotland) Act 1978, Part VI.
16 Health Service Commissioners (Amendment) Act 1996.
17 Parliamentary Commissioner (Consular Complaints) Act 1981.

could be or have been raised at a statutory inquiry held on behalf of a Minister, provided that the inquiry leads to an 'administrative' type of decision. The PCA's decisions are amenable to judicial review, although the courts will be slow to interfere with his exercise of the discretion which is conferred on him in wide terms by the 1967 Act.[18]

In any year the Department of Social Security and the Inland Revenue will together account for about half the number of complaints received by the PCA. Of such dry statistics it is indeed worth quoting the PCA.[19] 'The complaints which I have had to consider (in 1979) scarcely attained a national dimension . . . But to the complainants the grievance of each was important: and it is the mark of a great civilization that it believes in the importance of the individual and finds time for his concerns.'

Evaluation[20]

The Ombudsman was greeted by the sceptics as an Ombudsmouse. Following his special report on the Sachsenhausen case late in 1967,[21] when he found that Foreign Office officials had been guilty of procedural maladministration in dealing with an application by ex-prisoners-of-war for discretionary compensation for suffering caused by incarceration in a Nazi concentration camp, the ranks of Tuscany were cheering. The Foreign Secretary strenuously defended his officials and complained of an encroachment on the principle of ministerial responsibility, but still agreed to pay up.[22]

From him there have come no sensational exposures of bureaucratic turpitude or gross abuses of power. The general picture emerging from his reports is one of a high level of integrity (not to be confused with efficiency) in British central government administration.[23] There are other factors impossible to quantify. The Select Committee has asked whether, if the

---

18 R. v. *Parliamentary Commissioner for Administration, ex p. Dyer* [1994] 1 All ER 375.
19 Annual Report for 1979, HC 402 (1979–80), para. 4.
20 See Marshall [1973] *Public Law* 32; Sir Kenneth Wheare, *Maladministration and its Remedies* (1973), ch. 5; JUSTICE, *Our Fettered Ombudsman* (1977); Frank Stacey, *Ombudsmen Compared* (1978); R. Gregory and P. G. Hutchesson, *The Parliamentary Ombudsman* (1975); Gregory [1982] *Public Law* 49; G. Marshall, *Constitutional Conventions* (1984), ch. V.
21 HC 54 (1967–8).
22 758 HC Deb. 107–70 (5 February 1968); Fry [1970] *Public Law* 336.
23 This is not to say that official turpitude is non-existent. Occasional prosecutions, and revelations of financial malversation in reports of the Comptroller and Auditor-General, show that it does exist.

PCA is to be appointed from the civil service, a period of 'quarantine' between leaving the service and taking up office should be introduced, and also is strongly of the view that the House of Commons should be consulted before an appointment is made.[24] The Government has subsequently appointed to the office individuals who had not previously been full-time public officials. The 'MP filter' has not worked well. The PCA has placed a very high priority on cultivating good relations with heads of Departments, so as to obtain their cooperation in his investigations, but he is little known to the general public. He is a remote figure, neither seeking nor being accorded publicity.[25] His terms of reference are fairly narrow and have, on the whole, been conservatively interpreted,[26] despite the prodding by the Select Committee. Another possible reason for disillusionment or tepid enthusiasm is that a finding of maladministration does not necessarily lead to anything more than an expression of official regret or an undertaking that the Department will take another look at its procedures.

On the credit side of the balance, it is apparent that the PCA's investigations are extremely thorough. Departments have often rescinded decisions, made *ex gratia* payments or refunds, waived or modified tax claims in response to his adverse findings; they have been made more aware of the need for giving adequate and prompt explanations in response to requests and inquiries from members of the public. The Select Committee on the Parliamentary Commissioner, which has acquired a good deal of information about administrative procedures by considering his reports and examining senior departmental witnesses, has not been as inhibited as the PCA in passing judgment on the merits of a rule or decision. It has been instrumental in securing a relaxation in the Inland Revenue rules for remission of tax arrears in cases of hardship,[27] though it has been unsuccessful in persuading the Government to sponsor legislation enlarging the Com-

24 *Second Report from the Select Committee of the Parliamentary Commissioner for Administration, 1975–76* (HC 480 (1975–6)).
25 His reports on investigations go to MPs; he does not give them any publicity himself, except in special reports and his Annual Report. Lack of publicity for the office probably tends to cause fewer complainants to *take the initiative in asking* MPs to bring their own cases before him. But note the PCA's views on publicity in his Annual Report for 1975 (HC 141 (1975–6)), paras. 38–9, and for 1979 (HC 402 (1979–80)), paras. 11–12.
26 Subject to exceptions, some of which (the 'bad rule' and the type of case where there might also be a successful invocation of judicial review) are mentioned below. There are others – cases where an action for negligent misstatements might have been brought (but the law on this matter is still developing), and cases where the complainant shows a *prima facie* case of injustice but cannot point to an act of maladministration, in which event the PCA will often begin an investigation.
27 See Cmnd 4729 (1971).

missioner's terms of reference.[28] This is quite undramatic stuff, but those who would write the experiment off as a failure would do well to read his Annual Reports and the Reports (with Minutes of Evidence) of the Select Committee. Some people have obtained redress which they would almost certainly have been denied had these institutions not existed.

To assess the impact of his work on civil service efficiency is impracticable. As he cannot deal with personnel matters or the most politically sensitive issues, there is no obvious reason why the knowledge that he has access to files should inhibit civil servants in expressing their opinions. There have been isolated complaints that he has made officers in some departments too non-committal. Complaints that he has heavily increased departmental workloads are unsubstantiated. Civil Service morale does not appear to have suffered from his activities. He has been careful, as far as possible, to avoid identifying individual culprits in his reports, and in general he has shielded the service against sweeping and unwarranted aspersions. (This has indeed been the experience of Ombudsmen in several other countries.) Senior departmental officers, and Ministers, have been given a better idea of personal, organizational and procedural deficiencies at a lower level.

Although Departments cease to be monolithic under the PCA's scrutiny, the concept of individual ministerial responsibility to Parliament has not been undermined. The PCA's criticisms are indeed directed almost exclusively against officials, but the Minister remains politically vulnerable within the limits already explained;[29] and he is supplied with ample material for the meaningful discharge of his responsibility. There is no evidence at all that the PCA has detracted from the traditional functions of MPs in procuring the redress of individual grievances. MPs have a wide discretion whether or not to pass a complaint on to him for investigation, as has unfortunately been demonstrated. He is able to obtain access to materials closed to MPs and has coercive powers that they lack. His criticisms of individual administrative decisions cannot be brushed aside as superficial or politically motivated. They have provided opportunities for well-informed parliamentary questions and some well-informed debates.

When a Government of this country seriously addresses itself to administrative law reform, a primary source of information will be the reports of the Parliamentary Commissioner for Administration. In particular, he has

---

28 Cmnd 4661 (1971), where the Government rejected its recommendations for an extension of the PCA's jurisdiction to include various personnel matters in the public service and the forces.
29 See pp. 190–95.

exposed a number of situations in which administrative ineptitude has led to loss or hardship for which no legal redress may yet be obtainable as of right. Where it is proper to make an *ex gratia* award, it is often unjust that a remedy in the courts should be denied.

Table of Cases

Table of Statutes

Index